Online Dispute Resolution

Online Dispute Resolution

Theory and Practice

Daniel Rainey, Ethan Katsh and Mohamed S. Abdel Wahab
(Eds.)

Second edition

eleven

Published, sold and distributed by Eleven
P.O. Box 85576
2508 CG The Hague
The Netherlands
Tel.: +31 70 33 070 33
Fax: +31 70 33 070 30
e-mail: sales@elevenpub.nl
www.elevenpub.com

Sold and distributed in USA and Canada
Independent Publishers Group
814 N. Franklin Street
Chicago, IL 60610
USA
Order Placement: (800) 888-4741
Fax: (312) 337-5985
orders@ipgbook.com
www.ipgbook.com

Eleven is an imprint of Boom uitgevers Den Haag.

ISBN 978-94-6236-183-6
ISBN 978-90-8974-360-2 (E-book)

Table of Contents

Foreword

Richard Susskind

Is court a service or a place? When people or organizations are in dispute, must they congregate in physical courtrooms to resolve their legal differences?

Until March 2020, the answers to both of these questions were clear. It was deeply imbued in conventional Western thinking that when serious conflicts arise in society, the warring people become parties and it is to some physical courtroom that they should head. At law school, therefore, students were taught until recently that the court was the definitive forum and mechanism for settling all disputes. In our literature, likewise, the courtroom was the theatre in which many disagreements were played out. And the lay perception of the administration of justice was frequently captured in films and novels in terms of wood paneled hearing rooms, arcane procedures and judges in robes.

Then came Covid-19, physical court buildings closed around the world, and the justice community scrambled for ways to conduct hearings remotely with the support of some kind of technology. In turn, as technology-based alternatives to traditional courts were rolled out rapidly, legal minds were opened and legal minds were changed. In this way, in a few months in the middle of 2020, while the text of this book was being finalized, its subject matter became a central concern of judges, lawyers, policymakers, and academics around the world. More quickly than expected even by the most optimistic of this volume's contributors, online dispute resolution (ODR) has become a core topic for anyone who cares about the future of justice. This second edition could not, therefore, have been better timed. Its contents provide light for us all as we contemplate a future in the shadow of Covid-19.

There has been another major development since the first version of the book appeared and its authors can rightly claim that they played a part. Many of the ideas, systems, and processes discussed back in 2012 in the earlier edition are now steadily being embraced and implemented by various governments, embedding ODR in public dispute resolution services, as an integral part of courts rather than as a private sector alternative. The gradual emergence of these online courts will, in my view, help us to solve the global access to justice problem.

What, then, is ODR? The story that unfolds in the pages that follow answers that question fully. In truth, ODR itself is not an entirely new narrative, and nor was it in 2012, because critics of the court system have for long challenged whether courts are indeed the best placed institution and method for resolving many kinds of dispute. Opponents have for long argued, for example, that pursuing an action in the courts is too confrontational, too time-consuming and too costly. Many have gone further and called for the widespread adoption of ADR, alternative dispute resolution.

I regard this collection of essays – written by undoubted authorities in the field – as being largely concerned, therefore, with one crucial category of alternative dispute resolution and we call it ODR. When a conflict is handled using ODR, a traditional courtroom is not employed. Instead, the process of resolving a dispute is entirely or largely conducted through the Internet. Of course, as this volume shows, this snapshot of ODR is an oversimplification. In the pages that follow, it is made clear that many techniques fall under the umbrella of ODR, such as e-mediation, e-negotiation, and e-arbitration, and that these techniques can be deployed in sorting out a wide range of disagreements – from consumer disputes to problems arising from e-commerce, from quarrels amongst citizens to conflicts between individuals and the state, to peacebuilding more generally. The book also shows that ODR is already being deployed, albeit in varying degrees, in North America, Europe, Asia, Africa, and Latin America.

In a world in which the Internet is so firmly rooted, it should come as no revelation that online methods might be devised for sorting out at least some tensions and clashes that arise amongst human beings. And yet, most lawyers and many litigators, until this year, had not yet heard of ODR. Even now, when seasoned legal advisers are introduced to the notion, they often regard it with distrust and as a curiosity that they hope will remain forever on the edge of their world. The skeptics quickly question the fairness, openness, rigor and reliability of ODR. These misgivings are not to be dismissed lightly. Instead, in this book, measured, compelling and reassuring accounts of ODR are offered, addressing a wide range of related issues, including trust, justice, cultural context, and the interaction of ODR with traditional judicial systems. Even in the chapters that explore the potential of artificial intelligence and blockchain for ODR, the tone is measured and not evangelical.

Nonetheless, it is hard to digest the theory and case studies presented here and not feel a strong sense of optimism that we are on the threshold of a new era for dispute resolution; that we are being offered a glimpse of methods for settling disagreements that will incur costs that are, at last, proportionate to the amounts at issue. Even before Covid-19, the credibility of legal systems around the world was being challenged by disgruntled users – from impoverished individuals through to multinational businesses – who claimed that the courts were no longer an affordable or sensible forum for disposing of many of their conflicts. As we struggle to keep court service available in 2020, ODR now offers a tried and tested set of techniques to help people and organization resolves their legal problems while the virus remains at large.

ODR offers the promise of robust and yet radically less expensive dispute resolution. And while it may still seem alien or outlandish for some lawyers, policymakers and opinion formers of today, few of the doubters belong to the Internet generation. Future generations, for whom working and socializing online is second nature, may regard ODR as an entirely natural facility, much more so than conventional courts.

For long, I have described ODR as an example, in law, of a disruptive technology – one whose introduction can fundamentally challenge and change working practices of the past. For whom, though, is ODR disruptive? The harsh truth is that ODR is most disruptive for those who currently make a living from traditional litigation. For lawyers and public servants whose careers are in the courts, ODR may well be regarded as threatening. But this should not deter us from evolving techniques that better meet the needs of Internet-based societies. It is not the purpose of the courts to provide lawyers with a livelihood. Crucially, what may be disruptive for law firms may simultaneously be empowering for those who have problems to resolve.

As with all disruptive technologies, ODR is not therefore an uncontroversial field of theory and practice. That is why this book is so important. Beyond this collection and its contributors, much discussion of ODR is anecdotal and speculative. In gathering together the essays that follow, Daniel Rainey, Ethan Katsh and Mohamed Wahab once again take the debate and theory about ODR to a new level – a standard of discourse that is better informed, more systematic, and rooted more reliably in experience of live systems.

I wish the work every success.

Professor Richard Susskind OBE
Technology Adviser to the Lord Chief Justice of England and Wales
President of the Society for Computers and Law

Introduction

The first edition of this book was published in 2012. In 2011, we had witnessed the power of information and communication technologies ('ICTs') in a socio-political context as a tidal wave of revolutions in the Middle East was spurred through online communication between netizens and citizens. There was what can almost be described as euphoria surrounding the ability of ICTs to facilitate and catalyze change across all aspects of life. We had anticipated more than a decade ago that technology is destined to play a significant role in dispute avoidance, management and resolution.

There have been truly significant developments related to technology since our 2012 publication date: some developments have been benign, some have led to social change, and some are troubling. In 2014, for the first time in the United States, more people accessed the Internet using mobile technology than accessed the Internet using desktop or laptop computers. The number of social media outlets has exploded since 2012, and the subsequent fracturing of our public and private discourse has proceeded at a what feels like a dizzying pace. As this introduction is being written, discussion has begun about the use of facial recognition technology used with surveillance cameras to distinguish ethnic minorities in public gatherings – minorities that may be the object of oppression or mistreatment.

One thing has not changed – the increasing sophistication and use of ICTs to communicate, share information, and organize groups has created more opportunities for conflict and more opportunities to resolve those conflicts. To paraphrase a comment one of the editors of this volume made in the early 2000's, the capacity of the Internet to resolve conflict will be dwarfed by the capacity of the Internet to create conflict. This volume is dedicated to presenting the status of online dispute resolution, and to encouraging dispute resolvers to continue to find creative ways to apply the conflict *resolution* potential of ICTs and related artificial intelligence (AI) applications in our contentious cyber-environment, as the human race transitions into a new virtual chapter of human life.

Of course, the biggest change since 2012 has been the "Big Bang" of ODR – the COVID-19 pandemic. At the beginning of 2020, ODR was making slow and steady inroads into the practice of dispute resolution, moving out from e-commerce to justice systems around the world, peacebuilding, and private dispute resolution practice. The end of 2020 saw phenomenal growth in the use of ICTs and ODR applications as well as the increasing acceptance of ODR platforms and approaches as a legitimate and effective way to address conflict. As we noted in 2012, the ongoing proliferation and advancement of ICTs is having a profound impact in all regions of the globe in diverse socio-legal, economic, cultural, and political climates. As this book documents, ICTs and

AI applications are fundamentally changing institutions in every country, altering our shared world and our particular cultures and institutions.

Probably still the most well-known book on negotiations as a mode of dispute resolution, *Getting to Yes* by Roger Fisher and William Ury, was published in 1981, exactly forty years ago. It argued that a new approach to dispute resolution was needed because 'conflict is a growth industry' and courts were inadequate and inefficient in responding to disputes. During the last four decades, the Alternative Dispute Resolution ('ADR') processes of negotiation, mediation, arbitration, have grown in use and have become the primary forms of dispute resolution. The use of ODR technology in negotiation, mediation, and arbitration have become commonplace and is proliferating across the globe, to the extent that it was high time to establish the International Council for Online Dispute Resolution (ICODR). ICODR promotes worldwide standards for all forms of technology-assisted dispute resolution, including diagnosis, negotiation, mediation, arbitration and courts. It aims to drive the development, convergence, and adoption of open standards for the global effort to resolve disputes and conflicts using information and communications technology.

This book is intended to provide an in-depth analysis and overview of not only the past and present but also the future of ODR. It is intended to serve as a guide to scholars and practitioners having an interest in the interplay between dispute resolution, ICTs and AI applications. The book employs international, comparative, empirical, and interdisciplinary approaches to a myriad of legal and technical issues across the ODR spectrum. ODR is a field that lies at the intersection of dispute resolution and technology and our challenge has been to examine the many different areas that are being touched by these elements of modern life.

This book is divided into three main parts. The first part is dedicated to providing background and context for scrutinizing ODR, its applications, its interconnection with established legal and extra-legal doctrines and principles, as well as its past, present, and future. The second part addresses issues related to the practice of ODR, and the third part is dedicated to mapping ODR in Europe, North America, Asia, Africa, and South America.

Overall, the authors offer interdisciplinary analysis of contemporary and pervasive issues which remain in a state of flux.

By and large, ODR is considered a global phenomenon that requires due consideration and further integration of cultural practices, global and local norms, technical and technological standards, and regulatory initiatives. This will certainly pave the way for the development and progression of ODR schemes, applications, and initiatives on local, regional, and global levels.

Finally, the editors hope that readers, whether scholars, students, or practitioners, enjoy and appreciate the availability of this updated version of a leading treatise that combines a wealth of theoretical and practical approaches to a multifaceted phenomenon such as ODR. The chapters in the book represent a discussion of the key issues driving the development of ODR, and a lens through which readers may observe and understand the issues facing dispute resolution practitioners as we all struggle with how to integrate ODR and technology into 'mainline' dispute resolution theory and practice. The editors anticipate that ODR and technology will indeed transform the world of dispute avoidance, management, prevention, and resolution in ways that are beyond present comprehension and traditional wisdom.

Daniel Rainey, Ethan Katsh and Mohamed S. Abdel Wahab

Chapter 1 Online Dispute Resolution (ODR): A Look at History

Ethan Katsh

As technology changes, sneakiness finds new expressions
Clifford Stoll, The Cuckoo's Egg

1 The Early Years[1]

The internet was invented in 1969 with the linking of four sites, three in California and one in Utah. In the two decades following, the internet grew through the linking of many more sites, all focused on research and most connected to either the military or academia. During this period – which represents almost half the lifespan of the internet – there were relatively few disputes, largely because there were relatively few users. Those who had both access to the internet and were able to use it, belonged to a kind of restricted club; the restrictions were based on where one worked or studied, and whether one had sufficient technical skills.

Membership in this 'club' was limited not only in who could join, but in what one was permitted to do once one became a 'member.' Software for email and exchanging files online was the opposite of user friendly. The U.S. government also imposed restrictions on use of the network. In 1982, for example, when the internet was known as the ARPANet, MIT told its users that

> It is considered illegal to use the ARPANet for anything which is not in direct support of Government business ... personal messages to other ARPANet subscribers (for example, to arrange a get-together or check and say a friendly hello) are generally not considered harmful ... Sending electronic mail over the ARPANet for commercial profit or political purposes is both anti-social and illegal. By sending such messages, you can offend many people, and it is possible to get MIT in serious trouble with the Government agencies which manage the ARPANet.[2]

1 Parts of this chapter are discussed in more detail in E. Katsh and O. Rabinovitch-Einy, *Digital Justice: Technology and the Internet of Disputes* (Oxford University Press, 2017).

2 Christopher C. Stacy, *Getting Started Computing at the AI Lab* 9 (Mass. Inst. of Tech. Artificial Intelligence Laboratory, Working Paper No. 235, 7 September 1982).

A little later, when the National Science Foundation established NSFNet and began to manage the civilian part of the internet, it had a similar Acceptable Use Policy that prohibited its use for commercial purposes.[3] It is ironic, given the growth of social networks during the last 15 years, that during most of its existence the internet was a non-user friendly and, in a sense, an anti-social environment for ordinary citizens.

In this heavily restricted environment, disputes were few. When they did occur, the population was small and homogeneous enough that informal techniques for reducing friction were sufficient. Similarly, no one raised any First Amendment or other objections to the government regulating speech, perhaps because the relative few who were aware of the technology did not consider commercial communications over a government funded network to be protected speech, or because very few of its users could even imagine a successful commercial venture employing the network.[4] There was no supply of anything the public might want, and certainly no demand.

Opportunities for citizen access slowly began to change when the Apple II was introduced in 1977 and the IBM PC in 1981. A few years later, anyone could connect a modem to their computer and link to a private commercial online service not connected to the internet, such as CompuServe, AOL, Prodigy and a few more. Connection speeds were slow and users were often charged fees by the minute, but these services had a great deal of content, active topical discussion groups and the software employed was user friendly. The great drawback of these private online environments was that one could only communicate with subscribers to the network to which one belonged.[5] An AOL subscriber could send email to another AOL subscriber, but not to a CompuServe subscriber or to a faculty member at a university who had an email account linked to the internet.

The walled off nature of the private networks also helped to limit the reach of disputes. In 1985, a case came to light in which it was revealed that, for two years, a participant in a discussion group on CompuServe was a man pretending to be a woman. Offline, the individual was a male psychiatrist in New York. Online, he took on the persona of a woman named Joan, claiming to be a New York neuropsychologist in her late twenties who had been severely disfigured in a car accident which killed her boyfriend. Joan's story was that she herself had spent a year in the hospital, being treated for brain damage, which affected both her speech and her ability to walk. Mute, confined to a wheelchair, and frequently suffering intense back and leg pain, Joan had at first been

---

3 *The NSFNET Backbone Services Acceptable Use Policy*, Cyber Telecom (1995), www.cybertelecom.org/notes/nsfnet.htm#aup.

4 Milo Medin, *What I Saw at the Revolution (or) An Abridged History of the Internet*, NANOG (16 June 2011), www.nanog.org/meetings/nanog52/presentations/Monday/Medin-nanog-6-15.pdf.

5 AOL bought CompuServe in 1998. *See* Caitlin Dewey, *A Complete History of the Rise and Fall—and Reincarnation!—of the Beloved '90s Chatroom*, Wash. Post (30 October 2014), www.washingtonpost.com/news/the-intersect/wp/2014/10/30/a-complete-history-of-the-rise-and-fall-and-reincarnation-of-the-beloved-90s-chatroom/.

so embittered about her disabilities that she told the group that she had considered ending her life. Over the next two years, she became an active online presence who served both as a support for other disabled women and as an inspiring stereotype smasher to the able bodied. Through her many intense friendships and (in some cases) her online romances, she changed the lives of dozens of women.[6]

When Joan's true identity was discovered, there was an enormous outcry from CompuServe users. CompuServe was asked to provide warnings for newcomers to inform them they might encounter impostors. The company replied, "Blaming CompuServe for impostors makes about as much sense as blaming the phone company for obscene calls."[7] This may be true and, indeed, legal protection against liability was later granted to internet service providers.[8] On the other hand, it is not unreasonable to expect some kind of help from entities like the phone company to combat obscene phone calls or other illegal acts. However, the impostor was not committing an illegal act. In any event, a story that in all likelihood would have 'gone viral' 10 years later and become a network-wide controversy did not do so in the mid-1980s. There were not enough participants, forums, or links to spread the word about this story any further than the CompuServe group in which Joan participated. Without a growth industry of networks, there was not enough fuel to sustain a chain of disputes. The only reason we know of this incident was that a journalist happened to be a participant in the discussion forum and wrote a story, 'The Strange Case of the Electronic Lover,' that was published in Ms. Magazine in 1985.[9]

CompuServe's refusal to get involved was linked to the fear that accepting any responsibility would lead to legal liability. Ironically, CompuServe was, at the time, beginning to monitor and intervene in some discussion forums when problems arose. Its most notable action was the use of *Sysops*[10] or 'system operators' who oversaw certain CompuServe discussion forums and who could get involved in discussions and even remove participants. Their existence was recognition of the growing need of private network companies to try to encourage active discourse but also exercise some limits.

Like universities and government institutions connected to the internet, all of the private internet services had their own Acceptable Use Policies. However, those policies were often ignored or violated, particularly by the many high school students who were feverishly experimenting with what could be found and done online. When a service's Acceptable Use Policies were violated, as they often were, and accounts were cancelled,

---

6 Lindsay Van Gelder, *The Strange Case of the Electronic Lover*, Ms. Mag. (October 1985), http://lindsyvangelder.com/sites/default/files/Plinkers.org%20-%20Electronic%20Lover.htm_.pdf.

7 *Id.*

8 "No provider or user of an interactive computer service shall be treated as the publisher or speaker of any information provided by another information content provider." Communications Decency Act of 1996, 47 U.S.C. § 230(c)(1) (2012).

9 Van Gelder, *supra* note 6.

10 Short for 'system operator.' *SYSOP*, NetLingo, www.netlingo.com/word/sysop.php.

many of these individuals would contact me asking for advice on how to regain the account which had been taken from them. This was a very early indication of a future in which the growing online environment would need systems to resolve disputes. It was also a valuable lesson for students who would often tell me that their First Amendment rights were being violated. They learned that private companies, CompuServe then and Twitter and Facebook today, are not bound by the First Amendment and can limit expression. The few cases in which a public institution, such as a public university, restricted speech often did provide protection under the First Amendment.[11]

Discussion groups, more commonly called newsgroups, were also available on a service called Usenet. Created in 1979 by two Duke University students, Usenet was accessible to the public and did not have a 'centralized management authority.'[12] Between 1983 and 1993, "Usenet's growth continued to exceed the expectations of developers and site operators alike. The addition of more servers and their users led to disorder and chaos."[13] As described by Professor Jonathan Zittrain, co-founder of Harvard's Berkman Klein Center for Internet and Society and one-time CompuServe sysop, in the

> early days newsgroups simply ran themselves... bothersome members found their posts without audiences as other members configured their software to have a 'kill file' and filter out messages from those sources; without an audience the 'troublemakers' as often as not would move on to another group or beg forgiveness from the existing one. Social forces functioned brilliantly to maintain order so long as participants craved each other's respect.[14]

However, as Professor Zittrain, writing in 1997, also pointed out,

> [C]ommerce found the Internet. Given the current state of the Net it's hard to believe, even as one who saw it firsthand, that the old Net enjoyed an obeyed if unenforced ban on commercial solicitations and advertisements. Those who strayed into mass advertising in newsgroups were dealt with mercilessly, and the strayers cared enough about the views of their peers (or, if one is more cynical, about the overstuffing of their own email boxes with their peers' angry complaints) to desist. Indeed, it was a seismic event when an otherwise-obscure law firm explicitly decided to start advertising within newsgroups, complaints be damned. Normative forces are simultaneously

11 *See,* for example, *United States v. Alkhabaz,* 104 F.3d 1492 (6th Cir. 1997).

12 Andrew Anderson, *What is Usenet, Anyway?*, TLDP (7 March 1996), www.tldp.org/LDP/nag/node257.html.

13 *Giganews' Usenet History*, Giganews, www.giganews.com/usenet-history/.

14 Jonathan Zittrain, *The Rise and Fall of Sysopdom,* 10 Harv. J. L. & Tech. 495, 499 (1997).

> strong and vulnerable, perhaps unchallenged and dominant for years yet suited to near-instant unraveling in the presence of a few unchecked norm-flouters: once a few people cut in line or walk carelessly across the groomed Commons, a stampede is not far behind.[15]

Zittrain was discussing the online environment in the early to mid-1990s, but even in the late eighties several glimpses of future problems had begun to appear. In November of 1988, Robert Morris, a graduate student at Cornell University, released a computer worm that shut down the entire internet for more than a day.[16] This was a remarkable enough event to prompt a *New York Times* article, an article also notable for the paper's first reference to the 'internet.'[17]

At about the same time, distribution of pornography started to become an issue. In the words of one researcher,

> [t]ransmitting porn across the Internet was in violation of the NSF and Federal Acceptable Use Policies, but was quite popular when it uploaded, usually in a hidden location. We had to police it because we did not want to be written up about federal dollars being used to transport porn (and possibly have federal funding cut off because of it).[18]

2 The 1990s: More Users, More Disputes

As noted earlier, for its first 20 or so years, the internet was a limited network. It was limited in functionality, usability, and reach. In the mid-1980s, there were not enough links to generate the network effect necessary for most of the disputes we see today. The World Wide Web was not invented until 1989 and was purely textual in its original state. After 1989, the Web and a system called Gopher were helpful in linking information stored in different places, but it was not until the lifting of the ban on commercial activity in 1992, the development of Web browsers that could display colorful images in 1993, and the appearance of the first internet service providers shortly thereafter, that the proliferation of visually appealing and easy to access sites began to attract large numbers of new users.

---

15 *Id.*

16 Timothy B. Lee, *How a Grad Student Trying to Build the First Botnet Brought the Internet to Its Knees*, Wash. Post (1 November 2013), www.washingtonpost.com/news/the-switch/wp/2013/11/01/how-a-grad-student-trying-to-build-the-first-botnet-brought-the-internet-to-its-knees/.

17 John Markoff, *Author of Computer "Virus" is Son of N.S.A. Expert on Data Security*, N.Y. Times (5 November 1988), www.nytimes.com/1988/11/05/us/author-of-computer-virus-is-son-of-nsa-expert-on-data-security.html?pagewanted=all. It should be noted that editions of the *Times* in the late 1850s also used the word internet but it is not clear what the meaning of the word was then.

18 Medin, *supra* note 4, at 10.

As these new developments coalesced, a growth industry of users began in turn to establish a growth industry of disputes. Many students who had lost their AOL or CompuServe accounts while in high school were now enrolled in universities and eager and skillful enough to take advantage of their university's internet connectivity. A wave of issues around the use and access of the new technology, ranging from using the internet for personal emails to using it to send online chain letters, began to crest. Some of those students became involved in disputes as they violated their university's or the NSFNET Acceptable Use Policy.

As commercial activity on the internet – and the increasing size of the internet audience – began to grow, more attention was focused on those who violated norms. The beginning of spam, referred to earlier by Professor Zittrain, is generally attributed to a 1994 posting by Laurence Canter and Martha Siegel, two immigration lawyers seeking clients. If the posting had been to a Usenet newsgroup 10 years earlier, it might have been ignored or led to some name calling, and almost certainly forgotten relatively quickly. By 1994, however, times had changed enough so that Canter and Siegel are still remembered today by those who were online at the time. What they did was neither the first actual case of spam sent to Usenet[19] nor the first case of spam sent by email – but it was the first case that attracted considerable media attention and motivated large numbers of users to complain.

By the mid-1990s, certain types of internet activity did begin to 'go viral.' In October 1995, a student posted a message on a World Wide Web site for gay men. The message called for gay men to be castrated and 'die a slow death.' The person responsible – a student at Virginia Tech – was disciplined for violating a policy that prohibited the 'use [of] mail or messaging services to harass, intimidate or otherwise annoy another person.' The Dean of Students stated that the university's position was, "if you use our server, then you have some responsibilities because you associate the name of the institution with what you say."[20]

This was only the beginning of a rash of problematic behavior, the precedent to many misogynous, homophobic, and racist online acts to come. Another brand of transgressive communication, called 'flaming,'[21] was also commonplace on listservs. This kind of over the top verbal attack typically required the listserv moderator to manage the dispute, often by removing the offending party from the list. In 1994, I started a listserv called

19 *Newsgroup Spam*, Wikipedia, https://en.wikipedia.org/wiki/Newsgroup_spam (last modified 17 February 2016, at 03:33); Brad Templeton, *Origin of the Term "Spam" to Mean Net Abuse*, Templetons, www.templetons.com/brad/spamterm.html.

20 Michael D. Shear, *Free Speech Gets Tangled in the 'Net; Colleges Try to Balance Rights, Cybersensitivity*, Wash. Post (23 October 1995), www.highbeam.com/doc/1P2-861701.html.

21 Richard T. Griffiths, *Chapter Three: History of Electronic Mail, in History of the Internet, Internet for Historians (and Just about Everyone Else)*, Leiden U. (October 2002), www.let.leidenuniv.nl/history/ivh/chap3.htm.

Dispute-res. Somewhat ironically, during the very first week, a subscriber flamed the list, generating hostile exchanges for two weeks until the individual left the list.

As the population of users grew and more and more information rich, easily navigable Web sites appeared, the internet and the World Wide Web began to receive a lot of media attention. Not surprisingly, entrepreneurs were discovering it as well. In 1994, e-commerce was still in its infancy, talked about but not really practiced. In 1995, however, eBay (originally called AuctionWeb) and Amazon would make their debut on the Web, alongside the first search engines.

Ebay launched on Labor Day, 1995. Disputes about transactions were present almost immediately – and the "[o]ne thing [eBay founder] Omidyar[22] knew was that he did not want to arbitrate all of these disputes."[23] When receiving email complaints, Omidyar would himself write back to the buyer and seller together, asking them to 'work it out.'[24] Omidyar also recognized, however, that this was not a sustainable approach. In February 1996, he established a Feedback Rating system, where parties to a transaction could praise or criticize each other. This allowed users to acquire a reputation, thus establishing a level of trust, reducing perceived risk and, it was hoped, reducing the number of contested transactions.

This did not, however, cure the dispute problem. By May 1996, eBay was receiving 50 to 100 emails a day from users. The company selected an active user from Vermont, Jim Griffith, and invited him to be its first customer service employee. Griffith "spent a lot of time doing what Omidyar hated: stepping in and trying to resolve disputes."[25]

Coincidentally, during that same month, the National Center for Automated Information Research (NCAIR) sponsored the first conference on online dispute resolution.[26] The rationale for the meeting was stated as follows:

> System operators in today's online environment face a difficult choice when their subscribers, or third parties, bring to their attention allegations of tortious communications appearing on their system (e.g., messages alleged to infringe the rights of a copyright holder, defamatory messages, or the like). Taking no action at all in the face of such an allegation would appear to be unreasonable... At the same time, simply removing the allegedly tortious communication is equally unsatisfactory; the allegation may, of course, prove to be a false one, and the removal of the communications unfairly and unnecessarily impacts on the communication of third parties who have engaged in no wrongdoing. And determining whether the communication in

22 Pierre Omidyar, eBay's founder.

23 Adam Cohen, *The Perfect Store: Inside Ebay*. Back Bay Books, 2003. p. 27.

24 *Id.*

25 *Id.*, at 36.

26 Dispute Resolution Conference (22 May 1996), www.umass.edu/dispute/ncair/.

> question is, or is not, tortious may be extremely difficult; it may not be clear from an examination of any particular message whether it contains infringing, or defamatory, material.[27]

As a result of the meeting, NCAIR decided to fund three experiments: the Virtual Magistrate project at Villanova University Law School,[28] the Online Ombuds Office at the University of Massachusetts[29] and a family law project at the University of Maryland employing the internet.[30] This was, in effect, the beginning of the online dispute resolution movement.

Two years later, eBay had over 700,000 users and one and a half million items for sale. In December 1998, it asked the National Center for Technology and Dispute Resolution at the University of Massachusetts[31] to conduct a pilot project to see whether disputes between buyers and sellers could be mediated online. Starting in mid-March 1999, a link was placed on the eBay customer service page informing users that they could obtain assistance in transaction-related disputes by clicking on a link and filling out a complaint form, which went to an experienced mediator at the Center. Ebay did not, at the beginning, publicize the link, and the customer service page was two levels down on its site. Even so, during the first two week period, 225 buyers and sellers found the link and filed complaints. The mediator used email to communicate with the parties – a labor-intensive approach, but one that succeeded in reaching a positive resolution in more than half of the disputes.[32]

The growing population of internet users during the 1990s also led to an extraordinary increase in the registration of domain names. A domain name is a kind of address and, in the days before search engines, was useful in locating a particular Web site. The number of .com domain names increased from 1,151 in October 1990[33] to 1,301,000 in July 1997, to more than 20 million in November 2000.[34] Even in the middle of that period, however, many corporations were unaware of what a domain

27 Robert Gellman, *A Brief History of the Virtual Magistrate Project: The Early Months*, The On-Line Disp. Resol. Conf. (22 May 1996), www.umass.edu/dispute/ncair/gellman.htm.

28 *Id.*

29 Ethan Katsh, *The Online Ombuds Office: Adapting Dispute Resolution to Cyberspace*, The On-Line Disp. Resol. Conf. (22 May 1996), www.umass.edu/dispute/ncair/katsh.htm.

30 Richard S. Granat, *Creating an Environment for Mediating Disputes on the Internet*, The On-Line Disp. Resol. Conf. (22 May 1996), www.umass.edu/dispute/ncair/granat.htm.

31 The National Center for Technology and Dispute Resolution (NCTDR), originally the Center for Technology and Dispute Resolution, was established in 1997 by Ethan Katsh and Janet Rifkin with a grant from the Hewlett Foundation to the University of Massachusetts. Leah Wing became Co-director in 2018.

32 Ethan Katsh et al., *E-Commerce, E-Disputes, and E-Dispute Resolution: In the Shadow of "eBay Law"*, 15 Ohio St. J. Disp. Resol. 705 (2000) [hereinafter Katsh et al., *E-commerce, E-Disputes*].

33 *The Internet in 1990: Domain Registration, E-mail and Networks*, IAPS, www.iaps.com/internet-history-october-1990.html#email.

34 *History of gTLD Domain Name Growth*, ZookNIC, www.zooknic.com/Domains/counts.html.

name was or how valuable it might be. A company called Network Solutions was the sole source of domain names; the cost to register a domain name was one hundred dollars for two years. Today, there are 350 million domain names and registering one can cost as little as five dollars.

In October 1994, Joshua Quittner, a journalist for Wired Magazine,[35] registered McDonalds.com, then contacted McDonalds to see if they were interested in owning it. They did not seem to be aware of what domain names were or how they worked. Later, domain names grew in both number and value, and a relatively simple system for addressing trademark disputes over domain name registration and use was developed by Network Solutions' successor, the Internet Corporation for Assigned Names and Numbers (ICANN).

3 Post-2000

By the turn of the 21st century, the landscape of disputes on the internet was radically different from its earlier relatively tranquil and sparsely populated state. New types of disputes were emerging, often in large numbers, stemming from frequent interactions that took place virtually and globally, in very short time frames, often involving algorithms and thin textual communication. These were disputes for which traditional face-to-face dispute resolution mechanisms – courts and ADR – were, for the most part, unavailable. Novel means for addressing online conflicts were now needed, ones that could likewise handle masses of disputes, at a low cost, in short time frames.

The need for new dispute resolution approaches became all the more pressing in the first decade of the 21st century as internet use skyrocketed, social networks evolved quickly from a means for college students to interact with each other to worldwide phenomena, smartphones appeared and became a primary vehicle for online access for a growing number of people, and digital communication became the primary avenue for connecting with anyone anywhere. As this is being written at the beginning of 2021, conflicts of an enormous variety – relating to claims of 'fake news,' anonymous comments, intellectual property breaches, accuracy of edits to crowd sourced sites, harassment from trolls, invasions of privacy, manipulation of and an inability to avoid user generated reviews, phishing and ransomware, and large numbers of social media related conflicts – have all become an integral and familiar part of online activity, and, consequently, of most people's lives. We anticipate that Covid-19 will generate its own universe of disputes.

35 Joshua Quittner, *Billions Registered*, Wired (1 October 1994), http://archive.wired.com/wired/archive/2.10/mcdonalds.html.

4 THE EVOLUTION OF THE FIELD OF ODR: FROM 'ONLINE ADR' TO ODR

ODR emerged from an online environment that was rich with misunderstandings and disputes but deficient in avenues for effectively addressing them. Originally, the intent of ODR was not to displace, challenge, or disrupt an existing legal regime or familiar ADR processes. Rather, its goal was to fill the vacuum involving online disputes where the law's authority was absent or inadequate, and to provide 'new and better ways to resolve the disputes that arise in connection with [network] use.'[36] Developers of early ODR mechanisms, however, tended to mimic the dispute resolution channels of traditional ADR processes and offer online equivalents. 'When a new online technology is created for any process,' it has been noted, 'the initial impulse is to create online mirror images of the "live" or offline process.'[37] In such instances, "[s]ome agencies aim to replicate exactly their current processes online. Public agency staff may have been using the existing system for so long that it may be difficult for them to envision the new system as something other than an online replica of their offline process."[38]

In reality, however, attempts to copy ADR in the online setting proved to be a difficult task and ODR began to develop processes with features that were clearly different from traditional dispute resolution. First, in the pre-ZOOM time period, convenient, asynchronous substitutes for face-to-face interaction were needed. Second, new processes began to automatically record all dispute data; and third, new processes were based on the intelligence of the machine. Many of these features were initially viewed as shortcomings – a challenge of format to overcome. However, they are now seen as benefits. For example, while the lack of face-to-face interaction does reduce the richness of communication, it also conveys advantages for those who employ asynchronous communication, such as time to consult and conduct research before replying. Similarly, the decrease in privacy and confidentiality due to documentation can assist in quality control and dispute prevention efforts. Finally, the intelligence of the machine can enhance efficiency through automation and artificial intelligence (AI), allowing ODR systems to handle staggeringly large numbers of small scale conflicts.

36 David R. Johnson, *Dispute Resolution in Cyberspace*, Electronic Frontier Found. (10 February 1994), http://w2.eff.org/legal/online_dispute_resolution_johnson.article.txt.

37 Daniel Rainey and Ethan Katsh, *ODR and Government*, *in* Online Dispute Resolution: Theory and Practice: A Treatise on Technology and Dispute Resolution 248 (M. S. Wahab et al. eds., 2012).

38 Colin Rule and Mark Wilson, *Online Resolution and Citizen Empowerment: Property Tax Appeals in North America*, *in* Revolutionizing the Interaction Between State and Citizens Through Digital Communications 185 (Sam B. Edwards III & Diogo Santos eds., Hershey, Pennsylvania: I GI Global 2015).

5 From Tools to Systems

The eBay ODR system is probably the best known ODR system, and the one with the most impressive achievements in terms of volume and system design. As noted above, the need for addressing and anticipating problems was part of eBay culture from the start. Ebay was aggressive in establishing a user rating system to try to build trust and prevent disputes. The company was intent on creating an online community for its users, emphasizing the good intentions of most users and the need to communicate once problems arose.[39] Following the UMass pilot program in 1999, eBay contracted with the startup SquareTrade to develop an ODR system that would address the types of problems that arose on the site and that could handle large numbers of disputes. The end-product was a two-stage process of technology-assisted negotiation, using online forms as a first stage to make claims, exchange demands, identify options and explore settlement possibilities, then escalating to an online mediation involving a human mediator if no settlement were reached in the first stage. The SquareTrade system was revolutionary in that it represented a shift in attitude towards the digital medium. It was no longer considered necessary to mimic labor-intensive offline processes. Instead, the differences between communicating face to face and online were embraced, ultimately producing a new type of software-assisted process that had not existed in the physical environment.

By substituting software for a human, and breaking down the mediation process into small components, technology-assisted negotiation could, albeit in a different way, perform many of the tasks previously performed by a human facilitator and could easily scale to an extraordinarily large numbers of cases. These component tasks, presented parties with choices that included identifying dispute types; exposing parties' interests; asking questions about positions; reframing demands; suggesting options for solutions; allowing some venting; establishing a time frame; keeping parties informed; disaggregating issues; matching solutions to problems; and drafting agreements.[40] This kind of extracting, parsing and processing of information from the parties involved enabled SquareTrade to create a Web-based system which could quickly respond to large numbers of disputes in the same ways human mediators might address a single dispute in face-to-face mediation.

By 2003, when eBay hired Colin Rule to develop in-house systems for handling disputes, the SquareTrade system was handling several million disputes per year. By the time Rule (who also developed a system for PayPal) left in 2011 to start Modria.com, eBay systems were handling over 60 million disputes a year.

---

39 *About Community Member Spotlight*, eBay, http://community.ebay.com/.

40 Steve Abernethy, *Trusted Access to the Global Digital Economy/Square Trade International ODR Case Study*, UNECE Forum on Online Disp. Resol. (6-7 June 2002).

The eBay ODR process was notable in that it introduced the concept of an ODR *system* as opposed to an ODR *tool*. In an ODR *system*, data is generated that reveals patterns of disputes and provides opportunities to both facilitate and monitor consensual agreements, thus making disputes in the future less likely.[41] In all the situations described in this book in which very large numbers of disputes are managed, an organized communication and data processing system is employed.

Most contributions of technology to ODR to date have involved the development of tools: specific dispute resolution applications that can be used to help resolve disputes that arise both online and offline, often a specific task that can help a neutral to resolve such disputes. Cybersettle, for example, developed a blind bidding system that could be employed in all disputes over money. SmartSettle designed more elaborate blind bidding software that could be employed in a multi-part dispute. A National Science Foundation project at the University of Massachusetts developed software that produced a highly detailed model of the brainstorming process and could assist parties who wished to brainstorm at a distance. This replaced the use of paper flipcharts, the most common brainstorming tool employed in face-to-face negotiations.[42] Daniel Rainey, Chief of Staff of the U.S. National Mediation Board developed a variety of ODR tools that were employed in disputes occurring in the airline and railroad industries.

Many in the ADR field have assumed that the future of ODR lies in an expanding array of such tools that will open up new options for third parties to help reach agreement.[43] During the last 10 years, as mediators have become more comfortable with the use of technology, the demand for software applications that can perform a discrete function and can be plugged into their practice in some way has also increased.[44] A variety of ODR providers have, for some time, been operating online platforms that allow mediators and arbitrators, wherever they might be, to exchange documents and communicate with parties without having to meet face to face. These ODR tools are so effective that they are now used to facilitate the mediation process even when the disputants are in the same room and the conflicts have nothing to do with being online. In all likelihood, we can look forward to seeing an ongoing evolution of more and more powerful software tools that can be plugged into more and more complicated disputes

41 *Id.*

42 Ethan Katsh et al., *Process Technology for Achieving Government Online Dispute Resolution*, *in* Proceedings of the 2004 Annual National Conference on Digital Government Research 1-2 (dg.o '04 ed. 2004).

43 Katsh et al., *E-Commerce, E-Disputes*, *supra* note 32, at 90-116; David A. Larson, *Technology Mediated Dispute Resolution (TMDR): A New Paradigm for ADR*, 38 U. of Tol. L. Rev. 213, 215-217 (2006); Arno R. Lodder and John Zeleznikow, *Enhanced Dispute Resolution Through the Use of Information Technology*, 10 Harv. Negot. L. Rev. 287 (2010).

44 For example, the use of software for an online brainstorming process. *See* Ethan Katsh and Leah Wing, *Ten Years of Online Dispute Resolution: Looking at the Past and Constructing the Future*, 38 Tol. L. Rev 101 (2006). *See also* DebateGraph, http://debategraph.org (Debatagraph's visualization tools are used for exploring various aspects of a problem and potential solutions).

The most widespread recently adopted tool is the video conferencing app ZOOM. ZOOM facilitates video communication real time. It is user friendly and works with small and medium sized groups as well as with two individuals. It had been used occasionally before the pandemic closed physical court buildings but, as this is being written, it is probably the most used online tool. It does not, however, take advantage of the intelligence of the machine. Does simple online communication make ZOOM ODR? Is, for example, a pencil or a flipchart ADR because these simple offline tools can be employed to manage part of the offline dispute resolution process? Or, can email itself be considered ODR? One can argue both sides of this but to this author it seems that however valuable ZOOM is as a tool, communication alone does not transform it into ODR.

In the late 1990s, the developers of two ODR applications, Cybersettle and Smartsettle, identified elements of the traditional dispute resolution process where the use of information was inefficient, and aimed to improve it. Cybersettle developed a fairly simple application that facilitated 'blind bidding' online. It was originally aimed at malpractice claims but useable in any negotiation involving money, it enabled one party to instruct a machine as to how much that party was willing to pay, and the other party instructed the machine the minimum that party would accept. The parties agreed that if the offer and demand were within some percentage of each other, they would split the difference and settle. If they were not within range, there would be no settlement and the offer and demand numbers would not be revealed to either party.[45]

Blind bidding was a simple and creative way of doing something online that was relatively inefficient to do offline. It took advantage of the machine's capability for both calculating and communicating, and for following a programmed rule to decide whether there would be a settlement or not. This allowed parties to overcome tactics often employed in face-to-face negotiations that hinder the reaching of an agreement despite the existence of a 'zone of possible agreement.'[46] In later years, use of Cybersettle's software tool expanded beyond malpractice cases to include monetary claims against the City of New York. (Unfortunately, the company was never able to capture a large market and is no longer in existence.)

SmartSettle was developed by an engineer and computer scientist, Ernest Thiessen, who found that the introduction of technology into a *Getting to Yes* interest-based negotiation could increase the likelihood of parties reaching win-win outcomes. Building on the insights provided by game theory, Smartsettle software had parties list their interests and assign numerical values to them, thereby creating a weighted spectrum of issues along which the parties could negotiate. Based on the parties' input, the software

---

45 Paul Kirgis, *Cybersettle and the Value of Online Dispute Resolution*, Indisputably (7 July 2010), www.indisputably.org/?p=1456.

46 *See* Robert H. Mnookin et al., *Beyond Winning: Negotiating to Create Value in Deals and Disputes* 2004, pp. 18-22; Lodder and Zeleznikow, *supra* note 43, at 40, n. 3.

generated various 'packages' or combinations of issues and preferences that might satisfy both parties. The software created a graph as a visual display of the level of satisfaction each package of issues represented for the parties in light of their own initial ranking of interests. Furthermore, Thiessen built a unique optimization feature that suggested other combinations that might meet the needs of both parties better than the agreement they had negotiated.[47]

SmartSettle, which could even be used in complex multi-party and multi-issue disputes[48] used technology in a much more complex way than Cybersettle. What both shared was a design that could facilitate resolution in a context in which the parties might not meet. These software programs could operate as add-ons for a mediator or, on occasion, possibly even as a replacement for one. In Smartsettle's case, an algorithm supported an ODR system that could be adapted to many different types of disputes, that could be employed in large numbers of cases in different disputes, and that used the computer in a way that went beyond mimicking what a human mediator might do.

The Hewlett Foundation grant to the University of Massachusetts in 1997 for the establishment of the National Center for Technology and Dispute Resolution (NCTDR) was intended to foster the growth of the field of ODR. The following are examples of the framework for a new field has been put in place during the last two decades.

- Management of the ODR.info Web site.
- ODR courses, the initial ones taught by Leah Wing, Alan Gaitenby and Ethan Katsh at UMass, then by Daniel Rainey at Southern Methodist University and by David Larson at Mitchell Hamline Law School.
- The International Journal of Online Dispute Resolution was established in 2014.
- An online conference called ODR Cyberweek has been organized annually since 1998.
- Since 2002, an annual international ODR conference has been held in 19 different locations around the world.
- NCTDR has, via a Fellows program begun in 1998, participated in working groups with a variety of ADR and judicial organizations.
- Assisted in the establishment of the International Council of Online Dispute Resolution (ICODR) in 2019.
- Created an extensive ODR bibliography, accessible at ODR.info and supported publication of an award-winning book Online Dispute Resolution: Theory and Practice by Rainey, Katsh and Wahab. A second edition is forthcoming.

47 Ernest M. Thiessen and Joseph P. McMahon, *Beyond Win-Win in Cyberspace*, 15 Ohio St. J. on Disp. Resol. 643, 647-648 (2000).

48 *Id.*, at 648.

6 ODR Systems Design: The Dispute Resolution and Prevention Triangle

Katsh and Rifkin's early book on ODR, *Online Dispute Resolution: Resolving Conflicts in Cyberspace,*[49] pointed out that any successful dispute resolution system can be represented by a triangle. The three sides of the triangle each represent an essential element to a dispute resolution process: convenience and efficiency, expertise and intelligence, and trust. Any ODR system should include all three elements, but not necessarily to the same degree. All three are needed if the system is to attract users but the length of each side of the triangle can change and, by doing so, emphasize that more of one element is present than another.

The benefits of ODR in the 2000s and 2010s were mostly in the area of convenience: they allowed communication at a distance, and asynchronously – with participation at any time. These simple improvements removed many long established physical constraints or boundaries of time and space. Expertise, in the sense of taking advantage of the computer's processing capabilities, was yet to be fully exploited. Until recently, the 'convenience' side of the triangle in ODR was usually the longest. This is now changing as more systems, as opposed to tools, are being developed, as the possibilities of AI are being recognized, and as efforts to employ blockchain processes are being carries out.

A second contribution of the Katsh and Rifkin book is that it provided the field with the metaphor of the 'Fourth Party.'[50] The metaphor suggests that technology can be an aid to a human third party, or even to the first and second parties, in a dispute resolution process.[51] It originally emphasized the network's novel communications tools that enable a human third party to interact with parties at a distance.[52] In substituting online communication for offline, the network provided convenience to participants in that travel was avoided and more options for times to communicate were available. This represents the simplest use of technology tools. The Fourth Party now provides a conceptual framework for understanding the use of more complex tools and systems and also, in the process, of building trust in new ways.

The goals of convenience, expertise, and trust are, of course, also the goals of face-to-face dispute resolution. Gathering, evaluating, and communicating information are at the heart of all dispute resolution processes, online or offline. Digital tools that further these goals should be attractive no matter what kind of dispute has occurred. ODR, as a result, has, for some time, been more focused on the tools that are employed than on where the dispute originated. While use of ODR is still more common in disputes that emerged

---

49 Ethan Katsh and Janet Rifkin, *Online Dispute Resolution: Resolving Conflicts in Cyberspace.* 2001. pp. 73-92.

50 Katsh and Rifkin, *supra* note 49, at 73-92.

51 L. Wing, J. Martinez, E. Katsh and C. Rule, *Designing Ethical Online Dispute Resolution Systems: The Rise of the Fourth Party,* J. Negotiation. v. 31, 2021, p. 1.

52 Lodder and Zeleznikow, *supra* note 43, at 79 (introducing the fifth party, which represents the provider of the technology).

online, the future will involve ODR tools and systems used in both online and offline disputes, especially as this very distinction becomes more and more elusive.

An important catalyst for increasing the use of ODR will likely be the enhancement of the expertise side of the triangle. This will be the payoff of the increased use of algorithms, in the role of advisor or, in some instances, by replacing the human dispute handler. Such developments hold a promise for increased efficiency and capacity and, potentially, consistency. They also create the necessary data-based infrastructure required for studying the incidence of disputes, and therefore enable us to develop strategies for preventing conflicts from recurring.

Current ODR ventures are becoming more aggressive in using technology to enhance or substitute for the expertise of a mediator.[53] In the future, we will see increasingly intelligent machines using rich data that has been collected in various contexts to enable or suggest solutions to parties. We can also expect to see problems arising from increased use of algorithms. The evolution of the use, meaning, and impact of ODR is accelerating, as it needs to be in an era in which disputing is a growth industry and building consensus in a growing number of areas is increasingly difficult. Once focused on imitating ADR processes and specific only to addressing conflicts that arose online (mostly in the e-commerce setting or on online social media forums), the innovative applications and new features of ODR as they are being developed are increasingly being perceived as applicable to a broad range of disputes, including those that arise offline. The growing awareness of the type, variety, and potential of these tools has spurred the development and adoption of ODR in many new settings, including government agencies, courts, and international organizations. As experience with ODR grows, we can expect to see its integration into the dispute resolution field continue and expand.

While this chapter has focused on the past, it would be neglectful not to include some consideration of the present. The main reason for this is that Covid-19 has drastically changed the disputing and dispute resolution landscapes and, as a consequence, the ODR landscape. Covid-19 is most obviously a health emergency but it is creating other kinds of emergencies as various traditional institutions prove to be ineffective. In such a crisis, it is reasonable to expect Covid-19 to generate large numbers of disputes and employ dispute resolution of prevention processes that challenge the value of face-to-face dispute resolution processes.

As noted earlier, ZOOM's relationship to the convenience, trust and expertise triangle was largely convenience oriented. It was easy to use and widely available at fairly low cost. ZOOM, however, is not considered by some to be ODR because while it substitutes communications technology for human communication, none of the expertise or intelligence of the human is transferred. It is a tool, not a more pervasive system. Of

53 Wing et al., *supra* note 51.

course, ZOOM and its current or new competitors and emerging start-ups may evolve, add significant technological features, and become a more multi-faceted ODR system.

The main long term contribution of ZOOM to ODR at this point is that it was a demonstration or entry point for many in the dispute resolution field of what is possible with ODR. In the 2010s, many in the dispute resolution field were unaware of ODR and large numbers of others were skeptical of it. ODR now, it is fair to say, is universally known although many may still be skeptical. For many. ZOOM was an introduction to ODR by highlighting and facilitating online communication. ZOOM may not be ODR but it has contributed to the acceptance of ODR by traditional ADR and court communities that have long been resistant to ODR and processes that did not involve face-to-face communication. The experience with ZOOM during the pandemic has provided proof of concept for ODR and set the stage for greater use of ODR in traditional settings. As AI, blockchain and other multi-faceted ODR systems become available, ODR will be seen to be much more than a simple replacement for face to face.

If there is one clear lesson about our approximately 30 year history with ODR it is to be cautious about predicting the future. In 1990, no one would have anticipated the incredible growth of the World Wide Web or e-commerce or Google. In 2000, no one would have predicted the appearance of Facebook or Twitter. In 2015 and later no one would have predicted the impact of the internet on national elections. At the same time, we were and continue to be unprepared for the disputing environment these huge technology platforms will generate. The future of ODR may be hazy but one can be confident that there will be ever growing numbers and kinds of disputes in the future as well as an ever expanding role for technology in dispute resolution and prevention processes.

Chapter 2 Ethical Principles and Standards for Online Dispute Resolution

Leah Wing and Daniel Rainey

1 Introduction

After practicing mediation for more than 15 years, she decided to add online dispute resolution to her tool kit. She had already been using email of course, and had increasingly used a popular software for collaboratively writing agreements; but she hadn't considered adding a video conferencing option until the pandemic made it a necessity. But now she saw it made sense to continue to offer it even after social distancing is no longer necessary. After all, it seemed that almost everyone was becoming accustomed to communicating via video and her mediation practice needed to keep pace with changes in expectations for how people can connect. As she contemplated whether to use the same video conference platform she employed to chat with her friends and family, a set of concerns came to her mind: How will I know if someone else is in the room with one of the parties? How can I ensure that one party doesn't record the session and post it on social media? Even if they sign an agreement not to, what could be the implications for my practice if they do it anyway? What liability do I carry for the security of the data? While technology most often works smoothly, what if a feature of the system fails and what I thought was a private session can be viewed by another party?

He had never purchased from this website before. It had an overall good rating which he had checked out before he made the $105 purchase of a gorgeous bouquet of flowers. He was using his savings for this gift for his grandmother's 75th birthday so he wanted to ensure the flowers would arrive on time and as ordered. When they didn't, his birthday surprise was ruined. So, he immediately emailed customer service and received an automated response offering him a coupon for $25 off a future purchase. It was not likely he'd be purchasing flowers again any time soon and certainly not from that site! When he mentioned this to his manager, she said that when something similar had happened after purchasing flowers from that same website, she had gotten a full refund. Why was he offered a different solution to his problem? He began to wonder if his lack of having purchased from that site before had been a factor. Had the company used other information from his digital trail – his social media or credit card history, for example – to see how much money he spends? Were they able to tell how much his friends on social media spend on similar items in case he was to complain to them about the site? Why was his dollar worth less than his manager's – someone who appeared to have and spend more money than he did? Was the company's offer to resolve his dispute generated by machine learning algorithms? How could he find out? If he wrote to customer service to complain would he be communicating with a person or negotiating with a computer?

The role of technology in dispute handling has moved from the margins into the forefront of the field, and this chapter will explore the implications for ethical practice in light of the rapid and dramatic changes underway. While it is only relatively recently that a majority of dispute resolution practitioners have begun to innovate by including different forms of technology they use in their personal lives into their practice, certainly, businesses have long incorporated multiple forms of online dispute resolution (ODR) by including dispute prevention strategies such as reputational rating and platforms that facilitate negotiation between buyers and sellers in e-marketplaces. However, as online dispute resolution is moving into the middle of its third decade, it has finally begun to make significant headway beyond its usage in ecommerce,[1] in courts (as explored

1 *See* Thompson, A. "Design Approaches for Optimal ODR." *International Journal of Online Dispute Resolution*, 6(2), 2019, 212-218; van Gelder, E. "The EU Approach to Consumer ODR." *International Journal of Online Dispute Resolution*, 6(2), 2019, 219-226; Vilalta Nicuesa, A.E. "Reputational Feedback Systems and Consumer Rights: Improving the European Online Redress System." *International Journal of Online Dispute Resolution*, 5(1-2), 2018, 122-142; Katsh, E. and Rabinovich-Einy, O. *Digital Justice*. Oxford: OUP, 2017, 57-79; Schmitz, A.J. and Rule, C. *The New Handshake: Online Dispute Resolution and the Future of Consumer Protection*. Chicago, IL: American Bar Association Section on Dispute Resolution, 2017; Cortes, P. *The New Regulatory Framework for Consumer Dispute Resolution*. Oxford: Oxford University Press, 2016; Adamson, C. (Ed.) *Online Dispute Resolution: An International Approach to Solving Consumer Complaints*. Bloomington, IN: Net Neutrals, 2015; Mania, K. "Online Dispute Resolution: The Future of Justice." *International Comparative Jurisprudence*, 1(1), 2015, 76-86; Wang, F.F. *Online Dispute Resolution: Technology, Management and Legal Practice from an International Perspective*. Oxford: Chandos, 2009; Ponte, L.M. and Cavenagh, T.D. *CyberJustice: Online Dispute Resolution (ODR) for E-commerce*. Upper Saddle River, NJ: Pearson/Prentice Hall, 2005; Rule, C. *Online Dispute Resolution for Business: B2B, E-commerce, Consumer, Employment, Insurance, and Other Commercial Conflicts*. San Francisco, CA: Jossey-Bass, 2002; Katsh, E., Rifkin, J. and Gaitenby, A. "Ecommerce, E-disputes, and E-dispute Resolution: In the Shadow of 'eBay Law.'" *Ohio State Journal of Dispute Resolution*, 15(3), 2000, 705-734.

elsewhere in this book),[2] multiparty public dispute resolution,[3] the handling of labor disputes,[4] and increasingly in family mediation[5] and blockchain smart contract

---

2 In this volume *see*: "ODR and the Justice System," Larry Bridgesmith; "ODR and the Courts," Paul Embley; "ODR and Social Justice," Ben Davis. *See also* Susskind, R. *Online Courts and the Future of Justice*. Oxford: Oxford University Press, 2019; Katsh, E. and Rabinovich-Einy, O. *Digital Justice*. Oxford: OUP, 2017, 149-169; Manware, S.B. "Online Dispute Resolution in Traffic Courts and the Impact on Highway Safety." *International Journal of Online Dispute Resolution*, 6(2), 2019, 181-182; Rodrigues, M. "Access to Justice and the Role of ODR Inside and Outside Brazilian Courts." *International Journal of Online Dispute Resolution*, 6(2), 2019, 193-196; Acosta, M., Kulp, H, Marz, S. and Ruckel, J.C. "ODR Best Practices for Court-Connected Programmes from Our Experiences with Court-Based ODR Design Processes." *International Journal of Online Dispute Resolution*, 6(2), 2019, 134-137; Schmitz, A.J. "Expanding Access to Remedies through E-Court Initiatives." *Buffalo Law Review*, 67, 2019, 101-173; Martinez, J., Rule, C. and Yates, S. "Designing a System for the Online Resolution of Cross-Border Custody Disputes." *World Arbitration and Mediation Review*, 12, 2018, 45-69; Leong, O.Y.T. "Access to Justice and Innovative Court Solutions for Litigants-in-Person: The Singapore Experience." *International Journal of Online Dispute Resolution*, 5(1-2), 2018, 9-19.

3 *See* Linden, J. "Listening to the City: Eleven Years Later–Rebuilding the World Trade Center–New York City–ODR Helps Determine the 9/11 World Trade Center Memorial." In Edwards, S.B. and Santos, D. (eds.), *Revolutionizing the Interaction Between State and Citizens Through Digital Communications*. Hershey, PA: Information Science Reference, 2015, 176-199; Gershowitz, J. and Rule, C. *Applying Information and Communications Technology to Multiparty Conflict Resolution Processes*. Washington, DC: Association for Conflict Resolution, 2012; Eisen, J.B. "Are We Ready for Mediation in Cyberspace?" *Brigham Young University Law Review*, (4), 1998, 1305-1358.

4 *See* Katsh, E. and Rabinovich-Einy, O. *Digital Justice*. Oxford: OUP, 2017, 131-148; the American Arbitration Association, available at: www.adr.org/sites/default/files/document_repository/American%20Arbitration%20Association-International%20Centre%20for%20Dispute%20Resolution%20Online%20Clause-Building%20Tool%20Adds%20International%20Clause%20Capability.pdf Last accessed 7 February 2020; Bollen, K. and Euwema, M. "E-Supported Mediation: What Do We Learn From The Field?" National Mediation Conference: Emerging Dynamics in Mediation-New Thinking, New Practices, New Relationships, 10-13 September 2012, available at: www.slideshare.net/NationalMediationConference/e-supported-mediation-bolleneuwema Last accessed 21 June 2020; Clarke, L.A., Gaitenby, A., Gyllstrom, D., Katsh, E., Marzilli, M., Osterweil, L.J., Sondheimer, N.K., Wing, L., Wise, A., and Rainey, D. "A Process-Driven Tool to Support Online Dispute Resolution." International Conference on Digital Government Research, San Diego, CA, May 2006, 356-357; Rule, C. *Online Dispute Resolution for Business: B2B, E-commerce, Consumer, Employment, Insurance, and Other Commercial Conflicts*. San Francisco, CA: Jossey-Bass, 2002.

5 *See* Schmitz, A. and Wing, L. "Beneficial and Ethical ODR for Family Issues." *Family Court Review*, Forthcoming 2021; Ainsworth, N., Zeleznikow, L. and Zeleznikow, J. "Readiness for Family and Online Dispute Resolution." *International Journal of Online Dispute Resolution*, 6(2), 2019, 243-263; Cartwright, M.J. and Greiling, D. "Courts and Court Connected Online Dispute Resolution: Outcomes from Family, Civil, and Traffic Cases in the United States." *International Journal of Online Dispute Resolution*, 5(1-2), 2018, 4-8; Barsky, A.E. "The Ethics of App-Assisted Family Mediation." *Conflict Resolution Quarterly*, 34 (1), Fall 2016, 31-42; Lavi, D. "No More Click-Click in Here: E-Mediation in Divorce Disputes-The Reality and the Desirable." *Cardoza Journal of Conflict Resolution*, 16, 2014-2015, 479-542; Tyler, C., McPherson, M. and McPherson, M.W. "Online Dispute Resolution and Family Disputes." *Journal of Family Studies*, 12(2), 2014, 166-183.

management.[6] The incremental but consistent growth in ODR usage over the past 20 plus years, experienced an exponential leap forward in 2020 in response to the Covid-19 pandemic as dispute resolution entities and practitioners were forced to respond to quarantining and social distancing by employing technology. Now, more than ever, dispute resolution processes affecting virtually every sector of public and private life are being infiltrated by ODR;[7] those who were reluctant or inexperienced at applying technology to dispute handling now have had to experiment with it by force of necessity. Conversations with a variety of dispute resolution practitioners indicate a general feeling that we will not, ever, go back to the pre-Covid normal: technology is here with us to stay in dispute resolution.

Explosion in usage however, has taken place in the absence of sufficient ethical guidance and requirements for training, processes, platforms, and systems design for technology enhanced dispute resolution. While at the time of writing[8] a variety of public and private entities have produced[9] or are presently developing[10] ODR guidance and requirements, there remains no agreement within sectors or legal jurisdictions, or across them on what the governing standards should be for the integration of ODR into existing systems and practices or for its implementation in stand-alone platforms.[11] This leaves gaping holes into which both creative innovation and the worst of human behavior and technology's impact can flourish.

---

6 *See* Vilalta Nicuesa, A.E. "Smart Legal Contracts: A Shift in Conflict Prevention and Dispute Resolution." *International Journal of Online Dispute Resolution*, 6(2), 2019, 239-242; Katsh, E. and Rabinovich-Einy, O. "Blockchain and the Inevitability of Disputes: The Role for Online Dispute Resolution." *Journal of Dispute Resolution*, (2), 2019, 47-75; Metzger, J. "Decentralized Justice in the Era of Blockchain." *International Journal of Online Dispute Resolution*, 5(1-2), 2018, 69-81; Gurkov, A. "Blockchain in Arbitration Development: Multi-Signature Wallet Showcase." *International Journal of Online Dispute Resolution*, 4 (2), 2017, 63-65; van der Linden, T. "ODR and Blockchain." *International Journal of Online Dispute Resolution*, 4(2), 2017, 57-58.

7 The website Remote Courts Worldwide at remotecourts.org was established during the spring of 2020 as Covid-19 shut many courts globally. Within just a few weeks, it had listed dozens of nations' court systems that had begun to utilize video conferencing to handle hearings.

8 This chapter is being completed in summer 2020 as the Covid-19 pandemic is still raging in most of the world.

9 Examples that emerged in 2020 in the face of the pandemic include the International Council on Dispute Resolution guidelines for video usage in mediation and arbitration, ODR Training Components Guidelines, and ODR Standards for Payment Platforms; as well as guidance for Using Zoom to Conduct Online Mediation published by the Michigan Supreme Court Office of Dispute Resolution. References to these and other standards and guidance documents can be found at odr.info on the National Center for Technology and Dispute Resolution website. Last accessed 20 June 2020.

10 For example, at the time of writing, the American Bar Association, International Council for Online Dispute Resolution and the National Center for Technology and Dispute Resolution are collaborating on drafting standards for ODR systems, processes, and practitioners.

11 Acosta, M., Kulp, H., Marz, S. and Ruckel, J.C. "ODR Best Practices for Court-Connected Programmes from Our Experiences with Court-Based ODR Design Processes." *International Journal of Online Dispute Resolution*, 6(2), 2019, 134-137.

This chapter highlights the importance of such ethical guidance for the development and operation of online dispute resolution; and it explores questions about its implementation through principles useful for self-monitoring and the importance of standards or rules promulgated through policy, regulation and legislation by public and private entities for accountability. We explore questions central to the governance of dispute resolution processes that deploy information and communication technology (ICT); particularly with regards to ensuring that the core tenets of dispute resolution practice are not only protected, but can be enhanced by ICT use.

ICT and ADR (which together create ODR) are a natural fit. It has been argued that third parties

> engage in three activities on a regular basis: managing communication with the parties, helping the parties deal with information ... , and managing group dynamics.[12]

ICT is liberating, in that it expands the available communication channels, offers new, effective ways of dealing with information and data, and even helps redefine the concept of a working group. However, technology is also disruptive. It changes the perimeters of data collection, information exchange, and how we can organize and understand that data. Not only do communication patterns change through the use of ICT but so, too, do the way they can appear to us. For example, opportunities to communicate asynchronistically as well as simultaneously alter communication through access to multiple channels (such as visuals, text, and verbal). Technology-infused dispute resolution offers enhancements in the form of both new tools with which to work, and new spaces in which to communicate, but these inevitably also are tools and spaces in which to create conflict.[13] Therefore, it makes sense that innovative practitioners, theorists, and entrepreneurs have been conceptualizing new ways technology can be harnessed to help prevent and resolve disputes.

The first ODR experiment focused on handling disputes solely online[14] and developed further with reliance on algorithms and generally applicable dispute resolution models to handle cases that arose and were handled online. And eventually ODR technology came to be employed during face-to-face (f2f) sessions as well, so that now

> the idea of ODR as a fully self-contained online mode of work is ... really [only] a feature of ecommerce [and increasingly the courts] not mainstream ADR.[15]

---

12 Rainey, D., "Conflict Management and ICT: Evolution and Revolution." *The International Journal of Online Dispute Resolution*, 2(3), 2016, 78. *See also* Katsh, E. and Rifkin, J. *Online Dispute Resolution: Resolving Conflicts in Cyberspace.* San Francisco: Jossey-Bass, 2001.

13 For a more extensive discussion *see* Wing, L. and Rainey, D. "Online Dispute Resolution and the Development of Theory." In Wahab, M., Katsh, E., and Rainey, D. (eds.), *Online Dispute Resolution: Theory and Practice.* The Hague: Eleven International Publishing, 2012, 23-38.

14 Katsh, E. and Rifkin, J. *Online Dispute Resolution: Resolving Conflicts in Cyberspace.* San Francisco: Jossey-Bass, 2001.

15 Rainey, D. "Conflict Engagement and ICT: Evolution and Revolution." *The International Journal of Online Dispute Resolution*, 2(3), 2016, 77-83. *See also* Carrel, A. and Ebner, N. "Mind the Gap: Bringing Technology to the Mediation Table." *The Journal of Dispute Resolution*, 2019(2), Art. 5.

Early discussions about using technology for dispute resolution raised excitement about its capabilities for enhancing the core values of the field. For example, it could increase time and cost efficiency by reducing the need of parties and intervenors to take time away from work and family responsibilities to travel to the same physical space. ODR could provide a value add for those who needed time between hearing another's point of view and responding. The option of asynchronistic engagement enhanced the ability of mediators to provide a more needs-based process that could increase access to participation.[16] One of the most powerful perceived advantages to the use of online technology for dispute resolution was elucidated through National Science Foundation funded research on labor mediation. In this study participants stated that contributing ideas anonymously was both easier online than face-to-face and useful in building agreements. And specifically, it reduced anxiety and fear in participants, generating more ideas and more creative suggestions than in an attributed environment.[17]

The awareness of the value that technology can bring to dispute handling has grown consistently since the first experiments were undertaken in the 1990s[18] after the Internet became available to the public. And its success at becoming mainstreamed into some sectors and further institutionalized in others can be marked by a variety of factors. An early adopter of ODR, ecommerce has applied ODR to great effect: for example, ODR handles over 60 million disputes annually in one e-marketplace[19] and in 2020 ODR will likely manage over 1 billion disputes worldwide in ecommerce alone.[20] There are approximately 100 ODR platforms worldwide handling family, workplace, and business disputes[21] and an exploding number of courts and tribunals are employing ODR across

---

16 For specific examples *see* Schmitz, A. and Wing, L. "Beneficial and Ethical ODR for Family Issues." *Family Court Review,* Forthcoming 2021. For guidance on providing increased accessibility in ODR for those with disabilities, *see* Larson, D. and Feingold, L. "ODR for All: Digital Accessibility and Disability Accommodations in Online Dispute Resolution." Mediate.com, May 2018. Available at: www.mediate.com/articles/larsond2.cfm Last accessed 24 August 2020.

17 Unpublishing findings from research supported by National Science Foundation award #0429297. "Process Technology for Achieving Government Online Dispute Resolution." Available at: www.fastlane.nsf.gov/servlet/showaward?award=0429297. This interdisciplinary research project included the National Mediation Board, the Departments of Legal Studies and Computer Science at the University of Massachusetts Amherst and included both the authors as well as Ethan Katsh, Lee Osterweil, Norman Sondheimer, Lori Clarke, Alan Gaitenby, Alexander Wise, and Matt Mazzilli.

18 For an overview of the beginnings of the ODR field, the first experiments and early ODR software, *see* Katsh, E. and Rifkin, J. *Online Dispute Resolution: Resolving Conflicts in Cyberspace.* San Francisco: Jossey-Bass, 2001.

19 Statistics as of 2014, *see* Del Duca, L.F., Rule, C., and Rimpfel, K. "ebay's De Facto Low Value, High Volume Resolution Process: Lessons and Best Practices for ODR Systems Designers." *Arbitration Law Review,* 6, 2014, 205.

20 Colin Rule, ODR Forum, The Hague, 2016.

21 *See* the ever increasing ODR Provider list housed on The National Center for Technology and Dispute Resolution website: http://odr.info/provider-list/ Last accessed 24 August 2020.

the globe.[22] ODR has found a home in the academy as well, with an academic journal devoted entirely to ODR, *The International Journal for Online Dispute Resolution*, and course infusion in a number of law schools' curricula.[23] In addition, the International Council for Online Dispute Resolution was incorporated in 2017 as the first international membership organization dedicated to the advancement of ODR and its governance through standards.[24] In addition, mainstream ADR membership organizations have also recognized the importance of ODR, adding sections, committees and task forces to guide its usage and impact.[25] The incorporation of technology into ADR has clearly been increasingly well-received and continues to gain visibility, support, and institutionalization.

Simultaneous to the experimentation with and expansion of ODR have been ongoing expressions of concern about how its disruption could undermine core values and techniques central to dispute resolution practices. For example, the use of face-to-face (f2f) communication has been argued as crucial for humanizing the parties to each other and providing third parties with observational access to pick up cues from body language and tone that early text-only forms of ODR made impossible.[26] And ODR has been critiqued regarding accessibility and fairness for insufficiently addressing the realities of a digital divide and its impact on participation, and therefore outcomes.[27] While many of these concerns have been assuaged as video conferencing options have been added to ODR processes, the debate continues about loss of benefits of non-

---

22 At the time of publication ODR was being utilized or designed in courts in at least a dozen countries and almost two dozen U.S. states, for example; *see* the ever increasing number listed on Remote Courts Worldwide at remotecourts.org and the Courts Using ODR list housed on The National Center for Technology and Dispute Resolution website: http://odr.info/courts-using-odr/ Both last accessed 20 June 2020.

23 *See* the list of academic programs offering courses about ODR on The National Center for Technology and Dispute Resolution website: http://odr.info/courses/ Last accessed 24 August 2020.

24 "ICODR is an international nonprofit, incorporated in the United States, that drives the development, convergence, and adoption of open standards for the global effort to resolve disputes and conflicts using information and communications technology." *See* https://icodr.org/ Last accessed 24 August 2020.

25 This includes the ADR Institute of Canada, American Bar Association, Association of Conflict Resolution, ADR Institute of Canada, Indian Institute of Arbitration and Mediation, Mediate.com, and the International Council for Online Dispute Resolution among others.

26 For a more extensive discussion *see* Wing, L. and Rainey, D. "Online Dispute Resolution and the Development of Theory." In Wahab, M., Katsh, E., and Rainey, D. (eds.), *Online Dispute Resolution: Theory and Practice.* The Hague: Eleven International Publishing, 2012, 23-38. *See also* Raines, S. "Mediating in Your Pajamas: The Benefits and Challenges for ODR Practitioners." *Conflict Resolution Quarterly*, 23(3), 2006, 359-369.

27 Rifkin, J., Gaitenby, A. and Wing, L. Personal conversation with co-author, Leah Wing, 1998; Raines, S. "Mediating in Your Pajamas: The Benefits and Challenges for ODR Practitioners." *Conflict Resolution Quarterly*, 23(3), 2006, 359-369; Beal, B.L. "Online Mediation: Has Its Time Come?" *Ohio State Journal on Dispute Resolution*, 15(3), 2000, 735-768; Foxmyn, W. Personal Communication with co-author, Leah Wing, 2020.

technology-mediated f2f dispute resolution as well as issues of inaccessibility.[28] In addition, concerns about how ICT can be employed for repression have been raised along with warning against

the divorcing of [ICT] tools from the general socio-political, ethnic, economic, cultural and religious context. [That can lead to] delink[ing] the use of ICTs from those that have access to them, and the manner in which they are adopted.[29]

Thus, there is an argument for consideration of context for policy development and application of ICT. This has included bringing attention to the usage of mobile phones by activists for human rights, conflict transformation, and peacebuilding and thereby challenging the narrow definition of ODR as merely computer-bound and dispute resolution oriented.[30]

As infusion of technology into dispute resolution systems and practices flourished along with a growing set of concerns, so, too, have the calls for governance structures

28 Sternlight, J.R. "Pouring a Little Psychological Cold Water on Online Dispute Resolution." *Journal of Dispute Resolution*, (1), 2020, 1-29; Larson, D. and Feingold, L. "ODR for All: Digital Accessibility and Disability Accommodations in Online Dispute Resolution." Mediate.com, May 2018, available at: www.mediate.com/articles/larsond2.cfm Last accessed 24 August 2020; Wing, L. "Artificial Intelligence and Online Dispute Resolution Systems Design: Lack of/Access to Justice Magnified." *International Journal of Online Dispute Resolution,* 4(2), 2017, 16-20; Condlin, R. "Online Dispute Resolution: Stinky, Repugnant, or Drab?" *Cordoza Journal of Conflict Resolution,* 18, 2017, 717-759; Menkel-Meadow, C. "Is ODR ADR?" *International Journal of Online Dispute Resolution*, 3(1), 2016, 4-7; Wing, L. "Ethical Principles for Online Dispute Resolution: A GPS Device for the Field." *International Journal of Online Dispute Resolution*, 3(1), 2016, 12-29; Raymond, A.H. and Shackelford, S.J. "Technology, Ethics, and Access to Justice: Should an Algorithm Be Deciding Your Case?" *Michigan Journal of International Law*, 35(3), 2014, 485-524.

29 Hattotuwa, J. "Mobiles and ODR: Why We Should Care." In Wahab, M., Katsh, E., and Rainey, D. (eds.), *Online Dispute Resolution: Theory and Practice.* The Hague: Eleven International Publishing, 2012, 84.

30 Hattotuwa, J. "Mobiles and ODR: Why We Should Care." In Wahab, M., Katsh, E., and Rainey, D. (eds.), *Online Dispute Resolution: Theory and Practice.* The Hague: Eleven International Publishing, 2012, 83-84.

to oversee the quality of ODR implementation.[31] A relevant backdrop to these calls were active discussions about how ethics created for the litigious context could be adapted to alternative dispute resolution.[32] By the early 2000s, as the University of Massachusetts Amherst and the National Mediation Board began the first National Science Foundation study of the impact of technology on mediation, the debate about dispute resolution ethics was underway.[33] And by the end of the first decade of ODR's existence, the idea of creating an ADR ethical framework that included technology was being more widely

---

31 *See* Schmitz, A. and Wing, L. "Beneficial and Ethical ODR for Family Issues." *Family Court Review*, Forthcoming 2021; Wing, L. "Ethical Principles for Online Dispute Resolution: A GPS Device for the Field." *International Journal of Online Dispute Resolution*, 3(1), 2016, 12-29. Advisory Committee, National Center for Technology and Dispute Resolution, Online Dispute Resolution Standards of Practice, 2009, available at: www.icann.org/en/system/files/files/odr-standards-of-practice-en.pdf Last accessed 20 June 2020; Barsky, A. "The Ethics of App-Assisted Family Mediation." *Conflict Resolution Quarterly*, 34(1), Fall 2016, 31-42; Casanovas, P. and Zeleznikow, J. "Online Dispute Resolution and Models of Relational Law and Justice: A Table of Ethical Principles." In Casanovas, P. et al. (eds.), *AICOL IV/V 2013*, LNAI 8929, Berlin, Heidelberg: Springer-Verlag, 2014, 54-68; de Werra, J. "ADR in Cyberspace: The Need to Adopt Global Alternative Dispute Resolution Mechanisms for Addressing the Challenges of Massive Online Micro-Justice." *Swiss Review of International & European Law*, 26(2), 2016, 289-306; Ebner, N. and Zeleznikow, J. "No Sheriff in Town: Governance for the ODR Field." *Negotiation Journal*, 32(4), 2016, 297-323; The European Parliament and the Council of the European Union, "Regulation of the European Parliament and of the Council on Online Dispute Resolution for Consumer Disputes and Amending (EC) No. 2006/2004 and Directive 2009/22/EC (Regulation on Consumer ODR) ODR Regulation (EU) 524/2013." *Official Journal of the European Union*, 2013, L 165/63; Jani, S. and Getz, C. *Mediating from a Distance: Suggested Practice Guidelines for Family Mediators* (2nd ed.). Vancouver: Mediate BC Society, 2012, available at: https://www.mediatebc.com/sites/default/files/Guidelines_Mediating-from-a-Distance-%28Second-edition%29_0.pdf Last accessed 2021; Liyanage, K.C. "The Regulation of Online Dispute Resolution: Effectiveness of Online Consumer Protection Guidelines." *Deakin Law Review*, 17(2), 2012, 251-282; DeMars, J., et al. "Virtual Virtues: Ethical Considerations for an Online Dispute Resolution Practice." *Dispute Resolution Magazine*, 17(1), 2010, 6-10; Morek, R. "The Regulatory Framework for Online Dispute Resolution: A Critical View." *Toledo Law Review*, 38(1), 2006, 163-192; Rainey, D. "Third-Party Ethics in the Age of the Fourth Party." *International Journal of Online Dispute Resolution*, 1(1), 2014, 37-56; Shackelford, S.J. and Raymond, A.H. "Building the Virtual Courthouse: Ethical Considerations for Design, Implementation, and Regulation in the World of ODR." *Wisconsin Law Review*, 3, 2014, 614-657; Raymond, A.H. and Shackelford, S.J. "Technology, Ethics, and Access to Justice: Should an Algorithm Be Deciding Your Case?" *Michigan Journal of International Law*, 35, Spring 2014, 485-524; Rule, C. *Online Dispute Resolution for Business: B2B, Ecommerce, Consumer, Employment, Insurance, and Other Commercial Conflicts*. San Francisco, CA: Jossey-Bass, 2002; Sole, M.E. "E-mediation: A New Stage of Ethics." 2015, available at: www.mediate.com/articles/SoleME4.cfm Last accessed 6 October 2016; UNCITRAL, Online Working Group III: Online Dispute Resolution, 2016, available at: www.uncitral.org/uncitral/commission/working_groups/3Online_Dispute_Resolution.html (accessed 22 August 2016); Welsh, N. "ODR: A Time for Celebration and the Embrace of Procedural Safeguards." Conference presentation at the International Forum for Online Dispute Resolution, The Hague, May 2016, available at: www.adrhub.com/profiles/blogs/procedural-justice-in-odr Last accessed 7 October 2016; and Wiener, A. "Regulations and Standards for Online Dispute Resolution: A Primer for Policymakers and Stakeholders." 2001, available at: www.mediate.com/articles/awiener2.cfm Last accessed 22 August 2016.

32 *See* Menkel-Meadow, C. "Ethics in Alternative Dispute Resolution: New Issues, No Answers from the Adversary Conception of Lawyers' Responsibilities." *South Texas Law Review*, 38, 1997, 407ff.

33 *See* Charles Pao, Jr., "Embracing Limbo: Thinking About Rethinking Dispute Resolution Ethics." *Penn State Law Review*, 108(2003-2004), 199ff.

discussed in the field of practice.[34] More recently, there have been attempts to address the specifics of ODR ethics through annotations to the existing rules of practice for ADR with commentary about the impact of ODR technology in both the field of practice and the academic arena[35] as well as efforts to create separate ethical codes for ODR.[36]

We argue that the attention being paid to the role of ethical principles, standards and other forms of regulation and guidance are part of the typical progression of the development of a new field. Professor Carrie Menkel-Meadow, writing about the conflict resolution field in general, reminds us of these patterns, (with arguably a note of caution about their potential exclusionary effects as well):

As new competencies are created and studied, the progression from initial theorization, to the development of practice protocols, training and education, attempts at credentialing, and "monopolization of expertise," to the development of "best practices" and ethics codes, marches on to the eventual state of exclusionary practices, such as degree requirements, licensing, and formal professional discipline.[37]

And like the broader conflict resolution field which has ethical and legal implications for practitioners and participants, ODR can increase risks, raise legal and other liabilities, and facilitate harm.[38] The larger dispute resolution field has sought to address these concerns by engaging in the types of activities Menkel-Meadow highlights - but not yet fulfilling them regarding technology. On the whole, it has yet to formally incorporate technology into its systems of best practices, accountability, and governance structures. Even for ADR generally, there are still no consistent, universally accepted protocols,

34 *See* Advisory Committee, National Center for Technology and Dispute Resolution, Online Dispute Resolution Standards of Practice, 2009, available at: www. icann.org/en/system/files/files/odr-standards-of-practice-en.pdf Last accessed 21 June 2020; Memars, J., Exon, S.N., Kovach, K. and Rule, C. "Virtual Ethics: Ethical Considerations for Online Dispute Resolution Practice." *Dispute Resolution Magazine*, 17 (2010-2011), 17ff; Jani, S. and Getz, C. *Mediating from a Distance: Suggested Practice Guidelines for Family Mediators* (2nd ed.). Vancouver: Mediate BC Society, 2012, available at: www.mediatebc.com/sites/default/files/Guidelines_Mediating-from-a-Distance-%28Second-edition%29_0.pdf Last accessed 21 June 2020; Liyanage, K.C. "The Regulation of Online Dispute Resolution: Effectiveness of Online Consumer Protection Guidelines." *Deakin Law Review*, 17(2), 2012, 251-282; Morek, R. "The Regulatory Framework for Online Dispute Resolution: A Critical View." *Toledo Law Review*, 38(1), 2006, 163-192.

35 *See* Exon, S.N. "Ethics and Online Dispute Resolution: From Evolution to Revolution." *Ohio State Journal on Dispute Resolution*, 32(2017) 609ff and Rainey, D. "Model Standards of Conduct for Mediators: Annotated for Online Dispute Resolution Practice." *The International Journal of Online Dispute Resolution*, 1(3), 2016, 30-40.

36 *See* an ever increasing list of ODR principles, standards and guidelines housed on The National Center for Technology and Dispute Resolution website: http://odr.info/standards Last accessed 24 August 2020.

37 Menkel-Meadow, C. "Are There Systemic Ethics Issues in Dispute System Design? And What We Should [Not] Do About It: Lessons from International and Domestic Fronts." *Harvard Negotiation Law Review*, 14, Winter 2009, 195.

38 Consider the potential impact in cases that could involve threats of harm such as domestic violence, financial ruin, and data privacy breaches. Also consider the negative consequences if machine learning and other forms of artificial intelligence wittingly or unwittingly result in structurally determining unequal ODR processes and outcomes.

credentials, or ethics codes regarding technology. And as we continue to build the ODR field, we would do well to proactively heed Menkel-Meadows' warning about creating exclusionary practices as we consider ways of codifying ethics for technology-infused practices.

Interestingly, many of the first sets of ODR guidelines and regulations have emerged from outside the field. This may speak to both the importance of ODR and to its potential attendant risks as seen by those responsible for systems into which ODR is being institutionalized. For example, by 2009, not much more than a decade after the birth of ODR, organizations and public entities which had issued some form of regulation or guidance for ODR included: The US Federal Trade Commission, The Canadian Working Group on Electronic Commerce and Consumers, The Alliance for Global Business, The Global Business Dialogue on Electronic Commerce, The Transatlantic Consumer Dialogue, Consumers International, The European Consumers' Organisation, The International Chamber of Commerce, The Internet Corporation for Assigned Names and Numbers, The National Center for Technology and Dispute Resolution, The National Mediation Board, The Australian National Alternative Dispute Resolution Advisory Council, and The American Bar Association. And in the decade since, calls from within the field for self-governance and accountability mechanisms have increased[39] with productive developments proliferating.[40] Consideration of stakeholder involvement in their development[41] and of the intersections with other systems is valuable as technology has increasingly blurred the boundaries of forms of dispute resolution, and of jurisdictions, national boundaries, and disciplines.[42] Designing regulations and guidance to govern ODR demands innovations that account for both the present use of technology in dispute handling, but also the inevitability that future uses will look different. Inclusivity in the efforts to create governance mechanisms will strengthen the outcomes, making them more viable, ethical and responsive to the demands of stakeholders. Yet, while these efforts are underway, unregulated application of technology to dispute resolution continues to raise risks for disputing parties and ODR systems administrators and practitioners alike. Again, we see that in the abyss both risk and innovation can flourish. Rising to meet these challenges are a growing set of ODR ethics initiatives and collaborations, seeking to build an important ethical infrastructure for an ever-changing field in the

39 *See* reference in footnote 33.

40 *See* ODR principles, standards and guidelines listed on The National Center for Technology and Dispute Resolution website: http://odr.info/standards Last accessed 20 June 2020.

41 Ethical standards development can be viewed within the context of dispute system design and for a more in depth examination of stakeholder involvement *see* Amsler, L.B., Martinez, J.K. and Smith, S.E. *Dispute System Design: Preventing, Managing, and Resolving Conflict*. Stanford, CA: Stanford University, 2020.

42 For further discussion *see* Katsh, E. and Rabinovich-Einy, O. *Digital Justice: Technology and the Internet of Disputes*. Oxford: Oxford University Press, 2017; Rabinovich-Einy, O. and Katsh, E. "Digital Justice – Reshaping Boundaries in an Online Dispute Resolution Environment." *International Journal of Online Dispute Resolution*, 1(1), 2014, 5-36.

face of technological changes that outpace nascent and disparate governance mechanisms.

2 ODR Governance and Accountability Projects

A number of the leading projects about ODR governance and accountability – some completed and others underway at the time of writing – are outlined below. We discuss highlights of several and note that since attention to these issues has grown exponentially with the focus courts are now putting on ODR, we anticipate a plethora of new initiatives to emerge over the next few years.

We begin our overview with a series of initiatives undertaken by the National Center for Technology and Dispute Resolution (NCTDR), the birthplace of ODR, which published a set of Online Dispute Resolution Standards of Practice in 2009[43] which, significantly, were adopted by the Internet Corporation for Assigned Names and Numbers. In 2016 the Ethics Initiative of NCTDR presented the Ethical Principles for Online Dispute Resolution,[44] building the first document highlighting principles (values) to serve as ongoing guidance as well as for specific use in the development of standards for ODR regulation.

As noted, NCTDR created the International Council for Online Dispute Resolution (ICODR) in 2017, the field's first ODR membership organization, and incorporated it with the expressed purpose of furthering the development and use of ODR standards.[45] ICODR promulgated ODR Standards[46] based on the NCTDR Ethical Principles for ODR and has two committees working on ODR standards and accountability mechanisms, the

43 Advisory Committee, National Center for Technology and Dispute Resolution, *Online Dispute Resolution Standards of Practice*, 2009, available at: www.icann.org/en/system/files/files/odrstandards-of-practice-en.pdf Last accessed 21 June 2020.

44 *See* http://odr.info/ethics-and-odr/ and for an extensive exploration of the Ethical Principles for Online Dispute Resolution, *see* Wing, L. "Ethical Principles for Online Dispute Resolution: A GPS Device for the Field." *International Journal of Online Dispute Resolution*, 3(1), 2016, 12-29.

45 ICODR was founded by the administrators and 40 international Fellows of the National Center for Technology and Dispute Resolution: https://icodr.org/ Last accessed 24 June 2020.

46 *See* https://icodr.org/standards/ Last accessed 31 August 2020.

ODR Standards Committee[47] and the Training and Education Committee.[48] In 2020, in response to the explosion in use of video conferencing by courts and alternative dispute resolution practitioners in the midst of the Covid-19 crisis, ICODR sought to provide quick first level guidance for the thousands who were incorporating the use of video for the first time to mediating[49] and arbitrating.[50] In addition, ICODR issued guidelines for ODR Training Components to supplement mediation and arbitration training.[51]

We continue next with other efforts underway at the time of writing as well as a description of a number of such undertakings which are completed. In 2020, the website Remote Courts Worldwide was set up as a resource as courts were shifting from face-to-face to remote hearings in response to the pandemic. The site was designed to help the global community of justice workers – judges, lawyers, court officials, litigants, court technologists – to share their experiences of 'remote' alternatives to traditional court hearings...[and it] offers a systematic way of remote-court innovators and people who work in the justice system to exchange news of operational systems, as well as of plans, ideas, policies, protocols, techniques, and safeguards.[52]

The website is hosted by the Society for Computers and Law, while the UK LawTech Delivery Panel funds it, and Her Majesty's Courts & Tribunals Service (UK) provides support.

In the United States, the National Center for State Courts (NCSC) has conducted assessments during 2020 of ODR systems used by the courts. It will publish its findings with recommendations for ODR standards.[53]

---

47 At the time of writing, the ICODR Standards Committee has undertaken the collection and comparison of ODR principles, standards, guidance, and related regulation and legislation from entities across the globe as part of a joint project with the American Bar Association and the National Center for Technology and Dispute Resolution. The ICODR Standards Committee seeks to enhance ICODR ODR standards across sectors and type of actors, to develop recommendations for the board of directors regarding mechanisms for accreditation and auditing processes, and to create a mechanism to address inquiries on ODR ethical dilemmas; (based on Committee minutes, October 10 and 16, 2019).

48 This committee has a "primary mission: to develop, disseminate, and manage ODR training norms or standards that serve the community of 'trainers', 'third parties' and the 'primary parties' whom they may serve, as well as the developers and platform providers who constitute the corps of 'fourth parties' providing ICT platforms;" (ICODR Training and Education Committee Statement, National Center for Technology and Dispute Resolution blog, 26 October 2019). Last accessed 9 February 2020.

49 ICODR's Video Mediation Guidelines can be found at: https://icodr.org/guides/videomed.pdf Last accessed 22 June 2020.

50 ICODR's Video Arbitration Guidelines can be found at: https://icodr.org/guides/videoarb.pdf Last accessed 22 June 2020.

51 ICODR's guidelines for ODR Training Components can be found at https://icodr.org/guides/training.pdf Last accessed 22 June 2020.

52 Professor Richard Susskind, President, Society for Computers and Law, 27th March 2020, available at: https://remotecourts.org/ Last accessed 22 June 2020.

53 *See* www.ncsc.org/odr Last accessed 16 March 2020.

And also, in 2020, the ADR Institute of Canada ODR Task Force has begun exploring ethics and ODR. The ODR Task Force is recommending ADRIC adopt the Ethical Principles for ODR developed by the National Center for Technology and Dispute Resolution.[54]

The American Bar Association (ABA) ODR Task Force was set up in 2019 to, among other assignments, examine 'existing and suggested statutes, rules, principles and standards regarding ODR platforms and practice' and collaborate with other organizations, providing guidance on ODR standards efforts.[55] This work by the ABA ODR Task Force was undertaken in collaboration with the National Center for Technology and Dispute Resolution (NCTDR) and the International Council for Online Dispute Resolution (ICODR); with the ABA efforts concentrated on the U.S. and the NCTDR ethics initiative and ICODR Standards committees focused globally. The collaboration archive includes an e-library hosted on the NCTDR website[56] listing ODR principles, standards, and guidelines found throughout the world.[57]

The National Consumer Law Center (U.S.) promulgated a document in 2019 outlining guidance for courts regarding employing ODR in ways that protect consumers and prevent problems with implementation.[58]

The International Organization for Standardization (ISO) set up a Technical Committee (TC 321) in 2018 to begin working on standards for ecommerce, online consumer rights, and online dispute prevention and resolution.[59] Technical Committees, of which there are more than 300, are made up of technical experts, and have an assigned scope of work, such as the one for TC 321.

Standardization in the field of 'transaction assurance in e- [sic]commerce related upstream/downstream processes', [sic] including the following: ... Protection of online consumer rights including both prevention of online disputes and resolution process....[60]

In 2017, the United Nations Commission on International Trade Law (UNCITRAL) Working Group III on ODR issued its 'Technical Notes on Online Dispute Resolution.' The Working group focused on dispute resolution for cross-border ecommerce, and the Notes included a section on Principles, which begin in part: "The principles that underpin any ODR process include fairness, transparency, due process and

54 Péch, E. ADR Institute of Canada ODR Task Force; personal communication, email on file with one of the authors, Leah Wing, 20 March 2020.
55 American Bar Association ODR Task Force Term and Charge, 2019.
56 http://odr.info/ Last accessed 30 August 2020.
57 *See* http://odr.info/standards/ Last accessed 22 June 2020.
58 www.nclc.org/images/pdf/debt_collection/ib-odr-july2019.pdf Last accessed 21 March 2020.
59 *See* www.iso.org/committee/7145156.html Last accessed 16 March 2020.
60 ISO TC 321: www.iso.org/committee/7145156.html Last accessed 30 August 2020.

accountability." The UNCITRAL Technical Notes on Principles included commentary on each of the elements articulated above, plus notes on expertise and consent.[61]

In the beginning of 2016, the International Mediation Institute (IMI) undertook a project designed to establish standards for online mediator practice, and for online mediation training and education. They harnessed input from dispute resolution professionals and volunteers from a number of countries and organizations to examine the need and scope for credentialing, self and government regulation, as well as the creation of ODR standards and core competencies.[62]

The Association for Conflict Resolution, American Bar Association and American Arbitration Association collaborated on a survey of members about whether they thought their shared Model Standards of Conduct for Mediators should be updated to include use of technology and address specifics regarding ODR. Initial results were published in 2016.[63]

The Civil Justice Council ODR Advisory Group issued a set of recommendations in 2016 for the Courts and Tribunal Judiciary (UK) regarding online dispute resolution integration.[64]

In 2015, the Government of Mexico issued a Federal Law of Consumer Protection on ODR for the Federal Consumer Protection Prosecutor Office of Mexico.[65,66]

The Government of Brazil instituted an online platform in 2014, consumidor.gov.br,[67] with articulated standards for handling consumer-business disputes.[68]

In 2013, The European Union (EU) incorporated ODR into consumer dispute resolution processes within the EU enacting Regulation No. 524/2013 of the European Parliament and of the Council.[69] Woven into the regulation are a number of statements of principles or standards: e.g., the ODR platform 'should enable the secure interchange of data,' and 'should be made accessible.'[70] In light of this, in March 2019 the government

61 *See* UNCITRAL Technical Notes on Online Dispute Resolution, United Nations, April 2017. Available at: www.uncitral.org/pdf/english/texts/odr/V1700382_English_Technical_Notes_on_ODR.pdf Last accessed 16 March 2020.

62 www.imimediation.org/about/who-are-imi/odr-tf/ Last accessed 9 January 2020.

63 *See* Rainey, D. "Model Standards of Conduct for Mediators: Annotated for Online Dispute Resolution Practice." *International Journal of Online Dispute Resolution*, 3(1), 2016, 30-40.

64 www.judiciary.uk/wp-content/uploads/2016/04/cjc-odr-advisory-group-response-to-lj-briggs-report.pdf Last accessed 21 March 2020.

65 2015 Manual of Process for the SubProsecutor Office of Conciliation of Profeco (Federal Consumer Protection Prosecutor Office of Mexico). Arley, A. Personal communication 27 May 2020; email on file with co-author, Leah Wing.

66 The authors express thanks to Amada Arley for research and translation regarding this ODR legislation.

67 http://consumidor.gov.br/ Last accessed 29 March 2020.

68 The authors express thanks to Alexandre Augusto Fiori de Tella for research and translation regarding this ODR platform.

69 *See* https://eur-lex.europa.eu/LexUriServ/LexUriServ.do?uri=OJ:L:2013:165:0001:0012:EN:PDF Last accessed 16 March 2020.

70 *See* Sections 21 and 22 of the Regulation No. 524/2013 of the European Parliament and of the Council EU Regulation.

of France passed an Act providing rules on voluntary ODR certification for ODR platforms.[71]

In 2012, The Distance Mediation Project of Mediate BC (Canada) published guidelines for virtual mediation.[72]

Asia-Pacific Cooperation has articulated support for the development and utilization of ODR for cross-border trade. It outlined values for such processes and has determined that the "UNCITRAL Arbitration Rules and Technical Notes on Online Dispute Resolution [will] provide the framework for the APEC ODR Procedural Rules."[73]

It is notable, although perhaps not surprising, that those entities that already have governance responsibilities regarding dispute resolution (ie: practitioner membership organizations, legislative and regulatory bodies, and field-building organizations such as NCTDR) have promulgated mechanisms for ODR quality control and accountability before any led by stakeholders from disputant populations – including those who may be most heavily affected by the increased risks of infusing technology in dispute resolution processes. All disputants including populations that often experience access to justice barriers and highest risks in dispute resolution fora, such as victims of domestic violence, immigrants, and people with disabilities among others are stakeholders who may know little about the growth of ODR, and yet, their views could be instrumental in the development of ethical governance for ODR. Therefore, while there are many champions of access to justice and of ensuring that the foundational tenets of alternative dispute resolution are translated into this 21st century version of ADR – nothing beats participative justice – hearing from all relevant stakeholders and including them in decision making about new developments. ODR governance initiatives that are inclusive will bear fruit in creating the most useful, just, and sustainable forms of accountability and guidance for quality ODR systems and practices.

3 WHY DEVELOP ODR ETHICS GOVERNANCE MECHANISMS?

As we have noted, there are now many organizations discussing and playing a role in creating standards, principles, guidelines, etc., for online dispute resolution. Why pursue standards, ethics and guidelines with such apparent fervor? The International Standards Organization (ISO) in its description of the ISO mission gives the beginning of a very

71 *See* www.legifrance.gouv.fr/affichLoiPreparation.do;jsessionid=67461511805D3C45A7E68E1CC1CD736A.tplgfr35s_2?idDocument=JORFDOLE000036830320&type=general&typeLoi=proj&legislature=15 Last accessed 21 March 2020.

72 *See* Jani, S. and Getz, C. *Mediating from a Distance: Suggested Practice Guidelines for Family Mediators* (2nd ed.). Vancouver: Mediate BC Society, available at: https://www.mediatebc.com/sites/default/files/Guidelines_Mediating-from-a-Distance-%28Second-edition%29_0.pdf Last accessed 2021.

73 Dennis, M.J. "APEC's New Online Dispute Resolution Framework Could Be a Game Changer for Small Businesses." LinkedIn, 20 March 2019, available at: www.linkedin.com/pulse/how-apec-odr-framework-revolutionize-global-dispute-small-dennis/?published=t Last accessed 4 August 2020.

good answer: "ISO was founded with the idea of answering a fundamental question – what's the best way of doing this?"[74] It would seem obvious that finding the best way of doing 'this' – this being ODR – would benefit platform designers, service providers, practitioners, and parties in ways that uphold commitments to access to justice and other core values of dispute resolution. It is useful to think of the ways of developing ODR ethics governance mechanisms as diverse as well as comprehensive, existing in a cascading relationship. At the top are ethical considerations and general principles, often thought of as moral guidance and values. For example, the NCTDR ethical principles include ideals to strive to achieve for ODR systems and processes – such as accountability, accessibility, competence, etc., but the ethical principles do not suggest behavior that would lead to those ideal states. At the next level are rules or standards that tell us how to behave in a given situation. They can be thought of as defining, within a given circumstance, a triggering condition and a consequence; they provide, therefore, the ability to measure behavior and provide accountability. Rules or standards tend to be rather rigid, and once enacted by whatever body promulgated them, are often slow to change. Best practices, on the other hand define a set of options with a given circumstance – pointing to the 'best' way of doing something, based on the knowledge available when the best practice was articulated. And mere guidance can be outlined as well, providing suggestions that are practical and useful but not necessarily designed with the scrutiny of a best practice. It is in the nature of best practices and guidance that they are constantly reviewed and revised, making the notion of the 'best' way of doing something fluid and tied to developing knowledge and experience. Given the fundamental changes to disputes handling processes taking place within and between societies as well as the constantly evolving nature of technology, we argue for creation of all levels of ethics infrastructure – principles, rules/standards, best practices and guidance as well as mechanisms to routinely revisit them.

The examples from the opening of this chapter can help illustrate the value of implementing each level of this cascade of ODR governance mechanisms. The experienced mediator in the first example would be used to a set of best practices that are designed to uphold the core values of ADR, such as the principle of confidentiality, as well as related standards as outlined by the membership organization to which she belongs. Her strategies to uphold the principle and standard of confidentiality, for example, previously likely included keeping paper records in a locked file, not revealing confidential information stated by one party to another (or anyone else) without their permission, and stating to parties any exceptions to confidentiality she must adhere to. She may have utilized other behaviors based on best practices or other guidance suggestions colleagues shared about language to use in an intake or opening statement which reinforced to the parties how she as their mediator would live up to this principle

74 *See* www.iso.org/benefits-of-standards.html Last accessed 16 March 2020.

and standard. And, it is possible that her alternative dispute resolution membership organization may have a mechanism for consultation about dilemmas relating to standards and for holding members accountable if they are accused of violating them. Yet, while these practices are routinized in mediator behavior, taught in mediation trainings, and passed down through norms manifesting in scholarship and at conferences, they on the whole, have not yet sufficiently prepared her to undertake ODR – to harness its strengths while reducing its ever-changing risks. As one measure of the problem, at the time of writing, there are very few standard mediation training courses that 1) include guidance on how to integrate technology into a traditional practice and 2) provide related ethics guidance. The dearth of attention to how technology impacts ADR systems, processes and practices in our governance, guidance, and education mechanisms leaves practitioners and most importantly, parties, vulnerable to these unaccounted for risks.

Ethical Principles for Online Dispute Resolution[75] are part of the efforts to address this challenge. They were designed to incorporate the historical values of the ADR field with a direct focus on technology-infused dispute handling. They were written to be from a high enough order to provide flexibility for cultural, sectoral, and temporal interpretation as appropriate; although even they will need to remain a living document, engaged with by stakeholders over time to be adapted to changing circumstances and technologies. In addition, these principles highlight the need to see ethical values as interrelated, for example:

3.1 *Confidentiality*

The development and implementation of ODR systems, processes, and practitioners maintain confidentiality in accordance with all legal obligations and in a manner that is consistent, in particular, with the principles of Legal Obligation, Informed Participation, Security, and Transparency.[76]

In looking at just one of those principles with which confidentiality is linked we can see how they are interrelated. The Transparency ethical principle explicitly draws attention to the importance of data security and privacy policies and lays out related expectations with regards to transparency; and all of which can impact confidentiality. Consider our second example in the opening can illustrate the interconnectedness of ethical principles in ODR: the disputant raised concerns about data security, lack of transparency in the use of algorithms, and confidentiality, wondering how they could

75 *See* http://odr.info/ethics-and-odr/ and Wing, L. "Ethical Principles for Online Dispute Resolution: A GPS Device for the Field." *International Journal of Online Dispute Resolution*, 3(1), 2016, 12-29.

76 *See* http://odr.info/ethics-and-odr/ and Wing, L. "Ethical Principles for Online Dispute Resolution: A GPS Device for the Field." *International Journal of Online Dispute Resolution*, 3(1), 2016, 25.

or would impact the online dispute resolution process and outcomes provided to him by the company.

3.2 Transparency

All reasonable efforts are taken to make transparent the true purposes, risks, and legal obligations inclusive of but not limited to: the form and legal jurisdiction of dispute resolution processes; the identities, affiliations, obligations, and conflicts of interest of the parties, entities, and systems; and the data security, confidentiality, and privacy policies and systems involved.[77]

The inclusion of new ethical expectations, connecting historical foundational ADR ethics to the circumstances of new technologies and inter-relating these Ethical Principles for ODR will hopefully serve as an ongoing set of values relevant to our technology-infused dispute resolution terrain. However, these principles are insufficient as guidance for the mediator seeking to determine what platform to use and what criteria upon which to make that decision, and looking for useful strategies to address confidentiality, data security, and transparency in a technology-infused practice. They are also insufficient for membership organizations to hold practitioners accountable in what has become our new conditions of practice. And they are insufficient for stakeholders who, like the disputant in the second opening example, no doubt would like transparency about the use algorithms and of their digital trail – to be informed consumers, aware of their risks and empowered in both purchasing and in dispute resolution.

If ODR principles are useful but insufficient, this raises important and complex questions about standards development and oversight. How to develop standards based on ethical principles? How to effectively and meaningfully incorporate stakeholders in their development? Which standards should be designed to respond to sector-specific circumstances (ie: commerce, courts, family, labor, public policy) and which should be cross-cutting? How to best create standards that will have relevance across cultures and legal jurisdictions? What standards are important for dispute system design, platforms, software, algorithms, machine learning, and other forms of artificial intelligence (AI); for human neutrals utilizing technology? For example, should there be standards regarding the use of ODR software that require ensuring multi-media, multi-linguality, and a certain level of visibility for the ODR process within an ecommerce or court online ecosystem, for example? Should standards exist that ensure access and understanding for those with limited resources or limited experiences with technology? What or who is the target of such standards: the software, ecosystem, neutrals? What accountability

77 *See* http://odr.info/ethics-and-odr/ and Wing, L. "Ethical Principles for Online Dispute Resolution: A GPS Device for the Field." *International Journal of Online Dispute Resolution*, 3(1), 2016, 27.

measures are required and, importantly, how will they be employed and by whom? Adding to the consideration of the cascading relationship between principles, standards, best practices, and guidance, a rigorous examination of systems, AI, and intervenors is called for within each arena. Figure 4.1 provides a few examples of standards development and implementation strategies.[78]

78 Co-author Leah Wing developed these activities and templates in hopes they could contribute to stimulating utilization of the Ethical Principles for Online Dispute Resolution to create standards, best practices, and guidance for all actors within the ODR universe.

Figure 4.1 ODR Standards Development Activity[79]

ODR Standards Development Activity[1]

First presented at a workshop exploring ODR Standards development, this activity is not meant to be comprehensive in any respect, rather to serve as a stimulus for further engagements to that end. Inevitably, legislators, regulators, membership organizations and other stakeholders will have many additional jurisdictional and sector-specific criteria they will wish include in developing regulatory mechanisms; and they may also consider criteria for standards covering activities and actors that cross such boundaries.

Suggestions for ODR Standards Development

Utilize the Ethical Principles for Online Dispute Resolution[2] to guide the development of ODR Standards for the design, implementation, and accountability of ODR systems, software, and artificial intelligence for ODR; and the human neutrals utilizing ODR. The ODR Standards Development Grid below provides a visual to assist in thinking about the interrelationships between components within an ODR system and is recommended for consideration during standards development.

- Work with and consider a variety of stakeholders; include those with least ODR access
- Use ODR Ethical Principles as a GPS[3]
- Consider the target of the standard and whether it is for a particular sector or to cross sectors (ie: court, commercial, labor, family; public or private; etc.):
  - o dispute system design
  - o software/product
  - o algorithmic
  - o human ODR neutrals/practitioners
- Consider how each standard relates directly to one or more Principles[4]
- Ground the analysis through use cases: common, realistic (rather than only brainstorm in the abstract)[5]
- Consider matrices of measurability[6]
- Prior to completion, "ODR Principle-proof" the standard by examining additional relevant Principles. This can enhance the standard's applicability to the reality of complex ethical, legal and economic challenges.[7]

[1] This activity was presented in Wing, L. "Ethical Principles and Standards for Online Dispute Resolution." Workshop on Private International Online Dispute Resolution, Stanford University, April 19, 2017. Reproduced with permission based on slides 18-24, 30-31.
[2] See the National Center for Technology and Dispute Resolution http://odr.info/ethics-and-odr/ and Wing, L. "Ethical Principles for Online Dispute Resolution: A GPS Device for the Field." *International Journal of Online Dispute Resolution*, 3(1), 2016, 12-29.
[3] See Wing, L. "Ethical Principles for Online Dispute Resolution: A GPS Device for the Field." *International Journal of Online Dispute Resolution*, 3(1), 2016, 12-29.
[4] See example 1 below.
[5] See example 2 below.
[6] See ODR Standards Measurement Matrices Grid below.
[7] See example 3 below.

79 This activity was presented in Wing, L. "Ethical Principles and Standards for Online Dispute Resolution." Workshop on Private International Online Dispute Resolution, Stanford University, 19 April 2017. Reproduced with permission based on slides 18-24, 30-31.

ODR Standards Development Grid[8]

Principle	System / Software / Product Design	Algorithmic / Machine Learning / AI	Human Neutrals / ODR Practitioners
Accessibility			
Accountability			
Competence			
Confidentiality			
Empowerment			
Equality			
Fairness			
Honesty			
Impartiality			
Informed Participation			
Innovation			
Integration			
Legal Obligation			
Neutrality			
Protection from Harm			
Security			
Transparency			

[8] © 2017 Leah Wing.

Example 1: Some potential attributes of a standard based on the ODR Ethical Principle of Accessibility
This list is just a sample and will prove most useful through an examination by sector and context, across them, and by considering example use cases. That can provide the necessary specificity for the standards developers to consider if, for example, there are rules that should be the same for mandatory court ODR processes, voluntary community mediation use of ODR, and cross border e-commerce ODR. Should a specific standard under construction apply across all sectors and jurisdictions and if not, which should it apply to?

- Ability to choose types of dispute resolution processes
- Cost of participation in dispute resolution process(es)
- Assistance to understand and utilize the technology
- Length of time between complaint submission, acknowledgment, case assignment to algorithm and/or human for intervention, response, decision
- When/if ever required to use ODR (plaintiff/defendant, disputant, customer, vendor)
- Placement: integrated into customer service; required separate ODR track, etc.
- Visibility: when party is made aware of ODR system, location on website
- Availability of multi-lingual and multi-media engagement: sound, visuals, and text

Example 2: Sample of Users' Context and Concerns Impacting Standards Development
Use case: Two Small-Mid Size Enterprises (SME) located in different countries considering using ODR may have these types of questions and concerns:

- Data security: how data will be transmitted, stored, who can get access to it
- Confidentiality: protection from recording and text being uploaded by other party to social media or for another proceeding
- Artificial Intelligence (AI) usage: protection against bias; will it be used, when, how?

Standards creators need to ascertain if/how standards will address the fact that parties may have differences in these areas:

- Legal jurisdictions
- Primary languages
- Levels of experience with the ODR platform (ie: repeat player)
- Levels of fluency with the ODR technology
- Levels of familiarity with their legal protections
- Levels of knowledge about the risks they face
- Resources available to address these concerns

In this use case, relevant considerations should also be made in the standards development for e-commerce ODR providers and practitioners who would be engaged in handling the dispute. They would need to know what their legal, economic, and ethical responsibilities and risks could be, both within and across legal jurisdictions; ie:

- Should ODR providers or practitioners be required to offer technical support to parties?
- Should ODR ever be mandatory? Under what conditions? Who decides?
- What guarantees should be offered regarding no bias in use of AI?
- Who is legally responsible for the data security and confidentiality of the platform: The software developer? The e-marketplace? ODR platform provider? ODR human practitioner? A governmental agency?

Example 3: ODR Ethical Principle-proofing a standard under development

Only using one Principle may not address the reality of the interlocking nature of risks that a standard ought to reduce and protect stakeholders from. For example, an ODR standard based solely on Confidentiality could state that all ODR platforms and practitioners must require parties to agree at the start of a process that they will maintain the confidentiality of all the data exchanged (with necessary stated exceptions). However, this standard would not account for the reality of overlapping ethical issues (and legal and economic risks). Thus, such a limited ODR confidentiality standard would not ensure that parties are fully informed of related risks resulting in their vulnerability to:

- exposure to tools that include location features without their consent[9]
- other software they are not familiar with or skilled at using
- potential loss of right to access court by participating
- use of algorithms impacting options and outcomes without their consent
- data collection, even in the aggregate, for machine learning or commercial use without their consent

By examining use cases, specific contexts, and targets of a standard, its creators may find that more than one Principle is relevant for consideration in its formulation. In this use case example, applicable Ethical Principles beyond Confidentiality include:

- Informed Participation
- Legal Obligation
- Security
- Transparency

Matrices of Measurability for ODR Standards

Measures of accountability for systems, software, artificial intelligence and humans can be key to standards enforcement, building and maintaining trust with users, and ensuring ethical processes and practice. Below is an example to stimulate thinking about the development of tools for integrating ODR standards development with attention to accountability measures.

[9] This is not merely a confidentiality concern but can heighten risks in situations with domestic or workplace violence. This concern is explored in Barsky, A. E. "The Ethics of App-Assisted Family Mediation." *Conflict Resolution Quarterly*, 34(1), Fall 2016, 31-42.

ODR Standards Measurement Matrices Grid[10]

Accessibility
Accountability
Competence
Confidentiality
Empowerment
Equality

Fairness
Honesty
Impartiality
Informed Participation
Innovation
Integration

Legal Obligation
Neutrality
Protection from Harm
Security
Transparency

Standard (state target: system design, AI, ODR human practitioner, etc.)	Principles Used	Measurement Matrices

Multiple efforts are underway to develop each step in the cascade of mechanisms necessary for the ethical governance and implementation of ADR in an age of technological infusion. And the challenge remains about how to coordinate them and balance the need to both move forward efficiently to meet the challenges of the day while being inclusive through stakeholder input and shared decision making. More innovative ideas about how to accomplish this will undoubtedly emerge as long as we keep a commitment to both on our radars. Standards are crucial to develop and yet, once they have been formed, we can still continue to utilize ethical principles as a touchstone for responding to the rapid technological innovations that will undoubtedly emerge faster than efforts to change the rules.

4 Reflecting on ODR Ethics for the Future

Perhaps the most significant and far reaching development in the evolution of ODR is the apparent cultural shift within the dispute resolution community regarding the efficacy of technology based or assisted processes. Before the Covid pandemic forced the use of online tools, it was common for many practitioners to use only very limited forms of technology and not fully appreciate that its inclusion introduced ethical issues to their practices. Through the 2000s, up until Covid, it was common for those who were engaged in the study and practice of ODR to ask at ADR conferences, 'how many are currently using technology in your practice,' and to have no one respond that they were using technology. But when followed by more specific questions, e.g., 'how many are using cell phones/email/etc.,' nearly all would acknowledge the use of technology. The inclusion of forms of technology were incremental and seemingly invisible. And yet, it raised risks just as it expanded benefits to practitioners and disputants. And now, with the explosion in the application of a much broader range of types of technologies to dispute handling systems and by ADR practitioners, the risks and benefits, too, are multiplying.

Why do we need ethical standards? Because even using technology at the level of mobile phones and email introduced significant ethical issues to dispute resolution practices: oral communication over a mobile link can be hacked or recorded, and sending a document using email can be hacked and unintentionally shared. Adding web video and other more advanced types of ODR technology heightens the impact on our ethical obligations as practitioners and system designers and managers.

The cultural shift goes beyond acknowledging that ODR tools are available and useful: it includes the assumption that 'normal' practice has been changed going forward. A recent exchange with a well-established mediator/arbitrator demonstrates:

> Before COVID, I just did not believe that using technology would work. Things had to be done face-to-face to be effective. I have completely changed my mind.

> I've been using online tools and I now know they work for most of the cases I have – we are not losing anything by using the technology. It's part of the future. It's here to stay.[80]

As we have discussed earlier in this chapter, there are now many organizations addressing the need for ethical standards in ODR, although there are only a few engaged in a strict standards development process at the time of writing. A great challenge for the field over the next few years is to construct a rigorous governance infrastructure for ODR ethics. Perhaps ways will be found to consolidate all of the separate ethics rules and guidance that are being developed into a unified set of principles and standards; or perhaps we will need to acknowledge that there are many approaches to governance of ethical ODR systems, software, and practice. If the latter remains the course of action, we will need to find a way to operate effectively within that fractured universe. If we do not successfully achieve one or the other, can we fairly argue that we are providing parties, let alone present and future practitioners, any degree of certainty about ethical practice?

As an example of the problem, we could cite the United Nations Convention on International Settlement Agreements Resulting from Mediation (also known as the Singapore Convention).[81] Article 5 (1) e of the Convention states that relief may be granted from a mediated settlement if:

> There was a serious breach by the mediator of standards applicable to the mediator or the mediation without which breach the party would not have entered into the settlement agreement … .[82]

There are no published standards in the Convention, nor are any specific standards cited in the Convention, so one might reasonably ask how a serious breach would be determined if there was no baseline set of standards against which to judge the mediator's behavior. A recent article in the *International Journal of Online Dispute Resolution* suggests using a standard code of disclosure as a way to address this issue,[83] but until there is some accepted cross-jurisdictional approach to defining standards or to reconciling different standards, practitioners and participants will exist in a murky

80 A comment made by a participant in a practitioners' dialogue conducted by one of the authors after the Covid pandemic had become widespread in 2020.

81 https://uncitral.un.org/en/texts/mediation/conventions/international_settlement_agreements Last accessed 21 July 2020.

82 *United Nations Convention on International Settlement Agreements Resulting from Mediation*, United Nations, New York, 2019, Art. 5, Section 1e, 6.

83 Goncalves, A.M.M., Bogacz, F. and Rainey, D. "Beyond the Singapore Convention: The Importance of Creating a Code of Disclosure to Make International Commercial Mediation Mainstream." *International Journal of Online Dispute Resolution*, 6(2), 2019, 164-169.

landscape; one without a clear ethical infrastructure for cross-border and technologically enhanced dispute resolution.

Thus, merely having a rule, such as an international Convention, does not an ethics infrastructure make. Beyond filling the gaps in the cascade of ODR ethical standards and guidance needed to govern the field, mechanisms for accountability are needed, including those that can feasibly handle cross-jurisdictional ethics complaints. And all aspects of our ODR ethics landscape should be designed to respond to the inevitable updates that will be needed due to ongoing technology development.

APPENDIX[84]

ODR Principles and Standards

Disputes in Cyberspace 2001: Update on Online Dispute Resolution for Consumers in Cross-Border Disputes, Office for Developed and Transition Economies, Consumers International, 2001.

Ethical Principles for Online Dispute Resolution, The National Center for Technology and Dispute Resolution. http://odr.info/ethics-and-odr/.

European Commission Recommendation on the Principles Applicable to the Bodies Responsible for the Out-of-Court Settlement of Consumer Disputes (98/257/CE). https://eur-lex.europa.eu/legal-content/EN/TXT/?uri=LEGISSUM:l32031.

European Committee for Standardization Workshop's Standardization of Online Dispute Resolution Tools. www.cen.eu/news/brochures/brochures/WorkshopODR.pdf.

Federal Law of Consumer Protection on ODR for the Federal Consumer Protection Prosecutor Office of the Government of Mexico, 2015.

French legislation and decree on voluntary ODR platform certification:

- LOI n° 2019-222 du 23 mars 2019 de programmation 2018-2022 et de réforme pour la justice. www.legifrance.gouv.fr/affichLoiPreparation.do;jsessionid=67461511805D3C45A7E68E1CC1CD736A.tplgfr35s_2?idDocument=JORFDOLE000036830320&type=general&typeLoi=proj&legislature=15.
- Décret n° 2019-1089 du 25 octobre 2019 relatif à la certification des services en ligne de conciliation, de médiation et d'arbitrage. www.legifrance.gouv.fr/eli/decret/2019/10/25/JUSC1922391D/jo/texte.

Government of Brazil standards for ODR platform, 2014. https://consumidor.gov.br/pages/principal/?1592940584830.

International Council for Online Dispute Resolution Guidelines for ODR Training Components. https://icodr.org/guides/training.pdf.

International Mediation Institute Competency Criteria for E-Mediators.

84 These are the ethical principles, standards, and guidelines for online dispute resolution identified at the time of publication.

International Mediation Institute e-Mediation Certification, Annex 1 and 2.

Mediating from a Distance: Suggested Practice Guidelines for Family Mediators by Mediate BC. www.mediatebc.com/sites/default/files/Guidelines_Mediating-from-a-Distance-%28Second-edition%29_0.pdf.

OECD's Guidelines for Consumer Protection in E-Commerce, 2016. www.oecd.org/sti/consumer/ECommerce-Recommendation-2016.pdf

Online Dispute Resolution Standards of the International Council for Online Dispute Resolution. https://icodr.org/standards/.

Online Dispute Resolution Standards of Practice, 2009, The National Center for Technology and Dispute Resolution. www.icann.org/en/system/files/files/odr-standards-of-practice-en.pdf.

Online Dispute Resolution Technical Interface Standards; Working Draft 3; February 2019, National Center for State Courts (USA). https://www.ncsc.org/__data/assets/pdf_file/0025/16756/odr-technical-interface-standards-wd-03.pdf.

Recommended Best Practices for Online Dispute Resolution Service Providers developed by the American Bar Association Taskforce on ECommerce and ADR.

Standards for ODR Platforms for Court Program Pilot of the American Bar Association Section on Pro Bono and Public Service and Technology and Dispute Resolution Committee 2018.

UNCITRAL Technical Notes on Online Dispute Resolution, 2017 by United Nations Commission on International Trade Law, UNCITRAL secretariat, Vienna, Austria. www.uncitral.org/pdf/english/texts/odr/V1700382_English_Technical_Notes_on_ODR.pdf.

Video Arbitration Guidelines of the International Council for Online Dispute Resolution. https://icodr.org/guides/videoarb.pdf.

Video Mediation Guidelines of the International Council for Online Dispute Resolution. https://icodr.org/guides/videomed.pdf.

Chapter 3 Lessons from Online Dispute Resolution for Dispute System Design

Orna Rabinovich-Einy and Ethan Katsh

1 Introduction

This chapter addresses a need to integrate two bodies of literature in the ADR field – that relating to 'disputes system design' (DSD) and that relating to 'online dispute resolution' (ODR). In the eight years that have passed since the first edition of this book was published, ODR has grown and the interconnections between the DSD and ODR fields have strengthened. Nevertheless, there is still significant room for enhanced integration. To date, technology in dispute resolution has been relegated to the ODR field, viewing it as a niche area relevant mostly to disputes that arose online or are substantively connected to technology. As we will show, the reach of new technologies is far more pervasive and holds a promise for transforming in a very deep sense some of the ADR field's most deep-rooted assumptions in the area of DSD. Indeed, the stark distinctions between ADR and ODR on the one hand, and between formal litigation and alternatives on the other hand, are being blurred with online processes becoming a design choice across the entire dispute resolution landscape.

While our main focus is on the lessons of ODR for the DSD field, we believe that the merging of ODR and DSD provides important insights for both the DSD field and the ODR field. In terms of DSD, technology has been challenging some of the field's most basic assumptions, but has also generated new means for addressing and preventing disputes systematically. For ODR, the DSD perspective highlights the need to think of dispute resolution in a systematic way and emphasize the prevention of disputes, rather than concentrate on tools for addressing individual disputes on an ad hoc basis.

In the sections that follow, we describe the rise of both ODR and DSD in recent decades, as well as the impact technology has had and can be expected to further have on the evolution of DSD in the future.

2 Lessons of ODR: DSD Meets Technology

2.1 The Rise of ODR

In the late 1990s, with the proliferation of internet communications, it became apparent that the online environment was fast becoming an arena that was rich with disputes but deficient in avenues for effectively addressing them. The unique features of online communication made traditional, face-to-face dispute resolution processes irrelevant. Since communications could be conducted over distances (oftentimes crossing legal jurisdictions) and identities could be easily masked, familiar means for engendering trust and ensuring the effectiveness of dispute resolution mechanisms were typically missing.[1] Even where some of these difficulties could be mitigated, courts and traditional ADR processes typically remained inaccessible due to the high costs associated with face-to-face processes that required long distance travel and legal representation for dealing with what were often small-scale conflicts (in monetary terms).

The realization that the very features that have contributed to the emergence of disputes online – mainly the communication over geographical, cultural and linguistic differences – also served to make traditional dispute resolution avenues ineffective, gave rise to the development of what has been termed 'online dispute resolution,' or ODR. Originally, the term referred to processes for dispute resolution that relied on ICT or were being offered through the internet for addressing conflicts that arose online (namely in the e-commerce setting or on online social forums) or were related to the digital environment (such as copyright abuse). Over time, use of such processes expanded, and these mechanisms are increasingly being offered for the resolution of offline disputes (although interestingly some of the very early ideas for using ODR targeted offline conflicts, offering online processes for addressing family disputes). Indeed, in recent years, ODR has been embraced by the court system for various offline claims and proceedings, including small claims, traffic violations, family conflicts, neighbor disputes, foreclosure suits and motor-vehicle accidents.[2]

The contemporary ODR landscape can be divided into two principal domains – *tools* and *systems*. The first area has involved the development of specific dispute resolution applications that can be used to resolve both online and offline disputes. The future of

1 O. Rabinovich-Einy, 'Technology's Impact: The Quest for a New Paradigm for Accountability in Mediation', *Harv. Neg. L. Rev.*, Vol 11, 2006, pp. 257-258.

2 A. Mentovich, J.J. Prescott & O. Rabinovich-Einy, 'Are Litigation Outcomes Disparities Inevitable? Courts, Technology and the Future of Impartiality', *Ala. L. Rev.*, Vol 71, No 4, 2020, pp. 893-979.

ODR is assumed by many to lie in an expanding array of tools that will open up new options for third parties.[3] Perceived in this way, ODR is not in itself a distinct field but more like a support system for mediators and arbitrators addressing individual disputes. As mediators have become more comfortable generally in the use of technology, they have increasingly been looking for software applications that could perform a discrete function and could be plugged into their practice in some way.[4] From such a perspective, the future of ODR would seem to lie in an ongoing evolution of more and more powerful software that could be employed in more and more complicated contexts.

One example of ODR tools is the development of processes for 'automated negotiation.'[5] In automated negotiation, a human third party such as a mediator or arbitrator is substituted with software-based decision-making. Prominent examples of such processes can be found in SquareTrade's[6] or eBay's[7] preliminary stage of dispute resolution, as well as in Smartsettle's blind bidding process.[8] Another tool consists of 'negotiation support systems' – software that assists negotiating parties in determining their own interests as well as reaching a mutually accepted resolution that maximizes joint gain for all parties.[9] A variety of ODR providers including The Mediation Room,[10] CREK,[11] WIPO[12] and Modron[13] have been for some time operating online platforms that allow mediators and arbitrators to exchange documents and communicate with parties without having to meet face to face. These ODR tools are now being used to facilitate the mediation process even when the disputants are in the same room and the conflicts emerged in the offline setting. While the appeal of ODR for online disputes is often obvious and is related to the lack of real alternatives, in the case of the application of ODR tools for offline disputes the main advantages of ODR have been perceived to be the accessibility, low cost and speed of communication through such

3 *See* E. Katsh & J. Rifkin, *Online Dispute Resolution: Resolving Conflicts in Cyberspace*, 2001, pp. 90-116; D. Larson, 'Technology Mediated Dispute Resolution', *U. of Toledo L. Rev.*, Vol 38, 2006, pp. 215-217.; A.R. Lodder & J. Zeleznikow, 'Developing an Online Dispute Resolution Environment: Dialogue Tools and Negotiation Support Systems in a Three-Step Model', *Harv. Negot. L. Rev.*, Vol 10, 2005, pp. 287-337.

4 For example, the use of software for an online brainstorming process (*see* E. Katsh & L. Wing, 'Ten Years of Online Dispute Resolution (ODR): Looking at the Past and Constructing the Future', *Univ. of Toledo L. Rev.*, Vol 38, 2006, pp. 19-45; *see also* Debatagraph's visualization tools used for exploring various aspects of a problem and potential solutions (*see* http://debategraph.org/) (last visited on 9 May 2011)).

5 *See* E. Katsh & O. Rabinovich-Einy, 'Technology and the Future of Dispute Systems Design', *Harv. Neg. L. Rev.*, Vol. 17, 2012, pp. 153-199.

6 Rabinovich-Einy 2006, *supra* note 1, at 258.

7 https://resolutioncenter.ebay.com/ (last visited on 19 March, 2021).

8 https://info.smartsettle.com/products/smartsettle-one/smartsettles-visual-blind-bidding/ (last visited on 19 March 2021).

9 https://info.smartsettle.com/products/smartsettle-infinity/ (last visited 19 March 2021).

10 https://www.themediationroom.com/ (last visited on 19 March 2021).

11 www.crekodr.com/ (last visited on 24 May 2020).

12 www.wipo.int/amc/en/arbitration/online/index.html (last visited on 24 May 2020).

13 www.modron.com/spaces (last visited on 24 May 2020).

tools.[14] During the Covid-19 outbreak in the winter and spring of 2020, ODR became the only means for resolving disputes both in- and outside the court context at a time when physical meetings were forbidden and many of these communications relied on Zoom, a widely available and easy to use video-conferencing tool.

Over the years, additional advantages beyond accessibility and efficiency of ODR have been recognized, which relate to the potential of new technologies to overcome disputant biases and facilitate parties in reaching better, pareto-optimal resolutions.[15] These qualitative advantages are perhaps even more salient in the second domain in which ODR has developed over the last two decades – the realm of ODR systems.

ODR *systems* include ODR tools (such as those described above) used in a coordinated way within a closed setting by a limited (but potentially very large) number of users who are engaged in ongoing interactions with other users and may experience similar types of problems over time. Originally, ODR systems were developed for online disputes and, in the case of systems, for online communities. The paradigmatic example of an ODR system is the eBay dispute resolution mechanism, which is well-known for its high usage rate (now handling well over 60 million disputes annually) and impressive success rates (over 80% of the disputes are satisfactorily resolved through automated mechanisms without a need for any human involvement).[16] eBay, by studying patterns of disputes and developing a system that can handle large numbers of repetitive types of conflicts, has managed to resolve such disputes early and at a low cost (an essential feature given the low dollar value of many, although certainly not all, eBay transactions). No less important, however, has been the contribution of eBay's ODR system to the realm of dispute prevention. By studying the data uncovered in the dispute resolution processes, eBay has managed to uncover common sources of problems and to structure information and services on its site so that these problems do not recur.[17]

Another elaborate ODR system that has emerged in another online context, is the one established on Wikipedia.[18] The system offers its users a variety of online parallels to traditional ADR processes (*e.g.*, negotiation, mediation, and arbitration), as well as some new variants (such as online polling). Alongside its dispute resolution efforts, Wikipedia is focused on dispute prevention, drawing on technological tools not only for studying patterns of disputes and effective resolution strategies, but also for

14 O. Rabinovich-Einy, 'Balancing the Scales: The Ford-Firestone Case, the Internet, and the Future Dispute Resolution Landscape', *Yale J. Law Technol.*, Vol 6, 2006, pp. 29-30.

15 E.M. Thiessen & J.P. McMahon, 'Beyond Win-Win in Cyberspace', *Ohio St. J. on Disp. Resol*, Vol 15, 2000, pp. 643-667.

16 Katsh & Rabinovich-Einy 2012, *supra* note 5. For an analysis of the eBay ODR system, *see also* A. Schmitz & J. Martinez, *ODR and Innovation in the United States*, Chapter 21.

17 Katsh & Rabinovich-Einy 2012, *supra* note 5.

18 http://en.wikipedia.org/wiki/Wikipedia:Dispute_resolution (last visited on 7 May 2011).

automatically detecting such problems as illegitimate editing of content on its site and deleting such content immediately, even before abuse has been reported by users.

What both eBay and Wikipedia understood early on was that by offering effective dispute resolution mechanisms that were integrated with the site's (or community's) principal mission, they not only satisfactorily address individual disputes, but are also able to prevent problems thereby enhancing trust in the site and improving its content and performance. In this mission, technology was not only a byproduct of such sites' online operations, but proved to be an invaluable tool in detecting problematic patterns and instituting effective, often automated, solutions.

More recently, ODR systems have developed on social media sites, such as Facebook and 'gig economy' platforms such as Upwork.[19] While Upwork deals with a relatively small variety of disputes that have to do with scope and quality of work performed and payment due, Facebook has to address a wide range of conflicts that arise among users, as well as between Facebook and its users. In recent years, 'content moderation' – Facebook's attempts to screen user generated content that is not in line with Facebook guidelines and values – has received heightened attention. As Facebook's influence on political speech, commercial activities and social engagement continues to grow, critiques have also become more and more vocal questioning the standards according to which content is being censored as well as the role played by algorithms and humans in performing such important and excruciating tasks. In response, Facebook announced that it would establish a global a Facebook Oversight Board referred to as the 'Facebook Supreme Court.' The Board will hear appeals on Facebook's 'policy-formation and enforcement processes,' as well as provide policy recommendations.[20] While it remains to be seen how the Facebook Oversight Board will perform, its launch is bring received with mixed reactions, with critics highlighting the shortcomings of the Board due to its limited mandate and powers, while others underscore the significance of this step which introduces enhanced transparency, oversight and accountability to public values to the operation of one of the most powerful private institutions in modern day society.[21]

As can be seen from the eBay, Wikipedia, Facebook and Upwork examples, companies that operate exclusively online have enjoyed a head start in understanding how influential a communications and information processing capability can be in

---

19 https://support.upwork.com/hc/en-us/sections/360002713853-Disputes (last visited on 31 May 2020).

20 E. Douek, 'What Kind of Oversight Board Have you Given Us?', *U. of Chicago L. Rev. Online*, available at https://lawreviewblog.uchicago.edu/2020/05/11/fb-oversight-board-edouek/ (last visited on 31 May 2020).

21 *Id.*; B. Gilbert, 'Facebook is Spending $130 Million to Create a "Supreme Court" that Can Overrule Mark Zuckerberg – Here's What We Know About It,' *Business Insider*, 16 February 2020, available at www.businessinsider.sg/meet-the-first-20-members-of-facebook-supreme-court-2020-5 (last visited on 31 May 2020). Facebook referred its decision to indefinitely suspend former President Trump's Facebook account to the Board. *See* https://about.fb.com/news/2021/01/referring-trump-suspension-to-oversight-board/ (last visited on 19 March, 2021).

shaping the nature and quantity of disputes that occur and the options for dispute resolution that will be needed. They have demonstrated the value of not treating disputes as isolated events and of treating the information generated by a functioning dispute system as something that needs to be attended in order to understand how disputes surface and to identify approaches in how they might be resolved.

The lessons learned by the all-online entities that had no choice but to think in terms of a dispute system are already extending to the offline setting. As all institutions adopt communication over the network as a significant part of their operating models, and as online interactions replace many traditional offline interactions, institutions in the physical world are confronting many of the forces, capabilities, and opportunities that the all-online entities have already identified. This process has already begun with some offline organizations, companies and, most notably, the courts, starting to integrate ODR systems. One past example was the adoption of an online arbitration system for the resolution of fender-bender subrogation claims for property damages in the insurance industry in Israel.[22] At the time, an entire industry shifted from litigating these claims to addressing them systematically through an exclusively online system. Beyond the effective and satisfactory resolution of individual disputes, the online system led to the refinement of the rules governing such claims, thereby enhancing clarity and preventing similar problems from recurring.[23] While the Benoam system has since collapsed due to the emergence of new insurance companies who objected to the arrangement that preceded them, Benoam's success continues to inspire new initiatives to adopt ODR mechanisms in this context, as evidenced by the growing adoption of ODR for a variety of claims in the court setting.

As we can see from the brief description of the evolution of the ODR field, the line between on- and offline activities is constantly shifting, with activities that were considered in the past to be the domain of face-to-face interaction becoming an inherent part of online communication. Parallel to these developments, the distinct characteristics of online communications have been blurred, with digital avenues becoming a primary means for communication between close friends who are based near one another as well as a means for connecting with distant strangers. These changes have meant that the domain of ODR has also expanded, relaxing many of the assumptions about what is and is not appropriate for online resolution. In the following section, we explore another development in the ADR field that emerged around the same time as internet communications began to spread – the growth of DSD. Despite both

22 O. Rabinovich-Einy & R. Tsur, 'The Case for Greater Formality in ADR: Drawing on the Lessons of Benoam's Private Arbitration System', *Vermont L. Rev.*, Vol 34, 2010, p. 542; O. Rabinovich-Einy & R. Tsur, 'Unclogging the Collision Course: The Evolution of Benoam, an Online Private Court', *ACResolution*, 2010, p. 8.

23 *See generally*, Rabinovich-Einy & Tsur 2010, *supra* note 22.

developments being grounded in the broader field of ADR and other connections that exist between them, they had for many years occupied distinct spheres, with occasional references to one another, but with only limited systematic effort to think about the deeper connections that exist between them.

2.2 *The Emergence of DSD*

In the late 1980s, Ury, Brett & Goldberg published a book entitled: "Getting Disputes Resolved: Designing Systems to Cut the Costs of Conflict."[24] This book would later be recognized as signaling the birth of the field of DSD. The authors' principal insight was that patterns of disputes can be found in closed settings and, therefore, by institutionalizing avenues for addressing disputes conflict will be handled more effectively and satisfactorily than through ex-post measures.[25] From the very beginning, it was clear that the emerging field marked a shift from an individual perspective (that was typical of ADR up to that point) to a structural one.

Ury *et al.*'s research was based on empirical data concerning wildcat strikes in the mining industry, but they also hoped to provide new perspectives on both dispute resolution and prevention systems in organizations and institutions. They were intrigued by the fact that different mines suffered from different kinds of strikes. The explanation lay in processes and levels of communication between union and management. Communication that focused on interests of the parties and that took place continuously was believed to help prevent strikes. This realization led Ury *et al.* to

> [d]istinguish three major ways of resolving disputes: to reconcile the disputants' underlying interests, to determine who is right, and to determine who has more power. Problem solving negotiation exemplifies the interests approach; going to court, the rights approach; strikes and wars, the power approach. We argue that, in general, an interests approach is less costly and more rewarding than a rights approach, which in turn is less costly and more rewarding than a power approach. The goal, then, is to design a system that provides interests-based procedures for disputants to use whenever possible and low-cost rights procedures (such as advisory arbitration) or low-cost power procedures (such as voting) as backups.[26]

---

24 W.B. Ury *et al.*, *Getting Disputes Resolved: Designing Systems to Cut the Costs of Conflict*, 1988.

25 *See id.*, pp. xii-xiii.

26 *See id.*, p. XV.

In addition, Ury *et al.* offered a four-stage communications-intensive design process comprised of diagnosis, design, implementation, and finally exit, evaluation and diffusion.[27]

Several years later, Costantino & Merchant published the second major building block in the evolution of the DSD field.[28] The Costatino & Merchant book focused attention on the value of identifying patterns of disputes. Where patterns can be identified, the dispute resolution system can move beyond the resolution of individual disputes and enhance prevention on a system-wide basis.[29] In addition, Costantino & Merchant highlighted the benefits of including in the design process those who would be affected by the processes developed.[30] Such practices are clearly relevant to dispute resolution systems which employ the new capabilities embedded in digital technology.

In recent years, two comprehensive books on dispute system design have come out, reflecting the changes the field has undergone over the last three decades, in its broad view of what constitutes dispute systems design, which extends well beyond the original framework of addressing conflicts within an organization, institution or industry.[31] DSD is defined as the 'intentional creation of a system or a process to achieve some end or set of goals.'[32]

What have the extensive experience and literature in the DSD area taught us about design activities? Admittedly, as stated in the DSD literature, 'it is difficult to come up with many useful generalizations,'[33] but several broad themes can be extracted from the writing on DSD.

One over-arching principle that comes across clearly from the various writings in the field is that 'one size or one process does not and cannot fit all,'[34] and there are no pre-made quick solutions. The success of the end-product is strongly linked to the process through which it was produced, ensuring the involvement of a broad range of

27 *See id.*, pp. 65-83.

28 *See* C. Costantino & C. Merchant, *Designing Conflict Management Systems: A Guide to Creating Productive and Healthy Organizations*, 1996.

29 *See id.*, p. 168.

30 *See id.*, p. 49.

31 N.H. Rogers *et al.*, *Designing Systems and Processes for Managing Disputes*, 2013; L.B. Amsler, J. Martinez & S. Smith, *Dispute: Preventing, Managing and Resolving Conflict*, 2020.

32 Rogers *et al.* 2013, *supra* note 32, at 5.

33 *Id.*, p. 4.

34 C. Menkel-Meadow, 'Are There Systemic Issues in Dispute System Design? And What We Should [Not] Do About It: Lessons from International and Domestic Fronts', *Harv. Negot. L. Rev.*, Vol 14, 2009, pp. 195, 228.

stakeholders,[35] whose interests are uncovered, articulated and addressed through process choice and structure.[36]

In addition, systemic goals, values and interests need to be articulated,[37] and potential conflicts of interests (between the various systemic goals on the one hand, and between systemic goals and individual interests on the other hand) need to be managed through the design of the dispute system.[38] Furthermore, process design must be attuned to the specific relational,[39] cultural[40] and legal[41] environment into which the system is being introduced, as well as the power[42] and incentive[43] structure such environment creates. Designers and third parties involved must meet predefined professional and ethical standards, criteria and principles, and uphold predefined values and goals.[44]

Finally, the system must be committed to ongoing assessment, learning and improvement, so as to ensure that the system meets its goals, while performing in a fair and efficient manner (which may require revisiting and refining some of these goals in light of the system's performance).[45] The tasks associated with the design of a dispute system are performed by a professional, who tailors the process to the context, while offering flexible and confidential avenues that are offered alongside familiar formal and public avenues of redress.

DSD can be viewed as an activity of setting, or resetting, professional, physical, and conceptual boundaries. These different kinds of boundaries can all be linked to, and affected by, processes of communication. In terms of professional boundaries, a new profession of dispute system designer emerged. Designers were often trained in ADR or/and organizational development and possessed expertise in conducting the organizational dispute analysis that would underlie the dispute system design and evaluation. While the literature emphasized the need to consult those affected by the process being designed, the use of an expert designer was generally also seen as

---

35 *Id.*, at 229-230; Rogers *et al.* 2013, *supra* note 32, at 20 (referring to 'those people whom a conflict affects or could affect implementation as "stakeholders"'), 69-73; S. Smith & J. Martinez, 'An Analytic Framework for Dispute Systems Design', *Harv. Negot. L. Rev.*, Vol 15, 2009, pp. 123, 131 (stating that 'Stakeholders may be the immediate parties in conflict, individuals or entities subsidiary to or constituents of those parties, or others directly or indirectly affected by the dispute's outcome' and that 'it is usually best to identify as many stakeholders as possible'); Schmitz & Martinez, *supra* note 16.

36 Menkel-Meadow 2009, *supra* note 35, at 129-130; Rogers *et al.* 2013, *supra* note 32, at 20; Smith & Martinez 2009, *supra* note 36, at 129-133.

37 Smith & Martinez 2009, *supra* note 36, at 129; Rogers *et al.* 2013, *supra* note 32, at 74-79; Schmitz & Martinez, *supra* note 16.

38 Rogers *et al.* 2013, *supra* note 32, at 22-24, 79-84.

39 Smith & Martinez 2009, *supra* note 36, at 130; Schmitz & Martinez, *supra* note 16.

40 Menkel-Meadow 2009, *supra* note 35, at 229-230; Rogers *et al.* 2013, *supra* note 32, at 23, 31-35, 86-91.

41 Menkel-Meadow 2009, *supra* note 35, at 229-230.

42 *Id*; Rogers *et al.* 2013, *supra* note 32, at 110; Smith & Martinez 2009, *supra* note 36, at 131-132.

43 Smith & Martinez 2009, *supra* note 36, at 131.

44 Menkel-Meadow 2009, *supra* note 35, at 229-230; Rogers *et al.* 2013, *supra* note 32, at 62-63.

45 Menkel-Meadow 2009, *supra* note 35, at 229-230; Rogers *et al.* 2013, *supra* note 32, at 352-353; Smith & Martinez 2009, *supra* note 36, at 132-133.

necessary. In this environment, internal dispute handlers, such as ombudsmen, became more widely used to oversee these newly established systems.

An important goal of DSD was the separation of the dispute resolution system from the other parts of the organization. The rationale was that a secure space was needed for employees to voice concerns and complaints. Confidentiality needed to be provided to those using the system in order to build trust in the system and in the neutrals who were often employees of the organization.[46] This is, of course, important but confidentiality also came at a cost to quality control efforts as it led to very little documentation being preserved about the operation of the dispute resolution process.[47]

Lastly, DSD has had an impact on conceptual boundaries relating to dispute resolution typologies. The establishment of distinctions among ADR processes was necessary to distinguish internal conflict management systems from the litigation process, something that was important in justifying their establishment and use. Dispute resolution literature tended to view the freedom and flexibility to select one's own dispute resolution process as a principal advantage of ADR. The framework offered by UB&G emphasized the advantages of internal systems and the value of deliberate design. Dispute system designers have often opted for one or more processes, including mediation, arbitration, and counseling. Clear lines were drawn between interest and rights-based processes and within each category, processes such as mediation tended to have set, predetermined characteristics.

In the course of the last three decades, the DSD field has generated a significant scope of writing on the topic and many conflict management systems have been established in many different organizations and institutions.[48] What originally was applied to the workplace setting has expanded and is being employed in additional areas, such as courts,[49] compensation facilities and funds,[50] constitution-drafting,[51] and the

46 *See* H. Gadlin & E.W. Pino, 'Neutrality: A Guide for the Organizational Ombudsperson', *Neg. J.*, Vol 13, 1997, pp. 17-35; M.P. Rowe, 'The Corporate Ombudsman: An Overview and Analysis', *Neg. J.*, Vol 3, 1987, pp. 128-129.

47 *See* H. Gadlin, 'The Ombudsman: What's in a Name?', *Neg. J.*, Vol 16, 2000, p. 41.

48 *See E.g.*, J.P. Conbere, 'Theory Building for Conflict Management System Design', *Conflict Res. Q.*, Vol 19, 2001, pp. 215-236; C.A. Costantino, 'Using Interest-Based Techniques to Design Conflict Management Systems', *Neg. J.*, Vol 12, 1996, pp. 207-214; D.M. Kolb & S.S. Silbey, 'Enhancing the Capacity of Organizations to Deal with Disputes', *Neg. J.*, Vol 6, 1990, pp. 297-304; M.P. Rowe, 'The Ombudsman's Role in a Dispute Resolution System', *Neg. J.*, Vol 7, 1991, pp. 353-360; A prominent example is Lipsky, Seeber & Fincher's comprehensive book on conflict management systems, published in 2003 (*See* D.B. Lipsky *et al.*, *Emerging Systems for Managing Workplace Conflict: Lessons from American Corporations for Managers and Dispute Resolution Professionals*, 2003).

49 *See* Menkel-Meadow 2009, *supra* note 35, at 201; O. Rabinovich-Einy, 'Beyond Efficiency: The Transformation of Courts through Technology', *UCLA J. L. & Tech.*, Vol 12, 2008, pp. 1-45.

50 *See* R.M. Ackerman, 'The September 11th Victim Compensation Fund: An Effective Administrative Response to a National Tragedy', *Harv. Negot. L. Rev.*, Vol 10, 2005, pp. 135-229; E. Eiran, 'Politics and the 2005 Gaza and North West Bank Compensation and Assistance Facility', *Harv. Negot. L. Rev.*, Vol 14, 2009, pp. 101-121.

51 *See* Menkel-Meadow 2009, *supra* note 35, at 219.

international sphere.[52] In all these contexts, it has been recognized that the heart of both dispute resolution and dispute prevention lies in the communication between parties as part of a decision-making process. Rather than waiting for disputes to occur, dialogues conducted by potential parties in organizational settings can lead to the design of processes for facilitating information exchange and information processing in other arenas and between different types of stakeholders. Such efforts also had the effect of dimming the distinction between formal and informal dispute resolution,[53] and between dispute resolution and norm generation.[54]

As part of the growth of the field, the Ury *et al.* and Costantino & Merchant models have been revisited in an attempt to address 'second generation' DSD issues.[55] Yet, the impact and potential of digital technology on the traditional framework of DSD has not been rigorously studied,[56] With some notable exceptions that have been published in the course of the last decade, where technology was discussed, it was assumed that the role of technology in DSD would be to move the field in the same direction it has been heading rather than being a force that represents a change in direction. Technology however, is often 'disruptive,' in that it may require a reorienting of accepted practices at the same time that it brings new ways and new ideas about how to achieve goals.[57] It is our view that the introduction of digital technology is generating a highly significant and perhaps radical shift, under which DSD is transformed from a boundary-setting activity to one in which boundaries are constantly being challenged, becoming more diffuse and flexible. One example is the way in which technology has allowed the breaking of traditional distinctions that have long existed within ADR between interest- and rights-based processes, as well as the blurring of boundaries within each process type. This involves

52 *See* A.K. Schneider, 'The Intersection of Dispute Systems Design and Transitional Justice', *Harv. Neg. L. Rev.* Vol 14, 2009, pp. 289-315.

53 For the application of DSD principles to courts: *See* Menkel-Meadow 2009, *supra* note 35, at 201; Rabinovich-Einy 2008, *supra* note 50.

54 With the application of DSD principles in consensus-building processes, they were often being used to generate new norms and shared understandings as opposed to addressing a concrete conflict in accordance with preexisting norms: *see* C. Menkel-Meadow, 'Peace and Justice: Notes no the Evolution and Purposes of Legal Processes', *Geo. L. J.*, Vol 94, 2006, pp. 572-576.

55 *See* C.A. Costantino, 'Second Generation Organizational Conflict Management Systems Design: A Practitioner's Perspective on Emerging Issues', *Harv. Neg. L. Rev.*, Vol 14, 2009, pp. 81-100; F.E. McGovern, 'The Second Generation of Dispute System Design: Recurring Problems and Potential Solutions', *Ohio St. J. on Disp. Resol.*, Vol 24, 2008, pp. 53-79.

56 Notable exceptions are the Bordone article (R.C. Bordone, 'Electronic Online Dispute Resolution: A Systems Approach – Potential, Problems, and a Proposal', *Harv. Neg. L. Rev.* Vol 3, 1998, pp. 175-211) and the Lipsky *et al.* book (Lipsky *et al.* 2003, *supra* note 49, at 329-331), which refers to the emergence of ODR. The following are some additional exceptions where ODR is mentioned: *See* L.B. Bingham *et al.*, 'Dispute System Design and Justice in Employment Dispute Resolution: Mediation at the Workplace', *Harv. Neg. L. Rev.*, Vol 14, 2009, pp. 14, 17; *See* Menkel-Meadow 2009, *supra* note 35, at 208; Smith & Martinez 2009, supra note 36, at 145, 150, 154-156; Eiran 2009, *supra* note 51, at 121. More commonly, however, the DSD literature ignores technology.

57 E. Katsh, *The Electronic Media and the Transformation of Law*, 1989, pp. 3-5; R. Susskind, *The End of Lawyers*, 2008, pp. 93-100.

generating new types of processes and variations within each familiar category of processes, each with its own qualities and traits. We expand on the blurring of boundaries in DSD in these and other realms in the following section.

2.3 The Impact of New Technologies on DSD: The Blurring of Traditional Boundaries

2.3.1 Professional Boundaries

The traditional DSD paradigm lay the foundation for both the creation of a new profession of dispute system designers and a new arena for the delivery of dispute resolution services by professional ombudsmen internally within organizations. The proliferation of digital technologies seems to challenge these professional categories and the boundaries they created on several levels. For one, our understanding of dispute system designer capabilities, qualities and training can be expected to undergo significant change.[58] While traditionally, both designers and ombudsmen were trained in such areas as organizational development and dispute resolution, the digital environment requires familiarity with the new opportunities and dangers that are associated with digital communication and the use of digital tools for locating, addressing and preventing conflicts. As digital technology becomes an inherent part of the way people interact and organizations function, it is also increasingly being incorporated into the way people communicate about their differences. We can expect a similar development to occur in terms of the spread of ODR systems (either as standalone systems or as an addition to face-to-face ones), requiring designers to better understand the qualities of these technologies and the new opportunities they open up (as well as the barriers and costs they entail).

As part of these changes, dispute system designers will need to learn to cooperate with technical experts in the development of ODR systems. Working together does not translate into a mere aggregation of perspectives but may very well result in a product that is altogether different, as a result of the commingling of the very different viewpoints, work processes and orientations each of the disciplines has.

An important new perspective that is bound to deeply impact the DSD field is that of computer scientists who will inevitably be drawn to ODR. Online dispute resolution and DSD have attracted the interest of computer scientists who have recognized that ODR is software-based and, like all forms of dispute resolution, is focused around the management of communication and information. There are many sub-fields of computer science, such as artificial intelligence, process modeling and software

58 *See* Costantino 2009, *supra* note 56, at 96-97 (raising the question what knowledge, skills and competencies dispute designers should possess).

engineering, that are likely to find that ODR and DSD provide opportunities for research and practical contributions.

As processes that were conducted entirely face to face in the past are joined by processes that are software-based, modes of analysis and presentation are likely to change. Verbal and textual applications, for example, are likely to be joined by visual and graphical resources, by tools for reflection and even by games that provide behavioral insights. In an early example of some of this, the University of Massachusetts Departments of Computer Science and Legal Studies, along with a federal agency, the National Mediation Board, worked together for seven years with an initial focus on the use of technology in labor disputes.[59] Computer scientists' input in the design phase proved crucial. Their role extended beyond that of mere executioners, uncovering assumptions underlying the ADR-trained designers' choice of goals and means, and, consequently, in refining the goals of these new tools as well as playing a key role in shaping their form. At the same time, computer scientists will need to better understand due process requirements and the ways in which procedural values can and should be translated into the design of ODR, which presents a real shift and could prove to be a significant challenge for such discipline.[60]

In addition, user input also has the potential to transform the way in which DSD is understood and practiced. Digital technology can make participation by stakeholders much more meaningful than it has traditionally been by allowing a wide array of voices to be heard. This is due to the capabilities for synthesizing input from a large number of participants,[61] the ability to offer input at convenient times and from afar and, in some cases, the opportunity for anonymous input that comes with digital communication in this day and age.[62] Interestingly, courts designing ODR processes are also changing their traditional approach and employing human-centered design, engaging with the population these systems are supposed to serve and those entities working with such population. This is a novel approach for courts and creates an opportunity for often those belonging to disempowered groups to play an active role in shaping the interface of the justice system.[63]

Furthermore, users can become actual designers of the dispute resolution systems on which they rely. Wikipedia's informal 'mediation cabal' dispute resolution avenue, now

59 Katsh & Wing 2006, *supra* note 4, at 33-35.

60 Indeed, with the expansion of ODR into new settings, some are warning about the dangers of translating due process into code and the ability of engineers to do so. *See* D.K. Citron, 'Technological Due Process', *Wash. U. L. Rev.*, Vol 85, 2007, pp. 1249-1313.

61 *See* B.S. Noveck, *Wiki Government: How Technology Can Make Government Better, Democracy Stronger, and Citizens More Powerful*, 2009, pp. 14, 18, 181 (for a more general discussion of the phenomenon of "crowd sourcing").

62 *See* Katsh & Wing 2006, *supra* note 4, at 40-41.

63 This has been the approach at the Civil Resolution Tribunal at British Columbia, where members of civil society and the individuals they serve have had a voice in the design and improvement of the ODR process offered there.

disabled, was one example of a bottom up dispute resolution mechanism that existed alongside parallel processes offered by the site.[64] This is another clear manifestation of the threats technology poses for professional boundaries, as individual users, with no background in DSD (nor ADR for that matter) can establish dispute resolution processes and systems. We can expect a layperson's design to differ from that of a professional dispute system designer, resulting in an end-product that resembles familiar processes, but also departs from some of the basic prevailing assumptions among ADR professionals. It is perhaps not surprising therefore that the mediation cabal process did not offer confidentiality to disputants and all mediation records were widely available online, much more in line with the spirit of current conventions of internet users than the assumptions and policies practiced by ADR professionals. Interestingly, the formal mediation process that was conducted on Wikipedia, which was a product of 'top down' design, was a discrete, closed process.

In the novel arena of ODR for the blockchain arena, we likewise see innovative processes designed to emulate the qualities of that particular environment, with crowd-sourced decision-making and game theory-inspired incentives. Thus, ODR providers such as Kleros, operating exclusively in this realm, offer resolution of disputes through crowd-sourced jury voting.[65] Jury members are driven to participate and to vote together with the majority through tokenization, which incentivizes appropriate conduct and qualitative decision-making while penalizing misconduct and errors.[66]

As we realize the ease with which users and other non-professional dispute system designers can set up a site for receiving and handling complaints, the question arises as to the value added by a dispute system designer. One important role for professional dispute system designers lies in their duty to ensure the fairness and effectiveness of such systems. While technology opens the door for greater user involvement and input, it is also true that the manner in which large organizations currently operate may undermine the ability of certain stakeholders to participate in the design process.[67] Technology can subject stakeholders to power, not only empower them. When evaluating these issues, designers need to be aware of the fact that new technologies represent more than a change in arena for the performance of dispute resolution processes; digital technology is transforming the very nature of these processes and changing their characteristics in ways that are bound to have an important impact on stakeholders and the organization alike. As others have demonstrated, technology is by no means neutral and a particular

64 http://en.wikipedia.org/wiki/Wikipedia%3AResolving_disputes (last visited on 7 May 2011).
65 C. Lesaege and F. Ast, *Teaching with Technology White Paper* 1 (2018), https://kleros.io/.
66 *Id.*, at 6-7. *See also* Schmitz & Martinez, *supra* note 16 for an analysis of Kleros' ODR process.
67 J. DeMars *et al.*, 'Virtual Virtues: Ethical Considerations for an Online Dispute Resolution (ODR) Practice', *Disp. Res. Mag.*, Vol 17, 2010, pp. 6-11.

software design reflects a preference for certain values over others.[68] While this is certainly a concern, it should be borne in mind that the danger for misconduct, negligence or incompetence by a third party conducting a private and flexible ADR process in a face-to-face setting can be of similar, if not greater concern.[69] The same software that promotes a particular value choice also can make design choices more visible, minimize third-party discretion due to enhanced structure, and allow for more ex-post study of the impact of design choices and quality control of decision-making where discretion is employed through data documentation and analysis. At the same time, as mentioned above, there are concerns about the ability to translate due process requirements into code given the proprietary and opaque nature of algorithmic decision-making, which presents a real hurdle to transparency and accountability.

Some of the pressures ODR can generate can be expected to impact dispute resolution professionals more generally, not only those designing these systems. Ombudsmen, mediators, arbitrators and others will have to feel comfortable with technological applications of dispute resolution processes and learn to incorporate these tools and systems either as a principal avenue for addressing conflict or as a supplement to more traditional channels. Undoubtedly, many dispute resolution professionals will find these developments threatening, as they will require additional training and learning. Indeed, in the recent Covid-19 pandemic, there was a dire need for wide availability of training programs to sensitize dispute resolution professions to the ethical, technological and procedural implications of the shift in medium.

The threat posed by ODR to some dispute resolution professionals, however, may run deeper than the mere need to learn new skills. As described above, some ODR tools are based on automated negotiation, which allows for the displacement of the third party. As we have seen, for simple, repetitive types of disputes, these tools can be extremely effective in resolving disputes. eBay reports an impressive 80% success rate for its automatic processes. Similarly, Cybersettle reported that its product was

> proven to reduce average claim cycles by reducing time spent in the negotiation and settlement stage of claim handling. The process provided claims management with enhanced control over of loss payments, avoided litigation costs, and lowered administrative expenses.[70]

More recently, AI is being introduced into dispute resolution. This development is still in its infancy and is relevant mostly outside the scope of decision-making, but the use of AI

68 *See generally* H. Nissenbaum, 'Values in Technical Design', *in* C. Mitcham (ed.), *Encyclopedia of Science Technology and Ethics*, 2005, pp. ixvi, ixvi-ixx (discussing the challenges of integrating values into the design of technology).

69 *See* Rabinovich-Einy 2006, *supra* note 1, at 266-267.

70 *See* www.cybersettle.com/pub/home/products.aspx (last visited on 7 May 2011).

in this realm will undoubtedly take place in the coming years.[71] Although many remain skeptical that an automated process can be effective in addressing more complex and idiosyncratic conflicts, these developments could prove significant over time for two reasons. First, the scope of what constitutes simple, repetitive and mold-like disputes for which automated processes could provide an effective response may prove to be substantial. Second, with the evolution of technological tools, the reach of automated processes may expand to include situations that today seem too complex for automated tools. Indeed, the expansion of court ODR from small-scale simple disputes to motor-vehicle and family disputes is a vivid demonstration of such trend, and even early AI uses seem to indicate that such developments are not far off.

Clearly, then, dispute system designers and other dispute resolution professionals will have to demonstrate their relevance in an era in which access, use and control of information is changing, the nature of expertise is shifting, and some functions of the traditional intermediaries are being displaced. They will have to gain a deeper understanding of the impact the shift to digital communication is having on their field and be able to identify what is changing and what is not new.

2.3.2 Physical Boundaries

Traditional DSD theory advocated the separation of the dispute resolution system from the other parts of the organization to ensure that a secure space was created for stakeholders to voice concerns and complaints. In the digital era such rigid separation often seems impossible, even undesirable. The fear that access to dispute information may impact the integrity of the dispute resolution process when it is conducted internally can be compensated in the online setting through increased documentation and transparency regarding the content and enforceability of dispute resolution outcomes. The same technology that makes confidentiality more difficult to sustain, can also provide us with alternatives to ensure that organizations or companies do not abuse the dispute resolution data that is now made increasingly accessible to them, and can be mined and used in much more significant ways than in the past.

To understand why ODR may be attractive to disputants despite the cost in terms of confidentiality, we need to reexamine the rationale for ensuring confidentiality in ADR and the reasons behind the establishment of a 'Chinese Wall' between internal dispute resolution units/processes and the rest of the organization's operations. Confidentiality is considered to be a key advantage of ADR processes over formal avenues, drawing disputants to take part in these voluntary processes and allowing them to participate more openly and meaningfully. In terms of confidentiality of proceedings within the organization, the idea was to ensure the independence and impartiality of the dispute resolvers, who were sometimes both employees of the organization and neutrals

71 *See* our article on this topic in the book.

addressing disputes that relate to the organization, or in which the organization had some indirect interest. The introduction of ODR has challenged the common expectations regarding confidentiality in ADR in general and in internal dispute resolution processes in particular on three levels – the individual level of the disputants, the organizational level (separation between dispute resolution data and other units of an organization), and the intra-organizational level (translating into greater ability and willingness to share dispute resolution data across institutions).

On the individual level, because most ODR processes are based on textual communication, disputants obtain a copy of all communications exchanged as part of the process (with the exception of private communications between the dispute resolver and the other party/ies to the dispute). This means that it can be more difficult to contain the flow of dispute resolution information than in a face-to-face oral process. While parties may commit to maintaining such information secret, the difficulty of regulating party actions over such data has led at least some ODR services, such as SquareTrade when handling eBay disputes already in the early days of ODR, to forego such demands altogether.[72]

But with this risk, also comes an important benefit in terms of quality control over the process, its fairness and effectiveness. Since communications are documented and parties (as well as others) can access them in real time as well as later on, this serves as a check on third-party intervention. Through in depth study of particular cases as well as aggregate data on the outcomes delivered under specific third parties or ODR providers, improper conduct, poor performance and problematic process design can be quite easily uncovered.[73] In many instances, current use of ODR has been restricted to 'simple,' non-emotional disputes where the reduction of privacy has been viewed as insignificant. Our view, however, is that over time we can expect the privacy barrier to use of ODR to further decline. Already, social attitudes towards privacy are changing dramatically with the younger generation willing to disclose an abundance of personal, sensitive information online. While some have viewed these developments as a consequence of ignorance, it seems that the trend is a strong one, most likely irreversible, and its impact will inevitably be a dramatic change in our attitudes towards privacy. In terms of third-party neutrality then, while we may be sacrificing the original means for ensuring independence (mainly through separation and distance), we have opened the door for a different kind of quality control mechanism, operating on both the individual and aggregate levels.

New practices that rely on online communication and information processing are generating and potentially capturing more information during the online dispute

72 Rabinovich-Einy 2006, *supra* note 1, at 274-276. Nevertheless, parties are often requested to respect such expectation of confidentiality. *See* the standards promulgated by the International Council for Online Dispute Resolution (ICODR), available at https://icodr.org/standards/ (last visited on 31 May 2020).

73 Rabinovich-Einy 2006, *supra* note 1, pp. 278-280.

resolution process than had occurred when everything was conducted face to face. DSD had previously emphasized looking for patterns of disputing conduct and addressing them during the DSD process. ODR will challenge institutions developing dispute systems as efforts are made to build trust in the process and, at the same time, use the information and value that are generated as the parties interact with each other and with the mediator.

In the introduction to *Getting to Yes*, Fisher and Ury note that 'conflict is a growth industry.'[74] If that was true almost four decades ago, it is even more true today. Disputes are a byproduct of transactions and relationships and when such interactions are novel and also complex, even more disputes are likely to occur. If institutions are to be trusted as they use the new media widely, the trust enhancing value of ODR will need to be recognized in contexts in which disputes do not occur or rarely occur.

As one example, the U.S. government for some years now has been aggressively trying to increase use of electronic health records.[75] As patients acquire electronic access to records that were rarely accessed when they were in paper form, they are increasingly discovering errors in the records and questionable diagnoses and characterizations in doctor's notes.[76] It is to be expected that online systems for challenging and correcting information in the record will arise. In addition, these records are perceived not only to be helpful in improving individual health but in improving understanding of public health needs. The government has required that some data on the record be in a structured format that will facilitate the data, without the patient's name included, being transferred to the government for public health purposes. This has privacy implications, since there have been many cases of data being lost in the U.S. and there is evidence that with some effort, almost any data can be re-identified and the patient's name revealed. With growing use of such records, patient concerns require online resources for responding to them. These avenues of redress have yet to become widely available in this context.

Similarly, payment systems are undergoing radical change with the growth of cryptocurrencies and while initial expectations were for a 'dispute-less' environment, these hopes soon dissipated. With problems ranging from people forgetting their passwords to smart contract-related disagreements, the need for effective online avenues for the quick and enforceable resolution of such disputes between distant (and often anonymous) strangers has become urgent.[77] Indeed, various ODR providers for

---

74 R. Fisher & W. L. Ury, *Getting to Yes: Negotiating Agreement Without Giving In*, 1981, p. xvii.

75 D. Blumenthal & M. Tavenner, 'The "Meaningful Use" Regulation for Electronic Health Records', *New Eng. J. Med.*,Vol 363, No. 6, 2010, pp. 501-504.

76 For a recent article on the types of problems that such records can create, *see* J. Hecht, 'The Future of Electronic Health Records', *Nature*, 25 September 2019, available at www.nature.com/articles/d41586-019-02876-y (last visited on 31 May 2020).

77 O. Rabinovich-Einy & E. Katsh, 'Blockchain and the Inevitability of Disputes: The Role for Online Dispute Resolution', *J. Disp. Resol.*, 2019, p. 47.

these types of conflicts have emerged offering a range of online processes, many of which rely on crowd-sourced tokenized juror voting.[78]

2.3.3 Conceptual Boundaries

As described above, the field of DSD has been premised on the existence of a conceptual boundary separating ADR from what is not ADR and has established additional internal conceptual boundaries within ADR, defining a fixed set of processes, each with their own commonly accepted features. Despite the rhetoric of ADR being comprised of individually tailored processes, leaving much room for creativity and imagination, the reality has been one in which these processes have tended to fit a preexisting mold which is rarely revisited and questioned.

However, developments in the ODR field have undermined what have seemed like firm distinctions between process types, dispute resolution system goals and third-party activities. Digital technology is transforming the nature and characteristics of the different dispute resolution processes, blurring prevailing conceptual boundaries within DSD. Dispute system designers need to realize that the way they have done things in the past is not the only way. Dispute resolution processes can be structured differently than they have been, not only because of constraints related to the shift in medium, but because it may actually prove to be a better way to design the process in a given context. This realization has blurred conceptual boundaries on several fronts: (1) accepted distinctions between ADR process types and the set of characteristics and assumptions each of these processes has been associated with; (2) common distinctions between formal and informal, confidential and public, flexible and structured are revisited as new hybrid combinations emerge; and (3) the line between the different goals of the system – dispute resolution vs. dispute prevention – are increasingly being blurred with intervention taking place very early on, often without being prompted by a complaint.

In terms of conceptual boundaries between the different ADR processes offered, the emergence of ODR, and more specifically the introduction of technology into the design of the process in the form of the 'fourth party,'[79] have both generated completely new types of processes unimaginable in the face-to-face era and have separated some familiar dispute resolution processes from qualities and traits previously considered significant, if not essential, to their design and operation. A clear example of a new process is the emergence of automated negotiation ODR schemes which include, as described above, problem identification processes (eBay), mechanisms for matching problems and solutions (SquareTrade), automated negotiation support systems (SmartSettle), blind

78 *Id.*

79 Katsh & Rifkin 2001, *supra* note 3, at 93-95.

bidding tools (CyberSettle), diagnosis of legal problems (Civil Resolution Tribunal) and crowd-sourced dispute resolution (eBay and blockchain ODR).

Some of the above processes escape the previously existing clear-cut distinction between direct negotiation and third-party dispute resolution giving rise to another *sui generis* category in which the fourth party displaces the third party. In these instances, dispute system design has a crucial role, perhaps more so than in those cases where a human third party is later involved, because in many ways it determines the power allocation between the parties and the manner in which opportunities and challenges are shared by them.

In other cases, ODR processes are offered under the same title as their offline equivalents but may in fact possess very different qualities. The evolution of the Wikipedia dispute resolution system offers several examples with a somewhat non-traditional arbitration process in terms of mandate and procedures for reaching a decision,[80] and what used to be an open informal mediation process which also challenges the widespread current notion that mediation should and needs to be offered confidentially.[81]

In court ODR, the entry point to litigation is altered with parties starting their process through self-diagnosis tools, interacting with an algorithm before turning to automated negotiation and additional ODR processes and tools.[82] The court fulfils a different role than it has thus far, providing parties with information on their legal situation and options for redress, as well as various means for negotiating and mediating which are offered through technological means under the umbrella of court proceedings, rather than being outsourced to external entities and professionals. In some ways, these proceedings become less public than physical in-court hearings, but in other respects they are more accessible and open for use, making courts a closer and friendlier options. Indeed, as this last point reflects, there is another conceptual boundary, perhaps several boundaries, that have been blurred by the shift to digital technology. Not only have dispute resolution processes changed, but our perceptions of what constitutes formal versus informal or private as opposed to public dispute resolution have been challenged by developments in the ODR field. Benoam, a former online arbitration provider, provides a compelling demonstration of these trends.

As stated above, for some time Benoam handled the vast majority of property damages claims between insurance companies in Israel ('fender-bender' claims), which were contractually referred to it *in lieu* of the courts. During its operation Benoam had,

80 D. Hoffman & S. Mehra, 'Wikitruth through Wikiorder', *Emory L. J.*, Vol 59, 2010, pp. 174-175.

81 Of course there are exceptions to this rule offline as well, but they are rare. Mediation is defined and understood to be a confidential process and indeed one in which confidentiality constitutes an essential feature. *See* for example, Section 8 of the Uniform Mediation Act, available at www.mediate.com/articles/umafinalstyled.cfm (last visited on 7 May 2011).

82 *See* S. Salter & D. Thompson, 'Public-Centered Civil Justice Redesign: A Case Study of the British Columbia Civil Resolution Tribunal', *McGill J. of Disp. Resol.*, Vol 3, 2016-2017, p. 113.

therefore, in effect displaced the court system in this particular domain of disputes. While Benoam emerged as a means for providing a more efficient alternative to the court system, the system and its rules have evolved significantly over time, rendering this private system increasingly formal and less private by offering more nuanced understandings of both flexibility and confidentiality than those typically held in the dispute resolution arena. Benoam found that in order to preserve its users trust, it had to both regulate their conduct closely through elaborate rules and by providing consistency on a substantive level.[83] In terms of restricting user conduct and options on such matters as time extensions and choice of arbitrator, Benoam was limiting somewhat the flexibility of the process and the control of the parties but compensated for such loss through ongoing learning of the impact of its rules on participants and outcomes.[84]

Benoam also decided to revisit its initial decision to maintain complete confidentiality of its arbitrators' rulings both internally and externally so as to enhance predictability of the system and, consequently, the consistency and fairness of resolutions rendered. While it chose to sustain external confidentiality, it curtailed somewhat the confidentiality of awards within the system by creating a space in which previous landmark decisions were published and adopted *res judicata* rules and a practice of binding precedents in the system.[85]

In the recently launched Facebook Oversight Board, we see a similar trend. A private entity adopting the 'look and feel' of a public entity in search of legitimacy and in what seems to be a sincere attempt to share some of its responsibility for the need to balance free speech against competing values in a global setting. The entity is privately funded, but its independence is ensured through secured funds, reputable members and a commitment to transparency. The board's mandate is limited, and the governing rules and principles are located in Facebook internal guidelines and bylaws, but international law is clearly expected to permeate the Board's decision-making. How this comingling of private and public structures, principles and values will play out remains to be seen, but this structure already represents a novel attempt to provide a 'third way.'

Indeed, we can see how these examples, largely due to the way in which technology has shaped these systems and their design, have undermined the sharp dichotomies between flexible and structured systems on the one hand and between private and public systems on the other hand that have typically accompanied the ADR-court divide.

While DSD has traditionally been more focused on full-blown disputes and what is happening downstream, the capability to obtain information from persons or groups who do not yet perceive themselves as parties is a valuable-by-product of enhanced communications capabilities and, hopefully, a contributor to much more effective dispute prevention strategies. Technology can contribute to this effort in several ways.

83 Rabinovich-Einy & Katsh, *supra* note 5, at 184-185.
84 *Id.*, at 182.
85 *Id.*, at 184.

For one, it can assist in the automatic detection of problems obviating the need to passively wait for complaints to arrive and allowing proactive remedying of a problem, even before a potential complainant has been made aware of its existence. This example can be evidenced in Wikipedia's use of bots that locate instances of infringement of its policies by editors who abuse content and harm the accuracy and reputation of the content on its site,[86] as well as by effective content moderation by Facebook. At the same time, where prevention efforts are erroneous, they can themselves generate disputes, as the Facebook example also exemplifies.

Another, perhaps more subtle way in which digital technology promises to enhance prevention efforts is by lowering barriers for voicing complaints and concerns, allowing them to stream in at an early stage, perhaps even before they have materialized into full-fledged disputes or prior to being experienced by additional potential claimants. Indeed, this is what eBay did when they began intervening very early on in addressing problems, often alerting one of the parties to the potential dispute even before the other party was aware of it. ODR is generally viewed as an alternative to ADR or the courts and is generally evaluated in the same way, largely in terms of numbers of disputes successfully resolved. Our experience with eBay and other ODR platforms suggests that evaluation of an ODR effort may be more complex in that the seeds of an effort to prevent disputes may lie in the technology employed to resolve disputes.

At the same time that technology provides new tools to prevent disputes, it lowers the barriers to complaining and initiating a dispute resolution process. Merely placing forms online or providing easy access to customer service phone numbers will increase the number of filings. Amazon will facilitate the return of books, something it can automate, but makes it extremely difficult to speak to someone. The only way one can find an Amazon phone number is through a search engine, not through the Amazon Web site. Another way of looking at this is that Amazon can respond to grievances by technology and, by doing so, prevent a grievance from evolving into a dispute.[87]

While the success of ADR entities that simply resolve disputes may be properly measured by the size of caseload and the manner in which disputes are resolved, bodies using ODR in a way that can impact the larger system that generates disputes may need to be looked at differently. A reduction in caseload in such instances may actually be a sign of success and improving communication may have more long term benefits than responding to individual cases. It is reasonable to assume that the use of technology provides ODR with more opportunities to identify systemic contributors to conflict and systemic opportunities to reduce conflict. In this sense, it is appropriate to characterize ODR processes as being more involved in conflict management than are ADR systems focused on resolving individual cases. The growth in use of ODR can therefore be

86 Hoffman & Mehra 2010, *supra* note 82, at 207-208.

87 W.L.F. Felstiner, R.L. Abel & A. Sarat, 'The Emergence and Transformation of Disputes: Naming, Blaming, Claiming ...', *L. & Soc'y Rev.*, Vol 15, 1980, pp. 631-654.

expected to shine more light on the variables that underlie the emergence of conflicts and lead to efforts to respond to causes of problems.

Finally, digital technology allows those who offer dispute resolution services on- and offline to systematically study patterns of disputes and the effectiveness of avenues for addressing them due to the ease of gathering data and analyzing it through multiple lenses on an ongoing basis. While online entities offering ODR services have had a head start in recognizing this potential (as can be seen in the eBay example described above), there is no reason why these benefits should not be extended to those offering ADR services face to face and indeed, more broadly, to courts, who have also been increasingly adopting technology into their case management and filing operations, and in some cases as a substitute to the proceedings themselves. Indeed, those courts employing ODR could study the impact of the diagnosis phase – is it contributing to resolution 'upstream'? Whose problems are being referred out of court? Are certain types of disputes more effectively resolved through particular types of ODR processes or by employing different means of online communication (writing, audio or video)? Are parties belonging to different social groups faring better or worse in different procedural avenues? As ODR is being introduced into public settings, more and more research is being conducted and these questions are gradually being addressed.[88]

The blurring of conceptual boundaries on all three fronts described above calls for an ongoing reevaluation of the assumptions and conceptions that underlie current design of dispute resolution systems and processes, opening up new possibilities and options tailored to particular circumstances.

3 Conclusion

Alternative dispute resolution processes have become the primary form of dispute resolution during the last several decades. In the late 1980s, after approximately a decade of growth, it was realized that ADR needed not only skilled practitioners but systems. These systems either assisted practitioners as caseloads increased, or identified causes of disputes and reduced the levels of disputing. After several decades of growth in the use of ODR, something very similar is occurring. An array of online tools has been developed to assist practitioners and parties to resolve both online and offline disputes. As we point out in this chapter and elsewhere,[89] ODR needs to orient itself to systems as well as tools and ADR needs to incorporate new technologies into the theory and practice of dispute system design.

The attraction of ADR at its origins lay mostly in the hope for the resolution of disputes more efficiently, effectively and conveniently than occurred in court. Over

88 *See* for example, Mentovich, Prescott & Rabinovich-Einy 2020, *supra* note 2.
89 Katsh & Rabinovich-Einy 2012, *supra* note 5.

time, the value of ADR in being able to generate outcomes that were also more flexible and responsive to the disputant's needs and interests became clear. ODR, in its original form, was also perceived to be largely aimed at providing disputants, often located in different jurisdictions, with a convenient and efficient alternative when no face to face alternative was feasible. Increasingly, however, ODR applications are being linked to powerful information machines, machines that either enhance the face-to-face process or provide parties with alternatives not possible in face-to-face processes.

Dispute system design which employs technology and also embeds technology in the system created is likely to lead ODR down a path that will generate new options, new challenges, new roles and new expectations. DSD oriented around ADR highlighted new professional roles and conceptual frameworks, and technology-oriented DSD will likely do the same. The use of technology tends to lead both to the emergence of more complex processes and to the technological resources to manage these more complex processes. Information machines should be particularly adept at preventing disputes by tracking cases and identifying causes of problems. Technology can not only reinforce processes but change them and this is something that is inevitable as the field of DSD itself is transformed by information and communications technologies.

Chapter 4 The Human Touch in ODR: Trust, Empathy, and Social Intuition in Online Negotiation and Mediation

Noam Ebner

1 Introduction

Online Dispute Resolution will never work.

So I've been told, a million times. Others working in the Online Dispute Resolution (ODR) field during its formative period, I'm sure, have heard this at least as often as I have.

Why not? Because, I've been informed, its cornerstone processes of online negotiation and mediation will never work. Negotiation and mediation are built on a foundation of interpersonal dynamics that are impossible to replicate online. The back-and-forth flow of the negotiation table, and the magic of the mediation room, can never transfer to the cold, impersonal, interaction at-a-distance ODR offers. Successful negotiation and mediation are *fundamentally dependent* on the human touch.

While I did not always argue the point, I never agreed with it, either. Empirically speaking, of course, it has been wrong for many years, as demonstrated by those successfully practicing negotiation and mediation online since the late 1990s. In practice, negotiation and mediation 'worked' online in the same anecdotal sense that in-the-room processes did. More substantively, ODR's preemptive death knell was flawed in that it related to negotiation and mediation as static phenomena rather than interactional processes between humans, who change with the times and are changed by their times.[1] Often, it seemed as if this statement actually stemmed from personal preference,[2] fueled by a very natural human response to change: resistance.[3]

I preface this in recognition of the sharp, sudden reversal in attitudes and practice that has occurred over the course of the writing of this chapter. In early 2020, Covid-19's rapid

1 *See* Ebner, N. (2017). Negotiation is changing. *Journal of Dispute Resolution,* 2017(1), 99-143 [hereinafter – Ebner (2017 CHANGE)].

2 Carrel, A. & Ebner, N. (2019). Mind the gap: Bringing technology to the mediation table. *Journal of Dispute Resolution,* 2019(2), 1-45.

3 Ebner (2017 CHANGE).

spread shut down government offices, courts, schools, businesses, law firms and all other venues for economic and social interaction not deemed absolutely vital. In response, the world over, any activity that could transition online did so, including all negotiation and mediation activity.

This quantum shift online has immense implications for the field of negotiation and dispute resolution, as it does for many fields. Before looking ahead, though, I'll note that it clearly exposed much of the objection to ODR, and in particular, to conducting negotiation and mediation processes online, for what it was: resistance to change. Resistance to change is human; the capacity to stave off change *over time*, however, is a luxury and a privilege few can afford. Ask any seismologist: Shift happens. In the early weeks of the Covid-19 era, resistance to online practice of negotiation and mediation was swept away in a heartbeat, and the entire field shifted online. And, even as practitioners scrambled to learn to use Zoom, they promised their clients and employers that while there may be some technological hiccups now and then, they had no doubt that these processes could, practically speaking, be conducted online. Anecdotally, I'm not familiar with a single professional mediator who decided to cancel all their sessions and wait the pandemic out. Neither am I familiar with a single practitioner who reduced their fees in recognition of providing a product of diminished quality. Institutionally speaking, court activity, business activity, court-connected mediation, university-based mediation clinics, and community-based mediation programs transitioned online as well, signaling their belief that, in a pinch, online negotiation and mediation process 'work'.

Moreover, still anecdotally, while many mediators continue to voice a general preference for in-person processes, many acknowledge that online mediation not only 'works', but it 'works' just fine; in fact, it 'works' in the ballpark of how the in-person process 'works'.[4] Breaking that down into outcome and process, it works not only by that measure by which mediation has too often been assessed, for better or for worst: settlement rates.[5] It also works for issues that are deep in the 'human touch' zone: engagement, comfort, warmth, trust, and sense of immediacy.[6]

While the 'pinch' of Covid-19 was not anyone's preferred way to settle this issue, recognizing that we have moved far beyond the 'online mediation and negotiation can't

4 *See, e.g.*, Creo, R.A. (2020). Zoom, Zooming, Zoomed into the future! Moving to optimist from skeptic on online mediation. *Alternatives to the High Cost of Litigation*, 38(8), 119.

5 On the macro level of 'working', eight months into online pandemic-era practice, JAMS reported that "Settlement rates have been at least as high as they were for in-person mediations." Singer, L.R. (2020). Updates on remote mediation and the virtual evolution of ADR. Available at www.jamsadr.com/blog/2020/update-on-remote-mediations-and-the-virtual-evolution-of-adr. For an example of online mediation 'working' at the individual case level, *see* O'Sullivan, J. (2020). Hybrid mediation and Zoom. *Mediation Theory and Practice*, 5, 55-62.

6 *E.g.*, Singer (2020): "Mediators… skeptical about our ability to connect with parties on a screen have been proved wrong. Using speaker view on a videoconferencing platform can bring us even closer to parties than when they are seated across a conference room table."

work' or 'they will never be as good' stage is a necessary and helpful part of this chapter's frame.

And yet, old slogans of resistance to ODR gain value, once reframed (significantly): To facilitate online negotiation and mediation 'work'ing, practitioners would do well to mindfully instill elements of the human touch in their processes. In fact, viewing the human touch issue as an area for mindful practice rather than a barrier to practice poses an inspiring challenge: *How might we achieve more with the human touch online than we have traditionally attained in the room?*

2 The Human Touch

At this point, any scientific publication would provide a definition, or at least a definition-for-the-purposes-of-this-publication, of the human touch in mediation. I will not.

2.1 What is This Human Touch, Anyway?

It's not that I have not tried. Rather, I've reached the conclusion that any definition I'd suggest would be superfluous *and* pointless, given that the people who have decried the lack of human touch in online mediation, as well as people who seek to augment the human touch in their processes, have not been working off of any agreed upon definition. Indeed, the human touch is more simply invoked than defined. Efforts to define it call to mind two elephants. The first originates in the Indian sub-continent to remind people that our definitions rely on our limited entry-points and perceptions.[7] The second, occasionally conjured in British courts, facilitates judicial decision making when legal arguments fall short of defining ineffable concepts by reminding the court that while it might be difficult to define, you most certainly know an elephant when you see it.[8] Such, I think, is the human touch in mediation and negotiation.

Table 4.1 lists different phrases and terms negotiators mediators have often used in relating to the human touch in one-on-on conversations and workshops. This is not

7 There are many sources for this tale, parable, or metaphor in the literature of Eastern religions. *See, e.g.*, Ashliman, D.L. (2014) (ed.). The blind men and the elephant. In Folktales of Aarne-Thompson-Uther type 1317. Available at www.pitt.edu/~dash/type1317.html. In each, this elephant encounters several visually disabled people who attempt to characterize it. Of course, each person's description is inducted from the particular part of the elephant their hands encounter – its feet, ears, mouth, tail, or tusk – and so are quite different from each other.

8 *E.g.*, a 'realistic' contractual offer: "This seems to me to be an application of the well-known elephant test. It is difficult to describe, but you know it when you see it." Lord Stuart-Smith in *Cadogan Estates Ltd v. Morris*; EWCA Civ 1671, available at www.bailii.org/ew/cases/EWCA/Civ/1998/1671.html.

intended to provide any pseudoscientific delineation of the term, but rather to demonstrate its scope and to invite readers their own connotations of human touch.

Table 4.1 Human Touch Associations

Human Touch Associations		
Warmth	Mutual reactions	Jokes
Energy	Discussing the 'real stuff'	Connection
Emotional focus	Really 'getting into it'	Togetherness
Emotional expression	Working together	Smiles
Seeing their faces	Being authentic	Feeling 'it'
Looking them in the eyes	Spontaneity	Compassion
Being in-synch	Handshakes	Genuineness
Like we're in a bubble	Small talk	Understanding

Some of these terms are specific, while others are fuzzy. Practitioners likely recognize and understand many of both types, and relate some from each to their own notion of human touch.

Having loosely identified negotiators' and mediators' intent when discussing 'the human touch', though, what do they mean when they say it is *missing?*

2.2 The Human Touch: AWOL, or Elusive?

When negotiators say that they miss the human touch, they require the human touch to succeed, or the online environment does not support the human touch, what do they mean? Do all online media inherently robotize all aspects of an interaction? Do they automatically shut down all support to human touch issues? And, do they all affect human touch?

In pursuing the human touch online, across-the-board statements muddy the waters. Instead, we can further our understanding of the human touch by considering not only what it is, but how we imbue our processes with it. In doing so, we transform the discussion about whether the online arena is devoid of humanity to a nuanced exploration of the tools and methods that different media offer or deny us for supporting, conveying, and operationalizing the human touch.

To begin this process, Table 4.2 species a range of human-touch conveying elements that are affected in online interactions. Comparing email interactions to videoconferencing demonstrates how different media share some limiting elements and have others unique to them. Note how some elements are fully denied by the medium, whereas others are merely constrained.

Table 4.2 Missing Elements

Missing / Constrained Human Touch – Impacting Elements	
Email	**Videoconferencing**
Tone	Co-speaking
Facial Expressions	Natural eye-contact
Body Language	Out-of-the-video-box cues
Synchronicity	Perfect, non-lag, synchronicity
Quick clarification/verification questions	Directing joint attention, pointing
Immediate feedback look	Limited ability to adjust distance and space
Touch	
Smell	
Taste	
Hosting	
Sharing food	
Sharing space	
Motion around space	
Rituals related to all the above	

The literature on negotiation and mediation tends to discuss online processes in much the same way depicted in Table 4.2: focusing on *what is lost*. An appreciative look at online media, however, allows us to ask what tools, methods and medium features can support or even enhance our capacity to bring the human touch to bear. Once again using videoconferencing and email to demonstrate the different characteristics of media with regards to human touch conveyance, we offer an appreciative approach to communication media and the human touch in Table 4.3.

Table 4.3 Elements to be Used

Human Touch – Impacting Elements Afforded by the Medium	
Email	**Videoconferencing**
Words	
Subject line	Tone
Length of message	Pitch
Timing	Pace
Emoji/emoticons	Body language
Name, title, signature line	Changing perceived distance

Human Touch – Impacting Elements Afforded by the Medium	
Attachments	Perceived eye contact
Hyperlinks	Elements of surroundings and background
Uninterrupted transmission	Accessories
Ability to reset tone with each iteration	Synchronicity
Time to consider and reflect	Real-time feedback look
Consultation	Interruptions (dogs/children joining the interaction)
Record of the other's precise words available	Multichannel cue reinforcement (e.g., video + audio)

2.3 *Human Touch: From Associations to Tools to Process Elements*

Having complemented the typical glass-half-empty outlook on online media and the human touch with a glass-half-full perspective, we have a clear picture of what tools and capacities are missing and which remain in (or have been added into) our toolbox. We now return to the terms associated with the notion of human touch discussed above.

Table 4.4 revisits the terms introduced in Table 4.1. It shifts discussion of the human touch from the intuitive language in which it is so often expressed (left-hand column) to specific elements, actions, tools, and dynamics of negotiation and mediation in which it manifests (center column). These are then categorized as relating to three key areas in negotiation and mediation (right-hand column). Given the interconnectedness of the terms and of the areas, several terms (located at the bottom of the chart) are noted as relating to all three areas. Table 4.4 maps the relationships between intuitive language, scientific professional tools and terms, and the manifestation of the human touch in the mediation and negotiation areas of trust, empathy, and social intuition.

Table 4.4 The Human Touch: From Intuitive Language to Negotiation and Mediation Areas

Intuitive language	Associated terminology	Area
Warmth	Presence Listening Containing Recognizing Holding space empowerment	Empathy
Compassion		
Energy		

Intuitive language	**Associated terminology**	**Area**
Understanding		
Feeling 'it'		
Reaching the 'real stuff'	Discussing interests Broad / Narrow issue definition Motivation Commitment Affect Vulnerability Truth, bluffing, lying Negotiators dilemma Cooperation	Trust
Really 'getting into it'		
Emotional expression		
Emotional focus (more/less)		
Genuineness		
Working together		
Being authentic		
Spontaneity	Timing Touch Nonverbal communication Physical proximity and distance Hosting rituals Humor	Social Intuition
Handshakes		
Smile		
Eye contact		
Jokes		
Small talk	Rapport Bonding Hosting rituals Informal interactions Inclusion	Trust Empathy Social Intuition
Connection		
Togetherness		
Being in-synch		

Intuitive language	Associated terminology	Area
Like we're in a bubble		
Mutual reactions		

2.4 *Human Touch-Supported Elements of Negotiation and Mediation*

Accordingly, in this chapter, we will introduce and discuss 'human touch' issues in negotiation and mediation under the broader domains of these three areas:[9]

Trust: One person's assumption that another is benevolent toward them and will not do them harm even if they have the opportunity to do so.

Empathy: One person's ability to be aware of, sensitive to, and caring about, what another person is feeling or experiencing, from their point of view – and to express this to the other.

Social Intuition: One person's capacity to harness their self-awareness and other-awareness in order to bridge between themselves and another.

Each area will be introduced, followed by discussion of the challenges and opportunities that they face in the online environment, and suggestions for working with them in negotiation and mediation processes conducted online. The goal is not to provide a full manual of best practices, but rather to demonstrate how working with the varied tools each communication media offers (drawing on those specified in Tables 4.2 and 4.3) can enhance and convey the human touch.

Of these three areas, trust will be presented in the most detail, given its centrality to negotiation and mediation processes and the relatively large extent of research that has been focused on it. Moreover, trust's effects carry over to the other two elements. To express this at an intuitive level: the more trust is built between people, the greater the opportunity for authentic empathy expression and appreciative empathy reception, and the better our ability to employ social intuition to bridge between our self and another. To be sure, these areas all spill into one another, as will be noted along the way: empathy affects trustbuilding, and social intuition does as well.

One challenge in writing this piece is my attempt to discuss, and still distinguish, between two sets of issues that should not be muddled together:

The first, is discussing negotiation and mediation, two very different processes (particularly, when comparing the negotiator and the mediator's viewpoints, roles, and goals). In each section, I will clarify whether the practical suggestions are being made from the perspective of the negotiator negotiating with counterpart, of a mediator

9 Of course, human touch issues pertain to many other areas in negotiation and mediation. This chapter's discussion of these three areas should serve to expose and explain the human touch's role and functions in other areas.

working with disputing parties, or both. While many human touch elements affect both types of interactions, these are two fundamentally different relationships and interactions, and conflating or mishmashing them would not be helpful or accurate.[10]

The second, is discussing issues encountered in each area whilst interacting both via email and videoconferencing; two very different types of communication media, with very different impacts on processes. The need to discuss both reflects the shift in the field catalyzed by the Covid-19 era. Previously, online negotiation and mediation processes were predominantly text based, with video's entry into the practice arena slow and gradual. In the pandemic-normal, videoconferencing is ubiquitous. Both are likely to remain common modes of interaction in the post-pandemic normal. Moreover, discussing processes as if they take place through a single medium does not accurately reflect practice. In-person meetings, videoconferencing, emails, and other media might all be used as main channels for different parts of a process, or as supporting channels for a single main channel. Understanding all these modalities of interaction is necessary for conducting media choice and for successful employ of different media at different points in any process.[11] I will strive to indicate clearly which medium's impact is under the lens at different points, and provide separate advice for each medium.

3 Trust

> The existence of trust between individuals makes conflict resolution easier and more effective. This point is obvious to anybody who has been in a conflict. A party who trusts another is likely to believe the other's words, assume that the

10 In that same vein of mishmash avoidance, note that in this chapter, human touch elements are discussed from the perspective of human participants in negotiation and mediation processes conducted through use of online technology as a communication channel, rather than focusing on technology developed to actively facilitate a process or enhance parties' outcomes. Our focus is on *online replication of traditional negotiation and dispute resolution processes* (*see* the distinction articulated in Ebner, N. & Greenberg, E. (2020). Strengthening ODR justice. *Washington University Journal of Law and Policy*, 63, 65-118). In terms introduced by Ayelet Sela, our focus is on *instrumental* ODR platforms that facilitate interparty communication (such as email or Zoom), rather than *principle* ODR platforms in which artificial intelligence proactively intervenes to improve processes or outcomes. *See* Sela, A. (2016). Can computers be fair? How automated and human-powered *Online Dispute Resolution* affect procedural justice in mediation and arbitration, *Ohio State Journal on Dispute Resolution*, 33, pp. 91, 100. However, while written for mediators and negotiators working online, this chapter may also be helpful to ODR platform designers, system designers, and programmers seeking to imbue intelligent agents, created for the purposes of mediating between or negotiating with humans, elements of the human touch.

11 For analysis of characteristics of a broad array of communication media, *see* Mor, S. & Suppes, A. (2014). The role of communication media in negotiation. In M. Benoliel (ed.), *Negotiation Excellence: Successful Deal Making* (2nd ed.). Singapore: World Scientific Publishing. For discussion of conducting choice between different media, and of the multiple choice points of a single process, *see* Schneider, A.K. & McCarthy, S. (2017). Choosing among modes of communication. In C. Honeyman & A.K. Schneider (eds.), *The Negotiator's Desk Reference (Vol. 2)*. St Paul, MN: DRI Press.

> other will act out of good intentions, and probably look for productive ways to resolve a conflict... The level of trust or distrust in a relationship therefore definitively shapes emergent conflict dynamics...[12]

Trust is on the rise. Perhaps not in practice,[13] regrettably, but certainly as an area of interest and research in the fields of negotiation, dispute resolution, conflict management, and ODR. However, what do people mean when they talk about trust? As trust is best defined in context, we preface specific definition of the term with a map of its different in the context of ODR.

3.1 Seven Trust Areas in ODR

Zooming in on specific uses of the term with regards to ODR, it would seem as if seven different issues (at least) crowd together under trust's umbrella:[14]

1. *ODR as a trust-provider/facilitator*: Incorporating ODR into systems such as e-commerce is one measure intended to raise the consumer's level of trust in the system.[15] Internet development, from an economic perspective, relies to no small extent on the continued success of e-commerce, which is *absolutely* dependent on users' trust.[16] While e-commerce has survived threats to trust in the form of account-hacking, fly-by-night sales websites, and leaked personal information, maintaining user trust will always be a challenge. As Colin Rule has summarized this issue: "Transactions require trust, and the Internet is woefully lacking in trust."[17] The availability of redress, in the form of ODR, continues to bolster users' trust in online markets, online banking, and more. As increasing quantities of transactions and verifications occur via blockchain, ODR is anticipated to play a similar role.[18]

---

12 Lewicki, R.J. (2006). Trust, trust development and trust repair. In M. Deutsch, E.C. Coleman & E.C. Marcus (eds.), *The Handbook of Conflict Resolution*. San Francisco, CA: Jossey-Bass, p. 110.

13 Far from it, in fact. *See* Ebner, N. (2019). Begun, the trust war has: Teaching negotiation when truth isn't truth. *Negotiation Journal,* 35(1), 207-210.

14 Types 1, 2 and 7, were first introduced in Ebner, N. (2012). ODR and interpersonal trust. In M.S. Abdel Wahab, E. Katsh & D. Rainey (eds.), *ODR: Theory and Practice*. The Hague: Eleven Intl. Publishing. Type 3 was added in Ebner, N. & Zeleznikow, J. (2015). Fairness, trust and security in Online Dispute Resolution. *Hamline Journal of Public Law and Policy,* 36(2), 143-160. Types 4, 5, and 6 are articulated here as discrete ODR trust areas for the first time.

15 *See* Rule, C. & Friedberg, L. (2005). The appropriate role of dispute resolution in building trust online. *Artificial Intelligence and Law*, 13, 2.

16 Wang, Y.D. & Emurian, H.H. (2005). An overview of online trust: concepts, elements, and implications. *Computers in Human Behavior*, 21, 1.

17 Rule, C. (2002). *Online Dispute Resolution for Business: B2B, E-Commerce, Consumer, Employment, Insurance, and Other Commercial Conflicts.* San Francisco, CA: Jossey-Bass, 98.

18 *See* Rabinovich-Einy, O. & Katsh, E. (2019). Blockchain and the inevitability of disputes: the role for online dispute resolution. *Journal of Dispute Resolution* 2019(2), 47-75.

2. *Users' trust in ODR itself*: ODR must be designed and introduced in such a way that the public will trust it as an efficient and effective way of managing their disputes.[19] This is not something to be taken for granted. In addition to the low level of trust all forms of alternative dispute resolution have encountered at one point or another (up to, and including, the present moment), ODR as a field faces additional challenges. Each potential participant in ODR will need to be convinced they can trust that mediators can overcome distance-related challenges and that they have the skills required to help them online. They must feel able to rely on the technology being employed: that it is up the task, is sufficiently user-friendly to accommodate them, and will not freeze up mid-process, crash their computer, or otherwise affect them or the interaction detrimentally.
3. *Trust in content offered by the system:* While some variations of ODR replicate familiar negotiation and mediation processes via online communication platforms such as videoconferencing or email, other forms involve dedicated systems offering parties substantive advice or information. For example, basic legal diagnostics,[20] information about how similar disputes have been resolved, or suggestions for tradeoffs for optimizing agreements.[21] Some systems even provide parties with an outcome (e.g., the result of automated blind bidding). These ODR platforms depend on parties' trust in the information, advice, and outcomes they provide.[22]
4. *Trust in the platform/system's designer/operator*: Whether an ODR process convenes via Zoom or takes place a dedicated platform designed by an ODR service, the platform designer/operator becomes, in essence, an additional 'party' with which all involved have a trust relationship. Are they acting only in participants' best interests? Do participants suspect them of advancing their own interests, or even of malevolence? For example: do parties trust the system's operators to keep their information secret? Not to use it for their own ends? Not to record an ostensibly

19 *See* Abdel Wahab, M. (2004). Does technology emasculate trust? Confidentiality and security concerns in online arbitration. *ICC Bulletin Special Supplement on* Using Technology to Resolve Business Disputes, No. 667; Gillieron, P. (2008). From face-to-face to screen-to-screen: real hope or true fallacy. *Ohio State Journal on Dispute Resolution,* 23(2), 301-343.

20 *See, e.g.,* the Civil Resolution Tribunal's Solution Explorer, available at https://civilresolutionbc.ca/how-the-crt-works/getting-started/.

21 For examples, *see* Brams, S. J., & Taylor, A. D. (1996). *Fair division: From cake-cutting to dispute resolution.* Cambridge University Press; Bellucci, E. and Zeleznikow, J. (2010). Decision support in interest based Negotiation Support Systems: The AssetDivider system. In Yearwood, J. and Stranieri, A. (Eds.) *Technologies for Supporting Reasoning Communities and Collaborative Decision Making: Cooperative* Approaches, IGI Global. Information Science Publisher, 319-339; and Thiessen, E. M., & McMahon, J. P. (2000). Beyond Win-Win in Cyberspace. *Ohio State Journal on Dispute Resolution* 15(3), 643.

22 This trust can also be related to parties' perception of 'fairness': Does the system treat them evenhandedly? Is any bias unintentionally coded into its algorithms? *See* Ebner & Zeleznikow (2015); Welsh, N. (2019). Dispute resolution neutrals' ethical obligation to support measured transparency. *Oklahoma Law Review,* 71, 823, 862-863; Sternlight, J.R. (2020). Pouring a little psychological cold water on online dispute resolution. *Journal of Dispute Resolution,* 1, 24.

unrecorded videoconference conversation even for something as benign as 'quality control?'[23]

5. *Institutional trust*: When an ODR process is conducted under the auspices of an organization whose reputation and areas of activity are far broader that its ODR activity, parties have a trust assessment toward that institution that is independent of (although it certainly might affect their trust assessment of) its ODR activity. This is true when ODR is offered by eBay or Alibaba; its importance as an independent trust area sharpens when ODR is offered by court systems or other government agencies.
6. *Peer trust*: This newly evolving form of trust leverages a general acceptance of the wisdom of the crowd for making individual decisions involving risk.[24] Our trust in a broad group of strangers causes us to favor one restaurant over another based on its Yelp reviews; to get into a car driven by yet another complete stranger based on their Lyft ratings; or to entrust much of the budget we've painstakingly saved for our annual vacation to a stranger a thousand miles away based on their Airbnb stats.[25] The notion of ratings systems has already been explored through a perspective coupling trust and ODR dispute systems design;[26] as online processes become more ubiquitous, online rating systems for practitioners and service providers will impact parties' trust in them.
7. *Interpersonal trust*: Parties utilizing ODR experience not only the low levels of trust and high levels of distrust in one another inherent in most conflict situations, they are also hindered by challenges to trust generated and maintained by the nature of online communication and of the online environment.

While there are some commonalities to these uses of the term trust, there are conceptual differences between them. Not all of them are relevant to all areas of ODR. For example, the issue of trust in content provided by a tailored system might not pertain to the work of a mediator conducting a process via Skype or Zoom that provides no such information. Additionally, each usage there are fundamentally different players doing the trusting and being trusted. As our focus in this chapter on the human touch (as opposed to all aspects of trust) in online negotiation and mediation processes (as opposed to the broader area of ODR) our discussion will focus *primarily* on the seventh

23 In Ebner & Zeleznikow (2015), a previous effort at clarifying terms in ODR, we categorized these as 'security' rather than 'trust' concerns, showing connections between these buckets even as we distinguished between them.

24 *See* Botsman, R. (2016). Technology is making it easier to trust strangers. *Wired*. Available at www.wired.co.uk/article/trust-networks. *Also see* Ebner (2017 CHANGE).

25 *See* Brooks, D. (2014). The evolution of trust. Available at www.nytimes.com/2014/07/01/opinion/david-brooks-the-evolution-of-trust.html.

26 Rule, C. & Singh, H. (2012). ODR and online reputation systems. In M.S. Abdel Wahab, E. Katsh & D. Rainey (eds.), *ODR: Theory and Practice*. The Hague: Eleven International Publishing.

type of trust, interpersonal trust between parties to negotiation and mediation processes conducted online, and only occasionally note trust issues related to another trust area.[27]

The goal of this section is to enable online negotiators and mediators to understand the vital role that trust plays in these interactions, to identify process-junctures ripe with potential for trust-building (or trust-breaking), and to apply, at these critical junctures, tested methods for trustbuilding which facilitate these processes and improve their outcomes.

We begin by defining the notion of interpersonal trust in the context of online mediation and negotiation processes, Next, we will review the research exploring the effect that trust, or lack thereof, has on these processes. Having established the beneficial effects of trust, we will explain the challenges that characteristics of online communication channels pose to trust's formation and maintenance. We will break these media effects down into discrete elements, identifying eight specific challenges to building and maintaining trust in online interactions. Each will be broken down into a dual perspective: challenges, opportunities and best practices for the online negotiator, and challenges, opportunities and best practices for the online mediator. Combined, these will provide an initial set of guidelines for bringing the human touch into online negotiation and mediation processes.

3.2 Defining Trust

Many attempts have been made to define trust, across a wide range of disciplines. It has been suggested that trust can only be defined in context, yet even the literature on negotiation and dispute resolution provides varying definitions of trust. For the purpose of a shared understanding of 'trust' as it is used in this section, I will adopt a definition I've previously posited,[28] combining three elements suggested in the literature:

- *Risk*: The existence of risk is a precondition for trust. Only when one is at risk, dependent or vulnerable can his/her behavior or expectations demonstrate trust.[29]
- *Uncertainty*: Trust can manifest only when there is a degree of uncertainty regarding another's future behavior; if their behavior is preordained or controlled, trust is unnecessary and moot.[30]

---

27 That is not to say that the seven types of trust do not affect each other. On the contrary, I subscribe to the notion that a type of a penumbra effect causes trust and distrust to spill over from one type to another. For example, trust in a system will affect trust in the human at its other end, and trust in humans will affect our trust in the technology we use to engage with them. This will be briefly discussed at the end of this section.

28 Ebner, N. (2007). Trust-building in e-negotiation. In L. Brennan & V. Johnson (eds.), *Computer-Mediated Relationships and Trust: Managerial and Organizational Effects.* Hershey, PA: Information Science Pub.

29 Boyd, J. (2003). The rhetorical construction of trust online. *Communication Theory*, 13(4), 392-410.

30 Gambetta, D. (1988). Can we trust trust? In D. Gambetta (ed.), *Trust: Making and Breaking Cooperative Relations.* Oxford: Blackwell Publishing.

- *Expectations*: One expects that his/her cooperation, or other trust-indicating action, will be reciprocated by the other.[31]

Taken together, these elements portray trust in the context of negotiation and dispute resolution as *an expectation that one's cooperation will be reciprocated, in a situation where one is vulnerable to loss, should the other choose not to cooperate.*

To bring that into the world of practice, from the viewpoint of online negotiators and then from the perspective of online mediators:

As negotiators, we need our counterparts to trust us every time we ask them to bet on our unguaranteed cooperation. We ask them to do so at multiple points during any given process, not only when we seek their agreement at its conclusion. Throughout the process, we request they share information, even though they cannot be certain we will not use it to their detriment. We require them to invest their time in discussing ways to achieve our goals, even though they are not guaranteed we will reciprocate regarding their own issues. And, at a process' end, we often request our counterpart's agreement to a particular solution requiring some concession on their part, and to do so without absolute certainty that we will deliver on whatever promises we've made in return. Each of these requires a certain leap of faith; leaps of faith are generated by trust.

In mediation, multiple trust relationships exist. The process' simplest form, one mediator assisting two parties, involves a triangle of trust relationships: two mediator-party relationships, and the interparty relationship.[32] Any discussion of trust in mediation needs to take into account, the distinction between party-party and mediator-party trust dynamics. At its core, mediation is facilitated negotiation; therefore, its interparty trust dynamics involve all the elements discussed in the preceding discussion of inter-negotiator trust. The mediator-party trust relationship serves different purposes and involves different dynamics.

Some mediators abstain from intervening in or affecting the interparty trust relationship. Others suffice with naming or explaining trust dynamics as they see them unfold in the room, adding a trust perspective to parties' own considerations as they plan their next move. Some mediators are more hands-on in efforts to increase parties' trust in each other. Whatever a mediator's outlook on this issue is, many common mediator tactics utilized even by mediators not seeking to directly impact the parties' trust relationship, are, essentially, trust-impacting moves. For example, mediators may ask parties to deal fairly and openly with each other, to have an open and candid

31 Pruitt, D.G. & Kimmel, M.J. (1977). Twenty years of experimental gaming: critique, synthesis, and suggestions for the future. *Annual Review of Psychology*, 28, 363-398.

32 *See* Ebner, N. & Thompson, J. (2014). @Face value? Nonverbal communication and trust development in online video-based mediation. *International Journal of Online Dispute Resolution*, 1(2), 103-124. Additional participants (*e.g.*, multiple parties, attorneys, accompanying friends, or a co-mediator) compound the number of trust relationships.

conversation, to remember that the process is confidential, to discuss their interests with each other, or to desist from unilateral actions for the interim, all in order to advance or protect the mediation. Under the definition we've adopted, all these suggestions impact trust.

In the mediator-party trust relationship, mediators are more uniform in actively and directly seeking to increase parties' degree of trust in them. In fact, as mediators, we bank on parties' trust to a high degree. We ask them to trust *us* and to trust the mediation *process*, despite the risk and uncertainty involved, and despite the fact that their substantive expectations cannot, ultimately, be satisfied by us but rather by the other party. We ask them to desist, delay, or act in parallel to alternative processes for solving their problems, while at the same time explaining that there is no certainty regarding the outcome of the mediation process. We might invite them to divulge information, to explore their interests, and to reconsider their assessments and offers, even at points when they are hesitant or uncomfortable doing this with the other party present. We might ask them to do so in a private meeting with us alone. Party agreement to any or all of these requests are at least partly predicated on their degree of trust in the mediator.

These examples - only the tip of the iceberg, really - demonstrate the practical importance of understanding, and learning to work with, trust - as negotiators and as mediators. To do so, we turn to the literature to explore in higher resolution just how trust works in these processes.

3.3 Specific Roles of Trust in Negotiation and Mediation

Trust is essential for conducting any successful negotiation or mediation processes. The professional and academic literature on negotiation and mediation devotes enormous effort to understanding how trust is built, maintained, broken and reconstructed.

3.3.1 Negotiation

Trust plays a key role in promoting cooperation,[33] problem solving,[34] information exchange,[35] negotiator effectiveness,[36] and achieving integrative solutions.[37] Trust is a

33 Deutsch, M. (1962). Cooperation and trust: some theoretical notes. In *Nebraska Symposium on Motivation*, Lincoln, NE: University of Nebraska Press.

34 Pruitt, D.G., Rubin, J.Z. & Kim, S. (2004). *Social Conflict: Escalation, Stalemate, and Settlement* (3rd ed.). London: McGraw Hill.

35 Kimmel *et al.*, M.J. (1980). Effects of trust, aspiration and gender on negotiation tactics. *Journal of Personality and Social Psychology*, 38, 1.

36 Schneider, A.K. (2002). Shattering negotiations myths: empirical evidence on the effectiveness of negotiation style. *Harvard Negotiation Law Review*, 7, 143-233.

37 Lewicki, R.J. & Litterer, J.A. (1985). *Negotiation: Readings, Exercises and Cases*. Burr Ridge, IL: Irwin; Lax, D. & Sebenius, J.K. (1986). *The Manager as Negotiator: Bargaining for Cooperation and Competitive Gain*. New York, NY: Free Press.

vital precondition for information sharing, which arouses generosity and empathy and reciprocation. When our counterpart does not trust us, they fear that we will use information they share with us against them.[38] By creating a trust-filled environment, we reduce this fear-factor which causes negotiators to playing their cards close to their chest. With heightened trust in their counterpart, negotiators no longer focus on perceived catastrophic results in the negotiation process; they recognize that the worst outcome of the process will be a mutually agreed-upon 'no-deal', with the underlying premise of a continued relationship and potentially future interactions. This shift in perspective allows for cooperative behavior in the negotiation process. *Dis*trust, on the other hand, causes parties to focus on how their cooperative behavior can be used against them, triggering defensive behavior. Distrusting their counterpart, parties withhold information from them, attack their position and statements, threaten them, and lock themselves into positions from which they cannot easily withdraw.[39] These research findings have translated into practice through their centrality in professional training; with negotiation trainees advised to seek out and create opportunities for trust-building whenever possible, as early as possible in the course of a negotiation process,[40] and or even before its formal inception.[41]

3.3.2 Mediation

These findings on negotiation certainly inform the role of trust in mediation as well, in both the party-mediator and the party-party relationships. The mediation literature makes it clear that managing these trust-fronts well facilitates resolution, whereas their mismanagement can derail a process. In addition to suggesting trust's general contribution to promoting dispute resolution[42] the literature on mediation suggests specific beneficial impacts of trust. Parties' trust in the mediator is an important factor in the question of whether they agree to mediate their dispute in the first place, as well as that of whether they settle it.[43] The ability of a mediator to form rapport with parties has been found to be the most important ability or skill as mediator can possess.[44] A primary

38 Nadler, J. & Shestowsky, D. (2006). Negotiation, information technology, and the problem of the faceless other. In L.L. Thompson (ed.), *Negotiation Theory and Research*. New York, NY: Psychology Press.
39 Lewicki & Litterer (1985).
40 *Id.*
41 *See* M. Morris *et al.* (2002). Schmooze or lose: social friction and lubrication in e-mail negotiations. *Group Dynamics: Theory, Research, and Practice*, 6, 1.
42 Moore, C. (2014). *The Mediation Process* (4th ed.). San Francisco, CA: Jossey-Bass.
43 *See* Carnevale, P.J. & Pruitt, D.G. (1992). Negotiation and mediation. *Annual Review of Psychology*, 43, 1.
44 Goldberg, S.B. (2005). The secrets of successful mediators. *Negotiation Journal*, 21(3) 365-276; Goldberg, S.B. & Shaw, M.L. (2007). The secrets of successful (and unsuccessful) mediators continued: studies two and three. *Negotiation Journal*, 23(4) 393-418.

element of this rapport, as the term was used in this study, was parties' trust in the mediator, also discussed as the mediator gaining the confidence of the parties.[45] The flip side of that coin is that a lack of integrity (including trust-breaking behavior) has been found to be widely viewed as a cause of mediator failure.[46] Regarding the interparty trust relationship, successful mediators utilize a range of approaches for encouraging interparty trust, or circumvent distrust by suggesting solutions that are nondependent on trust.[47]

3.4 *What Makes Disputants, or Negotiators, Trust Each Other?*

Trust does not appear out of thin air. It is the outcome of cognitive and interactional processes.

3.4.1 Routes to Interparty Trust

In negotiation (both direct and mediated), interparty trust develops along three routes:

Deterrence-based or calculus-based trust is premised on the assumption that people act in accordance with their rational self-interest. While this is in itself a questionable assumption,[48] we still base some of our trust-decisions on it: we conduct a subjective cost/benefit analysis estimating our opposite's own self-interest, and trust them to act as they committed only insofar as this promotes this self-interest. Our counterpart will keep trust only if their payoff is greater that way. If breaking trust would lead them to

45 On the close relationship between trust and rapport, *see* Nadler, J. (2004). Rapport in legal negotiation: how small talk can facilitate e-mail deal making. *Harvard Negotiation Law Review*, 9, 223-251; Braeutigam, A.M. (2006). What I hear you writing is... issues in ODR: building trust and rapport in the text-based environment. *University of Toledo Law Review*, 38, 101.

46 Goldberg (2005).

47 *Id. Also see* Cristal, M. (2017). Negotiating in a low-to-no trust environment. In C. Honeyman & A.K. Schneider (eds.), *The Negotiator's Desk Reference (Vol. 1)*. St Paul, MN: DRI Press.

48 Rational self-interest guides parties' decisions and actions far less than traditionally assumed. *See*, Ebner, N. & Kamp, A. (2010). Relationship 2.0: Mot setting students up for failure (this time). In C. Honeyman, J. Coben & G. De Palo (eds.), *Venturing Beyond the Classroom: Vol. 2 in the Rethinking Negotiation Teaching Series*. St. Paul, MN: DRI Press. Other drivers have powerful effect even running counter to rational self-interest, such as: process dynamics and cognitive biases (Bazerman, M.H. & Neale, M.A. (1994). *Negotiating Rationally*. New York, NY: Free Press); emotions (*see, e.g.*, Fisher, R. & Shapiro, D. (2005). *Beyond Reason*. London: Penguin Books); subjective value (Curhan, J.R., Elfenbein, H.A. & Xu, H. (2006). What do people value when they negotiate? Mapping the domain of subjective value in negotiation. *Journal of Personality and Social Psychology*, 91, 493-512; and negotiator personality traits (Sharma, S., Elfenbein, H.A., Foster, J. & Bottom, W.P. (2018). Predicting negotiation performance from personality traits: a field study across multiple occupations. *Human Performance*, 31(3), 145-164.). The diminished role of rational or economic self-interest in negotiation, combined with our focus on human touch issues, underpin this section's expansion on relational trust issues (deriving from knowledge and identification-based trust), rather than sufficing with tips on drafting a really good punitive damage clause in any contract.

larger gain (for example, if we lack the ability to punish them for violating trust), they may choose to do so.[49] We can directly affect or create this form of trust, such as by contracting punitive repercussions for trust-breaking behavior.[50]

Knowledge-based trust is grounded in the other's predictability, based on an assessment specific to them (as opposed to general assumptions such as that of generic rational self-interest). So far as our knowledge of our negotiation opposites allows us to predict their responses and behaviors, we can estimate the degree to which they can be trusted. This form of trust might result from study of negotiation opposites, or develop over time as we come to know them through a series of interactions.[51] The 'knowledge' involved includes, for example, our counterpart's reputation, the networks they belong to, the values we know them to hold, their behavior in previous interactions with us or with others we consult with.

Identification-based trust develops when one party perceives that their counterpart shares characteristics, traits, or backgrounds with them. We tend to trust negotiation counterparts in whom we (often subconsciously) identify perceived similarities with ourselves.[52] These can be as innocuous as one can imagine: eye color, hometown, college attended, or love (or hate) of the same sports team. Irrelevant though these similarities may be to the interaction at hand, they nonetheless spark a sense of trust in our counterpart, whether warranted or not.

3.4.2 Whom Do Negotiators Trust?

Translating the previous sections into practical terms, in the relationship between Negotiator A and Negotiator B (whether working on their own, or as Party A and Party B negotiating across a mediation table), Negotiator B is more likely to trust Negotiator A if:

a. Negotiator B perceives Negotiator A to be similar to her;
b. Negotiator B holds power of reward or sanction over Negotiator A;
c. Negotiator A displays a positive attitude toward Negotiator B or initiates trusting, cooperative behavior, which invites reciprocation;
d. Negotiator A makes concessions, signaling motivation for finding a joint solution;[53]
e. Negotiator B anticipates having future interactions with Negotiator A;[54]
f. Negotiator B has helped Negotiator A in the past (creating expectations of reciprocity);

49 Paulson, G.D. & Naquin, C.E. (2004). Establishing trust via technology: long distance practices and pitfalls. *International Negotiation*, 9(2), 229-244.
50 *See* Axelrod, R. (1984). *The Evolution of Cooperation*. New York: Basic Books; Schelling, T.C. (1980). *The Strategy of Conflict* (2nd ed.). Cambridge, MA: Harvard University Press.
51 Lewicki (2006).
52 *Id.*
53 Lewicki & Litterer (1985).
54 Thompson, L.L. (2019). *The Mind and Heart of the Negotiator* (7th ed.). London: Pearson.

g. Negotiator A is known to have been helpful and cooperative in the past, whether toward others or toward Negotiator B;[55]
h. Negotiator B feels she knows and understands Negotiator A to a degree granting her insight into Negotiator A's system of needs, norms, and values.

These inter-party trust dynamics will play out in unassisted negotiation processes, as well as in processes facilitated by third parties. Mediators who trigger, promote, or highlight these dynamics (depending on their approach and process model), will affect interparty trust.

However, what affects the level of trust between parties and mediators?

3.4.3 What Engenders Parties' Trust in Mediators?

Regarding the party-mediator trust relationship, a survey of mediators and parties clearly showed that both groups agreed that the ability to gain a party's trust is *the* most valuable skill of an effective mediator. What operationalizes this 'ability', though, practically speaking? It seems to depend who you ask. *Mediators* suggested that trust was most effectively built though the mediator's empathic listening, and to a lesser extent by the mediator displaying honesty, and adhering to ethical standards.[56] *Parties* to mediation stressed mediators' friendliness, likability, integrity, neutrality, maintaining of confidentiality, and preparedness.[57] Note the mixture of human touch issues (friendliness, likability) with professional issues (e.g., neutrality, confidentiality). These in-depth studies show that not only do many mediator moves *depend* on trust, as discussed above – many (or most) mediator moves *affect* trust as well.

3.5 Trustbuilding Tough? Wait Till You Get Online!

After clarifying the nature of trust and its role in negotiation and dispute resolution, we next explore why this concept is challenged in online negotiation and mediation processes. First, we explain why the internet, in general, is a trust-adverse environment. Next, we conceptualize how online communication media impacts these processes by affecting interparty trust. This prepares us to identify specific trust issues challenging ODR processes, through exploring the trust effects of the communication media utilized for ODR.

55 Pruitt & Kimmel (1977).
56 Goldberg (2005).
57 Goldberg & Shaw (2007).

3.5.1 Trust in the Online Environment

Before getting into the nuts and bolts the trust effects of particular media, we should note the overarching sense of distrust many people have toward the internet. Patricia Wallace, an early writer on internet psychology, noted how rampant exploitation has caused users to approach with a pre-emptive filter of distrust in place.[58] One might have generally expected that with time, we would develop our warning sensors, Spidey-senses, and personal degree of comfort online, enabling us to function well in the hazardous online environment just as naturally as we transverse an unpaved road. However, this has not fully materialized and, its benefits and opportunities notwithstanding, the internet remains similar to a bad neighborhood after dark. We watch where we are going, try and stay close to familiar sites, complain about the lack of competent policing and repeatedly warn our children not to speak to strangers or take candy from them. And yet, we ourselves are but babes in the internet woods, facing threats intensifying in quantity, stealth, and sophistication. Even as we bank, shop, and date online, we endure (or, hear of others enduring) identity theft, fraud, catfishing, and other forms of trust-breaking activity. In the battle for control of opinions and worldviews, the sophistication with which fake news is disseminated is unprecedented. The degree to which we are targeted, individually, by legitimate businesses evokes concerns for our privacy. How did that platform offer me certain news or products only minutes after I had spoken about them? More concerning is when these offers arrive after I merely *thought* about something related to them! Recently, movies such as *The Big Hack*[59] and *The Social Dilemma*[60] have exposed just how manipulative Big Tech companies are toward individual internet users, how responsive we are to the beckoning call of our devices, and how susceptible we are to the information they display.

The online environment, then, is rife with distrust, even as its use depends on it. Any internet use requires us to place trust in a software platform, an informational website, an online vendor, or another individual. And indeed, consciously or not, we place a remarkable amount of trust in all these, as we bank, shop, and date online. And yet, even as we do so, and even as the internet has further developed its potential as a global library, a world of opportunity, and a connecting medium for meaningful interactions between everyone on the planet, some part of our mind tags it as a hunting ground for predators prowling for prey.[61] Predators out for profit are joined by pranksters out for

58 Wallace, P.M. (1999). *The Psychology of the Internet.* Cambridge: Cambridge University Press.

59 Amer, K. & Noujaim, J. (2019). *The Great Hack.* Netflix.

60 Orlowski, J. (2020). *The Social Dilemma.* Exposure Labs.

61 While more sinister examples exist, this might be most easily exemplified by the phenomena of spam e-mail. In 2020, an estimated 53.5% of 300 billion emails sent daily were spam. *See* Clement, J. (2020). Spam: share of global email traffic 2014-2020. Available at www.statista.com/statistics/420391/spam-email-traffic-share/.

thrills; by countries, governments, and political parties out to influence our social and political behavior and voting decisions;[62] and by others mixing these motivations.[63] Knowing this primes us to some level of caution or suspicion, perhaps a threat warning level of pale yellow, whenever we open a browser or click on our inbox.

3.5.2 It Gets Worse Once We Start Talking

Communication, seemingly the great trust builder, was found to be, in itself, a *hazard* to trust, when conducted at a distance. Even in pre-internet times, comparing face-to-face with telephone-based communication found the former to foster rapport, trusting behavior, and cooperation; the latter fosters distrust, and competitive and contentious behavior.[64]

As researchers began exploring the 'bad neighborhood' of the internet, they discovered that while communicating online, people develop disinhibition; they ignore possible adverse consequences of interactions, due to physical distance, reduced accountability, and a sense of anonymity.[65] Online, people tend to act more contentiously than face-to-face communicators, causing more frequent occurrences of swearing, name calling, insults, and hostile behavior.[66] Focusing on trust, online communicators find it difficult to build the trust necessary for their opposites to perceive them, and construe their intentions, positively. As a result, they lose control of interactions or even of relationships. Why does this happen? What is it about online communication that makes building or maintaining trust so difficult?

3.5.3 Media Effects

To explain this, we need to understand a basic principle in communications theory: *the medium matters.* Messages do not just 'happen', they are transmitted from one communicator and received by another, via a medium. For convenience's sake, we

62 *See* Mueller, R. (2019). Report on the investigation into Russian interference in the 2016 presidential election ('The Mueller Report'), available at www.justice.gov/storage/report.pdf, detailing Russia's employ of troll farms and bots to manipulate social media debate and real-world events to influence the 2016 U.S. presidential election. Also, *see The Great Hack* (2019), detailing arrangements between the Trump campaign in the U.S. (and the Leave.EU movement in the U.K), and Cambridge Analytica. This company analyzed citizens' social media data, identified susceptible individuals, and targeted them with messaging designed to capture their vote for their client campaign.

63 As perhaps evidenced by the huge number of computer viruses circulated; currently, over 1,000,000 new codes are released *daily*. *See* Harrison, V. & Pagliery, J. (2015). Nearly 1 million new malware threats released every day. Available at https://money.cnn.com/2015/04/14/technology/security/cyber-attack-hacks-security/index.html.

64 Drolet, A.L. & Morris, M.W. (2000). Rapport in conflict resolution: accounting for how face-to-face contact fosters mutual cooperation in mixed-motive conflicts. *Journal of Experimental Social Psychology*, 36(1), 26-50. Also *see* Raiffa, H. (1982). *The Art and Science of Negotiation*. Cambridge: Harvard University Press.

65 Wallace (1999).

66 Kiesler, S. & Sproull, L. (1992). Group decision making and communication technology. *Organizational Behavior and Human Decision Making*, 52(1), 96-123.

often assume the medium to be a neutral vehicle for the essence, which is the message we intended to transmit or receive. As a result, when we hear a message from another, we assume that we understand them as they meant to be understood. When we say something in response, we assume they understood us as we intended (or, we blame their filters or shortcomings for distorting our intent). What we often fail to take into account, as we text, phone, email, Tweet, and videoconference our way through life, is that the messages we transmit and receive, and the way we transmit and receive messages, are affected – sometimes, fundamentally altered – by the medium we choose to convey them through.

In fact, the communication channel through which negotiations and mediations are conducted is neither passive nor neutral. Any communication medium influences both ends of the communication loop, affecting *what* information negotiators share and *how* that information is conveyed,[67] as well as how that information is received and interpreted. These effects – the specific ways in which the medium affects the message – are called 'media effects'.

Why is some information easily communicated face-to-face, yet difficult to convey by e-mail? Why might we respond in one way to something we are told face-to-face, but a very different way to a text-message containing essentially the same content? Underlying these differences are two dimensions of communication media:[68]

3.5.3.1 Media Richness

A media's capacity to convey 'contextual cues': body language, facial expressions, tone of voice, etc. Face-to-face communication is a 'rich' medium: it allows for all of these, which account for a significant proportion of a message's meaning.[69] E-mail is often considered a 'lean' medium because it conveys neither visual nor audio cues; we cannot see the other's gestures or facial expressions, nor hear their tone of voice. Denied these contextual cues, negotiators both transmit and receive information differently. Text messaging is often portrayed as even leaner. Videoconferencing, while considered leaner than face-to-face interactions, is richer than email.

On the transmitting side, media richness affects presentation style: e-mail negotiators, as opposed to face-to-face or videoconferencing parties, rely more heavily on logical argumentation, share less personal information and are more task oriented than in-

67 Carnevale & Pruitt (1992); Friedman, R.A. & Currall, S.C. (2001). *E-Mail Escalation: Dispute Exacerbating Elements of Electronic Communication.* Nashville, TN: Vanderbilt University; Valley, K.L., Moag, J. & Bazerman, M.H. (1998). 'A matter of trust' effects of communication on the efficiency and distribution of outcomes. *Journal of Economic Behavior & Organization*, 34, 2.

68 Barsness, Z.I. & Bhappu, A.D. (2004). At the crossroads of technology and culture: social influences, information sharing, and sense-making processes during negotiations. In M.J. Gelfand & J.M. Brett (eds.), *The Handbook of Negotiation & Culture.* Palo Alto, CA: Stanford University Press.

69 DePaulo, B.M. & Friedman, H.S. (1998). Nonverbal communication. In D.T. Gilber, S.T. Fiske & G. Lidzey (eds.), *The Handbook of Social Psychology.* Boston, MA: McGraw Hill.

person negotiators tend to be.[70] On the receiving end, further media effects kick in: Information exchanged in e-mail tends to be less nuanced than information exchanged face-to-face,[71] and the elimination of important back-channel and clarifying information such as speech acknowledgements (e.g., 'uh-huh' or 'huh?') and reactive body language (e.g., nods)[72] compounds this. Communicating through lean media, negotiators focus on the actual *content* of messages,[73] granting more importance to the words that are chosen, and their interpretation.

3.5.3.2 Interactivity

This is the potential of the medium to sustain a seamless flow of information between two or more negotiators.[74] Interactivity has two dimensions:

The first, a temporal dimension, captures the *synchronicity* of interactions. Face-to-face communication and videoconferencing are synchronous and co-temporal. Each party receives a message just as it is produced, resulting in speaking 'turns' occurring sequentially. E-mail is often asynchronous: negotiators can read and respond to others' messages whenever they happen to open their inbox or choose to reply. Responses are not necessarily sequential; reading messages out-of-order commonly causes misunderstandings. However, while early research categorized email as asynchronous, this is no longer the way we often use it. Most of us now walk around with our inboxes in our pocket, hyper-alert to notifications of incoming messages.[75] While we sometimes put off responding in pursuit of focus or of deliberation, we often respond immediately to email messages we receive. This has led me to suggest previously that email had transformed from asynchronous to semi-synchronous,[76] and perhaps the best way to capture how we use it in practice is 'sometimes synchronous'. This raises the notion

70 *See* Ebner, N. (2014). Negotiating via (the new) e-mail. In M. Benoliel (ed.), *Negotiation Excellence: Successful Deal Making* (2nd ed.). Singapore: World Scientific Publishing.

71 Friedman & Currall (2001); Valley, Moag & Bazerman (1998).

72 O'Connaill, B., Whittaker, S. & Wilber, S. (1993). Conversations over video conferences: an evaluation of the spoken aspects of video-mediated communication. *Human Computer Interaction*, 8(4), 389-428.

73 Ocker, R.J. & Yaverbaum, G.J. (1999). Asynchronous computer-mediated communication versus face-to-face collaboration: results on student learning, quality and satisfaction. *Group Decision and Negotiations*, 8, 5. Also *see* Sokolova, M. & Lapalme, G. (2012). How much do we say? Using informativeness of negotiation text records for early prediction of negotiation outcomes. *Group Decision and Negotiation*, 21(3), 363-379.

74 R. Kraut *et al.*, (1992). Task requirements & media choice in collaborative writing. *Human Computer Interactions*, 7, 4.

75 So alert, in fact, that we now experience phantom phone vibrations leading us to constantly check our screen for incoming calls and messages. *See* Rosenberger, R. (2015). An experiential account of phantom vibration syndrome. *Computers in Human Behavior*, 52, 124-131.

76 Ebner (2014).

that our actual patterns in using a medium is more important than how it is usually used or how others tend to regard it.[77]

The second dimension of interactivity is *parallel processing*, which describes a medium's ability to allow negotiators to *simultaneously* transmit messages. In face-to-face communication, parallel processing is overt and part of the familiar communication loop. As you speak, I nod, or hold a hand up in protest. In text messaging or email communication, feedback is never in-real-time and is only sometimes near-instant. Moreover, simultaneous exchange of messages, or 'crossing messages', often causes confusion.

3.5.3.3 Media Richness and Interactivity: For Better and for Worse

In summary, media richness and interactivity account for important differences across media in the structure, style, and content of negotiation information exchanged.[78] The research generally holds out face-to-face communication as the gold standard for interaction – and we know that even when this mode is employed, as Bernie Mayer has written about us all, 'We are very imperfect communicators.'[79] The further a communicative interaction departs from this familiar communication mode along spectrums of lean/rich media and high/low interactivity, the greater the challenges posed by media effects to the human touch areas of trust, empathy, and social intuition.[80] We now turn to discussing specific media effects of online communication on trust, and how to best work with this element – such a critical element of the human touch – in online negotiation and mediation processes.

77 Indeed, this is one thrust of another theoretical approach the field of communications offers for understanding communication media. For more on Channel Expansion Theory, *see* Ebner, N. (2017). Negotiation via text messaging. In C. Honeyman & A.K. Schneider (eds.), *The Negotiator's Desk Reference (Vol. 2)*. St Paul, MN: DRI Press [hereinafter – Ebner (2017 TEXTING)].

78 For more detail, *see* N. Ebner *et al.* (2009). You've got agreement: Negoti@ting via e-mail. In C. Honeyman, J. Coben & G. De Palo (eds.), *Rethinking Negotiation Teaching: Innovations for Context and Culture*. St. Paul, MN: DRI Press; Ebner, N. (2017). Negotiation via email. In C. Honeyman & A.K. Schneider (eds.), *The Negotiator's Desk Reference (Vol. 2)*. St Paul, MN: DRI Press [hereinafter – Ebner (2017 EMAIL)].

79 Mayer, B. (2012). *The Dynamics of Conflict* (2nd ed.), 11.

80 As noted above, Media Richness Theory is not the only theory explaining differences in media effects across media. However, it is the most commonly referenced in the negotiation literature and offers the most straightforward explanation for commonly encountered phenomena. For other theories helping to explain specific media, *see* Ebner, N. (2017). Negotiation via videoconferencing. In C. Honeyman & A.K. Schneider (eds.), *The Negotiator's Desk Reference (Vol. 2)*. St Paul, MN: DRI Press [hereinafter – Ebner (2017 VIDEOCONFERENCING)]; and Ebner (2017 TEXTING). *For an overview of other theoretical perspectives for understanding online communication in negotiation, see* Geiger, I. (2020). From letter to twitter: a systematic review of communication media in negotiation. *Group Decision and Negotiation* 29, 1-44.

3.5.4 Trust Reduction in Online Negotiation and Mediation: Are We Sure?

The previous section would suggest that interparty trust would be challenged by media effects. Is this borne out by research findings? The answer is generally yes, but not all media impacts it equally. In this section, we will review the answer provided by the research on each medium, and note some of the limitations of research into this question.

3.5.4.1 Trust Reduction in Text-Based Interactions

Early in the era of negotiation via computer-based text messaging or email, researchers realized that in this environment, negotiators feel less normatively bound; they are more contentious and less cooperative. From a trust-perspective, this suggests email to be a particularly trust-challenging communication channel. Is this conclusion warranted? Absolutely. It is supported by both indirect and direct measurements of trust in email-based negotiation processes.

Indirect measurements examine process cooperation and integrative outcomes. Both are known to be facilitated by interparty trust enabling negotiators to discuss their true needs, preferences, and priorities; and assisting them to refrain from unconstructive posturing, escalation, or walk-outs.[81] Reduction in them would indirectly indicate a diminishment of trust. The majority of experiments measuring these two indicators have, indeed, reported lower rates of process cooperation, and lower rates of integrative outcomes in email as compared to face-to-face negotiation.[82] While these findings are only partially directly mediated by the issue of trust, other possible explanations, such as increased contentiousness and the difficulty of forming rapport online,[83] are themselves indirect measures of trust-diminishment, as will be discussed below.

Researchers have also directly asked negotiators to assess their degree of trust in counterparts. Unsurprisingly, given the research we've surveyed thus far, negotiators

---

81 *See* Ebner (2007).

82 Arunachalam, V. & Dilla, W. (1995). Judgment accuracy & outcomes in negotiation: a casual modeling analysis of decision-aiding effects. *Organizational Behavior & Human Decision Processes,* 61, 3; Valley, Moag & Bazerman (1998); Nadler & Shestowsky (2006). For contrasting research, *see* Galin, A., Gross, M. & Gosalker, G. (2007). E-negotiation versus face-to-face negotiation what has changed – if anything? *Computers in Human Behavior,* 23, 1; Nadler & Shestowsky (2006); Naquin, C.E. & Paulson, G.D. (2003). Online bargaining and interpersonal trust. *Journal of Applied Psychology,* 88, 1.

83 Ebner (2014).

interacting via email experienced lower levels of trust in their counterparts than did face-to-face negotiators.[84,85]

3.5.4.2 *Trust Reduction in Videoconferencing*

Set alongside the wealth of research on email negotiation, the research on negotiation via videoconferencing is starkly meager.[86] What little there is offers somewhat mixed results, which, taken altogether, present far less evidence of trust-reduction in videoconference-based processes.

Early experiments focusing on trust formation in tasks involving collaboration and competition (although not, specifically, negotiation or mediation) have shown videoconferencing to support trust better than text, as could be expected from our discussion of media effects. For the purposes of the task examined in those experiments, videoconferencing supported trust as well as telephone and face-to-face communication.[87]

Recent experiments on negotiators have also found videoconferencing to support higher levels of interparty trust between parties than text-based communication.[88] However, how does its support of trust match up with face-to-face communication? Dominick Sondern and Guido Hertel of the University of Munster experimented with 160 negotiation dyads, half of whom negotiated an issue via videoconferencing and the other half negotiating the same issue in-person. They found no significant reduction in

---

84 Naquin & Paulson (2003).

85 Less research has been conducted directly on trust in email-based mediation. However, a recent study comparing parties to in-person mediation to those participating in a process conducted via a text-only, chat-like communication platform showed that participants in the text-only condition experienced lower mutual feelings of understanding and trust, and considered their mediator to be less trustworthy, than those participating in the in-person processes. *See* Damen, D., van der Wijst, P., van Amelsvoort, M. & Krahmer, E. (2020). The effect of perspective-taking on trust and understanding in online and face-to-face mediations. *Group Decision and Negotiation*, 29, 1121-1156. Of course, even two text-based media have different characteristics (*e.g.*, the nature of the chat in the experiment was synchronous or in real-time; email interaction can have a lower level of interactivity), and will therefore have different media effects.

86 This is particularly interesting, given that videoconferencing, as a technology, has been around for far longer than email. Commercially available since the 1930s, videoconferencing only truly began spreading in the mid-2000s (*see* Ebner (2017 VIDEOCONFERENCING)). Use of videoconferencing for professional activities including mediation and negotiation only became truly ubiquitous during the Covid-19 era in 2020. Videoconferencing's lack of adoption probably explains the dearth of research on the its media effects and impacts on trust.

87 For the purposes of the task under examination in those experiments, videoconferencing supported trust as well as telephone and face-to-face communication. *See* Bos, N. *et al.*, (2002). Effects of four computer-mediated communications channels on trust development. *Proceedings of SIGGHI Conference on Human Factors in Computing Systems: Changing the world, changing ourselves*, ACM.

88 Kurtzberg, T.R., Kang, S. & Naquin, C.E. (2018). The effect of screen size and e-communication richness on negotiation performance. *Group Decision and Negotiation*, 27, 573-592. Note, that the text-based negotiators used Skype's chat function, rather than email, and recall that even two text-based media have different media effects. This experiment did not compare videoconference negotiators to face-to-face negotiators.

trust between videoconference-based negotiators and those conducting face-to-face interactions. Interestingly, from our human-touch perspective, their work pinpointed the decrease in trust between videoconferencing negotiators (statistically insignificant though it was) as resulting specifically from diminishment of social presence. When negotiators sensed diminished social presence of their counterpart, they trusted them less.[89] They also noted that the issue of whether the negotiation was recorded or not had no impact on interparty trust.[90]

In the mediation context, Susan Nauss Exon and Soomi Lee of the University of La Verne[91] compared 30 mediation parties participating in a face-to-face simulation to 30 parties engaging in a mediation simulation conducted via telepresence (a suite of cameras, lighting, and screens resulting in a more immersive sense of co-presence than videoconferencing). All the simulations were conducted by the same mediator. In post-simulation surveys, parties reported the degree to which they trusted the mediator, and the degree to which the mediator was trustworthy. Both questions received high rankings by participants, and there was no significant difference regarding trust between the in-person and telepresence conditions.

These findings suggest that the richer the medium, the more tools negotiators and mediators have at their disposal for trust-building. They establish quite convincingly that even working largely intuitively, negotiators and mediators are likely to do better at establishing and maintaining trust via videoconferencing as opposed to email or other text-based platforms.

However, has this research established that videoconferencing is, for negotiation and mediation trust purposes, 'the same' or 'as good' as face-to-face interactions? Hardly. Beyond their sparsity, other issues limit any conclusions we might draw: media differences, measurement differences, and ceiling effects, to name but a few.

I suggest that, until a considerable body of research finds negligible impacts of videoconferencing on trust, we should continue to consider videoconferencing, in

---

89 Interestingly, a somewhat contrary result was found in experiments comparing (not face-to-face with videoconferencing but rather) two forms of videoconferencing allowing different degrees of body language *availability*. Participants negotiated in two camera conditions: one showed head and shoulders only; the other, the full upper body. In these experiments, participants reported higher social presence in the full upper-body view, with body-language availability being the significant factor. However, those negotiating in the full upper-body view condition reported slightly *lower* degrees of trust compared to those viewing head-and-shoulders. *See* Teoh, H.L. (2012). Body language availability in videoconferencing (Ph.D Thesis, U. of Otago). Available at http://hdl.handle.net/10523/2592. Does this indicate that while social presence generates trust, too much of it is counterproductive? Might other issues mediate the trust differences? This is a good example of how we are only just beginning to scratch the surface of understanding the mechanisms at play in generating trust via videoconferencing.

90 Sondern, D. & Hertel, G. (2020). Negotiations in the digital age: effects of communication media and information reprocessability on negotiator trust. Paper presented at the *33rd Annual Conference of the International Association for Conflict Management.*

91 Exon, S.N. & Lee, S. (2019). Building trust online: the realities of telepresence for mediators engaged in Online Dispute Resolution. *Stetson Law Review,* 49, 110-147.

practice, to be a trust-changing, and probably-diminishing, channel. Maintaining this approach, negotiators and mediators will be mindful when working through the medium, assisting them to avoid unforeseen trust-diminishing incidents, and potentially to uncover ways in which the medium can be used to enhance trust even beyond levels typical to face-to-face interactions.

If anything, I think it is the assumption that videoconferencing is close enough to face-to-face interactions as to make no difference that is likely to be most harmful to those working with trust via this channel. As Jeff Thompson and I have written:

> (R)eading through the literature, one gets the sense that there is an assumption, spoken or unspoken, that in video-based communication trust would not pose any more of a challenge than it does in face-to-face communication.
> Indeed, research has found video interactions to be almost as good as face-to-face
> interactions for trust emergence. However, even if trust can emerge to the same degree through video interactions in a quantitative sense, qualitative differences with regard to trust development and resilience persist. We suggest that video presents new challenges to trust formation precisely owing to this intuitive assumption that video and face-to-face communication are largely the same. In reality, video-based communication does not fill in the full range of cues and psychological impacts lacking in text-based communication. It only fills them in partially, and alters others – while giving the impression of providing them in full. Communicators' expectations that video would be the same as in-person may lead them to forgo conscious filtering of the unique set of contextual cues provided by online video communication. These could pose even greater challenges to mediators aiming to build trust, given the opportunities for misreading these cues by all communicators involved.[92]

Similarly, researchers So Yeong Park (Stanford) and Mark Whiting (U. of Pennsylvania) have recently warned:

> Video-conferencing can provide a false affordance of visibility – it tricks us into thinking we know more than we actually do about what the other person means. This can lead users toward an illusion of transparency and overestimation of their perceptions, which could be misled…

92 Ebner & Thompson (2014), at 118-119, citations omitted.

> In aggregate, this situation suggests that video chat remains in a perceptual uncanny valley – it works well enough to trick us into thinking it works better than it does, which leads to emotional fatigue.[93]

There is much we do not know about videoconferencing; particularly, with regards to its effects on trust in negotiation and dispute resolution. So many of its features and characteristics potentially posing challenges to trust in negotiation and mediation have not yet been explored. Specific examples of these challenges are detailed in the discussion below; at this point I will suffice with one acute example that has surfaced as this chapter was being written.

A meta-analysis conducted by Serena Lu of Singapore Management University and her colleagues in 2017 showed that a party's affect (the combined state of their mood and emotions) impacts their degree of trust in their counterpart. Parties with positive affect trust the other more; experiencing negative affect decreases trust in another party.[94] How does videoconferencing impact affect? This question was yet to be asked as I began writing this chapter. As it goes to press, the issue is pressing and emergent, with tentative answers already put forth.

It was only during the Covid-19 era and its attendant natural experiment in videoconferencing that the syndrome dubbed Zoom fatigue emerged. Previously, individuals engaging regularly in videoconferencing may have blamed personal or contextual causes for their experiencing a rough day. At the beginning of the Covid-19 lockdowns Zoom fatigue surfaced as a widespread response to videoconferencing. By mid-2020, scientists had explained some of the mechanisms through which videoconferencing imposes an unusually high cognitive load, triggers biological responses we are unaware of, and generally sends our brains into exhausting spin. Brains aside, consider the physical effects of sitting rigidly in a chair for extended periods of time.

We know recognize that by the middle of a videoconference (or right from its inception, if it is our third call of the day) participants might experience a host of reactions that all feed directly into negative affect: depletion, exhaustion, enhanced self-awareness, cognitive dulling, physical discomfort, restlessness, and more. All the while, we are denied some of the neurobiological and physical affect-*improving* elements of in-person interaction. From a trust perspective, combining Lu *et al.*'s findings on affect and

---

93 Park, S.Y. & Whiting, M.E. (2020). Beyond Zooming there: understanding nonverbal interaction online. Paper presented at the Microsoft New Future of Work 2020 Symposium, Available at www.microsoft.com/en-us/research/uploads/prod/2020/07/NFW-Park-Whiting.pdf, pp. 3-4, citations omitted.

94 Lu, S.C., Kong, D.T., Ferrin, D.L. & Dirks, K.T. (2017). What are the determinants of interpersonal trust in dyadic negotiations? Meta-analytic evidence and implications for future research. *Journal of Trust Research*, 7(1), 22-50. Note, that in these studies, trustor's levels of trust were unrelated to their counterpart's trust behavior. In other words, dips or highs in affect level were unrelated to a counterpart keeping or breaking trust.

trust with the literature on Zoom fatigue would suggest a negative correlation between videoconferencing and trust: an increase in Zoom fatigue would result in a decrease in interparty trust, mediated by negative affect. However, even just designing a valid experiment to explore this hypothesis would require us to understand the mechanisms of Zoom fatigue – presently, another elephant – far better than we do.

3.6 *Eight Challenges to Trust in Online Mediation and Negotiation*

We now break these wider issues down to frame eight specific challenges to interparty trust in online interactions. After generally portraying each challenge, we reframe the literature into practical recommendations to negotiators on coping with that obstacle. Next, we make similar recommendations to mediators.[95] To avoid repetitiveness, it should be said, once and up front, that *all* of the implications for negotiators are important for mediators to keep in mind as they help parties to negotiate. Separate recommendations to mediators focus, for the main part, on enhancing mediator-party trust. Each recommendation specifies whether it applies to email or videoconferencing, or both. Table 4.5 introduces eight trust-challenges discussed in this section.[96]

Table 4.5 Challenges to Trust in Online Processes

Challenge	Detail
1. Low expectations of trust	*Parties* have low expectations regarding the other's trustworthiness walking into an online process, and this becomes a self-fulfilling prophesy.
2. Lack of contextual cues	Online communication constrains many of the non-verbal cues we rely on for assessing another person's trustworthiness.
3. Increased attribution and misinterpretation	The tendency to put the worst possible face on another's intentions and meanings increases in online communication. As a result, parties will perceive the other's intentions through the most distrusting lens possible.
4. I am anonymous, the other is faceless	The mutual invisibility inherent in online interactions facilitates trust-breaking behavior.
5. Physical distance and interpersonal 'otherness'	The sense of separation inherent to online processes results in reduced identification with the other, challenging identity-based trust.

95 While there is a wide body of literature addressing online communication and online negotiation, relatively few pieces have been written on online mediation (*see* Ebner & Rainey, Chapter 17 in this book), and only a handful have directly addressed the issue of trust. As a result, some of the recommendations addressing mediators in this chapter are admittedly less grounded in existing literature than is desirable; they combine practical experience and observations with an adaptation of negotiation-related literature to the third-party role.

96 This list incorporates, updates, and sharpens previous lists; *e.g.*, Ebner (2007), Ebner (2012).

Challenge	Detail
6. Increased contentiousness: a vicious cycle	People are more apt to lash out at each other online. It is difficult to trust someone treating you this way – or to gain someone's trust, after doing this yourself.
7. Privacy	In online processes, parties can never know who is 'in the room' with them, in real-time or after the process concludes, eroding trust.
8. Diminished parties	Negotiating online, parties might experience diminished commitment, investment, and focus.

3.6.1 Low Expectations of Trust

Communicating via e-mail, negotiators experience lower levels of trust in their opposites than those experienced by negotiators in similar face-to-face interactions – at *all* stages of the process.[97] Before the process' inception, parties negotiating via email report lower levels of trust in their opposite than do participants in face-to-face negotiations.[98] This prophesy self-fulfills: low trust-levels persists throughout the course of the negotiation, resulting in diminished process cooperation and information sharing,[99] and heightened suspicion: email are more likely to suspect their opposite of lying, even when no actual deception has taken place.[100] The cycle culminates in email negotiators showing lower post-negotiation trust levels and less desire to engage with their counterparts in future interactions with them than do face-to-face dyads – even when there is no objective difference in the negotiation outcome.[101]

One recent experiment has indicated that these findings regarding trust expectations may not apply in negotiation via videoconferencing.[102]

3.6.1.1 Implications for Negotiators

Begin early: Trustbuilding attempts need to begin before your opposite's initial expectations turn into a self-fulfilling prophesy through attribution. Begin these efforts right at the negotiation's launch, and even before the 'official' kick-off by means of informal, off-task communication.[103]

97 Ebner (2007).
98 Naquin & Paulson (2003).
99 *Id.*
100 Thompson (2019).
101 Naquin & Paulson (2003). This trust-degradation cycle concerns not only one's negotiation opposite, but also one's self-perceptions of satisfaction and efficacy: email negotiators are less satisfied with their outcome and less confident in their performance's quality than in-person negotiators. In other words, they lose trust in themselves.
102 In a comparison of face-to-face and videoconferencing negotiators, pre-testing showed no difference in trust expectations. Moreover, in both conditions, trust increased from pre- to post-testing. *See* Sondern & Hertel (2020). However, as noted earlier, more experimentation, focused specifically on expectations rather than on setting baseline levels of trust, is required to determine whether there are differences in trust expectations.
103 Morris *et al.* (2002).

Be prepared for rejection: Your opposite may expect you to be untrustworthy. Do not be surprised, or discouraged, if your early trustbuilding moves are rejected, misconstrued, unnoticed or ignored. Keep trying.

Do not stop at success: Initial trust needs building, but that is not enough. Trust must then be maintained in order to see the process through to its conclusion, and in a manner that naturally extends beyond the negotiation to support you in a future interaction with the same counterparty.

3.6.1.2 Implications for Mediators

Tech Tour: Parties' trust expectations regarding their online mediators is yet to be been explored. Taking the inter-party dynamics discussed above to heart, it would seem wise to assume that it is never too early to begin trustbuilding. As parties enter the platform the first time, give them a guided tour, explaining how its main features work and everything they need to know in order to navigate it effectively. If anything goes wrong and you can fix it right there in front of them, so much the better. Your skill with the platform will engender parties' trust in you.[104]

Preempt distrust: Help parties recognize, perhaps by means of a comment in your introduction to the process, that any initial misgivings they feel entering an online mediation process are normal. They are a part of the playing field, and *not* (as they may be telling themselves) some intuitive insight into your intentions or those of their counterpart.[105]

3.6.2 Lack of Contextual Cues

Perhaps underlying our low trust expectations is our intuitive sense that, negotiating online, our trust sensors are operating in the dark. Communicating with one another, people rely on contextual cues to interpret others' messages: their facial expressions, body language, tone of voice and other non-verbal hints 'padding' the words themselves. We infer most of a message's meaning through these cues, in fact, rather than its words.[106] In the rich medium of face-to-face communication we are so overcome with cues that we allow ourselves to ignore some of them (such as by looking away from our counterpart). Communicating through leaner media, however, we seek out such cues more actively. Unable to see our interlocutor's face over the phone, we strain to infer meaning from their tone of voice. Text-based online communication, including e-mail and other communication systems common to ODR providers, is a very lean media for conveying

104 Hammond, A.M.G. (2003). How do you write 'yes'? A study on the effectiveness of online dispute resolution. *Conflict Resolution Quarterly*, 20, 3.

105 Ebner (2007).

106 Thompson (2019). Also *see* Thompson, J., Ebner, N. & Giddings, J. (2017). Nonverbal communication in negotiation. In C. Honeyman & A.K. Schneider (eds.), *The Negotiator's Desk Reference (Vol. 1)*. St Paul, MN: DRI Press.

contextual cues. Our usual methods for transmitting our trustworthiness to others are rendered valueless, and the senses we have developed to analyze another's cues for assessing credibility are neutralized. Text-based communicators are denied many of the cues that have been found to inspire trust in face-to-face settings: facial expressions, vocal inflections, physical proximity, and touch.[107] Indeed, in experiments comparing interactions through face-to-face, audio, video and text-based communication, found the last to be the *least* supportive of trust-building.[108] Videoconferencing provides participants with more contextual cues in audio and visual form, and is therefore more supportive of trust building. Still, given the limitations of the video box and other constraints, these are still not the full array of cues provided in face-to-face communication (as detailed in Table 4.2).[109] These reduced cues may diminish trust in ways that have yet to be identified.

3.6.2.1 Implications for Negotiators

Learn to read: Text communication is full of cues – just not those we are used to. Never skim through a message, assuming you will get the gist of it. You will get the wrong gist. Read messages carefully, paying attention to details such as specific wording and phraseology.

Use what you've got: You can enhance your communication by utilizing every option your medium offers. In email, consider writing a new subject line each time instead of leaving the initial subject written three exchanges ago. In video communication, if you tend to communicate with your hands, make sure they are visible in the video box for your counterpart to see.

3.6.2.2 Implications for Mediators

Forewarn and forearm: Comment on the challenges of reduced cues in your introduction. Mediating via email, request parties to be as clear as they can, including regarding the tone of voice they are 'speaking' in. Ask them to be descriptive regarding their frame of mind, and that mentioning they are writing something angrily, or sarcastically, is more helpful than being ambiguous.

---

107 In text-based interactions these cues are at best expressed using emoticons and emoji. These can either assist or interfere; much as with "real" terms, people use and interpret emoticons differently, paving the way for misunderstanding. While in the past, many (including myself; *e.g.*, in Ebner (2014) have recommended against using emoticons in formal communication, I suggest that changing attitudes and use now warrant viewing emoticons as any other form of communicative device: if it can serve a positive communicative purpose, use it. And, if your capacity for expression grows when you are able to use this device, strive to create an overall interactional environment in which its use will seem natural and acceptable rather than norm-breaking or unprofessional.

108 Bos *et al.* (2002).

109 For detail of such cue-diminishment, *see* Ebner & Thompson (2014).

Ask questions: If one party sends another an ambiguous message, help clarify the author's intentions before the response arrives. In joint communication, you might ask directly, hoping the answer will clarify things to the receiver. You might write back a reframed, clear message, asking the author if this is their intent. Alternatively, you can use either method in a caucus with the author via private communication, seeking understanding the author's frame of mind before deciding how to handle the situation.

Assume the 'explainer' role: Often, you will identify, in real-time, a message or situation ripe for misconstruction. For example, you might notice one party's video freezing for a couple of seconds as the other spoke (causing them to miss what was said) or ambiguous language in an email. You might step in to reframe the message or directly explain (e.g., 'It sounds to me as if John is saying….' or 'I think you froze there for a second, so I'll just repeat what Gina said…')

3.6.3 Increased Attribution, Increased Misunderstanding

Any medium diminishing in contextual cues causes parties to focus on the actual *content* of their counterpart's messages. At the same time, it denies them the means to interpret them accurately. Meaning ambiguity increases the tendency toward the fundamental attribution error:[110] parties perceive negative actions or statements of their counterpart, and attribute these to the other's negative intentions and character rather than to any unmalicious circumstance. Reduced social presence, paired with few contextual cues, imbue a sense of distance and vagueness, which are compounded by lack of interactivity. Email negotiators ask fewer clarifying questions than face-to-face negotiators, leaving more room for parties to make and reinforce assumptions.[111] Attribution dynamics nudge assumptions toward negativity and distrust. Failed e-mail negotiations tend to include unclear messages, irrelevant points, and long general statements,[112] each an attribution breeding ground. Given the impact of the fundamental attribution error on interparty trust, email negotiators are more likely to suspect their counterpart of lying than are face-to-face negotiators, even when no actual deception took place.[113] It is yet to be discovered whether interacting via video (which allows for on-the-spot clarification, yet nudges parties toward one-at-a-time speaking rather than instantaneous response) has a similar effect.[114]

---

110 Kramer, R.M. (1995). Power, paranoia, and distrust in organizations: The distorted view from the top. *Research on Negotiation in Organizations* 5, 119-153; Thompson (2019).

111 Thompson, L.L. & Nadler, J. (2002). Negotiating via information technology: theory and application. *Journal of Social Issues*, 58, 1.

112 Thompson (2019).

113 Thompson & Nadler (2002).

114 For a survey regarding actual online deception, suspicion of online deception, and accuracy of online deception detection, *see* Toma, C.L., Bonus, J.A. & Van Swol, L.M. (2019). Lying online: examining the production, detection, and popular beliefs surrounding interpersonal deception in technologically-mediated environments. In T. Docan-Morgan (ed.), *The Palgrave Handbook of Deceptive Communication*. London: Palgrave Macmillan.

3.6.3.1 *Implications for Negotiators*

Slow down: Asynchronous text communication enables negotiators to slow down the pace of message crafting and improve their quality, preempting lack of clarity and misunderstandings.

Increase your social presence: Remind the other, repeatedly, that there is a real person opposite them. Use physical imagery in your writing, to reinforce this issue – for example, mention the city you are in, your surroundings (your office, hotel), a place you went to, a physical sensation, etc. In video conferencing, refer to real-world imagery and places beyond the video screen.

Communicate clearly: Preempt negative interpretations by enhancing clarity. In emails, clarify *much* more than you would face-to-face. In video interactions, be on the lookout for opportunities to verify your understanding or the others, even when you would not do so in an in-person encounter Here are several suggestions for enhancing clarity:

a. In emails, avoid unnecessary length; do not overload your opposite. Interacting via video, pause to ask your counterpart if they have any questions before you go on.
b. If you are writing a message on a smartphone, be alert to the changes this brings to your writing style. If it causes you to respond in short messages, or constrains the way your email is laid out, consider how it might be read by your counterpart.
c. Use the email subject field intentionally. It introduces your letter (preparing your counterpart for the content), sets a frame through which it will be read (diminishing negative interpretation), allows your counterpart to easily find it for reviewing it before responding, and helps organize messages bundling multiple issues.
d. Use 'In summary' sentences to highlight your main points, in both emails and video.

Don't read too much intent into their style: Even as you mind your own writing style and framing, try not to read too much into stylistic issues in your counterpart's email. They may not be mindful, or skilled with the medium. Do not overanalyze the length or brevity of their messages, either. Many factors affect the length of your counterpart's emails that have little to do with you or with the negotiation, including their age, gender, the device they are using, the day of the week, the time of day, and their email traffic volume.[115]

Avoid delays, but do not sweat them: Waiting and perceived delay cause anxiety, which is, in turn, conducive to formation of negative attribution. Manage both sides of this cycle: Do not expect immediate responses to your emails, and try to provide prompt responses to your counterpart's.[116] In video interactions, arrive a couple of minutes

115 Kooti, F., Aiello, L.M., Grbovic, M., Lerman, K. & Mantrach, A. (2015). Evolution of conversations in the age of email overload. Proceedings of the 24th International World Wide Web Conference (WWW'15), Florence, Italy, May 2015. Available at http://arxiv.org/pdf/1504.00704v1.pdf.

116 *See* Thompson & Nadler (2002).

ahead of time, rather than having your counterpart wait for you as you troubleshoot your equipment.

Clear bottom line: More so than anything else, your basic message, offer, or statement must be kept clear. End every email message with a very clear 'to summarize' paragraph.

Save by the Bell: Concerned that all the intentionality and caution in the world might not suffice? Do not entrust the situation to text communication, if this is possible. If misconstrued messages threaten to derail the process, simply pick up the phone, or arrange a videoconference or an in-person meeting with your counterpart.

3.6.3.2 Implications for Mediators

Clarify: Both in email and in video actions, ask clarifying questions, even if parties do not. By asking for clarification after an unclear message is transmitted, but before it is answered, you will slow down the process a bit, as the original receiver will wait for the author's clarification. This prevents misunderstanding expanding quickly or knee-jerk responses.

Educate: When attribution seems to be rearing its head, consider relating to its effects head on, by writing or saying something such as 'I think we're missing out on something that would be very clear if we were all sitting together in a room…' or 'We all know how things get misunderstood in e-mail communication, so let me be as clear as possible on this point….'[117]

3.6.4 I Am Anonymous, the Other Is Faceless

A major challenge to one party's desire wish to generate trust in their opposite arises from the setting of the encounter itself. Parties sit behind their computers, far away from their counterparts. In email negotiation, remoteness and intervening technology is augmented by facelessness, which only heightens the sense of anonymity, distance, and remote detachment. This engenders assumptions that one can get away with trust-breaking behavior at the same time as it lowers moral inhibitions against doing so. This, even when the process takes place between identifiable and accountable parties! The degree of effect this has on negotiation depends on how much effort parties put into 'unmasking' each other – or, more pro-actively, unmasking themselves *toward* the other. The more one party perceives the other as an *identifiable other*, as opposed to an anonymous, faceless e-mail address, the more likely they are to share information, rely on them and trust in them.[118] The more one party perceives the other as human, rather than just a face on the other side of a video connection, the more likely they are to maintain and uphold any promised or implied benevolence toward them. To allow trust to develop, we must

117 Summers Raines, S. (2005). Can online mediation be transformative? Tales from the front. *Conflict Resolution Quarterly*, 22, 4.
118 Nadler & Shestowsky (2006).

incorporate unmasking dynamics into online processes – and the earlier on, the better. In fact, there is no need to wait for the main show to begin.

3.6.4.1 Implications for Negotiators

Meet if you can: The challenge of online bonding has led to recommendations that you would do well to hold a preliminary face-to-face meeting with your opposite before beginning an online process, given the potential for trust formed in one venue to spill over into the other.[119]

Schmooze, and schmooze ahead: If a face-to-face meeting is impossible or impractical, as will often be the case in online processes, try to reach out, before initiating a negotiation process, in a short e-mail or phone call, to introduce yourself and to conduct some very basic 'schmoozing'.[120] Of course, in some processes this might seem impractical or at odds with the dynamics or essence of the process. In such cases, an in-process unmasking process is necessary.

Work at rapport (rapport before work): In-person negotiators have always been advised to pre-personalize processes, using pre-negotiation interaction for 'bonding'[121] and 'building rapport'.[122] Such light social interactions do not manifest as intuitively or play out as smoothly in online conversations.[123] In both emails and in videoconferencing, people tend to jump straight to the point. *Sans* rituals of handshakes and small talk, even introductions are more utilitarian than relationship building. Remember that even one lighter, bond-oriented sentence embedded in a businesslike e-mail can have great effect. Similarly, including a bit of personal information or commenting on your surroundings as you introduce yourself by video might elicit reciprocation.

Unmask yourself: As counterparts perceived as distant and faceless are less trusted, act intentionally to make yourself appear human, present, and real to the other. In email negotiation, self-unmasking might involve sharing personal information, or reducing perceived distance through shared language, or shared geographical or cultural references. In videoconferencing, attention to camera quality, angle, and background can further assist you to in providing your counterpart a humanized and engaging perspective of you and your surroundings. Express interest about an item in your counterpart's environment, and arrange your own background to provide fodder for such conversations.

---

119 Rocco, E. (1998). Trust breaks down in electronic contexts but can be repaired by some initial face-to-face contact. *Proceedings of the SIGGHI Conference on Human Factors in Computing Systems*, ACM Press; Zheng *et al.*, J. (2002). Trust without touch: jumpstarting long-distance trust with initial social activities. *Proceedings of the SIGGHI 2002 Conference on Human Factors in Computing Systems*, ACM Press.

120 Morris *et al.* (2002); Nadler & Shestowsky (2006).

121 Shapiro, R.M. & Jankowski, M.A. (1998). *The Power of Nice: How to Negotiate so Everyone Wins – Especially You!* New York, NY: John Wiley.

122 Drolet & Morris (2000); Thompson (2019).

123 Ebner (2007).

Unmask the other: Remember, there is a person behind the other screen, whether they have had the foresight unmask themselves or not. They are not computers or inboxes; they will respond to your messages on emotional, cognitive, and behavioral levels which you will then have to deal with.[124] Encourage them to engage in unmasking by normalizing such behavior, by asking questions, and by providing references or cues for them to latch on to.

3.6.4.2 Implications for Mediators

Jump-start your own rapport: Pre-process communication with parties is your opportunity to begin rapport-building. Your introductory remarks set the tone for the mediation, and should combine of rapport building and professionalism, promoting parties' confidence in you on multiple levels.

Keep working at it: Continue to seek rapport-forming opportunities as the process continues. Just as in in-person mediation, online caucuses offer an environment conducive to rapport as well as to other elements of trustbuilding.[125] However, rapport-building can be done in joint email messages and video sessions as well. Mention the weather in your area, or share local events. A party's reciprocation of these comments indicates their own desire to build rapport.[126]

Model unmasking: Some mediators share information and stories about themselves and their backgrounds as a means to connect with parties, whereas others consider this inappropriate. This human touch behavior might have particular value in online interactions, in countering the interpersonal masking effects of distance and technology. Sharing some personal information humanizes yourself and models open communication. Likely, at least one of the parties will respond to this, allowing you to continue a mutual unmasking dynamic.

3.6.5 Physical Distance and Interpersonal 'Otherness'

In the previous section we explained how online communication transforms online parties' distance into a sense of being faceless (via email) or fuzzy and disembodied (via video) with a dash of (oft-unsubstantiated) sense of anonymity. We now add to this a related yet distinct challenge: Distance, facelessness and anonymity causes a perception of *difference*, of '*otherness*' between the two parties, exacerbating the regular potential for 'otherness' effects to confound negotiation and conflict resolution. The structure of negotiation typically casts our counterpart in the role of the 'other' or 'opponent' – different from us and at odds with us. This poses significant challenges to identity-

---

124 *See* Mayer (2012).

125 Poitras, J. (2013). The strategic use of caucus to facilitate parties' trust in mediators. *International Journal of Conflict Management*, 24(1), 23-39.

126 Braeutigam, A.M. (2006). "What I Hear You Writing Is ... Issues in ODR: Building Trust and Rapport in the Text-Based Environment", *University of Toledo Law Review* 38, 101.

based trust, which relies on perceived *similarities*. Given our unfamiliarity with many of our online counterparts, this deficit in identification-based trust cannot be counterbalanced by knowledge-based trust. Indeed, the only thing we may know about them is that we need something from them, and/or that they need something from us. This can spiral parties into identification-based *dis*trust, as we subconsciously assume that our mutual demands are manifestations of more fundamental dissimilarities; our opposites are *nothing* like us, and their attitudes, personality, and interests *conflict* with ours.

3.6.5.1 Implications for Negotiators

Do not just unmask, team up! Through initiating an unmasking process, you can potentially begin to dispel the 'otherness' obstacle and close distances perceived between you and your counterpart by tapping a particularly powerful source of identification-based trust: shared group membership. When we perceive ourselves as belonging to the same group as another, our perceptions of the other become more positive and our level of trust in them increases. This counteracts the 'otherness' obstacle, which essentially boils down to you and your counterpart perceiving yourselves as belonging to different 'out-groups', whose members are prone to mutual distrust. Development of positive attitudes and identification-based trust toward in-group members plays out online much as it does offline,[127] resulting in a greater likelihood of agreement between in-group members.[128]

A new way of reading: Tune in closely to the other's messages, in order to discover things to connect to as members of a joint in-group. This involves a different type of message reading beyond the usual content-assimilation process. Glean any information you can from your counterpart's introduction and note personal information conveyed in later messages.

Link yourselves together: Use verbal mimicry of your counterpart's words to connect between you, particularly in the early stages of a negotiation.[129]

3.6.5.2 Implications for Mediators

Create a team: Create an *ad-hoc* mediation process in-group, by using joining terms such as 'we have all come here to work on this', 'we are not giving up on this'.

Careful with caucusing: One effect of caucusing is reinforcing mutual out-group thinking. At best, it reinforces a false in-group dynamic of one party (and, perhaps,

127 Wallace (1999).

128 Moore, D.A., Kurtzberg, T.R. & Thompson, L.L. (1999). Long & short routes to success in electronically mediated negotiations: group affiliations & good vibrations. *Organizational Behavior & Human Decision Processes*, 77, 1.

129 Swaab, R.I., Maddux, W.W. & Sinaceur, M. (2011). Early words that work: when and how virtual linguistic mimicry facilitates negotiation outcomes. *Journal of Experimental Social Psychology*, 47(3), 616-621.

their attorney) and the mediator, 'against' the other party. These effects may be exacerbated in online interactions.

Borrow from the future: By discussing parties' futures in terms of a successful relationship (when relevant), you are, in essence, discussing a future state of in-groupness. Try importing that sense into the current discussion. For example,

> Let's assume we've worked this out, and three years from now, working together on an important project, you encounter disagreement between you. How would you handle that, while protecting your project and your relationship?.

3.6.6 Increased Contentiousness: A Vicious Cycle

As media richness is diminished, social presence is reduced[130] and perceived social distance between parties increases.[131] Negotiators feel disinhibited, less bound by normatively appropriate behavior than face-to-face negotiators. They ignore adverse consequences of negative online interactions, owing to physical distance, reduced social presence, reduced accountability and a sense of anonymity.[132] Such disinhibition is expressed in varied ways: an increased tendency of negotiators to threaten or voice ultimata,[133] to adopt contentious, 'squeaky wheel' behavior, and to engage in flaming,[134] that particularly rapid conflict escalation phenomenon unique to online text-based communication. Email and other text-based interactions are particularly prone to disinhibition-based contentiousness. However, you might recall angry statements you've made over the phone that you would not have voiced to your counterpart's face; clearly, even richer media encourages some of these dynamics. Of course, medium notwithstanding, it is difficult to trust someone who has treated you in any of the contentious ways described above, or to gain back their trust after treating them poorly yourself.

In email negotiation, the path to contentiousness is further smoothed by the medium's low synchronicity, which encourages what Anne Marie Bülow has dubbed a 'double monologue' style of interaction: Cherry-picking elements of a message to respond

130 Short, J., Williams, E. & Christie, B. (1976). *The Social Psychology of Telecommunications*. New York, NY: John Wiley and Sons Ltd; Weisband, S.P. & Atwater, L. (1999). Evaluating self and others in electronic and face-to-face groups. *Journal of Applied Psychology*, 84, 4.

131 Jessup, L.M. & Tansik, D. (1991). Decision making in an automated environment: The effects of anonymity & proximity with a group decision support system. *Decision Science*, 22, 2; Siegel, J., Dubrovsky, V. & Kiesler, S. (1986). Group processes in computer-mediated communication. *Organization Behavior & Human Decision Processes*, 37, 2.

132 Griffith, T.L. & Northcraft, G.B. (1994). Distinguishing between the forest and the trees: media, features, and methodology in electronic communication research. *Organization Science*, 5, 2; Wallace (1999); Thompson (2019).

133 Morris *et al.* (2002).

134 Thompson & Nadler (2002).

to while ignoring others, and relating to them in long, argumentative statements. Parties work simultaneously to *persuade each other that they are right*, rather than jointly *exploring ways to work together*. This conversational pattern prefers declarations over questions, reducing information-sharing. It also diminishes information-intake: I'm too busy rejecting your stance to relate to the information you have provided. That information might go undiscussed and unclarified. Even those queries employed tend to be short and specific, extracting specific information yet not inviting elaboration. One might extract a factual detail from the other, but not the interest underlying it.[135]

In this state of affairs, parties have little incentive to work at trustbuilding. *Au contraire*, they are led down a path of competition if not downright aggression. Not only do parties to lean-media negotiation behave more competitively,[136] they feel *justified* for choosing this behavior.[137] Iterated rounds of contentious moves are likely to be mirrored in a cycle of trust-diminishment, and repeatedly justified by 'Well, they started it! I *knew* they couldn't be trusted.'

3.6.6.1 Implications for Negotiators

Use cooperative language intentionally: In both video and email, an intentional shift from contentious to cooperative language, such as by using the terms 'cooperation', 'agreement', or 'relationship' might ward off escalation. They remind parties (yourself included) what they are here to do, and steer them back toward trust-building, rather than trust-breaking, dynamics.

Step out, step in: Use your distance from the other to take time to 'step out' of the discussion in order to respond thoughtfully, rather than instantly reacting to the other party's moves. Encourage your counterpart to do the same (e.g., 'I realize my "No" wasn't what you had hoped for; why not take some time to think it over, and get back to me tomorrow?'). Email's asynchronicity accommodates this quite naturally. Video negotiations are more easily broken down into several sessions than co-located negotiations; there are no travel costs and scheduling is simpler. Consider asking to take a break and reconvene at your counterpart's convenience, if things seem to be spiraling in a negative direction.

3.6.6.2 Implications for Mediators

Check in often: Keep a close eye on your inbox. Conflict can escalate very quickly in text-based communication. A quick response or reassurance can be the difference between a

135 Bülow, A.M. (2011). The double monologue principle: argumentation in email negotiation. Working Paper, Copenhagen Business School Press. Available at http://papers.ssrn.com/sol3/papers.cfm?abstract_id=1899225.

136 Barsness & Bhappu (2004).

137 Naquin, C.E., Kurtzberg, T.R. & Belkin, L.Y. (2008). E-mail communication and group cooperation in mixed motive contexts. *Social Justice Research*, 21, 4.

routine discussion and extreme trust-breaking behavior from which there may be no recovery.

Initiate cool-off periods: Parties engaging in flaming can demolish months of painstaking trustbuilding efforts in a matter of minutes or hours. You might recommend parties refrain from writing each other for a day or two, to cool off and think about things. Keep your eye on your inbox, though; as they might not be able to withstand the urge to reach, or lash, out.[138]

Shuttle Diplomacy: If parties lack the requisite trust to engage in constructive conversation with each other, consider writing to each separately, rather than having them write each other. In videoconferences, you can create separate breakout rooms and caucus with each separately.

Grow thick skin: With online interactions so rife with contentiousness, it should come as no surprise that parties occasionally act contentiously in dealing with their mediator. Remember the nature of the process and the effects of the media: do not get insulted, and do not get sucked in.

3.6.7 Privacy

Maintaining a negotiation process' privacy is never an easy task. In face-to-face negotiation, absent a confidentiality agreement (and too often, in practice, even when one exists!) parties can and do share information about the negotiation with anyone they like. However, meetings can at least be held behind closed doors, and sensitive information can be related in a lowered voice. Anything shared with external parties will always be subjective, after-the-fact, secondhand (and in legal terms, hearsay). The same extends to mediation: Mediators are bound to maintain parties' privacy. In many locales, details of their conversations are precluded from being admissible in court. Outside of the mediation room and courthouse, however, parties generally can and do share their experiences as they choose.[139] This balance between in-the-room privacy, and out-of-the-room sharing, is a familiar structural aspect of these processes.

In online processes, however, parties never know who is 'in the room' with them. Will my counterpart forward my message to their boss or colleagues? It my counterpart alone in the room, or is someone listening in, off-camera? Beyond immediate privacy issues is that of privacy over time. Messages transmitted via email are recorded, forever archived on your counterpart's computer, beyond your control. Similarly, there is no way for one party to prevent another from recording a videoconference session without their

138 Summers Raines (2005).

139 A few jurisdictions have confidentiality laws prohibiting parties from sharing any information about mediation communications or agreements. For example, *see* Florida Statues (2020), Title V, Section 44.405 (1) stating "Except as provided in this section, all mediation communications shall be confidential. A mediation participant shall not disclose a mediation communication to a person other than another mediation participant or a participant's counsel."

knowledge or consent. Both records might even be tampered with, altering what you wrote or said. Private information might become public – due to the other's bad intentions, or just a technical mishap. Who amongst us has never clicked 'reply all' instead of 'reply', sending a personal message into a public domain? All this might easily lead to the reduced information-sharing and risk-taking associated with low trust.

3.6.7.1 Implications for Negotiators

Before sending emails: Consider each address field carefully. To whom should a message be sent? Should anyone appear in the 'cc' field? Do you want anyone invisibly lurking on the conversation, from the 'bcc' field?

When receiving mails: Use these information fields in reverse, alert for breaches of privacy. Review the address fields and tracking information visible in messages you receive, and read through previous messages recorded in the e-mail. Has your opposite included any internal correspondence you might want to see? CC'd someone on this latest message to you?

Consult: Unless you have agreed not to, share messages with anybody you feel can help you strategize and plan your responses.

Watch it: Increasingly, individuals' online activities are becoming public, widespread, sought out by future opponents and admissible in court. Be cautious of what you write in an e-mail, particularly before trust is established. A good rule of thumb might be: Do not write anything in an e-mail that you would not want shown on the news.

3.6.7.2 Implications for Mediators

Do not promise what you cannot keep: Be explicit about what you can promise, in terms of confidentiality, and what you cannot. Promise you will not divulge information, and describe any security measures your platform incorporates. However, refrain from promising 'We will all be keeping this secret'. Promise 'I am not recording this,' but not 'This is not being recorded.'

Ask parties: If parties raise privacy concerns, use this as an opportunity for trustbuilding. Discuss their concerns, explore their interests, ask for their recommendations, accommodate them as best as you can, and never coerce them into participating in a process they are uncomfortable with. Such transparent handling of the issue will have significant trustbuilding implications on both the mediator-party and on the party-party fronts.

3.6.8 Diminished Party Commitment, Investment, and Focus

Parties to online processes might be somewhat less motivated than those participating in face-to-face processes, given investment's role in human motivation. In-person meetings involve preliminary coordination, dressing, and travel time, cost, and effort. Videoconferencing requires only coordination and dressing (and reduces investment in these areas as well); email eliminates all these completely. With no sunk costs in the process, online communication provides an easy option for 'shot in the dark' approaches with little follow-through. This might provide partial explanation for reports of higher rates of impasse in e-mail negotiation[140] and for the phenomena of parties to text-based and email mediation and negotiation processes simply disappearing. From a trust perspective, one party's agreeing to participate may not induce a trust effect in the other, and a lack of constant, active participation might easily be interpreted by a counterpart opposite as untrustworthiness.

Even highly-committed parties are likely to suffer media-related effects including confusion, low cognitive retention of previous messages and diminished concentration.[141] In email interactions, this is due to several factors, including time passage between exchanges, the tendency to answer e-mails in spurts and sections rather blocking out time to write full messages, and the fact that we often read and write email in less-than-optimal surroundings and circumstances (e.g., on a train, in a meeting, or *while driving*). In addition, email is often not something we train our full attention on, but rather something we do as part of our media multitasking. Consider how often you've checked your email, as you've read this chapter! More generally, we read an email, check the news, read a different email, check on our stocks, click into Facebook to make sure everything is fine with the world, and return to respond to the first email. We might do all this while holding in-person or phone conversations at the same time. Videoconferencing would seem to be a medium that draws and hold our attention better. However, read the list of 'multi-tasking' activities (as these self-distracting activities are often called) above, and ask yourself: have you ever done any of these during a videoconference meeting? The draw to do so is similar: these other sources of gratification are literally at your fingertips, on the very same device you are using for videoconferencing. The tendency to engage in other activities (work and non-work related) during phone conferences[142] has clearly carried over to videoconferencing,[143] driving platforms and employers to seek technological means to

140 Croson, R. (1999). Look at me when you say that: an electronic negotiation simulation. *Simulation & Gaming*, 30(1), 23-27; Bülow, A.M. (2010). Argument, cognition and deadlock in email negotiation. Working Paper, CBS. Available at http://openarchive.cbs.dk/bitstream/handle/10398/8239/Email%20working%20paper.pdf?sequence=1.

141 *See* Ebner (2014).

142 Gavett, G. (2014). What people are really doing when they're on a conference call. *Harvard Business Review*. Available at https://hbr.org/2014/08/what-people-are-really-doing-when-theyre-on-a-conference-call.

143 *See, e.g.*, Li, S. (2020). Admit it, you do laundry during work video calls. *Wall Street Journal*. Available at www.wsj.com/articles/admit-it-you-do-laundry-during-work-video-calls-11597246242.

prevent such behaviors,[144] and multitasking participants to push back against this[145] as well as innovating to avoid detection of their lack of attention.[146] Multitasking during videoconferencing may be one of the causes contributing to Zoom fatigue,[147] the sense of depletion and physical and mental exhaustion one experiences after spending extended time in videoconference.[148] Moreover, it stands to reason that Zoom fatigued people might tend to *increase* their multitasking, hoping for a lift.

In general, research suggests that in the digital age, human attention span is decreasing.[149] Proud of our ability to multitask, we fail to realize that we are not as good at this as we like to think we are. Heavy multitaskers suffer a range of shortcomings as opposed to 'focusers', many of which are pertinent to negotiation and mediation. They tend not to filter out irrelevant information, and are easily distracted. They often have low detail-recall, and despite their ability to switch between tasks rapidly, their performance of each suffers as their brain is always somewhat focused on the task they are *not* doing.[150] Multitasking negotiators or mediators, or those working in crowded places or noisy work environments, might be cognitively overwhelmed, confused, or unfocused, without being aware. So too, might be parties participating via smartphone in noisy or crowded environments, without considering the effects their surroundings may have on their capacity to focus. In particular, the multi-screen environment presented by many home, work, and entertainment venues primes our brains to latch onto new stimuli.[151] While the impact of multitasking on online negotiation interactions has not been researched, it is hardly likely to be more positive than its impact on in-person negotiations: negotiators multitasking (in the form of

144 For example, WebEx can sense whether users have minimized the meeting window, or have opened messaging or browser windows on top of it. It provides that information to meeting hosts. *See* https://help.webex.com/en-us/st7tr1/Track-Participant-Attention-in-Cisco-Webex-Training#ID_2703_00001140.

145 For example, an outpouring of user pushback early in the Covid-19 era migration to remote work caused Zoom to eliminate its 'Attention Tracker' feature, which notified meeting conveners of multitasking participants. *See* Yuan, E. (2020). A message to our users. Available at https://blog.zoom.us/a-message-to-our-users/.

146 *See, e.g.*, Cole, S. (2020). Vice. People are looping videos to fake paying attention during video calls. Available at www.vice.com/en/article/7kzq5x/looping-videos-to-fake-paying-attention-in-zoom-meetings.

147 Lee, J. (2020). A neuropsychological exploration of Zoom fatigue. *Psychiatric Times*. Available at www.psychiatrictimes.com/view/psychological-exploration-zoom-fatigue.

148 On the phenomena of Zoom fatigue and other factors contributing to it, *see* Greenberg, E. & Ebner, N. (2020). Designing binge-worthy courses: Pandemic pleasures and COVID-19 consequences. *Negotiation Journal*, 36(4), 535-560; Bailenson, J. N. (2021). Nonverbal overload: A theoretical argument for the causes of Zoom fatigue. *Technology, Mind, and Behavior*, 2(1). https://doi.org/10.1037/tmb0000030.

149 Newell, L. (2017). Reclaiming attention in the digital generation negotiator. In C. Honeyman & A.K. Schneider (eds.), *The Negotiator's Desk Reference (Vol. 2I)*. St Paul, MN: DRI Press. Also *see* Ebner (2017 CHANGE).

150 Ofir, E., Nass, C. & Wagner, A.D. (2009). Cognitive control in media multitaskers. *Proceedings of the National Academy of Sciences* 106(37), 15583-15587. Also *see* Microsoft (2015). Attention Spans: Consumer Insights. Microsoft Canada, Winter 2015. Available at https://dl.motamem.org/microsoft-attention-spans-research-report.pdf.

151 Microsoft (2015), *Id.*

reading messages on a smartphone while negotiating face-to-face) have been found to achieve lower outcomes than those ignoring messages.[152]

3.6.8.1 *Implications for Negotiators*

Stay on top of things: To keep your counterpart engaged, maintain regular email contact, without being too pushy.[153] Offer breaks to replenish during videoconferencing, or ask for one yourself.

Bridge time gaps: In email communication, use literary style to create the sense of uninterrupted conversation. For example, write 'As I wrote you...', followed by a quote pasted from your previous email.

Stay focused: The greater the importance of the negotiation to you, the more it pays to concentrate on it. Read and write messages in an environment that allows you to concentrate. Close your browser, and leave other devices out of reach, while negotiating via videoconference.

3.6.8.2 *Implications for Mediators*

Adapt your style: Parties to online mediation will have lower commitment to the process than face-to-face parties. Learn to identify low-commitment parties, and adapt a style that engages them rather than providing them with reasons to walk.[154]

Responsibility for pace, momentum, and engagement: Offer parties breaks, and call one when you need one yourself. Shift between breaks, joint sessions, caucuses, and other activities more often that you might do in-person, to stimulate parties' cognitive engagement. Be mindful of one party's attention wandering while you engage the other in caucus. Consider setting separate appointments with parties, if you need to caucus, to have your conversation with each while they are relatively focused, and without needing to keep the other's time and attention span in mind.

3.7 *Trust in Online Negotiation and Mediation: Looking Ahead*

In writing this chapter, I enjoyed the moment I decided to leave out one issue that has challenged trust in online negotiation and mediation right from the start. This is, as Josh Boyd has put it, the medium's 'novelty, and its attendant mystery'.[155] He suggests that

152 Krishnan, A., Kurtzberg, T.R. & Naquin, C.E. (2014). The curse of the smartphone: electronic multitasking in negotiations. *Negotiation Journal,* 30(2), 191-208.

153 *See* Shipley, D. & Schwalbe, W. (2007). *Send: The Essential Guide to E-Mail for Office and Home*". New York, NY: Alfred A. Knopf.

154 Summers Raines, S. (2004). The practice of mediation online: techniques to use or avoid when mediating in cyberspace. Paper delivered at *The Third Annual Forum on Online Dispute Resolution*, Melbourne, Australia 2004.

155 Boyd (2003), at 394.

this is a particularly powerful challenge, due to its spillover effects: a user's distrust of the medium, due to inexperience, can lead to that user harboring suspicions toward a website's credibility or a human counterpart's trustworthiness. The flip side of this suggestion is that each successful online experience will result in progressively *lower* trust thresholds in assessing online actors and technology, causing positive spillover between trust in technology and trust in humans. In addition, *optimism* resulting from past experiences will facilitate the forming of trust during subsequent interactions. This is where the seven types of trust listed at the beginning of this section come together, and affect one another, for better or for worse.[156]

While the novelty of the internet has worn off over the years, the novelty of its use for negotiation and dispute resolution has been slow to fade. It is only in the Covid-19 period that one can identify fieldwide educational coverage on conducting online processes, and broad acceptance of online process conduct in practice. While I doubt that the next medium to come along will be met with fully open arms by negotiators and mediators, I believe that the deep inherent distrust of technology for mediation and negotiation has subsided, and that knee-jerk novelty-based distrust will not be as much of an issue in the past as it has been in the future. It is good to be able to cross one trust challenge off the list.

Trust, so valuable in negotiation and dispute resolution, is hard enough to come by under the best of circumstances. Online, for reasons ranging from technological to psychological, trust is extremely challenging to develop and to maintain. However, intentional, skilled use of online communication media by negotiators and mediators can overcome many of these challenges, and even provide new methods for trustbuilding. The human touch, at the core of this new capacity, also paves the way for development of other areas such as empathy and social intuition.

4 Empathy, Online?

Empathy is similar to trust, in that it is hard to pin down and define. This, not only due to any such effort being preceded (or supplanted) by lengthy distinctions between empathy and sympathy, but because the very notion of empathy is amorphous. To start off with, it

156 Consider how structural solutions have connected these in a positive way. For example, eBay's rating system provides potential buyers the opportunity to view the degree to which previous clients were satisfied with a vendor. The buyer's interpersonal trust in specific users, combined with their peer trust in the broad assessment of the crowd, generates interpersonal trust in a seller. The knowledge that sellers are held accountable by reviews increases user's trust in the system's overall operators, eBay Inc., which, in turn, increases their trust in the technological platform eBay Inc. has deployed (*e.g.*, that it records things properly, payment is secure, and ratings are not manipulated). While this has been successful in creating the environment of trust required to hold the eBay marketplace together, no web-wide rating system is so widely accepted as to constitute an integral part of the internet's commercial infrastructure, to say nothing of the social media environment. *See* Rule & Friedberg (2005).

is unclear whether empathy is a cognitive mechanism or an emotional response. Additionally, it is discussed in different terms in different contexts. For example, *dispositional empathy* relates to the degree to which a person is 'chronically' empathic, whereas the notion of *situational empathy* focuses on whether a particular set of circumstances elicits an empathic response from someone (their empathic 'set point' notwithstanding).[157] In other words, empathy can be discussed as a tendency, a capacity, a reaction, a mode of thinking, or a mode of interaction.

4.1 Walking the Empathy Tightrope in Negotiation and Mediation

Negotiators often walk an empathy tightrope. A basic directive in any book or course on negotiation is that a negotiator should show empathy for their counterpart.[158] And yet, doing so is counterintuitive, in practice. It may be that breaking empathy down into discrete components might be helpful for understanding negotiators' employ and avoidance of empathy. For example, one helpful distinction might be between these two elements of empathy:[159]

Perspective taking: Seeing things from your counterpoint's point of view, often described as walking in their shoes, seeing the world as they do, or seeing the situation from their perspective.

Empathic concern: Accurately identifying what your counterpoint is feeling, while separating this from your own emptions.

The former tends toward the cognitive side of empathy, and the latter toward its affective elements. Both are tricky to navigate. While perspective-taking can contribute to a negotiator's gains through enabling them to identify their counterpart's interests, it can threaten their sense of certainty in the absolute Rightness of their own demands and goals. Similarly, while empathic concern is often key for understanding your counterpart's nonverbal cues or emotional priorities, it causes you to recognize the emotional costs the other will bear if they do not achieve their own goals. This might soften your resolve to achieve your own goals. Walking the empathy tightrope is challenging. Parties attaining the right balance of empathy can make an end-run around their own absolutes of positions and truth to reach differentiated and thoughtful solutions that are responsive to the complexities of each situation.[160]

---

157 Newell, L.A. (2019). Rebooting empathy for the digital generation lawyer. *Ohio State Journal on Dispute Resolution*, 34(1), 1-96.

158 Ury, W. (1991). *Getting Past No*. New York, NY: Bantam Books; Mnookin, R.H., Peppet, S.R. & Tulumello, A.S. (2004). *Beyond Winning: Negotiating to Create Value in Deals and Disputes*, Cambridge: Harvard University Press; Schneider (2002).

159 *See* Newell (2019).

160 Reynolds, J. (2017). Truth and the trial lawyer. *Trial Lawyer Magazine* (Summer), 13-17.

Finding this balance will enhance negotiators' joint gains,[161] improve communication and information flow,[162] and enhance interparty trust.[163] Individual negotiators missing that balance can wind up hobbling themselves.[164]

A second important distinction is between *empathic tendency* or *skill*, and *empathic expression*. The former might involve a general tendency to see things from another's perspective or the skill to do so, on-demand, in a given situation. It might involve the tendency to recognize other's emotions or the skill to accurately interpret and name them to one's self. However, what should a negotiator do with this information, once gained? That is where the latter comes in. Should negotiators express what they've learned through empathic channels to their counterpart? Should they demonstrate their ability to see the world from their point of view? Should they express understanding or concern for their counterpart in response to their emotional reading of them? While negotiators might find perspective-taking expression to a counterpart to be somewhat intuitive, easily anchored in joint pragmatic thinking, many find expression of empathic concern counterintuitive, and worry that showing empathy might be perceived as a display of weakness.

Mediators walk a different, yet equally challenging, empathy tightrope. They are taught to demonstrate empathy toward parties for multiple purposes: providing what they are not receiving from the other party, giving parties the support necessary to engage in a difficult process, and modeling constructive communication patterns. Besides its other beneficial effects in mediation, there is no doubt as to its effect on trust: both mediators and parties to mediation name empathy as a core element in building party-mediator trust.[165] That is not to say, that mediators always tend (or, always feel free) to lavish empathy on parties, or that this would always have a positive effect on the mediation. Walking the empathy tightrope mediators balance benefits of empathy with other issues. For example, they might be concerned that displays of personality and emotion undermine their professionalism. More generally, they may restrain empathic expression in an attempt to walk the fine line between empathy and impartiality, two elements that feed into trust only if the right balance between them is struck.[166] Here, too, we might consider distinctions between perspective-taking and empathic concern, and considerations of mediators' degree and style of empathic expression.

---

161 Galinsky A.D. *et al.*, (2008). Why it pays to get inside the head of your opponent: the differential effects of perspective taking and empathy in negotiations. *Psychological Science*, 19, 378, 383.

162 Lax, D.A. & Sebenius, J.K. (2006). *3-D Negotiation: Powerful Tools to Change the Game in Your Most Important Deals.*Boston: Harvard Business Press.

163 Mnookin, Peppet & Tulumello (2004).

164 Newell (2019).

165 Goldberg (2005).

166 Poitras (2013)

4.2 Challenges to Online Empathy

Navigating and employing empathy is therefore challenging in any negotiation or mediation encounter. Constraints imposed by online channels pose new challenges to empathy's forming, interpretational accuracy, expression, and reception by (or impact on) a counterpart.[167]

4.2.1 Challenges to Empathy Formation

As noted previously regarding trust, online communication involves real or perceived distance, anonymity, and 'otherness'. People tend to be less empathic toward strangers.[168] Additionally, their tendency to be less empathic toward people they consider as 'outgroup' members;[169] is exacerbated by anxiety,[170] an emotional state commonly experienced by parties to negotiation[171] and conflict.[172] To continue this spiral, many people experience heightened anxiety related to communication via

167 In this discussion, we focus on how online channels affects empathy in the here and now. A separate, important, issue is the longitudinal effects of increased online (and decreased in-person) interactions on empathic capacity. Newell (2019) explains that digital natives are showing a decline in dispositional empathy, and suggests that we probably all are, to some extent. I've suggested this to be one the most plainly evident areas in which negotiators are changing in response to our new, technologically-immersed environment. *See* Ebner (2017 CHANGE).

168 Tesser, A., Pilkington, C.J. & McIntosh, W.D. (1989). Self-evaluation maintenance and the mediational role of emotion: the perception of friends and strangers. *Journal of Personality and Social Psychology*, 57, 442-456.

169 Fourie, M.M., Subramoney, S. & Gobodo-Madikizela, P. (2017). A less attractive feature of empathy: intergroup empathy bias. In M. Kondo (ed.), *Empathy: An evidence-based interdisciplinary perspective*. London: IntechOpen

170 Todd, A.R., Forstmann, M., Burgmer, P., Brooks, A.W. & Galinsky, A.D. (2015). Anxious and egocentric: how specific emotions influence perspective taking. *Journal of Experimental Psychology*, 144(2), 374-391. Also *see* Arceneaux, K. (2017). Anxiety reduces empathy toward outgroup members but not ingroup members. *Journal of Experimental Political Science*, *4*(1), 68-80.

171 *See, e.g.*, Wheeler, M. (2004). Anxious moments: openings in negotiation. *Negotiation Journal*, 20(2), 153-169.

172 de Dreu, C.K.W. (1997). Productive conflict: the importance of conflict management and the conflict issue. In C.K.W. de Dreu & E.V. de Vliert (eds.), *Using Conflict in Organizations*. London: SAGE.

email[173] and videoconferencing.[174] Finally, certain aspects of empathy development are dependent on seeing the other; email cannot provide the necessary cues and videoconferencing provides only a limited portion of them.

4.2.2 Challenges to Empathetic Accuracy

Empathy is not a blunt tool. To utilize it for effect, it needs to be accurate. This entails, in terms of empathic concern, not only recognizing that our counterpart has an emotional response to an issue on the table, but understanding just what that emotion is. We might recognize it as a positive or a negative emotion; however, in order to reap the benefits of empathy, we must discern it is happiness, acceptance, elation, or satisfaction; or, whether it is frustration, anxiety, fear, or anger. Similarly, in the realm of perspective taking, we must be able to truly see things as our counterpart does, not merely recognize that they have a different opinion or other priorities. Denied some or many of the cues providing information via videoconferencing or email, how can we possibly attain this level of accuracy?

Regarding empathic concern, research has found verbal input to be more important than visual input for attaining empathic accuracy.[175] Indeed, psychotherapists conducting therapy via phone, videoconferencing, and in-person meetings all attained

173 For discussion of the general sense of anxiety permeating use of email, as well as specific communicational anxiety triggers, *see* Glei, J.K. (2016). *Unsubscribe.* Public Affairs. Additionally, the 'always on' nature of email means that email negotiators, parties, and neutrals are never fully out of each others' reach or free of their expectations of response. On this source of anxiety (in the wider context of work's encroachment into the home and private lives of professionals), *see* Becker, W.J., Belkin, L.Y., Conroy, S.A. & Tuskey, S. (2019). Killing me softly: organizational e-mail monitoring expectations' impact on employee and significant other well-being. *Journal of Management.* https://doi.org/10.1177/0149206319890655.

174 'Videoconference anxiety' or 'Zoom anxiety' is sometimes noted as an aspect of Zoom fatigue and other times as a standalone phenomenon. Like Zoom fatigue, it surfaced only during the Covid-19 era surge in videoconferencing and has yet to be studied. Workplace psychologists note that it seems to develop along two pathways. The first, is heightening social anxiety in individuals with social anxiety disorder. *See* Schmidit, M. (2020). A psychologist explains how to cope with video chat when you're socially anxious. *Discover.* Available at www.discovermagazine.com/technology/a-psychologist-explains-how-to-cope-with-video-chat-when-youre-socially. The second, is affecting people who are not ordinarily susceptible to social anxiety. In one U.K. survey, 73% of people working from home reported experiencing Zoom anxiety. *See* Buffalo7, Triggered: What is Zoom Anxiety, and what can we do about it? Available at https://buffalo7.co.uk/zoom-anxiety/. It may be that, amongst the general population ordinarily not coping with social anxiety disorder, certain subgroups are more prone to experience Zoom anxiety than others: introverts (*see* Degges-White, S. (2020). Dealing with Zoom anxiety. *Psychology Today.* Available at www.psychologytoday.com/us/blog/lifetime-connections/202004/dealing-zoom-anxiety) and people who struggle with technology (*see* Anderson, K. (2020). Have you experienced video conference anxiety? Here are 4 ways to cope. Available at www.singlecare.com/blog/zoom-anxiety/).

175 Gesn, P.R. & Ickes, W. (1999). The development of meaning contexts for empathic accuracy: channel and sequence effects. *Journal of Personality and Social Psychology*, 77, 746-761; Zaki, J., Bolger, N. & Ochsner, K. (2009). Unpacking the informational bases of empathic accuracy. *Emotion*, 9, 478-487.

similar levels of empathetic accuracy.[176] This suggests that empathetic accuracy is less dependent on a full array of communicative cues as one might suppose. Note, though, that this only relates to empathetic concern (and not perspective taking). Moreover, experiment participants were all professional psychotherapists. While most negotiators and mediators often work with empathy and emotions, few are rigorously trained for this. The experiment included telephone and video, but not email; other research on emotion detection in email negotiation has shown that even trained coders focused solely on emotion reach very different conclusions in identifying emotional expression.[177] Empathetic accuracy, therefore, might remain an issue for them to be concerned in online processes.

4.2.3 Challenges to Empathy Expression

We've previously discussed the ways that communication channels affect the content we decide to communicate. The medium does not only constrain *what* we choose to say, but *how* we say it. How do we show empathy for another person via a communication channel with limited contextual cues? We cannot nod understandingly via email, or use our signature empathic tone. While videoconferencing is more conducive to some expressions of empathy, it is still a limited channel, with unintended effects, confounding of precise nuance. Time-lag can make gestures appear clumsy or out-of-place, and – with most web cameras currently in use – there is little sensation of eye-contact. We cannot seize an opportune moment in which, certain the other is seeing us, we give them an empathic smile or encouraging nod, as we never know what our counterpart is actually looking at. We certainly cannot lay a supportive hand on our counterpart's own. On an unconscious level, lag and video quality diminish our precise view of our counterpart's subtle facial expressions of emotion. As a result, we do not mirror these expressions in movements of our own facial muscles. This diminishes our empathic formation and accuracy, as this mirroring is a mechanism for emotional intake; we recognize emotions by embodying them.[178] This also diminishes our empathic expression, given that the other is just as likely to miss our own reflexive or carefully chosen facial expressions. The same goes for other body language expressed outside of the video box on either end: we do not see our counterpart move or position most of their body, our body does not mirror them, and they do not see or mirror us.[179] Clearly,

176 Reese, R.J., Mecham, M.R., Vasilj, I., Lengerich, A.J., Brown, H.M., Simpson, N.B. & Newsome, B.D. (2016). The effects of telepsychology format on empathic accuracy and the therapeutic alliance: An analogue counselling session. *Counselling and Psychotherapy Research,* 16(4), 256-265.

177 Laubert, C. & Parlamis, J. (2019). Are you angry (happy, sad) or aren't you? Emotion detection difficulty in email negotiation. *Group Decision and Negotiation*, *28*(2), 377-413.

178 Dimberg, U., Thunberg, M. & Elmehed, K. (2000). Unconscious facial reactions to emotional facial expressions. *Psychological Science*, 11(1), 86-89.

179 For more on the role of nonverbal mirroring and mimicry, *see* Thompson, Ebner & Giddings (2017).

expressing empathy over online communication media is challenge; just as clearly, we must develop special methods for showing e-empathy.

4.2.4 Challenges to Empathy Reception by (Or Impact on) the Other Party

Empathy reception by our counterparts has two components: perception, and response.

First, our counterparts need to perceive the empathic signals we send them, and *identify* them for what they are. This is challenged by the negativity bias surrounding all conveyance of tone and emotion via online media.[180] If you think you've sent a positive message; the other will think it is neutral. If you've composed a neutral message, the other will perceive it as negative. Applying this to empathy, we must to convey enough empathic 'stuff' through the channel we are using for it to resonate as empathically as we intended on the other end. The 'empathy premium' we must add does not come naturally; this significantly alters the empathy tightrope we walk.

Second, in order for an empathic cycle to have any of its intended effect, our counterparts need to be able to *respond* to our empathic signals somehow. Your counterpart's positive affirmation of your empathic expression might be as minor as a glance, a nod, or a 'yeah, that's it.' It serves both to affirm to themselves that they have been empathized with, and to transmit to us that our empathic expression has hit its mark. If they do not send such a signal, or if we are in doubt as to whether it has hit its mark, the conversation can fizzle, or the topic might be changed, rather than follow the constructive path your empathy might have intended to blaze. In other words, the process goals of empathy expression, cannot be achieved through empathy formation and expression, due to empathy's *interactional* quality.[181]

Not only do all of the media effects challenging your accurate transmission, and your counterpart's accurate reception, of messages challenge their understanding of your empathic message, the same challenge applies to the affirmation or rejection message they return to you via the affirmation feedback loop. As discussed above, media effects of online communication can challenge this loop from forming. In email communication, the transmitter does not receive any immediate micro-feedback as they speak, as they are provided in face-to-face communication. And, your counterpart may never relate to your empathic expression in their response email to you, so you may not know if it struck the chord you intended. In video communication, lags and delays undermine the impact of

180 This has been specifically discussed in the context of email. *See* Glei (2016). The discussion of media effects in this chapter should enable readers to recognize the more muted effects of this bias in videoconferencing.

181 This aspect of empathy, developed in the realm of psychotherapy, applies handily to empathy's use in negotiation and conflict settings. In the psychotherapeutic relationship, the positive effects of empathy will fully manifest only if t therapist's accurate expression of empathy has been received and perceived as such by the patient, and responded to by the patient in some way that the therapist can recognize as an affirmation, recognition, or acceptance of the empathetic expression. Wynn, R. & Wynn, M. (2006). Empathy as an interactionally achieved phenomenon in psychotherapy: characteristics of some conversational resources. *Journal of Pragmatics*, 38(9), 1385-1397.

your best empathic intentions. In experiments conducted on phone conferences, brief transmission lag caused communicators to misattribute the technical degradation to their interlocutor's engagement and personality, considering them to be less attentive, friendly, or active.[182] All of these feed into your counterpart's perception of your degree of empathy, care, and rapport. On the feedback side of empathy reception, many of the challenges noted in the previous section regarding empathy expression pertain to the response messaging your counterpart transmits to you as feedback.

4.3 *Implications and Recommendations for Practitioners*

My observation, contrasting practice with the literature surveyed above and the broader literature on negotiation and mediation, is that online practitioners of negotiation and mediation underinvest in empathizing. This had not been particularly surprising, in processes conducted via email, despite empathy playing the same roles of enhancing relationship and communication in text-based interactions as it does in face-to-face encounters.[183] Aside from its potential for sharp conflict escalation, email communication tends to be constrained and veers away from emotional expression. However, I've been surprised to observe, particularly in the surge of online mediation in the Covid-19 era, that mediators tend to underinvest in empathy when mediating over video as well. With some empathy-building behaviors and channels inherently out of their reach, such as touch, one might expect them to intuitively harness features of videoconferencing supporting empathic expression to compensate. And yet (again, based only on my observations and conversations with mediators and trainers), like any other media, videoconferencing covertly impacts mediator behavior, including diminishing empathy-conveying activities.

My first overall recommendation is to do more, rather than less, to express empathy toward parties and counterparts. My second is to remember that the 'regular' empathy toolbox remains available, even online, just waiting to be employed. While displaying empathy via body language might be constrained by the medium, we can adapt most of our tools for use online. These include online versions of those basic communication tools negotiators and mediators employ with empathy-showing in mind: Active listening, reflecting, and asking relevant, productive, and to-the-point questions showing interest in your counterpart and their needs and concerns.[184]

---

182 Schoenenberg, K., Raake, A. & Koeppe, J. (2014). Why are you so slow? Misattribution of transmission delay to attributes of the conversation partner at the far-end. *International Journal of Human-Computer Studies*, 72(5), 477-487.

183 Specifically, in text-based exchanges, negotiators conveying accurate empathy were found to be trusted by their negotiation counterparts more than those who do not. *See* Feng, J., Lazar, J. & Preece, J. (2004). Empathy and online interpersonal trust: a fragile relationship. *Behavior and Information Technology*, 23, 2.

184 Ury (1991).

Below, I'll make some more specific recommendations for online adaptations of these and other suggestions for conveying e-empathy across email and videoconference communication. These apply both to negotiators and mediators seeking to show empathy for their counterparts and to increase the mutually empathic levels of the interaction.

4.3.1 e-Empathy in Practice: Videoconferencing

It's not about you: One of the most unnatural things about videoconferencing is that we see ourselves. This causes self-absorption; naturally drawn to our own image, we view our self at the price of focusing on others. Self-focused attention maintains or heightens social anxiety, whereas diminishing self-focused attention can prevent it.[185] Eliminate or diminish self-view as best you can, using your videoconference platform's settings. Mediators might recommend this to parties.

Focus on gaze: Our instinctive and trained tendency to transmit interest and empathy to a counterpart via eye contact falls flat in videoconferencing. Directing our eyes toward theirs on screen, in fact, backfires; we appear to them as if we are looking down, *away* from their eyes. There is no real solution to the lack of eye contact in videoconferencing. The best you can do is for the purposes of conveying empathy, it to artificially give counterparts or parties the *sense* you are looking in their eyes even though you are not. To do so, choose a view setting placing your interlocutor's face adjacent to your camera. If your platform allows you to arrange the video boxes on your screen, drag your interlocutor toward your camera. Looking at your counterpart, you are now looking nearly directly into the camera. To your counterpart's brain, this will give the sensation of looking in their direction, and occasionally, if somewhat randomly, the full sense of eye contact. Research conducted in the context of psychotherapists working with patients (professionals whose need to convey empathy to clients matches that negotiators' and mediators') via such simulated eye contact has reinforced the notion that eye-contact – conveyed empathy results from one person's brain recognizing that the other's eyes have made contact with their own. Perceived eye contact causes your interlocutor's brain to feel you have conveyed empathy even if no actual eye contact took place.[186] To trigger a full eye-contact reaction in a counterpart's brain, tear your eyes away from the faces on the screen, and look directly into the camera, despite the extreme artificiality of doing so.[187]

---

185 Vriends, N., Meral, Y., Bargas-Avila, J.A., Stadler, C. & Bögels, S.M. (2017). How do I look? Self-focused attention during a video chat of women with social anxiety (disorder). *Behaviour Research and Therapy*, 92, 77-86.

186 Dowell, N.M. & Berman, J.S. (2013). Therapist nonverbal behavior and perceptions of empathy, alliance, and treatment credibility. *Journal of Psychotherapy Integration*, 23(2), 158.

187 For more on eye contact and camera positioning in online mediation, *see* Ebner & Thompson (2014).

Show thyself: Including the upper body in the video frame (head, torso, and hands), as opposed to the face only or primarily, increases empathy development. In fact, videoconferences using upper-body views have been found to be equivalent to face-to-face interactions, from the perspective of empathic development.[188] Negotiators and mediators might model this behavior hoping that other participants will follow along; mediators can also suggest this outright.

Lean in: Therapists forward body-trunk lean was found to enhance their patients' perception of the therapists' empathy toward them.[189] Changing bodily direction and proximity seem to be less intuitive when communicating over videoconferencing, but their effects are still potent.

4.3.2 E-Empathy in Practice: Email

Paint them a picture: In your writing, be more descriptive of your actions and thoughts than you would ordinarily be. This demonstrates listening, and puts the 'active' back in active listening. For example, to demonstrate online listening you might stress the (seemingly trivial) fact that you have read what your counterpart wrote, Writing 'I read your message carefully' or 'Reading your email last night, I realized…' might seem like casual opening lines, but they convey a powerful covert message to your interlocutor: 'I read your message, you have been heard'.[190]

Accurate and specific clarifying questions demonstrate listening: Copy and paste an ambiguous message right back to your interlocutor, highlight an unclear element, and ask for clarifications. 'When you wrote "XYZ" I wasn't clear if you meant… or… Could you please clarify?' This will not only help you avoid mistakes; it continues to convey active listening through its subtext of 'I am listening to you, and it is *very* important for me to make sure I understand you'.

See, feel, write: Make sure to express elements of both perspective taking and empathic concern in your writing. This may cause you to explicitly write things that you would have expressed in a facial expression in a face-to-face conversation, so do not be surprised if your 'voice' sounds a little different to you when you read your own messages.

Do I dare ask? Ask questions. Take advantage email's low interactivity, which allows you to ask multiple questions in a single e-mail without the other breaking in to respond or stopping the flow. This facilitates a show of interest and engagement and can be worded to show empathy. For example:

---

188 Nguyen, D. & Canny, J. (2009). More than face-to-face: empathy effects of video framing. *Proceedings of the SIGCHI Conference on Human Factors in Computing Systems,* 423-432. It is unclear, from this experiment, whether it is being seeing by, or seeing, the other more fully that develops one's sense of empathy for the other.

189 Dowell & Berman (2013).

190 *See* Ebner (2007).

> Before we delve into the issues you've raised, I'd like to ask you to respond to three questions, to make sure I've understood how you feel about the events you've described and how you see the issue resolving from your point of view.

Model empathic communication: In communicating empathically, you are modeling empathic communication to your interlocutors, nudging them to follow suit. Promote this further, by calling attention to what you are doing. For example, write 'I'll summarize what I heard you say, just to make sure I'm clear on your intent', instead of jumping straight to the summary itself.

4.4 *Empathy's Wider Role*

Understanding empathy and the dynamics of its generation and exchange online is important to negotiators and mediators in its own self. It is trebly important, given empathy's contribution to trustbuilding, and role in social intuition. We now turn to explore this last human touch area.

5 SOCIAL INTUITION

Much of the negotiation and conflict resolution literature focuses on the cognitive realm of interaction. This realm is concerned with identifying interests, communicating positions, seeking new information, considering alternatives, assessing offers and crafting counteroffers, generating options for agreement or resolution and evaluating the benefits.[191]

Certainly, all these elements are important factors in our overall ability to influence and affect others. However, in navigating the process or determining the outcome, negotiators and mediators draw upon a broader, and more covert, array of interactional elements.

While questions such as 'Does my counterpart trust or suspect me?' receive attention in the literature, others, such as 'Does my counterpart like me? Does she enjoy our time together?' do not – and yet, they are key negotiation process issues. The same goes for 'Do parties feel comfortable in the office with me, or not?' or 'Are parties intimidated by my questions, or appreciative of them?' in mediation. All these questions reflect the impact of 'flow' in interpersonal channels that are as intangible as they are crucial.

---

191 The emotional realm is also often addressed via cognitive frames, as demonstrated in the discussion above. The literature dedicates far more pages to 'identifying,' and 'dealing with' emotions than it does to 'feeling' them.

As Andrea Schneider and I have described this issue:[192]

> These channels provide the building blocks for many of the intangible, yet solidly important, elements that affect and control interactional patterns, overall strategic approach, and actual decision making. Core negotiation issues ... are all conveyed through intuitive communication. Other issues that pertain to people's ability and desire to work with one another, such as their perceived warmth, likability, and competency, are also affected by these elements. The degree to which one is adept at navigating this little-charted terrain is captured by the term social intuition.

What are these intangible channels? Some have been discussed in the negotiation literature directly, such as those channels provided by trust and empathy as well as others offered by rapport,[193] liking,[194] power,[195] relationship,[196] emotional intelligence, social intelligence, and more. When these channels flow well, we can affect the other regarding issues of process and substance; when they are blocked, or flow the wrong way, we find ourselves challenged.

Social intuition is a more comprehensive notion than any of these individual channels. Indeed, each channel provides building blocks for social intuition. In applying our social intuition, we aim not to *change the other's thinking* but to *engage their thinking patterns.* We are not intent on *precise* communication, but rather on communicating in a way *that speaks to our counterpart.* The focus is less on affecting our counterpart's *opinion* and more on affecting their *attitude.* It encompasses our ability to grasp an interactional situation and to affect it.

5.1 Three Elements of Social Intuition

To fully understand the nature of social intuition, it is helpful to relate to its discrete elements, and then consider the impact of applying them all together. Social intuition is the convergence of the following three elements of capacity:[197]

Self: Our general self-awareness to our own cognitive patterns, biases, and typical responses and reactions, as well as to our present emotional status and what we are

192 Schneider, A.K. & Ebner, N. (2017). Social intuition. In C. Honeyman & A.K. Schneider (eds.), *The Negotiator's Desk Reference (Vol.1).* St Paul, MN: DRI Press, at 128.

193 Thompson, Ebner & Giddings (2017).

194 Guthrie, C. (2017). Getting your way. In C. Honeyman & A.K. Schneider (eds.), *The Negotiator's Desk Reference (Vol.1).* St Paul, MN: DRI Press.

195 *See* Mayer (2012); Ury (1991).

196 Hollander-Blumoff, R. (2010). Building relationships as negotiation strategy. In C. Honeyman & A.K. Schneider (eds.), *The Negotiator's Desk Reference (Vol. 1).* St Paul, MN: DRI Press. Ebner & Kamp.

197 Schneider & Ebner (2017).

transmitting in the moment. What emotions am I feeling right now? Am I transmitting them to my counterpart? Are the words I'm speaking, or my nonverbal cues, congruent with my internal emotional map, or with the external façade I had planned to project?

Other: Our ability to read our counterpart via awareness to their signals, verbal and nonverbal, intentional or not. Do I sense for their attention span, when I speak? Can I distinguish between their laughs, volume levels, paces of speech? Do their signals match the words they speak?

Bridging: Actions we take via these intuitive channels to form connections with the other. Each connection offers a window into affecting them. While these windows do not often overlook our counterpart's opinion or stated position, they do allow us to access and engage with their underlying mechanisms, all of which combine to form process and outcome determinations: their mood, engagement with us, receptivity, curiosity, comfort, openness, suspicion, and more.

5.2 *Interactional Realms of Social Intuition*

In our first treatment on this topic, Prof. Schneider and I outlined eight interactional realms of social intuition (Table 4.6), noting these to be exemplary rather than a full list.

Table 4.6 Elements of Social Intuition

Elements of Social Intuition	
Physical proximity	Vocal tone
Body language and mirroring	Vocal and conversational pace
Eye contact	Humor
Physical contact	Metaphor and analogies

In the context of this chapter, each realm is recognizable as a way for people reach out and touch each other, with or without lifting a finger. Combined, the realms of social intuition are essentially a human-touch *smorgasbord.*

5.3 *Social Intuition, Online*

How is our capacity for social intuition be impacted online? And, how can we adapt to these changes? In our first effort at conceptualizing the nature and impact of social intuition, we largely kicked this can down the road:

> Social intuition also helps us figure out the most effective way to communicate. Given the multiple modes of communication available, it is social intuition about our counterpart, the context, and ourselves that helps guide us to get up and walk down the hall rather than email – or to text a quick note rather than leave a phone message. While this chapter has discussed social intuition in face-to-face encounters, our social intuition now needs to be developed for, and employed over, any medium we are using for negotiation.[198]

This section provides initial responses to these questions. In fact, we've already discussed some of social intuition's component realms, their online manifestations, and their impact on the intuitive channels of trust and empathy. Here, we map social intuition out as a human touch area and consider how our capacity to wield it is impacted online.

5.3.1 Social Intuition and Channel Constraints: Videoconferencing

Of the realms listed above, we are denied only physical in videoconferencing-based processes. While we can avail ourselves of all the other elements, most are impacted and constrained.

Most constrained is the element of eye-contact. As discussed above, true eye-contact is not possible via videoconference; we can only generate the perception of eye-contact in our counterpart's brain, and sense it in our own. Considering such artificial interaction through frames of self, other, and bridging reinforces the advice given above to intentionally enact such perceived eye-contact. This serves to exemplify mindful application of the three elements of social intuition. Aware of our own unquenched thirst for eye-contact, we can remind ourselves not to judge the other's degree of connection, engagement. or empathy based on this as we naturally tend to do. Aware of our own in-person techniques for providing our counterparts with eye-contact, and recognizing the other's need for our eye-contact, we can recognize that these will not fill their need. This awareness to self and other enables us to design the new bridging mechanism of artificially gazing into the camera to give our counterpart the sense of eye contact.

Videoconferencing impacts other elements in subtler ways. For example, we've noted how video/audio lag affects vocal and conversational pace. Other impacts, yet to be studied, may resonate with experienced videoconferencers. For example, issues of motion and proximity.

Many people remain fairly static while videoconferencing, though they might demonstrate far more motion in an in-person setting. This might be unconscious conforming to the limited video square. It may stem from awareness of being on camera, or from the lack of another's presence to trigger mirroring responses.

198 *Id.*, at 140-141.

Whatever the cause, these changes to individuals' motion patterns warrant awareness in terms of self, and may change the effects of our communication on the other. If your ordinarily animated communicative style is constrained online, you must intentionally develop new bridging mechanisms.

Similarly, videoconferencers largely seem to maintain a constant distance from their camera. Perhaps we unconsciously assume that, three thousand miles away from our counterpart, our leaning forward six inches will not make much of a difference. Remember, though, that physical proximity's effects as a communicative tool rely, at least in part, on *perceived* rather than actual proximity. For this reason, leaning in or back can have largely the same impact on your counterpart via video as it does in person.[199] Awareness of our own new habits, and of our counterpart's likely responses to proximity changes, will cause us to counterintuitively maintain bridging mechanisms of leaning in or back just as we would do in a room.

Social intuition offers another perspective on why mindful camera placement is so important. Beyond preparing your camera to capture body language and changes of proximity you intend to use for bridging purposes, placement also brings unexpected, unique-to-the-medium issues into play. Imagine someone standing unusually close to you while speaking to you. Even if they are speaking entirely benevolently, your body will likely assume a defensive or evasive posture. If their tone is more belligerent (as might easily occur in mediation and negotiation), your full fight-or-flight mode will be activated. For this reason, people who do not intend to be aggressive simply stay out of others' triggering range of space.[200] In videoconferencing, however, people often place their camera close to their faces, or their camera provides a zooming-in effect. The visual outcome is that they appear to their counterparts as giant faces; the psychological impact is that, to some primal part of their counterpart's brain that ignores the virtuality of the interaction, they are literally 'getting in their face' aggressively.[201] Awareness to self will allow us to name any sense of unease created by our counterpart's camera placement, and remind us not to read too much into it. Awareness to other will lead us to recognize their response to our own placement, whether they are aware of it or not. Bridging mechanisms will involve camera placement and camera-face proximity such that we will avoid triggering the other (or, trigger them, if that is our intention). As a mediator, we can counsel parties on camera placement, thus removing one covert source of friction from the interaction.

These issues exemplify how videoconferencing impacts our capacity for social intuition and our intuitive use of it. They also demonstrate that intentional

199 *See* Dowell & Berman (2013).

200 *See* Kennedy, D.P., Gläscher, J., Tyszka, J.M. & Adolphs, R. (2009). Personal space regulation by the human amygdala. *Nature Neuroscience*, 12(10), 1226-1227.

201 Miller, R. (2020). What's 'Zoom fatigue'? Here's why video calls can be so exhausting. *USA Today*, 29 April. Available at www.usatoday.com/story/news/nation/2020/04/23/zoom-fatigue-video-calls-coronavirus-can-make-us-tired-anxious/3010478001/.

implementation of social intuition's framework of self, other, and bridging considerations will help negotiators and mediators in successfully applying the human touch.[202]

5.3.2 Social Intuition and Channel Constraints: Email

In email communication, our capacity for social intuition is not just impacted, it is fundamentally constrained. Not only are communicators denied the opportunity to use (or avoid) physical touch; their interaction is also totally bereft of key elements of social intuition: physical proximity, vocal tone, vocal and conversational pace, eye contact, body language, and mirroring.

Skilled email communicators recognize that some of these elements have proxies or surrogates, to which applying the social intuition framework of self, other, and bridging could be helpful. For example, vocal tone can be recreated in text form by use of language, italics, underlining, bolding, or emoji. The pace at which you might have voiced your thoughts can be indicated in writing style such as through choosing to use short sentences or expounding at length without using periods. The pace of message exchange (whether you responded to an email promptly or letting it sit in your inbox for a week) partially reflects the element of conversational pace. Each of these can be considered through self, other, and bridging considerations.

Humor and metaphor remain available via email, but their use entails new challenges.

Humor is a powerful bridging mechanism in negotiation. Indeed, what is more human-touch than one person causing another to laugh, and joining in themselves? Successfully employing humor in email negotiation increases trust and satisfaction as well as joint gains. It pays off, directly, in higher individual gains to the initiators of humorous events.[203] Before you laugh it up, though, remember that use of humor can backfire. Humor is more likely to fall flat, to be misunderstood, or to be mistakenly perceived as earnest communication via email than in a face-to-face setting.

While metaphors might go over well, we are denied the recognition reflex or the befuddled look in our counterpart's eyes that show us, in real time, whether a metaphor, simile, or analogy we use hits the bullseye, strikes true like as a well-thrown dart, or is as incomprehensible to them as a Lonely Planet guidebook to Spain is to a polar bear.

---

202 While social intuition elements of humor and metaphors are not directly impacted by videoconferencing, one caveat pertains: Lockdown situations aside, we are more likely to videoconference with people at a distance than those next door to us. As distance increases, so too does the likelihood for cultural difference. It would be prudent to remember that humor and analogies are very much social and cultural constructs, and can fall flat outside of their cultural birthplace. Of course, generally speaking, all elements of social intuition (e.g., conversational pace, and norms regarding physical proximity or physical touch) are culturally dependent. See Schneider & Ebner (2017).

203 T.R. Kurtzberg, C.E. Naquin & L.Y. Belkin, 'Humor as a Relationship-Building Tool in Online Negotiations', *International Journal of Conflict Management* (2009) 20, 4, 2009.

5.3.3 Online Social Intuition: General Practice Suggestions

Recognize that your capacity to read the other has diminished: Remind yourself of this often, during a negotiation or mediation process. This will help you to avoid knee-jerk inferring or attributing in order to fill the vacuum.

Recognize that the other's capacity to read you has diminished: If your core or go-to attributes for leading conversations in the direction you wish flow through intuitive channels such as warmth, humor, charm, empathizing, and so forth, business is not as usual. You must find new ways to express and convey these, allowing you to bridge toward the other in ways that overcome obstacles the medium poses to some of your traditional moves.

Resurrect missing realms: In email or in videoconferencing, evoke missing elements by painting a verbal picture. 'I wish we could shake hands right now' and 'If we were shaking hands right now, you'd get the full sense of my enthusiasm' both evoke that most elusive (online) realm of social intuition, physical contact, in negotiation. 'If you were to shake on this proposal now, how enthusiastic would your handshake be, on a scale of one to ten?' or 'I think that if you were in a room together, that last idea would receive not only a handshake, but a high-five!' are verbal pictures you can paint around the same element in mediation.

6 Looking Ahead

Completing this chapter on the last day of 2020, I will heed one lesson this year has gifted us all: Do not cast too far ahead. Another lesson we've all learned this year is that – in a pinch, at least – technology provides us with tools through which we can reach out and touch each other, significantly and meaningfully. Professionally, negotiators and mediators have learned that online communication enables us to do so to the extent that we can entrust our clients' welfare, our reputations, and our professional satisfaction to.

Without projecting what the new normal of negotiation and mediation will be in 2021 and beyond, the default has irreversibly changed. Dismissing online mediation and online negotiation as bereft of the human touch will be replaced by pursuit of ever-improving methods for conducting online processes rich in human-touch elements. This is a new, exciting, starting line for anyone involved in creating and improving human connections thorough online mediation and negotiation.

Chapter 5 ODR and the Justice System

Larry W. Bridgesmith

1 Introduction

We live in a world of online everything. The Sars-Cov-2 (Covid-19) pandemic has accelerated a journey to on-demand products, services and expectations of fairness in our dealings with others, businesses and the governments that serve us.

Our world also is one which is in a desperate search for justice. Charles Dickens' ***A Tale of Two Cities*** is the terrifying story of what happens to individuals, communities, and nations when injustice reigns. It is a story of extremes and of the havoc wreaked by such extremes, as the famous opening lines suggest:

> It was the best of times, it was the worst of times, it was the age of wisdom, it was the age of foolishness, it was the epoch of belief, it was the epoch of incredulity, it was the season of Light, it was the season of Darkness, it was the spring of hope, it was the winter of despair, we had everything before us, we had nothing before us, we were all going direct to Heaven, we were all going direct the other way … .[1]

Many decades later, technology has accelerated commerce, social interaction and a perception of injustice that might exceed the era about which Dickens wrote: the French Revolution. Can technology advances also serve the interests of justice and help avoid civil unrest? Can Online Dispute Resolution bring both efficient conflict management as well as address the deeper needs of justice in a technology driven culture? These are essential questions for the ODR community.

The global pandemic radically transformed business as usual in virtually every sector of the economy. Work from the office transitioned to work from home for 25% of the entire workforce, a trend that had begun prior to the pandemic.[2] Telehealth services exploded in number as contagion threatened even the customary office visit in health care. Between March 2019 and March 2020, remote healthcare consultations increased

---

1 Dickens, Charles. (1989). ***A Tale of Two Cities.*** New York: Bantam Classic, 1.

2 CIPD. (2020). *Working from Home: What's Driving the Rise in Remote Working?* London: Chartered Institute of Personnel and Development.

4,347% in the US.[3] All but non-essential services halted and face to face encounters were viewed as life threatening.

Zoom Communications Inc. users zoomed from 10 million daily meetings in December 2019 to 300 million per day in April 2020.[4] On 2 January 2020, Zoom traded its stock at $68.72.[5] On August 21, Zoom shares were trading at $289.68:[6] a micro-indicator of the impact of Covid-19 on business as usual.

Most office work transitioned to the work from home mode almost overnight. Some businesses reported as many as 85% of their employees were exclusively working from home.[7] The transition to a virtual economy, workforce and even social encounters will survive the pandemic. It is projected that as much as 20% of the workforce will permanently and exclusively remain work from home employees, or at least half those employees whose work would allow it.[8]

The courts were less responsive to the remote work environment. Access to justice by way of judicial relief almost ceased immediately after the pandemic hit. Courts closed and only gradually resorted to virtual meeting technology to conduct some elements of their business. Jury trials, the foundation of American justice, were delayed for many months creating enormous backlogs in US courts for the remainder of 2020.[9] Although hopeful voices are heard, justice dispensed through the courts remains inertia bound in its traditions.[10]

Immediately following the pandemic of 2020, mediated disputes were also postponed or canceled until mediators began to learn the techniques of remote work with virtual meeting tools like Zoom, Microsoft Teams, WhatsApp, GoogleMeets, WebEx, GoToMeeting and others. Like many forms of remote work, online dispute resolution (ODR) grew exponentially in the wake of Covid-19.

This journal has promoted, illustrated and educated ODR users in the principles and techniques of online dispute resolution long before the pandemic. Is justice being served?

---

3 Robin Gelburd, J.D. (2 June 2020). "The Coronavirus Pandemic and the Transformation of Telehealth". *US News & World Report.*

4 Warren, Tom. (3 April 2020). "Zoom grows to 300 million meeting participants despite security backlash." *The Verge*, www.theverge.com/2020/4/23/21232401/zoom-300-million-users-growth-coronavirus-pandemic-security-privacy-concerns-response.

5 www.google.com/search?client=firefox-b-1-d&q=zoom+share+price.

6 *Ibid.*

7 McKinsey & Company. (20 August 2020 Thursday). "Critical communications infrastructure and COVID-19: an interview with Ericsson's CEO". *McKinsey & Company.*

8 Thompson, Derek. (6 August 2020 Thursday). "The Workforce Is About to Change Dramatically." *Atlantic Online*, www.theatlantic.com/ideas/archive/2020/08/just-small-shift-remote-work-could-change-everything/614980/; Cain Miller, Claire. (20 August 2020 Sunday). "The Office Will Never Be the Same." *New York Times*, www.nytimes.com/2020/08/20/style/office-culture.html?referringSource=articleShare.

9 Timms, Maria. (13 August 2020). "Jury trials in Davidson County pushed back again, some to 2021 as COVID-19 cases continue." *The Tennessean*, www.tennessean.com/story/news/local/2020/08/13/davidson-county-no-jury-trials-nashville-until-2021/3365611001/.

10 Susskind, Richard. (July/August 2020). "The Future of Courts." *Remote Courts*, Harvard Center on the Legal Profession 6(5), https://thepractice.law.harvard.edu/article/the-future-of-courts/.

When measured by universal notions of justice, has ODR realized it potential? What more must be accomplished for ODR to become an access to justice tool trusted globally?

This chapter will attempt to address these issues.

2 What is Justice?

Aristotle observed that justice is 'the whole of virtue.'[11] He further states that the most excellent citizen is one whose virtue is perfected in relationship to others.[12] Justice is always expressed 'in relation to another person.'[13] Justice is the mean between selfishness and selflessness. This relative sense of justice has implications within political, economic, social, and racial realms. For the social fabric of a nation and globally to avoid disintegrating into chaos and civil revolt, perceptions of fairness in human interactions reign paramount.

Black's Law Dictionary defines justice as:

> 1 The fair treatment of people. 2. The quality of being fair or reasonable. 3. The legal system by which people and their causes are judged; esp., the system used to punish people who have committed crimes. 4. The fair and proper administration of laws.[14]

The core concept of justice in Western thought is 'fairness' experienced by people, especially in the context of legal rights and remedies available through the administration of laws. Dispute or conflict resolution need not involve legal rights (such as in personality conflicts). However, 'dispute resolution' more commonly includes legal disputes regarding rights and remedies. Ironically, Black's definition of this key term refers to alternative dispute resolution (ADR) without defining what the alternative is.[15]

There must be critical meaning to be derived by the definition of ADR: "Any procedure for settling a dispute by means other than litigation, as by arbitration or mediation."[16] Only by inference can it be argued that litigation is the primary means of resolving disputes and its alternatives are mediation and arbitration.

Regardless of the semantics, the three core processes of dispute resolution in law (litigation, mediation and arbitration) are all managed by third parties. Negotiation,

---

11 Aristotle. (2014). Nicomachean Ethics (Edited by Roger Crisp, revised Ed.). Cambridge: Cambridge University Press, 81. BN.V.1.1130a8-10.
12 Aristotle, 81. BN.V.1.1130a8-10.
13 *Ibid.* BN.V.I.1129b26-28.
14 JUSTICE, Black's Law Dictionary (11th ed. 2019).
15 DISPUTE RESOLUTION, Black's Law Dictionary (11th ed. 2019).
16 ALTERNATIVE DISPUTE RESOLUTION, Black's Law Dictionary (11th ed. 2019).

avoidance and self-help, in which the disputants determine how to resolve the dispute themselves, appear to be excluded from the application of the concept of fairness. Accordingly, fairness is a critical component of dispute resolution in which third parties are engaged to assist the disputing parties resolve their conflict.

Whether the third party is a judge, mediator or arbitrator, this outcome is appropriate. Online Dispute Resolution is the applicable term when any third party takes part in the administration of justice using the tools of Internet based communication, collaboration, meeting and information sharing. This chapter is limited to those instances in which mediators, arbitrators and any hybrid version of these processes are involved.

2.1 Fairness

Fairness comes in many forms. The concept of fairness might seem subjective. However, there are identifiable characteristics of fairness which in combination engender trust in a person or a process. It may be that objective fairness can be maximized by insuring as much as possible that its identifiable traits are promoted and demonstrated in the ODR process. Some of the key characteristics of fairness include the following:

2.1.1 Outcomes

When disputes are resolved (agreed to or decided by others), a key question is whether or not the outcome was considered to be fair. Obviously, fair outcomes when decisions are made by others (arbitrators or judges) will be determined largely by how close to a party's desired outcome the decision hews. In agreed outcomes (negotiation and mediation) fairness might be measured by an external comparison to how reasonable the agreement when viewed in light of legal, cultural or industry specific acceptable standards.

When outcomes are decided by others, appeals may be available to dissatisfied litigants in judicial proceedings under limited circumstances.[17] However, attacks on the legal correctness or fairness of an arbitral award are far more restricted.[18] In both instances, great deference is given to decision makers responsible for deciding outcomes for the disputes of others. This is the case especially because the parties have chosen an arbitral process and decision maker through consensual agreement. Because arbitration is

17 *State v. Williams*, 286 P.3d 195, 295 Kan. 506 (Kan. 2012).

18 *Robbins v. Day*, 954 F.2d 679 (11th Cir. 1992) (Under the US Federal Arbitration Act applicable to commercial disputes great deference is afforded the arbitration process and an award will be vacated only upon a showing of misconduct attributable to the parties or the arbitrator. Legal error alone is not enough.) Other courts have imposed a 'manifest disregard for law' standard. *National Wrecking Co. v. International Broth. of Teamsters*, 990 F.2d 957 (7th Cir. 1993) (Requiring proof the arbitrator knew the correct law and consciously disregarded it.).

a 'creature of the contract' between the parties, arbitral limitations can also be imposed by the terms of the agreement to arbitrate.[19]

However, mediation is even more removed from judicial review. Subject matter or outcome fairness is doubly insulated from court inspection due to 1) the terms of the agreement to mediate and 2) the consensual basis of the mediation process. Mediation outcomes are presumed to be fair by virtue of the fact that the parties agreed to resolve the mediated dispute on terms which are satisfactory them.

A US federal court discounted allegations of outcome unfairness offered in defense of a party's action to enforce an agreement reached in mediation.[20] Judicial reactions like this show how little focus a court gives to allegations of an unfair mediation outcome. Because of the voluntary and consensual nature of mediation, attacks on substantive (outcome) fairness are seldom successful in the legal context.

Nonetheless, substantive fairness remains a factor in how participants themselves view mediation outcomes and may impact the sustainability of agreements reached. Ironically, notions of outcome fairness have prompted complex rules attempting to regulate the mediation process of which the United States is the standard bearer. Global commentators are not convinced of the necessity for these regulatory restrictions on mediation.

If one combines the comparison of mediation laws with a comparison of empirical data on mediation, it is striking that the success of mediation as an institution does not depend on whether it is subject to a comprehensive and detailed set of rules or whether the norm creators confine themselves to selective regulation … .[21]

Instead, the flexibility, informality and consensual principles which underlie mediation as a dispute resolution process suggest the benefits of less regulation rather than more as it relates to outcome fairness.[22]

2.1.2 Processes

Process fairness involves a different set of variables and criteria than outcome fairness. In part because mediators and arbitrators are the masters of the process, greater scrutiny justifiably is focused on the third party's conduct in how the proceedings are conducted.

Judicial review of mediation and arbitration outcomes are focused more often on the procedural fairness than the outcome.[23] If the parties have chosen the process, the courts

---

19 *Sound Inpatient Physicians Inc. v. Carr*, 2:19-cv-02034-TLP, ROSS 13556150 (W.D. Tenn. 20 August 2020).

20 *Olam v. Congress Mortg. Co.*, 68 F.Supp.2d 1110 (N.D. Cal. 1999).

21 Mediation: Principles and Regulation in Comparative Perspective 110 (Klaus J. Hopt & Felis Steffek eds., 2013).

22 Sarah R. Cole, Craig A. McEwen, Nancy H. Rogers, James R. Coben, Peter N. Thompson, Mediation: Law, Policy and Practice, Chapter 2.7 Dilemmas Presented by Institutionalization of Mediation, December 2019 Update.

23 In re Atlantic Pipe Corp., 304 F.3d 135 (1st Cir. 2002) (Challenge to substantive and procedural fairness of court ordered mediation determined on the basis of its procedural fairness.)

seem to presume they have agreed on the impartial party as "process master". However, if a party perceives that the third party fails to provide "fundamental fairness" in the administration of the process, greater scrutiny of the outcome is possible.

Of course, mediation and arbitration agreements are the primary source to which the courts look for guidance regarding the parties' expectations of appropriate process. Third party dispute resolution providers must regularly review and appropriately revise the terms of their agreements to maximize the enforceability of procedural provisions. It might be argued that no two mediation or arbitration procedures are identical and that each agreement should be tailored to the specifics of the parties' expectations to minimize fairness arguments.

The US federal court ADR process has proven to be a remarkable tool to reduce the need for trials to less than 1% of all cases filed.[24] However, the perceived lack of fair processes has lead commentators to call for rule changes that would prohibit trial judges from conducting settlement conferences in their own cases and imposing an objective standard for 'good faith' assessments of process appropriateness.[25] Procedural fairness remains a significant concern in the face of perceived power imbalances in third party dispute resolution.

2.1.3 Restitution/Recovery

Parties confronted with a dispute for which they desire resolution may be more focused on the degree to which they can obtain restitution for injured interests and recovery for lost value. In most settings, litigation and arbitration differ markedly from mediation when a dispute turns on the scope of recovery or restitution. Legal analysis and/or contractual terms may limit the degree to which litigation and arbitration outcomes are customarily reached. In contrast, mediation often encourages the search for creative solutions on which the parties can agree which may be neither legally nor contractually required.

Some commentators and jurisdictions have experimented with an integration approach by which ADR is incorporated into the judicial process and a multi-level access to a justice model is proposed or formally instituted.[26] In such systems, ADR including mediation and arbitration becomes a mandatory component of the search for solutions in addition to judicial relief. However, staging these dispute resolution processes and mandating them also carries the potential for coercion and inefficiency that ADR is designed to limit. This is turn creates concerns about fairness and unnecessary cost.[27]

---

24 Lynch, William P. (2019). "Why Settle For Less? Improving Settlement Conferences In Federal Court." *Washington Law Review* 94(3).

25 *Ibid.*

26 Cohen, Hadas. (December 2019). "Multilevel access to justice in a world of vanishing trials: a conflict resolution perspective." *Fordham Urban Law Journal.*

27 Conley, Amberlee B. (November 2018). "You Can Have Your Day in Court – But Not Before Your Mandatory Non-Binding Arbitration: Balancing Practicalities of State Arbitration." *Iowa Law Review*, 325+.

Some commentators have addressed the common perception that compulsory arbitration serves to disadvantage employees to the benefit employers in terms of recovery amounts.[28] These commentators make the 'apples to oranges' comparisons when the nature of arbitration claims (primarily contractual) is viewed in light of the nature of litigation claims (primarily statutory). They note that recovery comparisons require much more sophisticated empirical analysis is needed than is commonly applied to this question.

The consensual nature of mediation outcomes leaves the question of the adequacy of recovery and restitution to the parties. In the absence of mediator bias or the exploitation of less powerful parties, mediation outcomes are presumed to be satisfactory because they have been agreed to. However, implicit (unconscious) mediator bias can infect the perception of just recovery in mediation.[29]

2.1.4 Transformation

Some ADR proponents seek transformative resolutions in which the outcome provides more than mere economic recovery. Instead, when relationships, social fabric or personal dignity have been injured, transformative outcomes seek to mend the relationship as well as transform the social fabric and restore the injured self-image.

Transformative Justice seeks to provide people who experience violence with immediate safety, long-term healing and reparations; to demand that people who have done harm take accountability for their harmful actions, while holding the possibility for their transformation and humanity; and to mobilize communities to shift the oppressive social and systemic conditions that create the context for violence.[30]

Transformative justice principles move beyond recovery and restitution between victim and offender in order to reform both the offender and the societal norms which may have engendered the offense. Needless to say, despite the lofty aspiration of these goals, this outcome much more difficult to achieve.

In ADR processes, the principles of transformative justice have become a staple in many forms of mediation, and even in some forms of arbitration.[31] In disputes which are grounded in shared values among the parties, transformative ADR justice can perform a vital and valued function.

---

28 Sherwyn, David, Estreicher, Samuel and Heise, Michael. (April 2005). "Assessing the case for employment arbitration: a new path for empirical research." *Stanford Law Review*, 1557+.

29 Izumi, Carol. (2010). "Implicit bias and the illusion of mediator neutrality." *Washington University Journal of Law & Policy* 34, 71+.

30 Generationfive. (2017). *Ending Child Sexual Abuse: A Transformative Justice Handbook*, 45. http://www.generationfive.org/wp-content/uploads/2017/06/Transformative-Justice-Handbook.pdf.

31 Helfand, Michael A. (June 2015). "Feature: Arbitration, Transparency, and Privatization: Arbitration's Counter-Narrative: The Religious Arbitration Paradigm." *The Yale Law Journal* 124, 2994.

3 ODR and Justice

As observed by commentators:

> The role of fairness and justice in negotiation and other ADR processes is complex. Fairness includes several different aspects, with the foremost divide being that between distributive (or outcome) fairness, and procedural fairness. In the environment created by the Internet, these complexities are compounded.[32]

If ODR is to provide justice to the parties, it must anticipate the unique environment created by the Internet and adopt the features of justice recognized as appropriate in ADR over the course of its advent and growth.

The Internet environment is noted for its immediacy (on demand), security/privacy issues and the lasting nature of the digital footprint left by its users. ODR practitioners must be aware of and adjust to these challenges with no less vigilance than ADR professionals learned to deal with paper trails, face to face meeting rooms and user expectations of security and confidentiality.

A starting point for ODR proponents is to assess how courts have adjusted to the global pandemic of 2020. Just as the judicial system was forced to transform to an online reality, ODR practitioners must retain the essential elements of trustworthy ADR practices as it evolves into an Internet meeting and collaboration space.

Commentators have analyzed the lasting values of the judicial administration of justice which are expected to survive into the advent and growth of remote courts. These essential attributes of the common law system are identified as open justice, procedural fairness and impartiality.[33]

Unlike the courts, ADR and its technological sibling ODR are expected to be just, fair and impartial, but not open to the public as is the case in a nation's judicial system. To the contrary, confidentiality is a norm unique to ADR which is challenged by the ODR Internet environment. Likewise, fairness and impartiality must be preserved in ODR proceedings no less than in judicial processes.

---

32 Ebner, Noam and Zeleznikow, John. (2015). "Fairness, Trust and Security in Online Dispute Resolution." *Hamline University's School of Law's Journal of Public Law and Policy* 36(2), Article 6, 152.

33 Legg, Michael. (2021). "The COVID-19 Pandemic, the Courts and Online Hearings: Maintaining Open Justice, Procedural Fairness and Impartiality". Forthcoming (2021) Federal Law Review, UNSW Law Research No. 20-46, available at SSRN: https://ssrn.com/abstract=3681165. Same: https://papers.ssrn.com/sol3/papers.cfm?abstract_id=3681165.

3.1 ODR Fairness

Professor Amy Schmitz, a leading scholar regarding ODR processes, concludes her call for more research and empirical study on ODR fairness with the following observation:

ODR holds great promise for advancing A2J but only if properly deployed, improved, and monitored. This depends on research, along with transparency, to help inform best practices and means for monitoring. Hopefully, this research will also expand to provide better and more informed ideas for advancing A2J broadly and enhancing social and legal justice in the United States and beyond.[34]

Clearly, one of the major challenges of the current state of ODR applications is the degree to which meaningful and relevant data can be generated to provide the depth of empirical research Prof. Schmitz calls for. Those who are developing ODR platforms and those using them must be attentive the degree to which this data is created, collected and analyzed while maintaining the confidentiality which ADR/ODR must assure its users. Otherwise, the 'psychological cold water' to be thrown ODR enthusiasm well might be warranted.[35]

One empirical research experiment on the perceptions of fairness in ODR applications studied user reactions to online mediation, arbitration and mediation/arbitration processes. Whether principal (human facilitated outcomes) or instrumental (machine driven outcomes) the user experiences were uniformly positive under the controlled conditions of the experiment.[36]

Most of these admonitions and experiments preceded a global pandemic which rapidly moved ODR into the mainstream of dispute resolution practices. The forward movement of ODR practices can ill afford to await the in-depth research and empirical study results to improve the users' legitimate expectations of justice and fairness.

Practitioners would do well to follow and learn from the community of ODR specialists who are engaged in the pioneering work of exploring these new territories each day. Non-profit entities such as the Pew Charitable Trusts and the National Center for State Courts (NCSC) are living in the trenches of ODR deployment in real time. ODR practitioners will benefit from periodic review of the work of the NCSC on its ODR webpage.[37] The site is updated regularly with examples of how many have started

34 Schmitz, Amy J. (18 May 2020). "Measuring 'Access to Justice' in the Rush to Digitize." *Fordham Law Review* 88, 2381, University of Missouri School of Law Legal Studies Research Paper No. 2020-15, available at SSRN: https://ssrn.com/abstract=3604717.

35 Sternlight, Jean R. (Winter 2020). "Pouring a Little Psychological Cold Water on Online Dispute Resolution." *Journal of Dispute Resolution*, at 1, UNLV William S. Boyd School of Law Legal Studies Research Paper Series, available at SSRN: https://ssrn.com/abstract=3446140.

36 Sela, Ayelet. (2018). "Can Computers Be Fair? How Automated and Human-Powered Online Dispute Resolution Affect Procedural Justice in Mediation and Arbitration." *Ohio State Journal on Dispute Resolution* 33, 91, available at SSRN: https://ssrn.com/abstract=3074311 (20 December 2016).

37 www.ncsc.org/odr.

the ODR journey,[38] the importance of stakeholder input and involvement,[39] the steps that many have taken to insure fair and impartial processes[40] and how program developers have measured success.[41]

3.2 *Technological Trust and Competence*

One of the most visible US state court ODR initiatives is that of Utah, a widely promoted and highly publicized Utah Supreme Court program. An exhaustive user focused evaluation of its groundbreaking progress makes five actionable recommendations for the program's continued growth and success:

1. Ease the transition from paper to platform using website design and user interface standards of useful Internet access.
2. Streamline the registration process by applying the best practices of web form design.
3. Simplify document upload and review with intuitive design choices.
4. Improve ODR information and assistance on the site with effective FAQ design.
5. Clarify legal information and user options with best practices for presenting visual information.[42]

One of the few post-pandemic ODR research projects, the report on the Utah experience concludes:

> Users are ready for online courts: when asked if they had the option, nearly every study participant said they would prefer to use a website over physically going to a courthouse to resolve a dispute. The challenge – and opportunity – now is to integrate human-centered design into the expansion of ODR so the technologies employed are useful and intuitive for all users. The findings from this research study demonstrate that ODR users want accessible and transparent information about how ODR works and what their legal rights and options are within an ODR platform. They also want a platform that is responsive, simple, and has the look and feel of other mobile-first online consumer spaces they use on a regular basis. With the national trend toward ODR accelerated by the unanticipated shift to remote courts in response to the COVID-19 pandemic, it is more important than ever that courts commit to

---

38 www.ncsc.org/odr/home/startup2.

39 www.ncsc.org/odr/home/stakeholder-engagement.

40 www.ncsc.org/odr/home/ensuring-a-fair-and-impartial-process.

41 www.ncsc.org/odr/home/measuring-success.

42 Butler, Stacy, Mauet, Sarah, Griffin, Christopher L., Jr. and Pish, Mackenzie S. (8 September 2020). "The Utah Online Dispute Resolution Platform: A Usability Evaluation and Report." The University of Arizona James E. Rogers College of Law Innovation for Justice Program, www.law.arizona.edu/i4j.

creating fair, just, and equitable online legal environments that meet the needs of all users.[43]

Clearly, if ODR is to make its way into the mainstream of consumer focused dispute resolution, it will need to focus far more on the user experience (UX) and the user interface (UI) in order to function and appear like the thousands of other web based tools we have all come to use. Human-centered design must leave its mark on the ODR experience for it to meet user needs.

ODR practitioners must also become coaches and trainers for the best uses of online products and tools. Mediation preparation in the face to face world was too often given short shrift by ADR professionals. Consumers of mediation services faulted mediators for their lack of preparation in the American Bar Association 2008 survey which identified numerous shortfalls in the practice of commercial mediation.[44] Preparation is even more critical in the ODR Internet environment.

Whether mediation or arbitration, ODR practitioners must assure their own technical competence with the tools to be used and orient their users to the systems, techniques and challenges of ODR tools. Among other issues, process fairness will be measured by the degree which the ODR service provider and the users they introduce to ODR technology are equipped to utilize the required Internet tools easily, confidently and securely.

4 Conclusion

The standards and expectations of our on-demand world are shaping the features of access to justice and ODR services as much as they do our Internet shopping experiences. ODR practitioners owe it to the demographic we serve to pay heed to these expectations and maintain the highest levels of outcome and procedural fairness as well as impartiality in the manner Internet based dispute resolution is conducted.

ODR professionals must 'up their game' to bring satisfactorily the established standards of ADR justice into the complications introduced by the Internet environment. As technologically advanced as our society of Internet users may be, ODR practitioners can neither assume technological competence on the part of ODR customers nor themselves.

---

43 *Ibid.*, pp. 91-92.

44 American Bar Association Section of Dispute Resolution, Task Force on Improving Mediation Quality Final Report (2008), www.abanet.org/dch/committee.cfm?com=DR020600.

CHAPTER 6 ODR ACCESSIBILITY FOR PERSONS WITH DISABILITIES: WE MUST DO BETTER

David Allen Larson

1 INTRODUCTION[1]

I am completing this chapter in April 2020 as Covid-19 continues to sweep across the United States and the world. Covid-19 is causing damage and loss at a stunning speed. The confirmed and probable deaths attributed to Covid-19 in New York City alone, for example, were reported as 18,909 as of 4 May 2020.[2] The only currently available preventive measure is social distancing – staying at least six feet away from everyone else. Almost all the states in the United States have issued stay-at-home orders, and only essential services remain open.[3] We remain isolated in our homes, and most of our interaction with the outside world is taking place online. As a result, businesses are struggling to survive, and governments are trying to determine how they can provide their desperately needed goods and services online as quickly as possible.

People need to be able to resolve disputes peacefully during this stressful time. Court systems, government agencies, and private businesses are feeling tremendous pressure to provide online dispute resolution (ODR) systems. As they rush to design and implement ODR systems, however, it is critical that all the institutions make digital accessibility a priority. Persons with disabilities were not always able to effectively access internet websites before Covid-19. But because many more aspects of our lives are now moving online and may remain online for the long term, it is even more important that persons with disabilities are not excluded from our 'new normal' version of life. Effective access to

1 The author thanks editor Mary Trevor and Mary Dunnewold for their invaluable editorial suggestions, and Mitchell Hamline law student Reverend Hannah Cranbury for her excellent assistance. This chapter is a significant revision of an article published last year, David Allen Larson, *Digital Accessibility and Disability Accommodations in Online Dispute Resolution: ODR for Everyone*, 34 Ohio St. J. on Disp. Resol. 431 (2019), which in turn expanded upon a shorter, conversational piece co-authored with Lainey Feingold, a nationally recognized disability rights attorney who can be contacted at https://www.lflegal.com/.

2 NYC Health, https://www1.nyc.gov/site/doh/covid/covid-19-data.page (last visited 4 May 2020).

3 Stephen Sorace, *Coronavirus Stay-at-Home Orders: What States Have Issued Directives so Far?* (reporting only Arkansas, Iowa, Nebraska, North Dakota, and South Dakota have not issued any stay-at-home orders. Partial orders have been issued locally by cities or counties in Oklahoma, Utah, and Wyoming.), https://www.foxnews.com/us/coronavirus-stay-at-home-orders-what-states-have-issued-so-far (last visited 19 April 2020).

dispute resolution processes is one part of life that must remain accessible to persons with disabilities.

Although we can hope and expect that eventually we will discover an effective vaccine or treatment for Covid-19, it is unclear when that will occur and whether we will experience second and third waves of this disease. When the day finally arrives when we can be confident that it is safe to go out into the world, the world will not look the same as it did before this pandemic. Services that moved online may never again be offered face-to-face. Consequently, much of the online environment we now are rushing to build may stay in place permanently. Understanding that we need to provide services as quickly as possible, we still must not overlook design features that ensure accessibility for persons with disabilities. We cannot dismiss these features as mere details that can be added later. It is more efficient to include accessibility features when an online platform is first being designed and constructed. And more importantly, if the plan is simply to add those design features later, sometimes 'later' never arrives.

Accessibility is a civil and human right of persons with disabilities, as discussed below. Yet accessible ODR platforms and content do not provide benefits only to people with disabilities. While accessibility is essential for some individuals, many accessibility design features will be helpful and useful for everyone. People with 'temporary disabilities' such as a broken arm or lost glasses, those confronting situational limitations such as sensitivity to bright light or loud audio, or individuals with slow, limited, or expensive bandwidth internet connections may all benefit from accessible website design.[4] Similarly, captioned video content benefits anyone in a noisy environment as well as individuals who are deaf or have limited hearing. A well designed, easy-to-navigate website may benefit aging baby boomers in addition to people with cognitive and other disabilities. In fact, one can safely assume most people will appreciate a website that has an intuitive design, tasks that are easy to learn, that can be completed quickly, and steps that are memorable and easily performed again when users return to the website.[5] Universally designed digital content can benefit everyone.

Digital accessibility is achievable. Regardless of whether compliance is mandatory, substantial guidance is available. Websites, mobile applications, software platforms, and other technologies will be accessible when developed and designed to internationally recognized accessibility standards. A host of best practices related to business processes and training are available to ensure accessibility for ODR systems.

ODR systems have been available for at least 20 years. Until recently, they functioned primarily as alternative dispute resolution (ADR) processes that were separate and

4 AKE, *Why Web Accessibility Matters*, https://www.akeaweb.com/why-web-accessibility-matters/ (last visited 21 March, 2021).

5 *Id.*

distinct from court systems.[6] Even before the appearance of Covid-19, however, a rapidly expanding number of court systems had adopted, or were designing, court-integrated ODR processes.[7] Because the number of ODR systems is guaranteed to increase, we must be especially careful to ensure that ODR systems are accessible to persons with disabilities. Individuals who use computers and mobile devices but cannot see a screen, hear a video, or hold a mouse, or who have other disabilities, may not be able to use an ODR system unless we pay close attention to digital accessibility.

The success of any ODR system is contingent upon accessibility. It is obvious that users must have access to computers, tablets, or smartphones that have the technological capacity to interact with an ODR platform. Just as importantly, that ODR platform must be designed so individuals are not excluded because of their disability.

The purpose of this chapter is to offer ODR system designers, practicing neutrals such as mediators and arbitrators, information technology professionals, private and public decisionmakers, and policymakers essential information and tools to build and

---

6 *See* Ethan Katsh, *ODR: A Look at History*, https://www.mediate.com/pdf/katsh.pdf (last visited 29 April 2020).

7 The author presently is serving as the System Designer for the New York State Unified Court System to create an ODR process that will become a fully integrated component of that court system. Other court systems that were already using ODR as of June 2019 include: (1) British Columbia Civil Resolution Tribunal, Province-wide; (2) Clark County Family Court, Las Vegas, NV; (3) Franklin County Small Claims, Columbus, Ohio; (4) Fulton County Small Claims, Atlanta, GA; (5) New York State Unified Court System Consumer Debt, Statewide; (6) Ohio Court of Claims, Statewide; (7) Ottawa County Family Court Compliance, Grand Rapids, Michigan; (8) Travis County Small Claims, Austin, TX; (9) Utah Courts Small Claims, Statewide; (10) Tlaxcala Supreme Court, Mexico; (11) Faulkner and Van Buren County District Courts, Faulkner and Van Buren County, AR; (12) Sherwood District Court, Sherwood, AR; (13) DeKalb County State Court - Traffic Division, DeKalb County, GA; (14) Village of Ford Heights, Cook County, IL; (15) Jefferson County District Court, Louisville, KY; (16) 15th District Court, Ann Arbor, MI; (17) 74th District Court, Bay County, MI; (18) 10th District Court, Calhoun County, MI; (19) 65A District Court, Clinton County, MI; (20) Clinton Township, MI, 41B District Court; (21) 54B District Court, East Lansing, MI; (22) 21st District Court, Garden City, MI; (23) 20th Circuit Court, Grand Haven, MI; (24) 61st District Court, Grand Rapids, MI; (25) 31st District Court, Hamtramck, MI; (26) 32A District Court, Harper Woods, MI; (27) 30th District Court, Highland Park, MI; (28) 55th District Court, Ingham County, MI; (29) 22nd District Court, Inkster, MI; (30) 12th District Court, Jackson County, MI; (31) 4th Circuit Court, Jackson, MI; (32) 62B District Court, Kentwood, MI; (33) City of Lansing - Income Tax Division, Lansing, MI; (34) 54A District Court, Lansing, MI; (35) 16th District Court, Livonia, MI; (36) 1st District Court, Monroe County, MI; (37) 50th District Court, Pontiac, MI; (38) 46th District Court, Southfield, MI; (39) 23rd District Court, Taylor, MI; (40) 14A District Court, Washtenaw County, MI; (41) Washtenaw County Friend of the Court, Washtenaw County, MI; (42) 29th District Court, Wayne, MI; (43) 14B District Court, Ypsilanti Township, MI; (44) Cleveland Municipal Court, Cleveland, OH; (45) Franklin County Municipal Court, Franklin County, OH; and (46) Farmers Branch Municipal Court, Farmers Branch, TX. *Courts Using ODR*, The Nat'l Ctr. for Tech. and Dispute Resolution, http://odr.info/courts-using-odr/ (last visited 29 April 2020) (list of courts as of 21 June 2019). Eleven courts were added to the list since 21 June 2019 but before the Covid-19 pandemic. (47) Hartford and New Haven (Connecticut, USA); (48) Orange County Small Claims (California, USA); (49) New Mexico Courts, (USA); (50) Yolo County Courts (California, USA); (51) Hangzhou Internet Court (China); (52) Zhejiang Court ODR Program (China); (53) Guangzhou Court of the Internet (China); (54) The Beijing Internet Court (China); (55) Michigan Supreme Court (USA); (56) e-Court Canada; (57) The Condominium Authority Tribunal (CAT) (Ontario, Canada).

maintain systems that work for everyone. It is my hope that readers will be encouraged to share ideas for making ODR a model of accessibility across the globe.

2 Digital Accessibility: Required or Merely Desired

Digital accessibility

> is the ability of a website, mobile application or electronic document to be easily navigated and understood by a wide range of users, including those users who have visual, auditory, motor, or cognitive disabilities.[8]

Monitoring digital accessibility, however, involves unique challenges. Unlike the situation when someone builds or remodels a physical structure, there is no need to acquire permits or licenses. No one will be reviewing a website to ensure compliance with a set of standards. Individuals who want to build a website can do it alone. They do not need a general contractor or specialists like plumbers and electricians.[9] And, unlike with physical structures, little has been done as a matter of law or policy to ensure access to websites.

The Americans with Disabilities Act of 1990 (ADA) was enacted almost 30 years ago because

> historically, society has tended to isolate and segregate individuals with disabilities, and, despite some improvements, such forms of discrimination against individuals with disabilities continue to be a serious and pervasive social problem.[10]

One of the primary purposes of the ADA was to make certain that buildings and their means of access were navigable for persons with disabilities. That focus made sense in 1990 and remains an important concern today. Tremendous amounts of time and energy have been spent providing specific instruction concerning disability-accessible architectural design. The 2010 ADA Standards for Accessible Design update to the original 1990 standards, for instance, includes 279 pages of very specific design requirements for a wide variety of facilities and accessories that include drinking

8 Margaret Rouse, *Digital Accessibility*, Tech Target: WhatIs.com, https://whatis.techtarget.com/definition/digital-accessibility (last updated May 2016).

9 Individuals can build physical structures by themselves. For example, determined individuals can and have built homes by themselves. That is the rare exception, however. And those structures are almost always modest. I am not aware of any individuals who have built a 70-story office building by themselves.

10 Americans with Disabilities Act, 42 U.S.C. § 12101(a)(2) (1990).

fountains, carpet pile height, locker rooms, clear floor or ground space, knee and toe clearance, holding cells, parking places, saunas, fishing piers, and miniature golf courses.[11] This detailed concern with physical accessibility has provided opportunities for persons with disabilities that were never previously available.

When the Americans with Disabilities Act of 1990 was passed, it was national news, and the goal of making physical structures accessible was a conspicuous concern. The emergence of the internet, however, was not accompanied by an equivalent concern for digital accessibility. It obviously requires far less money and time to create a website, mobile application, or electronic document than it takes to build a physical structure. Although access to the necessary hardware can be a barrier, the cost to create a website can be quite minimal. Everything one needs may be available without charge at public libraries and other venues.

Consequently, ensuring digital accessibility for every website requires either regulation or the cooperation of millions of individuals. The task may appear overwhelming, but a conscious effort to achieve digital accessibility will result in an online environment that is inviting and more understandable for all users, regardless of whether they have a disability. Digital accessibility ensures that persons with disabilities can participate in our online world, which soon may be the only place to access an increasing variety of goods and services.

The Americans with Disabilities Act was written to ensure access to a physical world, but we now must ensure access to a virtual world. We must take an expansive perspective in our search for helpful guidance that includes both national and international resources. We need to be purposeful and proactive about identifying succinct guidelines and standards that can easily be understood and applied. This chapter is a modest effort in that direction.

One might hope that concerns about equity and inclusion alone would be sufficient motivation to guarantee digital accessibility. That hope has not materialized, and many websites continue to be inaccessible. WebAIM explains there are primarily three reasons why people might be motivated to create accessible web content:

> (1) to improve the lives of people with disabilities (human-centered motivations), (2) to capitalize on a wider audience or consumer base (marketing or economic-centered motivations), and (3) to avoid lawsuits and/or bad press (public relations and punishment-centered motivations).[12]

11 2010 ADA Standards for Accessible Design, 65-67, 68, 81, 90-91, 97, 98, 102, 104-05, 107-11, 206 (Dept. of Justice 2010), https://www.ada.gov/regs2010/2010ADAStandards/2010ADAStandards.pdf.

12 WebAim, *Motivations to Create Accessible Web Content,* https://webaim.org (last visited 19 April 2020).

Despite these accessibility incentives, many websites remain inaccessible.

In November 2017, for example, the Information Technology and Innovation Foundation noted that of the 468 most popular federal websites, only 60% were accessible to users with disabilities.[13] Problems ranged from poor contrast to a lack of labels, which makes it difficult for persons with vision impairments who rely on a screen reader to navigate those websites.[14] That same Foundation reported in October 2018 that 41% of 400 state government websites had a substantial number of problems that could have prevented someone with a disability from using the site.[15] Consequently, there is a rapidly increasing possibility that websites not digitally accessible will be sued. A 6 January 2020 Seyfarth Shaw report confirms this possibility by noting that lawsuits alleging inaccessible websites and mobile apps accounted for at least a fifth[16] of the 11,053[17] ADA Title III[18] lawsuits filed in federal court in 2019. Thus, plaintiffs filed more than 2,000 ADA Title III website accessibility lawsuits in federal court last year.

> Most plaintiffs in these cases are blind and claim that the websites in question do not work with their screen reader software which reads website content aloud. A much smaller number of plaintiffs are deaf and are suing about the lack of closed captioning for online videos.[19]

One obvious question, given the fact that the ADA was enacted almost 30 years ago, why has it taken so long for a significant number of lawsuits to be brought against websites that are not accessible?

> For years, many potential plaintiffs were waiting for the U.S. Department of Justice to issue their interpretation of the ADA about websites. That never happened.
>
> And after the DOJ once again extended its deadline in 2015, "it felt like that clarification was never going to come," Helland said. A wave of lawsuits hit the federal court system that year and the next.

13 Daniel Castro et al., *Benchmarking U.S. Government Websites*, Info. Tech. and Innovation Found (4 November 2017), https://itif.org/publications/2017/11/27/benchmarking-us-government-websites.

14 *Id.*

15 Daniel Castro, *Designing Accessible Government Websites*, Info. Tech. and Innovation Found (1 October 2018), https://itif.org/publications/2018/10/01/designing-accessible-government-websites (last visited 19 April 2020).

16 Minh Vu et al., *ADA Title III Litigation: A 2019 Review and Hot Trends for 2020*, Seyfarth Shaw (6 January 2020), https://www.adatitleiii.com (last visited 19 April 2020).

17 Minh Vu, et al., *2019 Was Another Record-Breaking Year for Federal ADA Title III Lawsuits*, Seyfarth Shaw (20 February 2020), https://www.adatitleiii.com (last visited 19 April 2020).

18 42 U.S.C. § 12182.

19 Minh N. Vu et al., *supra* note 16.

> Others point to the way websites have developed. In many cases, as websites have become more sophisticated, access to them has actually worsened.[20]

In this continually evolving area of website accessibility, it is difficult to define liability exposure clearly. On 20 June 2018, 103 members of the House of Representatives wrote a letter requesting that Attorney General Jeff Sessions

> state publicly that private legal action under the ADA with respect to websites is unfair and violates basic due process principles in the absence of clear statutory authority and issuance by the department of a final rule establishing website accessibility standards.[21]

The letter asserts that

> unresolved questions about the applicability of the ADA to websites as well as the department's abandonment of the effort to write a rule defining website accessibility standards, has created a liability hazard that directly affects businesses in our states and the customers they serve.[22]

On 25 September 2018, the U.S. Department of Justice Office of Legislative Affairs responded to the Congressional request by first reminding Congress that on 26 December 2017, the Department of Justice published a Notice of Withdrawal of Four Previously Announced Rulemaking Actions in the Federal Register and that two of those rulemakings related to website accessibility.[23]

> The first withdrawn rulemaking (RIN 1190-A61) covered accessibility of web information and services of public accommodations. The second withdrawn rulemaking (RIN 1190-AA65) covered accessibility of web services of state and local governments.[24]

The Office of Legislative Affairs letter further explained that the department first articulated its interpretation that the ADA applies to public accommodation websites

---

20 Ted Vezner, *Minnesota Sees First Website Access Suit*, Pioneer Press (29 April 2020), https://www.twincities.com/2018/10/07/minnesota-websites-sued-lawsuit-disability-advocates/.

21 Letter from the Congress of the United States, to Attorney Gen. Jeff Sessions (20 June 2018), https://www.adatitleiii.com/wp-content/uploads/sites/121/2018/06/ADA-Final-003.pdf.

22 *Id.*

23 Letter from the U.S. Dep't of Just., Office of Legis. Aff., to Rep. Ted Budd (25 September 2018), https://www.adatitleiii.com/wp-content/uploads/sites/121/2018/10/DOJ-letter-to-congress.pdf.

24 *Id.*

over 20 years ago, which is consistent with the ADA's Title III requirement of equal accessibility for persons with disabilities.[25] The letter, however, then stated:

> Absent the adoption of specific technical requirements for websites through rulemaking, public accommodations have flexibility in how to comply with the ADA's general requirements of nondiscrimination and effective communication. Accordingly, noncompliance with a voluntary technical standard for website accessibility does not necessarily indicate noncompliance with the ADA.[26]

Thus, for the moment, noncompliance with commonly accepted, but privately promulgated, web content accessibility standards[27] may not necessarily result in ADA liability. With the recent confirmation of Supreme Court Justice Brett Kavanaugh, I believe that the Court has become more firmly conservative. As a result, the Court may not require businesses to comply with currently available, privately promulgated digital accessibility standards. This chapter will revisit the question of what digital accessibility standards are legally required. But suffice it to say that the sands are continually shifting.

I prefer the carrot to the stick, however. Although the threat of legal liability for failing to satisfy well-respected privately promulgated standards is still real, making a website digitally accessible will make it easier for everyone to use and may attract new users. It is simply a good business decision.

3 People with Disabilities May Need to Access Technology Differently

Any discussion of accessibility must start with the people who depend on it: individuals with disabilities. Technology provides unprecedented potential for social and civic participation and engagement by persons with disabilities. Persons with disabilities can use digital tools, but only when websites, mobile applications, conferencing platforms, and other technologies are designed and developed with accessibility in mind.

One of the challenges when it comes to accommodating disabilities is the range of differences among disabilities. People with disabilities need to access ODR systems in a variety of ways. For instance:

- Not everyone can hear. Accessible websites and mobile apps must provide captions for all video content.

---

25 *Id.*

26 *Id.*

27 One example of standards is the WCAG 2.1 Guidelines developed by the Web Accessibility Initiative (WAI) of the World Wide Web Consortium (W3C). *Web Content Accessibility Guidelines 2.1*, World Wide Web Consortium (5 June 2018), https://www.w3.org/TR/WCAG21/.

- Visually impaired individuals may be able to hear video content, but they may not be able to find the video player on the page, operate the controls, or adjust the volume. Video will be useless for visually impaired individuals unless it is accessible.[28] If equivalent alternative text ('alt text') is not provided for all images, then any information communicated through images will be inaccessible for persons who use screen readers.[29] Individuals without vision impairments who turn off video and images because they have low or expensive bandwidth also will benefit from alt text.[30] Audio description is another valuable accessibility service that will augment the audio portion of a presentation with essential information when the video portion is not available.[31]

During existing pauses in dialogue, audio description provides information about actions, characters, scene changes, and on-screen text that are important and are not described or spoken in the main soundtrack.[32]

- Many people have difficulty using a mouse. Instead, they rely on a standard keyboard or on a specialized keyboard that allows characters to be entered with one hand like a chord on a piano. Some people with disabilities cannot use their hands but instead rely on a mouth stick or eye tracking to input data. Voice recognition software (like Dragon Dictate) allows for voice-activated input. A variety of assistive technologies are available.[33] These alternative input methods may not work unless a site (including an ODR system) is designed and developed with accessibility standards that, among other things, require all functionality to be available without use of a mouse.[34]
- Some people with visual impairments either cannot see color at all or cannot distinguish between certain colors. In fact, one out of every twelve men is color blind.[35] Developers and designers should not use color as the only means of conveying information. When using color to differentiate elements, provide additional identification that does not rely solely on color perception. Use an asterisk in addition to color to indicate required form fields, for example, and use

28 *Id.*

29 *Id.*

30 Tim Berners-Lee, *Accessibility*, World Wide Web Consortium (W3C), https://www.w3.org/standards/webdesign/accessibility (last visited 29 April 2020).

31 *Understanding Success Criterion 1.2.5: Audio Description (Prerecorded)*, Web Accessibility Initiative, https://www.w3.org/WAI/WCAG21/Understanding/audio-description-prerecorded.html (last visited 29 April 2020).

32 *Id.*

33 *See Motor Disabilities: Assistive Technologies*, WebAIM, https://webaim.org/articles/motor/assistive#intro (last visited 12 October 2012).

34 To experience what inaccessibility feels like, readers are encouraged to put away a mouse for 15 minutes and use only the space bar; tab and enter keys; and up, down, left, and right arrows to navigate a webpage. Readers will quickly discover which site owners have thought about accessibility.

35 *Colour Blindness*, Colour Blind Awareness, http://www.colourblindawareness.org/colour-blindness/ (last visited 29 April 2020).

labels to distinguish areas on graphs.[36] Light gray text on a white screen may be difficult to read for many viewers. Accessibility principles embrace color contrast requirements that enhance readability for everyone.[37]

- Accessible websites are well-advised not to have blinking and flashing content, simply because many users find it distracting or annoying.[38] More importantly, a website with these features may be unusable for people with epilepsy or certain cognitive disabilities.[39]

Around the world, consistently higher numbers of people will access ODR systems from mobile devices than traditional home broadband service. An impressive 95% of Americans now own mobile phones, 77% own smartphones, and among those 77%, one-in-five accesses the internet only through his or her smartphone.[40] As they can with computers, disabled people can access mobile devices – even without a keyboard – assuming websites and applications are designed to mobile accessibility standards.

Both Apple and Android publish accessibility standards so developers can build applications that work for everyone. General guidance and specific information about building accessible websites are available at Accessibility on iOS[41] and Accessibility on Android.[42]

4 Accessibility in ODR

Regardless of whether ODR systems are developed by large corporations, small businesses, neutrals who work independently, or courts, all systems should become aware of, and comply with, generally accepted digital accessibility standards. Sir Tim Berners-Lee, inventor of the World Wide Web, put it succinctly when he spoke at the 1997 launch of the web accessibility initiative: "The power of the Web is in its universality. Access by everyone regardless of disability is an essential aspect."[43] Every

36 *Tips for Getting Started Designing for Web Accessibility*, Web Accessibility Initiative (9 January 2019), https://www.w3.org/WAI/tips/designing/.

37 *See Accessible Technology: Providing Sufficient Color Contrast*, Univ. of Wash., https://www.washington.edu/accessibility/checklist/contrast/ (last visited 29 April 2020).

38 *Id.*; *Accessible Technology: Avoiding Flashing or Flickering Content*, Univ. of Wash., https://www.washington.edu/accessibility/checklist/flashing-content/ (last visited 29 April 2020).

39 *Accessible Technology: Avoiding Flashing or Flickering Content*, *supra* note 38.

40 *Internet & Technology: Mobile Fact Sheet*, Pew Research Ctr. (5 February 2018), http://www.pewinternet.org/fact-sheet/mobile/.

41 *Accessibility on iOS*, Apple Inc., https://developer.apple.com/accessibility/ios/ (last visited 29 April 2020).

42 *Accessibility Overview*, Android, https://developer.android.com/guide/topics/ui/accessibility/ (last visited 29 April 2020).

43 *World Wide Web Consortium Launches International Program Office for Web Accessibility Initiative*, World Wide Web Consortium (22 October 1997), https://www.w3.org/Press/IPO-announce.

element of ODR information and communications technology – systems, content, and processes – must be accessible for ODR to be truly universal.

Although many of us may think about alternative dispute resolution (ADR) and ODR as distinct processes, ODR is merely a form of ADR. In fact, the label 'Online Dispute Resolution (ODR)' is a little misleading. When most practitioners use the term ODR, they typically are referring to dispute resolution processes that not only rely on the internet but also may be supported or assisted by other technologies. This so-called ODR process may be supplemented by face-to-face contacts. A more accurate term may be 'technology-assisted dispute resolution,' but the term ODR is typically used.[44]

'Technology' includes everything from telephones to websites, mobile apps, electronic meeting rooms, fax machines, mobile devices, and Near Field Communication. Dispute resolvers have been using some of these technologies 'offline' for decades and they are an essential part of dispute resolution practices.

ODR system designers may encourage parties to keep every communication on the ODR platform for reasons such as confidentiality and accountability. Dispute resolution professionals, however, may prefer to use online tools along with 'offline' technologies, such as the telephone or even a possible in-person meeting. Although a dispute resolution process may combine online and offline communications or have several stages that progress from negotiation to mediation to arbitration, there nonetheless are ODR systems that allow parties to complete the negotiation stage entirely online.[45]

All technologies and communication options, whether offline or online, must be accessible. One advantage of a dispute resolution process that is entirely online is that all the online interactions can be designed and monitored for accessibility.

One of the goals of ODR has been improving access to justice. I am the System Designer currently working with the New York State Unified Court System to create an ODR process that will be fully integrated into the official court system. We began working on this project because the New York state courts recognized that the default judgment rate in credit card debt collection cases was disturbingly high. The New Economy Project has reported, for example, that the default judgment rate in several New York City zip codes was more than 90%.[46] Several reasons contribute to the low debtor participation rate, including allegations of 'sewer service' (false claims of legal service) and massive 'robo-signing' of fraudulent documents that are submitted to the

---

44 Another acronym I proposed years ago is TMDR (Technology Mediated Dispute Resolution). *See* David Allen Larson, *Technology Mediated Dispute Resolution (TMDR): A New Paradigm for ADR*, 21 Ohio St. J. on Disp. Resol. 629 (2006); David Allen Larson, *Technology Mediated Dispute Resolution (TMDR): Opportunities and Dangers*, 38 U. Tol. L. Rev. 213 (2006).

45 *See* Modria, https://www.tylertech.com/products/modria (last visited 6 November 2018); Smartsettle, https://smartsettle.com/ (last visited 6 November 2018).

46 *The Debt Collection Racket in New York*, New Economy Project 5 (June 2013), https://www.neweconomynyc.org/wp-content/uploads/2014/08/DebtCollectionRacketUpdated.pdf.

court.[47] The Office of Court Administration was directed to explore the possibility of designing an ODR system that would increase debtor participation rates in debt collection cases. The hope was that an official online court process would address and improve some of the fraudulent service and document-signing concerns. In addition to these benefits, an ODR system would also encourage debtors who do not have vacation days and could not afford to attend a court hearing, or who were intimidated by the prospect of appearing before a judge, to participate in the debt collection process.[48]

Some of the same reasons for integrating an ODR process into the New York State Unified Court System apply when we consider whether an ODR process can improve access to justice for persons with disabilities. Persons with disabilities may have the same lack of vacation time, financial concerns, transportation challenges, and intimidation challenges facing credit card debtors and, in fact, many other types of civil justice defendants. Just as we must ensure that an ODR system has a literacy level appropriate for the vast majority of the population, we must ensure that any ODR system is digitally accessible for persons with disabilities.

There are distinct aspects of an ODR system that require attention so that 'everyone regardless of disability' will be able to fully participate.

- **Home Page**: The home page is the landing page – the user's first interaction with the ODR system. It must be understandable and engaging. If any users cannot understand the first steps that must be taken, or if persons with disabilities immediately are confronted with inaccessible features, then users quickly may abandon the process and never return.
- **Dashboard**: The dashboard is the control center for an ODR platform, where information needed to understand the platform is organized and presented. Just as a driver cannot safely drive a car without understanding its dashboard, an ODR participant will not be able use the platform without understanding its dashboard. An inaccessible dashboard means the ODR system will fail.
- **Participants**: Accessibility is too often thought of only in terms of the end user – in our case, the parties to a dispute. But any system participant may need accessibility. Neutrals, court clerks, attorneys, or systems administrators may be disabled. Computer users with disabilities may be anywhere (and everywhere) in the process.
- Authentication: Security and confidentiality require that each person on the ODR platform is the person that he or she claims to be, or is someone authorized to act on that person's behalf. Authentication is a critical issue when we use technology to resolve disputes. The process or procedures we use to confirm identity must be accessible. Alternative authentication processes must be available. An ODR system

47 *Id.*, at 1.

48 *See* David Allen Larson, *Designing and Implementing a State Court ODR System: From Disappointment to Celebration*, 2019 J. Disp. Resol. 77 (2019), available at http://ssrn.com/abstract=3399778.

cannot rely only on items or documents that persons with disabilities may not possess, such as a driver's license.

- **Conferencing Platform**: Conferencing accessibility may be essential to an ODR system. Careful attention must be paid to ensure that everyone has an equal opportunity to participate in video or audio-only conferences. Key aspects of platform accessibility include:
- Effective communications for deaf and hard of hearing participants, including captions and/or sign language interpreters. Video remote interpreting, if used, must be carefully monitored and follow best practices.[49]
- Audio description, for blind participants, to describe visual elements of any video content introduced during the conference.
- Accessibility of the video conferencing platform itself. All functionality must be accessible, including chat windows, sign-in, volume control, and mutability.

Specialized vendors are available to assist with ensuring accessible conferencing platforms.[50] Careful vetting for experience is critical and references should always be obtained.

- **Email:** As with all forms of communication that comprise ODR systems, email systems must be coded to accessibility standards and tested as per the best practices, such as those identified by Email Monks.[51]
- **Chat Programs**: Any chat program used to share or provide information must be accessible. (This may be either within or independent from the conferencing platform.)
- Digital Signatures: If parties are expected to sign documents as part of an ODR process, care must be taken to ensure that electronic signature software is usable by everyone. eSign Live, for example, enables blind and visually impaired signers to review and sign documents in accordance with WCAG 2.0 Level AA.[52]
- Electronic Documents: Documents are essential to most legal processes, and ODR is no exception. If system users and administrators can download documents, the downloading tool must be usable by all. The documents themselves must be

49 *See Remote Interpreting Guide for Courts and Court Staff*, National Center for State Courts (June 2014), http://www.courts.ca.gov/documents/COS-VRILAP-MDS-080816-attachment-7.pdf.

50 *See, e.g.*, Zoom, https://zoom.us/accessibility (last visited 6 November 2018); BlueJeans, https://www.bluejeans.com/accessible-online-video-conferencing-features (last visited 6 November 2018).

51 *See* Kevin George, *Accessible Emails: How to Design and Code Them the Right Way*, Email Monks (11 January 2018), https://emailmonks.com/blog/email-design/accessibility-in-emails/.

52 Harris Haidary, *eSignLive Release 11.2: Accessibility Support*, eSignLive (7 March 2008), https://www.esignlive.com/blog/esignlive-release-11-12-accessibility-support *see ESRA Recommendation: The ADA and Electronic Signatures*, Elec. Signature and Records Ass'n, https://esignrecords.org/esra-recommendation-ada-electronic-signatures/ (last visited 29 April 2020).

readable by all participants. PDF/UA is the ISO standard for universal accessibility ensuring PDF documents are available to the largest audience of readers possible.[53] Documents generated in Word, Excel, and of course HTML can be made fully accessible – including all aspects of those documents such as complex data tables and other visual elements.[54]

- **Phone Systems:** As mentioned earlier, ODR processes may rely on web-based communications as well as older technologies such as telephones. All participants must be familiar with Telecommunication Relay Services (TRS) – federally established communication systems that allow deaf and hard of hearing people, as well as people with speech disabilities, to place, receive, and participate in phone calls. As the U.S. Federal Communications Commission states on its website:
- If you hear, 'Hello. This is the relay service …' when you pick up the phone, please don't hang up! You are about to talk, through a TRS provider, to a person who is deaf, hard-of-hearing, or has a speech disability.[55]
- To allow deaf and hard of hearing individuals and people with speech disabilities calling via TRS to have full and equal participation in telephone discussions, all ODR participants must be mindful of the time lags that naturally result when spoken English is being translated into ASL or transcribed into English, and vice versa.
- **Architectural Accessibility**: When ODR mediations, arbitrations, or meetings are held in the physical environment, that environment must be accessible to people with physical disabilities. This not only means that the meeting room(s) must be wheelchair accessible, for example, but also that the restrooms must be. If the meeting host (mediator, lawyer, etc.) does not typically operate in an accessible space, policies must be in place to hold the meeting, mediation, or arbitration in an accessible space.[56]
- The physical location, the documents, and the technology employed at that location must all be accessible. If a mediator, arbitrator, or other third-party neutral hands out a paper copy of a confidentiality statement, for example, or uses technology to summarize or illustrate progress that is being made during an in-person meeting, that information must be presented in an accessible manner.
- Given the difficulty one often encounters when trying to locate and reserve a meeting place, this obviously should not be left to the last minute. Arrangements should be in place in advance.

53 *PDF/UA: The ISO Standard for Universal Accessibility*, PDF Ass'n, https://www.pdfa.org/pdfua-the-iso-standard-for-universal-accessibility/ (last visited 29 April 2020).

54 *Id.*

55 U.S. F.C.C., *Telecommunications Relay Service – TRS* (8 September 2017), https://www.fcc.gov/consumers/guides/telecommunications-relay-service-trs.

56 *See A Planning Guide for Making Temporary Events Accessible to People with Disabilities*, ADA National Network (2015), https://adata.org/publication/temporary-events-guide.

- Sign Language Interpreters and Other Communication Services: It was previously explained that ODR systems often rely upon both online and offline communications and that it is crucial for digital conferencing platforms to be accessible for participants who are deaf or have hearing limitations. When meetings are held in a physical location as part of a primarily ODR process, disability accommodations also must be provided. Sign language interpreters or Real-Time Captioning, known as CART (Communication Access Real-time Translation), must be available to those who need it.[57]
- Alternative Formats for Paper Copies: When ODR interactions occur in person, anything distributed in paper format must be made accessible to people who cannot read standard print. Alternatives to print (known as alternative formats) include Braille, large print, and accessible electronic formats. The person needing the accommodation should be consulted to determine effective alternative formats.[58]

5 Relevant Law

The Introduction already described the most recent developments concerning ADA Title III web accessibility litigation. A complete analysis of the legal foundation for accessible ODR platforms, systems, and content is beyond the scope of this chapter. The following material provides examples from around the world of laws and policies mandating accessibility that apply to ODR systems design.

5.1 *International Efforts*

The United Nations Convention on the Rights of People with Disabilities (CRPD)[59] is a treaty ratified by more than 170 nations (although not by the United States) that includes obligations for digital accessibility. Among other things, Article 9 requires signatories to "promote access for persons with disabilities to new information and communications technologies and systems, including the Internet."[60] Article 21 includes the obligation of

> [a]ccepting and facilitating the use of sign languages, Braille, augmentative and alternative communication, and all other accessible means, modes and formats

57 *See, e.g.*, QuickCaption, http://www.quickcaption.com/.
58 *See generally* June Kailes, *Accessible Meetings, Events, and Conferences, A Guide to Planning Accessible Meetings*, The Mid-Atlantic ADA Center and TransCen Inc., https://www.adahospitality.org/accessible-meetings-events-conferences-guide/book (last visited 21 March 2021).
59 G.A. Res. 61/106, annex, United Nations Convention on the Rights of Persons with Disabilities (CRPD) (24 January 2007).
60 *Id.* at Art. 9.

of communication of their choice by persons with disabilities in official interactions.[61]

Article 13 ensures effective access to justice for persons with disabilities.[62]

Governing bodies around the world increasingly are mandating that digital properties and content be accessible. The Accessibility for Ontarians with Disabilities Act,[63] for example, which applies to both private and public sectors in Ontario, Canada, requires websites to meet WCAG 2.0. WCAG 2.0 identifies three different levels of adherence (A, AA, AAA), and by 21 January 2021 covered entities must meet essentially all the requirements of AA.[64] The Web Accessibility Initiative of the World Wide Web Consortium (W3C) maintains a list of international accessibility laws and policies.[65]

5.2 ADA Title III

In addition to the recent ADA Title III litigation and regulation developments discussed earlier, it is important to recognize that United States courts have determined that the Americans with Disabilities Act (ADA) does apply to websites. The United States District Court for the Eastern District of New York, for example, could not have said it more clearly than it did in *Andrews v. Blick Art Materials, LLC* when it stated that "[i]t is unambiguous that under Title III of the ADA, dickblick.com [the retailer's website] is a place of public accommodation."[66] *Andrews* relied in part on *National Federation of the Blind v. Scribd Inc.*, which held that Title III of the ADA covers the website of a company without any physical locations.[67]

Andrews reveals that there is a disagreement among United States courts, however, as to whether a website must be affiliated with a physical location to be covered under ADA Title III.[68] In *Magee v. Coca-Cola Refreshments USA, Inc.*, the United States Court of Appeals for the Fifth Circuit noted that the First Circuit and Seventh Circuit have interpreted the words 'public accommodation' in ADA Title III to extend beyond

61 *Id.* at Art. 21.

62 *Id.* at Art. 13.

63 Accessibility for Ontarians with Disabilities Act, 2005, O.S. 2005. C. 11, https://www.ontario.ca/laws/statute/05a11 (last visited 29 April 2020).

64 Integrated Accessibility Standards, Ontario Regulation 191/11, s. 14(3), https://www.ontario.ca/laws/regulation/110191#BK14 (last visited 29 April 2020).

65 *Web Accessibility Laws & Policies*, World Wide Web Consortium (21 March 2018), https://www.w3.org/WAI/policies/.

66 *Andrews v. Blick Art Materials, LLC*, 268 F. Supp. 3d 381, 393 (E.D.N.Y. 2017).

67 *Nat'l Fed'n of the Blind v. Scribd Inc.*, 97 F. Supp. 3d 565 (D. Vt. 2015).

68 *Id.* at 388-394.

physical places.[69] In contrast, the Third, Sixth, and Ninth Circuits have determined that a physical location is a requirement for ADA Title III coverage.[70]

I believe that the better view is that ADA Title III should cover all websites, regardless whether they are affiliated with a physical location. As Americans continue to depend more frequently on websites to deliver services and goods, those websites increasingly will be perceived as 'places.' In addition to our common understanding of what constitutes a 'place,' we cannot forget that the ADA is a remedial statute that must be given a broad interpretation.[71]

The *Andrews* court provided additional reasons as to why a physical location is not a prerequisite. The court observed that Title III is called 'Public Accommodations and Services Operated by Private Entities,' not '*Places* of Public Accommodation and Services Operated by Private Entities.'[72] Additionally, the title of Section 42 U.S.C. § 12182, which prohibits discrimination, is 'Prohibition of Discrimination by Public Accommodations,' not 'Prohibition of Discrimination by or in *Places* of Public Accommodation.'[73] Furthermore, the categories of private entities covered by 42 U.S.C. § 12181(7) are listed under 'Public accommodation,' not '*Places* of public accommodation.'[74] On the one hand, when ADA Title III describes the public accommodations covered by the law, it uses a variety of words, including 'place,' 'office,' and 'establishment.'[75] On the other hand, when describing the entities that sell goods and provide services to the public, the statute never uses the word 'place,' making it evident that it covers every 'sales or rental establishment' and 'service establishment.'[76] Although the statute defines 'public accommodation,' it never defines 'place' nor 'place of public accommodation.' This difference indicates that the word 'place' was not intended to limit the statute's reach, but 'that Congress likely used the word "place" because there was no other less cumbersome way to describe businesses that offer those particular goods or services to the public.'[77]

As convincing as that may sound, as President Donald Trump continues to appoint new federal judges who are more conservative, those judges may adopt a narrow version of the ADA Title III 'public accommodations' definition and decide that a website must be affiliated with a physical location. *National Federation of the Blind* summarizes the argument as to why the term 'public accommodations' must require a physical location:

---

69 *Magee v. Coca-Cola Refreshments USA, Inc.*, 833 F.3d 530, 534 n.23 (5th Cir. 2016).

70 *Id.*

71 *Noel v. New York City Taxi & Limousine Comm'n*, 687 F.3d 63, 68 (2d Cir. 2012).

72 *Andrews v. Blick Art Materials, LLC*, 268 F. Supp. 3d 381, 393 (E.D.N.Y. 2017) (citing 42 U.S.C. subch. III).

73 *Id.*

74 *Id.*

75 *Id.*

76 *Id.* (citing 42 U.S.C. § 12181(7)(E)–(F)).

77 *Id.* (citing Nat'l Fed'n of the Blind, 97 F. Supp. 3d at 572).

> [T]he canons of *noscitur a sociis* and *ejusdem generis* compel the Court to conclude that Congress did not intend to cover businesses unconnected to any physical space open to the public under Title III. The former doctrine permits the meaning of doubtful terms and phrases to be determined by reference to other associated phrases. The latter suggests that where general words are accompanied by a specific enumeration of persons or things, the general words should be limited to the persons or things similar to those specifically enumerated. ... [B]ecause all of the specific examples in the statute operate at concrete physical locations open to the public, the statute must be construed to apply only to such places.[78]

5.3 WCAG

While specific digital accessibility regulations have not yet been incorporated into the Americans with Disabilities Act, the Web Content Accessibility Guidelines (WCAG) 2.0 and 2.1[79] offer detailed information that can help online dispute resolvers adhere to ADA obligations.[80] At one point there was a possibility that the WCAG would be adopted as regulatory standards. As *Gathers v. 1-800-Flowers.com, Inc.*[81] explains, in 2010 the Department of Justice published an Advanced Notice of Proposed Rulemaking to revise the regulations implementing Title III.[82] In that Advanced Notice of Proposed Rulemaking, the DOJ requested public comment on whether and how the agency should adopt the WCAG as its standard for website accessibility for Title II and III entities.[83] No rule or regulation was ever adopted as a result of the Advanced Notice of Proposed Rulemaking, and in 2015, the DOJ announced that it would pursue separate rulemakings addressing web accessibility for websites falling under Title II and Title III.[84] DOJ added that it planned to address rulemaking for Title II first.[85] Today, there still are not any rules for Title III, because in 2016 the DOJ withdrew the Advanced Notice of Proposed Rulemaking and issued a Supplemental Advanced Notice of Proposed Rulemaking seeking input only regarding websites of entities covered by Title II.[86]

---

78 *Nat'l Fed'n of the Blind v. Scribd Inc.*, 97 F. Supp. 3d 565, 572 (D. Vt. 2015) (citing *City of New York v. Beretta U.S.A. Corp.*, 524 F.3d 384, 401 (2d Cir. 2008)).

79 *Web Content Accessibility Guidelines (WCAG) 2.0 Level AA*, World Wide Web Consortium (11 December 2008), https://www.w3.org/TR/WCAG20/.

80 *See Markett v. Five Guys Enters. LLC*, No. 17-cv-788 (KBF), 2017 WL 5054568 (S.D.N.Y. 2017).

81 *Gathers v. 1-800-Flowers.com, Inc.*, No. 17-cv-10273-IT, 2018 WL 839381, at *2 n.3 (D. Mass. 2018).

82 75 Fed. Reg. 142, 43460 (26 July 2010).

83 75 Fed. Reg. 142, 43465 (26 July 2010).

84 *Gathers*, 2018 WL 839381, at *2.

85 *Id.*

86 *Id.*

The United States District Court for the Southern District of New York did, however, refer to the WCAG standards when denying a motion to dismiss, stating, 'Plaintiff has identified steps that defendant can take to ensure equal access to its website by the blind, such as by using the Web Content Accessibility Guidelines 2.0.'[87] And the DOJ has, at least twice, required entities subject to Title III to adopt measures to ensure that their websites and mobile applications conform, at a minimum, to certain WCAG 2.0 success criteria.[88] But in *Robles v. Domino's Pizza LLC*, the Central District of California noted that in one settlement, the DOJ required the defendants to fashion their website and mobile applications to conform to WCAG 2.0 Level AA Success Criteria, but in the other settlement the DOJ obligated the defendants to comply instead with WCAG 2.0 Level AA or Level A Success Criteria.[89]

The plaintiff in *Robles* had claimed that Domino's website and mobile app did not support screen-reading software and that he and other visually impaired individuals could not customize their pizza toppings, browse, shop, or complete a purchase.[90] Dismissing the plaintiff's cause of action without prejudice, the court explained that the two cited examples highlighted, rather than dispelled, the vagueness concern asserted by defendant and demonstrated why a lack of formal guidance in this complex regulatory arena places those subject to Title III in the precarious position of having to speculate which accessibility criteria their websites and mobile applications must meet.[91] Obviously frustrated with the lack of guidance and the consequent need to dismiss the case, the court called on Congress, the Attorney General, and the DOJ to take action to set minimum web accessibility standards for the benefit of the disabled community, those subject to Title III, and the judiciary. Confronted with the same lack of guidance, other courts may feel constrained to reach the same conclusion. A 25 September 2018 letter from the Office of Legislative Affairs appears to support the position that courts should not adopt privately promulgated standards in the absence of action by the DOJ, but one must keep in mind that at this point it is only a letter.

Significantly, in January 2019, a three-judge panel of the United States Court of Appeals for the Ninth Circuit rejected the Central District's conclusion that Domino's due process rights were violated because the DOJ had not issued online accessibility standards or provided technical assistance to implement those standards. It instead declared that, "[T]he Constitution only requires that Domino's receive fair notice of its legal duties, not a blueprint for compliance with its statutory obligations."[92] The court

87 *Markett*, 2017 WL 5054568, at *2.

88 *Robles v. Domino's Pizza LLC*, No. CV 16-06599 SJO (SPx), 2017 WL 1330216, at *7 (C.D. Cal. 1 August 2017).

89 *Id.*

90 Complaint at 11, Para. 34, *Domino's Pizza*, 2017 WL 1330216, *available at* https://www.courthousenews.com/wp-content/uploads/2019/01/Dominos-Lawsuit.pdf.

91 *Id.*

92 *Robles v. Domino's Pizza LLC*, 913 F.3d 898, 908 (9th Cir. 2019).

stated the DOJ's position that the ADA applies to websites is clear, and that it "does not matter that the ADA and the DOJ fail to describe exactly how any given website must be made accessible to people with visual impairments."[93] The absence of specific guidance is not problematic

> because the ADA and its implementing regulations are intended to give public accommodations maximum flexibility in meeting the statute's requirements. This flexibility is a feature, not a bug, and certainly not a violation of due process.[94]

The court added that its precedent clearly states an absence of specific regulations cannot eliminate statutory obligations.[95] The case was remanded to the district court to determine "whether Domino's website and app provide the blind with effective communication and full and equal enjoyment of its products and services as the ADA mandates."[96]

The United States Supreme Court denied Domino's Pizza's Petition for Certiorari on 7 October 2019, deciding not to review the Ninth Circuit's decision that holding businesses liable under ADA Title III for failing to have an accessible website does not violate the due process rights of public accommodations despite the lack of website accessibility regulations.[97]

5.4 *Section 508 of the Rehabilitation Act*

Section 508 of the Rehabilitation Act of 1973 requires that all United States government technology purchases be accessible.[98] Individual states in the U.S. may have similar procurement statutes. Government purchases of ODR systems, including purchases by court systems, will only increase in the coming years.

6 Best Practices for Digital Accessibility in ODR

Regardless of the exact legal requirements for accessibility to websites generally, it is extremely important that the ODR community focus on digital accessibility at this moment. ODR systems are not only being implemented in the United States; they are

---

93 *Id.* (citing *Reed v. CVS Pharmacy Inc*, No. CV 17-3877-MWF (SKx), 2017 WL 4457508, at *5).
94 *Id.*
95 *Domino's Pizza*, 913 F.3d at 909 (citing *Fortyune v. City of Lomita*, 766 F.3d 1098, 1102 (9th Cir. 2014)).
96 *Id.* at 911.
97 *Domino's Pizza LLC v. Robles,* 140 S.Ct.122, 205 L.Ed.2d 41 (2019).
98 U.S.C. § 794d(a)(1)(A) (2000).

being adopted around the world. The British Columbia Civil Resolution Tribunal (CRT), for instance, accepts small claims cases under five thousand dollars and condominium disputes.[99] The CRT offers two distinct stages. It first offers a 'Solution Explorer,' which is an expert system that educates users about their dispute by asking progressively more detailed and focused questions.[100] Once users are educated about the nature of their dispute, it suggests options for resolution.[101] By August 2018, there had been 43,719 explorations by users attempting to resolve their disputes online.[102] The second stage offered by the CRT is an ODR process where the parties engage with each other to resolve their dispute. By August 2018, the CRT had accepted 7,142 disputes and resolved 4,574.[103] With this level of user engagement, we can expect that ODR increasingly will be used to resolve disputes that previously were addressed in the traditional civil court system.

The following practices will help to make certain ODR systems are accessible:

- **Adopt an Accessibility Standard:** The international standard for web, mobile, and document accessibility is the Web Content Accessibility Guide (WCAG) 2.0 Level AA and 2.1, which both offer the most complete and specific guidance for an ODR system.[104] System authoring tools must also be accessible. The Web Accessory Initiative's authoring tools address this important component of ODR systems.[105]

  The Web Accessibility Initiative – Accessible Rich Internet Applications (WAI-ARIA) was built by W3C to support javascript-generated HTML with semantic meanings to improve the user's experience by, for instance, enabling a button to declare that it will launch a pop-up when pressed.[106]
- **Read and Comply with ODR Principles and Standards:** Although ODR is still in its early stages, significant work is already being done to ensure that ODR increases access to justice for everyone. Much of the attention has focused on differences in power and sophistication that may exist between the disputing parties. Understanding and addressing these concerns will protect everyone, including persons with disabilities.

---

99 Civil Resolution Tribunal, https://civilresolutionbc.ca/ (last visited 29 April 2020).

100 *Getting Started*, Civil Resolution Tribunal, https://civilresolutionbc.ca/how-the-crt-works/getting-started/ (last visited 29 April 2020).

101 *Id.*

102 *CRT Statistics Snapshot, August 2018*, Civil Resolution Tribunal (12 September 2018), https://civilresolutionbc.ca/crt-statistics-snapshot-august-2018/.

103 *Id.*

104 *See Web Content Accessibility Guidelines (WCAG) 2.0 Level AA*, World Wide Web Consortium (11 December 2008), https://www.w3.org/TR/WCAG20/.

105 *Authoring Tool Accessibility Guidelines (ATAG) Overview*, World Wide Web Consortium Web Accessibility Initiative (24 September 2015), https://www.w3.org/WAI/standards-guidelines/atag/.

106 Jack Merideth, *Web Accessibility AKA a11y, and Why It's not Enough to Say "ADA Compliant"*, Callibrity (25 January 2019), https://www.callibrity.com/blog/web-accessibility-why-its-not-enough. Merideth explains that it is preferred to use semantic HTML tagging (*e.g.*: <h1>, <table>) when available, as defined in the very first rule of using ARIA. *Id.*

The International Council for Online Dispute Resolution (ICODR), building on The National Center for Technology and Dispute Resolution's 'Principles for ODR Practice,' has identified Ethical Standards for ODR.[107] Many of these Standards provide support for digital accessibility design features. ICODR believes that quality ODR programs must be:

- **Accessible:** ODR must be easy for parties to find and participate in and not limit their right to representation. ODR should be available through both mobile and desktop channels, minimize costs to participants, and be easily accessed by people with different physical ability levels. (I recommend that the term 'accessible' as traditionally used in the ODR field be expressly expanded to include digital accessibility for persons with disabilities.)
- **Accountable:** ODR systems must be continuously accountable to the institutions, legal frameworks, and communities that they serve.
- **Competent:** ODR providers must have the relevant expertise in dispute resolution, law, technical execution, language, and culture required to deliver competent, effective services in their target areas. ODR services must be timely and use participant time efficiently.
- **Confidential:** ODR must maintain the confidentiality of party communications but also must be transparent regarding (1) who will see what data, and (2) how that data can be used. (I would add that 'there cannot be confidentiality for people with disabilities without accessibility.')
- **Equal:** ODR must treat all participants with respect and dignity. ODR should enable often silenced or marginalized voices to be heard and ensure that offline privileges and disadvantages are not replicated in the ODR process.
- **Fair/Impartial/Neutral:** ODR must treat all parties equally and in line with due process, without bias or benefits for or against individuals, groups, or entities. Conflicts of interest of providers, participants, and system administrators must be disclosed in advance of commencement of ODR services.
- **Legal:** ODR must abide by and uphold the laws in all relevant jurisdictions. (This, of course, includes laws relating to accessibility and nondiscrimination.)
- **Secure:** ODR providers must ensure that data collected and communications between those engaged in ODR is not shared with any unauthorized parties. Users must be informed of any breaches in a timely manner.
- **Transparent:** ODR providers must explicitly disclose in advance (1) the form and enforceability of dispute resolution processes and outcomes, and (2) the risks and benefits of participation. Data in ODR must be gathered, managed, and presented in ways that ensure it is not misrepresented or out of context.

107 ICODR Standards (Int'l Council for Online Dispute Resolution 2011).

- **Designate a Digital Accessibility Coordinator:** Assign someone responsibility for accessibility and think carefully about where they are placed in the management structure. This individual must have the capacity to reach – and be readily available to – all the different departments and geographic locations in the enterprise. To achieve the best possible outcome and move beyond compliance, think broadly and avoid automatic placement in the legal or risk department.
- **Include accessibility in all requests for proposals involving digital content and technology:** The Americans with Disabilities Act prohibits discrimination 'directly, or through contractual, licensing, or other arrangements.'[108] In the context of the digital world, this means making certain all vendors understand accessibility. A simple request that technology vendors 'comply with applicable law' is not enough. Organizations must specify accessibility standards in every request for proposals (RFP) and require testing by disabled people before product delivery. Identify roadmaps or strategic plans for accomplishing accessibility goals before implementing any proposals.[109]
- **Include Accessibility in All Technology Contracts:** Once a contract is awarded, accessibility requirements must be described with specificity. Consider the level of detail demanded for security and privacy requirements, and use that same high standard with accessibility. In *Gil v. Winn-Dixie Stores, Inc.* (currently on appeal and stayed pending a bankruptcy filing), the judge found:

> [T]he fact that third party vendors operate certain parts of the Winn-Dixie website is not a legal impediment to Winn-Dixie's obligation to make its website accessible to the disabled. First, many, if not most, of the third-party vendors may already be accessible to the disabled and, if not, Winn-Dixie has a legal obligation to require them to be accessible if they choose to operate within the Winn-Dixie website.[110]

---

108 42 U.S.C. § 12182(b).

109 *E.g., 2016 Roadmap to Web Accessibility in Higher Education*, 3PlayMedia (2016), https://uwm.edu/adaaac/wp-content/uploads/sites/374/2016/08/2016-Roadmap.pdf.

110 *Gil v. Winn-Dixie Stores, Inc.*, 257 F. Supp. 3d 1340, 1346 (S.D. Fla. 2017); *see also* Lainey Feingold and Eve Hill, *Technology Vendor Contracts and Accessibility: What Every Business Lawyer Should Know*, Business Law Today (19 April 2018), https://businesslawtoday.org/2018/04/technology-vendor-contracts-accessibility-every-business-lawyer-know/.

- **Train Staff (and Maintain Training):** Training staff about digital accessibility is not only about educating coders, designers, and content writers about accessibility standards and accessible design principles. Individuals who design, manage, and maintain ODR systems must also understand how persons with disabilities use computers and other digital devices. Further, they must know how to direct issues to the appropriate person. In her book, *Structured Negotiation, A Winning Alternative to Lawsuits*, Lainey Feingold shares stories about a common problem that leads to structured negotiations and lawsuits: consumers receiving poor customer service from untrained staff. Not surprisingly, staff training was an element of the *Winn-Dixie* court-ordered injunction.[111]
- **Test Your Website:** Use available tools to test for accessibility. WAVE,[112] for example, is a helpful web accessibility evaluation tool developed by WebAIM.org that provides visual feedback about accessibility by inserting icons and indicators into your webpage. Because the analysis is done entirely within the Chrome browser, the valuation of intranet, local, password protected, and other sensitive webpages is secure.[113] Colorblinding[114] simulates the website as a color vision impaired person would see it. This Chrome extension can simulate Red-Blind/Protanopia, Green-Blind/Deuteranopia, Blue-Blind/Tritanopia, Red-Weak/Protanomaly, Green-Weak/Deuteranomaly, Blue-Weak/Tritanomaly, Monochromacy/Achromatopsia, and Blue Cone Monochromacy.[115] Freedom Scientific's Access with Speech (JAWS)[116] can be used to test website accessibility.
- **Adopt Testing Protocols that Include Disabled People:** Ongoing testing is critical to make certain accessibility is maintained. Automated tools can provide useful data but should never be used alone – human input is critical to any testing program. Additionally, testing by individuals with disabilities must be a regular aspect of a digital accessibility testing program.
- **Hire a Consultant when Needed:** Public and private entities must treat accessibility as they would any other aspect of their organization. If in-house expertise is lacking, hire someone to help. Always interview at least two or three potential consultants and check their references. Depending on your specific needs, it may be necessary to hire more than one individual.

---

111 *Winn-Dixie Stores*, 257 F. Supp. 3d at 1351.

112 "WAVE Evaluation Tool," *Chrome Web Store*, Chrome (search performed 29 April 2020), https://chrome.google.com/webstore/detail/wave-evaluation-tool/jbbplnpkjmmeebjpijfedlgcdilocofh?hl=en-US.

113 *Id.*

114 "Colorblinding," *Chrome Web Store*, Chrome (search performed 29 April 2020), https://chrome.google.com/webstore/detail/colorblinding/dgbgleaofjainknadoffbjkclicbbgaa?hl=en-US.

115 *Id.*

116 *JAWS*, Freedom Scientific, http://www.freedomscientific.com/Products/software/JAWS/ (last visited 29 April 2020). Jack Merideth suggests using WAVE, Colorblinding, and JAWS. Merideth, *supra* note 106.

- **Have an Easy-to-Find Accessibility Information Page Linked to Every ODR Page:** An Accessibility Information Page (AIP), also known as an Accessibility Statement, demonstrates an organization's commitment to accessibility. It gives persons with disabilities who encounter a problem a way to address that problem within the organization rather than calling a lawyer or simply being excluded from participation. The European Union Web and Mobile Accessibility Directive requires public sector bodies to publish Accessibility Statements.[117] The UK has recently published requirements for what is needed in the statement.[118]
  Among other things, the page(s) should clearly state the organization's digital accessibility policies and services and include both a phone number and email address (or a simple and accessible form) for a site visitor to report a problem or get help. Most importantly, the person on the receiving end of the phone call or email must be prompt and responsive. Examples of Accessibility Statements in public, private, and academic settings can help ODR providers compose pages.[119]
- **Put Accessibility Enhancements in Release Notes:** ODR providers can let the public know of their accessibility commitment by including enhancements in standard release notes. In a 2016 settlement agreement reached through a structured negotiation, E*Trade agreed to 'include information about accessibility improvements, as applicable, in the release notes for new E*Trade Mobile App releases.'[120]
- **Make Accessibility Part of Appropriate Job Descriptions and Evaluations:** If someone's job includes accessibility responsibility, accessibility should be included in that person's job description and evaluations. This raises consciousness concerning disability and demonstrates to employees that accessibility is an important aspect of their work. If employees understand that accessibility is a component of their job performance evaluations, they will be motivated to identify and remedy problems before they become legal issues.
- **Evaluate Systems:** Digital accessibility concerns go beyond websites and mobile applications. Every stage of an ODR system can raise disability concerns because a person with a disability may be the next ODR disputant, mediator, lawyer, judge, or court or company personnel. Emails often contain accessibility barriers and are overlooked when thinking about website access. Digital services, including services

117 Council Directive 2016/2102, Art. 7, 2016 O.J. (L 327) 1 (EC).

118 *Consultation Information and Questions*, U.K.'s Gov't Dig. Serv. (11 September 2018), https://www.gov.uk/government/consultations/accessibility-of-public-sector-websites-and-apps-new-duties-and-regulations/consultation-information-and-questions#what-organisations-will-have-to-do-to-comply-with-the-directive.

119 *See* Lainey Feingold, *Accessibility Information Pages Show Commitment to All Site Users*, Law Office of Lainey Feingold (12 February 2013), https://www.lflegal.com/2013/02/access-info-pages/.

120 *E*Trade Digital Accessibility Settlement Agreement*, Law Office of Lainey Feingold (21 June 2016), https://www.lflegal.com/2016/06/etrade-agreement/#notes.

increasingly being offered in courthouses and government agencies (that may soon include ODR systems), are typically part of stand-alone kiosks – kiosks that must be accessible.[121]

Different teams may be responsible for different digital aspects of an ODR system, but a holistic approach to accessibility saves money, leverages resources, and ensures that the public is not inadvertently left out of any aspect of the dispute resolution process.

- **Study and Compare Other Plans:** Reviewing plans from other institutions can be helpful and informative.[122]

The goal of these best practices is to create a culture where accessibility becomes an inherent part of all ODR systems. As each new type of technology or information is introduced in the ODR community, accessibility must be present from the beginning as an integral way of doing business and providing both private and government services.

7 HELP IS AVAILABLE

Many accessibility improvements can be implemented by website operators themselves. It is reassuring, however, to know that helpful assistance is readily available. The following is not intended as an endorsement of one consulting service over another, but it is helpful to look more closely at a few providers to become better informed regarding the types of services that consultants offer.

WAVE is a very useful accessibility tool that can be used free of charge. WAVE identifies many accessibility and WCAG errors while also encouraging critical evaluation of web content. WAVE focuses on issues that impact end users, facilitates web content evaluation, and educates about web accessibility.[123] WAVE is developed as a free community service by WebAIM at Utah State University and has been used to evaluate millions of web pages' accessibility.[124]

WAVE Firefox and Chrome extensions can be used to test accessibility directly within your web browser. WAVE Runner service, subscription WAVE API and a stand-alone WAVE API can be used to collect data on many pages. Enterprise-level reporting and tracking of accessibility can be accomplished using the Pope Tech accessibility tool.[125] Further evaluation and consultation will be priced depending on the size and complexity of the task. WAVE is a non-profit organization connected with the Center for Persons

121 *See ADA Kiosks: Accessible Kiosks for Everyone*, Kiosk Group, Inc., https://www.adakiosks.com/ (last visited 21 March 2021).

122 *E.g., Accessibility at PPCC*, Pikes Peak Community College, https://www.ppcc.edu/accessibility-at-ppcc (last visited 29 April 2020).

123 https://wave.webaim.org/ (last visited 29 April 2020).

124 https://wave.webaim.org/about (last visited 29 April 2020).

125 *Id.*

with Disabilities at Utah State University. It is not flashy or sophisticated, but it is cost effective.

UsableNet describes itself as 'a driving force in the world of accessibility and digital transformation.'[126] It reports that it has 500 global engagements and more than 250 clients.[127] It allows clients to test their sites using UsableNet AQA for free.[128] UsableNet builds, repairs, and maintains accessible digital experiences in accordance with the most current accessibility standards from the World Wide Web Consortium, WCAG 2.0 or 2.1. It conducts accessibility audits, remediates inaccessible features, facilitates user testing with the disability community, and certifies digitally accessible companies. UsableNet's accessibility quality assurance team tests user journeys using the most popular screen readers every month or on every new release.[129] It offers an informative, continually updated blog.[130] UsableNet offers two platforms: AQA and Assistive. AQA is a cloud-based platform that identifies accessibility issues and provides tools that clients then can use for remediation.[131] Assistive is a full-service platform that performs all the digital accessibility work for the clients.[132] UsableNet is a highly sophisticated, for-profit organization that has numerous high profile corporations in its portfolio. While very thorough, UsableNet's AQA and Assistive platforms are not cost free.

accessiBe is a fully automated ADA and WCAG compliance solution using AI technology.[133] accessiBe promises compliance with both United States and international standards (WCAG 2.1, ADA, Section 508, AODA, EN 301549, and IS 5568).[134] Using contextual understanding and image recognition, acessiBe's AI scans and analyzes websites to learn what elements and functionality they include and adjusts them to blind users' screen readers. After installing the program on the target website, accessiBe scans and repairs the website every 24 hours to ensure compliance with WCAG 2.1, ADA, and other accessibility standards. Because accessiBe is automated, the cost is significantly lower (currently starting at $490 per year) than programs that are not fully automated, such as UsableNet, and can be fully operational within 48 hours.[135] While the accessiBe website touts high success rates, as a general rule one is well advised to be careful when relying on automation.[136] Incomplete reviews or missed accessibility

126 https://usablenet.com/about-us (last visited 29 April 2020).
127 *Id.*
128 https://usablenet.com/automated-accessibility-testing-tool (last visited 29 April 2020).
129 https://usablenet.com/services/digital-accessibility (last visited 29 April 2020).
130 https://blog.usablenet.com/ (last visited 29 April 2020).
131 https://usablenet.com/technology/aqa (last visited 29 April 2020).
132 https://usablenet.com/technology/assistive-technology-services (last visited 29 April 2020).
133 https://accessibe.com/ (last visited 29 April 2020).
134 *Id.*
135 *Id.*
136 *Id.*

issues are a possibility, although those concerns also are present with non-automated systems.

Monsido combines accessibility compliance with quality assurance and branding management in a single platform.[137] Like many other consulting services, Monsido offers a free scan. Monsido's three service packages include Content Optimization (Ongoing Quality Assurance and Time-saving Error Detection), Optimize & Collaborate (Compliance Solution for Teams and Individuals), and Accessibility & Compliance (The Complete Web Governance Solution).[138] Only the Accessibility and Compliance package provide tools for complying with WCAG.[139] An automated tool scans the site for accessibility concerns and alerts clients of any issues. Monsido then is available for advice via chat, phone, or a 'support request button' regarding remediation.[140] Monsido does not provide the full-service accessibility support available through UsableNet, but it may be more attractive to those looking to consolidate digital tools.

AudioEye will evaluate your website with its machine learning engine built on data from over 40 million remediations.[141] It states that its embedded script will improve and continually track WCAG and ADA compliance.[142] AudioEye offers automated scans, managed services, and integrated third-party platforms to enhance digital accessibility. One unique tool offered by AudioEye is an accessibility toolbar that allows end-users to adjust the client's website to meet the end-user's own specific accessibility needs. An end-user can change contrast and color, font size, and text spacing, for example.

Siteimprove offers both a global website and a website for the United States.[143] Siteimprove describes itself as 'a people-centric software company driven by the desire to simplify website management and make the internet a better place.'[144] It was founded in Copenhagen, Denmark, expanded into ten offices around the world (with more in the works): Amsterdam, Berlin, Copenhagen, London, Minneapolis, Oslo, Paris, Singapore, Sydney, Tokyo, Toronto, Vienna, and Zurich. It has 500 employees working in 14 distinct markets.[145] Like Monsido, Siteimprove offers multiple tools in one platform, including accessibility compliance, data privacy, quality assurance, ads, analytics, search engine optimization, and performance improvement. Siteimprove has automated accessibility testing for websites to identify issues. The platform prioritizes the issues based on severity and responsibility and monitors progress towards accessibility compliance.

137 https://monsido.com/ (last visited 29 April 2020).
138 https://monsido.com/solutions (last visited 29 April 2020).
139 *Id.*
140 *Id.*
141 https://www.audioeye.com/marketplace (last visited 29 April 2020).
142 *Id.*
143 https://siteimprove.com/ (last visited 29 April 2020).
144 *Id.*
145 https://siteimprove.com/en/company/about-us/ (last visited 29 April 2020).

Siteimprove does not appear to provide the full-service accessibility support available through UsableNet, for instance. But it does provide a wide range of supplemental digital tools that may be attractive to clients seeking to consolidate tools.

Although it is a resource focused on education, the National Center on Accessible Educational Materials[146] (AEM Center) offers easy-to-understand suggestions for making websites accessible for everyone. The AEM Center was created to 'support students who need accessible materials and technologies while learning remotely during the COVID-19 crisis.'[147] The AEM Center notes that the Website Content Accessibility Guidelines (WCAG) version 2.1 provide detailed guidance, but also that the guidance is technical in nature and may be difficult to understand and implement.[148] Those Guidelines can be summarized, however, using the acronym POUR. Accessible user experiences should be Perceivable, Operable, Understandable, and Robust.[149]

The AEM Center explains that websites should be designed for accessibility with POUR.[150] A Perceivable website provides alternative text to images and other visuals, transcripts or closed captioning for videos, strong color contrast between text and background, and, importantly, content that does not rely solely on color.[151] An Operable website has a clear structure with properly marked-up headings, descriptive links that explain context, adequate time for interaction and response, and no content that can trigger seizures.[152] An Understandable website clarifies expectations with clear directions and models, ensures a predictable and consistent experience, uses plain language, and identifies the language used for any content.[153] A Robust website will work well with current and future technologies. This can be accomplished by adding metadata that makes content easier to find and use, and by performing accessibility checks and basic assistive technology testing.[154]

The AEM Center provides two helpful documents titled, 'Getting Started with Document Accessibility' and 'Getting Started with Presentation Accessibility.'[155] Both documents advocate using the mnemonic SLIDE, which incorporates the POUR suggestions but also adds that empathy should always drive design.[156]

The AEM Center also provides a list of website accessibility consultants with their contact information. The list does not include all consultants, and web-based service

---

146 http://aem.cast.org/ (last visited 28 April 2020).
147 *Id.*
148 http://aem.cast.org/creating/designing-for-accessibility-pour.html (last visited 28 April 2020).
149 *Id.*
150 *Id.*
151 *Id.*
152 *Id.*
153 *Id.*
154 *Id.*
155 *Id.*
156 http://aem.cast.org/binaries/content/assets/aem/creating-aem/getting-started-with-document-accessibility.docx-2.pdf (last visited 28 April 2020).

providers should invest time to learn what these, as well as other, website accessibility consultants can offer. The AEM Center list includes Accessiblity.Works[157] (ADA and Section 508 WCAG web accessibility compliance consultants), Aditus[158] (accessibility audit for ADA, WCAG, or Section 508), Bender Consulting Services, Inc.[159] (employment of people with disabilities and accessible disability solutions), Bureau of Internet Accessibility[160] (industry-specific solutions to website accessibility since 2001), Deque Systems Inc.[161] (accessibility for good - assessment, remediation, and training), Falling Leaf Productions[162] (campus accessibility liaison for the University of Illinois at Urbana-Champaign; Champaign County, Illinois; Yakima County, Washington), Interactive Accessibility[163] (ADA compliance, Section 508 compliance with VPAT® certification, and WCAG 2.0 compliance), Level Access[164] (secure SaaS platform, developer integrations, analytics and monitoring; ADA, Section 508, WCAG compliance; training), MicroAssist Inc.[165] (accessible e-learning, accessibility audit, training management and curriculum design), Perkins Access[166] (part of Perkins School for the Blind, access workshops, accessible design reviews, unique user testing network), Tech for All, Inc.[167] (web, mobile, and multi-platform applications; kiosk and self-service systems; training; planning and strategy), The Paciello Group[168] (accessibility testing and evaluation, WCAG/Section 508 audits, VPAT® analysis and production, training, user testing and research, design reviews and strategic planning, accessibility management platform ARC), WebAIM[169] (free WAVE web accessibility evaluation tool, accessibility training, strategic web accessibility workshop, technical assistance, evaluation and reporting), WeCo[170] (digital accessibility specialists and trained usability testers for cognitive, hearing, sight, and mobility disabilities, mission-based improving access, increasing awareness of persons with disabilities' capabilities, fostering independence for persons with disabilities, currently 100% of support staff live with a disability).

157 https://www.accessibility.works/ (last visited 28 April 2020).
158 https://www.aditus.io/accessibility-audit/ (last visited 28 April 2020).
159 http://www.benderconsult.com/ (last visited 28 April 2020).
160 https://www.boia.org/ (last visited 28 April 2020).
161 https://www.deque.com/ (last visited 28 April 2020).
162 https://falling-leaf-productions.com/accessibility/index.htm (last visited 28 April 2020).
163 https://interactiveaccessibility.com/ (last visited 28 April 2020).
164 https://www.levelaccess.com/ (last visited 28 April 2020).
165 https://www.microassist.com/ (last visited 28 April 2020).
166 https://www.perkins.org/access (last visited 28 April 2020).
167 http://www.tfaconsulting.com/ (last visited 28 April 2020).
168 https://www.paciellogroup.com/ (last visited 28 April 2020).
169 https://webaim.org/ (last visited 28 April 2020).
170 https://theweco.com/ (last visited 28 April 2020).

8 Conclusion

The Covid-19 pandemic has accelerated the transition of our daily lives to a virtual environment. Online communication may provide the only avenue for contact with the outside world for those of us sheltering at home. When the pandemic is finally under control, it is unclear how much of our former lives will return. It is highly unlikely, however, that our lives will be conducted as they were previously. We will not abandon many of the online behaviors with which we are becoming increasingly comfortable.

It is critical that we remain vigilant and proactive to ensure that everyone can interact effectively online. If we genuinely believe that access is an essential component of any dispute resolution system, then we must act now to ensure that persons with disabilities and other vulnerable populations are not excluded. When accessibility is an afterthought, it can become more expensive and ODR providers may not make the necessary changes. The ODR community must view disability accommodations and digital accessibility not as mere entries in a compliance checklist, but as crucial components of ODR system design.

Chapter 7 Online Dispute Resolution Data Security

Chris Draper

1 Introduction

This chapter provides a high-level introduction to the fundamentals of data security as it applies to online dispute resolution (ODR). It presents concepts, technologies, and techniques in a manner that should offer non-technical practitioners a starting point for understanding how to think about the complex issues within data security. This chapter is not intended to be an exhaustive investigation of any specific technology or technique and should instead be a framework for how to think strategically about data security. Understanding when to seek a more in-depth analysis of any data security technology or technique, versus pulling back to reexamine the fundamental goals and objectives of any technology-enable ODR system, is aided by framing the issues associated with dispute resolution technology (DRTech) more generally as follows:[1]

- **It Is Not Magic.** DRTech's primary utility is the acceleration of communication. There is both opportunity and danger when DRTech outpaces human dispute resolution.
- **The Creator Cannot Be Removed from Its Creation.** Technology can be perfectly and usefully ignorant. It always will learn as it is taught.
- **Technologies are Like Prescription Medications.** When technologies are combined correctly, they can be powerful. When we ignore possible interactions, they can be lethal.
- **Human Minds are Binary.** Our minds are designed to gloss over uncertainty so that we can make 'black and white' decisions in a world that is fundamentally gray. As Kahneman and Tversky found, even people trained to account for uncertainty must routinely fight the natural tendency to view the world in ways that can mimic computers that can see only '1' or '0.'
- **Intuition and Bias are Two Sides of the Same Coin.** Like computers, human minds use data recursively to develop rulesets that develop their paths of learning. When

1 Draper, C.H., "The Dispute Resolution Community Should Actively Craft a DRTech Roadmap to Produce Technology That Will Promote Collaborative Justice," *Theories of Change for the Dispute Resolution Movement: Actionable Ideas to Revitalize Our Movement*, John Lande, ed., 2020. pp. 123-127. Available at SSRN: https://ssrn.com/abstract=3533324 or http://dx.doi.org/10.2139/ssrn.3533324.

these rulesets make us falsely believe things, we label them as bias. When rulesets help us correctly identify problems, we label them as intuition.

- **Imperfect Technologies Can Be Useful.** Too often, people – including those in the dispute resolution community – assume that a technology must be 'perfect' before it can be used. Of course, perfection is not possible. Instead, when considering adopting new technologies, we should compare their relative utility to the human systems they would replace by using the same risks/benefit analysis and standards.

Given this scope and framing, at the end of this chapter one should be able to understand:

- The applicability, similarity, and differences between Data Security, Information Security, and Cyber Security for ODR applications;
- The legal, economic, and ethical relationships between data and information from the perspectives of security, privacy, and confidentiality;
- How to apply risk-based thinking toward the evaluation, operation, and protection of the software tools and packages that make up ODR systems; and
- How to evaluate when a technology selection, or the choice to not replace an existing technology, is ethical.

2 What Are ODR Systems?

This chapter follows the approach taken by organizations such as the International Council for Online Dispute Resolution (ICODR), National Center for Technology and Dispute Resolution (NCTDR), International Mediation Institute (IMI), National Center for State Courts (NCSC), and American Bar Association (ABA) to broadly define **ODR** as *the subset of dispute resolution processes that depend on one or more often internet enabled collaboration technologies.*[2] It is extremely important to note that this definition focuses on ODR as being a collection of technology-enabled human processes. No matter what processes are automated by any specific technology, this chapter considers an ODR system to include all parties involved in an ODR process. Figure 7.1 represents this concept using a squared Venn diagram showing ODR as the intersection of both dispute resolution processes and technology, which can support both distributed and face-to-face parties. An **ODR System** is defined as *any combination of collaboration*

2 It is not clear that the term ODR is appropriate for the modern interpretation of its uses or implementations, notably because there is very little community support for restricting the definition of ODR to only include those processes that occur 'online.' It is the position of this author that ODR as defined by this chapter should instead be considered Augmented Dispute Resolution (ADR) using the same arguments made by NCSC to define AI as 'augmented intelligence' versus 'artificial intelligence.' ODR is used in this chapter instead of ADR to avoid confusion with current practice and traditional community and industry nomenclature.

technologies and human processes that allow parties to meet their individual and collective obligations during ODR.

Figure 7.1 Online Dispute Resolution (ODR)

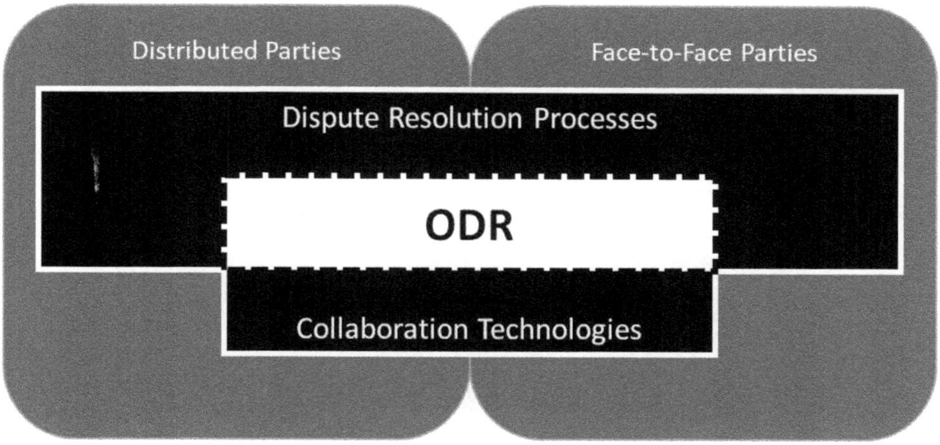

The term 'ODR technology' is purposely avoided to prevent efforts that would classify technologies based upon their usage. For example, Zoom is a video conferencing technology that became unavoidably popular during the 2020 Pandemic after slow adoption during the 2010s primarily by educational institutions and dispute resolution professionals. Zoom's core function is aiding real-time, multiparty collaboration by allowing users to manage video, audio, and text data streams. Zoom would be an 'ODR technology' when used as part of an ODR system during a dispute resolution process. Yet Zoom would not be considered an ODR technology when used for teaching an online class. To avoid confusion, Zoom is considered a **collaboration technology** defined in this chapter as *any tool or service that enables digital data management.*

Effective ODR Systems may be developed by working through the Functional Layer hierarchy presented in Figure 7.2. In this figure, nomenclature on various boundaries is provided to help define that ODR is considered the successful integration of all six functional layers, an ODR System is an assembly of collaboration technologies that meet the needs of the ODR process being automated, and Dispute Resolution Technology (DRTech) are those collaboration technologies within an ODR System that directly support the dispute resolution functions during an ODR process. The ideal development of a successful ODR System should starts by defining the Dispute System Design needed before incorporating a strategy for selecting, integrating, and implementing the tools that meet the needs of the affected communities. Yet technology availability is too often the common driving factor in ODR System Design.

Figure 7.2 Functional Layer Hierarchy for Assessing ODR System Development

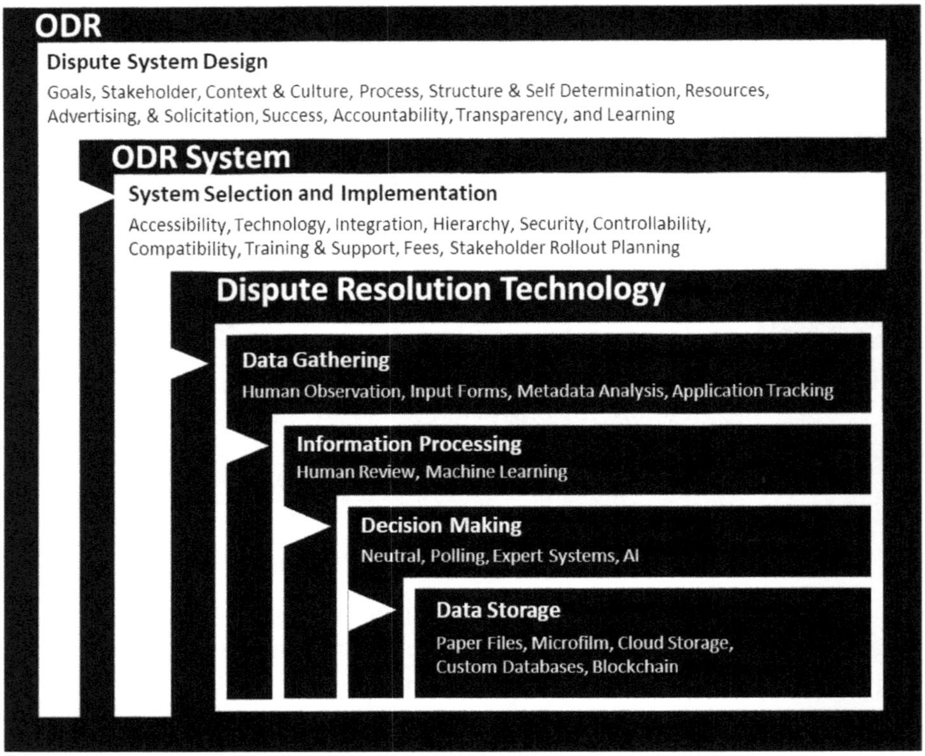

For example, most modern dispute resolution processes finish by writing any agreement down using a word processing software. Most commercially available word processing software, which was originally designed to replicate the creation of a paper file using a typewriter, is well suited for archiving clearly defined agreements. However, the drafting of what will become a final agreement with a word processing software often starts before the agreement is finalized. These draft proposals will often be sent back and forth via email or some other file sharing system. When these drafts are sent back and forth, with tracked changes helping both sides identify differences between drafts, a technology that was originally built to archive information is now being used as a negotiation tool. This use of word processing software to facilitate negotiation affects the following Functional Layers:

- Information Processing, since the parties assess data presented in the documents;
- Data Gathering, since the written proposals will provide data relevant to each party's positions; and
- System Selection and Implementation, since this technology would likely be the primary form of inter-party communication in situations where it is used.

This instance where an ODR System is developed around a specific communication technology will result in reducing the number of Dispute System Designs for which this ODR System could be appropriate. For example, multiparty brainstorming is so difficult to effectively facilitate using documents sent back and forth via email that any dispute system using this communication tool will essentially be unable to include a reasonable brainstorming component. However, fitting a dispute system to the technologies that are available is not uncommon in ODR.

ODR System Designs are currently so dependent on the DRTech used that they will tend to fall into one of the two general types presented in Figure 7.3: *filtering* and *facilitating*.

Figure 7.3 Filtering versus Facilitating ODR

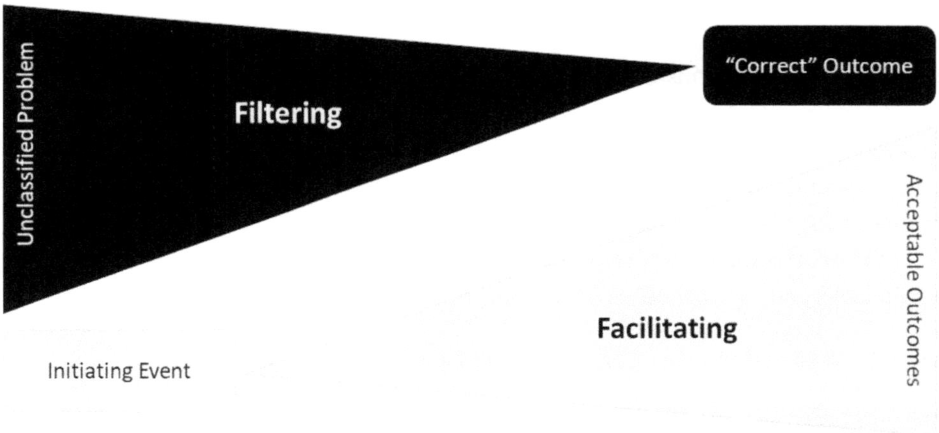

Filtering systems grew out of the ecommerce industry and are often the most recognized ODR technologies due to their court-based integrations by companies like Tyler Technologies or Matterhorn. Filtering systems are defined as *ODR systems that take unclassified problems and bin them into a correct outcome.* Filtering systems typically solve simple, low-value, high-volume monetary disputes involving such things as traffic tickets, eviction orders, or debt defaults. These systems are continually optimized to use expert systems or artificial intelligence (AI) to bin parties into acceptable outcomes[3] as quickly as possible. Filtering systems are most appropriate when the number of potential outcomes are limited, the primary element being disputed is the form of any monetary disbursements owed by one party to another, and all parties are willing and capable of completing any associated dispute resolution processes online.

3 It is important to note that 'acceptable' does not necessarily mean either correct or equitable. The issues that arise when a system constrains future possibilities to past outcomes is discussed more broadly in later sections on artificial intelligence.

Facilitating systems are defined as *ODR systems that take an initiating event and allow any number of parties to collaborate toward any acceptable outcome.* Facilitating systems use technology to help involved parties simply, safely, and securely codify agreements reached through open-ended ADR processes. While there are a few specialty facilitating ODR systems, most incorporate the same collaboration technologies and tools that are used when needed for the more than 98% of tort cases in the United States that do not go to trial in any given year.[4] Most settlement documents that end these tort cases start as standardized templates that, when needed, are modified through tracked-changes documents going back and forth via email or shared folders that are discussed over the phone or in a video conference. Despite the widespread understanding that using this collection of tools is not a secure way to relay sensitive digital data, tens of thousands of complex settlements are negotiated every year using processes enabled by these technologies which have effectively been assembled into rudimentary ODR systems.

These widely used systems are represented by the following hypothetical ODR System referred to as **Basic ODR**. This Basic ODR system is presented as a grounding point for illustrating the concepts discussed throughout this chapter. This type of ODR System is extremely common among small to mid-sized practitioners and often engrained in the operations of large law firms. Basic ODR is typically a collection of human processes and **commercial off the shelf (COTS)** software packages set up by the neutral for internal, permissionable, and external use (Figure 7.4).

Figure 7.4 Basic ODR using COTS software packages

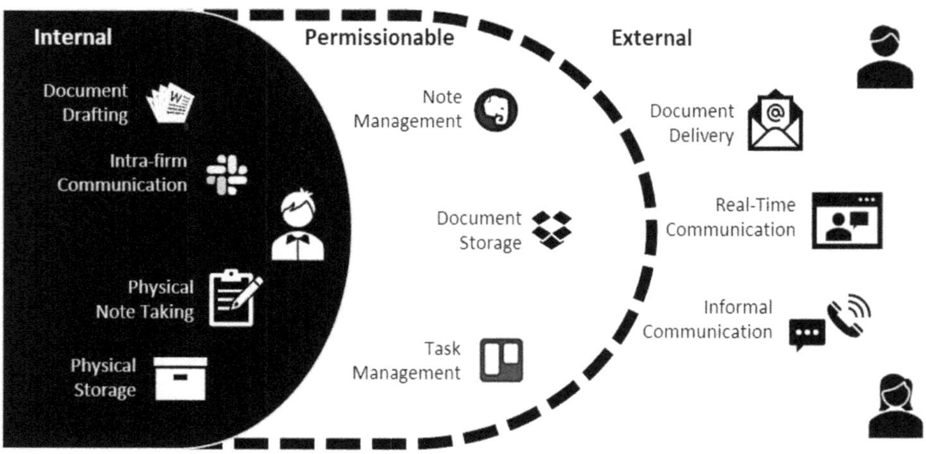

4 It is important to note that, while an ODR System may be made up of the same technologies used in the settlement of tort cases, the use of the same technologies does not make the settlement of a tort case an ODR process. As before, ODR is currently considered any technology enabled ADR process.

In the above diagram, the uses and their components can be summarized as follows:

- **Internal**. These are tools or centralized[5] software packages the neutral does not expect any other party to access. In the diagram above, commonly used examples could include software like Microsoft Word for document drafting, Adobe Acrobat for distilling PDF's, or Slack for communicating with other partners or associates. It also includes physical data collection and storage tools like paper notebooks and filing cabinets.
- **Permissionable**. These are centralized software packages where all parties are invited into a single web-based service with permission levels set by the neutral. In the diagram above, commonly used examples could include Evernote for gathering and sharing meeting notes, Dropbox for sharing files between parties and the neutral, or Trello for creating and assigning tasks or deliverables agreed to in a meeting.
- **External**. These are traditional or centralized communication tools through which parties expect to communicate externally. In the diagram above, commonly used examples could include email for sending documents or messages, Zoom for centralized real-time video-based conferencing, or text messaging for informal communication between one or more parties.

Many of the concepts discussed in this chapter will use data security as the basis for assessing the appropriateness of Basic ODR versus more specialized alternatives. In this chapter, an **ODR sub-system** is defined as *an independent process or software package or platform integrated into the wider ODR system*. The relationship between an ODR System and an ODR Sub-system is presented in Figure 7.5.

Figure 7.5 Relationship between an ODR System and an ODR Sub-system

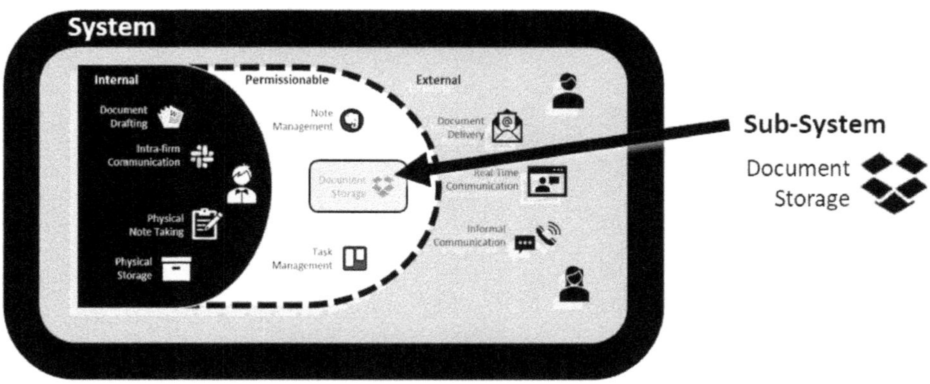

5 Centralized is used here to identify software that brings all parties into the same platform, even if the platform does not use a centralized computing architecture. For example, a software tool may use a distributed computing architecture yet here be considered a centralized software package if all parties are provided access by a single authority, like the neutral, who controls system permissions.

The use of 'independent … software package or platform' does not imply that data will be contained at the sub-system level by default. Basic ODR will rarely transfer data automatically from one ODR sub-system to another. In cases where data is automatically synchronized or linked between ODR sub-systems, it is usually user directed. For example, Dropbox has integration options for letting email services like Outlook reach directly into a Dropbox folder to access a file. Alternatively, Slack has integrations that allow any new file in Dropbox, document in Evernote, or task update in Trello to be shared into a Slack workspace.

These user-directed integrations are intentionally simple to set up and can be extremely useful when correctly managed. Yet their 'simplicity' often leads to syncing that the user may not have expected and can easily lead to accidental privacy or confidentiality breaches. For example, take Microsoft Teams, a software program that competes with Slack to integrate real-time messaging, file sharing, and video collaboration within an organization. If a mediator is using Microsoft Teams for multiple cases and has set up Teams to generate a notification any time an Office 365 file is modified, a simple misconfiguration could lead an uninvolved party to be notified of changes to a client's file. As of 2021, many users still have difficulty auditing the accuracy of sync settings for retail versions of commonly employed ODR sub-systems.

In addition to data sharing through integrations directed by users, independent or centralized systems will also share significant amounts of data in potentially unexpected ways for a variety of reasons. Figure 7.6 represents a generic data, processing, and analytics architecture that is common in independent, centralized platforms. In this example, the platform is available directly to retail users and through enterprise configurations for users controlled by that enterprise customer.

Figure 7.6 Generic Data, Processing, and Analytics Architecture for Common Software Platforms

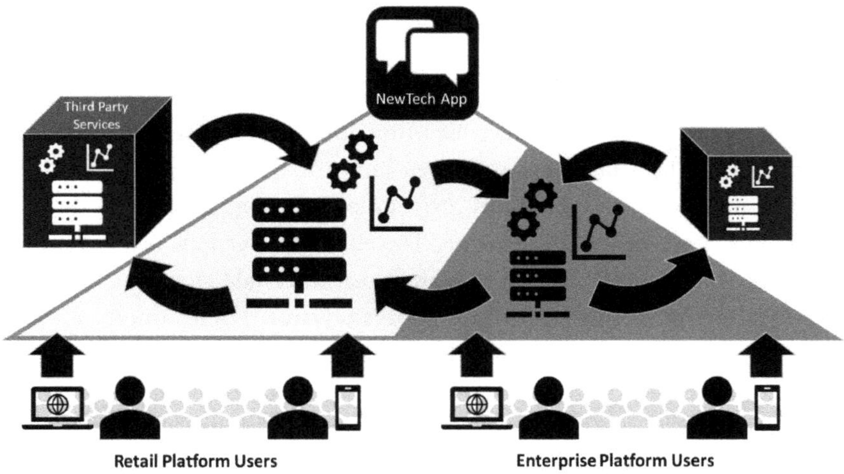

Modern commercial software rarely comes on a disk or CD that loads a piece of wholly contained software onto a single computer. Cloud-based software now routinely offloads processes to third-party services, sending data out to be processed before taking actions based on the third-party outputs that are retuned. For example, 2020 estimates of Amazon Web Services (AWS) adoption indicate that over 100,000 accounts represent enterprise-scale users making up "47.8% in the Infrastructure-as-a-Service sector, along with a share of 25.2% in the Platform-as-a-Service arena."[6] This use of third parties means significant amounts of data are routinely shared, much is at least temporarily stored, and an often unknown amount is retained for system performance analysis.

Very rarely are the data retention and analysis features of many platforms or the third-party services they use currently problematic. However, the extent of data retention and analysis employed by these tools often remains unknown. For example, reporting as of 2020 found that Amazon Alexa was recording and retaining conversations from thousands of homes across the world.[7] Google's "Project Nightingale" was found to have retained medical data on millions of Americans.[8] And for more than a decade it was known that Carrier IQ, whose intellectual property was

6 Saunders, B., "Who" Using Amazon Web Services? [2020 Update]", www.contino.io/insights/whos-using-aws (retrieved 28 March 2020).

7 www.washingtonpost.com/technology/2019/05/06/alexa-has-been-eavesdropping-you-this-whole-time/.

8 www.wsj.com/articles/google-s-secret-project-nightingale-gathers-personal-health-data-on-millions-of-americans-11573496790.

purchased and skilled personnel hired by AT&T in 2015, was logging all keystrokes on the majority of all phones used on American cellphone networks.[9]

Retail users have extremely limited opportunities for controlling where data flows for system performance purposes. Slightly more control is offered to enterprise customers. **Enterprise software** is defined as *software purchased by an organization for its members that is tailored to organizational processes or functions.* Functionally, enterprise software allows a client to modify the features or default settings of a retail software platform to its organizational needs. These tailorings will often limit the types of data the platform owner can retain and control, enabling privacy policies and strategies that are appropriate for the needs of the organization. The enterprise versions of the platform could also include the incorporation of organizational level data storage, analysis, or integration of alternative third-party tools or analytics. For example, a video conferencing tool that is used by an organization which also provides its members WiFi access may record and retain the location data of any cell phone connecting to a video conference for the purpose of optimizing that organization's WiFi network operations.

These unavoidable realities of data sharing and retention within modern technologies should not prevent neutrals from using commercial software as part of an ODR system. Instead, understanding the scope and impact of data control should factor into ODR sub-system selection. Many of the alternatives examined in this chapter may include both full replacements of the overall system, or replacement of sub-systems. For example, the following diagram replaces a mixture of four internal, permissionable, and external sub-system tools with one centralized, permissionable tool (Figure 7.7).

Figure 7.7 Example of Specialized ODR

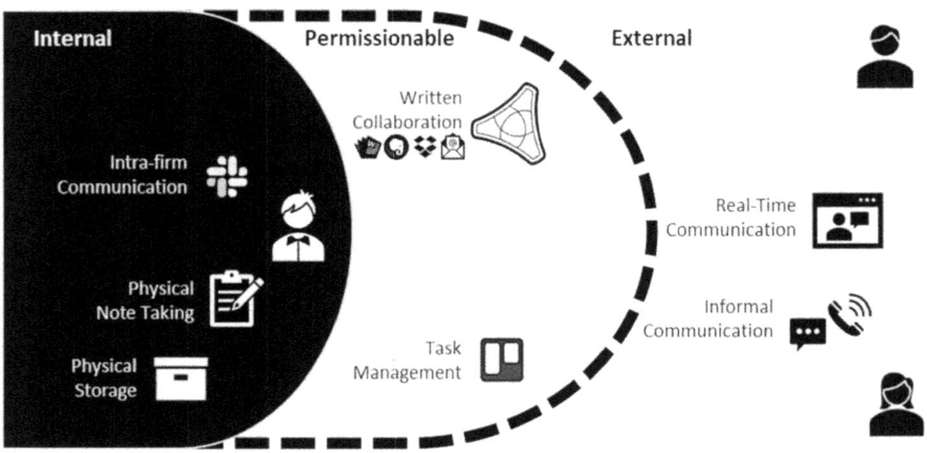

9 https://techcrunch.com/2015/12/30/att-snaps-up-assets-talent-from-carrier-iq-as-phone-monitoring-startup-goes-offline/.

The ODR System above is one example of a modification to Basic ODR that will be referred to in this chapter as **Specialized ODR**. Specialized ODR can vary from small modifications that can be enacted by practitioners like the one above, to custom platforms like those developed and deployed in court systems. This chapter will provide an overview of the principles, strategies, and analytical approaches to assessing when and how ODR Systems should be redesigned to meet modern data security standards.

3 What is Data Security?

Security is a term too often clouded in so much marketing jargon that few people can make meaningful assessments of specific security strategies or their effectiveness. In this chapter, **security** is defined as *the absence of significant, adverse consequences*. It is important to note this definition is not arguing that security can prevent all adverse consequences. This definition supports the argument that achieving security is a continual, iterative process of reducing the frequency and severity of adverse consequences.

Data security is defined as *a set of standards and technologies that protect data from intentional or accidental destruction, modification or disclosure.*[10] This definition addresses both the physical and electronic data commonly managed in Basic ODR. **Cybersecurity** is more limitedly defined as *prevention of damage to, protection of, and restoration of computers, electronic communications systems, electronic communications services, wire communication, and electronic communication, including information contained therein, to ensure its availability, integrity, authentication, confidentiality, and nonrepudiation.*[11] This chapter focuses on data security versus cybersecurity because very few ODR Systems exclusively use electronic files, and cybersecurity is more often associated with repelling malicious attackers than accounting for 'accidental destruction, modification, or disclosure.'

Computer scientists will often consider data security synonymous with **Information Security (InfoSec)**.[12] InfoSec is defined as *the processes and tools designed and deployed to protect sensitive business information from modification, disruption, destruction, and inspection.*[13] In 2020, Cysco considered InfoSec to include the following areas of specialization:

- **Application security** is a broad topic that covers software vulnerabilities in web and mobile applications and application programming interfaces (APIs). These

---

10 Forcepoint, "CYBER EDU," www.forcepoint.com/cyber-edu/data-security.

11 NIST, "Computer Security Resource Center Glossary," https://csrc.nist.gov/glossary/term/cybersecurity.

12 Determan, L., "No One Owns Data," www.hastingslawjournal.org/wp-content/uploads/70.1-Determann.pdf.

13 Cysco, "What is Information Security," www.cisco.com/c/en/us/products/security/what-is-information-security-infosec.html.

vulnerabilities may be found in authentication or authorization of users, integrity of code and configurations, and mature policies and procedures. Application vulnerabilities can create entry points for significant InfoSec breaches. Application security is an important part of perimeter defense for InfoSec.

- **Cloud security** focuses on building and hosting secure applications in cloud environments and securely consuming third-party cloud applications. 'Cloud' simply means that the application is running in a shared environment. Businesses must make sure that there is adequate isolation between different processes in shared environments.
- **Cryptography** is the field of security that includes encryption. Encrypting data in transit and data at rest helps ensure data confidentiality and integrity. Digital signatures are commonly used in cryptography to validate the authenticity of data. Cryptography and encryption has become increasingly important. A good example of cryptography use is the Advanced Encryption Standard (AES). The AES is a symmetric key algorithm used to protect classified government information.
- **Infrastructure security** deals with the protection of internal and extranet networks, labs, data centers, servers, desktops, and mobile devices.
- **Incident response** is the function that monitors for and investigates potentially malicious behavior. In preparation for breaches, IT staff should have an incident response plan for containing the threat and restoring the network. In addition, the plan should create a system to preserve evidence for forensic analysis and potential prosecution. This data can help prevent further breaches and help staff discover the attacker.
- **Vulnerability management** is the process of scanning an environment for weak points (such as unpatched software) and prioritizing remediation based on risk. In many networks, businesses are constantly adding applications, users, infrastructure, and so on. For this reason, it is important to constantly scan the network for potential vulnerabilities. Finding a vulnerability in advance can save your businesses the catastrophic costs of a breach.[14]

This chapter takes a data science view of the relationship between data and information. This data science perspective that differentiates between data and information prevents data security and InfoSec from being directly equivalent. This chapter defines **data** as *discrete, objective facts or observations that are unorganized, unprocessed and without*

14 *Ibid.*

any specific meaning; and **information** as *data that has been shaped into forms that are meaningful and useful*[15] *to human beings.*[16] These definitions mean that a **data breach**, which is defined here as *the intentional or unintentional release of protected data into an untrusted environment*, will not always lead to adverse economic consequences.

For example, an isolated string of nine numerical digits is a discrete data fragment that does not have any known meaning. When two dashes are added after the third and fifth digits, a human being could interpret this string as a United States Social Security number. As more data elements like a name, phone number, address, or personal identification number are associated with the Social Security number, the combination of data elements becomes information of increasing usefulness. The usefulness of these combined data elements could be economically defined in any number of ways. This chapter examines the usefulness of this combination of data elements from the perspectives of:

- the value of any assets associated with those data elements,
- the cost of ensuring access to the associated assets, and
- the cost of compensating anyone for any damages associated with misuse of that combination of data elements.

4 THE VALUE OF DATA

There is significant debate as of 2020 regarding data ownership and how ownership impacts the value of data. Debate focused on data as property generally ranges from interests like Internet of Things (IoT) advocates who argue data cannot be owned because it does not conform to either the letter nor intent of real, personal, or intellectual property rights;[17] to interests like municipalities who believe data is a taxable, tangible asset because it is an "arrangement of matter, physically recorded on some tangible medium, [that] constitutes a corporeal body."[18] For those who do not believe that data value derives from property rights, the European Union's General Data Protection Regulation (GDPR), the California Consumer Privacy Act (CCPA), and a wide range of 'digital dividend' concepts create data value by expanding individual control over reuse of personal data.

15 'Useful' is primarily measured as a function of the information's direct or indirect economic value.

16 Baškarada, S. & Koronios, A., "Data, Information, Knowledge, Wisdom (DIKW): A Semiotic Theoretical and Empirical Exploration of the Hierarchy and Its Quality Dimension," *Australian Journal of Information Systems* Vol. 18, 5, 7 tbl.1, 2013, https://pdfs.semanticscholar.org/5044/b2ae9934230bc336f0353927587d6aa5dc97.pdf?_ga=2.82724182.1184255695.1581964673-997965916.1581964673.

17 Determan, L., "No One Owns Data," www.hastingslawjournal.org/wp-content/uploads/70.1-Determann.pdf.

18 https://law.justia.com/cases/louisiana/supreme-court/1994/94-c-0499-6.html.

No matter the legal framework for why value exists, it is widely accepted that the economic value derived from data usage is now significant. With analyses of the internet and software sector estimating the percentage of corporate value attributed to intangible assets at 87%,[19] the January 2020 market capitalization of FAANG companies (Facebook, Amazon, Apple, Netflix, and Alphabet)[20] indicates the market value of their data alone exceeds $3.5 Trillion. This intangible asset ratio applied to Facebook's 2019 average revenue per user (ARPU) values without compensating for an appropriate percentage of fake user accounts[21] estimates the value that can be derived from just advertising to Facebook users is roughly worth $25 per year.

It is important to understand that these ARPU-based estimates do not represent the value of data from a data security perspective. These values only represent the advertising revenue potential for each user. When Facebook is no longer able to access a user's data, Facebook could estimate the economic impact due to lost advertising revenue as $25 per year. Yet that same data made accessible to the black market via a data breach could easily cost over $1,000 to resolve each instance of fraud or identify theft.[22]

Most data breach statistics focus on the cost of hacking large databases of personal information. During 2019, IBM estimates the average cost per data breach as $8.19 Million for American companies. The global average number of records lost per breach was estimated as 25,575, with data breaches costing organizations with between 500 and 1,000 employees approximately $3,533 per employee to resolve.[23]

Most ODR practitioners will immediately recognize it is extremely unlikely they will cause a breach that releases tens of thousands of personal client records. However, many ODR practitioners are still easily exposing their clients to similar financial risks. For example, it is extremely rare to see construction arbitrators using anything more sophisticated than Basic ODR. Yet in 2015, American Arbitration Association (AAA) panels managed over $5.5 Billion worth of claims and counterclaims at an average of $5.5 Million per case. Alternatively, the median cost of data sensitive intellectual property (IP) litigation in 2017 was over $1.7 Million per case, meaning one fragment of misdirected data could be as costly as the kinds of attacks that make the evening news.

---

19 https://brandfinance.com/news/press-releases/global-intangible-value-exceeds-us50-trillion-for-the-first-time/.

20 www.investopedia.com/terms/f/faang-stocks.asp.

21 www.cnbc.com/2019/11/01/facebook-towers-over-rivals-in-the-critical-metric-of-revenue-per-user.html.

22 www.iii.org/fact-statistic/facts-statistics-identity-theft-and-cybercrime.

23 IMB Guide, www.ibm.com/downloads/cas/ZBZLY7KL?_ga=2.88211291.1135849089.1582011121-615242018.1580845995&_gac=1.242477494.1580845995.EAIaIQobChMI4YuanNa45wIViLzACh3tzAVgEAAYASAAEgItbvD_BwE.

4.1 *Creating Value*

Data is valuable because it can offer useful information when examined in an appropriate context. In the earlier example, it was not until two dashes were added as context to a series of nine numbers that the seemingly useless integer string became a Social Security number. In human interactions, the internal process of applying context is often unconscious or unrecognizable. For example, when discussing an upcoming business trip to Des Moines, most people will associate Des Moines with the state of Iowa more often than they will think of Des Moines, Washington. Beyond these often static, subconscious associations, humans will often dynamically apply context to more complex situations. For example, if a team is mediating a labor dispute where 'Mr. Smith' is introduced as the individual who denied an overtime request, the immediately accessible context could lead the parties to believe that Mr. Smith is a manager with the authority to deny the overtime request being disputed. However, unless the parties recognize and challenge the assumptions made due to the context around Mr. Smith's introduction, the team could just a easily miss a key piece of the dispute once Mr. Smith turns out to be just a coworker who made a misinterpreted, passing comment.

The primary reason data is rapidly becoming more valuable is that its digitized form makes it far easier to contextualize. **Contextualization** is defined as *the process of connecting a data fragment to meaningful context.*[24] The issue above where Mr. Smith may not have actually had his assumed authority could have previously taken hours if not days to resolve. When personnel files were all paper held in filing cabinets, individuals would need to go to the correct filing cabinets and comb through paper files to figure out who Mr. Smith was, which role he was filling on the night in question, and what authority he had on that night. As illustrated in Figure 7.8, data in old, physical formats that must be manually processed it is difficult to combine into meaningful information.

Figure 7.8 Contextualization of Old, Physical Data versus New, Digital Data

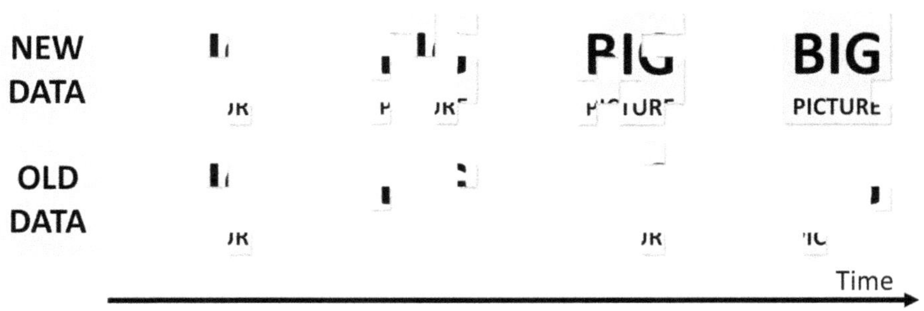

24 Draper, C.H. & Raymond, A.H. "Building a Risk Model for Data Incidents: A Guide to Assist Businesses in Making Ethical Data Decisions," *Business Horizons*, 2019, ISSN: 0007-6813, https://doi.org/10.1016/j.bushor.2019.04.005 (retrieved 7 July 2019).

Those same data fragments in digital form can quickly become breakthrough insights. Assembling digital data fragments into meaningful insight is routinely done with computer science disciplines like AI. AI uses a range of analytical strategies and techniques to rapidly cycle through large amounts of data, test data against a wide array of previously observed contexts, and predict the most likely meaning of new data given its similarity or fit to previously validated estimations.

AI has been generally considered 'the capability of a machine to imitate intelligent human behavior' since the term was coined by John McCarthy at the Dartmouth Summer Research Project on Artificial Intelligence (DSRPAI) in 1956. Broadly speaking, intelligent human behavior is often considered the making of reasonable decisions after gathering, processing, and testing new data against continually improving rules. A system is typically considered an AI system if it is able to generate insights, develop choices, or take actions that had previously required human decision making.

AI systems mimic intelligent human behavior by combining multiple layers of technologies, analytical methods, and learning strategies that allow an artificial system to make decisions regarding an often relatively narrow use case. The nested relationships between examples of technologies, methods, machine learning strategies, and artificial intelligence use cases are seen in Figure 7.9.

Figure 7.9 The Layers of Artificial Intelligence (AI)

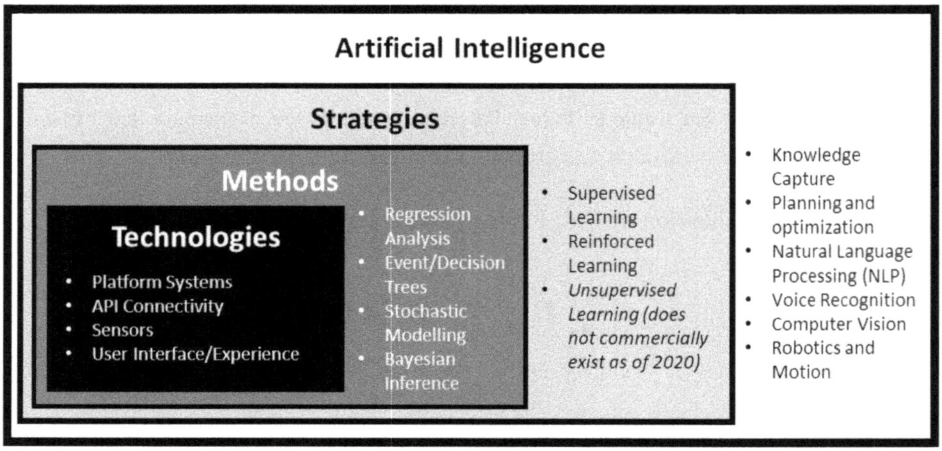

These different components can be combined into a wide range of tools or solutions. For example, a computer vision software (i.e. Artificial Intelligence use case) could use Reinforced Learning algorithms (i.e. Machine Learning strategy) based on Bayesian Inference (i.e. Method) to assess whether an image of a package traveling along a distribution center conveyor belt (i.e. optical Sensors) indicates that the package should be allowed to continue along its currently intended path.

Despite its ability to uncover previously unrecognized trends or relationships, neither AI nor human systems are perfect. Error rates are directly tied to the volume of data accessible to an AI system, yet the risk of inaccurate predictions cannot be overcome by data alone. For example, Figure 7.10 provides an illustration of the basic problem facing computer vision AI.[25] The figure shows two different scenarios where only 40% of the underlying image is visible. While the underlying image is the exact same in both scenarios, each sample showing only 40% of the image could lead to wildly different interpretations of the emotion expressed by the image. On the left side, the 10 out of 25 data points could be used to interpret that the image represents someone who is happy. On the right side, 10 different data points could be used to interpret that the image represents someone who is mad. In many scenarios, it is not clear how many data points are needed for AI to arrive at the 'correct' conclusion. In this example, even the full picture may allow the underlying emotional reality to remain unclear (Figure 7.10).[26]

Figure 7.10 Example of the Interpretation Challenges Given Limited Data

Many of the risks associated with contextualization come from how uncertain data is interpreted. The risks associated with misinterpretation of limited data are fundamentally the same for AI-enabled systems as they are for humans. Both humans and AI use observations of disparate data sources to refine analytical processes in order to make rational decisions. Both use observations of process outputs to make conclusions about unobservable processes. And both use data recursively to develop rulesets that develop their paths of learning. Yet where an AI system can be trained from a perfectly ignorant starting point, humans contextualization incorporates many under-identified data streams that go through under-defined analytical pre-processing. These under-

25 Draper, C.H., "The Pull of Unbiased AI Mediators," *International Journal of Online Dispute Resolution*, Vol. 6, 2019, 1.

26 This lack of clarity and the method of reducing it is not unique to facial recognition, where the interpretation of meaning in facial expressions is continually studied using large human surveys. These large surveys often calibrate a 'Weak' or 'Narrow' AI system that will use this data as the basis for making its decisions. These Weak or Narrow AI systems differ from 'Strong' AI systems that independently refine their analysis of the data, with the most important difference being that *Strong AI systems do not currently exist as of 2020.*

identified data streams that go through under-defined analytical pre-processing, as illustrated in Figure 7.11, are what may consider human intelligence.

Figure 7.11 Transparent AI Data Streams Versus Under-Defined Human Internal Processes and Data Streams

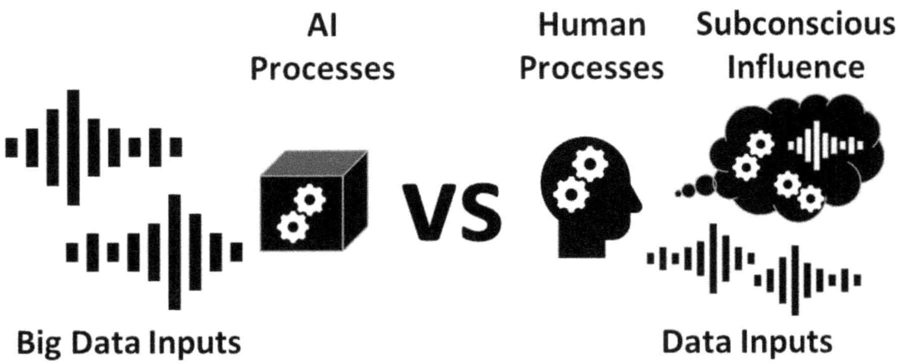

The risks posed by AI tools cause the most fear when discussing futuristic digital court systems run by robots.[27] In ODR, the risks from contextualization provided by AI tools are far more subtle yet just as important to consider. For example, the email tools that perform email searches, autofill additional emails that a user may want to add to a message, and propose ways to complete sentences are all AI enabled. These tools will work with varying degrees of quality depending upon the manner or extent to which its associated platform is used. For example, if a mediator has just finished a large case that had numerous emails sent to 'Chris,' the mediator must be extremely careful that emails intended for a 'New Chris' in the next case do not go to the 'Old Chris' from the last case.

This example of misdirected email recommendations is a feature of machine learning that could in other contexts result in bias. In this example, the email system does not know that the contract with one client has finished and another contract has started. The system only 'knows' that a significant percentage of emails have been going to 'Old Chris,' causing the system to predict that new emails going to 'Chris' are more likely intended to continue going to 'Old Chris.' The magnitude with which prior actions influence future outcomes will vary per AI system and is often protected as a proprietary trade secret.

27 China introduced its AI and blockchain enabled courts in 2019 with relative success, indicating that the push for autonomous dispute resolution technologies may be less futuristic with each passing year. A general article on the Chinese 'Smart Courts' can be found here: https://coinrivet.com/china-combines-ai-and-blockchain-to-be-judge-and-jury/.

The influence of AI predictions can become a bias if the conclusions produce unfair discrimination. In computer systems, **bias** is defined as *the systematic and unfair discrimination against certain individuals or groups of individuals in favor of others.*[28] Computer system bias can result due to:

- **Preexisting Bias** which has its roots in social institutions, practices, or attitudes;
- **Technical Bias** which results from technical considerations like computational tools, decontextualized algorithms, random number generation, or formalization of human constructs; or
- **Emergent Bias** which arises in the context of real users who either demonstrate new societal knowledge or a mismatch between actual users and those for which the system was designed.

Designers or operators of system that are dependent upon creating value through contextualization attempt to counteract computer system bias by incorporating human involvement in some manner. The three main types of human involvement strategies can be considered 'human-in-the-loop,' 'human-on-the-loop,' or 'human-out-of-the-loop,' as illustrated in Figure 7.12.[29]

Figure 7.12 Illustration of Human in-the-Loop, On-the-Loop, and Out-of-the-Loop Systems

These three strategies work in the following manner:

- **Human-in-the-loop** requires an operator to confirm an action before it can happen,
- **Human-on-the-loop** allows an operator to prevent an action that it believes is incorrect, and
- **Human-out-of-the-loop** relies upon safety measures designed into the system by humans.

---

28 Friedman, Batya and Nissenbaum, Helen, "Bias in Computer Systems" ACM Transactions on Information Systems. 14 (3): 330–347, 1996

29 Raymond, A.H., Draper, C.H. & Schubauer, J., "Artificial Intelligence Governance and Policy: A Practical Guide to Identifying, Understanding, and Mitigating Legal Risks Associated With AI Integration," Leading Legal Disruption: Artificial Intelligence and a Toolkit for Lawyers and the Law, Thomson Reuters, 2021, pp. 357-375.

Each of these safety measures assumes that human intuition is sufficient for identifying and avoiding computer system mistakes. However, **intuition**, which is defined as *the ability to understand something immediately, without the need for conscious reasoning*, is formed in the same manner as bias. The fundamental difference between bias or intuition is whether those observing agree with the outcome.

5 VALUE RETENTION

Upon creation, the value of digital data increases at a greater rate than physical data because it is far less expensive to prevent degradation. **Degradation** is *the process of an item breaking down over time.*[30] For example, a piece of paper upon which data is written will break down over time to the point where the data once written on it will no longer be legible, as illustrated by the old, physical data in Figure 7.13. That same data in digital form can now remain unmodified, endlessly replicable, and instantly transferrable without any significant economic investment. This elimination of any economic penalty for ensuring effective permanence of digital data makes each fragment easier to retain until there is a value that can be created through its contextualization.

Figure 7.13 Degradation of Old, Physical Data Versus New, Digital Data

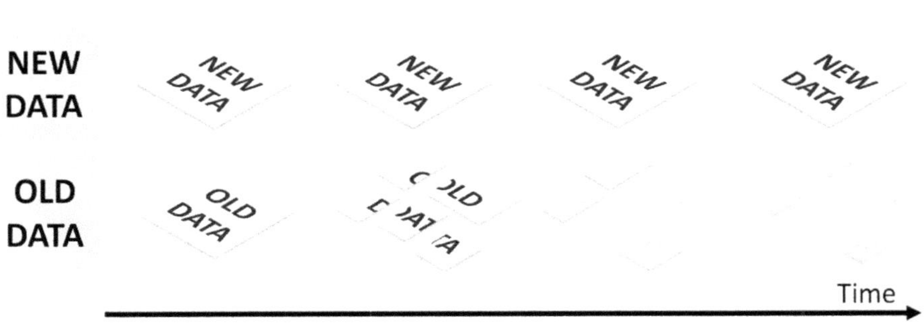

This ability for new, digital data to remain in a non-degraded state until it can be contextualized directly impacts the kind of breaches that ODR professionals must focus on protecting. Old data breaches were rarely costly unless the released data was immediately fully contextualized. Now, the non-degrading quality of digital data means that the kind of continual, small, random releases of old data that would not have survived long enough to be contextualized manually could now become extremely valuable. For example, many individuals write usernames and passwords on a Post-it

30 Draper, C.H. & Raymond, A.H. "Building a Risk Model for Data Incidents: A Guide to Assist Businesses in Making Ethical Data Decisions," *Business Horizons*, 2019, ISSN: 0007-6813, https://doi.org/10.1016/j.bushor.2019.04.005 (retrieved 7 July 2019).

Note stuck to the bottom of their laptops. If a Post-it Note falls into the street, these fragments of old data will typically unusably degrade or be non-contextualizable if found. When these same data fragments are retained digitally, their permanence means they can be held by the receiver at no prohibitive cost until their true value can be discovered.

This ability to create value from previously undervalued fragments is potentially best seen when considering 'anonymized' data. For example, technology giants like Facebook and Google routinely argue that broad use of the plentiful, anonymized data fragments they gather and create can be done without compromising privacy. However, more and more instances are emerging where data fragments that were intentionally anonymized can be directly tied to the individuals who provided it. Essentially 'de-anonymizing' data happened to those individuals identified with their anonymized data by the MIT Senseable City Lab project that was successfully able to "match up 17% of the users … to a 95% rate of accuracy."[31]

The fact that fragments of data which before could easily be lost now retain their ability to reveal valuable information creates new data retention considerations. ODR Systems must consider two instances of non-degradation defined here as:

- **Uncontrolled Retention** which occurs when the user has no control over how data is replicated or whether it can be fully destroyed, and
- **Inappropriate Permanence** which occurs when a user adds data that may need to be destroyed to a contextualized immutable system.

It is not clear as of 2021 whether any commercial cloud system available in the United States provides any user complete control over how stored data is replicated or whether it is ever fully destroyed. For example, revelations that Google inappropriately stored medical data or Amazon inappropriately stored verbal search histories gathered through Alexa raise well founded alarms about data privacy and control. However, as a user in an age when protections at least equal to GDPR and CCPA will likely become the law of the land, it is reasonable to build an ODR System under the assumption that a provider will honor the terms of its user agreement. ODR professionals assembling a Basic ODR or Specialized ODR system must be careful to understand the scope of a provider's stated data retention policy, the originality of any file that is stored in an ODR system, and make COTS choices accordingly.

These COTS choices with respect to data permanence must be made as a function of sub-system and the type of data it creates or protects. For example, digitally blended ODR Systems that have paper, scans of paper, and digitally created files must account for the value of each file in each form relative to its value in an alternative form. As the world

31 Campbell-Dollaghan, K., "Sorry, Your Data Can Still be Identified Even If It's Snonymized," *Fast Company*, 10 December 2018, www.fastcompany.com/90278465/sorry-your-data-can-still-be-identified-even-its-anonymized (retrieved 22 March 2020).

moves away from the belief that a piece of paper with handwritten, ink signatures is the preeminent test of originality, new standards are emerging to quantify the originality of digital files. This chapter views these types of files in three different ways:

- **Digital Replica** is defined as *a digital file that is able to convey all of the human readable information contained in the mimicked file.* A digital replica will not always share the same formatting or presentation style of the mimicked file. If the file being mimicked is also digital, running the same hash function[32] on both a digital replica and the file it mimics will not produce the same output. For example, a digital replica could be an Excel sheet that presents the data contained in a table from a PDF file.
- **Digital Copy** is defined as *a digital file that presents a visually identical representation of the mimicked file.* A digital copy will not always be presented in the same medium as the mimicked file. If the file being mimicked is also digital, running the same hash function on both a digital copy and the file it mimics will not produce the same output. For example, a digital copy would be a PDF scan of a paper document. ODR systems that use physical subsystems (e.g. taking notes on paper that are captured with a scanner or a camera) will often rely heavily on physical-to-digital (P2D) processes[33] like scanning a paper documents.
- **Digital Original** is defined as *an exact copy of the bits and bytes that make up the body of the mimicked file.* A digital original will not always share the same file name or properties as the mimicked file. Running the same hash function on both a digital original and the file it mimics will produce the exact same output. For example, a digital original would be a PDF that is copied, renamed, and saved in a different location.

The legal implications around each type of digital file based on its origin are still very much in flux across various jurisdictions. Yet understanding the kind of data that is being created, saved, and replicated is vital for understanding the risk each type of document poses.

In addition to understanding the originality of any digital document and the contractual obligations of cloud storage providers, it is vitally important to understand the fundamental limits of alternative data security architectures. The architectural elements that must be understood include how data is searched, saved, cataloged, and retrieved. For example, the fundamental, contextual architecture of traditional public blockchain should prevent it from ever being used for storing or pointing to legally

32 A hash function allows data of arbitrary size to be mapped to a fixed-size. Hash functions like SHA256 were developed so that two different files can be easily identified as being composed of the exact same sequence of 1s and 0s without needing to open or examine the files. Hash functions are a core feature of any digital forensic analysis that is attempting to prove that a file has not been modified in any way.

33 [missing text in this footnote]

sensitive data. Blockchain can be a powerful tool for validating and valuing distributed data, yet it can also be rapidly misused in a manner that violates an individual's rights.

The fundamental architecture of all blockchain exhibits the features of:

- **Decentralization** which means no single entity controls the network,
- **Transparency** which means everything seen in the core network is seen by everyone who has access to the core network, and
- **Immutability** which means no past records can ever be changed.

Figure 7.14 shows how these three features interact. First, (1) from a shared starting point (2) data is added in a block and (3) immutably blended into a new starting point (4) upon which each new data block (5) creates new links of a chain that is (6) replicated throughout the server Nodes that make up the decentralized network. These **blocks** build into a **chain** that is fundamentally a long string of values held on multiple computer servers called **nodes**.

Figure 7.14 Fundamental Architecture of Blockchain

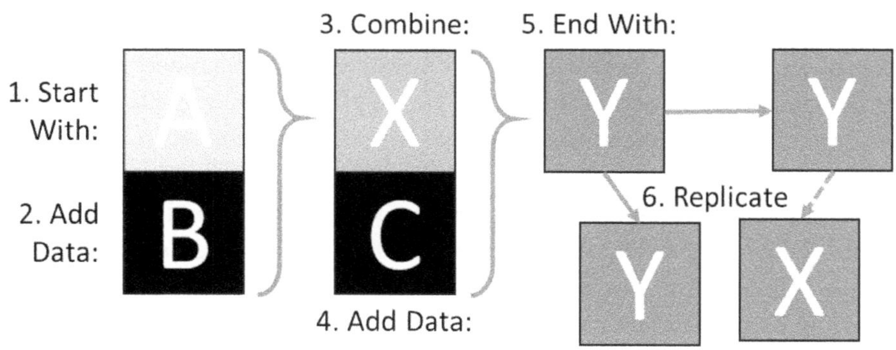

This architecture means that network data is shared with every server in the network, network data can be read by every user connected through any server, and the visible data that is shared can never be changed. In a traditional public blockchain, the entire network knows which 'anonymous' user is communicating with all other 'anonymous' users, the entire network sees a representation of the data being sent between the users, and that data becomes permanent once the users pay enough for specialty servers to write the data into the network. If a user does not pay enough to write its data into the network, it will not be saved; if the data being written is decryptable, any hacker has access to it; and if the anonymity of one user is compromised, the identity of any associated user could then also be at risk. This type of tool could become dangerous for ODR professionals if blockchain is misused as an encrypted storage system. Since all encryption is breakable given enough time and effort, any encrypted data accessible through a blockchain on, for example, juvenile records that will someday need to be expunged should be expected to become permanently, publicly accessible. Using the blockchain equivalently to a linear, public database would not only be inefficient, but it would also be unethical for a significant number of ODR use cases.

While using blockchain for storing sensitive information is inefficient and unadvisable, blockchain is a powerful tool for positive validation. This is because most blockchains are not strings of encrypted data, they are instead strings of data tokens. **Encryption** is *the process of encoding information into and back from an uninterpretable ciphertext using a cryptographic key*. While an extremely uncommon form of hacking, cryptographic keys can be recreated through various techniques that are quickly becoming less costly to run. If sensitive information is encrypted and the cryptographic key is recreated, the sensitive information is then usable to whoever want to access it using the cryptographic key.

Blockchain systems typically hold tokens. **Tokens** are *non-sensitive representations of sensitive data element that have no extrinsic or exploitable meaning or value*. The most commonly created token in blockchain use is a one-way data hash. A **data hash** is *the uninterpretable output of performing a hash function on a dataset*. When the same hash function is performed on the same data set, it will effectively always produce the same uninterpretable scramble of letters and numbers. However, this uninterpretable scramble does not contain the entirety of the data associated with the original dataset, so cannot be reversed like encryption.

This does not mean that all blockchain is inappropriate to use. Hybrid or consortia networks that only store data hashes can be valuable tools for validating sensitive files that are stored outside of the blockchain network. Incorporating any blockchain-based technology into Specialized ODR requires the decision owners to ensure the selected architecture does not create inappropriate data permanence.

The rapidly decreasing cost of data retention systems means data could easily or accidentally be more permanent that previously expected. An accurate understanding of permanence must factor into any assessment of the protection required for each data delivery system being used.

6 Privacy Versus Confidentiality

Privacy and confidentiality are two distinctly different legal and technological concepts in data security. The various issues associated with privacy and confidentiality are blended to create working definitions in this chapter that can be directly applied by ODR practitioners. **Privacy** is defined as *the state of preventing unapproved access to data*. For example, privacy would be violated if someone used another person's password to enter a protected folder and access data in that folder.[34] **Confidentiality** is defined as *the state of maintaining control over protected data or information*. Alternatively, confidentiality would be violated if data or information that was intended to only go from person A to person B was also sent to person C. The effective difference between privacy and confidentiality is presented in Figure 7.15.

Figure 7.15 Difference Between a Privacy Violation and a Confidentiality Violation

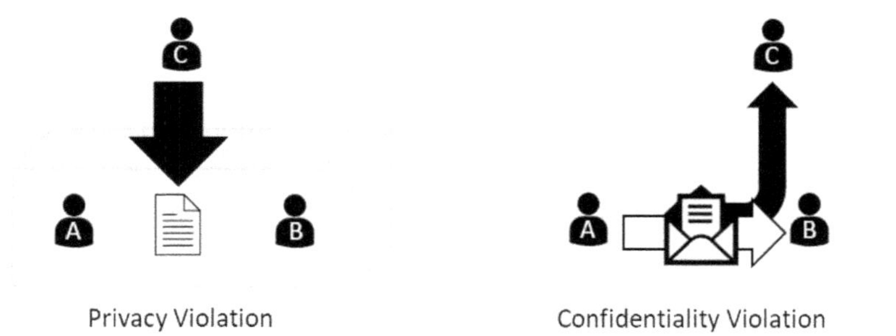

The primary focus of most data security awareness is privacy. This focus is what results in policies that require routine password changes, two-factor authorization, or minimum password complexity standards. Privacy is typically violated digitally following phishing efforts that steal passwords. The privacy of static records like credit card numbers or any associated personal data is extremely important in retail business processes. ODR rarely employs retail business processes that must account for these types of privacy concerns.

In ODR processes, the primary data security threat is misdirected data that violates confidentiality. It is widely agreed that 'practitioners and parties alike look to the third party's ... ability to maintain confidentiality, as a cornerstone of the intervention process' underpinning ADR. This responsibility for maintaining confidentiality rests with the neutral in Standard V of the Model Standards of Conduct for Mediators:

> A. A mediator shall maintain the confidentiality of all information obtained by the mediator in mediation, unless otherwise agreed to by the parties or required by applicable law.
> 1. If the parties to a mediation agree that the mediator may disclose information obtained during the mediation, the mediator may do so. ...

34 This concept of privacy is not counter to the intent of the privacy policies associated with various software licenses. Software licenses define the types of data that is stored or generated about the user, the processes the user is authorizing which may be performed with that personal data, and how software company will prevent unapproved parties from gaining access to that private data which has been licensed to the software company. Privacy policy clauses that discuss data selling or sharing with third-party applications are not wholly privacy issues, and instead blend elements of privacy and confidentiality.

> B. A mediator who meets with any persons in private session during a mediation shall not convey directly or indirectly to any other person, any information that was obtained during that private session without the consent of the disclosing person. …

And the impact of confidentially breaches is highlighted in the Code of Ethics for Arbitrators in Commercial Disputes, Canon VI as an event that could be used to inappropriately influence the outcome of an ADR process:

> A. An arbitrator is in a relationship of trust to the parties and should not, at any time, use confidential information acquired during the arbitration proceeding to gain personal advantage or advantage for others, or to affect adversely the interest of another. …

These standards highlight the importance of confidentiality in ADR and ODR. Where confidentiality is not defined and governed by Code like California Evidence Code §§1115-1128,[35] the scope and responsibilities of confidentiality are contractually defined. Therefore, confidentiality must be viewed from two perspectives: when we can expect it, and when we can enforce it.

An ADR practitioner is typically bounded by a confidentiality clause contained in the procedural rules all parties agree to when beginning the dispute resolution process. This element of confidentiality focuses the neutral's responsibilities within the dispute resolution process. For example, if the parties agree to use the *UNCITRAL Model Law on International Commercial Mediation and International Settlement Agreements Resulting from Mediation*, Article 9 requires "when a party gives any information to the mediator, subject to a specific condition that it be kept confidential, that information shall not be disclosed to any other party to the mediation."[36] UNCITRAL also addresses confidentiality with respect to what the parties can share about the proceedings or any products of a mediation in Article 10, yet protecting this aspect of confidentiality typically requires a protective order that has its own limitations.

Most scholars address the risks associated with managing an ADR process using an ODR system by expanding the responsibility of the neutral. This expansion makes the neutral responsible for ensuring the appropriateness of any 'ODR systems, processes, and

35 http://leginfo.legislature.ca.gov/faces/codes_displayText.xhtml?lawCode=EVID&division=9.&chapter=2.&article.

36 UNCITRAL Model Law on International Commercial Mediation and International Settlement Agreements Resulting from Mediation, 2018, United Nations Publication, No. E.05.V.4, ISBN 92-1-133730-5.

practitioners' as stated by the National Center for Technology and Dispute Resolution section on confidentiality:[37]

> The development and implementation of ODR systems, processes, and practitioners maintain confidentiality in accordance with all legal obligations and in a manner that is consistent, in particular, with the principles of Legal Obligation, Informed Participation, Security, and Transparency.

Neutrals must therefore understand the balance ODR Systems strike between the ease of transmitting confidential information and enforceable standards for appropriate protection. For example, if a party intentionally communicates confidential information by yelling it across a busy street or tacking a printed version of it to a light pole, both confidentiality and privacy are breached and therefore no longer exist. The question that must be answered with respect to ODR is: *when does an ODR system's design become the digital equivalent of tacking confidential information to a light pole.*

In a standard commercial contract, it is recommended that confidentiality agreements

> provide that the Receiving Party must take reasonable measures to keep the information confidential ... and require efforts from the Receiving Party that would – at a minimum – protect the information to the same degree that the Disclosing Party uses.[38]

And when assessing whether 'reasonable measures' to ensure confidentiality were taken prior to a breach:

courts will look at factors such as:
- the interests of the Disclosing Party in keeping the information secret;
- the period of time the information must be kept secret;
- the burden on the Receiving Party; and
- the interests of the public.

These intentions and standards mean there will be instances when confidential information is unintentionally released yet not considered a penalizable breach of enforceable confidentiality. These instances occur when courts deem that the cost of protecting the confidential information is misaligned with the value of any consequence

---

37 Wing, L., "Ethics and ODR: Ethical Principles for Online Dispute Resolution," National Center for Technology and Dispute Resolution, 2016, http://odr.info/ethics-and-odr/ (retrieved 4 September 2018).

38 Myers, R.K., "Confidentiality, Nondisclosure and Secrecy Agreements," *Lexus Practice Advisor Journal*, www.lexisnexis.com/lexis-practice-advisor/the-journal/b/lpa/archive/2015/11/30/confidentiality-nondisclosure-and-secrecy-agreements.aspx, Posted on 30 November 2015 (retrieved 5 September 2018).

arising from the information's disclosure. This economic balance between the resources that must be spent to maintain confidentiality and the consequences associated with confidential information being released is fundamentally characterized as risk.

7 ACCEPTABLE RISK

Risk in a data security context is an estimate of how often bad things happen. **Risk** is defined herein as *the probability of an event occurring multiplied by the event's consequence cost.* The **consequence cost** is defined as *the total economic burden associated with an adverse event occurring.* For example, a simplified application of these concepts could characterize the risk of driving a car during blizzard conditions where there is a 1% probability of totaling a $30,000 car. In this case, the 1% probability of the car being totaled is multiplied by the $30,000 consequence cost of totaling the car to produce a risk equal to 0.01 × $30,000 or $300. This type of simplification is rarely useful in isolation, since this type of calculation does not correspond to real world outcomes experienced by a single person. For this example, the driver will either make it through the blizzard at no cost, or the car will be totaled for a loss of $30,000. Expanding upon these fundamentals of risk, though, does allow for a reasonable approach to assessing the relativistic appropriateness at the heart of enforceable confidentiality and privacy protections.

Risk is most usefully applied regionally or relativistically. Graphically, Figure 7.16 shows event X defined by its probability of occurrence along the y-axis and the consequence cost of event X along the x-axis. This graphical representation groups high risk events as those in the upper right of the graph, and low risk events are those in the lower left of the graph.

Figure 7.16 High and Low Risk Regions Relative to Event X

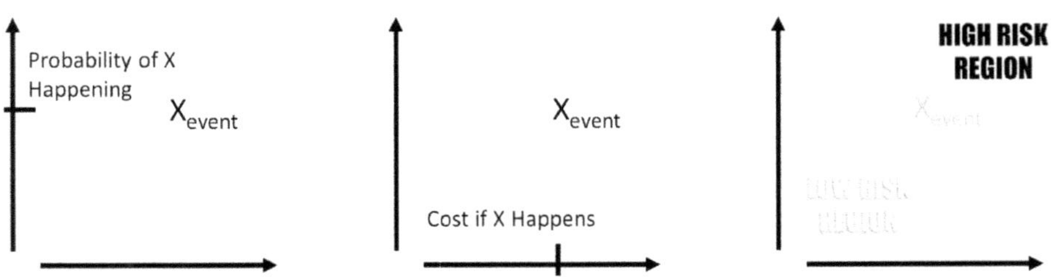

Fundamentally, risk cannot be eliminated. The goal of innovative system design is to take all economically reasonable steps to mitigate any undesirable outcomes and assess any residual risk. For example, a firm may use a shared Google calendar for scheduling the conference room. If the title of any scheduled meeting contains the names of the clients who will be in the room, there is an avoidable risk that this client data could create valuable information if released. This risk would be mitigated if the firm implements a policy requiring the name of any conference room meeting on the shared Google calendar to be an internal, anonymized billing code. This is a risk mitigation because the names of the individuals in the meeting are not immediately accessible. It does not eliminate the adverse consequence being protected against because someone with access to the accounting system could still take the time to link the code in the calendar to the names associated with the billing records. However, this type of a change will reduce system risk for essentially no economic cost, meaning this is an economically reasonably change.

The residual risk that is not economically reasonable to avoid through mitigation is then compared against legally or socially acceptable risk thresholds to determine whether the system is suitable to use for its intended application. For the above example, the residual risk would be approximated by estimating how likely it is for someone in the accounting department to want to steal from the firm, multiplied by the damage that would be done if the client identities became known. The ideal outcome is to ensure that any event which could happen using an ODR system would have a residual risk located in an acceptable region.

Most operational risks are not as narrow as that discussed above. For example, sending a confidential document via email is an event that could result in a wide range of potential outcomes, each with their own consequence cost. A data breach caused by a confidential document being misdirected via email could result in it being received by:

1. Someone who recognizes the document was sent in error and confirms immediate deletion;
2. Someone who does not recognize the document, does not acknowledge document receipt, yet deletes it without opening;
3. Someone who does not recognize the document, does not acknowledge document receipt, and takes no action on the document;
4. Someone who recognizes the value of the document, does not acknowledge document receipt, and retains possession of the document; or
5. A party who identifies the document and uses it for financial gain.

The consequence cost of each scenario above varies from no cost for the first scenario to a potentially significant cost for the fifth scenario. In the first scenario, the data contained in the confidential document is not spread or contextualized, meaning there is no cost to contain the data breach. By the fifth scenario, the consequence cost includes the legal fees required for a lawyer to assess and pursue actions that could limit the use of the data sent, the lost revenues gained by the receiving party, and any other intangible losses associated with releasing the intangible property contained on the document. None of these scenarios can be estimated as having exact consequence costs, so anyone analyzing this event would apply ranges to each scenario as represented graphically in Figure 7.17.

Figure 7.17 Assessing the Acceptability of the Consequences Associated with Event X

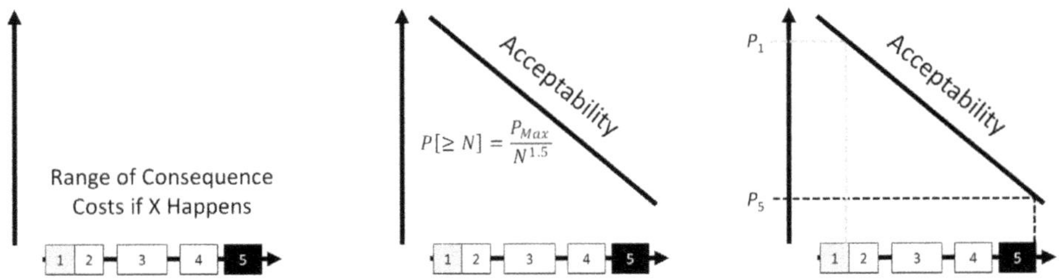

An ODR system is appropriate for use if the intersection of consequence cost and probability of occurrence for every outcome associated with event X falls below an acceptability boundary for residual risk. For many high-consequence industries, Acceptability is defined as the region under a 'catastrophe aversion curve' defined here as follows:[39]

$$P[\geq N]=P_{Max}/N^{1.5}$$

Where P[≥N] is the cumulative probability of all events capable of causing N or more casualties, and P_{Max} is the maximum acceptable probability of occurrence associated with a single casualty.

To define the legally and socially acceptable residual risk that would be reasonable for ODR systems, the Draper Catastrophe Value Curve (Draper CVC) was created by calibrating the catastrophe aversion curve methodology with value of life consequence cost models ranging from lost earnings,[40,41] *jury awards,*[42,43] *insurance settlements,*

39 Draper, C.H., "Ethical ODR Technology Selection Using the Catastrophe Value Curve," Working Paper 2018-140417-091, 30 September 2018.

40 King, E.M. & Smith, J.P., "Computing Economic Loss in Cases of Wrongful Death," RAND and The Institute for Civil Justice, R-3549-ICJ, 1988.

41 McClurg, A.J., "It's a Wonderful Life: The Case for Hedonic Damages in Wrongful Death Cases," *Notre Dame Law Review*, Vol. 66:57, 1990.

42 Peeples, R. & Harris, C.T., "What Is a Life Wroth in North Carolina? A Look at Wrongful-Death Awards," *Campbell Law Review*, Vol. 37:3, Summer 2015.

43 Peeples, R. & Harris, C.T., "Medical Malpractice and Wrongful Death: Some Lives Are Worth More Than Others," *Elon Law Review*, Vol. 8:461, 2016.

victim compensation methodologies,[44] *and value of statistical life*[45,46] *to identify three risk regions presented in Figure 7.18. These regions are considered acceptable in green, unacceptable in red, and requiring evaluation otherwise.*

Figure 7.18 Draper Catastrophe Value Curve

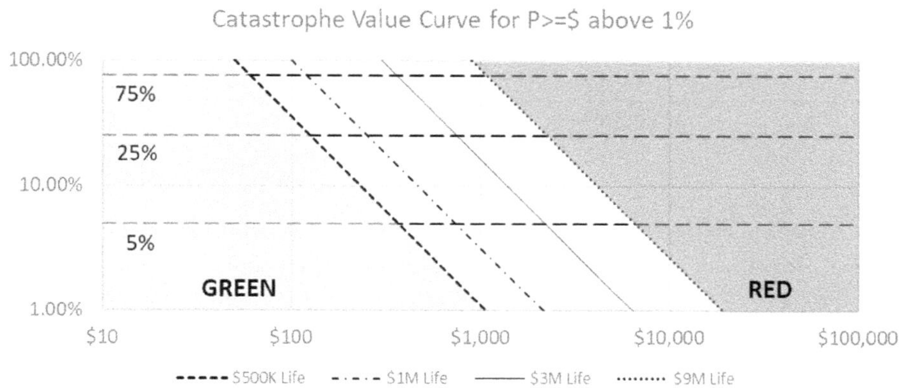

The regions presented in Figure 7.18 are based off of the intercept values presented in Table 7.1.[47] This table would be used to assess an ODR System by taking the probability that any scenario could occur and ensuring the value of that event occurring does not exceed the value identified. For example, using the above scenario of an email misdirection, if there is a 1% probability that the email could be received by an individual who could achieve a financial gain with the information being sent, that 1% misdirection rate is an acceptable risk if the value of the information sent does not cause an impact greater than $1,053. At the other end of the spectrum, it is unacceptable to use that same system with a 1% misdirection rate if the value of the data being transmitted could cause an impact that equals or exceeds $18,952.

44 Kip Viscusi, W., "The Value of Life in Legal Contexts: Survey and Critique", *American Law and Economics Review*, Vol. 2:195, 201-208, 2000.

45 Appelbaum, B., "As U.S. Agencies Put More Value on a Life, Businesses Fret," *The New York Times*, 16 February 2011.

46 Hirth, R.A., "Willingness to Pay for a Quality-Adjusted Life Year: In Search of a Standard," *Medical Decision Making*, Vol. 20.3, 332-342, 2000.

47 Many computer system reliabilities can be measured in the context of 99.99% or greater. However, most human-directed systems have error rates that are typically greater than 1%. Therefore, this representation of the Draper CVC offers reference lines for the 5%, 25%, and 75% probability of occurrence levels, with the specific intercept values for these different levels presented in the table.

Table 7.1 Values Associated with the Draper CVC in Figure 7.18

	Consequence Cost at Live Value Estimate			
	$500k	**$1M**	**$3M**	**$9M**
75%	$61	$121	$363	$1,090
50%	$79	$159	$476	$1,429
25%	$126	$252	$755	$2,265
5%	$368	$735	$2,206	$6,617
1%	$1,053	$2,106	$6,317	$18,952

These risk modeling strategies allow interpretation of the American Bar Association's discussion of 'reasonable protection' in *Model Standards Rule 1.6: Confidentiality of Information* to state that selecting or maintaining a system that produces unacceptable risks if an economically accessible alternative exists is unethical.[48]

8 OPTIMIZING PROTECTION

It is impossible for data security efforts to perfectly prevent access to adverse consequences. Data is useless if it is not used, and every process provides access to a consequential accident. At the same time, every risk reduction effort will be limited in resources, requiring practitioners to optimize the amount and type of protection that will be provided as a function of asset value. Optimizing protection requires acceptance that every piece of data does not need protected to the same level.

For example, there is a wide range of data that is collected, maintained, and used to develop sensitive information during the normal course of any dispute resolution practice. Some of these data fragments pose little economic threat if released, like calendar invitations that do not contain any personally identifiable information. Other data fragments can pose limited yet immediate and direct economic damage, like client billing details. The most risky data sets that could pose significant economic damage if released are often electronic files containing confidential case information that are sent using email or accessed via shared folders or file sharing. An hypothetical illustration of various ODR System Sub-Systems and their relative risk level is presented in Figure 7.19.

48 Draper, C.H. & Raymond, A.H. "Ethical Technology Risk: How to Identify What is Reasonable Data Protection for ODR," *International Journal of Dispute Resolution*, Vol. 12, pp. 144-153, 2019.

Figure 7.19 Relative Risk Assessment of Typical ODR System Sub-System Components Plotted Against the Draper CVC

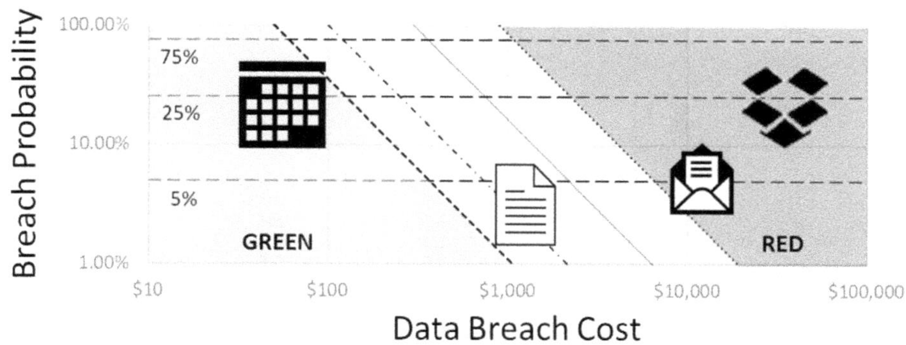

This hypothetical illustration presented in Figure 7.19 shows data sources that are appropriately protected (e.g. the calendar that does not contain any personally identifiable information in the Draper CVC Green Region), sources that are open to optimization (e.g. files managed by the Office 365 Suite in the Draper CVC Yellow Region), and sources for which it is unethical to not choose an economically accessible alternative (e.g. emailing or using unmodified file sharing software for sensitive documents in the Draper CVC Red Region). For sources where it would be unethical to not reduce their data risk, risk reduction strategies for data are not fundamentally different than for any other valuable asset. Risk is reduced through a combination of two strategies: *reducing the probability that an adverse event can occur* and *reducing the amount that can be lost per adverse event.*

Reducing the probability of an adverse outcome occurring is typically achieved for data by adding system access checks that serve the same function as adding locks to a door. These checks often include password complexity requirements, two-factor authorization, or periodic password resetting. These types of measures will shift the risk of a specific event downward on the Draper CVC as represented in Figure 7.19, yet it will also inhibit system use. If systems become too hard to use, they will not be used, which defeats their purpose.

Figure 7.20 Shifting Risk Down on the Draper CVC by Reducing System Access

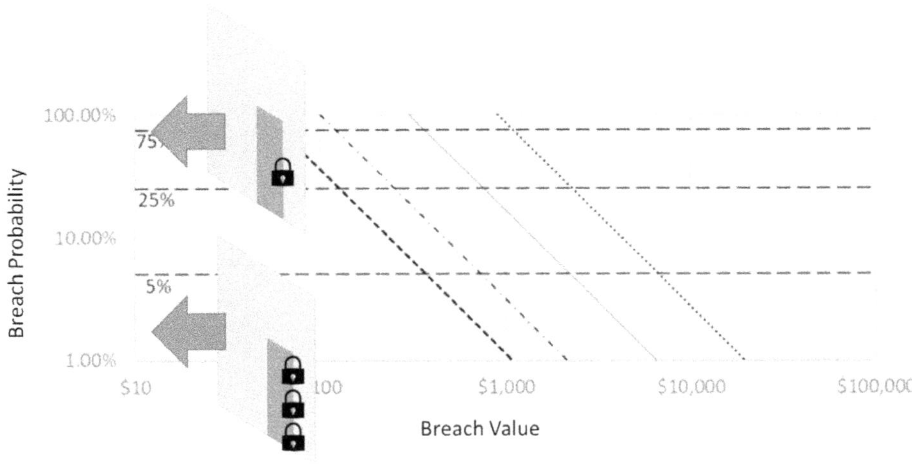

Reducing the cost of an adverse outcome is typically achieved through data segmentation strategies that serve the same function as spreading valuable assets across many different rooms. These practices often include database fragmenting or conditional permissioning practices so that a breach which compromises one data silo does not provide access to all protected data. These types of measures will shift the risk of a specific event leftward on the Draper CVC as represented in Figure 7.20, yet it will also increase data storage complexity. In blended systems that depend on individuals retrieving data consistently across multiple data repositories, the effectiveness of data fragmentation will be limited by the ability of the human users to retrieve data without security workarounds.[49]

Figure 7.21 Shifting Risk Left on the Draper CVC by Fragmenting Data Storage

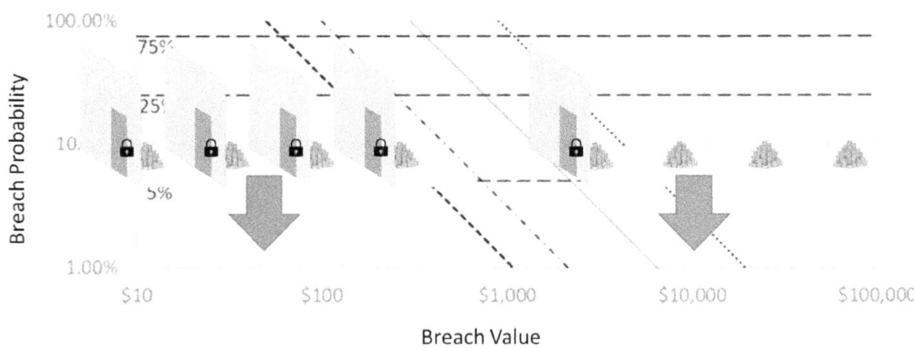

49 Security workarounds are 'tricks' that individuals will use to reduce inefficiencies cause by security requirements. These include basic workarounds like writing passwords on a Post-It note, or systemic workarounds like when Target turned off the security features that directly led to a data breach.

Ideally, an ODR system will employ a mixture of access and fragmentation measures that vary as a function of sub-system to appropriately protect the data contained or information accessible via that sub-system. This approach is metaphorically represented in Figure 7.22 as piles of gold distributed behind a range of doors secured with a varying number of locks.

Figure 7.22 Representation of Data Access and Fragmentation Optimization

9 ODR DATA BREACHES

IT Security has traditionally focused on privacy or confidentiality breaches caused by data theft. Yet experienced practitioners view ODR data security from the perspective where

> all of the egregious breaches of confidentiality and security [Rainey] has witnessed as a mediator came as a result of parties copying and passing around paper they should have not shared, not from hacking or losing information online.

This source of risk is caused by an intended user taking an unintended action with data the intended user has the right to possess.

Egregious data breaches are not the norm, however. ODR is rife with continual data breaches that are due to the unintended actions of well-intentioned actors inappropriately using Basic ODR tools. From misdirected emails to losing a Zoom recording, or sharing a cloud folder with the wrong person to sending the wrong data file, the primary cause of data breaches in ODR are operational human errors in the use of ODR technologies. These operational security threats represented in Figure 7.23 typically result in two types of data breaches that are most relevant to ODR system design: *misdirection* and *mischaracterization*.

Figure 7.23 Traditional IT Security Focus Versus Operational Security Threats

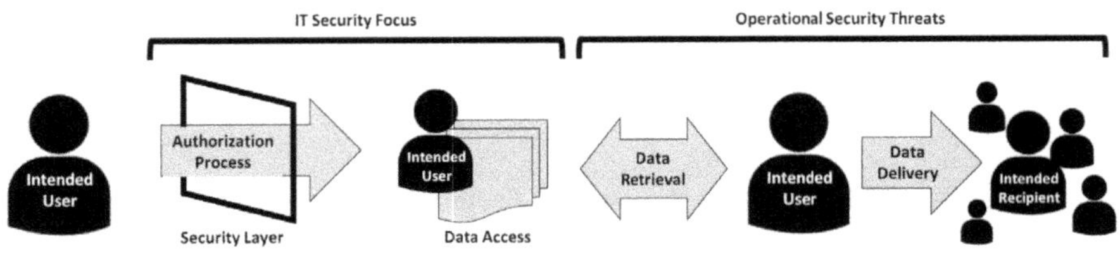

From an ODR perspective, a data breach caused by **misdirection** is defined as *data being sent to the wrong recipient.* For example, the scenario above where a confidential document is sent to the wrong person via email is a misdirection breach. The recipient did not seek out nor actively work to thwart any security systems containing the protected data received, yet the security protecting the sensitive data contained in the email was breached.

Email is an extremely common element of Basic ODR, yet there is limited data on how often misdirection breaches occur. The limited number of studies done provide strong indications that misdirection breaches are common with email. For example, a study that aggregated data obtained through interviews with professionals working in family care homes produced the data presented in Table 7.2.[50] This data does not provide access to any time-based error rate, yet does indicate that an extremely high percentage of people in an environment where constant, critical communication occurs will experience misdirection breaches when email or text messaging is a primary form of communication.

Table 7.2 Percentage of Workers at a Group Care Home Who Experienced Each Type of Data Security Issue

Difficulties	Email % Occurred at Some Point (2-5)	Text Message % Occurred at Some Point (2-5)
I received a message not intended for me	71.3	36.0
I sent a message to the wrong person(s)	63.2	19.1
My use led to a misunderstanding with other professionals	68.4	16.9
My use led to a misunderstanding with a client	44.1	16.9
I received a message that threatened, insulted, or harassed me	31.7	11.7
A client's confidentiality was violated	18.4	8.1

50 Breyette, S.K., "The Impact of Electronic Communication and Social Media on Child Welfare Practice", Master of Social Work Clinical Research Papers, Paper 295, http://sophia.stkate.edu/msw_papers/295, 2014.

A smaller study performed in 2019 arrived at nearly identical aggregate predications while providing slightly higher fidelity for time-based and send-rate projections.[51] The data on email misdirection rates is presented in Figure 7.24. Over the course of one year, more than 70% of all respondents had sent at least one misdirected email, increasing from 35% who sent at least one misdirected email over the course of a month, or 25% who sent at least one misdirected email over the course of a week. For the group analyzed, these misdirection errors represented approximately 4% of the total emails sent by respondents.

Figure 7.24 Rate at Which a Misdirection Breach Can Occur as a Function of Emails Sent

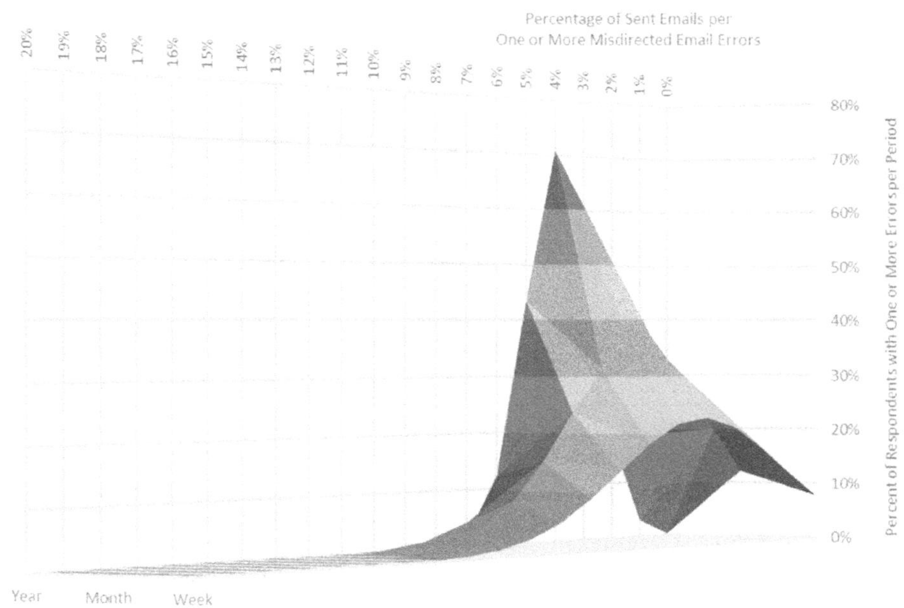

The other data security issue considered significant in ODR is data mischaracterization. **Mischaracterization** is defined herein as *an error in data delivery or presentation that prevents the recipient from accurately characterizing the data being sent.* Mischaracterization is considered a data breach for the purposes of ODR because it compromises the dataset being used by the collaborating parties. This type of error in a

51 Draper, C.H. & Raymond, A.H. "Ethical Technology Risk: How to Identify What Is Reasonable Data Protection For ODR," *International Journal of Dispute Resolution,* Vol. 12, pp. 144-153, 2019.

cybersecurity context would be equivalent to techniques like SQL Injection[52] that intentionally compromise a database so that it is unfit for use.

In ODR, this type of compromise is caused by human errors during communication. For example, if the neutral attempts to relay a proposal between parties using email and mischaracterizes the offer on the table, the information that will be used by the parties when considering their next steps is compromised. The above study looked at email misinterpretation and data misdirection rates in addition to email misdirection, with the summary results presented in Table 7.3. In the table, **normal** is defined as *the three-sigma boundary containing the variable estimate*, meaning there is a 0.27% probability that the specified range for each quality does not contain the true probability. The data presented in the table demonstrates reasonable stability regarding the probability associated with any particular breach type when email is the medium used to transmit data. This stability indicates that the limiting security factor in any email-dependent Basic ODR system is human error.

Table 7.3 Email Misdirection, Data Misdirection, and Email Misinterpretation Rates

	Week	Month	Year
Average Number of Emails Sent per Person	139 - 284	555 - 1,135	6,935 - 14,194
Normal Range for Email Misdirection	[0.000, 0.127]*mean = 0.042, std = 0.028*	[0.000, 0.112]*mean = 0.037, std = 0.025*	[0.005, 0.073]*mean = 0.039, std = 0.011*
Normal Range for Data Misdirection	[0.000, 0.134]*mean = 0.044, std = 0.030*	[0.000, 0.139]*mean = 0.047, std = 0.030*	[0.000, 0.124]*mean = 0.042, std = 0.027*
Normal Range for Email Misinterpretation	[0.000, 0.131]*mean = 0.044, std = 0.029*	[0.000, 0.131]*mean = 0.044, std = 0.029*	[0.000, 0.102]*mean = 0.034, std = 0.023*

This data on breach probability plotted against projected minimum legal costs for breach resolution based on AAA fees structures predict that Basic ODR systems which rely upon email are susceptible to communication events within the region plotted in Figure 7.25.

52 SQL Injection is one of many widely known techniques for compromising databases so is not discussed more in depth here, with many different resources suitable for providing background information on the technique.

Figure 7.25 Approximate Draper CVC Region Containing Email-based Communication Events

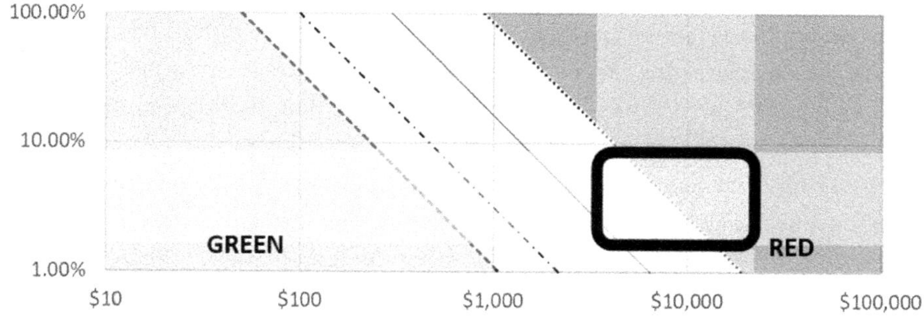

If a Basic ODR system is found to have communication event risks that can be characterized as in Figure 7.25, it is the ethical obligation of the neutral to seek out economically accessible alternatives.

10 ODR SYSTEM EVALUATION STRATEGY

Evaluating an ODR system or its alternatives from the perspective of data security starts with three main questions:

- Does the system type fit its purpose,
- Are its data security strategies suitable, and
- Where are the most important vulnerabilities?

Each of these questions will be discussed in turn, with examples provided to highlight the logic that should be used during any high-level system evaluation. None of the examples presented herein are exhaustive or indicate that other issues or concerns should not be explored or examined. For large, integrated, or highly complex systems, starting with this simple evaluation strategy may lead towards implementing a more rigorous evaluation process using tools like the NIST Cybersecurity Framework.

Does the system type fit its purpose? System type must be explored at both the overall system level and at the sub-system level. For example, an ODR system that is optimized to resolve traffic tickets is a direct outgrowth of ecommerce solutions. Someone using the system can often plead guilty and pay the ticket fine, no contest and pay the ticket fine, or fight the ticket. These types of systems are designed to increase the speed at which the user goes from a known sanction to a definitive resolution. Speed is increased in these systems using techniques like simplifying language, using expert systems or AI to funnel users along pre-defined use paths, integrating payment systems so that agreements can be immediately monetized, and reducing appeal options. These types of ODR systems are typically implemented as a single, fully integrated solution that does not have sub-system level options.

At a system level, it would be extremely difficult to see this system type being fit for resolving disputes like parenting orders. The potential mismatches between purpose and type when using a ticket resolution style system for something like parenting orders include:

- **Does issue simplification remove user understanding?** Many legally sensitive issues and options are difficult to summarize. Summarizations that are designed to relay complicated information faster may often enable uninformed choices, thus compromising the quality of the information, decisions, and agreements arrived at through ODR.
- **Can the full range of acceptable outcomes be pre-determined?** Many disputes that arise from human relations do not have a limited number of acceptable outcomes. Limiting the number of acceptable outcomes both compromises neutral objectivity and allows parties to gain insight into data that would likely otherwise be confidential based on transparent or interpretable decision points.
- **Does filtering a user onto a path most similar to those chosen by others best serve the current user?** Many filtering type systems use the decisions of similar, past users to influence the options available to a current user. Tools for assessing similarity have the ability to both contextually reveal confidential information and narrowly define similarity in a manner that prevents access to options appropriate for that user.

In the example of parenting orders, it may be concluded that using a pre-packaged, filtering type ODR system optimized for traffic tickets may not be appropriate. Neutrals that choose a Basic ODR system will still need to examine the suitability of COTS add-ons at the sub-system level. Some examples of sub-system appropriateness could include the following:

- **Grammarly.**[53] Grammarly is one of many tools that uses AI to help users optimize aspects like clarity, efficiency, or tone. Autocompletion technology has the ability to propose modifications to language that may alter the legal meaning of particular phrases or have unintended impacts upon communication.
- **TagSpaces.**[54] TagSpaces is a metadata management tool that allows users to add any number of tags to a file that are then saved in a hidden file with the tagged file. This tool will allow an individual to rapidly view groups of files across various storage mediums, yet sharing a folder with the hidden tags for a specific file has the potential to expose information about unshared, confidential files in other folders.

53 www.grammarly.com.
54 www.tagspaces.org.

Are its data security strategies suitable? Each ODR sub-system must be examined both independently and in the context of the wider system to determine whether it employs suitable security. This is done by examining each sub-system from the following roles it plays in ensuring data security.

- **Is it real?** Data quality in ODR systems is directly and primarily tied to communication effectiveness. For example, COTS tools like Zoom are now widely used for real-time, ODR collaboration, yet the technological and cultural comfort associated with this ODR sub-system varies widely. If the individuals using a tool are not comfortable effectively communicating given the system's technological or cultural restrictions (e.g. they are not comfortable interpreting the intentions of the other party without the non-verbal cues accessible when parties are face-to-face), then the data gathered or created with the tool will be anywhere from compromised to inappropriate for use. *All systems or sub-systems must be evaluated to ensure they can be used to create or relay reliable data and information.*
- **Is it permanent?** Data quality in ODR systems is directly impacted by the ability for data to remain appropriately permanent. For example, COTS tools like Google Docs allow for transparent collaboration by enabling many to all of the individuals in a single document to see and make edits to the document in real time. If the individuals using the tool do not have a strict, operational policy for collaborating in the platform, team members will be able to overwrite each other in a way that is difficult to audit. These auditability issues make it difficult or costly to prove a document's revision history. *All systems or sub-systems must be evaluated to ensure they can provide suitable control over the permanence required for the data being developed or transmitted.*
- **Is it (contextually) visible?** Confidentiality in ODR systems requires practitioners be able to control both system privacy and operational contextualization. For example, encrypted email is a popular method for ensuring that data packets sent by email are difficult to open by anyone who intentionally or accidentally intercepts them prior to their intended recipient. If the fact that communication is occurring between the sender and intended recipient provides insight to the value of their relationships (e.g. if an individual receives an encrypted email from a divorce attorney that was intended for her or his partner), confidentiality can effectively be violated without even opening the encrypted data contained within the email. *All systems or sub-systems must be evaluated to ensure the behavior of its users is not so transparent that the hidden value of the users' relationships can be determined through contextualization.*

The suitability of each strategy employed by an ODR system must then ensure its implementation protects each data fragment as intended. This is done by assessing system vulnerabilities from the perspective of data breach potentials.

Where are the most important vulnerabilities? System vulnerabilities are anywhere that data could be compromised, and the most important ones are where the consequence of any compromise are the most economically harmful. There are a wide range of techniques and tool for modeling threats to complex systems, typically starting with an Event Tree where each Event is modeled using a Fault Tree. An **Event Tree** (ET) is defined as *an inductive analytical diagram used to analyze the successive steps and consequences that occur following any event.* Where an ET uses Boolean logic to determine event sequence, the conditions and probability of each event occurring is found using a **Fault Tree** (FT) which is defined as *a top-down, deductive analytical approach for defining an event based on the combination of lower-level events that enable it.* The relationship between an ET and an FT is presented in Figure 7.26.

Figure 7.26 Example of Event Tree and Fault Tree Linking[55]

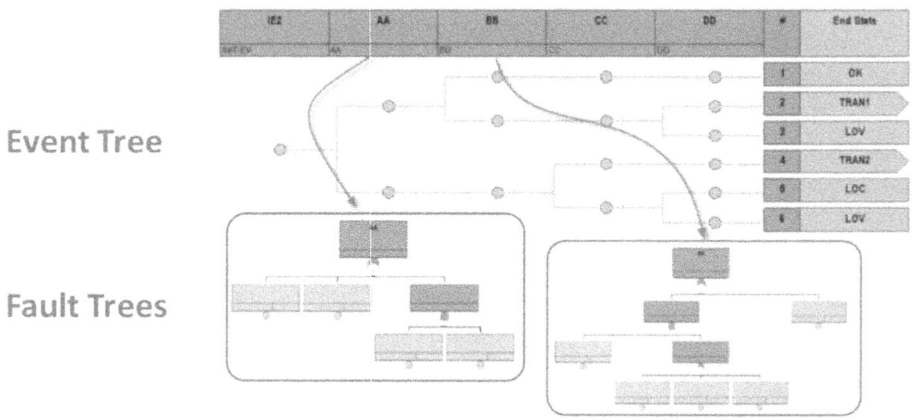

Using the type of data developed through ET/FT analyses, a Failure Modes Effects and Criticality Analysis (FMECA) allows practitioners to develop prioritized lists of vulnerabilities that need to be addressed through design or operational changes. A FMECA is defined as *an evaluation tool for analyzing each failure mode, the potential impact of each failure mode upon system performance, and the severity of each failure consequence in order appropriately mitigate or elimination risk.* A FMECA is typically performed on a worksheet like the one presented in Figure 7.27.

55 Probabilistic Risk Assessment Procedures Guide for NASA Managers and Practitioners, Second Edition, NASA/SP-2011-3421, December 2011.

Figure 7.27 FMECA Worksheet from Mil-Std-1629A

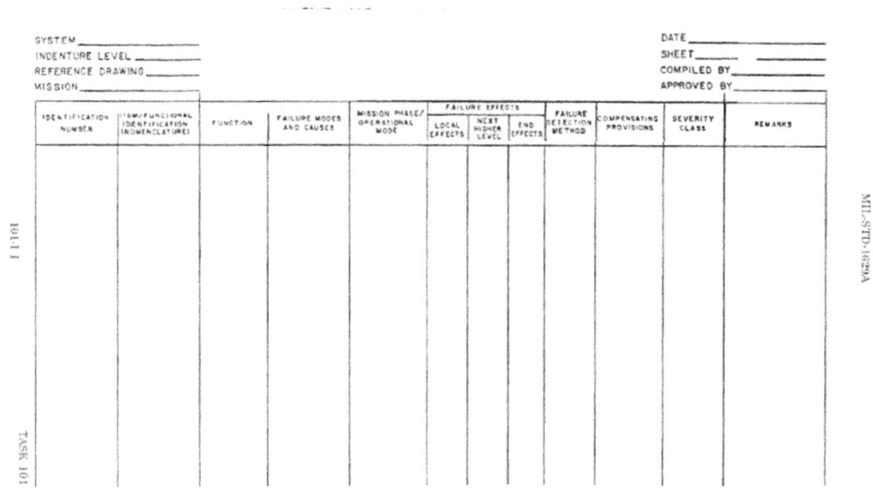
SYSTEM ______
INDENTURE LEVEL ______
REFERENCE DRAWING ______
MISSION ______

DATE ______
SHEET ______ ______
COMPILED BY ______
APPROVED BY ______

IDENTIFICATION NUMBER	ITEM/FUNCTIONAL IDENTIFICATION (NOMENCLATURE)	FUNCTION	FAILURE MODES AND CAUSES	MISSION PHASE/ OPERATIONAL MODE	FAILURE EFFECTS			FAILURE DETECTION METHOD	COMPENSATING PROVISIONS	SEVERITY CLASS	REMARKS
					LOCAL EFFECTS	NEXT HIGHER LEVEL	END EFFECTS				

Figure 101.3 Example of FMEA worksheet format

These combinations of tools and techniques are typically used in these formats for complex electromechanical systems in order to find, define, and prioritize risks that are difficult to otherwise see. The documentation associated with these techniques that is presented above will often be overkill for a practitioner who is attempting to assess whether one COTS sub-system is better than another for Basic ODR.

The FMECA process can be replicated at a level suitable for Basic ODR analysis by looking at each piece of data that is handled by each ODR Sub-System and stepping through questions like the following:

- How could data accidentally get out of this sub-system?
  - o Do I have to physically move it?
  - o Do I have to address and send it?
  - o Is it already shared with other people who can move or send it?
  - o Does it automatically sync with any other systems?

- Who could accidentally receive this data?
  - o Only people who have access to this computer?
  - o Anyone in my work email list?
  - o Anyone in my personal email list?

  - o Anyone in my phone address book?
  - o Anyone I have ever shared folders with?

- How often could this happen?
  - o When was the last time I mishandled data?
  - o How often do I get the wrong data from someone else?
  - o Is there bad data this system already?
  - o Am I really comfortable enough using this system to even understand how often I might make a mistake?

- What would happen if this data got out?
  - o Would I need, and how much would it cost, to engage my lawyer?
  - o Could I be professionally reprimanded for losing control of this data?
  - o Is there anyone in my address book who – if they got a hold of this data – could financially benefit from having it?
  - o Have there been any judgments against anyone like me for losing control of this type of data?

- How else could I do this?
  - o Do I need to store and send this data this way?
  - o Is there another platform, and at what cost, that could replace this process?
  - o Is anyone doing this differently?
  - o Do I know that everyone is doing this like me?

Asking these questions for every type of data that is being used or shared with every type of sub-system used for ODR will help a practitioner understand:
- Where is my data vulnerable,
- How costly would a data breach be, and
- Is there a better way to do this?

10.1 Example Evaluation: Summarizing Notes

The following example analyzes a process illustrated in Figure 7.28. In this process, the mediator has taken notes on paper during a face-to-face mediation, those notes are then typed up into a summary, that summary is shared with a partner for review, and then sent to the Red party. The following high-level analysis will step through the kinds of questions that a practitioner should ask or consider when analyzing this type of ODR system.

Figure 7.28 Example Data Security Process Evaluation for Summarizing Notes

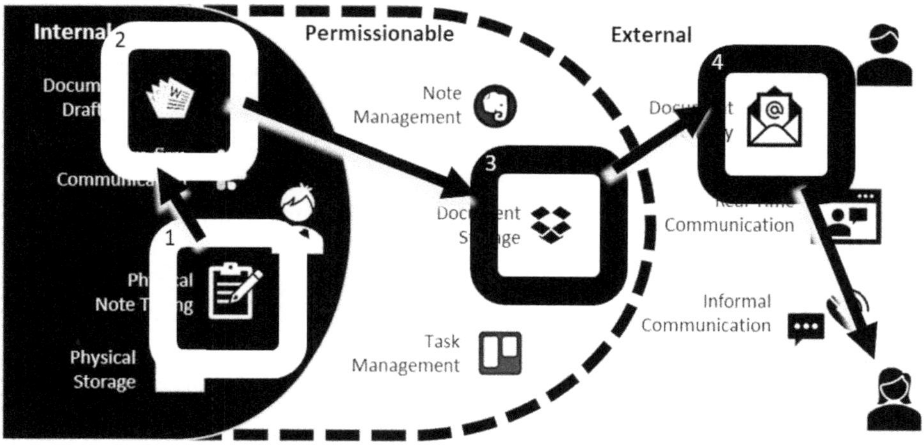

1. **Physical Notes**. The notes were taken on a standard legal pad, carried back to the office in a briefcase, and left on the desk to process in the morning. Questions to consider could include:
   - How did I control the visibility of my notes during the meeting?
   - How do I know that I have all the pages of my notes?
   - Are there any sections I am having trouble reading?
   - Are there any sections where I did not take as many notes as others?
2. **Word Processing**. The notes are used to draft up a summary of the face-to-face meeting that will eventually be shared with the Red party. Questions to consider could include:
   - Am I starting my new electronic document by opening an old file that may be attributed to a different author in the metadata?
   - Will the revision history show notes or comments that are not relevant or could be misinterpreted here?
   - Will I have any way of knowing who reads this document?
   - How can I be sure I don't have any placeholder comments still in the document that I do not want to send?
3. **Shared Storage**. The document draft is stored on Dropbox, where a partner goes to find the file, review it, and send any comments back as tracked changes or notes. Questions to consider could include:
   - Am I certain I uploaded the correct file to the correct folder?
   - How can I be sure my partner is looking at the correct version of the document?
   - Are my cloud files syncing up correctly to my laptop?
   - Does the metadata show anyone else who gets this file that my partner had access to this document?

4. **Email Delivery**. The revised document is sent via email to the Red party. Question to consider could include:
   - How often is an email misdirected?
   - Is my email restricted to work contacts, or is there a risk a work document could go to a personal contact?
   - Has everyone who needs to be informed been consistently included on all email threads?
   - Do I have an auto-archiving or auto-delete process running in my email?

10.2 Example Evaluation: Video Mediation

The following example analyzes a process illustrated in Figure 7.29. In this process, the parties are communicating via Zoom, the mediator is taking notes using Evernote, the parties assign follow up tasks via Trello, and a summary of the positions and progress of the mediation are generated in Word. The following high-level analysis will step through the kinds of questions that a practitioner should ask or consider when analyzing this type of ODR system.

Figure 7.29 Example Data Security Process Evaluation for Video Mediation

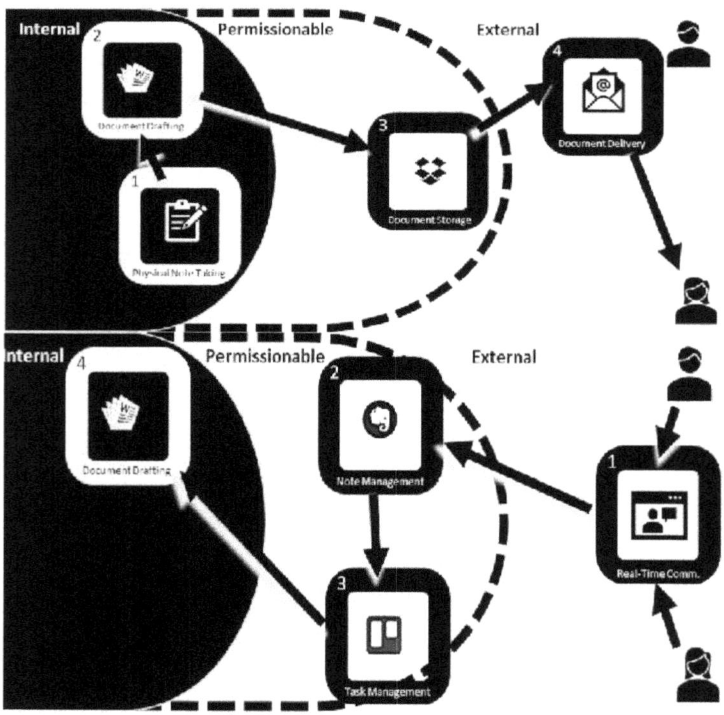

1. **Zoom Discussion**. The parties meet for a 'face-to-face' joint session using Zoom, and caucus with the mediator via telephone as necessary. Questions to consider could include:
   - Did we ensure that the camera and microphone were off whenever either side was caucusing?
   - How did we make sure that any non-verbal communication was correctly interpreted?
   - Do we know if everyone was adhering to the agreed to rules on recording?
   - Was there anything in the camera's view of my office that would have compromised privacy or confidentiality?
2. **Evernote Taking**. Evernote is used to draft up a summary of the face-to-face meeting that will eventually be shared with the both parties. Questions to consider could include:
   - Is my typing suitable for keeping up with the pace of the conversation?
   - Do I know where the notes are syncing?
   - Will anyone else have access to these notes?
   - Will these notes be linked to any other file or storage system?
3. **Task Tracking**. Next steps for all parties and the mediator are developed and tracked using Trello. Questions to consider could include:
   - Is everyone comfortable enough with Trello to not overwrite each other?
   - Who has access from each party to accept, move, or complete tasks?
   - Is the Trello board integrated with any other collaboration apps?
   - Are both parties restricted to just this Board, or do they have access to multiple Boards?
4. **Word Processing**. Progress throughout the mediation including summaries of the proposals discussed are developed in Word. Question to consider could include:
   - Did copy and pasting from Evernote save anything unexpected in Word?
   - How will I track and merge feedback from both parties confidentially?
   - Will the parties be able to tell who proposed new language first?
   - Is there a possibility that something was mischaracterized when transferring from Evernote to Trello to Word?

11 CONCLUSIONS

The world is going online, and its disputes are following. There is no option in the modern world except to become comfortable using ODR tools. This comfort with ODR tools cannot lead to complacency with respect to data security. ODR practitioners must be conscious of the threats posed by Basic ODR, thoughtful in their assessment of alternatives, and constantly working to reduce the risk to parties as the value of the data being protected continues to increase.

Chapter 8 ODR and Cultural Components of Dispute Engagement

Daniel Rainey and Alma Abdul-Hadi Jadallah

1 Preamble: What Has Changed?

The first edition of *ODR Theory and Practice* was published in 2012, and it contained 'ODR and Culture,' the precursor to this chapter.[1] At that time the use of technology in the practice of mediation, arbitration, and other forms of conflict or dispute engagement had made great strides from its beginnings in the 1990s. By 2012, every online commercial site worth its salt had an online approach to resolving disputes arising from exchanges among buyers and sellers, serious applications of artificial or augmented intelligence were being developed, and the courts were just catching a technology wave that would, by 2020, integrate online dispute resolution tools into judicial systems around the world. Even in the more traditional practices of dispute resolution – private mediation, arbitration, facilitation, etc. – ODR technology was gaining more and more traction. Then, in early 2020, everyone was faced with the Covid-19 pandemic. To borrow a phrase from the US automotive world, ODR went from zero to 60, seemingly in an instant. As one small example, Zoom, the web video application that became a staple of online work during Covid, increased its client base 30-fold almost overnight, and reported regular attendance at Zoom-hosted meetings by more than 300 million people each day.[2]

It has long been noted that the use of ODR technology impacts ADR practice: use of ICT for conflict engagement expands the opportunity for participation, and adds obvious benefits related to cost, convenience, and participant safety. It would be wrong, however,

---

1 Daniel Rainey, "ODR and Culture," in *Online Dispute Resolution Theory and Practice: A Treatise on Technology and Dispute Resolution*, Ethan Katsh, Mohamed S. Abdel Wahab, and Daniel Rainey, eds., Eleven International Publishers, The Hague, 2012, pp. 185-203.

2 BBC News, Natalie Sherman, "Zoom Sees Sales Boom Amid Pandemic," available at: www.bbc.com/news/business-52884782, last accessed September 2020.

to think of ODR as a mere analog of ADR, a set of processes for addressing conflict that happen to have been offered online.

In a set of experiments with software developed under a US National Science Foundation grant,[3] participants were divided into groups and asked to use an asynchronous online application to develop a problem statement, a set of interests, and a list of suggested options for resolving a problem. In the process of conducting that research at least two things became clear to the researchers. First, ODR technology works. After experiencing mediation using the ODR software, participants were asked to complete a survey in which two of the questions sought to discover if they felt 'heard' by the other party and the mediator. In these experiments, over 80% of the respondents indicated that they felt heard by both the other party and by the mediator. The overwhelming majority of the test subjects also indicated they would be willing to use this ODR application again for other conflict resolution efforts. Second, it became clear that ODR is not just an analog of ADR. Among other things, the impact of work at a distance on the conflict environment, the ability to generate truly anonymous input, and the ability to work asynchronously, all made clear that, to borrow a phrase, ODR are not your father's ADR.

Scholars and practitioners of ADR have long acknowledged that culture has an impact on efforts to engage in, resolve, and manage conflict. We will not replow that ground. In this chapter we will start with basic definitions of ODR and culture, discuss the impact of culture on communication, and then discuss some of the unique and significant impacts the online environment has on the cultural elements of conflict engagement. We will conclude the chapter by suggesting some of the issues related to culture that should be addressed by practitioners, application designers, and ODR service providers.

2 What Do We Mean by ODR?

There are competing definitions of online dispute resolution, with emphasis varying regarding how much of the practice of dispute resolution has to be actually online to be called ODR, and how much dispute resolution practices must rely on algorithms or artificial intelligence to be legitimately classified as ODR. In this chapter we will take a rather broad view of ODR. We agree with the approach to ODR included in the UNCITRAL report on cross border commercial dispute resolution:

3 Unpublishing findings from research supported by National Science Foundation award #0429297, "Process Technology for Achieving Government Online Dispute Resolution," available at www.fastlane.nsf.gov/servlet/showaward?award=0429297. This interdisciplinary research project included the National Mediation Board, the Departments of Legal Studies and Computer Science at the University of Massachusetts Amherst and included both the authors as well as Ethan Katsh, Lee Osterweil, Norman Sondheimer, Lori Clarke, Alan Gaitenby, Alexander Wise, and Matt Mazzilli.

> [ODR] can assist the parties in resolving the dispute in a simple, fast, flexible, and secure manner, without the need for physical presence at a meeting or hearing. ODR encompasses a broad range of approaches and forms (including but not limited to ombudsmen, complaints boards, negotiation, conciliation, mediation, facilitated settlement, arbitration and others), and the potential for hybrid processes comprising both online and offline elements.[4]

In addition, we will follow a definition of 'private ODR' to be offered in the forthcoming report of the American Bar Association ODR Task Force:

> the application of information and communication technology (ICT) directly to the performance of any of the functions central to the practice of dispute resolution[5]

Basically, we approach ODR as involving any online or offline technology that allows parties and third parties to do one or more of the basic functions of dispute resolution: managing and enhancing communication, facilitating the sharing and understanding of information, and the management of group dynamics. ODR may be used in dispute resolution practices that, it is hoped, lead to resolution and relationship building, or may be used in dispute engagement practices that do not seek resolution as an ultimate goal.

3 WHAT DO WE MEAN BY CULTURE?

In an essay prepared for the Fourth International Online Dispute Resolution Forum, Rainey and Jadallah argued that one key element of ODR platforms, perhaps particularly those not specifically designed for dispute resolution but being used in the practice of dispute resolution, was the fact that, inevitably, there is 'culture in the code.'[6] The basic argument was that when they create the code that drives apps used in ODR, designers and programmers will, consciously or subconsciously, build in assumptions about the way things should be done that: reflect their preferences or understanding regarding practice; reflect the things they value; and reflect approaches that fit with their worldview.

4 United Nations Commission on International Trade Law (UNCITAL), Working Group III – ODR, *Technical Notes on Online Dispute Resolution,* United Nations, New York, 2017, p. 1.

5 ABA, ICODR, NCTDR Report on Standards for ODR, forthcoming.

6 D. Rainey and A. Abdul-Hadi Jadallah, "The Culture in the Code", Proceedings of the Fourth International Online Dispute Resolution Forum, 22-23 May 2006, Cairo, Egypt.

It is tempting to echo Justice Potter Stewart's famous declaration about definitions, and simply say that most people know cultural differences when they see them.[7] In fact, this is probably not true: most experienced third parties can probably recognize or anticipate gross differences in culture, and, to some degree, prepare for those differences in a way that does not compromise efforts to resolve conflict. But subtle differences and 'micro-cultures' may be difficult or impossible to spot before they cause problems, if in fact they are going to cause problems. And basic differences in worldviews can be so overarching as to be invisible at 'ground level.'

So, what specifically is culture, or what do we mean when we talk about culture in this chapter? The very question invites an almost uncountable number of very direct, and sometimes pithy, definitions. There are anthropological definitions, sociological definitions, psychological definitions, etc., *ad infinitum*, most of which share some common features relating to values, beliefs, and behavior. Peter Black and Kevin Avruch discuss at length the relationship between culture and conflict, warning that there are a number of 'dead ends' inherent in looking at culture through a narrow lens.[8]

There are two basic definitions of culture that are more prosaic, and perhaps more utilitarian, than most academic definitions, but which may be useful in understanding how culture affects conflict engagement practice.

The first is a definition for which we have no seminal reference: *culture is the way we do things around here*. This definition of culture has been cited by many practitioners working in organizational change and development, and it is a good shorthand way of thinking about the behaviors that attend to mediation and negotiation.[9] The second definition relates to the extent that cultural habits and judgments are overt and conscious. Roy Wilkins has said, "culture is what happens when we stop thinking".[10]

These definitions suggest that culture may include factors that *seem* immutable (e.g., race, gender, and ethnicity) but which are in fact fluid. But cultural attributes also include behavior, relationships, and ways of thinking. In the words of a colleague, Janet Murdock, culture is "the operating system on which we load the *software* of our experience".[11]

Avruch warns that there are caveats involved in analytical thinking about the influence of culture in conflicts. It is possible to overplay or overestimate the role of

---

7 The full statement from Justice Stewart related to the definition of hard core pornography. His comment about the definition of pornography in the film *The Lovers* is as follows: "I shall not today attempt further to define the kinds of material I understand to be embraced within that shorthand description and perhaps I could never succeed in intelligibly doing so. But I know it when I see it, and the motion picture involved in this case is not that." Justice Potter Steward, concurring opinion in *Jacobellis v. Ohio* 378 U.S. 184 (1964).

8 P. Black and K. Avruch, "Cultural Relativism, Conflict Resolution, Social Justice", available at www.gmu.edu/programs/icar/pcs/BlackAvruch61PCS.html.

9 For example, this definition is used in T. Deal and A. Kennedy, *Corporate Cultures*, Perseus Books, New York, 1987.

10 This definition was offered during an NPR interview.

11 J. Murdock, *Culture in Mediation*, a training manual used by the Northern Virginia Mediation Service, 2010.

culture in interpreting what is happening in a given conflict. He defines these situations as Type I or Type II errors. In a Type I error, the third party undervalues culture in the analysis of the conflict and thereby appears to have what Avruch calls a tin ear'.[12] In Type II errors, one over-values culture and its impact on the conflict and the disputants, seeing problems where none may exist.

Another way we can think of culture takes a broader, umbrella view of culture and can be encapsulated in the term 'worldview,' which we will discuss in the next section.

Culture, in the context of this chapter, is the mix of values, beliefs, worldviews, and behaviors presented by parties in conflict, and which guide the thinking and behavior of third parties, fourth parties, designers, programmers, and service providers.

4 Culture and Communication

The introduction of ODR technology, providing new, non-face-to-face channels of communication, creates direct impacts on the process of dispute resolution, and on the cultural influences that attend to various dispute resolution or conflict engagement processes. Some of these impacts are related to micro-aspects of our identities – our race, our religion, where we grew up, how we were educated, etc. Some of the impacts stem from macro-aspects of our identities – literally how we see the shape of 'reality.'

As a way to understand how the use of these channels (audio, video, and text) influence our work as third parties, we suggest starting with understanding the exchange of information, and one hopes understanding, conveyed through a basic model of communication.

One way to conceptualize a communication model begins with and is drawn from the work of Claude Shannon, working at Bell Labs after World War II.[13] The model is composed of multiple actors (senders and receivers), multiple channels for the transfer of information (verbal, nonverbal, and environmental), feedback loops, and perhaps most importantly for conflict engagement practitioners, a set of perceptual filters.

---

12 K. Avruch, "Culture", in S. Cheldelin, D. Druckman, and L. Fast (eds.), *Conflict*, Continuum, New York, 2008, p. 362.

13 Shannon and his co-author, Warren Weaver, published a version of his work that goes beyond its application in engineering in 1949. It contains a basic approach to communication interchange, introducing terms like 'feedback' and 'noise' that have become standard in our discourse. Their work focused on communication in an increasingly technological environment, but is a good foundation for understanding the transfer of meaning generally. *See* Claude Shannon and Warren Weaver, *The Mathematical Theory of Communication*, The University of Illinois Press, Urbana, IL, 1949.

Figure 8.1 Communication Elements

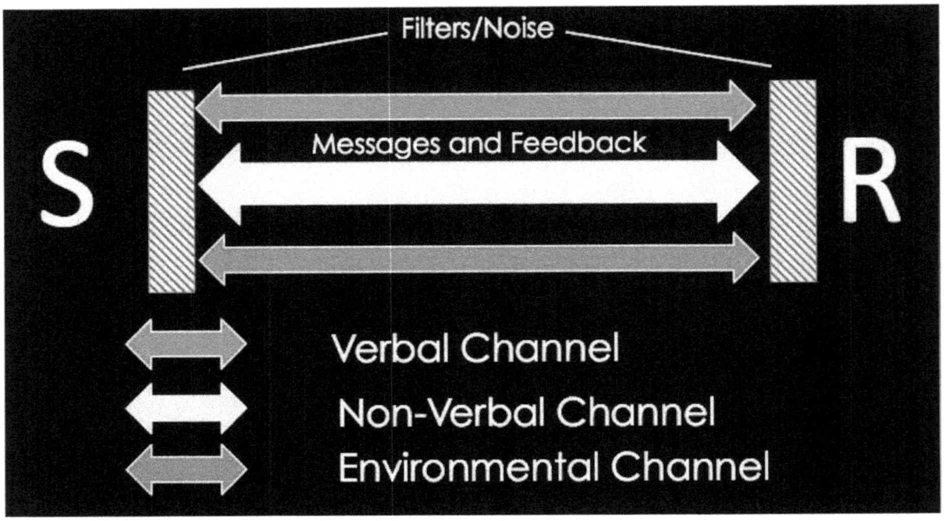

Messages are sent verbally – either orally or in writing – using symbols that conform to established grammar and syntax. The English language, spoken or written, is verbal, and the words chosen by the sender have a meaning that is *in part* independent of other factors. Nonverbal messages are conveyed through vocalization, body language, etc. The environment in which one is communicating – a pub, a law office, your living room – adds some elements to the overall message you are trying to convey. The use of technology affects all of these communication channels, and can in itself be a barrier to, or an enhancement to, the exchange of understanding. But when we speak about the impact of culture on conflict engagement, perhaps the perceptual filters that each of the parties carry with them have the greatest impact on understanding, resolving, or managing conflict.

If we are using a visual medium (face-to-face or video) I can see if you are white, wearing a head covering, are old, etc. If we are using an audio channel, I can still pick up some of the micro-elements of your culture – an accent, your choice and use of words, etc. Even if we are using a text channel, the words you choose, in the language of our exchange, can give me clues about your national origin, your level of education, etc. All of these micro-elements are important, insofar as they give some clues about who we are, and who are the people with whom we are dealing.

But the more important element in communication during conflict engagement is the impact of our perceptual filters. We can perceive race, sex, age, etc., but what gives them meaning, and what drives understanding or misunderstanding, and the way we interpret messages sent to us through any of the channels, is a matter of how our filters work to interpret and judge those cultural micro-elements. Those filters, and that process of judgment, is driven by a much larger cultural frame – our worldview. Our worldview works to create and operationalize the elements of our perceptual filters, creating, for example, the implicit biases we all carry around.

World view theory, generally, seems to have grown from questions about how we perceive reality, and how we develop a *weltanschauung*, that began in the field of cultural anthropology. Michael Kearney, writing in 1975, argued that "literature about world view and world-view-related subjects permeates anthropology."[14]

Later, writers addressing the place of worldview theory in conflict resolution, specifically addressed the dynamics of third-party work as influenced by worldview.

Historically, it has been argued that practitioners on all levels have to provide approaches that can address economic, social, political, and psychological dimensions of conflict – the range of micro-elements of culture. Nudler[15] criticizes this line of thinking and approach. He believes it failed to build bridges between the different disciplines and failed to address the inter-psychic level, or the micro and macro levels that cannot and should not be ignored when dealing with conflict. Nudler proposes an overarching concept to help address the dilemma of guiding the parties on how best to manage both the unconscious underpinnings of worldviews and turn them into explicit conscious elements of discourse. He proposes what he calls 'Worldview Analysis' an analysis that breaks the conflict domain into three different types: 1) conflict in which the parties share the same worldviews; 2) conflicts in which the parties partially share the same worldview; and, 3) conflicts in which there are no elements in common. He adds that most theoretical frameworks informing the models that practitioners use – mediation or facilitation – are informed by the first type. This is problematic as it ignores the existence of differences in worldviews – literally differences in the way parties may view 'reality.' Building on Nudler's work, Docherty[16] argues that what is needed is the ability of all those engaged in the process of conflict resolution to go beyond logical arguments and include the analysis of the symbolic, i.e. the stories that the individuals tell, the metaphors they use to explain their reality and context. Because these stories carry meaning, and because these stories contain the filters which the parties will use to interpret messages from other parties, they often express directly what is important and of value to the disputants. The stories allow listeners to ascribe intent and motives to the actors in ways that make sense to the narrator. In some cases, the stories may reflect the subjective reality of the narrator, but in other cases the stories may reflect the collective experience of a group, and this experience is often shared through a narrative that is passed on from one generation to the other. In either case and in our

14 Michael Kearney, "World View Theory and Study," *Annual Review of Anthropology*, Vol. 4, 1975, p. 247.

15 Oscar Nudler, "In Search of a Theory of Conflict Resolution: Taking a New Look at World Views Analysis," *ICAR Newsletter*, 5, 1993, p. 1.

16 Jayne Seminare Docherty, *Learning Lessons from Waco: When the Parties Bring Their Gods to the Negotiation Table*, Syracuse University Press, Syracuse, 2001.

perspective, Nudler and Docherty's approach may present an entry point to an enhanced understanding of the issues as articulated by the narrator. In addition, it presents practitioners with an additional dilemma. In an environment where ODR technology allows for easy access, and for more and more work across clearly different cultures and worldviews, the problem of how to deal with an increased awareness of cultural factors and with the multicultural nature of the parties, the mediators and the facilitators is critical.

In a later work, Campbell[17] and Docherty argue that the intervenors (or third parties) are often themselves engaged in the process of framing the stories, and that by doing so they thereby impact the intervention. This is direct acknowledgment that third parties bring to the table their own cultures, perceptual filters, and worldviews – they are not neutral players in the process. By framing the issues, occasionally at the expense of the inclusion or exclusion of the frame the parties bring to the conflict, the third parties can endorse or negate the views of the parties. It is the frame that determines the perception by which the parties make sense of the conflict, what it is, who is involved, how it should be resolved, and what is acceptable and unacceptable.

Fourth parties – the technology – are also not neutral players in the process of conflict engagement. To the extent that platforms enhance the ability to share stories and give parties the opportunity to exchange narratives and explain worldviews, ODR can enhance the process of dealing with cultural differences. To the extent that platforms limit the ability to exchange worldviews, they are likely to impede positive conflict engagement.

So how does a third party deal with the increasing likelihood that work online will be multicultural? Appiah, addressing identity, which is an important aspect of one's culture, speaks to the skill of working across divides, writing:

> You have to work with others inside and outside the labeled group in order to reframe [their identity] so they fit you better; and you can do that collective work only if you recognize that the results must serve others as well[18]

Again, to the extent that ODR platforms enhance working across divides, and find ways to compensate for the loss of message complexity that occurs when using video, audio, or text channels, the more they allow for positive intercultural interaction.

---

17 M.C. Campbell and J.S. Docherty, "What's in the Frame? (That Which We Call a Rose by Any Other Name Would Smell as Sweet)," *Marquette Law Review*, 87, Special Issue 4, 2004.

18 Kwame Anthony Appiah, *The Lies that Bind: Rethinking Identity*, Liveright Publishing Corporation, New York, 2018, p. 218.

5 ISSUES FOR THIRD PARTIES

Most definitions of culture address norms, beliefs, behaviors, and values held by groups, usually large groups. For a third party engaged primarily in face-to-face dispute resolution, there are some immediately evident problems with anticipating parties' behavior based on group beliefs and values. The problems vary between the extremes of dispute resolution. But whether it is face-to-face work among small numbers of parties, or online dispute resolution efforts allowing large groups, widely dispersed, to interact synchronously or asynchronously, cultural differences, at least our perceptions of them, can generate problems.

Perhaps the largest problem for both parties and third parties comes with the attempt to 'read' culture. Even when we are communicating immediately, in the room with someone who looks like us, speaks the same language, shares many social rules, shares a national history, etc., the opportunity for misunderstanding is present. As technology shrinks the world, it generates ever more opportunities for communicating with those of very different cultures, and it would seem reasonable to assume that the opportunity for misunderstanding and cultural disconnects are also increasing. The mediator or the parties may expect one set of beliefs and behaviors based on external signs – and be very wrong. We refer to this dilemma as the 'Colgate-Crest Caveat.' If you have 300 million people in the statistical universe, it is possible to use past behavior to predict within a couple of percentage points which toothpaste they will buy in the aggregate. But if the statistical universe is one person out of that 300 million – all bets are off. He or she may radically diverge from the 'norm.' A 70-year-old white Southern male may exhibit all of the cultural characteristics perceived to be common or 'normal' for his group. Or, he might be the aberrant individual who defies all of the group norms. There is no way of knowing without questioning and listening, which makes the ability to ask, listen, and paraphrase that are the center of third-party work. particularly important in dealing with cultural differences. If one takes as given that there is a loss of message complexity when using online communication channels, it makes compensating behavior by the third party (e.g., more frequent reframing, paraphrasing, reality checking, etc.) critical.

According to Jadallah[19] another major challenge for third parties is their ability or willingness to revisit working assumptions as they relate to culture, especially around deeply held values and beliefs (worldviews) when dealing with cross-cultural issues. Her study on the role of conflict engagement practitioners post-9/11 reported concerns over their inherent biases in dealing with different worldviews. They conveyed the need to shift their own thinking in relation to the operational and cultural assumptions of their

19 Alma Abdul-Hadi Jadallah, George Mason University, Ph.D., "Conflict Analysis and Resolution," Dissertation: Reflection on Practice: The Impact of 9/11 on Conflict Resolvers (unpublished), 2006.

work, and the usefulness of their tools when dealing with trauma and violence. They reported gaining additional insights into a culture – in this case the Arab and Islamic worldviews – that increased their realization that culture is a variable that warrants additional attention.

Basically, as third parties, we create problems when we assume that group culture is uniformly shared – when we ignore the Colgate-Crest Caveat. In fact, we are all multicultural, and although our cultural identities are rooted in tradition or custom, cultural identification remains fluid, flexible and based on specific situations in which we find ourselves.[20] With the advent of e-commerce and routine interaction among individuals from many countries, legal systems, and cultural groups, one could assume that intercultural misunderstanding would be a major feature of dispute resolution online. However, what appears to be happening in the world of international e-commerce is the development of an online culture into which individuals from many local cultures step into when they are working online. So, the behaviors or reactions that one might expect from parties if they were sitting at the table together, involved in mediation over an issue related to family or community, are put aside and replaced by appropriate behavior for the online commerce community the parties have joined voluntarily.

Even in social contexts, the increasing exposure to 'foreign' cultures through travel and international media has made it possible for individuals to be multicultural in a way that was not common a generation or two ago. A colleague suggests that his intercultural experience has created for him a 'cultural supermarket' allowing him to pick and choose which cultural attributes are dominant depending upon the circumstances in which he finds himself.[21] We suspect that this does not change his basic worldview – it may change his behavior, and his willingness to 'tolerate' the behavior of others. The rise of ODR and the attendant technology that enables work at a distance, across borders and across cultural divides, has made it more likely that conflict engagement efforts of all kinds will have to deal with three broad areas of cultural influence – in essence, a multicultural triangle: the culture of the third party, the culture of the parties, and the culture in the code. As we have suggested, using video, audio, and text channels for ODR call for adjustments in communication to describe, understand, and adjust to cultural differences. The addition of the Fourth Party culture means that the technology is both a participant and a channel.

20 Avruch (2008).

21 Dr. Mohamed S. Abdel Wahab, in communication with the authors.

Figure 8.2 Multi-Cultural Triangle

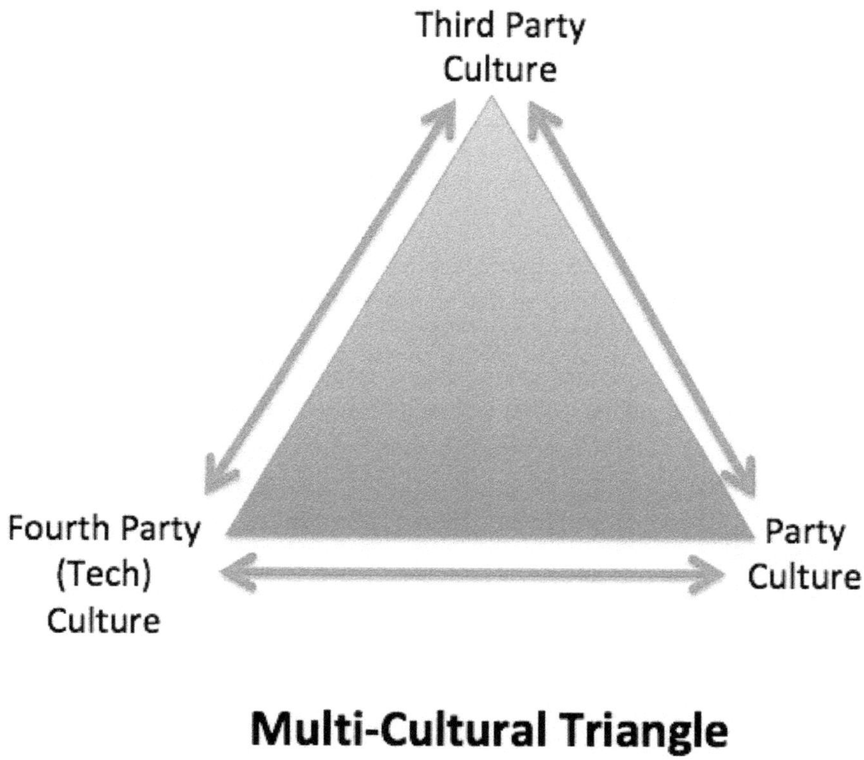

It may be that the increasing use of technology for dispute resolution will do for our online work what increased travel and cross-cultural exposure have done for our colleague in the cultural supermarket. But as of now, we have not seen the creation of an online venue that, in and of itself and without conscious work, offers a culturally safe place to go for online exchanges.

In addition to the cultural attributes of the parties, it is important to keep in mind the fact that third parties (and fourth parties[22]) bring to the table their own set of values, norms, assumptions, etc., which we can refer to as the 'culture of mediation'. The focus here is not on the culture of the *mediator* as it would traditionally be defined: the race, age, ethnicity, socio-economic status, worldview, etc., of the third party. Rainey refers instead to the *culture of mediation*, created by a complex of assumptions, values,

22 Ethan Katsh and Janet Rifkin, in their seminal book on ODR – Online Dispute Resolution: Resolving Disputes in Cyber-Space – offered the concept of the fourth party. It has come increasingly common to refer to the creation of artificial or augmented intelligence to assist third parties, or even take over third party actions as the Fourth Party, but initially, according to Katsh, the fourth party concept referred to the influence that any use of technology has on what was a traditionally face-to-face endeavor.

processes, and expectations that the mediator brings to the table as a result of her or his training and interaction with a body of seemingly like-minded professionals. *The Culture in the Code* argued that the North American Model of mediation, and the culture of mediation that it spawned, was a driving force behind much ODR development around the world. In short, the US was exporting the North American culture of mediation in the ADR and ODR work in which US-funded professionals were engaged. Fourteen years on from *The Culture in the Code,* the situation has significantly changed. The book for which this chapter is a part is evidence enough that third parties are working to create ODR platforms, and to adapt existing online tools to ODR work, in virtually every major international setting. To this work, they bring local and regional sensibilities and approaches to conflict that have stretched the boundaries of, and perhaps have basically redefined, the culture of mediation in online venues.

Discussions about culture in the context of dispute resolution or conflict engagement have tended to focus on the culture of the parties and the ability to adapt to the potential gulf between the third party and the parties. That seems to be changing. Schonewille and Schonewille have written about the 'variegated' nature of mediation practice around the world,[23] and the UN has organized the 'Singapore Convention on Mediation,'[24] which addresses the need to recognize some standards for mediation practice across borders. Rainey and Goncalves have argued that due to the variegated nature of practice across borders, it would be wise to create a universal code of disclosure to let parties know which mediation culture or process is being brought by the third party to her or his work.[25] Even so, it is still necessary to remember that each set of third parties, and developers of fourth party software, bring their own cultural biases.

6 ODR CAVEATS: WHAT SHOULD THE ODR COMMUNITY KEEP IN MIND?

Given the persistence of cultural differences and their impact on dispute resolution generally, there are some caveats that ODR practitioners, service providers, and system designers should keep in mind.

First, there is no truly 'uni-cultural' mediation or negotiation environment, online or face-to-face. The mediator and the parties may all be of the same race, from the same country, of the same age, of the same social class, etc., but no matter how homogeneous

23 M. Schonewille and F. Schonewille, eds., *The Variegated Nature of Mediation: A Comparative Study of Mediation Regulation and Practices in Europe and the World,* Eleven International Publishing, The Netherlands, 2014.

24 United Nations Convention on International Settlement Agreements Resulting From Mediation, UNCITRAL Secretariat, United Nations, New York, 2019.

25 Ana Goncalves, F. Bogacz, and D. Rainey, "Beyond the Singapore Convention: The Importance of Creating a 'Code of Disclosure' to Make International Mediation Mainstream," *The International Journal of Online Dispute Resolution,* Vol. 6, No. 2 (2019), pp. 164-169.

the group at the table (or online) may appear there will always be, at some level, cultural divergence. Obviously, the more heterogeneous the group, the more one would expect to find overt cultural elements at work in misunderstandings and confrontations. Unfortunately, what we assume to be obvious may, in fact, mask a level of complexity that could drive apparently homogenous groups to have more cultural conflict than apparently heterogeneous groups. Gaining cultural competency and fluency is a life-long journey: we cannot assume homogeneity among one cultural group nor that we have mastered such skills to a point where we can predict behaviors.

Second, for ODR practitioners this suggests that compensating for message loss is important. But it also means that taking advantage of some of the unique characteristics of ODR (the ability to offer time to think by using asynchronous platforms, or using anonymous input to take away perceived danger, or using non-visual platforms to remove immediate assumptions based on image) can be an important difference between ODR and traditional face-to-face practice.

Third, the culture of mediation is as important as the culture of the parties, and in some cases more important. Design of ODR systems should be undertaken with the understanding that creator biases will influence choices made in the design process, and designers should be aware that maximum flexibility in the configuration of online spaces will increase the 'culture-friendly' nature of ODR applications, by allowing for multiple approaches to process instead of being locked into one process that may be culturally inappropriate.

Fourth, designers and practitioners should be aware that online communication in general, including ODR, has created a 'third path' into which participants from divergent cultures may step when working together online. To some degree, the continuing pervasiveness of the Internet, and access to it through ever more 'smart' mobile technology, has begun to create a new culture, shared by what have come to be known as 'netizens'.[26] This notion was driven home to the authors by reflecting that a young relative who was born in 1992 has never lived in a world without commercial Internet. Interacting for one's entire life using ICT, as many of our colleagues and clients now have done, has made it possible, or unavoidable, to interact in obviously intercultural exchanges, and we think it has begun the process of changing their worldviews.

Historically, there has been what we perceive to be a 'fork in the road' for ODR, particularly as it applies to research and development of ODR tools. This split can be seen as a differing set of demands for e-commerce and the courts, and for more 'traditional' third-party work in social settings (family mediation, community mediation, etc.). E-commerce operates with huge input, disputes that are similar in nature, and disputes in which many cases need only access to information to resolve.

---

26 Netizen is a combination of InterNET and citIZEN, used to denote a person routinely using the Internet.

This is a 'wholesale' approach, and is based on the willingness and ability of large numbers of culturally diverse parties to step into the fourth party's structure. The courts, led in the US by the National Center for State Courts (NCSC), have adopted many of the fundamental elements of ODR from e-commerce. The courts also have a large caseload, and operate within a bounded universe controlled by the law. For the courts, a legitimate question is whether they are training staff in the role of culture in the various phases of interactions with the parties, and with sensitivity to the context and power dynamics imbedded in the court system especially as it relates to historically marginalized communities.

More traditional practitioners face fewer cases than e-commerce or the courts, more diverse cases, and cases in which there is often some expectation of an ongoing relationship among the parties. There are other differences, but these differences are the ones that really seem to drive research and development in ODR. Traditional third parties take a 'retail' approach to ODR, and one where, due to the number of participants and the nature of the issues, individual cultures are more likely to emerge as barriers or problems.

On the one hand, e-commerce (and to some degree, courts, the government or large multi-party venues) is pushing development of algorithm driven systems that can deal with massive input, sort cases, automatically offer information, and channel cases to live mediators when necessary. On the other hand, traditional ADR, after spending a lot of time borrowing applications from other endeavors (*e.g.*, group and team software) is beginning to push development of analytic and process tools designed to give live mediators information that assists in traditional settings. For both e-commerce and the courts, and ultimately for private ODR practice, there is the danger that algorithms and AI will be created using, and will learn from, data that is itself biased and culturally insensitive.

Stepping outside the world of online commerce and communication and into the world of social disputes brings with it a change in the perceived need for parties to flex out of their own cultures, and brings a different set of concerns and responsibilities for the third party. It may also allow for a deeper discussion of the context that informs their actions and decisions.

Given these observations, and the fact that a variety of trans-national dispute resolution processes, including a number of online processes, have been successful in handling a wide range of commercial and Internet-based disputes, insisting that cultural differences among commercial disputants will radically affect the willingness of parties to use ODR systems is almost surely a 'Type II' error. That is to say, arguing that cultural differences will doom commercial ODR or 'traditional' ODR to high failure rates, even where the disputant's cultures are quite different, is probably a case of seeing problems where none exist. However, not recognizing the impact of cultural differences in the application of online technology to social disputes is, it would seem, a Type I error.

It also seems clear that cultural influences on ODR will have an impact on international and trans-national disputes, but will perhaps be even more important in intra-national disputes where race, class, sex, tribal affiliation, identity and intersectionality, gender etc., are important.

The urge to create algorithm driven systems, and to create 'bespoke' systems for e-commerce, is not surprising. The growth of online dispute resolution is, as has been noted by many, tied to the growth of commerce and communication on the Internet. Ethan Katsh observed that:

> The decision by the National Science Foundation in 1992 to lift its ban on Internet-based commercial activity was highly controversial and enormously significant. After the ban's removal, disputes related to online commerce began to surface.[27]

A driving force behind the development of online systems was the inability of existing legal systems to cope with disputes among parties geographically dispersed and with no real hope of developing a proximate relationship. As Colin Rule argues:

> Legal systems are tied to geography almost by definition [...] It is obvious that transaction partners who meet on the Web can take little comfort from the redress options provided in the face-to-face world. You can't merely recreate offline judicial mechanisms online and expect them to work, with e-judges making e-rulings enforced by e-police running e-jails. The model doesn't work, on a fundamental level [...][28]

The elements of commercial and purely online disputes exist in a range that is narrower than disputes generated within the family or the community, or among political groups, and lend themselves more to bespoke, model driven, applications. For example, if party A buys something online from party B, it is likely that a dispute, if one exists, will fall into some predictable categories: I did not receive the item; it was not what you advertised it to be; it arrived broken or damaged; you did not pay me, etc. One may be a father, brother, son, elder, or leader, in one's home culture, but when operating as a seller or buyer of goods and services over the Internet there is a role one assumes that brings with it expectations and behaviors different from the ones at work in the home culture.

Finally, there is a tacit acknowledgment among most of the disputants involved in trans-national online commerce that, in lieu of a set of universal e-laws, e-judges, and

27 E. Katsh, "Online Dispute Resolution: Some Implications for the Emergence of Law in Cyberspace", *Lex Electronica*, Vol. 10, No. 3 (2006), https://www.lex-electronica.org/files/sites/103/10-3_katsh.pdf - Last accessed 2021.

28 C. Rule, *Online Dispute Resolution for Business*, Jossey-Bass, San Francisco, CA, 2002, p. 5.

e-police, both parties must, in order to resolve their dispute, find some mutually agreeable process to follow. Both parties step into a process that may not be what either party would prefer, but which is seen by both as an expedient way to reach the goal of resolving their conflict. Finding this middle ground approach is, at base, an exercise in managing worldviews and cultural differences.

The need for trust in conflict resolution systems is related directly to the fact that, in order to engage in conflict resolution at all, it is necessary to step forward and, on some level, expose one's self, identifying the issues causing conflict and identifying the other party in the conflict. This is not without risk. A range of fears running from anxiety at actually facing the other party to anxiety regarding information being gathered, stored, and possibly used to cause harm, affect the willingness of parties to use ADR/ODR systems. It is, then, first necessary that parties in dispute resolution trust that they will not be harmed, either by the other party or by the use of the dispute resolution process itself. Ethical guidelines should guide the process in all its phases.

In some locations, the trust in law and established systems does not exist, and by extension there is a tendency to distrust any process run by a powerful third party. Two examples will illustrate the problem. In Eastern Europe an ODR project sought to offer dispute resolution, including arbitration, to individuals involved in land ownership disputes. When asked about a pool of arbitrators who would be acceptable to the parties, the response was quick and clear: 'we want lawyers from anywhere in the world but here.' In Sierra Leone, an access to justice project with an ODR component sought to create intellectual property contracts for artists involved in community building and peace building. The local artists' initial response to rule of law and access to justice was, "we don't want contracts – contracts are just for the big guys to take advantage of the little guys."

In some way, both for online commercial disputes and for social disputes, the ODR provider must establish in her or his service a basic sense of utility and safety for potential users. Without the basic ability to trust the system, commercial disputants may be less willing to flex into the system, and social disputants may not be willing to risk attempts at dispute resolution.

This raises the issue of how parties feel they are being treated by the process, the other party, and the third party. Basic willingness to use dispute resolution systems is enhanced when parties feel they are respected and treated appropriately by the third party and the process. In a commercial context, the buyer/seller relationship and the assumed roles of the parties, drives the perception of appropriateness or respect. In social contexts respect may be related to social status, age, sex, or other factors that vary widely from culture to culture.[29] Online applications generally treat the parties as equals, with no deference given to either side. In a buyer/seller relationship where the primary issue is likely to be tightly focused and oriented toward a monetary exchange, this likely is not a problem, even across divergent cultures. However, when conflicts move outside the commercial context, treating every participant as an equal or approaching them in the same way may cause discomfort or a feeling of inappropriateness.

The desire to feel that communication is possible and appropriate, is a third constant that all dispute resolution systems must meet, no matter the context. Appropriate communication goes beyond the ability to understand the language being used by the other party, although that is a large factor in international online dispute resolution. Also involved in the concept of appropriate communication is the need for parties to feel that their voices, and their ideas, actually are being heard and understood by the other party. In fact, in some conflict resolution efforts, the ability to convince one party that he or she has been heard and understood may be all that is necessary to open the way to resolution.

Even if one accepts the idea that there are constants across cultures, and constantly required attributes for online and offline dispute resolution systems, there is still the problem of figuring out how to define and achieve trust, respect, and communication across cultures. What looks safe and fair to me may look risky and biased to you. This is where local cultural knowledge and competency, and reflective practice are truly key to the creation of successful ODR, and ADR, systems.

7 CONCLUSION

To state what we think is obvious, ODR is not just an analog of ADR. With the further development of artificial intelligence and the ability of third parties to use ever more sophisticated technological assistants, ODR will become even less an analog of ADR.

Even in the face of increased access by individuals of varying cultures and nationalities, constructive adaptation of conflict engagement processes will not come naturally and without thought. Recently one of the authors observed a joint online process involving mediators from Brazil, Kuwait, and the US. They were using the same online platform, but their approach to the mediation was remarkably different, and was driven, we think, by both their local culture of mediation and their own local culture and individual worldviews. It is unlikely that these three mediators, working with parties who were comfortable with their individual styles, would achieve maximum

29 *See* Amr Abdallah, "Principles of Islamic Interpersonal Conflict Intervention: A Search within Islam and Western Literature", *Journal of Law and Religion*, Vol. XV, Nos. 1 & 2, 2000-2001, pp. 151-184; and Mohammed Abu Nimer, "Conflict Resolution Training in the Middle East: Lessons to be Learned", *Journal of International Negotiation*, Special Issues on Conflict Resolution Training (Fall 1997), pp. 99-116.

success using exactly the same online tools and 'virtual room' configurations. Their practice is different, and their use of technology should probably be different.

Figure 8.3 Elements of Practice

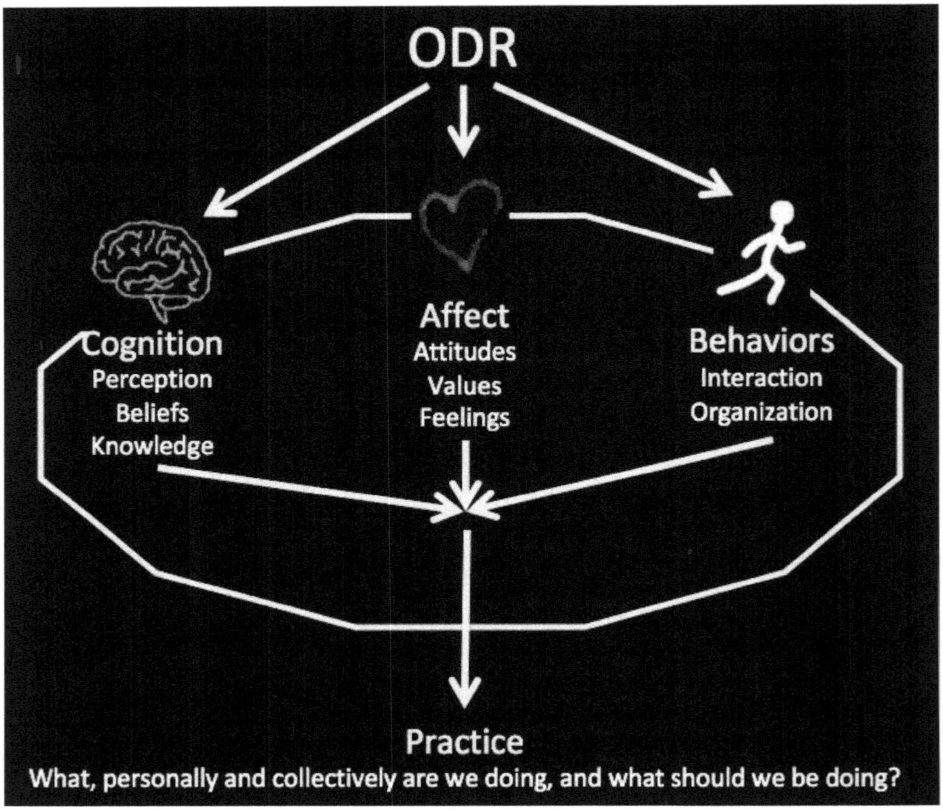

One way to look at the development of an appropriate online practice is to consider the impact of cognition, affect, and behavior.[30]

Cognition includes perceptions, beliefs, and knowledge (what we know or think we know). Introducing ODR technology may not radically affect what we believe or what we think we know, but it is likely to influence our perception of the conflict environment, the third party, and the parties across the table. As a practitioner, if I'm thinking clearly about practice – how to actually engage with the parties – I need to be aware of the parties (and my own) beliefs and knowledge, and be ready to address them in a positive way in a communication environment where some of the complexity of verbal/nonverbal/ environmental messages is lost. I also need to be conscious of the fact that working

30 The cognition, affect, behavior model was developed by Alma Abdul-Hadi Jadallah for her doctoral research on the role of conflict resolvers post 9/11. See footnote 19 for full reference.

with technology channels will have an impact on perceptions, and I need to develop approaches to practice that allow for expressing, testing, and adjusting perception of the context and the participants.

Affect involves attitudes, values, and feelings. Again, it is unlikely that working online will change our basic values. But it is likely that working online will have an impact on attitudes and feelings about the process and the venue. If I invite you to a mediation session in my office there are some things that I probably will not consider to be problems. For instance, I do not have to teach you to talk. If we speak different languages we may have to work out some form of translation, but the basic notion of walking into a room and directly addressing another party is one we all understand, whether we are comfortable with it or not. But if I invite you into a virtual room to work online, I may indeed have to teach you how to 'talk' effectively in that environment. The extent to which I coach you and prepare you to work in the online environment will have an impact on how you feel about the process, whether you feel heard by the other party, and whether you are seen as a competent third party. It takes some time and some work with the parties to address the non-rational, emotional components of conflict engagement. Ignored, those components, and the worldview the parties bring to the table, may cause their perceptual filters to be rather narrow and restrictive, and that may make it hard to reach any cultural convergence.

Behaviors, in this model, refer to the third party's interaction and organization. Both are, or should be, radically affected by working online. As we discussed earlier, the loss of channel capacity when sending messages makes the way one interacts successfully with parties online different from the way we interact in a face-to-face environment. The fact that I lose some or most of a message when I strip away nonverbal online means that I have to in some way shift my interaction patterns to compensate for that loss. It also means that because the 'normal' things I would do in a face-to-face environment to control or sequence the conversation (using nonverbal cues to indicate who should talk, etc.) have to be done more overtly, verbally, and in a more directive manner online. Organization is also affected. For a recent session, one of the authors made a test meeting two weeks prior to the session mandatory. In that meeting the parties were asked to 'touch' all of the aspects of the technology that would be used in the real session, and it was possible to test the connections, review the access to technology for each participant, and to answer any questions the participants had about how the session would be conducted. In addition, a written set of instructions was sent to each participant, and an open invitation to ask questions before the session began was offered. The result was that the participants had been taught 'how to talk' in the session, and they were familiar with all of the actions they would need to take during the session. Things went well, and everyone seemed satisfied after the session was concluded. Less organization would have risked more problems, and more negative perceptions by the parties. What does this have to do with culture? Organization and preparation done for online work, if done well, can give a third party some insight into the attitudes and worldview the parties will bring to the table, and can allow for adjustments to make parties more comfortable, or at the least forewarn the third party that there might be cultural issues.

Decades ago in the academic world of cross-cultural work there was a popular notion that it was possible to learn a taxonomy that would prepare an individual to operate successfully in a foreign culture: in certain places never use your left hand at the dinner table, do not look anyone directly in the eye when talking, never show the soles of your shoes, etc. The problem at the time was that those taxonomies ignored the fact that every person is an individual and in order to truly understand her or his worldview and cultural taxonomy, you have to deal with them as individuals. And, in the intervening years, the ability of anyone, anywhere in the world, to observe 'foreign' cultures through film, television, and now the Internet, have made most behavior, even if not appropriate in a particular area, at least not shocking.

As Edward Said argued:

> one of the great advances in modern cultural theory is the realization, almost universally acknowledged, that cultures are hybrid and heterogeneous and … that cultures and civilizations are so interrelated and interdependent as to beggar any unitary or simply delineated description of their individuality.[31]

What this means for ODR practitioners is that we have the exciting possibility of interacting across borders and across cultures in a way that has never existed in the history of the world.

It also means that we have to combine cognition, affect, and behavior to practice sensitively and effectively in this cultural supermarket.

31 Edward Said, *Orientalism*, Penguin Books, London, 2003, p. 346.

Chapter 9 ODR for E-Commerce: Legal Standards and Developments in Asia and Europe

Pablo Cortés, Aura Esther Vilalta Nicuesa and Chittu Nagarajan

1 Introduction

As electronic transactions and online sales continue to expand internationally and retail sales online increasingly surpass sales in physical stores,[1] effective online mechanisms for resolving online disputes are becoming more necessary. Inevitably, a growing number of transactions in e-commerce is leading to millions of complaints, many of which are related to buyers' dissatisfaction about late delivery and to non-conformity with the online description.

Online companies and marketplaces are progressively integrating internal online customer services, conflict avoidance tools[2] – namely, rating and reputation systems, chargebacks or money back guaranties, escrow accounts, account suspension or blocking – coupled with private Online Dispute Resolution (ODR) mechanisms that seek to provide quick redress and to avoid expensive and slow court litigation. The eBay and Alibaba complaint handling system are among the first and most remarkable ODR initiatives in the field of e-commerce.

Today, the delivery of goods and services are provided online on a regular basis. This shift to the virtual world is also happening in the dispute resolution arena, which is helping to reduce the barriers to access to justice. Indeed, access to justice is an internationally recognized fundamental right, that requires for its effectiveness to guarantee not only access to the courts, but also and more importantly, access to effective redress mechanisms through extrajudicial forms of dispute resolution – commonly referred as Alternative Dispute Resolution or ADR – that can offer simple,

---

1 In the US the total market-share of sales done with 'non-store' retailers, or online, was higher than general merchandise, including department stores sales, according to the US Commerce Department in 2019. *See* United States Census Bureau, U. S. Department of Commerce. Available at www.census.gov/retail/marts/www/marts_current.pdf [accessed 29 May 2020].

2 *See* more in A. E. Vilalta, 'Reputational Feedback Systems and Consumer Rights: Improving the European Online Redress System', (2019) 5(1) *International Journal of Online Dispute Resolution* 122.

fast, economical and reliable online resolution channels.[3] These ADR and ODR options are increasingly underpinned by legal standards from international organizations that have enacted guidelines, technical notes, codes of conduct and international conventions. This emerging legal framework has the twin aim of increasing access to justice and promoting competition, especially on a cross-border basis, by promoting suitable redress avenues. Accordingly, the European Regulation on ODR has acknowledged this twin aim, and together with the EU Directive on Consumer ADR, seek to increase trade within the EU, in particular through its digital market.[4]

Similarly, a number of international legal instruments is emerging from the United Nations with a view to boost online redress channels applicable to online commercial (B2B) and consumer (B2C) disputes, notably the UNCITRAL Technical Notes on Online Dispute Resolution 2017, the United Nations Convention on International Settlement Agreements Resulting from Mediation (the 'Singapore Convention on Mediation') 2018 and the updated United Nations Guidelines for Consumer Protection (UNGCP) 2015. Likewise, other international organizations have issued dispute resolution recommendations (e.g. The Organization for Economic Cooperation and Development Recommendation on Consumer Dispute Resolution and Redress),[5] collaborative services (e.g. The International Chamber of Commerce Dispute Resolution Services),[6] standards (e.g. The Standards for ODR of the International Center for Online Dispute Resolution or ICODR),[7] and competency criteria for

3 *See* Arts. 6-13 of the European Convention of Human Rights 1950. *See also* Council of Europe, Technical Study on Online Dispute Resolution Mechanisms CDCJ (2018)5 (1 August 2018). Available at https://rm.coe.int/cdcj-2018-5e-technical-study-odr/1680913249 [accessed 29 May 2020].

4 Directive 2013/11/EU on Alternative Dispute Resolution for Consumer Disputes O.J. (L 165) 63 and Regulation (EU) 524/2013 on Online Dispute Resolution for Consumer Disputes O.J. (L 165) 1.

5 Adopted on 12 July 2007, it is devoted to provide Governments with a framework to help consumers resolve domestic and cross-border disputes. This organization produced a previous Guidelines for Consumer Protection in the Context of Electronic Commerce in 1999 and a Guidelines for Protecting Consumers from Fraudulent and Deceptive Commercial Practices across Borders in 2003 that recommended further development of online dispute resolution redress for consumers. *See* OECD Recommendation on Consumer Dispute Resolution and Redress. Available at www.oecd.org/sti/ieconomy/oecdrecommendationonconsumerdisputeresolutionandredress.htm [accessed 29 May 2020].

6 The International Chamber of Commerce (ICC) launched in 2019 a mobile application for businesses – the ICC Dispute Resolution Services (DRS) app – that facilitates access to rules, standard clauses, guidance notes, commission reports, and a catalogue of dispute resolution tools and information from both ICC's International Court of Arbitration and Centre for ADR. Available at https://2go.iccwbo.org/icc-drs-app [accessed 29 May 2020].

7 ICODR is an international non-profit organization that drives the development, convergence, and adoption of open standards to resolve disputes using information and communications technology (ICTs). It promotes worldwide standards for all forms of technology-assisted dispute resolution to protect the right of free access to justice. Its Standards are devoted to ensure quality ODR programs and are built on previous works in 2016 by the National Center for Technology and Dispute Resolution (NCTDR) on ethical principles for online dispute resolution. It includes: accessibility, accountability, competency, confidentiality, equality, fairness, impartiality, neutrality, legality, security and transparency.

professionals dealing with online processes (e.g. The International Mediation Institute e-mediation competency criteria for e-mediators).[8]

In addition, an increasing number of consumer protection agencies are embedding ODR techniques to support the efficient resolution of mostly consumer and small claims, such as the Brazilian *Consumidor.gov.br.*,[9] the Mexican *Concilianet*[10] or the Canadian *Parle.*[11] The use of ODR is also reaching courts and tribunals, such as the British Columbia Civil Resolution Tribunal,[12] the Chinese Hangzhou Internet Court,[13] the English Civil Money Claim Online,[14] and the U.S. e-Courts pilot programs.[15]

This chapter discusses the recent legal developments in the field of e-commerce and ODR at national and regional level. To that end, the chapter starts first by discussing the

8 The Independent Standards Commission described the criteria for professional competency in online mediation in order to help to make informed decisions and help competent e-mediators promote their ODR services. The Criteria are presented in two categories: i) General requirements for the qualifying assessment programs (QAPs); ii) Substantive Criteria for e-Mediators that include: Experience of the e-Mediation, ensuring demonstrated experience of e-mediation, knowledge of the e-mediation, with theory and practical e-mediation skills, including a method for the performance-based assessment. Available at www.imimediation.org/about/who-are-imi/odr-tf/ [accessed 29 May 2020].

9 Public service offered by the Brazilian National Consumer Secretariat (SENACON) at the Ministry of Justice since 2014 Created by Decree No. 8,573, of 19 November 2015. It consists of a platform that allows customers to directly communicate with traders. Only applicable to consumers and traders that are registered on the site and the company must formally adhere to the tool. *See* website available at www.consumidor.gov.br/pages/principal/?1577491100593 [accessed 29 May 2020].

10 Government-sponsored conciliation platform in Mexico, created in 2008 by Profeco – public body of the Ministry of Economy of the Mexican Federal Government, responsible for carrying out conciliation and arbitration processes. Trader's participation is compulsory.

11 Public platform designed in 2016 by the University of Montreal and the Ministry of Justice in charge of the Consumer Protection Office devoted to online dispute resolution for customers of the Quebec's Consumer Protection Agency (CPA). This platform can be adapted according to different structured processes of negotiation, mediation and adjudication. *See* more in Report of Workshop for Developing an APEC. Collaborative Framework for Online Dispute Resolution. Available at http://mddb.apec.org/Documents/2019/EC/EC1/19_ec1_009.pdf [accessed 29 May 2020].

12 This public dispute resolution service has replaced their small claims court for disputes under $5,000 and condominium disputes with online dispute resolution. CRT has recently expanded to motor vehicle injury disputes under $50,000 and disputes of societies and cooperative associations of any amount. The process provides for online negotiation, mediation, and adjudication. In its first year of operation CRT closed more than 6,200 cases, with only 8% of the cases being resolved by adjudication. The majority (79%) of the participants would recommend CRT to others. *See* https://civilresolutionbc.ca/.

13 Combines ODR and court procedure for disputes related to online sales contracts, liability for defective products, online service contracts, financial loan agreements, online micro-credit contracts, copyright infringement and electronic service contracts. The system is embedding blockchain technology allowing access to transactions, communications, documents and testimonials so that they cannot be manipulated.

14 *See generally*, P. Cortés and T. Takagi, "The Civil Money Claim Online: The Flagship Project of Court Digitalization in England and Wales", (2019) 25(8) *Computer and Telecommunications Law Review* 207-212.

15 Such as the MI-Resolve in the Michigan district court that provides negotiation and mediation for small claims, the ODR Franklin County Municipal Court in Ohio for small claims providing negotiation, the New York Unified Court System providing e-tracking case service, the Texas Travis County Justice for the Peace Precinct, or the Utah Small claims ODR program. *See generally*, A. J. Schmitz, "Expanding Access to Remedies through E-Court Initiatives", (2019) 67(1) *Buffalo Law Review* 89-163.

main international initiatives – such as the United Nations Commission on International Trade Law (UNCITRAL) Technical Notes for ODR, the revised United Nations Guidelines for Consumer Protection, the United Nations Convention on the Enforcement of International Settlement Agreements Resulting from Mediation (Singapore Convention), and the Asia-Pacific Economic Cooperation (APEC) Collaborative Framework for Online Dispute Resolution. Secondly, the chapter provides updates on key regional and national developments in the field of ODR for e-Commerce in Asia and in Europe. Finally, this chapter critically discusses the EU ODR regulatory framework which sets up an ODR platform to facilitate the resolution of national and cross-border consumer disputes arising out of e-commerce transactions. It has been observed that the EU ODR platform is not carrying out the main function for which it has been designed the referral of unresolved consumer complaints to nationally approved ADR entities, and its design is currently undergoing significant changes that seek to increase the effectiveness for its users.

2 International Standards on ODR

2.1 The UNCITRAL Technical Notes for Online Dispute Resolution

Adopted in December 2017 by UNCITRAL, this international instrument is a non-binding document intended to foster the development of ODR. It compiles a number of guiding principles of a procedure for the settlement of online cross-border low-value disputes arising out of both a business-to-business (B2B) as well as business-to-consumer (B2C) transactions.[16] It also provides guidance for ODR platforms, systems, neutrals and third neutral parties. The Technical Notes recommend that all States and other stakeholders use this guide in designing and implementing ODR systems for cross-border commercial transactions to reach a uniform approach to ODR. Yet, they are not intended to impose any legal requirement binding on the parties or any persons and/or entities administering or enabling an ODR proceeding. Eventually, the Technical Notes did not include the accreditation of ODR providers, nor the enforcement of ODR decisions and the substantive principles for the resolution of e-commerce disputes. Below is a discussion of the main principles, the requirements for third neutral parties, and the two procedural tracks proposed to resolve cross-border online disputes.

16 *See* UNCITRAL Technical Notes on Online Dispute Resolution. Available at https://uncitral.un.org/sites/uncitral.un.org/files/media-documents/uncitral/en/v1700382_english_technical_notes_on_odr.pdf [accessed 29 May 2020].

2.1.1 Main Principles

- *Transparency*[17] The Notes recommend: i) to disclose any relationship between the ODR administrator and a particular vendor, so that users of the service are informed of potential conflicts of interest; ii) to publish anonymized data or statistics on outcomes in ODR processes, in order to enable parties to assess overall records, consistent with applicable principles of confidentiality; iii) to facilitate relevant information on the ODR administrator's website in a user-friendly and accessible manner; iv) and ODR proceedings be subject to the same confidentiality, due process standards and principles that apply to dispute resolution in offline contexts.
- *Independence.*[18] The ODR administrator should adopt: i) a code of ethics for its neutrals, in order to guide neutrals as to conflicts of interest and other rules of conduct; and ii) policies dealing with identifying and handling conflicts of interest.
- *Expertise.*[19] The Notes emphasize that the ODR administrator should: i) implement comprehensive policies governing selection and training of neutrals; and ii) establish an internal oversight/quality assurance process to ensure that a neutral conforms with the standards it has set for itself.
- *Consent.*[20] The ODR process should be based on the explicit and informed consent of the parties
- *Efficiency.*[21] The ODR process ought to be simple, fast, efficient, and it should not impose costs that are disproportionate to the economic value at stake. It is desirable that all communications in ODR proceedings take place via the ODR platform through an electronic address. It is considered also desirable that the ODR administrator promptly acknowledge receipt of any communication by the ODR platform, notify parties of the availability of any communication received by the ODR platform, and keep the parties informed of the commencement and conclusion of different stages of the proceedings. Furthermore, it recommends that a communication should be deemed to be received by a party when the administrator notifies that party of its availability on the platform, and the deadlines in the proceedings would run from the time the administrator has made that notification. Finally, the ODR administrator may be empowered to extend deadlines, in order to allow for some flexibility when appropriate. According to this principle, an ODR proceeding may be deemed to have commenced when the ODR administrator notifies the parties that the notice is available on the ODR platform. It is recommended that the claimant and respondent provide to the ODR administrator

17 *See* Section II – Principles, Paras. 10-12.
18 *Ibid.*, Para. 13.
19 *Ibid.*, Para. 15.16.
20 *Ibid.*, Para. 17.
21 *See* Section II – Principles, Para. 31 and Section X – Appointment, powers and functions of the neutral, Paras. 46 and 48 e.

some essential information.[22] Thus, for instance, parties should be able to indicate in the notice or response whether they wish to proceed in a different language, so that the ODR administrator can identify other language options that the parties may select.

2.1.2 Third Neutral Parties

With regard to the neutral, it is considered desirable that the ODR administrator appoint an expert, notify that appointment and provide certain details about the identity of the neutral. This neutral will communicate with the parties to try to achieve a settlement. If a facilitated settlement cannot be achieved within a reasonable period of time, the ODR administrator or the neutral will inform the parties of the nature of the final stage, and of the form that such final stage will take.[23] It is recommended that neutrals have the relevant professional experience as well as dispute resolution skills, but the ODR neutrals do not need to be qualified lawyers.[24]

With regard to the appointment, neutrals should confirm that they are available to take the case, declare their impartiality and independence, and disclose any facts or circumstances that might give rise to likely doubts as to their impartiality or independence. The ODR system should provide parties with a process for objecting to the appointment of the neutral, in which case the ODR administrator will be required to make a determination as to whether the neutral should be replaced. If the neutral resigns or has to be replaced, the ODR administrator will be required to appoint a replacement.

Regarding the functions of the neutral, the rules of an ODR process should allow the neutral to extend deadlines for a reasonable time. The neutral should be required to avoid unnecessary delay or expense in the conduct of the proceedings, provide a fair and efficient process for resolving disputes, remain independent and impartial, and make decisions based on the information submitted by the parties during the proceedings.[25]

2.1.3 Dispute Resolution Processes

These Technical Notes also reflect and integrate two different approaches to ODR processes or tracks. The multi-tiered process includes three stages: negotiation, facilitated settlement and a third (final) stage that may include recommendation or adjudication. Claimants may submit a notice through the ODR platform to the administrator, who informs the respondent of the existence of the claim. The first stage offers a technology-enabled negotiation in which the claimant and respondent negotiate directly through the ODR platform. If that negotiation process fails (i.e. does not result in

22 P. Cortés and F. Esteban, "Building a Global Redress System for Low-Value Cross-Border Disputes", (2013) 62(2) *International Comparative Law Quarterly* 407-440.
23 Section IX – Final stage, Para. 45.
24 *See* Section X – Appointment, powers and functions of the neutral, paragraph 47.
25 *Ibid.* Para. 49.

the settlement of the claim), the process can move to the second 'facilitated settlement' stage where the administrator appoints a third neutral party. If the facilitated settlement fails, a third and final stage of ODR proceedings may commence, in which case the administrator or the neutral will inform the parties of the nature of this final stage.

During the UNCITRAL discussions it became apparent that some challenges needed to be overcome in defining this final stage by using a two-track system, which would offer either arbitration or a non-binding recommendation. Difficulties derived from two approaches and sensibilities maintained by the States in the manner in which consumers have a higher level of protection. Thus, there were two groups of States: (i) States from 'Group I' whose legal frameworks allow that outcomes reached as a result of ex-ante arbitration agreements are binding and enforceable to all parties involved, irrespective to their nature (B2B or B2C); (ii) States from 'Group II' encompassing jurisdictions whose legal frameworks determine that decisions and awards based on pre-dispute agreements are not binding to consumers, and thus these decisions may be challenged before the courts. This 'Group II' however accepted that arbitral awards could be binding and enforceable on the consumer if the agreement to go to arbitration was reached after the dispute aroused.

The main obstacle to the integration of both approaches in the final stage of the ODR process has been the fact that States from 'Group II' were concerned that consumers would enter in ex-ante arbitration agreements without understanding the consequences of excluding their right to access their local courts. Moreover, these two separate approaches created additional challenges, including: (i) the development of a procedure for online merchants to identify whether or not a buyer is a consumer or a business; (ii) the setting up of two separate procedural tracks with physical technological barriers to account for two types of consumers, those that are based on a jurisdiction that allows for pre-dispute arbitration and those that are based on a jurisdiction that requires the agreement to be entered after the dispute arose. In addition to this, these approaches would require maintaining an updated list of countries pertaining to Groups I or II and also defining the identity of the International organization that should take on the task of keeping the list updated.[26] In fact, a proposal requiring vendors to put consumers on one or another track based on their geography would be impractical, and concerns were expressed as to the suggestion that the UNCITRAL Secretariat would maintain a list of States in which pre-dispute agreements to arbitration were not binding or enforceable according to the law of those States. Fundamental differences remained between States that allowed binding pre-dispute agreements to arbitrate and those that did not, despite

26 *See* Report of Working Group III (Online Dispute Resolution) on the work of its 27th session (New York, 20-24 May 2013) paras. 40-41, where questions were raised regarding who would maintain the list of jurisdictions, and what the consequence would be where a jurisdiction was added to the list after a consumer from that jurisdiction had already entered into an agreement specifying Track I. This proposal would require the provision of data from consumers and merchants that would be very difficult to implement in practice, and it might even contravene national public policy.

the Working Group's strenuous efforts to come to consensus. As no consensus was reached for this two-track approach due to the irreconcilable differences on pre-arbitration clauses and the Commission should terminate the mandate of the Working Group,[27] consensus was achieved on a three stage process including negotiation, negotiated settlement facilitated by a neutral and a final stage where the administrator or the neutral will inform the parties of its nature.

2.2 *The Revised United Nations Guidelines for Consumer Protection (UNGCP)*

The UNGCP is the most worldwide agreed upon document on consumer protection.[28] It establishes a set of principles for effective consumer protection: legislation, enforcement institutions and redress systems. It also promotes and encourages the adoption of international enforcement cooperation in consumer protection. The United Nations Conference on Trade and Development (UNCTAD) Guidelines in its last revision[29] stresses that electronic commerce, which includes mobile to consumers, has become increasingly relevant to consumers worldwide. Hence, Member States and businesses should devote special attention to consumer protection in electronic commerce. It stresses that access to justice goes beyond court redress and ought to be effective, observing that:

> the right of consumers to access dispute resolution and to obtain redress should be considered in the wider context of the right of consumers to access justice. For consumer rights to be effective, they need to be enforceable, and any damage suffered by consumers should allow for adequate redress. Aggrieved consumers should also be able to solve disputes with businesses in a fair, affordable and swift manner.[30]

27 *See* Report of Working Group III (Online Dispute Resolution) on the work of its 31st session (New York, 9-13 February 2015).

28 The Guidelines were first adopted by the General Assembly in resolution 39/248 of 16 April 1985, later expanded by the Economic and Social Council in resolution E/1999/INF/2/Add.2 of 26 July 1999, and recently revised by the General Assembly in resolution 70/186 of 22 December 2015.

29 *See* Intergovernmental Group of Experts on Consumer Protection Law and Policy from the Trade and Development Board, Third session, Geneva, 9-10 July 2018. Available at https://unctad.org/meetings/en/SessionalDocuments/cicplpd11_en.pdf [accessed 29 May 2020].

30 *See supra*, para. 2.

Accordingly, the Guidelines establishes benchmarks for conducting online and offline commercial activities.[31] Additionally, it also describes avenues for delivering resolution and redress: courts, collective redress, public regulatory and enforcement action, ombudspersons, alternative dispute resolution, online dispute resolution, business customer care and complaint functions – and provides policy options for member States implementing the guidelines on dispute resolution and redress, considering that access to justice relates to the responsibility of public authorities to act upon consumer complaints, either to undertake enforcement action to promote effective compliance with consumer protection laws and/or to obtain or facilitate redress for consumers. Finally, the Guidelines encourages the development of ODR mechanisms that meet the above standards when addressing consumer complaints through formal or informal procedures.

It should be noted that there is a distinction that the Guidelines highlights between the legal nature of dispute resolution and redress. Dispute resolution refers to the use of mechanisms designed to provide consumers who have suffered economic harm resulting from transactions involving goods or services, including transactions across borders, the opportunity to resolve their complaints against businesses and to obtain redress mainly, transactional settlement of disputes; 'redress' refers to compensation for economic harm, whether in the form of a monetary remedy (e.g. a voluntary payment, damages, restitution or other monetary relief) or a conduct remedy with a restorative element (e.g. exchange of a good or service, specific performance or rescission of a contract) and it usually presupposes enforcement of consumer rights that can be adopted through judicial, administrative or alternative dispute settlement procedures.[32]

The Report highlights that a vast majority of online businesses do not offer ODR services to consumers and there is no legal obligation for them to do so.[33] It also stresses the need for legal certainty and predictability in online dispute resolution.[34] The aim of this instrument is to invite State members to provide effective consumer dispute resolution and redress and to contribute to the achievement of the 2030 Agenda for Sustainable Development Goals.

---

31 Including consumer complaints and disputes, making available complaints-handling mechanisms that provide consumers with expeditious, fair, transparent, inexpensive, accessible, speedy and effective dispute resolution without unnecessary cost or burden. Businesses should consider subscribing to domestic and international standards and alternative dispute resolution services and customer satisfaction codes.

32 *See* paras. 10-11.

33 *Ibid.*

34 *See* para. 35.

2.3 The United Nations Convention on International Settlement Agreements Resulting from Mediation (the 'Singapore Convention on Mediation')

The Convention on the Enforcement of International Settlement Agreements (hereinafter 'Singapore Convention') of 2018 promotes mediation as an alternative and effective method of resolving trade disputes and provides for expedited enforcement of international mediation agreements. The Convention is consistent with the UNCITRAL Model Law on International Commercial Mediation (2018) that replaces the original Model Law on Conciliation.[35] The aim is to provide recognition and enforcement for settlement agreements resulting from mediation in the same vein as the New York Convention provides for international arbitral awards.

Yet, the scope of application is limited to agreements for commercial (B2B) disputes concluded in writing – which includes electronic agreements –[36] resulting from mediation which, at the time of its conclusion is international[37] and excludes agreements concluded to resolve disputes arising from consumer (B2C) transactions.[38]

This international instrument sets out a number of formal requirements for reliance on settlement agreements,[39] particularly on electronic agreements.[40] Additionally, the competent authority may refuse to grant relief at the request of the other party if that party furnishes proof that a number of limited circumstances have been met.[41]

That said, so far, United States of America, Chile, Colombia, Ecuador, Honduras, Paraguay, Uruguay, China, Ukraine, Turkey, Iran, Afghanistan, Republic of Serbia, Arabia Saudi, Kazakhstan, Nigeria, Chad, Democratic Republic of Congo, Uganda, Gabon, Benin, Armenia, Guinea Bissau, Belarus and a number of Asian pacific

35 *See* United Nations Convention on International Settlement Agreements Resulting from Mediation. United Nations Commission on International Trade Law. Available at https://uncitral.un.org/sites/uncitral.un.org/files/singapore_convention_eng.pdf [accessed 29 May 2020].

36 To be in writing includes electronic communications if the information contained is accessible so as to be useable for subsequent reference.

37 Which means essentially that at least two parties to the settlement agreement have their places of business in different States.

38 It excludes conflicts relating to family, inheritance or employment law as well as agreements approved by a court or concluded in the course of proceedings before a court and enforceable as a judgment. In addition to this, the Singapore Convention excludes agreements recorded and enforceable as an arbitral award. *See* Art. 1.

39 Art. 4. It could either be the mediator's signature on the settlement agreement, a document signed by the mediator indicating that the mediation was carried out, an attestation by the institution that administered the mediation or any other evidence acceptable to the competent authority.

40 Art. 4. Such requirements are met if: i) a method is used to identify the parties or the mediator and to indicate the parties' or mediator's intention in respect of the information contained in the electronic communication; ii) and the method used is as reliable as appropriate for the purpose for which the electronic communication was generated or communicated, in the light of all the circumstances, including any relevant agreement; or proven in fact to have fulfilled the functions described above.

41 Art. 5. *Cf.* Eunice Chua, "The Singapore Convention on Mediation – A Brighter Future for Asian Dispute Resolution", Singapore Management University 1(2019) *Institutional Knowledge at Singapore Management University Research Collection*, 5-6.

countries have already signed it. Remarkably enough, the European Union and its member States have not signed it yet and it is unlikely to happen any time soon. The EU has not declared the reasons for not signing the Convention, but the following factors seem to have influenced their refusal to sign it. First, some EU member States lack of clear and consistent domestic standards for the enforcement of mediated settlement agreements or for the mediator or mediation processes. Second, the EU Mediation Directive[42] already established that EU Member States should ensure that the parties to a written agreement resulting from mediation can have the content of their agreement made enforceable by a court or another competent authority in accordance with the law of the Member State where the request is made. Last, contrary to Article 6 of the EU Mediation Directive which prescribes the requirement for explicit consent of the parties for enforcement and the signature of the mediator, the Singapore Convention does not require such consent. This approach evidences that under the Convention mediation settlements do not require the mediator's signature and it limits the defenses that may be used to avoid their enforcement.

2.4 *The APEC Collaborative Framework for Online Dispute Resolution*

A number of States[43] are currently engaged in the elaboration of a Collaborative Framework for Online Dispute Resolution of Cross-Border B2B Disputes in order to establish an Asian Pacific sponsored initiative to help global businesses (especially SMEs) promote confidence by providing quick electronic resolution and enforcement of disputes across borders, focusing on low value disputes.[44] Considering that SMEs need a legal environment that promotes a seamless system for trade and dispute resolution that overcomes the significant hurdles of access to justice in cross-border transactions, the ODR Collaborative Framework and the Model Procedural Rules will provide quick and cheap dispute resolution and enforcement across languages and jurisdictions. It is a pilot partnering with ODR providers, including regional arbitration and mediation centers willing to provide platforms. Under this ODR Framework, a business may file a cross-border complaint online against another business if both

---

42 *See* European Union Directive 2008/52/EC of the European Parliament and of the Council on Certain Aspects of Mediation in Civil and Commercial Matters. Available at https://eur-lex.europa.eu/legal-content/EN/ALL/?uri=CELEX%3A32008L0052 [accessed 29 May 2020].

43 Currently the APEC's 21 Member Economies are the United States, Australia, Brunei Darussalam, Canada, Chile, China, Hong Kong, China, Indonesia, Japan, Malaysia, Mexico, New Zealand, Papua New Guinea, Peru, The Philippines, Russia, Singapore, Republic of Korea, Chinese Taipei, Thailand and Viet-Nam.

44 *See* the Report of Workshop for Developing an APEC Collaborative Framework for ODR held in Osaka Japan, in 8-9 November 2018 and the Report of the Second Economic Committee Meeting, Puerto Varas, Chile 26-27 August 2019. Available at http://mddb.apec.org/Documents/2019/EC/EC2/19_ec2_022.pdf [accessed 29 May 2020].

parties have consented to have such disputes resolved under the ODR framework (opt in).

It consists of a three tiered process that should be flexible, affordable and commensurate with the amount in dispute: i) During the first tier parties may exchange information and negotiate a binding settlement through electronic means ('Negotiation Stage'); ii) if the dispute remains unresolved, the ODR provider will appoint a qualified ODR neutral to mediate between the parties ('Mediation Stage'); iii) if the dispute is still unresolved, the neutral will be appointed to arbitrate the dispute and issue a binding award ('Arbitration Stage').

The Collaborative Framework for ODR embraces other private international law instruments relevant to ODR, including but not limited to: the 1958 Convention on the Recognition and Enforcement of Foreign Arbitral Awards; the 2006 UNCITRAL Model Law on International Commercial Arbitration; the 2005 UN Convention on the Use of Electronic Communications in International Contracts; and the 1996 UNCITRAL Model Law on Electronic Commerce. Surprisingly, although the ODR Framework and Report are not explicitly mentioning the UNCITRAL Technical Notes for ODR, it is apparent that the later has being inspirational to the former.

ODR providers are subject to a number of accountability and transparency measures. ODR providers are expected to request parties to complete a questionnaire at the end of the process, to gather some non-personal data and submit it on an annual basis and to publish such statistical data by themselves.[45] Finally, in case of non-compliance with the Procedural Rules, the ODR provider may be removed from the official list.

The exclusion of consumer transactions is due to their typically small amounts, the difficulty in enforcing decisions across borders due to the existing fragmentation of the legal framework applied for the protection of consumers. Not surprisingly, the rationale behind this effort is helping businesses, particularly SMEs, to engage in cross-border trade by lowering transaction costs and connecting businesses with Framework-compliant ODR providers.

45 This questionnaire includes: As the primary party accessing the system: (a) 'Do you think the process was fair or impartial?' (b) 'Do you think the dispute was handled in a reasonable timeframe?' (c) 'Do you think the neutral handled your case with dignity, fairness and impartiality?' (d) 'Do you think the system was easy to use?' (e) 'Would you recommend ODR to others?'.

3 Regional Developments: ODR for e-Commerce in Asia and in Europe

3.1 ODR Development in Asia

A number of large online marketplaces have emerged in recent times across Asia[46] – notably, *Alibaba, Flipkart, Paytm, Snapdeal, JD.com, Tencent, Pindu oduo, Haitao* – which are embedding cutting edge technology and offer innovative business models for e-commerce. There is not yet a legal framework or initiatives devoted to dealing with cross-border disputes arising from this region. Instead, there are several interesting national legal initiatives that seek to regulate and incorporate technology in dispute resolution processes.

In China, the Government has enacted the PRC E-commerce Law on 31st August 2018 with effect from 1st January 2019. This statute integrates consumer protection rules that include[47] i) the duty of e-commerce operators to disclose information in a timely and accurate manner about goods or services, to ensure consumers' right of information and right of choice;[48] ii) the duty of marketplace platform operators to assume joint liability if they fail to take necessary measures to stop sales after it is determined that they knew or should have known of any infringement of IP rights regarding items sold on their platforms;[49] and iii) a duty for marketplace platforms to establish a credit rating system for consumers, whose comments cannot be deleted by platform administrators and business users.

With the aim to facilitate ODR avenues in the public courts, China launched the first Internet Court in the city of Hangzhou in 2017. The whole process operates fully online and incorporates online mediation. Parties can register using their mobile phones allowing the system to have access to their identities, online transaction records and other relevant personal data. Hearings are conducted remotely, by means of video-conference or telephone, and payments are made through e-wallets.[50] The online process allows parties to apply for consultation, evaluation, mediation and arbitration

46 Before, the CIETAC Online Dispute Resolution Center to resolve electronic commerce disputes, stablished in 2010 by China International Economic and Trade Arbitration Commission (CIETAC). *See* more in J. Z. Zheng, 'The Role of ODR in Resolving Electronic Commerce Disputes in China', (2016) 1(3) *International Journal on Online Dispute Resolution,* 1 December 2016. Available at www.researchgate.net/publication/311669062_The_Role_of_ODR_in_Resolving_Electronic_Commerce_Disputes_in_China [accessed 27 May 2020].

47 M. Tan, "Tailor Wessing LLP 'China's New E-commerce Law, Good or Bad News for Business?'", (2019) 53 *EURObiz* (25 February 2019). Available at https://www.eurobiz.com.cn/chinas-new-e-commerce-law/ [accessed 29 May 2020].

48 Art. 17.

49 Art. 45.

50 *See* Y. Zhao, "Internet Courts in China, Asian-mena Counsel", (2019) *Dispute Resolution Special Report,* 2 August 2019. Available at www.inhousecommunity.com/article/internet-courts-china/ [accessed 29 May 2020].

instead of litigation via the Online Diversified Dispute Resolution Platform. Since 2018 the Beijing and the Guangzhou Courts follow the same structure. A number of AI assistant judges are starting to support human judges' tasks in various pilot projects that have been developed by Alibaba specifically for these Courts. Yet, some concerns have been expressed on whether these AI tools may be fully independent or may have been designed by an organization and individuals who have conflicts of interest and algorithmic biases.[51]

India is at the cusp of an ODR revolution. The Covid-19 pandemic has thrusted ODR to the forefront as a means of containing and resolving disputes. Many initiatives are underway all across India to create a conducive ODR ecosystem, in particular for payment and consumer disputes. A holistic vision of the development of ODR has been recently developed by the Government of India Think Tank NITI Aayog, which has brought together stakeholders from the Judiciary, the Government, the private sector and ODR startups with the goal of creating a coherent nation-wide ODR Policy.[52] The significance and scale of this initiative is unprecedented for a country with a 1.38 billion population.

A driving force for this ODR transformation has been the demonetization in India, which launch in November 2016 led to an exponential growth in digital payments. For 2021 the overall value of digital payments in India is estimated to be at US$160 billion and is expected to grow to US$267 billion by 2025.[53] Realizing that the Indian digital economy needs an effective way of resolving complaints in line with the digital nature of these transactions, the Reserve Bank of India – RBI (i.e., India's Central Bank and Regulatory Body) announced the introduction of ODR for resolving customer disputes and grievances pertaining to digital payments, using a system-driven and rule-based mechanism with zero or minimal manual intervention.[54] This resulted in the National Payments Corporation of India – NPCI (i.e., a combined umbrella organization of RBI and Indian Banks Association for operating retail payments and settlement systems in India) developing an ODR platform that can be plugged in by any bank and payments system provider offering digital payments. This service, called UPI-Help, was launched

---

51 *See* A. Mingay, "Size Matters: Alibaba Shapes China's First Court of the Internet" (2019) *Mercator Institute for China Studies*, 17 October 2019. Available at www.merics.org/en/blog/size-matters-alibaba-shapes-china s-first-court-internet [accessed 29 May 2020].

52 The NITI Aayog Expert Committee on ODR, "Designing the Future of Dispute Resolution: The ODR Policy Plan for India" (October 2020). Available at https://niti.gov.in/sites/default/files/2020-10/Draft-ODR-Repor t-NITI-Aayog-Committee.pdf.

53 Statista, "Digital Payments India". Available at https://www.statista.com/outlook/dmo/fintech/digital-payments/india.

54 Reserve Bank of India "Online Dispute Resolution (ODR) System for Digital Payments", RBI/2020-21/21 (6 August 2020). Available at https://m.rbi.org.in/Scripts/BS_CircularIndexDisplay.aspx?Id=11946.

on 15 March 2021 with a vision to show how technology and innovation can play a role in effective dispute resolution, providing consumer protection and enhancing their trust in digital payments.[55] This new ODR platform is available through the payment provider App and offers an end to end electronic dispute resolution that allows users to check the status of pending transactions, to raise complaints for transactions that have not been processed or money not credited to the beneficiary, and to raise complaints against merchant transactions.

In addition to digital payments, ODR is seen in India as an important piece of the puzzle for supporting the sustainable development of e-commerce, which is increasingly becoming an integral part of the Indian economy with an estimated annual value of US $137 billion for 2021.[56] With the aim of increasing consumer protection in e-commerce, the Ministry of Consumer Affairs has recently issued the Consumer Protection (E-Commerce) Rules 2020.[57] Notably, the Rules require all e-commerce businesses to offer a transparent grievance redressal mechanism and to appoint a grievance officer.[58] The Rules set a short time limit of 30 days for the resolution of complaints.[59] Moreover, online market places are required to issue a reference number to complainants, so that consumers can track the status of their claim, and to provide information about the redressal mechanisms as well as their sales policies (e.g. information relating to return, refund, exchange, warranty and guarantee, delivery and shipment, modes of payment).[60]

Meanwhile, at the time of writing a Draft National Ecommerce Policy was awaiting approval.[61] Section F of the Draft Policy states that the ecommerce sector requires a dispute resolution mechanism specific to this sector, which will be electronic, as this is what would be expected by e-commerce users. In this regard the Draft Policy observes: "It is only rational that a transaction completed online should have an online system of grievances redressal."[62] Lastly, an ODR handbook for business is being published.[63] All of the above initiatives leave no stone unturned in setting the stage to enable a big take off for ODR in Indian ecommerce.

---

55 National Payments Corporation of India, "UPI-Help for Digital Payments goes life on BHIM UPI" (15 March 2021). Available at https://www.npci.org.in/PDF/npci/press-releases/2021/NPCI-Press-Release-Online-Dispute-Resolution-for-Digital-Payments-goes.pdf.

56 Statista, above.

57 Consumer Protection (E-Commerce) Rules 2020. Available at https://consumeraffairs.nic.in/sites/default/files/E%20commerce%20rules.pdf.

58 Section 4.4.

59 Section 4.5.

60 Section 5.3(b) and (c).

61 Draft National e-Commerce Policy, India's Data for India's Development. Available at https://dipp.gov.in/sites/default/files/DraftNational_e-commerce_Policy_23February2019.pdf.

62 Section F.4.16.

63 Available at https://agami.in/odr/.

In Singapore the efforts made by the Government to adopt technology have also had a cascade effect in the Singaporean Courts. Specialized courts have emerged since 1996 adopting a wide variety of computer systems, latest audio-visual equipment, computer networks, multimedia tools, and computer-based transcription facilities that allow for testimonies to be digitally recorded. The Singaporean Courts also embrace ODR, electronic filing with paperless court document system and e-litigation system. Singapore's laws had already progressively made provisions for the use of technology in courts: Electronic Transactions Act 2010 recognizes the use of electronic records, electronic and digital signatures, and electronic contracts; Personal Data Protection Act 2012, governs the collection, use, disclosure and care of personal data; Payment Services Act 2019 regulates a number of payment services, including domestic and cross-border money transfers, digital payment tokens and electronic money issuance, wallets and cryptocurrency. In October 2018, Parliament passed amendments to the Supreme Court of Judicature Act enabling court hearings to be held via electronic means, such as live video link or live television link. Protection from Online Falsehoods and Manipulation Act 2019 regulates online fake news and provides remedies to private individuals and entities in respect of online falsehoods. Some marketplaces in Singapore also offer video conferencing solutions, providing even greater convenience to the lawyer and potential client. Currently, a two-year pilot program called FLIP 1 is supporting technology adoption and is building a community ecosystem with a national legal tech accelerator program (GLIDE) connecting high growth legal tech and tech entrepreneurs with law firms, law schools and legal industry professionals in a bid to revolutionize Asia's legal industry with artificial intelligence, blockchain, advanced analytics, machine learning and automated data collection and analysis.

In Japan the National Consumer Affairs Center (NCAC) continues to provide consumers information, advice and, in some cases, also encourages and supports online direct negotiations for B2C controversies.[64] If the case is considered an 'important consumer dispute', NCAC provides a service that includes mediation and arbitration. NCAC has a branch called Cross-border Consumer Centre Japan (CCJ) dealing with cross border disputes.[65]

3.2 ODR Developments in Europe

The European Union has also identified ODR as a crucial element to the development of e-commerce within the European boarders. To that end, it developed innovative rules on consumer ODR in the form of a Directive on Alternative Dispute Resolution for

64 Yet, NCAC is not providing service to C2C transactions or sharing economy.

65 *See* H. Habuka and C. Rule, "The Promise and Potential of Online Dispute Resolution in Japan", (2017) 2(4) *International Journal of Online Dispute Resolution*, Eleven International Publishing, 8-9.

Consumer Disputes[66] and a Regulation on Online Dispute Resolution for Consumer Disputes,[67] which took effect in July 2015 and January 2016 respectively. The European regulatory framework aims of stimulating trade, especially in the online arena, by requiring EU Member States to ensure that consumer complaints can be resolved online (through the EU ODR platform) by nationally certified ADR entities.[68] Together, these two legislative instruments set up a ground-breaking framework for consumer ODR to tackle both national and cross-border disputes within the EU and create a network of certified ADR entities. These ADR entities, which may be public or private bodies, can offer a variety of ADR techniques, including mediation, arbitration, complaint boards and ombudsman processes.

As a result, the EU framework has triggered an institutionalization process that is moving ADR and ODR schemes from unregulated models of redress to an increasingly important part of the Civil Justice System in the EU.[69] In doing so, it has ensured that businesses and consumers, regardless of their sectors, can agree to use quality ADR entities that have been publicly certified for complying with the EU and national procedural standards. Although the ADR Directive does not make participation in ADR compulsory, it requires, first and foremost, that all EU Member States ensure the availability of certified ADR entities that meet the procedural standards set in the Directive. Amongst these requirements, certified ADR entities must be able to process complaints online, be free of charge (or of low cost) for the consumer, and comply with the principles of independence, effectiveness (e.g. resolving disputes within 90 days), transparency (e.g. publishing annual activity reports), fairness (e.g. giving consumers a cooling off period before they agree to settle a claim), legality (e.g. ensuring that mandatory consumer law is respected)[70] and liberty (e.g. guaranteeing that consumers can only agree to arbitration, or any other procedure that precludes them from going to court, after the dispute arises – in other words, pre-dispute contractual agreements are only valid for consensual or non-binding ADR processes).[71] In addition, all businesses established in an EU Member States are obligated to inform a consumer resident in the EU about the availability of these certified ADR entities every time a trader has an unresolved dispute with that consumer or the consumer is not satisfied with the remedy offered by the trader.

---

66 *See* Directive 2013/11/EU on Alternative Dispute Resolution for Consumer Disputes O.J. (L 165) 63.

67 *See* Regulation (EU) 524/2013 on Online Dispute Resolution for Consumer Disputes O.J. (L 165) 1.

68 *Cf.* P. Cortés, "A New Regulatory Framework For Extra-Judicial Consumer Redress: Where We are and How to Move Forward", (2015) 35(1) *Legal Studies* 114-141.

69 P. Cortés, *The Law of Consumer Redress in an Evolving Digital Market* (2018, Cambridge University Press).

70 Moreover, this protection has been recently expanded by the CJEU which held that even when businesses choose a law different to that of the consumer jurisdiction, consumers cannot be led 'into error' of thinking that only the business' proposed governing law applies – i.e. implying that consumers do not have the protection afforded by the mandatory laws from their own jurisdictions. *See Verein fur Konsumenteninformation v Amazon EU Sarl* (C-191/15).

71 *See* Arts. 5-11 ADR Directive.

The ODR Regulation complements the Directive by requiring the European Commission to run an ODR platform to channel all consumer complaints arising from e-commerce to these certified ADR entities. The platform allows consumers (and traders, when the national law thus permits) to submit complaints related to online contracts in all the EU languages.[72] All traders operating online as well as online market places established within the EU, such as Amazon, have the obligation to provide an easily accessible link to the ODR platform. The European ODR Platform was launched in February 2016 with the goal of helping consumers and businesses to settle their disputes out-of-court through online communications via the multi-language ODR Platform, and when necessary, assisted by a nationally approved ADR entity.

In addition to the EU ODR Platform, there are a number of national ODR platforms in the EU and elsewhere, that are increasingly being used to resolve e-commerce disputes. A well-known example outside the EU is Consumidor.gov.br which operates in Brazil as a dispute resolution forum between consumers and businesses that have joined the scheme. Although the Brazilian platform only offers online negotiation, it boasts an impressive settlement rate for around 80% of the complaints.[73] However, in the remaining 20% of cases when parties cannot reach an amicable settlement, the complaints are left unresolved. In this sense, other platforms, such as the UK website Resolver.co.uk, provide a better service, as it directs consumers to ODR providers competent to deal with the unresolved dispute.

Resolver is an assisted complaints management system for consumers operating in the UK, but unlike Consumidor.gov.br, traders are businesses that have not opted into the ODR system of Resolver voluntarily. Resolver allows consumers to submit complaints in a broad list of categories, ranging from restaurants and legal services to energy or telecom suppliers. Once the consumer decides to bring a claim to the business, then Resolver assists the consumer in the process. Its complaint process is set out in five stages:

i. It explains the consumers' rights taking into consideration sectorial regulations.
ii. It helps consumers to draft a complaint letter or email and crucially, it provides the consumer with the correct trader's contact details to where the complaint should be sent.
iii. It records all written (and phone) communications between the consumer and the business.
iv. It creates a case file with all the information about the case, including emails and phone calls, which is accessible to the consumer at all times.
v. It provides consumers with useful information on how to scale a complaint, including to the ADR entities that operate in the traders' sector.

---

72 Online Dispute Resolution platform. Available at http://ec.europa.eu/odr [accessed 29 May 2020].

73 *See* C.L. Marques and P.G. Fonseca, "Consumer Protection in Brazil: The 2016 Report for the International Academy of Consumer Law", in H.W. Micklitz and G. Saumier (eds.), *Enforcement and Effectiveness of Consumer Law* (2018, Springer), 27.

Resolver processes a staggering 1.6 million complaints a year in the UK only and does it free of cost for consumers, who only have to register to use its services. Resolver assures consumers that they do not to pass the registration information on to anyone without the consumers' permission. Resolver business models rests on informing businesses what consumers complained about, while keeping data anonymous. Resolver covers more than 2,000 organizations from different sectors, including retail, pensions, energy, water, telecoms, motoring, insurance, restaurants, gyms, National Health System and leisure activities. It also contains the contact information of the complaints departments of all these organizations.

The digital transition in the framework of Justice is being carried out in light of the standards of responsibility, efficiency, transparency, compliance with due process, confidentiality and protection of personal data principles. The eJustice Portal is an example of the European Union commitment with the integration of ICT devoted to improve the access of European citizens to justice. The 2019-23 Strategy of the eJustice focuses on improving access to information, electronic communication and interoperability. Yet, this transition has not led yet to fully online judicial processes of dispute resolution.

In Germany, there is no homogeneous response among the different federal territories and the digitization process has not yield to the widespread adoption of videoconferences for hearings, nor have fully online procedures been developed. Something similar happens in Ireland and France, where videoconferencing is admitted only in exceptional circumstances. The lockdown due to the pandemic Covid-19 has struck the judicial activity and a number of countries has expanded, temporarily, its use. During this lockdown Norway has regulated the use of video conferencing as a default mechanism, previous acceptance of the parties and Court decisions are signed by means of electronic signature.

In Spain, the Civil Procedure Rules (*Ley de Enjuciamiento Civil* 1/2000) provides that Courts can use any technical, electronic, computer and electronic means available, and results are valid as long as their authenticity, integrity, compliance with the requirements of procedural laws, due identification of the parties, confidentiality, privacy, security and protection of personal data protection regulations are guaranteed. Software and apps ought to be approved in advance by the court's governing body (i.e. the General Council of the Judiciary and by the Technical Committee of the Electronic Justice Administration). Although many courthouses have specialized software such as Lexnet, eFidelius software, electronic signatures and videoconferencing, they have been underused. The state of alarm caused by the Covid-19 pandemic has trigged the

General Council of the Judiciary to issue a Protocol for telematic judicial proceedings which incorporates guidelines and recommendations for their use.[74] Similar guidelines have been issued elsewhere. For instance, the Judiciary of England and Wales also issued a Protocol providing guidance to conduct remote hearings.[75] The Protocol encourages the use of remote hearings to minimize the transmission of Covid-19, but lets the judge decide the method by which the hearings are conducted.

4 An Analysis of the Operation of the EU ODR Platform

4.1 *The Annual Reports of the EU ODR Platform*

This section critically discusses the annual reports of the EU ODR Platform published by the European Commission, which examine the journey of the complaints submitted to the Platform as well as the information obligations of traders, who are required to offer an accessible link to the Platform and to provide the consumer with an e-mail address for the Platform to send the consumer complaint.[76] It is observed that the Second Annual Report consolidates the findings of the First Annual Report, and discusses the improvements in the design that the Platform is due to implement in the near future.

The first annual report examined 20,000 websites of EU online traders and market places to establish their degree of compliance with their information obligations – i.e. listing on their website a link to the EU ODR Platform and an email address.[77] The first report found that while the majority of online traders (85%) provided an email address, only 28% of them had provided the link. The Commission averred that it is liaising with the Member States to support them in ensuring that online traders achieve a greater level of compliance with their information obligations. At the time of writing, the Commission has just published its most recent report where it found a significant

74 *See* Consejo General del Poder Judicial, "Guía para la celebración de actuaciones judiciales telemáticas" (27 May 2020). Available at https://www.poderjudicial.es/cgpj/es/Poder-Judicial/En-Portada/La-Comision-Permanente-aprueba-una-Guia-para-la-celebracion-de-actuaciones-judiciales-telematicas [accessed 29 May 2020].

75 Judiciary of England and Wales, "Civil Justice in England and Wales – Protocol Regarding Remote Hearings" (26 March 2020).

76 *Cf.* European Commission, Functioning of the European ODR Platform – Statistics 2nd year (December 2018), 2. Available at https://ec.europa.eu/info/sites/info/files/2nd_report_on_the_functioning_of_the_odr_platform_3.pdf [accessed 29 May 2020].

77 *Cf.* European Commission, 'Report on the functioning of the European Online Dispute Resolution Platform established under Regulation (EU) No 524/2013 on online dispute resolution for consumer disputes' COM (2017) 744 final. *See also* "Online Dispute Resolution: Web-Scraping of EU Traders' Websites" (November 2017). Available at http://ec.europa.eu/newsroom/just/item-detail.cfm?item_id=610445 [accessed 29 May 2020].

increase in the number of businesses providing the link to the EU ODR platform, which is now at 55% of all the websites screened by the European Commission.[78]

The web-sweep of the first annual report showed that in most cases (91%) the link was included in the traders' section of the website that contains the terms and conditions. Amongst those traders who included the link, only half (49%) had included a statement informing the consumer on whether they plan to use the ODR Platform. It also found that in approximately two thirds of those online traders investigated (64%) the ODR link was only moderately accessible; whereas in 26% of the websites the ODR link was, as required by the ODR Regulation, easy to access, and in the remaining 10% was difficult to access.[79]

The Commission reported that the ODR Platform received 24,000 online complaints in its first year of operation with an upwards trend in the number of complaints submitted as time passed by.[80] One third of the complaints lodged in the Platform were related to a cross-border issue. In terms of sectors, the most complained one was clothing and footwear (11.5%) followed by aviation disputes (8.5%) and information and technology goods (8%). As to the main reasons behind the complaints, these were most often linked to problems related to the delivery of goods (21%), non-conformity with the description in the order (15%) and defective goods (12%).

The report examined the life-cycle of complaints and it found that the majority of complaints (85%) were automatically closed 30 days after their submission because parties had not agreed to a competent ADR entity – this was typically because the trader has not replied to the complaint through the Platform. The Commission followed-up those cases through a survey and it found that 40%of those consumers whose complaints were automatically closed by the ODR Platform were contacted directly by the trader outside the Platform with the intention to settle the complaint. The Commission concluded that in these cases the Platform had helped to resolve the dispute without the need to escalate the complaint to an ADR entity.[81] According to the Commission, there were other technical factors that influenced in the lack of traders' responsiveness when receiving a complaint from the ODR Platform. The Commission noted that

> when a complaint is submitted against a trader for the first time and the trader is not yet registered on the Platform, the automatic notification [of the

78 *See* Online Shopping: Commission and Consumer Protection Authorities Urge Traders to Bring Information Policy in Line with EU Law (Press Release, 31 January 2020). Available at https://ec.europa.eu/commission/presscorner/detail/en/IP_20_156 [accessed 29 May 2020].

79 *Ibid.*

80 *Ibid.*, p. 4.

81 *Ibid.*, p. 6.

> complaint emailed by the Platform] may reach an incorrect email address ... or ends up in the spam folder.[82]

Of the 15% of complaints that were not automatically closed by the Platform after 30 days, the majority (9%) were closed because the trader refused to select an ADR entity, but in two thirds of these cases, the trader indicated that they made direct contact with the consumer and solved the issue, or that they were planning to do so.[83] In 4% of all the submitted complaints both parties chose the option of withdrawing from the ODR procedure before they had the opportunity to choose an ADR entity.

The data of the second year of operation of the ODR Platform were very similar to the first one: 81% of cases were automatically closed but the Commission survey amongst consumers found that 37% of these consumers had been contacted by the trader to settle the dispute outside the Platform.[84] Out of the 19% of complaints processed by the Platform, most of these cases (13%) were closed because the trader indicated they did not want to use the Platform, but the majority of these cases were resolved through bilateral negotiations. Lastly, 4% of cases were withdrawn from the procedure, which the Commission indicated was because parties were likely to have reached a solution, while the remaining 2% were referred to an ADR entity.[85]

Thus, in both years of operation it was found that only 2% of cases reached an ADR entity while only 1% the total complaints, were resolved by a third neutral party through an ADR/ODR entity. The Commission highlights that overall 44% of complaints were resolved successfully through bilateral negotiation outside the Platform. Therefore, whilst one can agree with the Commission's complacent conclusion that the EU ODR Platform is contributing to incentivize traders to cooperate on an amicable solution,[86] the Platform is clearly below its potential.

4.2 Forthcoming Changes in the EU ODR Platform

It has been discussed elsewhere that the EU ODR Platform should provide additional functions that support the resolution of the majority of disputes, such as the provision of a trustmark that encourages trader participation in the Platform, a negotiation tool that facilitates early settlements, the provision of automated online advice on consumer rights for the most common types of complaints, and automatic referrals to ADR/ODR bodies when traders are already adhered to an ADR entity.[87] The European Commission

82 *Ibid.*
83 *Ibid.*
84 EC Second Annual Report (2018), p. 4.
85 *Ibid.*
86 *Ibid.*
87 P. Cortés, *The Law of Consumer Redress in an Evolving Digital Market* (2018, Cambridge University Press).

has recently undergone a 'substantial overhaul' to make the ODR Platform 'more user-friendly, informative and engaging' and it continues to carry out awareness campaigns to promote its use amongst consumers and traders.[88]

Although the goals of the EU legislation have not been fully realized, the European legal framework for consumer ADR/ODR incorporates recognized best practices and an accreditation system, and in doing so, it has started a process of professionalizing a traditionally unregulated sector. The rationale behind this regulatory effort is the promotion of ADR/ODR as the primary form of dispute resolution for consumer disputes. Presently, the EU ODR Platform contains a network of over 400 certified ADR/ODR providers that have been publicly certified to resolve consumer disputes within the European Economic Area. This new structure has trigged an institutionalization process which is moving ADR from the unregulated models of redress to an increasingly important part of the civil justice system in the EU.

Moreover, from an EU view point, consumer ADR, like courts, is more than a mere tool of dispute resolution; it is an essential mechanism to widen access to justice by expanding the redress avenues to the online sphere, contributing to ensure better compliance with consumer protections laws. Accordingly, ADR/ODR entities are delivering a public service, the value of which goes beyond the provision of individual redress. Under the ADR Directive, these entities are now legally required to cooperate with the industry by identifying common causes of complaints as well as with enforcement bodies in improving standards and compliance with consumer law.[89]

Similarly, the recent Directive 2161/2019 reinforces the link between ODR and public enforcement.[90] This Directive provides that repeated violations of consumer laws by the same business represent an indication of the seriousness of the infringement and the need to raise the level of the sanction. It reinforces the duty of the national competent authorities to take all necessary enforcement measures in case of a widespread infringement. In addition, the Article 5 of the Directive 2161/2019 extends the functions of the ODR platform by requiring it to provide consumers with information on their rights that are tailored to their complaints.

Overall, the ODR Platform has received a very modest number of disputes if we take into consideration the size of the EU market which has half a billion EU consumers. Furthermore, only 2% of claims that go through the Platform, which has been designed as a referral website, are sent to nationally approved ADR/ODR entities – out of which only half of these are admitted or processed by the ADR/ODRs. This is because in the vast majority of cases the businesses do not engage with the consumer through the Platform,

88 EC Second Annual Report (2018), p. 5.

89 Arts. 17 and 19 of the ADR Directive 2013/11/EU.

90 Directive (EU) 2019/2161 of 27 November 2019 amending Council Directive 93/13/EEC and Directives 98/6/EC, 2005/29/EC and 2011/83/EU of the European Parliament and of the Council as regards the better enforcement and modernisation of Union consumer protection rules.

which currently requires both of them to agree in advance before the Platform can send the complaint to a nationally approved ADR entity.

Yet, as noted above, the European Commission has investigated what happened to those ignored complaints and found that in 44% of these claims, the businesses had contacted the consumer complainant outside the Platform and settled their complaints directly with them. After two years of operation of the EU ODR Platform the Commission has acknowledged that the Platform is not carrying out the main role for which the Platform was originally envisaged. That role consisted in operating as a referral website which ensured that EU consumers and traders would be able to identify a certified ADR entity that would assist them in resolving their disputes online through the ODR Platform. In light of the Annual Reports, the Commission has decided to make some changes in the design of the Platform. Once updated the new Platform will:

i. allow for direct negotiation between the parties inside the Platform, which goes beyond the present model that only allows to submit online the complaint and the response, whereas the negotiation at the time of writing can only be conducted outside the Platform;
ii. enable consumers to refer a complaint to an ADR entity without the prior agreement with the business in the Platform. Currently if parties do not agree to an ADR, the case is closed after 30 days, regardless of whether there is an ADR entity competent to process the complaint;
iii. provide automatically generated information on consumer rights for certain disputes where there is high volume of cases, e.g. airline complaints and for the online sale of IT goods;
iv. the Commission also plans to publish in the near future a call for grants to build new features in the EU ODR Platform, which amongst other things, it could help to interconnect the Platform with national courts dealing with small claims online.[91]

5 Conclusion

E-commerce continues to grow at a fast pace. Many international organizations are increasingly realizing that the development of effective and fair ODR processes are crucial elements for a sustainable and a competitive growth. The resolution of the typically low-value e-commerce disputes is nearly always more suited to extrajudicial redress mechanisms than it is to the courts, especially if disputes arise in a cross-border context.

International and regional organizations are developing guidelines that seek to stimulate the use of ODR for resolving online disputes, especially those arising from

91 2019-2023 Action Plan European e-Justice (2019/C 96/05) para. 24. Available at https://eur-lex.europa.eu/legal-content/EN/TXT/HTML/?uri=CELEX:52019XG0313(02)&rid=8 [accessed 29 May 2020].

online cross-border transactions where the courts cannot offer redress in a cost-efficient manner. ODR for e-commerce is an essential tool to guarantee access to justice and to foster a more competitive and sustainable online markets by promoting parties' trust in online transactions.

Accordingly, with the aim of fostering international trade, UNCITRAL has issued procedural guidelines for ODR processes and third neutral parties that deal with low-value cross-border disputes arising out of online sales. UNCITRAL recommends the use of a tiered process that seeks the resolution of these disputes as early and informally as possible. The online process commences with a negotiation stage, then moves to a facilitation stage, and those unresolved disputes escalate to a final stage where the third neutral party may issue an arbitral award or a recommendation depending on the model the parties have chosen or in the jurisdiction where the consumer is based. Although the UNCITRAL Technical Notes have not reached the consensus expected to deliver a more ambitious legal instrument, it has produced important guidelines that are expected to have a long lasting effect. Indeed, the UNGCP and APEC are already building on the UNCITRAL Technical Notes in order to enhance the redress avenues for consumer and commercial disputes respectively.

In recent years there has been important legal developments across the world. This chapter has noted some of the key changes in Asia and Europe. While the main economies in Asia, notably in China and India, have recently made important changes that sought to adapt their legislation and courts to embracing ODR, especially for ecommerce disputes, in the EU, which has a more integrated economy, has sought to promote cross-border trade through the launch of an out-of-court ODR platform. Although both regions considered ODR as an important tool to support the growth of e-commerce, the EU started earlier to offer ODR for e-commerce disputes.

Indeed, with the goal of stimulating the EU Internal Market, the EU has adopted legislation in 2013 that aimed to overcome the obstacles that have impeded the use of ADR and ODR: namely, gaps in coverage, the absence of legal standards, and a lack of awareness. While the ADR Directive has increased the availability of quality ADR processes for consumer disputes, the ODR Regulation has created an ODR Platform that acts as a signposting service, directing contractual disputes from online sales to ODR providers (called ADR entities) that meet the quality criteria set in the Directive and that have been certified by the national competent authorities (usually the administrative body overseeing a particular economic sector).

Albeit the EU ODR Platform is increasingly being used as the online vehicle to resolve many disputes that arise online, it is well below its potential. The updated ODR Platform is expected to encourage users to explore settlement options in its new online space for direct negotiation. The EU would do well to examine successful ODR platforms – such as Alibaba in China, Resolver.co.uk in the UK, and Consumidor.gov.br in Brazil – in order to identify how to empower consumers and engage traders in using the ODR platform, rather than – as it is often the case – refusing to participate. Nevertheless, under the new EU ODR Platform consumers will be better informed about their rights and obligations for the most common types of disputes, whereas unresolved disputes will be more easily escalated online to ADR entities and, one can predict in a non-distant future, to online courts which development has been accelerated worldwide in the aftermath of the Covid-19 pandemic and its consequential social-distancing measures.

Chapter 10 Online Dispute Resolution in US Courts Looking Back and Going Forward

Paul Embley and Lise Embley

As this book is prepared for publication, the world is in the throes of a pandemic. Not a tabletop exercise, but the real thing. Schools, stores, restaurants, theaters, and government offices have either closed or significantly restricted or altered operations. In some cities, residents had orders to 'shelter in place' for weeks. As a result, many daily activities are now happening online – college classes, doctor visits, staff meetings, and court sessions.

Coronavirus has done for court technology what more than two decades of concerted efforts could not. Overnight, courts have expanded virtual capacities to facilitate remote appearances and to accommodate teleworkers. Nearly every court in the nation has found a way to conduct essential business remotely. It is unlikely that things will ever be the same again, even after the dangers of the current pandemic are past. As Chief Justice Bridget Mary McCormack of the Michigan Supreme Court said in April 2020, 'This was not the disruption we wanted, but it was the disruption we needed.'[1] Her expectation is that many of the 'temporary' changes will become permanent. It remains to be seen how individual jurisdictions will go forward.

This chapter focuses on the history and future of online dispute resolution (ODR) in US courts. It begins with some successful ODR implementations already in place, which show the potential (and progress) for the concept. Then, we turn to obstacles that have slowed ODR implementations in the US state courts. In closing, we summarize with personal observations and encouragement for courts doing the important transformative work already underway.

1 Progress

The US is seeing a steady and encouraging increase in successful ODR implementations. Case types including small claims, landlord/tenant, traffic, and family law, as well as disputes over parenting time, property tax, and consumer satisfaction are currently

1 McCormack, Bridget Mary. "Call to Action." Coronavirus and the Courts, Webinar 1. National Center for State Courts. NCSC.org/pandemic. 7 April 2020. (Presentation begins at 23:06.)

being resolved via ODR. The following are representative ODR implementations and initiatives in US state courts, plus a noteworthy implementation north of the border.

1.1 British Columbia, Canada Civil Resolution Tribunal

Canada's Civil Resolution Tribunal (CRT) is a powerful success story in court connected ODR that has influenced efforts in the US and spawned similar initiatives across the globe. The CRT launched its Solution Explorer in late 2016 with a single case type: strata (condominium) disputes. Nearly four years later, it has grown to become the province's mechanism for resolving motor vehicle injury disputes up to CA$50,000, small claims disputes up to CA$5,000, and society/cooperative association disputes of any amount. Much of the CRT's success can be attributed to the thoughtful design of their Solution Explorer platform where the public can explore both legal and non-legal options available to them before taking any action. Like Utah, the CRT is opt-out. In addition to proceedings being remote for participants, most CRT staff work from home. As a result, the CRT was able to continue normal operations after the onset of the Covid-19 pandemic. As of August 2020, the system has facilitated more than 88,000 small claims, 34,000 strata (condominium), nearly 9,000 motor vehicle, and more than 1,500 society/association explorations.[2] The CRT is data-driven and highly transparent – monthly stats are readily available to the public on the CRT Blog.[3]

1.2 Connecticut Judicial Branch – Superior Court Online Ticket Review

This is an opt-in program developed in-house that allows the public to resolve most common traffic citations online. ODR is integrated with the state's Division of Motor Vehicles license and registration data, and the court's case management system. Crash information may also be available if the infraction was issued as the result of an accident. Before ODR, up to 200 traffic cases were decided during each three-hour hearing, with defendants who wished to go before the judge waiting in the courtroom until their particular case is called. The judge and prosecutor did not have ready access to the driver's history, subsequent infractions, and other public safety information. In 2019, more than 23,500 cases were resolved online.

2 *See* https://civilresolutionbc.ca/crt-statistics-snapshot-august-2020/.

3 *See* https://civilresolutionbc.ca/blog/.

1.3 *Franklin County (Ohio) Municipal Court (FCMC) ODR Negotiation Space*

In 2016, Franklin County, Ohio became the first court in the United States to implement ODR for civil small claims. The platform was developed in collaboration with a third-party vendor and was designed specifically to reduce default judgements in Columbus City Property Tax collection cases by making it easier for the public to participate. The process is opt-in and today, the platform can be used to resolve any civil dispute under the jurisdiction of FCMC. Plaintiffs, defendants, and the courts all experience quantifiable benefits from FCMC's ODR: increased defendant participation, fewer default judgements, reduced time to resolution, an increased percentage of voluntary dismissals, and less court staff time required to resolve cases. FCMC publishes ODR and non-ODR case data online at the FCMC Data Project.[4]

1.4 *Michigan Supreme Court – MI-Resolve*

Michigan recently completed the state-wide rollout of MI-Resolve,[5] the first complete state-level implementation of ODR in the United States. MI-Resolve is an opt-in third-party platform that adds anywhere/anytime access to Michigan's existing Community Dispute Resolution Program (CDRP). The platform can help users resolve complaints and disputes that would ordinarily become court cases. CDRP has provided community-based collaborative mediation since 1990, which has resolved more than 10,000 cases each year that otherwise might have been filed in District Court. The new ODR tool was piloted in 17 counties in August of 2019, prior to the onset of the Covid-19 pandemic. By 1 July 2020, the tool was available in all 83 counties.

1.5 *New Jersey Judiciary ODR*

In response to the Covid-19 pandemic, New Jersey courts expedited the development of an online traffic ticket review ODR platform. The initiative is part of a broader effort – unrelated to the pandemic – to make the court system more efficient and accessible. The software was developed in-house, expanding the capability of an existing 'plead guilty and pay' system. Before ODR, people could either plead guilty and pay online, or come to the courthouse to dispute a charge or explain mitigating factors. In-person visits with the prosecutor might lead to reduced charges, but that option was only available to individuals who had time and resources to come to court. ODR has now been implemented in 515 municipal courts. The public can resolve 37 minor traffic offenses

4 *See* https://sites.google.com/view/fcmcdataproject/data?authuser=0.

5 *See* https://courts.michigan.gov/Administration/SCAO/OfficesPrograms/ODR/Pages/MI-Resolve.aspx.

like speeding, failure to have an insurance card, failure to yield, etc.[6] Parking offenses and fish/game violations will soon be included. The system is opt-in, but planners anticipate the public will readily embrace the convenience. In the first few months, more than 3,700 cases were entered and more than 1,500 resolved through the system. The New Jersey (unified) courts handle more than 5 million traffic and parking cases annually.[7]

1.6 Utah Supreme Court – Small Claims ODR Pilot

The State of Utah launched its first small claims ODR pilot in September of 2018. An opt-out ODR implementation, Utah essentially re-engineered the state's small claims process into a website. All small claims cases must be handled through the ODR system unless someone qualifies for and seeks an exemption. To date, fewer than 2% of participants have sought exemptions. The ODR effort is another logical step in a more holistic approach that began years before with digitization and e-filing initiatives. Thoughtful business process analysis and in-house development lead to an intentionally stripped-down first attempt: a minimum viable product that could be pilot tested, adjusted, and enhanced over time. The tool was piloted in one high-volume court for a year; two small, rural courts were added a year later. With two years of usage data and a rigorous usability study[8] for guidance, Utah is reworking parts of the user interface in preparation for a state-wide rollout. This user-centric focus to designing both the legal process and the software to support it is unique among US ODR initiatives. Utah is making the code open source free to any court (domestic or foreign) that would like to customize and implement it.

2 Obstacles

Even as more courts embrace ODR, progress is surprisingly slow. To understand why, it is useful to examine some of the factors that impact the willingness of state and local courts[9] to embrace ODR and other technology-enabled approaches.

---

6 Crespolini, Russ. "NJ Courts To Resolve Cases Without In-Person Appearances." *Patch*, Mendham-Chester edition. 29 July 2020. Web.

7 Annual Report of the New Jersey Courts, Court Year 2018-2019. Administrative Director of the Courts. New Jersey Judiciary.

8 Butler, Stacy, et al. "The Utah Online Dispute Resolution Platform: A Usability Evaluation and Report." *University of Arizona*, James E. Rogers College of Law, 8 September 2020.

9 For more information about state court organizations, *see* NCSC's Interactive State Court Organization app at ncsc.org/sco.

2.1 US Court Structure

To assess the acceptance of ODR in state courts, it is important to understand the structure of US courts. There is one Federal court system, but in the states, there are literally *thousands* of courts; each court or court system is its own entity, with similarities, but even more idiosyncrasies and granular differences. In many ways, the US courts are awkwardly similar to a confederation of small countries/kingdoms that operate under similar but not identical rules and priorities with a judge or justice at the helm. State courts evolved individually from the ground up, rather than the top down (like Federal courts), which helps explain why there are so many differences in the various state court systems.

Broadly speaking, state and local courts work to provide impartial justice under the unique provisions of their individual state constitutions; 51 individual constitutions establish and govern the operation of state courts. In some states, judges are elected, while in others they are appointed. Some judges serve for a specific term, others for life.[10] In addition to presiding over cases, the chief justice or judge is often the court's administrative head. This individual can have a significant impact on the court's use of technology.

US state courts can be roughly categorized by whether some aspects of the court are administered by a central authority (centralized) or more locally (decentralized). Governance, funding, rules, organizational structure, and technical support are all dimensions of court administration that may be addressed differently depending on the state's overall court structure. There is no single model for how centralized or decentralized courts are administered. Some courts have characteristics of both centralized and decentralized systems. The way ODR is implemented can be impacted significantly by the state's level of centralization.

2.2 Centralized

States with centralized court systems may have centralized control over governance, funding, administration, judicial nominations, compensation, media coverage, the use of interpreters, technology, and other aspects of the judicial branch. The way those functions are managed can vary widely. States with highly centralized planning and authority are able to have more uniform operations and systems, and more consistent data. New Jersey, Utah, Alaska, and Hawaii have highly centralized court systems with strong Administrative Offices.

10 *See* Comparing Federal and State Courts, Administrative Office of the U.S. Courts on behalf of the Federal Judiciary, uscourts.gov and FAQs - Judges in the United States. Quality Judges Initiatives. Institute for the Advancement of the American Legal System, University of Denver. Iaals.du.edu. Web.

In centralized court systems, small courts generally have access to the same technology as large courts. New technology can be implemented state-wide with a single project plan and purchasing process. Centralized judicial systems may have the advantage of 'top down' momentum. An ODR solution can be identified, piloted, then rolled out uniformly across the entire state. Rule or statute changes required to adopt ODR would be initiated by the state's judicial council or supreme court instead of by a single court or county.

Recent ODR implementations by centralized state courts include New Jersey and Utah. Utah's opt-out small claims ODR system has been in pilot since August of 2018 with plans to roll it out statewide later this year. It is unlikely a decentralized court system would be able to do the same. New Jersey implemented its first ODR process in spring 2020 in response to limitations on in-person gatherings imposed by the Covid-19 pandemic. Their traffic citation review project launched after just three months of development and planning. This quick turnaround demonstrates another advantage of the unilateral implementation possible with a centralized court system.

2.3 Decentralized

In a decentralized court, each jurisdiction operates autonomously, although some more autonomously than others. Some, if not all, authority may be vested at the local level. Each court may determine some or all policies, processes, technology, and data requirements. Some states with decentralized court systems provide state-wide network infrastructure, specific applications, support, etc. Many do not. In states with decentralized court systems, smaller courts may not have sufficient resources to acquire and support the same solutions implemented in larger courts. Texas and Ohio are examples of highly decentralized court systems.

An obvious issue with decentralized court systems is that decisions made in one court may not align well with a neighboring court's technology. At risk are consistency in database structures, case types, demographic terminology, and more. The one or two-person court information technology departments may rely heavily on independent contractors or small vendors who ultimately make important IT decisions including whether or not to implement system updates or integrations. Very small IT departments likely lack sufficient cybersecurity resources to adequately protect public-facing systems (including ODR) that could inadvertently become an infection point impacting other courts and public agencies with whom they share information.

One-off systems may not integrate well (or at all) with other systems, including state-level systems. Individual courts may be silos of information that cannot easily be integrated to meet broader reporting and information sharing requirements. Integrating dozens (or in some states, hundreds) of disparate systems and consolidating their data is challenging and costly. System design, vendor selection, implementation, and support efforts are replicated across the state, resulting in inconsistency as well as inefficiency and added taxpayer expense. Overall costs to the state's taxpayers are likely to be higher than when technology is implemented uniformly, under bulk purchase agreements.

Decentralization is not all bad for ODR, though. Innovation can often be significantly constrained by hierarchies inherent in centralization. Individual courts can be more agile in their adoption of technology, and successes can be shared. An individual court can adopt ODR solutions for the area of greatest need without having to wait for the rest of the state. In January 2015, two Michigan counties pioneered an ODR solution for high-volume traffic cases. A year later, six more courts adopted the same platform, customized to their county's specific case type and requirements. Over time, more counties adopted the same platform. Five years after the first implementation, Michigan adopted the platform for a state-wide program, MI-Resolve,[11] for small claims and landlord/tenant disputes.

Texas, a highly decentralized court system, provides a statewide e-filing system through the Texas Administrative Office of the Courts (AOC). By the time the AOC implemented the state-wide solution, some counties had already implemented e-filing through a variety of for-profit vendors. Adopting and enforcing statewide standards made it possible for counties to choose to retain their existing solutions (so long as they conformed to the standard) while the AOC provided one for free. This approach was a unique and innovative solution to the complex issues presented by decentralized IT decision-making when e-filing was less common than it is today. Similarly, the Texas AOC is now exploring options for making a case management system available to counties.

This free-wheeling approach, made possible where courts are decentralized, carries one notable disadvantage. If one court's project – even a very successful one – runs counter to the state's technology plan (or if the state has no strategic technology plan), individual county projects could be costly 'one off' islands. Adopting platforms and development tools that differ from the state's IT could generate ill-will that ultimately scuttles opportunities for broader acceptance. Or worse, when a state lags behind an individual county in deploying a specific technology, the county may be forced to 'downgrade' to the state's solution (when it implements one) or face costly development to integrate with whatever the state deploys.

Some states with a decentralized court structure have pre-empted the different platform issues by covering the full cost of the ODR solution and providing it at no cost to each county. Michigan, a decentralized state with standardized statewide performance measures, is the first state-wide implementation of ODR with their MI-Resolve program. Ohio is beginning an effort to design and deploy ODR, but individual

11 *See* Matterhorn: Reaching New Heights in 2016 (February 2016) and MI-Resolve ODR now in Muskegon, Manistee, Mason, and Oceana Counties (July 2020).

counties must apply to participate and must commit both judicial and administrative support to the project.[12]

2.4 *Branding*

Another significant obstacle to US courts embracing ODR may simply be the name. Online Dispute Resolution in the US has suffered from a terminology disconnect – ultimately a 'branding' failure. The 'product' – ODR – has been tagged in a way that has not resonated with the public, the courts, or the legal profession. Neither courts nor the public commonly use the words 'dispute resolution' to describe what happens in court.

Figure 10.1 Pew Research Center chart of Americans' use of smartphones to access the internet (2019)

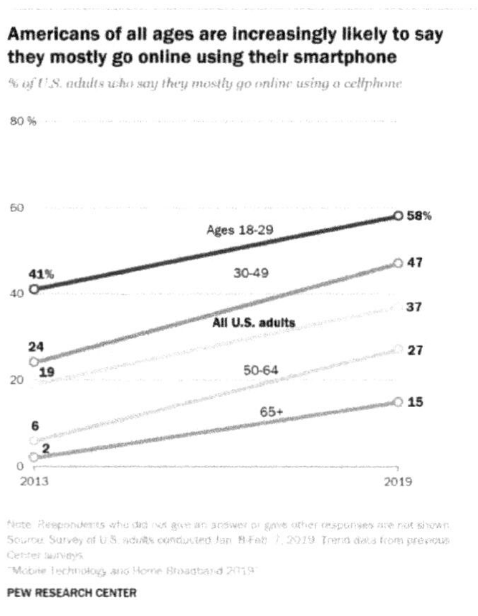

Names and titles are an important part of communicating to potential users or customers what something is or does, and why they should pay attention. Consider online banking, for example. How well accepted would it be today if that had been dubbed 'internet enabled transaction reconciliation'? The public has overwhelmingly embraced online banking, shopping, dating, and more. Noted author and legal/tech thought leader

12 Online Dispute Resolution Pilots. The Supreme Court of Ohio & The Ohio Judicial System, Dispute Resolution Section.

Professor Richard Susskind uses the term Online Courts. Possibly this shift in terminology could help expedite broader acceptance.

2.5 *Prevalence of Tech*

For courts to implement innovative solutions, they need innovative, tech-savvy staff. Often, technology adoption seems somehow influenced by the local 'drinking water'. Technical innovation and expertise often cluster into tech hubs and corridors. In some states, the geography's overall technology adoption/innovation significantly influence whether the courts are embracing or resisting court technologies including ODR. States with a vibrant private tech sector (e.g., California, Texas and Utah) tend to be more innovative in their use of technology initiatives to facilitate court processes.

At the same time, competing with the private tech sector can making recruiting and retaining tech staff challenging for courts. Typically, courts cannot meet private sector salaries required to attract the most qualified staff. However, high paying tech sector jobs draw well-qualified individuals to an area. Courts can offer 'quality of life' benefits and personal satisfaction that may offset some of the pay differential. Doing a job that matters is a decision-point for job-seekers.[13]

2.6 *Aging Judiciary*

Attitudes toward technology are tied closely to age demographics.[14] As of 2017, the average age of a federal circuit judge[15] was 64. Half of all circuit judges were older than 65; more than one in four were over 70.[16] At the same time, the median age of an American was 38.[17] Overlay the age demographics of US judges with technology

13 O'Connell, Brian. "The Search for Meaning – Employees value salary, benefits and company leadership, but meaningful work drives job satisfaction more than ever." The Society for Human Resource Management (SHRM), 23 March 2019.

14 *See* "Millennials stand out for their technology use, but older generations also embrace digital life." *FacTank.* Pew Research Center, 9 September 2019. Web.

15 State court judges tend to be somewhat younger than federal judges, but no similar national statistics for state court judges are readily available. Some states do publish judicial demographics. *See*, for example, Profile of Appellate and Trial Judges (Texas Courts). California Courts report Demographic data on gender, race/ethnicity, sexual orientation, gender identity, and veteran and disability status of California State Justices and Judges but do not report judges' ages.

16 McMillion, Barry J. "U.S. Circuit and District Court Judges: Profile of Select Characteristics." Congressional Research Service. 1 August 2017. p. 11. Web.

17 Rogers, Luke. "Counties Can Have the Same Median Age But Very Different Population Distributions." *American Counts: Stories Behind the Numbers.* United States Census Bureau. 20 June 2019. Web.

adoption statistics by age demographic,[18] and the disconnect becomes apparent: those who use the courts are primarily young and tech-savvy while those within the day-to-day operations of the courts and who make decisions about potential improvements are older and much less likely to embrace and therefore leverage technology.

There are notable exceptions to this age/tech adoption dynamic in the court community, but often the judiciary simply do not reflect the public they serve. For example, Americans age 65 and older (the age demographic for judges) use a smartphone to go online approximately 15% of the time. Contrast that with smartphone use in the 18-29 year-old category – 58% use a smartphone as their primary means of accessing the web.[19] The difference is striking.

2.7 *Judicial Attitudes Toward Technology*

At the intersection of technology and age demographics of the judiciary is the judiciary's attitude toward technology. A recent study of online hearings in Texas revealed that most judges, regardless of age, quickly became very adept at conducting a hearing online, taking on an additional tech support role if witnesses, lawyers, or other participants experience a technological issue during the hearing. However, a small number of judges took a distinctly 'hands off' approach to the technology. In the Texas study, when a judge failed to 'engage' and relied on others to resolve technology issues, the quality of the hearing was negatively impacted.[20]

2.8 *'Usability' and the Legal/Tech Disconnect*

In private industry, applications may be developed quickly over a period of weeks or months and adapted iteratively according to user feedback and changing requirements. The approach to government development, on the other hand, has generally been years-long procurement, design, and development efforts; systems are launched and remain mostly unchanged for years if not decades. A notable example in legal technology is PACER (Public Access to Electronic Records), which got its first significant facelift in June 2020 after initial launch *more than 30 years ago*.[21]

18 Auxier, Brooke, et al. "10 Tech-Related Trends That Shaped the Decade." FacTank: News in the Numbers, Pew Research Center, 20 December 2019, www.pewresearch.org/fact-tank/2019/12/20/10-tech-related-trends-that-shaped-the-decade/.

19 Auxier, Brooke, et al. "10 Tech-Related Trends That Shaped the Decade." *FacTank: News in the Numbers*, Pew Research Center, 20 December 2019, www.pewresearch.org/fact-tank/2019/12/20/10-tech-related-trends-that-shaped-the-decade/.

20 Thornburg, Elizabeth G. "Observing Online Courts: Lessons from the Pandemic", 21 September 2020, p. 10. Available at SSRN: https://ssrn.com/abstract=3696594 or http://dx.doi.org/10.2139/ssrn.3696594.

21 Judiciary Launches Redesigned PACER Website. *Judiciary News*. United States Courts. 26 June 2020. Web.

Banking, retail, education, and other industries continuously refine their websites to help users find information or complete tasks more quickly. Industries that compete for customers understand that if users are frustrated with the app/process, they very quickly 'bounce off' to look for something that works better for them. Users who do not remain on a site through to task completion represent lost revenue. Usability testing is a tool commonly used by the private sector in that refinement process.

> The goal of usability testing is to reveal areas of confusion, uncover opportunities to improve a user interface (UI) and enhance the overall user experience (UX). Broadly speaking, UX is the aggregate of a person's attitude, emotions, and reactions to using a product, service, or system.[22]

While courts doing ODR often track statistics including case filings, return of service, settlement agreements, default judgments, etc., they lack general usability testing. Usability testing looks at the system's overall effectiveness, efficiency, and how people actually interact with it. How successful are representative users at completing specific tasks? How long does each task take? Could users get to the right place with fewer clicks and less data entry? How satisfied are users are with the system?

Utah is the first court to commission a usability study to evaluate an ODR platform. The state's groundbreaking small claims ODR system has been in pilot since 2018; thousands of cases have been resolved using the platform. The court could easily have been satisfied with court-facing improvements in efficiency and a quantifiable reduction in default judgments. Instead, Utah contracted with the Innovation for Justice Program at the University of Arizona James E. Rogers College of Law for a formal usability evaluation prior to deploying the system state-wide.

The results of that study were made public in September 2020 as the Utah Courts were already in the process of implementing the study's suggestions. Designing an online court experience for typical users and testing to see how well it actually works for the public is a significant step in improving access to justice. Unfortunately, a legal publication that reported on the study missed the point.[23] Usability or user experience (UX) studies are not designed to be self-congratulatory; they identify where real people run into obstacles in successfully completing tasks. More importantly, usability studies foster improvement.

In private industry, a relentless focus on the user experience has helped create industry giants like Apple and Toyota. Apple's finely-honed customer out-of-box experience has generated almost cult-like loyalty. Consumers who buy one Apple

22 Butler, Stacy, et al. "The Utah Online Dispute Resolution Platform: A Usability Evaluation and Report." *University of Arizona*, James E. Rogers College of Law, 8 September 2020.

23 *See* Cueto, Emma. "Online Court Pilot Gets Low Marks Ahead of Wider Launch." *Law360*. LexusNexis, 13 September 2020. Web.

product often go on to buy five or more.[24] For Toyota, a careful study of how people actually drive influences everything about their car designs. Consumers appreciate the Toyota driving experience including very small details like the curve of seat backs, placement of radio controls and mirrors, etc.

> All this talk of advances in the automotive technology, it's really easy to lose sight of why we build cars ... We make them for people.[25]

Courts, like cars and computers, are ultimately made for people. Since the public cannot really choose whether or not to use most court services, courts have little incentive to adjust the 'user interface' of the processes people navigate. Failure to appear and default judgment rates are just one indicator that processes are not working for those required to navigate them.

2.9 *Digital Divide*

One of the consistent explanations for why some courts are not pursuing ODR is the 'digital divide' – the lack of adequate access to technology by some demographics/ communities.

Figure 10.2 Texas Poll of Potential Jurors' Access to Internet/Cell phone (2020)

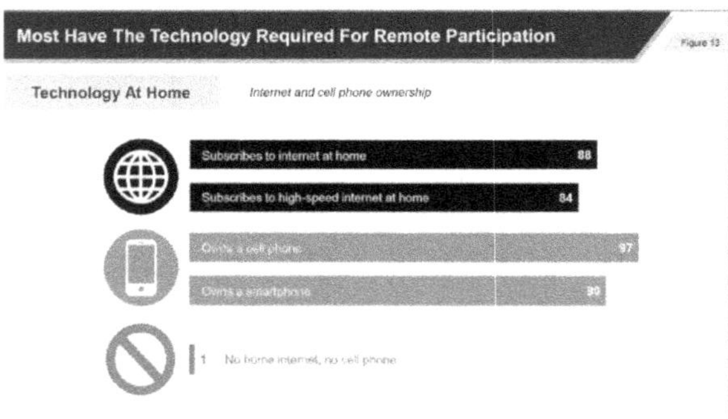

A spring 2020 poll of potential jurors in Texas found that only 1% of those who responded had no cell phone or internet access; 90% of potential jurors reported

24 Stibble, Matthew. "How Apple Wins at Brand Loyalty." *GeekBoss*. Web.

25 Bob Carter, Senior Vice President of Automotive Operations at Toyota, as quoted by Sheena Lyonnais in "The Key Thing UX Designers Can Learn From Toyota's Newest Concept Car." *Adobe Blog*. Creative Inspiration and Trends. 13 January 2017.

owning a smartphone and 88% had high-speed internet access. More than 75% of those with wireless service had data access plans with unlimited minutes and/or data.[26] Results from the 2020 National Public Opinion Poll are similar: 85% subscribe to the internet at home, 95% own a cellphone (85% own smartphones), 2.4% have no home internet or cell phone.[27]

Lack of access to broadband is an issue that does negatively impact rural communities, the poor, and others. This is a particularly troubling issue during the pandemic with schools closed and many children learning from home via Zoom or other conferencing platform instead of in the classroom. That said, the vast majority of people today have sufficient cell phone and/or Wi-Fi access to participate in a remote hearing or resolve a dispute via ODR.

Participating remotely has significant benefits for those same demographics/ communities that have greater technology access constraints. Several recent studies cite both anecdotal evidence of benefit as well as a quantifiable decrease in failure to appear rates when people can participate without having to take time away from work and traveling to the courthouse.

> One judge recounted the story of a witness who successfully testified from a Wal-Mart restroom, dressed in her Wal-Mart uniform, while on her break.[28]

In spite of cell phone and Wi-Fi limitations, technology generally makes court more accessible to the public, particularly to vulnerable communities. It may be that the real 'digital divide' is between the judiciary and the public.

2.10 *Legal Industry*

Possibly one of the more vexing issues is the hostility sometimes leveled by the legal industry toward legal tech innovations including ODR. Wielding the power of monopoly, the industry remains entrenched, with some state bar associations seemingly determined to block any effort to update antiquated regulations and practices.

Contrast the legal industry with the medical industry in the United States. Efficiencies are constantly implemented to improve healthcare. A variety of qualification levels balance training requirements against service complexity. A physician's assistant or nurse practitioner can deliver well-child and preventive care, as well as treat a wide variety of common ailments. The legal industry in the US, however, has no universal

26 Raftery, William. "Will Jurors Come Back to Courthouses?" *Judicature*. Bolch Judicial Institute and Duke Law School. Summer 2020. Volume 104 Number 2. Web.

27 "Most American's Have the Technology Tools for Remote Participation", *State of the State Courts in a (Post) Pandemic World*. National Center for State Courts. June 2020. Presentation Slide 12. Web.

28 Thornburg, p. 22.

equivalent. As a result, the common cold and well-child legal equivalents can only be dispensed by a lawyer who must have the same level of education whether preparing a will or appealing a death penalty conviction.

Law school is an investment of hundreds of thousands of dollars. With newly minted lawyers carrying law school debt the size of a mortgage,[29] paying that debt contributes to the scale of legal fees. As a direct result, legal services are prohibitively expensive even for low-risk/low-complexity cases. In most places, there is no legal equivalent to a 'midwife' or 'physician assistant'. The rise of AVVO and similar web sites (getting legal advice fast/cheap via web site) is indicative of the pent-up demand for more affordable legal services. To carry the medical analogy further, consumers have limited options to 'take their own temperature' to see if a case is worth pursuing. The cost of in-person consultation with a lawyer, with average hourly rates ranging from $284-637/hour,[30] is exponentially too high, particularly when set against potential legal remedies.

Some states have created non-lawyer legal roles that could mitigate this issue. In August 2020, the Arizona Supreme Court modified court rules to create a licensure process for a new kind of legal paraprofessional.[31] In 2018, the Utah Supreme Court established a paralegal practitioner role.[32] Under the rules governing the Utah State Bar, a Licensed Paralegal Practitioner can file forms, complete settlement negotiations, review court documents, and represent clients in mediation in family law, debt collection, and landlord-tenant cases.

At the same time, some states are either delaying such programs or withdrawing them. When the Washington Supreme Court announced its decision in June 2020 to 'sunset' their Limited License Legal Technician program,[33] they cited a lack of interest.[34] However, the bar created significant obstacles for candidates to obtain the required education and voted repeatedly to limit areas of practice.[35] The State Bar of California formed a task force in 2013 to explore options for non-lawyer legal roles, but no program was created. Seven years later, a new program – the Task Force on Access Through Innovation of Legal Services – is now underway in California. This January 2020 initiative broadens the scope of the earlier work and includes addressing the definition

29 "Which Law School Graduates Have the Most Debt?" *US News and World Report*, 2020 Report – Best Law Schools. Web.

30 USAO Attorney's Fees Matrix—2015-2020. Offices of the United States Attorneys. United States Department of Justice. Web. www.justice.gov/usao-dc/page/file/1189846/download.

31 Arizona Supreme Court, Administrative Office of the Courts. "Arizona Supreme Court Makes Generational Advance in Access to Justice." 27 August 2020.

32 *See* www.utahbar.org/licensed-paralegal-practitioner/.

33 Limited License Legal Technician Board, Washington State Bar Association. www.wsba.org/for-legal-professionals/join-the-legal-profession-in-wa/limited-license-legal-technicians.

34 Moran, Lyle. "Washington Supreme Court sunsets limited license program for nonlawyers." *ABA Journal.* 8 June 2020. Web.

35 Moran, Lyle. "How the Washington Supreme Court's LLLT program met its demise." *ABA Journal.* 9 July 2020. Web.

of the unauthorized practice of law as one of its three main tasks. A key difference between these two California task force initiatives is that the 2020 task force is made up primarily of non-attorneys.[36]

The legal regulations that proscribe and perpetuate these limitations are the same regulations that can be used to delay, curtail, or prevent ODR.

2.11 *Procedural Constraints*

Relatively simple things can stand in the way of some courts embracing more online processes: when wet signatures are required and paper is the court's official record, there is little room for digital innovation. While many US courts are fully digital, some are (unbelievably) not digital at all. Some organizations making early forays into ODR retained procedures that ultimately derailed the project, for example, requiring a case to be filed in-person at a courthouse or insisting that participants go before a judge to agree to participate in ODR.[37]

2.12 *Consumer Advocates*

Legal aid organizations and consumer advocates address some of the public's unmet legal needs. Increasingly, these organizations are turning to technology to help deliver services more efficiently.[38] Many state legal aid organizations have created legal aid 'portals' – a single point of access to information and assistance. Others are experimenting with ODR as front-end on-line mediation prior to court processes. These are appropriate and effective uses of technology but fall short of ODR's potential.

However, these same organizations have sometimes been unexpected opponents of ODR. For example, some consumer advocate groups fear ODR may facilitate an imbalance of power or simply expedite unfairness. Without an in-person experience, they fear the public would not fully understand their legal protections. In at least one instance, a legal aid organization effectively derailed a state's plans for ODR.

When ODR is done well, it can equip consumers with the legal information they need to respond appropriately and effectively to resolve many kinds of legal issues. For example, in inherently unfair situations where landlords and debt collectors are typically represented but tenants and debtors are not, ODR advocates see technology as

36 Fact Sheet. Task Force on Access Through Innovation of Legal Services. The State Bar of California. 28 January 2020. Web.

37 *See* "Case Studies in ODR for Courts: A view from the front lines." *JTC Resource Bulletin*. ncsc.org. 29 November 2017. Web.

38 *See*, for example, www.lawhelpmn.org/lawhelpmn-guide (Minnesota), https://michiganlegalhelp.org/, and www.illinoislegalaid.org/.

truly leveling the field. The Civil Resolution Tribunal[39] is an example of an effective combination of ODR tools that facilitate information gathering, triage, mediation, and adjudication.[40]

2.13 Purchasing Processes

Government organizations have long struggled with technology purchasing for a variety of reasons. Costs and risks are high, which should appropriately be tied to a higher level of constraints. A history of major IT failures in the public sector has created an environment of aversion to risk that stifles efforts to innovate. No one wants to be associated with the next big failure. Hence, highly restrictive procurement requirements.

In addition, purchasing is sometimes controlled within the executive branch, making those courts subject to the executive branch's purchasing rules and requirements. Almost always, purchasing is funded through appropriations by the legislative branch, which is influenced by a variety of things, including funding priorities, views of government (generally) and the judiciary (more specifically) and reaction to judicial opinions. Highly prescriptive requirements are common, and often the antithesis of innovation. Purchasing processes can also be lengthy up to a year or more while technology changes rapidly. Unique skillsets are required to effectively procure technology. But in smaller courts, the same individual(s) responsible for selecting an ODR solution may be accepting filings, overseeing human resources, setting policy, acquiring office supplies and furniture, and securing cleaning, trash and pest control services.

Even for courts with specialized, skilled court technology purchasing staff, selecting an ODR platform and vendor may be even more challenging. ODR is a relatively new sub-specialty within court technology. Capable vendors who qualify in every other category may not meet stringent requirements for the time in business or number and size of current implementations of their product.

While government purchasing is getting more progressive, it is not generally nimble and responsive to a dynamic marketplace. Ideally, purchasing staff can find ways to preserve the integrity of the process while responding to an evolving market.

39 *See* https://civilresolutionbc.ca/.

40 Canada's Civil Resolution Tribunal tracks 'explorations' (the pre-filing stage where the public can gather information anonymously before taking any action), as well as disputes resolved by agreement (mediation), and disputes resolved by adjudication. The Solution Explorer has resources such as complaint letter templates that can help the public resolve issues without making the matter a formal dispute.

2.14 *Implementation Failures*

Several recent court attempts at ODR have not gone well. This is not a fact any court is likely to broadcast, except possibly to place blame. Understanding what has gone wrong and why is very important for all courts – those who have experienced the setbacks as well as those still only considering an ODR implementation.

Responsibility for implementation failures can often be spread fairly across court administration, vendors, and even ODR proponents and non-profit funders, who may 'soften' tough messages to make them more palatable.

Adding a layer of technology to a complex process dictated by legal practices unfamiliar to all but the legal industry won't work. Creating online resources to help the public understand and respond appropriately to archaic legal terms and processes should not be the goal. Successful ODR implementations are the result of intentional efforts to overhaul processes to address the needs of users. Shannon Salter of British Columbia's highly successfully Civil Resolution Tribunal said this:

Do not pave the cow path … Even if you have very little technology or capital, you can start this re-design work by simply talking to the people in line at the court registry about their experience navigating the court system.

> How long did it take? How much has it cost? How much time off work have they taken? What was most confusing? How do they feel they have been treated? Ask them to fill out court forms and observe where they get stuck. Use this feedback to start designing new processes from the perspective, and with the help of, that person in the registry line-up.[41]

3 LOOKING AHEAD

Courts will face budget cuts from the economic impacts of the pandemic. At the same time, a backlog of cases is building, particularly evictions and debt collections, that will hit the courts like a tsunami once Covid-19 related protections expire. Pandemic-related unemployment and underemployment is impacting millions of US households financially, exacerbating the already problematic access to justice crisis. ODR presents a sensible solution that can help both the public and the courts.

With the initial shockwaves of the pandemic subsiding, more jurisdictions are doing serious ODR project work. Some courts are accelerating projects to provide permanent online offerings. Several states have initiated or accelerated ODR initiatives. Hawai'i,

41 Al Khayat, Joe. "ODR Interview with Shannon Salter." *Resolve Disputes Online/Blog*. 11 October 2019.

Alaska, Maryland, California, Iowa, New Hampshire, Colorado, Tennessee, and Vermont are all well underway with new ODR implementations for 2020/2021. These add to those solutions already being piloted or already implemented in Michigan, Texas, Ohio, Utah, Arizona, Connecticut, and New Mexico.

Change is hard, and there is a very real risk that some courts will attempt to return to business as usual when the pandemic danger finally retreats. For a variety of reasons, some states have slowed or halted ODR planning and pilot programs.

ODR in US courts is still very much in its infancy. Metrics to evaluate outcomes, A/B platform testing, qualitative and quantitative research are few or non-existent. Relevant statistics are difficult to gather and even more complicated to assess. For example, the ABA Center for Innovation's September 2020 report, *Online Dispute Resolution in the United States,* provides a map of jurisdictions with court-annexed ODR as of December 2019.[42] While the information provided is useful, it appears to be incomplete as well as misleading. The study treats ODR as a tick-box without differentiating between courts that have used ODR for a few dozen cases, and those that have successfully resolved thousands.

4 Observations

I close with some personal observations of implementation considerations and impacts based on my years of working within the court community to promote ODR.

The importance of a project champion

The single most important factor contributing to the success of court ODR implementation appears to be a strong, committed, tireless, and nearly bullet-proof project champion. The importance of involving stakeholders has long been recognized as key to success in IT initiatives. However, anecdotal evidence suggests that having the right project champion has a more significant impact with ODR. Conversely, the lack of such a champion can undermine a project's success, even if there are supportive stakeholders.

An effective ODR project champion can navigate organizational politics, unify the project team, persuade reticent stakeholders, and effectively negotiate unexpected obstacles. Notable examples include Justice Deno Himonas of the Utah Supreme Court; Doug Van Epps, Director of the Office of Dispute Resolution for the Michigan Supreme Court; Chief Justice Bridget Mary McCormack of the Michigan Supreme Court; Judge Glenn Grant, Administrative Director of the New Jersey Courts; and Shannon Salter,

42 "Online Dispute Resolution in the United States". ODR Visualization Report. American Bar Association Center for Innovation. September 2020. Web. www.americanbar.org/content/dam/aba/administrative/center-for-innovation/odrvisualizationreport.pdf.

Chair, Civil Resolution Tribunal. Both judicial and administrative leaders can play the project champion role effectively. In several jurisdictions, empowered leadership in combination with at least one strong technical resource and a capable, well-respected clerk has been pivotal to a project's success. In some cases, the project champion *is* the team, as with Alex Sanchez of Franklin County (Ohio) Municipal Court. Being undaunted may be the most essential technical skill.

Optional or mandatory?

Whether to make ODR optional/opt-in (where parties must agree to participate) or mandatory/opt-out (where only in certain circumstances can a party choose to use a paper-based or in-person process instead) is probably the most significant policy choice a jurisdiction will make regarding ODR, and likely the most emotional. Courts that make ODR *the* process (with appropriate options for unique circumstances) are able to craft an entirely new dispute resolution process without the constraints, inefficiencies, and power imbalances typical of existing processes. Resolving traffic citations as opt-in ODR works well enough because it is inherently advantageous for an individual to handle a citation without having to take time off work or away from other responsibilities. Most people happily choose to resolve citations without having to go into a courthouse.

Where there is likely to be an imbalance of power, opt-out (with limited justifications for doing so) is one way to truly level the playing field. ODR can prevent one party from having the power to make the process more inconvenient and costly for the other party. Opt-in ODR implementations for civil dispute resolution have not been as successful, likely because reducing that power imbalance is not attractive to those who benefit from the advantages of adversarial proceedings.

Reducing bias

The year 2020 brought not just a pandemic, but civil upheaval tied to an increased awareness of systemic racial bias in law enforcement and criminal justice. This heightened sensitivity is also drawing attention to unfairness rooted in biases with real, but less dramatic consequences. Because of time constraints and the sheer volume of cases, minor civil cases '... appear especially subject to implicit biases in judicial decision-making', according to a recent study.[43] Most courts genuinely want to ensure they deliver outcomes that are blind to race, gender, age, and any other bias. There is a new determination to do better.

ODR can help both expose and mitigate bias. Using data from both ODR and traditional court processes to compare outcomes, Mentovich, et al, found

43 Mentovich, Avital, Prescott, J. J. and Rabinovich-Einy, Orna. "Are Litigation Outcome Disparities Inevitable? Courts, Technology, and the Future of Impartiality." *Alabama Law Review*, 71(4) (June 2020), pp. 893-979, Available at SSRN: https://ssrn.com/abstract=3559773 or http://dx.doi.org/10.2139/ssrn.3559773.

'... substantial evidence that black litigants receive higher court fines and are less likely to receive charge reductions in face-to-face settings than similarly situated nonblack litigants'. The study also found '... strong evidence that younger drivers pay higher fines than their older peers in face-to-face courts'. However, statistics show those disparities disappear in cases resolved online.

Unanticipated benefits

Most notable in post-pandemic considerations, ODR keeps people out of the courthouse. For the foreseeable future, that protects both court staff and the public. Resolving as many cases as possible outside the physical structure of the courthouse will make it possible to focus resources on delivering justice outcomes that are both fair and safe for everyone involved: parties, court support staff, lawyers, judges and all of their families (especially extended family members who would never actually be in the courtroom but come into close proximity to those who do).

Even when issues cannot be resolved using an ODR platform, ODR is good preparation for the in-person process. Utah's West Valley City Justice Court judge Brendan McCullagh notes that self-represented litigants who appear before him with issues they could not resolve via ODR come prepared with necessary documents and a better understanding of both the issues and potential remedies. As a result, cases that in the past would likely have taken multiple court appearances have been settled in a single hearing.[44]

Courts will likely discover other unanticipated benefits such as savings in staff time, better access for ESL and disabled participants, less contentious hearings, and increased participant satisfaction as they implement ODR. There will likely be unanticipated challenges, but overwhelmingly, courts who implement ODR are discovering they had underestimated the advantages.

5 Where We Go from Here

Many believe the public is more than ready for additional online court processes. Stacy Butler, lead researcher on the Utah ODR usability study, summarized user feedback this way:

> Users are ready for online courts ... When asked whether they would prefer to access a website or physically appear at the courthouse to resolve a dispute, **all**

44 "Judicial Perspectives on ODR and Other Virtual Court Processes." *JTC Quick Response Bulletin.* 18 May 2020.

but one of the [35] participants ... responded with a preference for a website.[45]

NCSC's 2020 annual State of State Courts survey found a similar interest in videoconference court appearances, an approach that has been particularly useful during the pandemic.[46] The shift in public attitudes between 2014 and today portend an even greater interest in using online and remote court services going forward.

Figure 10.3 Attitudes towards remote court services (2020)

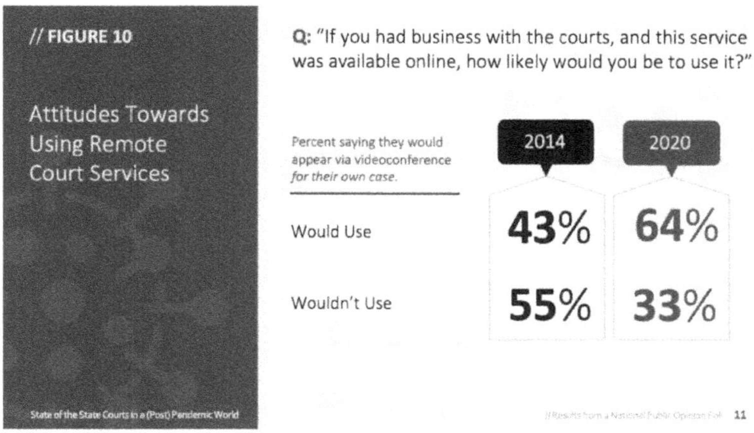

As courts gradually resume more normal operations, practical adjustments will be made to in-person processes: masks, physical distancing, hand sanitizer, better scheduling to limit the number of people in the courthouse at one time. These measures to prevent the spread of Covid-19 are likely to be necessary for at least a year and possibly two or more years. But at some point, these physical adjustments will no longer be needed. Could similar 'practicality' help prod more courts toward ODR and other online court processes?

Many thought-leaders like Chief Justice McCormack believe strongly that the shift to online court processes should be permanent. Instead of approaching the in-person/online question from the perspective of 'what could/should be done online?', it may be time for courts to assume court processes should be conducted online unless there is a compelling need to do them in person. In a July/August 2020 article on the future of courts, Richard Susskind expressed the need to look well beyond Zoom hearings.

45 Butler, Stacy, et al. "The Utah Online Dispute Resolution Platform: A Usability Evaluation and Report." *University of Arizona*, James E. Rogers College of Law, 8 September 2020. (emphasis added).

46 "State of the State Courts in a (Post) Pandemic World." *Public Trust and Confidence Resource Guide*. National Center for State Courts. Presentation slide 11. June 2020.

> Almost all the remote courts that have been set up in response to the virus are variations on the theme of traditional courts. But we should be clear: dropping our current court system into Zoom is not a shift in paradigm [...] The leap from physical courts to remote hearings has, of course, been remarkable, but it is very early ... and no one can sensibly claim that they are suitable for all cases and issues. We are at the foothills of the transformation in court services. The current array of remote courts is a valiant collection of ad hoc services, but much work and investment will be needed to industrialize these efforts, to build court capabilities that are scalable, stable, and, crucially, designed for use as much by lay people as by lawyers.[47]

The pandemic forced changes to the courts, many of which were arguably long overdue. Proven in the fire of necessity, courts have gained technical expertise through the pandemic that will hopefully expedite transformative efforts including ODR going forward. Visionary leadership will be required to ensure gains are solidified and innovation continues.

47 Susskind, Richard. "The Future of Courts" *Remote Courts,* 6(5) (July/August 2020). The Center on the Legal Profession, Harvard Law School.

Chapter 11 ODR and Social Justice: Technology Not Tricknology

Benjamin G. Davis

1 Introduction – Social Justice a Pejorative?[1]

In some quarters of the American polity, to describe someone as a Social Justice Warrior is an epithet[2]

> for someone who advocates liberal causes like feminism, racial justice or gay and transgender rights. It is also sometimes used to imply that a person's online advocacy of a cause is insincere or done for appearances. (Emphasis added)[3]

So to discuss *online* dispute resolution and social justice at a time where precisely *online* advocacy is derided in such a manner by some elements in society creates an initial burden on such a discussion. One must make sure to address all persons concerned without inadvertently playing into various critiques or celebrations of social justice whatever their origin.

To overcome this linguistic conundrum, we might first start with the idea of justice. Discussing justice is to be distinguished from discussing access to justice – a moniker we hear so frequently that it even has its own TLA[4] as A2J.[5] Having justice is more than access to justice – just like having a Lamborghini is more than having access to a Lamborghini[6] or having health care is more than having access to health care.[7]

---

1 The term Tricknology was brought to my attention by a member of the Central Park Exonerated 5 Dr. Yusef Salam, when he spoke at the University of Toledo on 11 January 2020.

2 Liam Stack, Alt-Right, Alt-Left, Antifa: A Glossary of Extremist Language, 15 August 2017 (New York Times), available at www.nytimes.com/2017/08/15/us/politics/alt-left-alt-right-glossary.html.

3 *Ibid.*

4 Three Letter Acronym.

5 Well two letters and a number.

6 One can buy one if one can afford one.

7 In counties without National Health Insurance, one can have health care if one can pay for it.

1.1 *Justice as a Concept in International and Domestic Law*

As succinctly proclaimed on the front of the United States Supreme Court building, the guiding principle is 'equal justice under law' not 'equal **access to** justice under law'. As we think of entities or persons as parties in some form of online dispute resolution and drilling down into this idea of justice, what are key features of justice? It was once noted by the late Supreme Court Justice Robert Jackson prior to becoming the Chief Prosecutor for the Nuremberg Tribunal,

> It is important that we do not allow the assumptions that lie at the foundation of any worthwhile international judiciary to become obscured in issues or pressures about details. These are not unimportant matters, but they are subsidiary to what I consider the great principles on which an international tribunal must be based.[8]

Justice Jackson went on to note the divergence of views on what tribunals are to do.

> Anglo-Americans and many others generally have adhered to the concept of a court as an independent body which neither serves nor controls policy and whose members owe a duty to truth in fact-finding and to the science of law in decision that transcends any duty to nation, to class, to governments, or to party.... It would, however, be unwise to overlook that this is quite contrary to the concept prevailing among nearly all of our enemies, among some of our allies and some neutrals, and beginning to have a considerable and influential school of thought in the United States. They think of courts as dependent and controlled arms of the policy-making part of government, as legitimate instruments to promote policy, and as bodies whose fact-findings and decisions may properly reflect the national interest, the class or party interest which is responsible for their creation, as the case may be.[9]

Given this lived dichotomy between independence and policy-making views of courts, his conclusion was that

---

8 Robert H. Jackson, The Rule of Law Among Nations, Address to the American Society of International Law, (13 April 1945), available at www.roberthjackson.org/wp-content/uploads/2015/01/Rule_of_Law_Among_Nations.pdf.

9 *Ibid.*

> It would be very difficult for an international court long to succeed if such irreconcilable conceptions of its character and function continued to divide the powerful constituents of our international organization.[10]

We might look at these views of tribunals as a tension between justice and power. Justice Jackson resolved this tension in a manner that might be of assistance to us as we create online dispute resolution as it was of assistance to him in the creation of the Nuremberg Tribunal. Justice Jackson identified several features of such a creation, to wit:

1. It seems to me that much hinges on acceptance of the concept of the Court as an independent body above obligation to any nation or interest.
2. It is a plain corollary of the principle that courts must not be swayed by policy, that they must not decide matters of policy.
3. We must not use the forms of judicial proceedings to carry out or rationalize previously settled political or military policy. Farcical judicial trials conducted by us will destroy confidence in the judicial process as quickly as those conducted by any other people.
4. [W]e will not suffer the worst of decision, but will benefit from the judicial process at its best if we insist upon the independence and intellectual integrity of any international tribunal which purports to arbitrate or adjudicate controversies between states.
5. I am pointing out hazards that attend such use of the judicial process-risk on the one hand that the decision which most of the world thinks should be made may not be justified as a judicial finding, even if perfectly justified as a political policy; and the alternative risk of damage to the future credit of judicial proceedings by manipulations of trial personnel or procedure to invest temporarily with judicial character what is in fact a political decision. I repeat that I am not saying there should be no trials. I merely say that our profession should see that it is understood that any trials to which lawyers worthy of their calling lend themselves will be trials in fact, not merely trials in name, to ratify a predetermined result.[11]

Other aspects of legitimate dispute resolution bodies might be gleaned from still another international source, Common Article 3 of the Geneva Conventions which states in relevant part that the following acts are and shall remain prohibited at any time and in any place whatsoever with respect to the relevant persons.

> Article 3 (d): the passing of sentences and the carrying out of executions without previous judgment pronounced by a regularly constituted court,

10 *Ibid.*
11 *Ibid.*

> affording all the judicial guarantees which are recognized as indispensable by civilized peoples.[12]

The importance of regular constitution and judicial guarantees which are recognized as indispensable by civilized people described here for courts finds its echo in still another international source in the New York Convention on the Recognition and Enforcement of Foreign Arbitral Awards. Article V(d) states in relevant part one of the grounds for which an arbitral award may be set aside is

> (d). the composition of the arbitral authority or the arbitral procedure was not in accordance with the agreement of the parties, or, failing such agreement, was not in accordance with the law of the country where the arbitration took place.[13]

This language inserts the arbitration into the legal regime of the place of arbitration with that state's vision of what is the appropriate manner to provide due process.

We might look to still another source of understanding what justice is to mean in the International Covenant on Civil and Political Rights which states in relevant part:

> Article 14
> 1. All persons shall be equal before the courts and tribunals. In the determination of any criminal charge against him, or of his rights and obligations in a suit at law, everyone shall be entitled to a fair and public hearing by a competent, independent and impartial tribunal established by law.[14]

Equal justice under law, independence and integrity, impartiality, competence, regularly constituted, judicial guarantees recognized as indispensable by civilized persons all are words these sources associate with legitimate processes of dispute resolution. For purposes of this discussion, I will incorporate all of these concepts in one concept I will succinctly call neutral dispute resolution. Is that synthesis a bridge too far? Surely these qualities described by these various sources are the essence of legitimate exercise of

---

12 Common Art. 3, Geneva Conventions, available at https://ihl-databases.icrc.org/applic/ihl/ihl.nsf/WebART/365-570006.

13 Art. V(d), Convention on the Recognition and Enforcement of Foreign Arbitral Awards (New York, 1958), available at https://uncitral.un.org/sites/uncitral.un.org/files/media-documents/uncitral/en/new-york-convention-e.pdf.

14 Art. 14(1), International Covenant on Civil and Political Rights, available at www.ohchr.org/EN/ProfessionalInterest/Pages/CCPR.aspx.

judicial power as it is done in some type of neutral forum by neutrals with a neutral procedure as between the protagonists.

Yet, such neutral dispute resolution providing all those guarantees does not provide them for free. To model online dispute resolution on such concepts may entail costs and mechanisms that in fact are cost ineffective relative to the types of disputes being resolved. So, as we are obliged by pragmatic constraints to consider how and where to diverge from this almost Platonic ideal of neutral dispute resolution we might move increasingly to dispute resolution without the attributes described above. In that less neutral or even non-neutral dispute resolution, we may get more cost-effective methods of dispute resolution in return for that departure from the ideal. And while it may not be perfect justice, it may be what we might describe as imperfect or good enough justice relative to the type of problems that are being addressed. And, as the adage says, the best can be the enemy of the good. Or should it be?

1.2 From Neutral Dispute Resolution to Customer Service Dispute Resolution

This no doubt less than perfect form of dispute resolution contrasts with neutral dispute resolution described above. Trying to come to understand the qualities of this imperfect form of dispute resolution, I have found the best analogy for this imperfect form of dispute resolution is a phrase with which most of us are familiar: customer service dispute resolution. When one goes to or calls customer service with respect to a problem one has with what a company has provided, one knows that the person to whom one is speaking is paid by that company, has been trained by that company, will be looking out primarily for the interests of that company in the manner that company describes its interests, and is neither independent nor impartial. Does that deprive them of the capacity to resolve disputes? On the contrary, subject to the limits they have at each level of authority, these customer services types form an important function of resolving disputes before they escalate too much.

1.2.1 A Wonderful Customer Service Vignette

A wonderful example of customer service dispute resolution occurred just last evening. My spouse was given a $100 Amazon gift card as a Christmas present which she applied to her Amazon account. She then proceeded to purchase three items that were for a total of $95.43. The technology (wags would say she made the mistake not the technology for technology is neutral) put her into my account where the gift card was not applied and a purchase was made. When I received a message on my cellphone (again technology providing information), I noted that it said that this private purchase had been made on behalf of the University of Toledo. Obviously this purchase was not so made and so the issue became what to do. The notice describing the purchase did not have a button one could click on to cancel the purchase, but did have a phone number to call (an Amazon technology choice to not have an automated process at the control of the customer, but have a screen of the need to make a phone call, deal with an Amazon professional (i.e. meaning speak to customer service)). So I called the phone number and very rapidly (another Amazon choice as to how many individuals work in this customer service space at any given time so as to have shorter or longer wait times) was put in touch with a live human being. After the Amazon system put me through a verification process (technology operating to send me a temporary verification code that I had to put in the screen that the Amazon person could observe), I explained the error and requested to cancel the order. Amazon immediately cancelled the order (again another Amazon choice as to the speed a cancellation would be made – immediately, 2 or 3 business days, etc). And, just as quickly I received an e-mail informing me that the order had been cancelled (another choice of having it sent out by technology to confirm the cancellation and whether it is sent to an e-mail or text messaged or both).

All this having been done, my spouse still wanted to purchase the items. We were unsure if it was an Ipad vs Iphone form of the Amazon website (another set of technological choices by Amazon as to how their website operates on different types of devices) on which to do the purchase so we tried both. After going through the relevant screens carefully making sure we were in my spouse's account, we came to the payment page which clearly indicated that there was a $100 gift card applied to her account. However, the orange 'continue' button was a lighter orange as compared to the prior screens where it was a darker orange and, when we clicked on it, nothing happened. So again we called Amazon and after their verification process showing that I was in fact calling on behalf of my spouse about her account (another technology process of verification), the person made some checks and informed us that we needed to add a credit or debit card to the account. We wondered why for a purchase of $95.43 to which she was applying a $100 gift card we would have to add such a credit or debit card. But, that was the solution required and so we added a credit or debit card to her account. At that point, the light orange 'continue' button became dark orange and operated to make the purchase. On the next screen, the summary of the purchase price was indicated and showed that to the $95.43 a sum was added for taxes that made the total price $102.40. Thus, the gift card had been insufficient to make the purchase and most likely it appeared that was why the orange continue button was inoperative until a credit or debit card was added. Or at least this seemed so to us.

1.2.2 This Little Vignette – Technology or Tricknology and Humans

For the information technology mavens who read the above vignette, they no doubt have a number of thoughts about the technology that Amazon created for my use and the manner in which the customer service person's screens would be set up to interact with me about the problem I was experiencing that could rise to a dispute. A colloquial technology description of this purchase might be that it was a 'dirty purchase'. That term dirty purchase is something I heard used by an officer of Cisco at a conference in Paris in the 1990s to describe purchase orders for routers in their on-line system that did not go through the automated purchase process well. Human intervention was needed to address the problem with the purchase so that it could be run through the system as adjusted or 'cleaned up'.

Now, according to the latest reports, Amazon is a nearly trillion dollar company in market value.[15] As it branches out to control every aspects of its system, it has the wherewithal to develop its technology and integrate the evolving technological advancements (whether we are talking about 4G, 5G or even OG[16]) in that technology to create value for its shareholders. But, even with all those investments in technology when a dirty purchase arises Amazon's systems needed that human interaction to smoothe the technological process. The customer service person was extremely competent and pleasant which means that some level of training for this kind of problem had been given them so that they could resolve the problem to my satisfaction and in a rapid manner. Those are investments in human capital. At the same time, as I worked with that human, I was fully aware that they were not neutral as between me and Amazon, but I was comfortable with that knowledge provided they were able to address my concern.

But, while working with that human, I did wonder a couple of things. First, I wondered why the manner in which the technology was set up made it so easy for my wife to come into my account. We had not agreed to some kind of joining of our accounts (we did that after all this) so I was curious whether the technology mumbo-jumbo system (I will probably call it the wrong thing but maybe it is cookies, maybe it is biscuits, whatever) would make that slide into error so easy. Next, when we were on the right page and when on the page before we had seen that the price was $95.43 why did that page not include in it the additional charges that appear to be taxes so that we could see the total amount that was actually to be charged. Third, even if the total price page did not show it, when we tried to apply the $100 gift card and the orange 'continue' button was light as opposed to dark, why did we not get or see some kind of pop-up message explaining the additional taxes and total amount of the purchase at that stage so we could understand that we needed to add a credit or debit card to the account? Fourth, were

15 Maggie Fitzgerald, Wall Street sees Amazon Rejoining the Trillion-Dollar Club Later this Year, 17 January 2020 (CNBC Markets), available at www.cnbc.com/2020/01/17/wall-street-sees-amazon-rejoining-the-trillion-dollar-club-later-this-year.html.

16 OG = Original Gangsta. I learned that the term refers to a person who either is very well-dressed or looks like they are a 'hard guy' who had survived a life on the wrong side of the law, possibly having been incarcerated (like Robert De Niro played in the movie the Irishman (www.imdb.com/title/tt1302006/).

those additional seven or so dollars actually taxes due from a Toledo, Ohio purchaser or were they in fact more additional profit to Amazon?[17]

Each of the Amazon decisions with respect to the manner in which this technology worked and what was provided to the consumer set up a path for that consumer purchase. At the same time, as the consumer walking down that path, I know that I am being channeled in a certain way by the website. I still wonder whether the need to add a credit or debit card having to be explained by the customer service person without the total being clear on the screen is set up that way to INDUCE me at the point of purchase to give Amazon a credit or debit card number that remains there for the foreseeable future. In addition, I still wonder whether the seven dollars or so was in fact taxes but the size of that amount is not enough for me to spend additional time with customer service on that point. Across the number of purchases on the Amazon site in any given day/week/year, those little seven dollars add up so that the total could be millions of dollars, if not more. Is the ordinary consumer just supposed to assume that the technology is accurate? Asking the question already provides one the answer because one knows without being paranoid that the website is not a neutral site but is there to encourage the consumer to make purchases and maximize Amazon's success.

I do not begrudge Amazon or any technology that desires to maximize shareholder profit, but what I think is important is for us to pause and think about these kinds of questions because I believe they are relevant to how we think together about creating and developing online dispute resolution. Put another way, are we discussing merely technological choices being made or is it more tricknology – meaning are we discussing taking advantage of the ordinary user to benefit the owner of the technology in a manner that the ordinary user cannot fathom? How far then are we diverging from neural dispute resolution becomes the urgent question.

1.2.3 Whither Divergence and Hello Complexity: From Customer Service Design and Online Dispute Resolution Design

Another vignette from early in the online dispute resolution development process was the story told by an early online dispute resolution provider who was contacted about setting up an online dispute resolution system for a large telecommunications company with over 32 million customers. After meeting with the top people at the telecommunications company, the fledgling online dispute resolution provider suggested that rather than have a pure online arbitration system, that a one-way system should be set up. The one-way system would allow the consumer to decide AFTER a dispute had arisen whether they would go to arbitration with the company or into court rather than be bound PRE-DISPUTE to arbitration whatever the case. On the

17 *Cf. Defontes v. Dell, Inc.*, Supreme Court of Rhode Island, 984 A.2d 1061 (2009) (service contract not taxable in Rhode Island yet amount characterized as tax on the service contract included in the price of the computer purchase.).

other hand, if the consumer wanted arbitration then the telecommunications company would be bound to arbitrate. The online dispute resolution technology could be designed to provide the type of process that was the idea of the online dispute resolution provider. However, when proposed to the telecommunications company the answer came back fairly rapidly that the online dispute resolution provider needed to set up a binding arbitration system – NOT a one-way system. If that online dispute resolution provider acceded to the request of the telecommunications company, that provider would be catapulted into a world of potentially 32 million customers' potential disputes – a lucrative possibility for them. That online dispute resolution provider had many people they trusted say to them that they should just accede to the request of the large telecommunications company for if they did not, some OTHER online dispute resolution provider would surely get that business (the pressure of competition).

Faced with such a decision, one can see the pressure on a relatively new entrant to the field of dispute resolution to accede to this one potential major customer's request, even if it goes against the online dispute resolution provider's sense of what would be a fair process or due process. Imagine that the online dispute resolution provider received angel funding or venture capital funding to set up their site, with the attendant contractual or statutory (such as Art. 9 of the Uniform Commercial Code concerning secured transactions) obligations conditioning the receipt of the funds. Imagine the meetings with the angel or venture capitalists going over the progress of the website at key points in its development as decisions are made as to whether a further tranche of funding would be granted. To say there are strings attached to such funding is to bring to one's attention the pressures on even the noblest of online dispute resolution providers. And, imagine such an online dispute resolution provider thinking of the ultimate exit strategy.[18] What is the time frame for success of that online dispute resolution provider is a reasonable question to ask.

To further emphasize this tension, we have the case with respect to the National Arbitration Forum settlement with the State of Minnesota.[19] In this case, the National Arbitration Forum held itself out to the public as an independent arbitration company. Yet, it was revealed that the same hedge fund that owned the National Arbitration Forum owned a major debt-collection enterprise, "which enterprise generated considerable business for the company."[20] So while the arbitrators who heard the cases could be completely independent, to the extent those arbitrators made decisions that tended to be more in favor of the debtor than the creditor, there was direct financial pressure to

18 Which frequently is in the going public and raising capital – cashing in and heading out. Not everyone stays on for the long haul like a Bill Gates or a Jeff Bezos.

19 National Arbitration Forum Settlement with Minnesota Attorney General, 11 August 2009, The Federalist Society, State AG Tracker, Vol. 1, No. 4, 2009, available at https://fedsoc.org/commentary/publications/national-arbitration-forum-settlement-with-minnesota-attorney-general.

20 *Ibid.*

not rename such arbitrators in future cases. Another variant on this kind of deception is the complaint made against the National Association of Security Dealers alleging

> In direct and flagrant violation of federal law, the NASD systematically evaded the Securities and Exchange Commission approved 'Neutral List Selection System' arbitration rule requiring arbitrators to be selected on a rotating basis. Instead, the NASD *secretly programmed its computers* to select some arbitrators on a seniority basis – just what the rule was designed to prevent. (Emphasis added)[21]

Or a further more recent issue is the vacating of an arbitration award by the Ninth Circuit due to evident partiality as one of the arbitrators failed to disclose sufficiently he was a co-owner of JAMS, the arbitration institution that administered the arbitration, which had administered 97 arbitrations for Monster over the past five years.[22] And still another variant is in the self-contained Uniform Dispute Resolution Process for domain names where selection bias as to who are the neutrals who hear the cases, the substantive criteria that are to be evaluated by the neutrals as opposed to the specificities of national laws in this arena, and other problems such as reverse domain name hijacking provide a plethora of concerns.[23]

All of these 'horribles' are presented to highlight the competitive and other pressures that may come to bear on an online dispute resolution provider entity and even the neutrals. These pressures can affect the design of the system, the neutrals, and maybe even the underlying criteria of decision making.

1.2.4 Two Other Layers of Complexity – Perversion and National Security

1.2.4.1 Zoombombing[24] – Perversion of the Online Dispute Resolution Space

With the rush to remote learning and dramatic increase in the use of technology for all variety of interactions in the Covid-19 pandemic, another perverse aspect of the online setting has reared its head. What I am discussing is third party entities with no role in the

---

21 Pam Martens, Judicial Apartheid: Wall Street's Kangaroo Courts (Part 1), 20 July 2009 (Wall Street on Parade), available at https://wallstreetonparade.com/judicial-apartheid-wall-streets-kangaroo-courts/.

22 *Monster Energy Co. v. City Beverages, LLC*, No. 17-55813 (9th Cir. 2019), available at https://law.justia.com/cases/federal/appellate-courts/ca9/17-55813/17-55813-2019-10-22.html.

23 J. R. Hildenbrand, A Normative Critique of Private Domain Name Dispute Resolution, 22 J. Marshall J. Computer & Info. L. 625 (2004); Benjamin G. Davis, Une magouille planetaire: The UDRP is an International Scam, 72 Miss L. J. 815 (2002).

24 Dakin Andone, FBI Warns Video Calls are Getting Hijacked. It's Called 'Zoombombing', 2 April 2020 (CNN), available at www.cnn.com/2020/04/02/us/fbi-warning-zoombombing-trnd/index.html ('The term refers to a form of cyber harassment reported by some app users, who have reported that some of their calls have been hijacked by unidentified individuals and trolls who spew hateful language or share graphic images.').

particular online space finding ways to come in and disrupt what is going on in those spaces. Part of this action is from the inventiveness of these third parties with their own perverse motivations, part comes from the lack of discipline or knowledge of the users new to the particular online technology's space, and part comes from the design decisions of the providers of that online space. I do believe that the German President best summarized the Covid-19 pandemic saying:

> [Covid-19 pandemic] does not pit nations against nations, or soldiers against soldiers. Rather, it is a test of our humanity. It brings out the worst and the best in people. Let us show each other our best side.[25]

Those persons who exploit weaknesses in technology for perverse reasons are endemic in online technology for the past 25 years. Whether they are called 'hackers' or 'griefers' (bad faith player in an online multiplayer game or community) or another term, they are constantly with technology and require the designers and users of technology to take appropriate steps to counter those intrusions so as to maintain the tranquility of the given online dispute resolution space. But, how open or how closed a given online environment is set up to be is a choice of the designers. From the point of view of social justice, it would seem that the provider of online dispute resolution should take into account the effect on social justice of its choices. Too much complexity may require levels of internet access that are not available to the least common denominator of users. Too little complexity may lead to perverse interventions by private entities in this brave new world of the Covid-19 pandemic.

1.2.4.2 National Security

We would not be complete unless we also addressed the issue that all of the discussion above and the tensions described operate in the context of states and their governments. And those states have their own concerns, one of them being national security. For behind the curtain of security clearances is a vast space of national security. An older dark example is noted,[26] and two current examples come to mind.

---

25 Imanuel Marcus, President Steinmeier: 'The World that Lies Ahead Will Be Different', 12 April 2020 (The Berlin Spectator), available at https://berlinspectator.com/2020/04/12/president-steinmeier-the-world-that-lies-ahead-will-be-different/; full text at Televised address by Federal President Frank-Walter Steinmeier on the coronavirus pandemic at Schloss Bellevue, on 11 April 2020, available at www.bundespraesident.de/SharedDocs/Downloads/DE/Reden/2020/04/200411-TV-Ansprache-Corona-Englisch.pdf?__blob=publicationFile.

26 Edwin Black, IBM and the Holocaust, The Strategic Alliance Between Nazi Germany and America's Most Powerful Corporation (Crown Publishers, New York, 2001) (The then new thing of card punch technology of IBM as it was used by the Nazis to organize the Holocaust). As we can see, concerns about state exploitation of technology and the willing servitors in the technology industry for that state oppression has a long and dark pedigree.

First, in the 1990s long before cybersecurity became a term bandied about, I remember a conversation with a Chair of an Arbitral Tribunal who had a difficult case with international implications settle just after the arbitrators completed their deliberations. He wondered whether his offices were bugged in some way or the technologies that can listen to what is going on in an office had been deployed. Of course, the easy answer would be that one of the arbitrators might have intimated the direction of the tribunal's decision, but the Chair was absolutely certain that had not been the case. The fact that he asked himself the question and shared this with me, shows that whether in a meeting room at a hotel, in an arbitrator's office, portable or landline phones, or other spaces beyond computers and smart phones, the powers that have access to the most sophisticated technologies are able to discern what is going on in ostensibly confidential proceedings.

Another example of these concerns in the negotiation space was the case of Mayer Brown and Platt in which it was discovered in the documents released by Edward Snowden that Australia had spied on Indonesia in its discussions with its lawyers Mayer Brown and Platt as Indonesia addressed a dispute Indonesia was having with the United States.[27] As part of the Five Eyes Alliance of the United Kingdom, the United States, Canada, Australia and New Zealand,[28] this Australian surveillance was described in

> [a] monthly bulletin from the NSA's (National Security Agency's) liaison office in Canberra (which) said the Australian Signals Directorate (ASD) was monitoring the talks and offered to share any information with the US. It offered up that "information covered by attorney-client privilege may be included". (Emphasis added)

No law firm, startup online dispute resolution provider, court system, or longstanding dispute resolution provider has the wherewithal to compete with the sophisticated technologies of the kind that nation-states can bring to bear on their process. Moreover, even for as anodyne a concept as attorney-client privilege, national views of what that means may vary and moreover, intelligence agencies definitions of what that term means may vary also.[29]

27 Bridie Jarbour and Martin Pengelly, Australia Spied on Indonesia Talks with US Law Firm in 2013, 15 February 2014 (The Guardian), available at www.theguardian.com/world/2014/feb/16/australia-spied-indonesia-talks-us-firm.

28 J. Vitor, Tossini, The Five Eyes – The Intelligence Alliance of the Anglosphere, available at https://ukdefencejournal.org.uk/the-five-eyes-the-intelligence-alliance-of-the-anglosphere/.

29 Does the term only apply to matters dealt with between an attorney and a client that do not cross-borders, for example? Does an e-mail within a country actually travel cross-borders so that communication would not be considered attorney-client privileged even if both ends of the transmission were in the same country.

I do not have a security clearance so I cannot know what goes on behind that the veil of national security. But what I do know is that issues like where you locate your server for your online dispute resolution system, the rules governing the protection of private data in that location, the use of encryption technology and if so are there known or unknown ways in[30] and no doubt other topics by far more sophisticated technology persons than me become part of the reflection on the dispute resolution system design. For when parties are sharing legal and confidential information as part of the dispute resolution process, should those parties and the neutrals need to worry about whether that information will somehow be captured by a state and used for its own purposes?[31]

And if persons think I am just paranoid, I should also mention the experience I had as a human rights observer at the military commissions in Guantanamo Bay when the court security light (similar to the red light when a goal is scored in professional hockey) went off in the middle of the sentence of a lawyer representing one of the defendants. The audio feed cut to the glassed-in gallery where I was sitting and the monitor from the courtroom into the glassed-in gallery went blank. But, all of the observers, the press, and the victims' families could see into the courtroom and it was quite apparent that something was amiss. After a few minutes, the feed came back up and the monitor came back to life at which point we heard a very angry military judge say that neither he nor the court security officer had cut the feed. So that meant that *someone else had access to the feed for the court and the military judge in his courtroom did not know who that someone else was.* Moreover, the issue of whether the microphones at the desks of the lawyers and their clients were *gated or ungated* immediately arose. For when a lawyer turned off the microphone or put a hand over the microphone to confer with their client, they were no longer certain that the microphone was in fact off. And another issue was in the meeting rooms where attorneys met with their defendant client and therefore ostensibly had conversations covered by the attorney-client privilege, it was discovered that *the smoke detector like devices were in fact listening devices.*[32]

Now some might readily see my concerns as being about *sui generis* situations and that such national security concerns should not impinge on our thinking about online dispute resolution design and social justice. I am perfectly happy to take that point as I am not a person with security clearance with access to requisite information about what goes on behind that veil. However, I have understood from my time on the ABA Standing

---

30 Backdoors in the parlance I believe.

31 I got the answer to that in a humorous way when I once was giving a conference on Big Data and Dispute Resolution at the Florida Bar Association. I had 20 minutes to speak and told Siri on my iphone to set the timer to 20 minutes. It responded as it always does and the timer started running. It turned out that I finished what I had to say about all these issues of Big Data and Dispute Resolution in about 18 minutes. So I asked Siri to stop the timer. Almost on cue, Siri said, "I am sorry Ben, I can't do that" (sounding like the HAL 9000 computer in 2001: A Space Odyssey), to enormous laughter in the room full of lawyers.

32 Benjamin G. Davis, The 9/11 Military Commission Motion Hearings: An Ordinary Citizen Looks at Comparative Legitimacy, 37 S. I. U. L. J. 599 (2013).

Committee on Law and National Security that with the tsunami of digitalization of matters and the internet one of the goals of at least the American national security establishment is to archive the tsunami.[33]

2 Online Dispute Resolution – No One Said It Was Going to be Easy to Provide Justice Let Alone Social Justice

Given the above discussion of neutral dispute resolution as contrasted with customer service dispute resolution with the overlay of national security concerns of states, one gets a slight sense of the complexity of the space within which online dispute resolution operates – whether or not as courts.[34] Yet, wonderful moments of social justice can arise with the simplest technology such as the *Ximenes-Lopes v. Brazil* of 2006 decision of the Inter-American Court of Human Rights wherein the plaintiff's first step was not through an online form. Rather the sister's application was through a simple e-mail from a cybercafé in Ceara in Northeastern Brazil to various human rights bodies that she had found in her online research as she sought justice for her murdered brother.[35]

Online courts and other providers can demystify and improve access to dispute resolution for all persons and entities within a polity. However, underlying such improved access are the legal rules that prevail in that polity. The question becomes whether the substantive rules as applied and the procedural rules in place provide for equal justice in a manner that the online dispute resolution enhances. Or, is the playing field for justice as a substantive law matter and/or procedural law matter tending to favor certain types of participants in the system as opposed to others. For example, very strict standing rules would tend to reduce the potential plaintiffs in courts. Arbitration clauses prohibiting class-actions in court or arbitrations, tend to impact the number of arbitrations being filed in smaller denomination cases.[36]

As part of my modest view of online dispute resolution's role in social justice, I am increasingly agnostic as to whether technology is deployed to automate (whether courts as broadly defined or in dispute resolution processes), disrupt or transform such current processes.[37] I am also agnostic as to whether in court or otherwise the result is some kind

33 "General Michael Hayden: Threat, Responses, Law, and Liberty" *General Michael V. Hayden*, former Director, Central Intelligence Agency, and former Director, National Security Agency, ABA Standing Committee on Law and National Security, Washington, DC, 2 September 2015.

34 For a more optimistic view of the prospects for online courts in a tour de force, *see* Richard Susskind, Online Courts and the Future of Justice (Oxford University Press, Oxford, 2019).

35 *Inter-American Court of Human Rights, Case of Ximenes-Lopes v. Brazil*, Judgment of 4 July 2006 (Merits, Reparations and Costs), available at www.corteidh.or.cr/docs/casos/articulos/seriec_149_ing.pdf.

36 For an inventive way around this issue see Charlotte Garden, Doordash's Multimillion Dollar Arbitration Mistake, 16 February 2020 (Washington Post), available at www.washingtonpost.com/opinions/2020/02/16/doordashs-multimillion-dollar-arbitration-mistake/.

37 Richard Susskind, The End of Lawyers 99-145 (Oxford University Press 2010).

of functional privatization of dispute resolution.[38] Technology is like water and will flow to its highest level. That flow is however dependent on adequate investment both in the inception of the technology and in a sustained manner over years.

For example, back in 1989-1993 I led the putting in place of the first case management system of the ICC International Court of Arbitration. Said effort first required a definition of just what we do in the physical world. Second we had to understand the data flows for what we did. Third, we had to build a system that properly provided the management system we sought across four languages in the context of the then current technology. Even then, disruptive technology occurred (a shift from MS-DOS to Windows operating systems happened in the middle of the project) that had to be addressed. The process was not just one of automation because the review of systems tended to encourage harmonization of approaches that diverged across the Secretariat. Another reason it was not JUST automation is that one key aspect of the design process was becoming aware of what were design choices that merely were trying to emulate physical processes but were actually unnecessary (we called them physical fossils). The elimination of physical fossils and the reflection on design could lead to altering case management processes in an electronic environment without at the same time deviating from the goal of providing a neutral dispute resolution process.

The data identification part of this process in itself is significant. There must be enough data to capture what the system wants to currently cover (automation) while trying to imagine what kind of data could be added to make the system be even better (modest to significant transformation) than the past. For example, for any form of alternative dispute resolution in courts in the United States, I recently attempted to do a survey of all federal and state courts in the United States as to the basic information of number of cases and neutral diversity. The variety of approaches to providing alternative dispute resolution at courts around the country was staggering both across states and within states. Moreover, it was apparent that actual collection of data was in some cases more about setting dates and times for mediations, without having any or little thought to doing the kind of analytics of the experience that could be built into the system. Thus, a clear understanding of the data flows and conditions of presence that is sufficiently robust with an eye toward its evolution in successive generations of the system is optimal rather than having to remake the wheel at each new generation.

Beyond the technological set-up there is the investment in human capital necessary to keep the systems properly working. While a totally automated system can be imagined, are we sufficiently comfortable with that being made a reality? And, if we are going to allow a role for humans in resolving these human disputes, how are we to ensure that those humans are oriented more toward neutral dispute resolution as opposed to customer service dispute resolution and at what cost. For investment is a never ending

38 Judith Resnik, A2J/A2K: Access to Justice, Access to Knowledge, and Economic Inequalities in Open Courts and Arbitrations, 96 North Carolina L. Rev. 101-178 (2018).

requirement requiring a commitment for a longer term. Whether in courts or otherwise, one can worry that such commitment can be fickle rather than sustained as allocation of scarce resources are changed due to pressing needs that vary in different periods.

In sum, reducing barriers to a system of justice that may be experienced as unequal is providing access to that unequal justice, but no social justice. When one thinks of online dispute resolution being asked to do more than better provide the justice the system provides – something that many experience already as very hard in the various polities – it seems a bridge too far in my view. It should be quite obvious that online dispute resolution cannot be the magic bullet to get us to social justice. At most, it can assist the providing of justice if its forms protect the kinds of norms we have described above. Put another way, it would be wonderful if online dispute resolution did not exacerbate social injustice that may be endemic to the laws and norms of a given polity. To ask online dispute resolution to cause that polity to change those unequal laws and norms is to require a methodology to impact powerful groups in a polity and change them. That kind of change being a movement derived from online dispute resolution as opposed to some other wellspring of discontent would appear unlikely.

3 From Justice to Social Justice

One way that online dispute resolution might not play a role in social injustice I would suggest comes in the manner in which it is deployed. A simple way to describe the difficulties in making sure online dispute resolution is technology that does not exacerbate inequalities in the surrounding legal regime is to ask whether the technology choices made tend to enhance neutrality or seem more like customer service in favor of the dominant groups in that polity including the national security state. If there is some kind of tilting of the playing field in the technology, once revealed, the sense of being fooled by the use of the technology will engender alienation. One will feel tricked and the technology viewed as tricknology.

Thus, we may deploy Artificial Intelligence but it should not be in a manner that amounts to Artificial Imperialism. We may have matters stored in the cloud, but it should not be done in a fog that leads to vulnerability of those whose data is stored there. We certainly should keep in mind cybersecurity without creating cyberinsecurity. While algorithms may assist, we should make sure they are not tools to create algowrongs.[39] For if there is a need for black boxes, at the same time surely we should make sure those are not in fact anti-black (or other human) boxes.[40] Even if we are developing internet of things in this arena, we must make sure that it serves human

39 Cade Metz, An Algorithm that Grants Freedom or Takes It Away, 6 February 2020 (New York Times), available at www.nytimes.com/2020/02/06/technology/predictive-algorithms-crime.html.

40 *Ibid.*

needs and does not make it an internet for things. If we are looking at block chain disputes, we should make sure it is done in a way that does not lead to a perverse block unchained result departing from meaningful neutral dispute resolution. If we think that encryption technology should be part of it, we must think also that it is not encryption tricknology[41] providing a false sense of cybersecurity. Whatever the type of technology included, these kinds of tensions between justice and power in the shaping of online dispute resolution technology are pervasive.

I take comfort from the fact that people from around the world are working on ways to design online dispute resolution systems that might provide access to justice, may provide justice, and may at least modestly contribute to social justice.[42] This decades long effort to get online dispute resolution 'right' worldwide with new actors coming as others like me fade away is a mechanism to make sure that the dialogue continues and deepens as to why and how to do or not do online dispute resolution. Excellent work by scholars and practitioners[43] is drawing on the past, developing the present, and building the future.

But let me circle back to the series of vignettes provided at the beginning and the challenges of neutral dispute resolution versus customer service dispute resolution with an overlay of national security concerns. No one says it will be easy, but I am certain that those who make online dispute resolution work well MAY be contributing to help humanity progress. But, at the same time, let me encourage online dispute resolution to be modest in its proclamations of its likely contribution to social justice. If online dispute resolution can ameliorate at the margins the social inequalities, all the better. If, on the other hand, online dispute resolution is deployed in a manner that tends to encourage social injustice it will create or exacerbate contradictions that will be insufferable. And, in such a case, the human rebellion – chanting 'confuse the algorithms!' as a wonderful colleague described the human spirit in a digital age – may be irresistible as it brings down the digital walls of social injustice.

41 Grant Gross, Debate Over Access to Encryption is Not Going Away, 9 January 2020 (The Washington Examiner), available at www.washingtonexaminer.com/policy/technology/debate-over-access-to-encryptio n-isnt-going-away.

42 International Council for Online Dispute Resolution, available at https://icodr.org/.

43 I refer you to the work of all the members of the International Council for Online Dispute Resolution as a rich source of what is going on and to the periodic ODR (Year) events that have gone on for 20 years and will continue in the future around the world in which the latest thinking is brought together.

Chapter 12 Online Dispute Resolution and Ombudsmanship, Observations on the Use of ODR by Ombudsman Practitioners

Frank Fowlie, Clare Fowler and Herb Waye

In the Online Dispute Resolution and Ombudsmanship chapter in the first edition of this treatise, we looked at a wide range of issues such as the differences between technology-assisted and technology-based ODR, the role of a practitioner in ODR, what an Ombudsman is and what they do, and the various types of Ombudsmen, and we discussed the possible roles for and limitations of ODR in Ombudsman programs.

In this second edition, we decided to conduct a survey amongst Ombudsman practitioners to determine to what extent, if any, internet-based technologies have been embraced by Ombuds and to gauge what sorts of technologies are used and what the resistance points might be for their adoption.

Following the survey, consultations were conducted with two experts in the Ombudsman/ODR field. One being an internet-based Ombudsman practitioner and the other an academic who has developed ODR software. These experts provided their opinions on a variety issues impacting ODR – Ombudsman work.

1 Methodology

1.1 Survey Design

The survey methodology started with designing the survey. The online platform, 'Survey Monkey' was selected as the survey tool.

The survey consisted of eight questions. We found that the average time to complete it was three minutes or less. It was to be a quick and to the point look into how Ombuds were, or were not, using ODR technologies to conduct conflict resolution.

We will deal with the eight questions in greater dealing later in this paper. Here is a summary of the questions:

- Do you use ODR technology in your practice?
- Which ODR technology(ies) do you use?

- How long have you been using ODR tools?
- What type of Ombudsman practice do you have?
- Where are your clients located relative to your practice?
- What are the identifying characteristics of your clients?
- An open-ended question soliciting comments, and
- A question that identifies where the Ombudsman practice is located.

Most of the questions also provided text boxes for respondents to add additional comments.

1.2 Circulating the Survey

A key goal of the survey was to receive responses from as wide a range of practitioners as possible. We sought answers to determine the type of Ombudsman (whether classical or governmental Ombudsmen, executive Ombudsmen, or organizational Ombudsmen),[1] but also to determine their geographic representation.

Once the survey was drafted, introductory emails were sent to several Ombudsman associations and to one Ombudsman blog. The invitations were sent to:

- The International Ombudsman Institute (IOI), members including classical or governmental Ombudsmen around the globe;
- The International Ombudsman Association (IOA), members including organizational ombudsmen around the globe;

1 Ombudsmen are generally classed in one of three categories: *classical or legislative*, *organizational*, and *executive*.
Classical or legislative ombudsmen are appointed by a national, state or provincial, or municipal legislative body to ensure the fair treatment of the population by the administration. There are numerous examples of classical ombudsmen around the globe. These would include the many municipal, state, provincial, or national ombudsmen appointed by the appropriate level of government. They are located outside of the structure of the agency they oversee, and receive complaints from the external users of services provided by the agency. Classical ombudsmen receive wide-ranging powers to investigate complaints, make reports, make recommendations, and resolve matters.
Organizational ombudsmen are appointed by their respective agencies to receive complaints about fairness issues within the organization. These internal ombudsmen service a community within an organization, such as staff, patients, or students. Organizational ombudsmen are an informal resource and do not conduct investigations, nor do they make reports or recommendations.
Executive ombudsmen are appointed by their agency as an internal dispute resolution resource for complaints generated by an external community. Examples of executive ombudsmen would be bank or insurance ombudsmen, newspaper ombudsmen, and, in the case of ICANN, an Internet Ombudsman.
While executive ombudsman are located within specific agencies, they are different from organizational ombudsmen because the executive ombudsmen deal with an external public and conduct investigations, and may make reports and recommendations, as do classical ombudsmen (Frank Fowlie, Online Dispute Resolution and Ombudsmanship, in *Online Dispute Resolution: Theory and Practice*, Eleven International Publishing, The Hague 2012).

- The United States Ombudsman Association (USOA), members including classical Ombudsmen in the United States, Canada, and internationally;
- The Forum of Canadian Ombudsmen (FCO), members including Canadian classical, organizational, university, and executive Ombudsmen;
- The Ombudsman Association, formerly the British and Irish Ombudsman Association (BIOA), members including British and Irish Ombudsmen;
- The United Nations and Related International Organizations Ombudsman Network (UNARIO), whose members are organizational Ombudsmen;
- The European Ombudsman Network (EON), members including organizational or executive Ombudsman; and
- The Ombuds Blog.

The invitations were aimed at including Ombuds organizations across the world and covered the span of Ombudsman practice types.

The reception and circulation of the survey request varied. The IOI kindly published a blog post about the survey, which was distributed to all of its members and blog subscribers worldwide.[2] The USOA, UNARIO, EON, and Ombudsman Association all forwarded copies of the survey invitation to their members.

The IOA refused to circulate the survey stating, "Unfortunately we are not able to distribute a survey link on your behalf as distribution of surveys and other materials is a benefit reserved for our members."[3,4] The FCO also declined to circulate the survey as it was in the midst of a policy development process on website postings, and could not send out an external link until the policy was completed. No reply was received from The Ombuds Blog. The lack of circulation by the IOA and FCO likely removed over a thousand potential respondents from the survey.

The author is grateful to those organizations who did distribute and promote the survey.

1.3 Data Collection

The survey remained 'live' for over a month. This allowed a reasonable time for emails to be received by respondents and for respondents to complete the survey. Judging from the survey completion dates, the survey was completed in close proximity to the IOI blog posting and the mailings by the several Ombudsman associations. Leaving the survey open for a month also allowed for 'word of mouth' invitations.

---

2 www.theioi.org/ioi-news/current-news/online-survey-for-new-publication-on-odr-and-ombudsmanship.

3 Email from IOA business office dated 25 November 2019.

4 'IOA is the largest international association of professional organizational ombuds practitioners in the world, representing almost 900 members across the globe.' www.ombudsassociation.org/learn-about-ioa (accessed 16 January 2020).

The survey received 32 responses. When one considers the overall membership of all of the above associations, the potential survey pool could have been as a high as two thousand people; bearing in mind that some practitioners could be members of multiple organizations. For example, an international organization's Ombudsman working in Europe could be a member of the UNARIO, the EON, and the IOA; a provincial Ombudsman in Canada could be a member of the FCO, the USOA, and the IOI.

A key question then becomes, 'Is the volume of responses statistically significant to give merit to the survey results?' In the author's opinion, one cannot, with any degree of certainty, state that the results of the survey are definitive. However, if we change the lens slightly and look at the results as being anecdotal evidence of the state of the ombudsman profession relating to ODR as expressed by interested practitioners; then the survey is of some value.

2 THE SURVEY RESULTS

Question 1 – Does your Ombuds practice use technology such as online telephone or video conferencing, online communication with parties, an online case management system, etc?

All of the respondents agreed that they used some degree of ODR technology in their practices. 30 out of 32 answered the question with a 'yes'; however, upon looking at the individual answers the two respondents who had answered 'no' each identified five or more ODR tools that they used in their practices. These 'no' answers were therefore considered to be in error. Thus, 100% of respondents use some ODR technologies.

Question 2 – If you do use online technology to conduct dispute resolution, please indicate what technology or methods you use. Please select as many as apply to your practice:

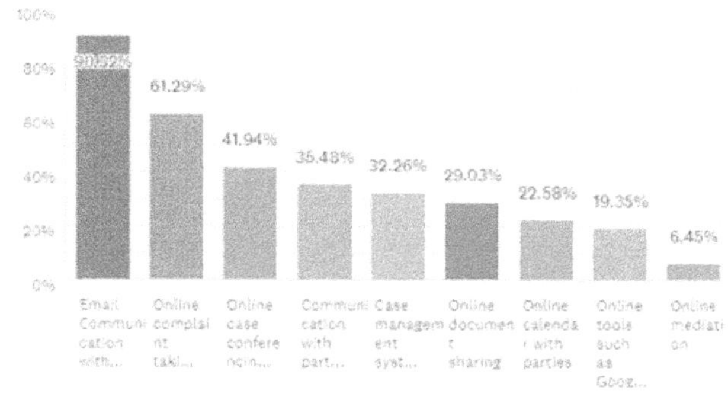

ANSWER CHOICES	RESPONSES	
Email Communication with parties	90.32%	28
Online complaint taking or complaint form filling	61.29%	19
Online case conferencing such as Zoom or Skype	41.94%	13
Communication with parties through a case management system	35.48%	11
Case management system with integrated features such as document sharing, case calendars, voice conferencing,	32.26%	10
Online document sharing	29.03%	9
Online calendar with parties	22.58%	7
Online tools such as Google Translate	19.35%	6
Online mediation	6.45%	2

Total Respondents: 31

We learned from the answers to this question that Ombudsmen use technology assisted ODR tools with a high degree of prevalence. More than 50% or respondents use email correspondence and/or online complaint processes in their practices. One practitioner commented that they also used a website and Facebook as ODR tools.

The survey received no responses concerning technology-based ODR tools such as blind bidding. None answered positively to the statement 'We do not use technology'.

Thus, on an anecdotal basis, we can say that Ombudsman practices use technology on a routine basis, and in particular, communications tools such as complaint forms, emails, or voice or video conferencing systems.

Question 3 – Please identify how long your practice has been using Online Dispute Resolution tools?

Answer Choices	Responses
I do not know	6.25% 2
We do not use any, and have no plans for ODR	3.13% 1
We do not use any presently, but plan to implement ODR in the future	6.25% 2
Less than one (1) year	6.25% 2
More than one (1) year and less than five (5) years	15.63% 5
More than five (5) years and less than ten (10) years	37.50% 12
More than ten (10) years	28.13% 9
Total respondents:	32

Question 4 – Please identify your type of Ombuds practice:

Classical or legislative Ombudsman	**43.75%** **14**
Organizational Ombudsman	28.13% 9
Executive Ombudsman	25.00% 8
None of the above	3.13% 1
Total respondents:	32

Given the support provided by the IOI and the USOA in circulating the survey, it is not surprising that classical Ombudsmen provided the greatest number of responses. The 'none of the above' respondent commented that they were an advocate ombudsman, which is a form of practice identified by the American Bar Association.[5]

5 'An advocate ombudsman serves as an advocate on behalf of a population that is designated in the charter.' www.americanbar.org/content/dam/aba/migrated/leadership/2001/107d.authcheckdam.pdf (accessed 16 January 2020). The document is available as a download here: https://www.google.com/url?sa=t&rct=j&q=&esrc=s&source=web&cd=&ved=2ahUKEwjTwOr3tabvAhXRop4KHRqRClEQFjACegQIBBAD&url=http%3A%2F%2Fwww.usombudsman.org%2Fsite-usoa%2Fwp-content%2Fuploads%2FABA_Standards.doc&usg=AOvVaw33d7td9nujSNDguo7kN8Z9.

Question 5 – Please identify the characteristics which best describe your practice:

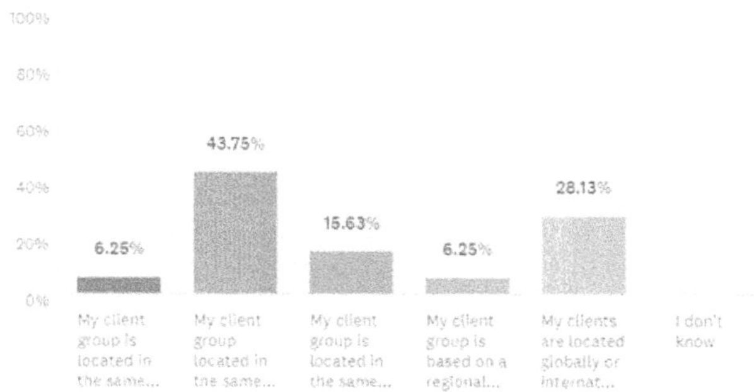

ANSWER CHOICES	RESPONSES	
My client group is located in the same location as my practice	6.25%	2
My client group located in the same city, state, or province as my practice	43.75%	14
My client group is located in the same country as my practice	15.63%	5
My client group is based on a regional or continental practice	6.25%	2
My clients are located globally or internationally	28.13%	9
I don't know	0.00%	0
TOTAL		32

Twelve respondents used the comments box to identify their locations:

London, United Kingdom
Catalonia Spain
King County Washington
Washington State
Phoenix, AZ, USA
Northern Hemisphere
Snohomish County, Washington State
Indiana
Iowa
Ohio
Geneva Based
Geneva

This question again portrays that classical or governmental Ombudsman comprised the greatest number of the respondents, with 44% of the respondents indicating that they were in the same city, state, or province as their clients. 28% of the respondents answered that their clients are located globally or internationally; these would likely be the responses from the UNARIO members.

Question 6 – Please identify characteristics about your client group:

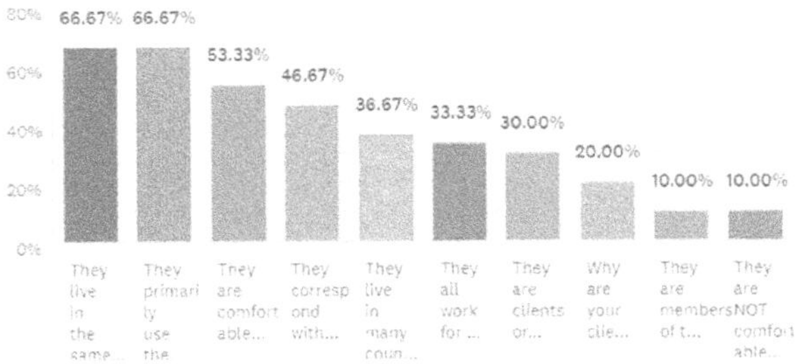

ANSWER CHOICES	RESPONSES	
They live in the same same city, state, province, or country	66.67%	20
They primarily use the same language	66.67%	20
They are comfortable in using technology in dispute resolution such as complaint form filling, email communication, voice or video conferencing such as Skype or Zoom	53.33%	16
They correspond with my practice in more than one language	46.67%	14
They live in many countries	36.67%	11
They all work for the same company as I do	33.33%	10
They are clients or outside stakeholders of the entity I work for	30.00%	9
Why are your clients not comfortable in using technology? Responses	20.00%	6
They are members of the armed services	10.00%	3
They are NOT comfortable in using technology (please explain in the comment box)	10.00%	3
Total Respondents: 30		

This question provides a portrait of the characteristics of Ombudsman clients. Again, remembering that the most of the responses come from classical or governmental Ombudsman, and bearing in mind the information found in the previous question about the location of the clients, there are no surprises with the first two high percentage responses – that clients lives in the same city, state or province, and that they primarily use the same language.

There is a multi-lingual and multi-national aspect to the responses, and one assumes that this is reflective of the UNARIO and EON members.

Interestingly 10% of the responses indicate that their clients were not comfortable in using technology. Comments about this lack of comfort included:

- Distrust
- The public has varying degrees of comfort with technology.
- It depends of the profile, some colleagues are very much computer literate but not others. This is the reason why we still continue having visits in countries of our operations to give all staff an opportunity to connect with the Ombuds Office.
- Some (mainly factory) struggle with technology but that is less and less
- We are responsible for receiving and reviewing constituent complaints regarding those who have involvement of some type with the Indiana Department of Child

Services. Complainants are not required to be residents of Indiana, the requirement is that at some point (after 2005) the constituent has had some involvement/concern with DCS (Parent, grandparent, other relative, foster home, service provider, attorney…). Complainants may file formal complaints on-line. However, many complainants do not have access to technology and/or may not feel comfortable as users.
- Huge range of comfort levels.

These issues around language and computer literacy were discussed in the first edition:

> Ombudsmen must be aware of the languages in which system users may wish to communicate, and ombudsmen must also take into consideration both the general literacy and computer literacy of their client group. If Ombudsmen serve a multi-lingual client group, the ODR system should be designed to accommodate system inputs in all the languages served, or to take into consideration translation services. Translations may be accomplished by using online translation tools, or by using native language translators. Ombudsmen must take translation as a matter of concern for both incoming correspondence from complainants and for outgoing correspondence to them.
>
> Ombudsmen must include the use of language and idioms as part of the general literacy factor. For example, is a client group that usually communicates in slang or patois well served in a written environment?
>
> Ombudsmen, when considering the implementation of ODR, must evaluate the general literacy level of their client group, and their computer literacy. If clients or Ombudsman staff lack either general literacy or computer literacy skills, Ombudsmen should reconsider the implementation of ODR.

All of this leads to the inevitable conclusion that the successful implementation of ODR strategies lies in fundamentally understanding of the client group needs and capacities.

Question 7 – Any general comments about ODR and Ombudsmanship?
The survey included an open-ended question to draw out specific concerns from practitioners. Twelve comments were posted in response to the open-ended question, three of which simply said 'No':
- 'How to file a complaint' website (English version): www.sindic.cat/en/page.asp?id=65.
- Implementation can often times be slow (high demand for IT resources) and usually always expensive.

- Skype and e-mail are sufficient. 'More' makes things complicated and can even annoy parties.
- We are still trying to strengthen internal technology system to support the Ombudsman office.
- Due to financial constraints and capacity measures.
- It makes intake a lot more secure.
- The Department of Child Services Ombudsman Bureau is beginning to explore technology options to support and streamline practice. This includes all mentioned above. Of course cost will be the deciding factor on when and how these needs will be met.
- We use technology internally mostly. Our clients are older adults and individuals with disabilities who live in facilities and have less access to technology than most people.
- If focusing strictly on Ombudsmanship ODR is an interesting tool. For mediations ODR is a stop-gap measure at best, person-to-person interaction needs to be privileged.

These several answers point out that Ombudsman practitioners wrestle with costs, competing demands for resources, client capacity issues, and, for some, a concern that face to face contact is the appropriate way to do business. All of these issues must be carefully considered by practitioners as they decide on the level and type of ODR implementation in their practices.

Question 8 – Where is your Ombudsman practice located? Check all that apply:

Answer Choices–	**Responses–**
North America	62.07% 18
Europe	37.93% 11
Asia	20.69% 6
Africa	17.24% 5
South America	13.79% 4
Oceania	13.79% 4
Total Respondents:	29

Two of the goals of this survey, as identified above, were seek out information from a) organizational, classical or governmental, and executive Ombudsman and b) to receive information from around the world. In question 4 we identified responses from all types of Ombudsman practitioners, including from an advocate Ombudsman. In question 8 we see that while a majority of responses come from North America, responses were also received from all other regions of the world. The many responses from North America were no doubt as a result of the assistance of the USOA is circulating the survey invitations.

3 What did We Learn from the Survey?

As discussed earlier, in comparison to the number of Ombudsman practitioners, the volume of respondents to the survey request is quite small. The author does not believe that the number of respondents provides statistical significance to the use of ODR in Ombudsmanship. However, the author does believe that the survey provides reasonable anecdotal evidence with respect to: a) the overall adoption of technology assisted ODR in Ombudsman practice; b) a sense of what sorts of tools are being used; c) a view of the acceptance of ODR in the various types of Ombudsman practice and by location; and, finally, d) barriers to using ODR.

The author finds that ODR tools, in particular tools that promote the ease of communication, including emails communication, online complaint forms, voice or video conferencing platforms, and online case management systems, are being used regularly by Ombudsmen. The adoption of these tools is seen in all forms of Ombudsman practices, and in Ombuds practices across the globe.

Barriers to the uptake of ODR in Ombudsman practice include: the lack of fiscal or information technology resources; the general and computer literacy of the client group; the specific need to be face-to-face with clients on specific types of conflicts, i.e. children's issues; trust issues on behalf of the client group; and, in some cases a lack of practitioner capacity in or training on using such technologies, such as online mediation platforms.

4 Second Step – Consultations with Ombudsman ODR Experts

4.1 Herb Waye

Herb Waye, MB, MALT, Ombudsman at the Internet Corporation for Assigned Names and Numbers

Herb, the ICANN Office of the Ombudsman is considered the first 'Internet Ombudsman' program, and was a very early adopter of ODR. As the Ombudsman program for the global agency that manages the domain name system for the internet, it is ideally placed to be a leader in ODR and Ombudsmanship. Can you tell us a little about the history of the Office, and your own role within the program over the years?

> I believe the ICANN Office of the Ombudsman is an excellent example of how online dispute resolution can facilitate conflict resolution in a global organization. The office was formed to act as a one-stop shop to address unfairness, action or inaction by Board members, organizational staff, or leaders and members a global multi-stakeholder model of policy development. The ICANN community, organization and Board have participants and staff from around the world with regional offices in every continent. The community, organization and Board comes together three times a year to meet face-to-face to work on global policy for the domain name system and the Internet in general. The Ombuds team consists of the Ombudsman, Herb Waye, and an Adjunct Ombuds, Barbara Curwin.

Your Office has used several iterations of ODR systems over its 15 years of existence. It began very simply as an email filing system based on Outlook, and since then there has been a couple of purpose built case management systems; and you are now using the Mediate.com system, which is an off the shelf program customized for your particular institution. Based on that long history of using various tools, what advice would you given to Ombudsman institutions who are considering starting an ODR-based practice?

> The new case management system offers current tools to handle cases, store documents, and develop reports. Email is the practical and common communication platform outside of the three regional meetings held annually. The Office of the Ombudsman uses the same online tools used by the organization and the community for holding online meetings, VOIP calls, video conferencing and document sharing. An interesting tool that has recently become popular includes an online meeting space (or office) that accepts visitors and places them in a waiting room until the Ombuds team allows access. This mitigates privacy issues by preventing two potential complainants from meeting in the same virtual space unless authorized by the Ombuds team.

As the ICANN Ombudsman, what sort of issues do you get involved with?

> The most frequent issue raised with the Office is abusive or disruptive discourse in the online environment: email, virtual meeting chat, public messaging platforms. This varies between bullying, name calling, filibustering, and goes to the rare incident of racism, discrimination and sexual harassment. The Office is also responsible for monitoring elections, policy implementation, Bylaw and Rules of Procedure enforcement, and promotion of the ICANN Expected Standards of Behavior and promotion and enforcement of the ICANN Community Anti-Harassment Policy.

You literally serve a global audience of stakeholders. There must be obvious benefits to the program in the use of asynchronous communications. Do you see any downside to the use of ODR as an Ombudsman?

> The greatest advantage in ODR in my environment, is the extensive use of email for communication with clients. This email environment offers the unique opportunity to 'pause' and 'reflect' when communicating. An ability to reread one's words before hitting send. To take the opportunity to think about a response for a few hours or overnight. Face-to-face interaction cannot be replaced by online interaction which is why ICANN meets three times a year throughout the globe, giving the Ombuds team an opportunity to, despite living on different continents, meet the people and sit down with them to discuss in person.

As an Ombudsman do you see any barriers for people who want to make complaints to Ombudsmen using ODR tools, and do you think that there is an barrier for the different types of Ombudsman programs (Organizational, Executive, or Classical) to integrate ODR into their practices?

> I have not faced any challenges in the online environment I work in. The community, organization and Board live and breathe 'Internet' and are very comfortable in this online environment. I believe the biggest challenge will be to overcome fears that confidentiality will be breached with the use of emails. This is a cultural challenge that can be overcome simply by acceptance of email as an accepted practice.

In your opinion, what is the easiest thing that Ombudsman practitioners can do start using ODR tools in their practice, online complaint forms, email communications, video conferencing, web sites, etc?

> I believe the promotion of technology as tools will facilitate acceptance of an online environment. As more and more people take to online learning, video conferencing, email communication and remote working, the ODR tools will fall into place naturally. There is a cost factor an Ombuds Office must consider and that may be limited by organizational budgets as not all Ombuds offices are adequately financially funded by organizations.

If you had crystal ball, what would the future of ODR and Ombudsmanship look like?

> It will continue to expand and become popular as people accept globalization, organizations become more and more internationally focused, and people become more comfortable with technology. I would do my utmost as a new ODR Ombuds practitioner to avoid automation and keep the human factor as close as possible to face-to-face until the clients become comfortable with a virtual Ombuds office.

Is there any other advice you would give to your Ombudsmen colleagues about using ODR tools?

> Keep your pulse on technology and try to keep ahead of your client's needs. If automation and artificial intelligence is creeping into your environment the interpersonal or systemic issues you are used to dealing with may become complainant vs. machine in the future. How will you evaluate a machine's behavior when it has been unfair to a member of your community?

4.2 Clare Fowler

Dr. Clare Fowler, Caseload Manager Director, Mediate.com

Dr. Fowler earned her Doctorate in Dispute Resolution at Pepperdine University. She works at Mediate.com and in the staff member responsible for their Caseload Dispute Resolution case management system, and teaches at University of Oregon Law School.

Dr. Clare, you are not only an expert in dispute resolution, you have brought that expertise to designing and sharing case management software. What do you see presently in how the Ombudsman field uses ODR tools, and what do you see happening in the future?

> We live in a world that expects immediate and thorough answers. There are some situations where those answers can come from a spontaneous

conversation. But for an increasing number of situations, those answers need to be augmented by an ODR tool. If a company has an issue with an overseas vendor, they cannot walk up and ask a question. With differing time zones, it is doubtful that they can pick up the phone. What they can do is an arrange an early morning video conference or a chat-based resolution. Once people have initiated a resolution attempt, they expect an answer, or at least some progress, within 24 hours. This is made possible by having a variety of tools at your disposal. The more versatile ombuds are with using online tools, the faster they can help their clients to resolve their dispute.

People also expect immediacy of data, meaning they will no longer wait for an annual report. They want to see a snapshot of standings and trends at any time. This cannot be obtained by traditional Post-it notes and Excel spreadsheets. To track trends as they are happening, and prevent problems before they grow, ombuds offices must be examining data in the moment. This requires keeping track of data in an integrated system that tracks a variety of issues, compares them with demographics, and can point out trouble spots.

I see the curve heading exponentially in this direction over the next few years. An increase in options for managing disputes and ADR data. Employees are expecting to be involved in resolving their dispute, as well as designing their dispute resolution process. This means that the ombuds office that has multiple options for resolving a dispute and allows the employee to be involved in choosing the process is reinforcing the ideals of ADR right from the beginning. Employees are expressing self-determination and taking ownership when they are invested in designing the process. If a manager forces an employee to mediate, every employee will be resistant – simple human nature. But if the employee sees mediation as one option, sees videoconferencing as an option, sees text-based negotiation as another option, and designs a hybrid that fits their issue and their schedule, then the employee will be much more committed to the process – and the outcome.

Do you think that ODR should be an integrated part of an Ombudsman practice? Is there any circumstance where ODR would not be helpful?

To me, dispute resolution is a menu. Everyone does not need everything. Some things are just not right for certain people and at certain times. But to provide the best service, we still want to make sure that we have quite a few options to meet people's needs.

For situations where people can meet quickly face-to-face, and will continue to work together face-to-face, I agree that resolving disputes in-person is still a very powerful option. However, when people are far apart, have busy schedules,

> have an abusive history, have no need for a continued relationship, or are resolving fact- and data-based disputes, it helps our clients to have processes to meet those needs. When we are analyzing trends, reviewing the wording of a contract, or trying to understand data, my clients find it much easier to do that via screensharing then to try to have everyone crowd around a conference table. Every department in an organization needs to justify their existence and expense. IT needs to report why they choose a certain brand of computer and what the benefit as well as the cost-saving potential is to a company. I believe an ombuds office is no different. And when other departments are using online tools to track data and run reports that provide instantaneous, detailed data that prove their worth, it will become hard for ombuds offices to compete with that if they are not able to show data to also prove their worth. Keeping track of this data online allows for the demographic and trends data to be available for reviewing, yet kept in a separate space from other data to support confidentiality.

There are a number of different options available for Ombudsman practitioners for ODR tools. These range from simply using email or video conferencing tools, to 'off the shelf' ODR products, to designed platforms which can be customized for the specific practice, and finally to completely purpose-built platforms. You deal with the predesigned and then customized platforms. What would you recommend that Ombudsman bear in mind as they consider ODR as part of their practices?

> This question is the reason why we built Caseload Manager 10 years ago. There were options out there for resolving disputes that kind of worked, but they just weren't right. They simply did not track the data that we needed. They didn't keep track of clients and meetings the way most ADR offices do. We were using volunteer-management, CRM, and legal software, which was close, but not close enough.
>
> So we built a software that has all of the basic functions that an ADR office needs, and then allowed customizations for every office's unique process (does the client need parking validation? history of violence/need to be in separate rooms? do they need an interpreter?).
>
> Most of the people that I work with find this is the best approach on the market right now. Trying to cobble together 20 different pieces (Outlook, Quickbooks, SurveyMonkey, Dropbox, etc.) is just too redundant and time-consuming. Trying to design your own software is also too time-consuming, and often is outdated by the time it is released (Washington and California have tried a few times, and ended up going back to off-the-shelf software, as an example.). The key to finding software is to begin by mapping out the steps in your workflow

> and your desired reports. Then find a software that has the basic elements you need AND is customizable. Being able to customize is key, and this is why designing your own static process often does not work, because companies grow and needs change. You cannot anticipate what reports you will need next year, or what demographics you will need to track, so make sure that you have the ability to update your system. Also, having a wicked cool support staff doesn't hurt.

Data security, in terms of threats, data protection systems, and legal frameworks around data protection are ever changing. From virus management, to the European Union's General Data Protection Regulation, to national law, there appears to be a great deal of information for practitioners to keep up to date on. How do you perceive the impact on that for Ombudsman practitioners ranging from sole practitioner offices, to state or national level institutions?

> Ombuds offices have always done a wonderful job of being aware of confidentiality and data concerns, and so they are more prepared than many offices to protect client data. My recommendation for most offices is to place a reminder on your calendar twice a year to examine your data safety practices. Is your case management tool, or client data password-protected? Is it encrypted? Where is it being stored? The big question: are you using software from reliable sources that are continually upgrading their security features? I think that for the majority of Ombuds practices if they make safety standards a daily habit (sign-out of software, strong passwords, use programs from reliable software), and then they examine these habits once or twice a year, then they are achieving the right balance of convenient data storage and protecting client information.

As with all technology, the price points vary with the product, and prices usually fall over time. What's the right timing in the life an Ombudsman's Office to consider the use of ODR tools? Would you say that ODR or interactive case management programs are a long-term money saver for Ombudsmen?

> I would not say they are a money saver – because most Ombuds offices could run on Post-it notes if they need to. Instead, I would say most case management tools are time savers. Many Ombuds offices report that our pre-designed reports are saving them the week of work that it used to take them to conduct an annual report. This is a week that overworked Ombuds can now spend on catching up on other tasks. And it means providing the type of data

that will show management their extreme value to the organization, and thus safe-guarding the life of the ombuds office for another year.
However, if an Ombuds office has moved past the Post-it notes phase, then I see integrated case management tools as being a huge money saver. The average price per month is just above the same price as a Pro-account of Dropbox, and case management should include the same services as Dropbox, SurveyMonkey, training management, anonymous data retention and a variety of other software that they are likely purchasing a la carte.

Any other advice you would care to share with Ombudsman practitioners or organizations?

I have seen a few Ombudsman offices fail and have looked into the reasons. The Ombuds at these institutions provided needed services and had excellent skills. However, they were forcing employees to use antiquated approaches that were not empowering the employees. For instance, they were forcing employees to use the skills that the Ombuds wanted, instead of finding out what would make the employees the most comfortable. I recommend to Ombuds offices to make sure that you are providing services that truly provide a safe space for employees. Make sure the process fits the substance, instead of trying to force the substance to fit your process.
When I was researching disputes, I found the 3 most common were:
1) Group-related disputes.
2) Confusion over job responsibilities/boundaries/scope
3) Everyday communication disputes
For Ombuds offices to stay ahead of the curve, I strongly recommend proactively finding answers for addressing these concerns. Prepare a recorded or online training for different departments for addressing communication concerns. Create a survey for employees to begin identifying their job responsibilities. Create online group roundtables using pollev (www.polleverywhere.com) or similar software where everyone is able to contribute, or train people in offices to take turns facilitating their departmental meetings.

5 CONCLUSION

Online Dispute Resolution is a functionality that most Ombudsmen practitioners use, to some degree. From simple tools, such as interactive or searchable websites, and email exchanges, to video conferencing, to integrated case management and communication platforms, Ombudsmen, in all types of practices, use online technology to augment their capacity to deal with cases and to meet the needs of their clients.

Technology continues to move, improve, and become more pervasive in our roles. Technology, both hardware and software, has become less expensive and more powerful. The way clients use technology continues to morph, as more and more people rely on mobile devices as their primary technology tool, and these devices become more faster, have greater capacity, and support many, and more diverse apps and programs.

The Cloud, and cloud-based programs and software, will continue to revolutionize ODR capacity for Ombudsmen. The cloud reduces costs for hardware such as servers, and also ensures data relevance, and program or platform update processing.

Chapter 13 The Wake-Up to the Virtual Space in Arbitration

*Mirèze Philippe and Mohamed Abdel Wahab**

1 Introduction

Start a movement[1] or a discussion, make noise about it, gather people around a single idea or cause, and it will soon become a trend. When such movement or discussion is initiated by recognised practitioners, the trend will grow faster. This has been the case of the discussions on virtual hearings in international dispute resolution since March 2020.

The trend of the virtual space has succeeded to make its way through the dispute resolution community which was rather opaque to using technology and move procedures or parts of them online. The sudden viral outbreak has been the triggering event that has generated popularity in the use of technology in dispute resolution and the need for avoiding disruptions. From every misfortune good things may derive. This situation has been the ideal opportunity to raise awareness about the necessity to be prepared for any unexpected circumstance that may prevent us again from meeting and travelling. We are not immune from an untimely interruption which may be caused by viruses, storms, floods, volcano irruptions, safety at the venue due to war or riots, temporary closure of airports, strikes, and any other cause. The location may also happen to be inconvenient because not well connected, in which case parties and arbitrators may consider moving the location of the meeting or hearing elsewhere, or hold it online.

From the economic perspective, the need for a virtual space for holding meetings and hearings remotely is all the more indispensable since this year, due to the fact that the economic crisis generated by the worldwide outbreak has impacted every sector, firm and individual. It is therefore crucial for the users to continue being able to bring their disputes to arbitration while reducing costs; technology offers this possibility.

---

* The views expressed by the authors are their own and do not reflect those of any institutions with which the authors are affiliated in any way.

1 How to Start a Movement That Changes the World, 24 September 2017, https://writingcooperative.com/the-quick-and-dirty-guide-to-leading-a-movement-9a8eddc870c7.

"Necessity is the golden chord that lies at the base of every innovation and invention" observed some authors.[2] 'However in this instance, innovation is rather about changing our traditional way of working as opposed to innovation in tools that already existed' remarked one of the authors of this chapter, who observed that "We are living in fascinating times!"[3]

Although virtual meetings and hearings are not a panacea and may not be adapted to all types of hearings or circumstances, they offer the advantages of saving time and costs for travelling, and saving the environment. Climate change being at the centre of the world's preoccupation, reducing travelling contributes to reducing the travel footprint. Some difficulties remain to be overcome, but we are learning how to better use the tools available to us. Further technology developments may probably contribute to holding hearings so seamlessly, that travelling to a hearing may become unnecessary in some instances. Practitioners have experienced different ways of working from the traditional approaches and will likely build on this momentum to continue evolving the working methods.

Technology in dispute resolution has been around for over two decades with pioneers who built platforms to settle disputes online and who published extensively about their research and their work. They gathered in two organisations, the National Center for Technology in Dispute Resolution (NCTDR)[4] and the International Council for Online Dispute Resolution (ICODR),[5] and organised conferences and trainings around the world to explain how technology could be used in resolving disputes and how the platforms they built could assist in dispute resolution procedures. They persevered in highlighting the need for moving public and private justice as much as possible online to afford to a bigger number of people the possibility to have access to remedy. They faced reluctance in general because it is hard to move people from their zone of comfort and to have them believe in this innovative way of working.

Using technology in public and private justice is a normal continuity of the evolution that led us to use technology in our daily lives. Courts are familiar with using technology to hear a witness incapable of travelling to the court, either because the witness is old or ill, or because the witness is imprisoned or in a conflict zone and unable to travel. Some courts around the world are being pioneers in using technology to hear cases entirely

2 Abayomi Okubote and Mohamed Abdel Wahab, *Africa Arbitration Academy Takes Over the Baton on Thought Leadership. Launches Virtual Hearing Protocol in Africa, for Africa*, Kluwer Arbitration Blog, 7 May 2020, http://arbitrationblog.kluwerarbitration.com/2020/05/07/africa-arbitration-academy-takes-over-the-baton-on-thought-leadershiplaunches-virtual-hearing-protocol-in-africa-for-africa/?doing_wp_cron=1594752787.8024549484252929687500.

3 Mirèze Philippe, *Offline or Online? Virtual Hearings or ODR?*, Kluwer Arbitration Blog, 26 April 2020, http://arbitrationblog.kluwerarbitration.com/2020/04/26/offline-or-online-virtual-hearings-or-odr/?doing_wp_cron=1595548750.7013959884643554687500.

4 National Center for Technology in Dispute Resolution (NCTDR), http://odr.info/.

5 International Council for Online Dispute Resolution (ICODR), https://icodr.org/.

remotely. The National Center for State Courts (NCSC)[6] that promotes the rule of law and improves the administration of justice in state courts and courts around the world, also promotes and uses technology in courts. A few states in the United States work entirely remotely, such as the Utah State Court, and others have implemented pilot projects to settle a variety of types of disputes online.[7] Other countries around the world either work entirely remotely, such as Singapore that has probably been a pioneer in this regard, or use technology to hear witnesses like in Germany. Some courts are entirely electronic, for instance in Lithuania, Estonia and Norway. Therefore the courts, the public justice, have tested and used technology. It is time for the private justice to follow this path.

While using platforms in dispute resolution to hold hearings is nothing new, the lockdown has put the spotlight more than ever before on the assistance that technology brings to the legal community. A judge recently said that it is

> immensely ironic that the coronavirus crisis will do more for virtual courts than decades of work by NCSC. I'm glad to see it come, even if this is not the way I would wish it to happen.[8]

Ironically and suddenly, many people now proclaim to be experts in ODR!

'Are people waking up to online dispute resolution?' was a question discussed in a blog post in which it was observed that there has been a surge of interest in the legal community to discuss online dispute resolution (ODR).[9] Three years later, following the outbreak forced by Covid-19, dispute resolution practitioners are waking up to the virtual space as a means available to them to proceed with their arbitrations and hold virtual hearings. Since March 2020, a plethora of webinars were held and articles and blogs were published about virtual hearings, including guidelines and protocols on holding virtual hearings. A book was recently dedicated to the virtual procedure in arbitration following the Covid-19 crisis.[10]

---

6 The National Center for State Courts (NCSC), www.ncsc.org/.

7 Amy J. Schmitz, *Expanding Access to Remedies through E-Court Initiatives*, 67(1) Buffalo Law Review 89 (2019), pilot projects were for example implemented in the States of Michigan, Ohio, New York, Texas, Utah. The city of Columbus seems to have saved on costs of negotiating and mediating income tax small claims and has increased its collection of recovered unpaid taxes.

8 Colin Rule, one of the two fathers of ODR with Ethan Katsh, posted a message on LinkedIn at the beginning of April 2020, quoting Tom Clarke from NCSC.

9 Mirèze Philippe, *Are People Waking Up to Online Dispute Resolution*, Global Pound Conference Blog, 22 May 2017, www.imimediation.org/2017/05/22/people-waking-online-dispute-resolution.

10 Maxi Scherer, Niuscha Bassiri, Mohamed Abdel Wahab, *Arbitration and the Covid-19 Revolution*, Kluwer Law International, November 2020, https://lrus.wolterskluwer.com/store/product/international-arbitration-and-the-covid-19-revolution.

Virtual hearings and ODR are however two different matters.[11] The use of technology to hold hearings remotely is meant to connect people, affording an opportunity to replace the real world, the offline space, which may not be available to them for some reason (such as difficulty to travel, illness), by an online space. The arbitration procedure is not conducted online, but technology is used to proceed with hearings remotely. ODR consists in using information and communication technology to negotiate, mediate, arbitrate, conduct proceedings, and settle disputes exclusively or primarily online. When platforms used make a significant contribution to resolving disputes, such online resolution equates to ODR. Using a platform for virtual hearings does not meet that purpose, unless other parts of the procedure are conducted online through a dedicated dispute resolution platform. The UNCITRAL Technical Notes on Online Dispute Resolution[12] issued in 2016 defined ODR as "a system for dispute resolution through an information technology-based platform and facilitated through the use of electronic communications and other information technology".

This chapter will address issues related to the perception of parties and their willingness or lack of willingness to use virtual hearings, and how parties' concerns can be reconciled with arbitrators' duties to proceed expeditiously: practitioners must strike the balance between the arbitrators' duties and each party's rights (I). It will then discuss best practices established by dispute resolution organisations and other firms and organisations, which may assist parties and arbitrators in organising virtual conferences and hearings (II).

2 Striking a Balance Between Arbitrators' Duties and Parties' Rights

Life and business froze during a few days around March 2020 when many countries around the world declared an official lockdown and closure of their bordures, with the hope to stop contamination by Covid-19. Such measures had immediate impact on meetings and hearings planned in arbitration cases. Practitioners were suddenly faced with a situation which was intended to be a temporary lockdown but which extended to a several months. The dispute resolution community had to organise the continuity of its activity. Dispute resolution organisations swiftly reacted to respond to the users' expectations. They provided best practices and sometimes also virtual room facilities to enable parties and arbitrators proceed with their arbitrations efficiently and expeditiously.

Despite the availability of techniques for conducting proceedings, which will be discussed in the second part of this chapter, some practitioners were reluctant to move

11 *See* note 3, Mirèze Philippe, *Offline or Online? Virtual Hearings or ODR?*.

12 UNCITRAL Technical Notes on Online Dispute Resolution, https://uncitral.un.org/sites/uncitral.un.org/files/media-documents/uncitral/en/v1700382_english_technical_notes_on_odr.pdf.

online and preferred to adjourn the scheduled meetings or hearings. How can parties' concerns and expectations be reconciled with arbitrators' duties to proceed with their arbitrations expeditiously? Are awards protected from potential annulments if hearings are held online (a)? A few parties have been pro-active and immediately raised the importance of proceeding with the arbitration without delaying it. While others, either considered that holding meetings and hearings in a virtual forum is not adapted to their arbitrations, or were concerned by due process and the necessity of being present 'in person' at a physical location (b). Is adjournment the only solution? (c)

2.1 *Arbitrators' Duties – Efficiency and Rapidity – Recognition and Enforcement of Awards*

In a significant number of arbitrations where meetings and hearings were scheduled before the lockdown, parties requested their adjournment. Arbitrators were faced with the dilemma of avoiding delaying the procedure while respecting due process and protecting the award. Arbitrators must thus assess whether adjournment is justified. The right of a party cannot be at the detriment of the other party or parties' right to proceed with the arbitration, as long as all parties are given an equal and reasonable opportunity to be heard. The parties' rights to be heard is 'impliedly limited by considerations of reasonableness and fairness' as recently decided by the Singapore Court of Appeal.[13] A necessary balance needs to be struck between both parties' competing interests on the one hand, and the arbitrators' duties to proceed efficiently and expeditiously on the other hand, thus, a balance between procedural fairness and efficiency.[14]

The party reluctant to appear virtually must provide substantiated reasons that justify delaying the proceedings and generating unnecessary costs. Some arbitrators who were not willing to delay the procedure, made the point – where applicable – that nothing in the law of the seat of arbitration prevented holding meetings and hearings remotely, and ordered to proceed with a virtual hearing. The European Court of Human Rights

13 Yvonne Mak, *Do Virtual Hearings Without Parties' Agreement Contravene Due Process? The View from Singapore*, Kluwer Arbitration Blog, 20 June 2020, http://arbitrationblog.kluwerarbitration.com/2020/06/20/do-virtual-hearings-without-parties-agreement-contravene-due-process-the-view-from-singapore/?doing_wp_cron=1593397834.5463769435882568359375. The author discussed in her blog the interesting decision of the Singapore Court of Appeal in *China Machine New Energy Corp v. Jaguar Energy Guatemala LLC and another* [2020] SGCA 12.

14 Mohamed Abdel Wahab quoted by Sylvia Tee and Andy Lau in a summary on the webinar of 18 June 2020, organised by Lipman Karas, on *Case Management in Virtual Hearings*, www.lipmankaras.com/2020/07/case-management-in-virtual-hearings/. The webinar featured speakers from four continents: Julia Dreosti (Lipman Karas, Adelaide), Mirèze Philippe (ICC, Paris), Mohamed Abdel Wahab (Zulficar & Partners, Cairo), and Kevin Kim (Peter & Kim, Seoul).

considered that hearings held by videoconference are compliant with due process provided that the technology can guarantee such due process.[15]

Moreover, as observed a practitioner,[16] at the time the UNCITRAL International Commercial Arbitration Model Law was drafted in 1985, the hearing referred to in Article 24 was clearly understood as being in person at the same physical location. Times have changed and we are now dealing with virtual hearings, albeit in person without being at the same physical location. The practitioner concluded that a virtual hearing is a hearing. He went on with the reasoning and noted that it would be surprising if virtual hearings are not accepted by national courts or tribunals, considering that in many national courts virtual hearings are taking place.

The arbitrators must examine the legal framework governing the arbitration, namely the parties' agreement, as well as the arbitration rules applicable to the procedure and the law of the seat of arbitration (*lex loci arbitri*), most of which provide for remote hearings in permissive terms.[17] They must also verify if any precedents justify not holding a virtual hearing, and whether there may be any risk jeopardising the recognition and enforcement of an award, which represents the major concern of any arbitration procedure. Article V (1)(b) of the New York Convention on the Recognition and Enforcement of Foreign Arbitral Awards defines violation of due process as one of the five grounds upon which recognition and enforcement may be refused.

Should a party or all parties refuse holding a virtual hearing, the tribunal may approach the parties to understand their concerns and if there are ways to address them. Sometimes the parties are not very familiar with technology and do not feel confident to present their arguments in a virtual space. It may happen that the parties have no logistics to ensure a proper participation remotely. They may feel concerned with cross-examining witnesses without being sure that answers are not being dictated to them. The various logistical issues will be addressed in the second part of this chapter.

Where the rules of arbitration or the procedural law are silent, the arbitrators may use their discretionary power to decide whether to hold a virtual hearing, unless their powers were restricted in the parties' agreement. The powers of arbitral tribunals are an

---

15 Aline Tanielian Fadel, Virtual Arbitration Hearings and Due Process: Two Sides of the Same Coin?, www.linkedin.com/posts/dr-aline-tanielian-fadel-a90a4728_my-newest-article-activity-6712986739566272512-mkcx. The author referred to several disputes in Italy: Visioconférence et Droit à un Procès Equitable, RDLF 2011, chron. n°08, citing: ECtHR, 5/10/2006, n°45106/04, *Marcello Viola v. Italy*; ECtHR, 27/11/2007, n° 35795/02, *Asciutto v. Italy*; ECtHR, 27/11/2007, n°58295/00, *Zagaria v. Italy*, Laure Milano.

16 Alvaro Galindo, *Arbitration Unplugged Series – Virtual Hearing: Present or Future?* Kluwer Arbitration Blog, 23 May 2020, http://arbitrationblog.kluwerarbitration.com/2020/05/23/arbitration-unplugged-series-virtual-hearing-present-or-future/?doing_wp_cron=1595676009.6175599098205566406250. The blog is about Gary Born's presentation on the subject of virtual hearings.

17 *See* Maxi Scherer, *Remote Hearings in International Arbitration and What Voltaire Has to Do With It,* Kluwer Arbitration Blog, 26 May 2020, http://arbitrationblog.kluwerarbitration.com/2020/05/26/remote-hearings-in-international-arbitration-and-what-voltaire-has-to-do-with-it/?doing_wp_cron=1595672568.7934119701385498046875.

important aspect of the arbitral process in international arbitration. In addition to the powers expressly conferred by the parties' agreement and by the laws and rules governing the arbitration, the arbitrators' powers have been defined in the International Law Association Resolution of 2016 on international commercial arbitration, as implied, discretionary and inherent powers.[18] The powers are implied by the parties' agreement and the rules governing the arbitration, discretionary over procedure, and inherent which is necessary to preserve jurisdiction, maintain the integrity of proceedings, and render an enforceable award.

While no law seems to exist that specifically precludes proceedings from taking place in a virtual format, and some laws and arbitration rules expressly permit hearings to be held through audio or video conferencing, if parties continue refusing a virtual hearing despite the tribunal's efforts to address their concern and avoid disruption of the proceedings, it will be ill-advised for arbitrators to hold such virtual hearing which may lead to the annulment of their award.

When the tribunal decides to hold a hearing despite a party's objection or all parties' refusal, it must make sure to motivate its decision and explain all measures duly considered before deciding against one's or all parties' objections. Thus, if a losing party attempts to challenge an award on the ground of the hearing not held in a physical location but virtually, the courts are unlikely to set aside an award on this ground.

One of the requirements expected from arbitrators appointed on a tribunal is the necessary availability allowing them to conduct the proceedings expeditiously. Such requirement exists in most of the arbitration rules, like in the ICC Rules of Arbitration which require that, after consulting the parties, the arbitrators may take into account their broad procedural authority under the Rules, (i) to "adopt such procedural measures as they consider appropriate, provided that they are not contrary to any agreement of the parties" (Art. 22(2)), (ii) to "proceed within as short a time as possible to establish the facts of the case by all appropriate means" (Art. 25(1)), and (iii) to "hear the parties together in person if any of them so requests" (Art. 25(2)).

The ICC Guidance Note on Possible Measures Aimed at Mitigating the Effects of the Covid-19 Pandemic ("ICC Guidance Note")[19] provides that in deciding on the appropriate procedural measures to proceed with the arbitration as expeditiously and efficiently as possible, arbitrators should take account of all circumstances (i) including those caused by the pandemic, (ii) the nature and length of the conference or hearing, (iii) the complexity of the case and the number of participants, (iv) any need to proceed without delay, (v) whether rescheduling the hearing would entail unwarranted or

18 International Law Association Resolution of 2016 on international commercial arbitration, www.ila-hq.org/images/ILA/docs/No.4_Resolution_2016_InternationalCommercialArbitration.pdf.

19 ICC Guidance Note on Possible Measures Aimed at Mitigating the Effects of the Covid-19, dated 9 April 2020: https://cms.iccwbo.org/content/uploads/sites/3/2020/04/guidance-note-possible-measures-mitigating-effects-covid-19-english.pdf.

excessive delays, and (iv) the need for parties to properly prepare for the hearing. Furthermore, the ICC Guidance Note provides that, should a meeting be necessary in a single physical location, parties and arbitrators should make efforts to reschedule in a way that minimises delays, and should discuss the appropriate sanitary measures to ensure the safety of all participants. If it is decided to proceed with a virtual hearing, arbitrators and parties should discuss and plan for special features of proceeding in that manner. If a tribunal decides to proceed with a virtual hearing without the parties' agreement, or over a party's objection, it should carefully consider all relevant circumstances, namely, assess whether the award will be enforceable at law and provide reasons for that determination.

In an arbitration where respondent was attempting to put the case in abeyance, the tribunal indicated to the parties that it is difficult to understand why respondent would need to gather together face-to-face in a physical location to prepare for an oral argument of motions that were already very well presented in their papers. The tribunal indicated to the parties that teleconference and video facilities are available and that parties can participate wherever they are if they have access to phone or internet. The tribunal further observed that the request for re-scheduling was made without any attempt to explore available options for a virtual hearing, and that there was no constitutional due process right to a face-to-face hearing at the arbitration seat. The tribunal added that it has been holding hearings telephonically without anyone insisting that the process is prejudicial or lacking in due process, and also that even evidentiary hearings are being held virtually. It informed the parties that it was not inclined to grant a half-year extension, as the hearing format provides each party a reasonable opportunity to make its case, as it did at the case management teleconference during which all parties made detailed submissions. Furthermore, the tribunal was satisfied that each party can supplement its detailed written arguments during an audio or a video conference. It concluded that the scheduled hearing was maintained and that it expected all parties to cooperate expeditiously in the organisation of a virtual hearing. Directions were provided to the parties to make their best efforts to accommodate video and/or teleconferencing solutions, which may require purchase of hardware and/or software.

In another case, after discussing with the parties and rolling out for them the various aspects to address their concerns, the tribunal issued a procedural order amending the procedure for expert witness examination at the hearing on the merits for the reconvened hearing by video conference. It provided directions on each of the sequences, their timing, and on the technology to be used to allow each side to show PowerPoint presentations and exhibits, in addition to seeing the tribunal, the experts, the attorneys conducting the cross-examination, and the real-time transcript. The videoconference accommodated attorneys for both sides, as well as for the tribunal, the experts, and the court reporter, most of whom connected from different locations. During cross-examination all other individuals present in the room with the expert were visible on camera. The parties' concerns were appropriately addressed in this case and the tribunal succeeded to overcome the parties' refusal to proceed with a virtual hearing. Interestingly, before starting the hearing, the tribunal took note that the parties conducted a test of the platform and confirmed that the platform performed satisfactorily in order to proceed with the hearing. The tribunal also noted that the parties had no objections to proceed with the hearing in the virtual forum.

The Hogan Lovells Protocol for the Use of Technology in Virtual International Arbitration Hearings[20] ('Hogan Protocol') suggests a useful measure under Article 2(10) on the agreement not to challenge the award on the basis of virtual hearing. It provides that:

> a) Prior to the hearing, the parties shall sign a joint agreement that: (i) videoconferencing constitutes an acceptable means of communication permitted by the applicable rules, including those at the juridical seat of the arbitration; (ii) the parties have agreed to the use of videoconferencing as the means for conducting the arbitral hearing; (iii) no party will seek to vacate any resultant arbitral award on the basis that the arbitral hearing was not held in person; and
> b) In order to minimize any risk of vacatur in certain jurisdictions where virtual hearings may be viewed as infringing on due process rights, it is recommended that the parties sign the above-referenced agreement and present it to the tribunal at the pre-hearing conference described above. (the pre-hearing conference is referred to under Art. 1(1) of the Hogan Protocol).

Likewise, the CPR Annotated Model procedural Order for Remote Video Arbitration Proceedings[21] ('CPR PO') provides a model clause dedicated to the enforcement of awards.

Although such agreement may sometimes be difficult to obtain, and does not 'protect against a risk of *vacatur*, it provides an additional security blanket for the award' as stated by an arbitrator.[22]

20 Hogan Lovells Protocol for the Use of Technology in Virtual International Arbitration Hearings, April 2020, Protocol for the Use of technology in Virtual International Arbitration Hearings.

21 CPR Model Annotated Model Procedural Order for Remote Video Arbitration Proceedings ("CPR PO").

22 Samaa Haridi quoted in the Global Arbitration Review of 6 May 2020, in *What If Parties Don't Agree on a Virtual Hearing? A Pandemic Pathway*, https://globalarbitrationreview.com/article/1226483/what-if-parties-dont-agree-on-a-virtual-hearing-a-pandemic-pathway.

2.2 *Parties' Rights – In Person Hearings – Physical and Virtual Location – Due Process*

One of the allegations raised by parties reluctant to convene virtually is that hearings must be held in person. The issue of the 'in person' hearing was never a concern until the lockdown, but the fact of being compelled to move meetings and hearings from offline space to online space became an issue. 'In person' was interpreted by some people as being in the presence of all stakeholders at a physical location. Are there justifiable arguments for excluding the presence of persons virtually?

If we draw a parallel with the way we moved from paper communication to virtual communication, communications were made in paper format and through 'snail mail' before the use of telecommunications, they were made possible during the 20th century through telex machines and then through telefax, until internet allowed communications through emails by the end of the 1980s. Almost all written communications today are made by email in all domains. It is hard to believe that the emails we receive are no valid communications. Evolution and technology allowed for a swifter means of communication and sharing information. It permitted reaching people we may not be able to reach otherwise because of postal difficulties. With the lockdown, we were prevented from using postal and courier services, but luckily internet afforded us to continue business almost as usual. Likewise, we were forbidden from travelling, but virtual meetings and hearings contributed to avoid total disruption.

Considering further the 'in person' interpretation, this issue generated some discussions in the working group who drafted the ICC Guidance Note, but we had enough elements to reach a logical conclusion. Article 25(2) of the ICC Rules of Arbitration is structured to regulate whether the tribunal can decide the dispute based on written submissions and documents only, or whether there must also be a live hearing. Article 25 does not preclude a hearing taking place in person by virtual means. The French version of Article 25(2) refers to the 'contradictoire', meaning that parties must have the opportunity of an adversarial debate to ensure that their arguments are heard in the presence of all parties:

> Après examen des écritures des parties et de toutes pièces versées par elles aux débats, le tribunal arbitral entend contradictoirement les parties si l'une d'elles en fait la demande; à défaut, il peut décider d'office de leur audition.

The Secretariat's Guide to ICC Arbitration provides that 'whether the tribunal construes Article 25(2) as requiring a face-to-face hearing, or whether the use of video or teleconferencing suffices, will depend on the circumstances of the case.' The fact that persons appear at a physical location or through a virtual location makes no difference, provided such persons are all present at the meeting or hearing and are heard, whether their appearance is physical or virtual, due process is respected. Moreover, the literal meaning or interpretation of 'in person' is contrasted with the provision of Article 26 (4) of the ICC Rules of Arbitration, which provides for 'participation through authorised representatives'. 'Physical location' is purposefully used in this chapter considering that a person is physically present at a virtual hearing when connected remotely.

The Rules of Arbitration of the London Court of International Arbitration provide in article 19(2) that '... a hearing may take place by video or telephone conference or in person (or a combination of all three)'.

With the evolution of working methods compared to when laws, rules, and conventions were drafted before technology became common place, new laws and rules are now either making explicit reference to information and communication technology, or referring implicitly to such technology means, and they sometimes refer to the tribunals' powers in this respect. The UAE Federal Arbitration Law of 2018 for example explicitly refers to the use of new technologies.[23]

Basing the examination on the governing procedural rules and the applicable law ('rules and/or law'), one of the authors of this chapter has established a tree on how to assess the possibility of holding a virtual hearing despite a party or all parties' objections by providing a pathway and considering four scenarios.[24]

The first scenario looks at situations where the rules and/or law expressly refer to the need for an in person physical hearing on the merits, and where the in person is synonymous with appearance at a physical location. In such scenario, the tribunal will not be able to impose a virtual hearing without the parties' express consent, failing which the award risks to be set aside.

The second scenario considers the situation where the rules and/or law expressly refer to the possibility of holding virtual hearings or using technology. Such scenario is the most straightforward, permitting the tribunal to proceed as it deems appropriate after consulting the parties.

Where the rules and/or law are silent and no direct inference may be drawn is the third scenario considered. Most legal systems consider that the applicable legal principle is that a matter is permissible unless prohibited. There are two possible approaches: the absence of a permissive provision to proceed virtually does not allow the tribunal to

---

23 UAE Federal Arbitration Law No.6 of 2018, https://u.ae/en/information-and-services/justice-safety-and-the-law/litigation-procedures/alternative-methods-to-settle-disputes-/uae-federal-law-on-arbitration.

24 Global Arbitration Review of 6 May 2020, *What If Parties Don't Agree on a Virtual Hearing? A Pandemic Pathway*, Mohamed Abdel Wahab's 6-point pathway about the possibility of holding a virtual hearing, https://globalarbitrationreview.com/article/1226483/what-if-parties-dont-agree-on-a-virtual-hearing-a-pandemic-pathway; Mohamed Abdel Wahab, Exculpating the Fear to Virtually Hear – A Proposed Pathway to Virtual Hearing Considerations in International Arbitrations", 13(2) NYSBA New York Dispute Resolution Lawyer, *Summer 2020, Vol. 13(2) p.18-24.*

decide in favour of virtual hearings without the parties' express consent; or the absence of a prohibitive provision equates to using the tribunal's discretionary power to proceed virtually without the parties' express consent unless otherwise stated. The tribunal's power to decide in favour or against a virtual hearing is moreover dependent on various factors:

- whether the rules and/or law include an express provision giving it such power to manage the proceedings as it deems appropriate;
- whether the rules and/or law refer to the parties' right to a 'full' or 'reasonable' opportunity to present their case;
- whether according to the rules and/or law hearings are a mandatory requirement or whether they permit tribunals to proceed with a case on a documents-basis only, which would not normally put an award at risk if a virtual hearing is held despite a party's objection;
- whether all parties object to the virtual hearing, which would risk vacating an award if a virtual hearing is held, as explained above;
- whether in the terms of reference or the procedural order it was agreed to limit the tribunal's power to proceed in certain matters without the parties' consent;
- whether the rules of evidence and civil procedure at the seat recognise the possibility of using technology in legal proceedings;
- whether the proceedings are subject to strict time limits and a hearing must take place, and where the tribunal's jurisdiction *ratione temporis* cannot be extended should the hearing be postponed; in this difficult instance, being compelled to hold a virtual hearing where no hearing in a physical place is possible will likely expose the award to be set aside;
- whether the circumstances of the case make it appropriate to hold a virtual hearing (for example participants' access to reliable technology, nature and volume of the evidence and lack of any serious risk of prejudice).

Any decision in any scenario the tribunal may face must be reasoned as explained above, whether the tribunal is in favour or against holding a virtual hearing, provided due process is not affected.

Finally, the fourth scenario is whether the applicable law is inconsistent with the governing procedural rules including any institutional rules, and whether such applicable law is a mandatory or a non-mandatory rule.

2.3 *Adjournment of Meetings and Hearings is Not the Only Solution*

Parties and arbitrators must consider all opportunities available to them to move arbitrations forward. Irrespective of the stage of the procedure, arbitrators must first examine potential factors which may disrupt the procedure should an adjournment or an extension of time limit be decided. Adjournments and extensions are not the only solution, other options are available. Practitioners benefit from many instruments and techniques ('toolkits') to assist them in ensuring effective case management, which they can adopt any time during the arbitration. The toolkits are not new but are not sufficiently utilised. They are unrelated to virtual hearings although they include such option as one of the techniques. The outbreak that the world has gone through in 2020 was hopefully an opportunity to discover or re-discover and use the toolkits, to contribute to getting procedures back under control, as well as to try to limit time and costs. Subject to any constraints of legal requirements as discussed above, the potential impediments to travelling generated by any phenomenon, whether natural or otherwise, must be seriously considered to avoid further disruptions. A practitioner recently observed that tribunals would ideally have already considered existing techniques, but that "the pandemic has moved from '*nice to try*' to '*need to use*'."[25]

The International Chamber of Commerce (ICC) Commission on Arbitration and ADR is one of the organisations that issued a few reports providing parties and arbitrators guidance on how to conduct procedures in an effective and cost-efficient manner. Such reports remain very relevant and useful to avoid disruptions.

The first one, published in 2004 and updated in 2017, concerns the Use of Information Technology (IT) in International Arbitration.[26] This report was the first publication that addressed all issues which need to be considered when using technology in arbitration and remains particularly relevant. It is intended to provide arbitrators, outside counsel, and in-house counsel with an overview of issues that may arise when using technology in international dispute resolution and how those issues might be addressed. It encourages arbitrators and counsel to analyse, as a matter of routine and not exception, whether and how IT might be used. It also helps users to address practical issues they may not think of, such as IT capabilities of each person involved in the case, data integrity issues, or coherent file naming which is important to retrieve documents easily and quickly. It addresses various logistical issues, like hearing room technologies, multimedia presentations, translations, and real-time electronic transcripts.

---

25 Michael McIlwrath quoted in the Global Arbitration Review of 6 May 2020, in *What If Parties Don't Agree on a Virtual Hearing? A Pandemic Pathway,* https://globalarbitrationreview.com/article/1226483/what-if-parties-dont-agree-on-a-virtual-hearing-a-pandemic-pathway.

26 ICC Commission on Arbitration and ADR Report on the 'Use of Information Technology in International Arbitration', https://iccwbo.org/publication/information-technology-international-arbitration-report-icc-commission-arbitration-adr.

The second report published in 2007 and re-issued in 2012, addressed Techniques for Controlling Time and Costs in Arbitration.[27] Some of the techniques proposed in the report were added as Appendix IV as of the 2012 version of the ICC Rules of Arbitration, including an important provision related to an early case management conference. It was recommended in the report since that time, that telephone and videoconferencing may be considered for procedural and other hearings where attendance in person is not essential. Another very helpful report, issued in 2015, provided further guidance for Effective Management in Arbitration,[28] such as maintaining realistic schedules, and raising awareness about potential settlement opportunities. The Techniques for Managing Electronic Document Production,[29] published in 2011, is another useful report.

The ICC International Court of Arbitration also issued two useful notes. The Note to Parties and Arbitral Tribunals on the Conduct of Arbitration under ICC Rules of Arbitration[30] mentions a few techniques recommended in the various reports and also provides new solutions, like disposing expeditiously of certain claims or defences, or the possibility of signing not only the terms of reference in counterparts, but also signing awards in counterparts, of course subject to any mandatory requirements of relevant applicable laws.

The second practical note is the ICC Guidance Note. Article 8 of such Note provides that to ensure continued effective case management, Article 24(3) of the ICC Rules of Arbitration provides that the tribunal may adopt appropriate procedural measures or modify the procedural timetable by means of a further case management conference or otherwise. The tribunal may discuss with the parties about potential measures aimed at reducing time and costs, and also mitigating disruptions. The measures may include:

- disposing expeditiously of certain claims or defences;
- resolving the issues in dispute in stages by rendering one or more partial awards when doing so is likely to result in a more efficient resolution of the case;
- identifying whether the entirety of the dispute or discrete issues may be resolved on documents-basis only, with no evidentiary hearing;
- identifying issues that may be resolved by agreement between the parties, as the case may be with the assistance of their experts;

27 ICC Commission on Arbitration and ADR Report on the 'Techniques for Controlling Time and Costs in Arbitration', https://iccwbo.org/publication/icc-arbitration-commission-report-on-techniques-for-controlling-time-and-costs-in-arbitration.

28 ICC Commission on Arbitration and ADR Report on the 'Effective Management in Arbitration', https://iccwbo.org/publication/effective-management-of-arbitration-a-guide-for-in-house-counsel-and-other-party-representatives.

29 ICC Commission on Arbitration and ADR Report on the 'Techniques for Managing Electronic Document Production', https://library.iccwbo.org/content/dr/COMMISSION_REPORTS/CR_0043.htm?l1=Commission+Reports.

30 Note to Parties and Arbitral Tribunals on the Conduct of Arbitration under ICC Rules of Arbitration, https://iccwbo.org/dispute-resolution-services/arbitration/practice-notes-forms-checklists.

- organising mid-stream procedural conferences in order to assess with the parties the most relevant issues and to consider possibilities for focusing on the most efficient means to resolve those issues;
- considering whether potentially dispositive issues, such as the application of a contractual limitation of liability or the inclusion of a non-signatory in the proceedings, can be decided without a phase for the production of documents, or with a highly limited production of documents that are deemed to be material only to the issue(s) to be decided;
- identifying issues that may be resolved without witness and/or expert evidence or on the basis of written questions from the opposite party or the tribunal and written answers from the witness or expert;
- considering whether site visits or inspections by experts can be replaced by video presentations or joint reports of experts;
- considering whether direct recourse to a tribunal-appointed expert as opposed to party-appointed experts is appropriate;
- using either audioconference or videoconference for conferences and hearings where possible and appropriate;
- requesting that the parties establish an agreed chronology of facts, joint lists of issues in dispute or other similar jointly produced documents that help define and narrow the range of issues in dispute;
- considering whether and how the number and size of submissions can be limited; and
- considering whether the parties would agree to opt-in to the ICC Expedited Rules Provisions.

The Institution's role is to establish best practices and effective tools. Parties and arbitrators are likely to adopt them naturally once they have discovered their benefits.[31]

3 Assisting Dispute Resolution Practitioners in Organising Virtual Hearings

The flexibility that the users of international dispute resolution showed during the sudden outbreak beginning 2020 was immediately supported by the dispute resolution organisations that swiftly offered guidance to users and practitioners in organising their online meetings and hearings. Firms and practitioners have also shared their experience. A significant number of material was issued in a few weeks, from protocols, checklists, guidelines, guidance notes, best practices (collectively referred here as

31 *See* note 14, Sylvia Tee and Andy Lau quoting Mirèze Philippe in a summary on the webinar of 18 June 2020, on *Case Management in Virtual Hearings*, www.lipmankaras.com/2020/07/case-manageme nt-in-virtual-hearings/.

'recommendations') and model procedural orders, to articles in which practitioners shared their experience. The recommendations provide a roadmap guiding practitioners in this new setting. They do not intend to be exhaustive as practice may evolve on the one hand, and on the other hand, each case is different from the other which requires specific adaptations.

Interestingly, an African dispute resolution community has benefited from the opportunity of the shift to virtual platforms to provide guidelines and best practices for arbitrations within Africa. They published an African Arbitration Academy's Protocol on Virtual Hearings in Africa[32] ('African Academy Protocol'). The objectives of such Protocol are noteworthy as they deal with general issues related to arbitration and not only virtual hearings, namely, in Articles 1(2), 1(3), 1(4), and 1(9):

> 1.2. To foster security and predictability in the management of arbitrations in the continent.
> 1.3. To promote the use of reliable technology in arbitral proceedings, and where appropriate, to reduce the cost of arbitrations and enhance the efficiency of arbitral proceedings.
> 1.4. To encourage African governments, businesses, institutions and other users of arbitration to invest in information and communication technologies that would facilitate access to reliable technology, and enable virtual hearings.
> 1.9. To encourage African institutions and governments to make express references to virtual hearings in arbitration rules and laws, and to serve as guiding standards, principles, and provisions to be adopted by arbitral institutions or governments in Africa when drafting their arbitration rules and laws.

The various recommendations, procedural orders and material about virtual hearings were usefully listed and made available on two websites: Delos Dispute Resolution[33] and Virtual Arbitration.[34] To enable readers retrieve information referred to, it will be indicated which parts of the recommendations are discussed below, namely from the following material:

32 African Arbitration Academy's Protocol on Virtual Hearings in Africa, April 2020 ("African Academy Protocol").

33 A very informative table was created by Delos Dispute Resolution https://delosdr.org/ and can be found here: https://delosdr.org/index.php/2020/05/12/resources-on-virtual-hearings/. The table compiles relevant resources on remote and virtual arbitration and mediation hearings, organised under the following headings: (i) Guidance & Checklists; (ii) Protocols; (iii) Model Procedural Orders; (iv) Case Materials & Legislation Reviews, (v) Survey Reports; (vi) Webinar Recordings; and (vii) Other Resources. The authors thank Hafez Virjee, Delos President, and Mihaela Apostol, Delos Team, for having prepared this useful list.

34 Virtual Arbitration, https://virtualarbitration.info/.

- ICC Guidance Note on Possible Measures Aimed at Mitigating the Effects of Covid-19 ('ICC Guidance Note')[35]
- CIArb's Guidance Note on Remote Dispute Resolution Proceedings ('CIArb Guidance Note')[36]
- African Arbitration Academy's Protocol on Virtual Hearings in Africa ('African Academy Protocol')[37]
- Vienna Protocol – A Practical Checklist for Remote Hearings ('VIAC Protocol')[38]
- HKIAC Guidelines for Virtual Hearings ('HKIAC Guidelines')[39]
- KCAB International's Seoul Protocol on Video Conferencing in International Arbitration ('Seoul Protocol')[40]
- Hogan Lovells Protocol for the Use of Technology in Virtual International Arbitration Hearings ('Hogan Protocol')[41]
- International Council for Online Dispute Resolution Video Arbitration Guidelines ('ICODR Guidelines')[42]
- CPR Model Annotated Model Procedural Order for Remote Video Arbitration Proceedings ('CPR PO')[43]
- Stephanie Cohen Draft Zoom Hearing Procedural Order ('Cohen PO')[44]
- Delos' Checklist on Holding Arbitration and Mediation Hearings in Times of Covid-19 ('Delos' Checklist')[45]

Dispute resolution organisations, legal organisations like the American Bar Association, law firms, universities and other groups organised webinars to offer users and practitioners the possibility to learn about the recommendations or hear practitioners who have experience in virtual hearings. Many of these webinars are available on YouTube.[46]

---

35 ICC Guidance Note on Possible Measures Aimed at Mitigating the Effects of COVID-19, April 2020 ("ICC Guidance Note").
36 CIArb's Guidance Note on Remote Dispute Resolution Proceedings, April 2020 ("CIArb Guidance Note").
37 African Arbitration Academy's Protocol on Virtual Hearings in Africa, April 2020 ("African Academy Protocol").
38 VIAC Vienna Protocol – A Practical Checklist for Remote Hearings, June 2020 ("VIAC Protocol").
39 HKIAC's Guidelines for Virtual Hearings, May 2020 ("HKIAC Guidelines").
40 KCAB International's Seoul Protocol on Video Conferencing in International Arbitration, March 2020 ("Seoul Protocol").
41 Hogan Lovells' Protocol for the Use of Technology in Virtual International Arbitration Hearings, April 2020 ("Hogan Protocol").
42 ICODR International Council for Online Dispute Resolution Video Arbitration Guidelines, April 2020 ("ICODR Guidelines").
43 CPR Annotated Model Procedural Order for Remote Video Arbitration Proceedings ("CPR PO").
44 Stephanie Cohen, *Draft Zoom Hearing Procedural Order*, www.transnational-dispute-management.com/journal-advance-publication-article.asp?key=1815, April 2020 ("Cohen PO").
45 Delos' Checklist on Holding Arbitration and Mediation Hearings in Times of COVID-19.
46 *See* for instance Erik Schäfer, *Virtual Hearings and Remote Evidence – Technology in Arbitration*, 7 October 2019, www.youtube.com/watch?v=vzp1p_kg5es.

In the second part of this chapter, some of the recommendations provided in the various best practices (a), and a few difficulties arising from virtual hearings (b) will be discussed.

3.1 Recommendations for Virtual Hearings

Conducting virtual meetings and hearings online has proven to be efficient to move cases forward and circumvent further delays in arbitration. Preparation of a hearing whether offline or online is key for its success. However, the virtual setting requires a different type of organisation and further adaptations than a hearing in a physical location where all players sit in the same room.[47] Experiences in virtual hearings have been successful when parties were cooperative, no matter the number of participants and the variety of locations from where they are connected.

Some practitioners succeeded to save time and costs. Others shared different views and indicated that they incurred extra costs to ensure that they are properly equipped with the required devices. Any extra costs invested in appropriate equipment are probably opportune given that we may be faced with impediments to travel for any reason as mentioned above, therefore preparing for any future potential disruption is useful.

Where parties have no access to technology or proper equipment for virtual hearings, they may use the services of arbitral institutions or hearing centres which are reliable and can provide the necessary equipment, software, bandwidth connection, and minimal risk of signal interruptions (African Academy Protocol, Art. 2.1.6).

Organisations and practitioners shared practical views and their experiences on issues to be considered before holding a virtual hearing and during such hearing. They mainly concern logistical and procedural issues which will be discussed in the various points raised below, and which need to be considered in order to ensure that parties are treated equally and given full opportunity to present their case during a virtual hearing. The sophisticated recommendations may assist parties and arbitrators who may take inspiration from such recommendations and tailor them to any given case. Whatever recommendations are adopted, none is intended to supersede any agreement between the parties and any arbitration rules governing the procedure.

3.1.1 Technology, Technical Support, Connectivity, Testing

The technology to be used constitutes a major part of the elements that come into play when a virtual hearing must be organised. Technology capabilities of all participants are fundamental. The support of computer technicians is thus indispensable from the outset

---

47 *See* for instance "Preliminary checklist prior to conducting remote dispute resolution proceedings" in Appendix I to the CIArb's Guidance Note on Remote Dispute Resolution Proceedings, April 2020 ("CIArb Guidance Note").

to assist the parties and the arbitrators in the choice of the platform and the technology best suited for the hearing. The platform must offer sufficient protection against unwanted third-party access. In addition, the conditions of use of the platform for data protection must be reviewed considering that some platform providers may assume ownership rights of the data transmitted through their platform (section II of the VIAC Protocol). The legal access to the platform and the technology selected must be verified to ensure that each participant may access it, given that some platforms are forbidden of use in some countries. Useful recommendations are provided under Article 2(5) of the Hogan protocol.

Needless to say that the selection of secure and stable platforms is essential (Art. 2(4) of the Hogan Protocol) to protect the integrity of the proceedings, and that consideration should be given to the level of encryption a platform offers, the types of security measures in place (e.g. whether the platform offers password protected meetings), and the potential cyber-risks presented by the platform. Article 2(4) of the Hogan Protocol also refers to some potential proprietary high-end teleconference systems password-protected, and to document sharing platforms. An annex to the Seoul Protocol provides technical specifications about video conferencing equipment with the common industry standards recommended by the International Telecommunications Union to serve as a guideline. The platform selected must enable the participants to have everyone on the screen at the same time as opposed to only highlighting the speaker (ICODR Guidelines).

A wired network connection should be preferred over a wireless connection, and no public Wi-Fi should be used without being password-protected (Art. 2(5) of the Hogan Protocol). The connection and the bandwidth may work fine at a time where not many people are connected, but the streaming can become slower if many people are connected and depending on their use of internet. During the lockdown and considering that activities and travelling were suspended, all people were connected through internet, to work remotely, to connect to their schools and universities, to access administrative services, to purchase online products and services, to download films, to organise meetings or webinars. The significant number of people connected made it sometimes hard for some people to be seamlessly connected from their homes without disconnections. Therefore testing the connection of participants at a time during the day where the hearing is scheduled to take place should be preferred to another time during the day where traffic on internet may be lower.

Tutorials may be needed and are an important support for participants who are unfamiliar with any platform, technology, plug-in, and any equipment to be used during the hearing.

Moreover, at each venue, the parties must jointly designate at least one person with adequate technical knowledge to be present virtually or in the physical room, at the pre-hearing conference and during the actual hearing for any troubleshooting. It is also recommended that the computer technicians cooperate with each other and report any issues promptly to the tribunal (Art. 2(3) of the Hogan Protocol).

The technical support staff assistance throughout the hearing is essential for any troubleshooting, and back-up facilities are equally indispensable in case of sudden disconnection, power outage which may happen especially in some countries, or technical failures. Alternatives must be available, namely dial-in numbers to connect and any other communication channels. Additional equipment in each location may be needed to ensure a proper back-up, namely back-up computers, telephones, connectivity boosters/extenders, any other equipment or audio-visual aids as deemed necessary (ICC Guidance Note, Checklist, section B).

The testing phase is one of the main components to ensure a successful connection and a successful use of all needed features. A virtual hearing can run smoothly and usually does, if proper verifications are conducted before the hearing. Running a minimum of two mock sessions is recommended within the month preceding the hearing, with the last session being held one day before the hearing to ensure everything tested the first time or times, continue working properly (ICC Guidance Note, Checklist, section B). All technical functionalities must be tested, namely: successful connection to the platform for all participants; secured connection to the breakout rooms; use of the mute and un-mute function; use of the audio and lack of background noise and echo; pop-up notifications disabled on the device in use (clause 2 (9) of the Hogan Protocol); use of the video with adequate lighting in the physical rooms (ICC Guidance Note, Checklist, section B) and back-lighting to avoid, such as sitting in front of a window or bright light (HKIAC Guidelines). Likewise, the screen or screens on which documents are shared must be tested and the smooth travelling from a document to another must be verified.

Finally, a decision on which party bears the costs must be made, pending the final decision on costs to be determined by the tribunal in the final award (section III of the VIAC Protocol).

3.1.2 Hearing Date and Duration

Parties and arbitrators must agree on the hearing date, the duration and the daily timetable to take into account the different time zones, as well as the number of breaks. In case of competing preferences, parties must defer to the wishes of the tribunal. Electronic calendaring invites must be limited to authorised attendees (Art. 2(1) of the Hogan Protocol).

Practitioners suggest that in selecting a time zone, the office hours of the seat of arbitration should be the default, with adjustments to be made to accommodate the time zones of the parties' representatives and the members of the tribunal.[48] Parties may consider travelling to locations that minimise time zone differences, and where travelling is not practical, to give preference to individuals and witnesses with health, family or other circumstances that raise special concerns as to the location from which they will testify (Art. 2(2) of the Hogan Protocol).

Similarly, and considering the different time zones, the start and the finish times must be considered to avoid starting too early and proceeding with the hearing too late. No party shall be expected to partake in a hearing at an unreasonable time based on their individual time zones (Art. 2(2) in the Hogan Protocol).

Furthermore, hearings need to be shorter than a normal hearing day, and limiting the number of hours per day has proven to be vital given that concentrating several hours on a screen and often on several screens is different from concentrating on what happens in a physical room. In a virtual room the attention can be much more limited, and participants sometimes spend several hours alone, connected to screens. Whereas in a physical setting, participants move, lawyers can present their arguments sitting or standing, they can walk to a board to present charts, they can show demonstratives and hand them potentially to arbitrators, lawyers can exchange short notes with the members of their teams or with their clients, arbitrators may have short discussions among themselves; the action and inter-action in a physical location is entirely different and more dynamic. The advocacy skills may need to be adapted to the virtual setting. Some practitioners consider the screen as 'an obstacle to their traditional tools of persuasiveness'.[49] Incidentally, as reported by some authors, sustained concentration and focus during video conferencing, the gap between the physical and the virtual, and the feeling of isolation may impact the mental health.[50] Although virtual hearings need to be shorter to avoid exhausting participants, the advantage of virtual hearings is to avoid the costs incurred by travelling and the accommodation, including the time wasted for the travelling.

Taking into account that virtual hearings need to be shorter than offline hearings, parties and arbitrators need to identify whether and which issues are essential to be on the hearing agenda and those which can be dealt with on a documents-basis only. Efficiency dictates that identifying such issues and concentrating on essential matters is a good practice, whether the hearing is offline or online.

---

48 *See* note 14, Sylvia Tee and Andy Lau quoting Kevin Kim in a summary on the webinar of 18 June 2020, on *Case Management in Virtual Hearings*, www.lipmankaras.com/2020/07/case-management-in-virtual-hearings/.

49 Sophie Nappert and Mihaela Apostol, *Healthy Virtual Hearings*, Kluwer Arbitration Blog, 17 July 2020, http://arbitrationblog.kluwerarbitration.com/2020/07/17/healthy-virtual-hearings/?doing_wp_cron=1595002045.9255509376525878906250.

50 *See Ibid.*

3.1.3 Participants in the Rooms and Breakout Rooms

Although the determination of the number of participants must be agreed upon whether hearings are held offline or online, the electronic setting is a constraint that needs to be addressed differently. In a physical room, it probably less matters how many people are in the room once parties and arbitrators agree on who should be in the room: arbitrators, parties, counsel, witnesses, experts, administrative secretaries, interpreters, stenographers. The situation is different when the participants connect remotely and from various locations. The number of participants potentially multiplies the number of virtual rooms, unless several persons connect from the same physical location. To the extent practicable, it is recommended that parties appear with their counsel in a single venue (Art. 2(8) of the Hogan Protocol), but it is discouraged that one of the parties attend the hearing in the same physical venue as the tribunal if the other party can only attend remotely, unless expressly agreed (African Academy Protocol, Art. 2.2.6). The single hearing room in a physical space that became multiple in a virtual space, requires a bigger control. The tribunal needs to see all persons present at the hearing through the various screens, so do the parties, and also the interpreters and the stenographers who need to know who is speaking.

Agreeing on the number of participants per virtual room is equally important as the number of rooms connected, and may need to be reviewed and limited to ensure that participants can be visible. Parties must endeavour to have no more than two individuals in the camera frame at once and at all times the tribunal and at least any speaking participant(s) shall be visible (Art. 2(8) of the Hogan Protocol). Moreover, parties and arbitrators need to agree on whether a 360° view for all participating rooms is required; normally, it would be necessary only for the rooms from which witnesses and experts will connect.

The tribunal is encouraged to ask parties to confirm that the only persons permitted to attend the hearing are those noticed or approved by opposing counsel and the tribunal, that no unauthorised parties shall attend in violation of that agreement, and that any witness who is giving evidence shall not be assisted during the course of his / her evidence (Art. 2(12) of the Hogan Protocol).

The rooms from which participants connect, whether from their homes, offices, or in special hearing venues, should be completely separate from non-participants to the remote hearing, and soundproofed where possible. The use of headsets is recommended to increase both privacy and audibility of participants (CIArb Guidance Note).

Similarly, identifying all log-in locations and points of connection is paramount for security. The arbitrators must have control over allowing in the room not only the participants agreed upon, but also the locations from which they will be logging into the platform chosen for the virtual hearing. Once all participants are allowed in the virtual room and before the start of the videoconference, measures should be taken to orally identify all individuals present at each venue, including any technical support (ICC

Guidance Note, Checklist, section A). The same procedure may need to be repeated after each break to confirm again who is present in each room, including the witnesses and experts during certain parts of the hearing (Delos Checklist, Art. B6). When all participants allowed in the room have joined, the tribunal must lock the room so others cannot join in.

With respect to breakout rooms, at a hearing or conference centre, participants can use several rooms to meet separately from the other participants. Usually, arbitrators want to have a breakout room to allow them to confer privately amongst themselves either during the hearing or during a break. Each side also needs a room to have private discussions between the counsel and the party or parties they represent. The technology permits today to use platforms that offer virtual breakout rooms, where arbitrators can mute themselves if all three are sitting in the same location, and if they are connecting from various locations to go to a virtual room offering them the opportunity to confer privately. Parties and arbitrators may need to select a platform that offers breakout rooms password-protected to ensure total privacy of the discussions, and to avoid that no person who is not allowed in the room access such room. If their hearing is hosted by a hearing centre offering virtual settings, virtual breakout rooms are available. The tribunal must decide who controls the breakout rooms, whether an administrative secretary or themselves will have control, or whether the hearing centre will manage such rooms.

3.1.4 Confidentiality, Privacy and Security

Cybersecurity and data protection have been in the last two decades among the major concerns of all communities or institutions. With the increased use of internet and the professional hackers who are capable of breaking through almost any system, significant care should be taken for all steps, from selecting platforms and plug-ins (for example live notes), to communicating the connection details enabling the participants to enter the virtual room. One typical mistake is the fact of communicating the URL address to the platform, together with a username and a password in the same unencrypted email to one or several participants. Annex 1 to the African Academy Protocol provides also some minimum cybersecurity standards, such as avoiding unsecured connection, ensuring encryption set-up and password-protected accounts. The connection of all devices to a secure and password-protected network is of paramount importance, so do compliance with all data protection laws and regulations which are generally of mandatory application. All cloud-based video conferences should be password-protected.

Dispute resolution users will find very useful recommendations in the ICCA-NYC Bar-CPR Protocol on Cybersecurity in International Arbitration.[51] As indicated in the

---

51 *See* the ICCA-NYC Bar-CPR Protocol on Cybersecurity in International Arbitration, www.arbitration-icca.org/media/14/52278078693299/icca-nyc_bar-cpr_cybersecurity_protocol_for_international_arbitration_-_electronic_version.pdf?mc_cid=8bb910d616&mc_eid=0d618241b1.

foreword of the Protocol, it includes procedural and practical guidance to assess security risks and identify available measures that may be implemented, and is intended to increase awareness about information security in international arbitrations. Likewise, the ICCA-IBA Joint Roadmap to Data Protection in International Arbitration Proceedings[52] has been developed to help arbitration professionals better understand the data protection and privacy obligations to which they may be subject in relation to international arbitration proceedings.

Parties and arbitrators must use a secure videoconferencing platform with end-to-end encryption. They must use no apps or software that requires location information to be shared, and must inform the parties that they have the ability to turn that off and explain how to do so. They must ensure that the videoconference will not time out or close down after a certain duration of time (ICODR Guidelines).

Tribunals should ensure with the parties that any videoconference platform and documents sharing platform for electronic bundles are licensed and set to maximum security settings. Customised or licensed fee-based platforms may offer greater security, confidentiality and data protection, than free-to-use, public platforms (ICC Guidance Note).

Parties and arbitrators must decide whether the virtual hearing will remain private and confidential to participants, and agree on an access and confidentiality undertaking that binds all participants. Likewise, they must agree on the recording of the hearing and whether it will be an audio or an audio-visual recording, as well as on the confidentiality and the value of the recording compared to any produced written transcript. Any overriding privacy requirements or standards that may impact access or connectivity of certain participants must be discussed, including the minimum requirements of encryption to safeguard the integrity and security of the virtual hearing against any hacking or illicit access (ICC Guidance Note).

3.1.5 Online Etiquette and Due Process Considerations

The parties shall provide the tribunal and opposing counsel a list of all anticipated attendees at least 48 hours in advance of the hearing. Participants to a hearing shall be limited to party representatives, counsel, witnesses, tribunal members, interpreters, reporters, and such logistical, technical, or other support as may be required to assist in the presentation of evidence; and if a party wishes to include an additional person not noticed in advance of the hearing, such person may participate only with the agreement of all parties or at the direction of the tribunal. In any event, no individual shall be in attendance who is not announced and to which all parties have not agreed.

52 *See* the ICCA-IBA Joint Roadmap to Data Protection in International Arbitration Proceedings, www.arbitration-icca.org/media/14/18191123957287/roadmap_28.02.20.pdf.

To achieve the necessary level of cooperation and coordination for a successful hearing by videoconference, parties and arbitrators must agree on the practices needed to safeguard the rights and obligations of participants in a virtual environment. This includes among others, identifying the lead speakers, refraining from interrupting any speaker, observing reasonable and responsible use of the platform and bandwidth, avoiding use of equipment that interferes with connectivity, refraining from any non-authorised recording, and taking whatever measures to support the procedural efficiency of the hearing (ICC Guidance Note).

After consulting the parties, the tribunal must set the mechanism for objections on the first hearing day during the introductory discussion of housekeeping matters. The parties must within a fixed period of time confirm in writing that (i) they have conducted the test runs envisaged and (ii) that the service provider, equipment, technical specifications and requirements are adequate for their participation in the hearing. The tribunal must finally advise the parties on their duty to cooperate on technical matters prior to and during the virtual hearing (ICC Guidance Note).

At the outset of any virtual proceedings, the presiding arbitrator or the tribunal-designated assistant shall be made the host and moderator of the meeting to the extent possible. If multiple parties and/or witnesses are speaking at the same time, it shall be the role of the presiding arbitrator or the tribunal-designated assistant to operate the mute function on the audio feed, to pause the proceedings and determine the appropriateness of any participants' contribution at the time in question. If disagreement or uncertainty regarding the application of the protocol agreed upon by the parties and the arbitrators and other procedures arise during the course of the proceedings, the tribunal shall resolve such a dispute.

In case one of the parties or the person speaking loses connectivity, it should be immediately reported to the rest of the attendees using a designated messaging system. This is especially relevant where there is only an audio connection (clause 2(9) of the Hogan Protocol). If one party disconnects, the tribunal must request that the rest of the attendees remain silent until the connectivity is restored. If a party's audio disconnects or becomes distorted, once the audio resumes, the tribunal must ask the participants to repeat what has been said during the outage (ICODR Guidelines).

There shall be no *ex parte* chat window communication with the tribunal. Similarly, there shall be no *ex parte* chat window communication between testifying witnesses and counsel offering their testimony. Each party should identify a member of their team to monitor the chat room and flag any relevant issues to their team (Art. 2(9) of the Hogan Protocol).

A single procedure for recording and a single individual responsible for the recording should be agreed upon (Art. 2(6) of the Hogan Protocol). It is also recommended that, with the exception of reporters, no separate recordings be made by the participants, unless otherwise agreed. The person responsible for the recording must circulate the recording to the parties and the arbitrators as soon as possible, within 24 or 48 hours of the close of the proceedings, depending on the time limit agreed upon. Likewise, if the parties agree to transcribe the proceedings, they shall agree to a single reporter who should remain available at all times to ensure integrity and ease of communication with the parties (Art. 2(7) of the Hogan Protocol).

3.1.6 Presentation of Evidence and Examination of Witnesses and Experts

Whether the hearing is held offline or online efficiency dictates to utilise a common bundle during the hearing including for cross examination of witnesses and experts. The use of electronic bundles also allows participants to share content concurrently in a share screen mode (CIArb Guidance Note).

Discussion on the applicable rules for examination of witnesses and experts is likewise important, in particular whether a representative of one party should be present in the room with the witness or expert for the other party who is being cross-examined, and what documents will be available to the witness or expert during their examination (Delos Checklist, Art. 6).[53] The Hogan Protocol provides from the outset under Art. 1 (c) that counsel shall arrange for all relevant documents to be transmitted to the testifying witnesses in advance of the preparation sessions so that the witness may prepare to be examined with documents during the hearing.

The modalities for submitting and showing demonstrative exhibits must also be discussed, namely: the order of calling and examining the witnesses or experts; the connection time and duration of availability; their virtual sequestration; the permission or prohibition of synchronous or asynchronous communications between witnesses or experts and parties or counsel in chat rooms or through concealed channels of communications; the interaction between the examiner and the witness or expert in an online environment and whether s/he will be assisted by anyone whilst giving his/her testimony (ICC Guidance Note, Checklist section E).

Moreover, an arrangement may be needed where a witness or expert will require the assistance of an interpreter to ensure that the interpreter is able to provide his/her services virtually. It must also be determined whether interpretation will be simultaneous or consecutive (ICC Guidance Note, Checklist section E), which may require adjusted time frames as consecutive interpretation is commonly used in remote proceedings (CIArb Guidance Note). If the parties do not reach an agreement on any or all items, they should communicate their proposals to the tribunal who will decide about the organisation (ICC Guidance Note, Checklist section E).

53 Delos checklist on holding arbitration and mediation hearings in times of Covid-19, March 2020, https://delosdr.org/index.php/2020/03/12/checklist-on-holding-hearings-in-times-of-covid-19/.

When presenting a witness, counsel shall ensure that both the table in front of the witness and the top of the witnesses' head are in the frame (Art. 2(8) of the Hogan Protocol).

Where parties intend to use during the oral pleadings demonstrative exhibits and presentation of certain evidence on record, they should ensure that the demonstrative exhibits will be clear and visible on a screen to all tribunal members, the other party or parties and any participants authorised to attend that portion of the hearing. If multi-screens are required for the presentation of demonstrative exhibits and evidence, the parties should ensure that such multi-screens are included in the list of required equipment (ICC Guidance Note, Checklist section E). The witnesses must be provided with an unmarked copy, no annotations, notes or mark-ups, of the agreed bundle of documents at the start of the examination of the witness (Seoul Protocol, Art. 4(2)).

Parties need to agree on whether real-time transcript or another form of recording, as well as live notes will be used, in which case and where practicable, to use a different screen than the one used for the videoconference. Procedures for the taking of evidence from fact witnesses and experts must also be agreed upon to ensure that the integrity of any oral testimonial evidence is preserved.

3.1.7 Model Procedural Orders

Finally, hugely useful model procedural orders are provided in various materials, such as in the CPR Model Annotated Model Procedural Order for Remote Video Arbitration Proceedings,[54] the Draft Zoom Hearing Procedural Order,[55] the Practical Law's Procedural Order for Video Conference Arbitration Hearings,[56] and the ICC Checklist for a Protocol on Virtual Hearings and Suggested Clauses for Cyber-Protocols and Procedural Orders Dealing with the Organisation of Virtual Hearings,[57] which serve as basis for discussion between the arbitrators and the parties. In the latter, in addition to issues to consider during the pre-hearing plan including scope and logistics, drafting is proposed and organised in four sections related to technical issues, specifications, requirements, and support staff; confidentiality, privacy, and security; online etiquette and due process considerations; and presentation of evidence and examination of witnesses and experts.

Useful checklists are made available and annexed to the CIArb Guidance Note, the VIAC Protocol, the African Academy Protocol, and the ICC Guidance Note.

---

54 CPR Model Annotated Model Procedural Order for Remote Video Arbitration Proceedings ("CPR PO").

55 *See* note 44, Stephanie Cohen, *Draft Zoom Hearing Procedural Order*, Transnational Dispute Management, April 2020.

56 Practical Law's Procedural Order for Video Conference Arbitration Hearings ("Practical Law PO").

57 ICC Checklist for a Protocol on Virtual Hearings and Suggested Clauses for Cyber-Protocols and Procedural Orders Dealing with the Organisation of Virtual Hearings, https://iccwbo.org/publication/icc-checklist-for-a-protocol-on-virtual-hearings-and-suggested-clauses-for-cyber-protocols-and-procedural-orders-dealing-with-the-organisation-of-virtual-hearings/.

3.2 Difficulties with Virtual Hearings

A few practitioners considered that preparation for online hearings may be more time consuming than hearings held in a physical location. This may be true considering that it could be harder to have a similar interaction between the members of a team present side by side at a hearing in a physical location and able to communicate.

Despite the evolution of the technology and the fact that many practitioners around the world have had the opportunity to use virtual hearings during the lockdown, some uncomfortable situations seem to indicate that remote hearings may not be suited to all circumstances and that there needs to be some adaptation; there are pros and cons to practically all situations.

A virtual setting may be considered as disproportionately unfair for one or several parties who do not benefit from the same technology capabilities and support that other parties enjoy. Access to technology and the necessary facilities are paramount to ensure an equality of arms and that all parties are in a position to present their case.

The lack of willingness to participate in a virtual hearing may not necessarily be due to the absence of cooperation of a party or several parties. Sometimes, the bandwidth connection of their location is not sufficient to hold a video conference during several hours. In addition, many computers may be connected and may thus slow down the connection for all persons present in such location.

Conciliating several time zones with significant difference is another example of difficulties that parties and arbitrators may be faced with. If a participant is joining at an uncomfortable hour for him or her, the efficiency of appearing might be limited. One way to remedy this impediment is to have some people travel to join one of the virtual spaces from which participants will connect, reducing thus the time zones.

Staying focused on a screen during several hours of hearings may be difficult. Moreover, there still needs to be adaptation with regard to the multiplicity of screens to see everyone in the virtual rooms and more specifically the witnesses during cross-examination.

The effectiveness of demonstratives produced at a virtual hearing may be limited when arbitrators cannot touch them or verify them by themselves.

As raised by a practitioner, how will 'the concern about real-time witness coaching' be addressed, and how will it be ensured 'that witnesses are sequestered where this is appropriate'?[58]

---

58 Janet Walker discusses whether virtual hearings can rise to the challenge, in *Virtual Hearings – The New Normal*, Global Arbitration Review, 27 March 2020, https://globalarbitrationreview.com/article/1222421/virtual-hearings-%E2%80%93-the-new-normal.

4 Conclusion

To conclude, the lockdown has given impetus to the use of technology in arbitration and to travelling other avenues. The way people now interact with technology has removed barriers which were difficult to remove before the outbreak. Practitioners have become more familiar with virtual meetings and hearings and will soon consider them as one of the techniques in their business toolkit to conduct proceedings more efficiently and expeditiously.

More importantly, the flexibility demonstrated by many practitioners is a positive game changer on which we need to build. Having addressed the lockdown with the resilience that people showed in general, should encourage us to develop different practices in a field that has proven to be constantly evolving and adapting to all situations and needs of the users. It is the ideal opportunity to revisit some of our current practices and streamline procedures.

The positive impact includes learning to work differently, saving time and costs on travelling, reducing the footprint generated by travelling and thus saving the environment, the climate change being at the centre of the world's preoccupation. Whereas the negative impact demonstrated by scientists concerns the isolation and the gap between the physical and the virtual, which have proven to be potentially detrimental to our mental health. We must necessarily strike a balance between the practical usefulness of virtual conferences and hearings, and the need for meeting in the same physical room and inter-acting in a more dynamic way.

We also learned to take more time for ourselves and our families, technology permitting to meet remotely without investing time in transportation, and rather using that time more efficiently. We are therefore unlikely to be willing to return to some practices which we now may consider as constraints that we are capable of overcoming by using other means to continue our activities.

Practitioners recognise in general the great opportunity offered to us to change some methods and continue improving.

Chapter 14 ODR and Negotiation

Michael Wolf

1 At the Intersection of ODR and Negotiation[1]

Negotiation is the heart and soul of most online dispute resolution (ODR) applications. At the intersection of negotiation and ODR lies a collection of skills, processes, and technology, the combination of which can be far more powerful than the sum of its parts.

This chapter begins with descriptive material about negotiation, appropriate dispute resolution (ADR), and ODR. Readers then gain greater insight into how ODR can boost the value derived from negotiations and ways that negotiators can use a diverse collection of ODR tools. This chapter concludes with a brief look at the origins of ODR in negotiations and a more in-depth examination of how we can carve a path toward future opportunities, albeit wrapped in real world challenges, together with ways some of the challenges might be addressed.

1.1 Negotiation

For purposes of this chapter, negotiation is a voluntary method people use to strategically engage each other about matters of mutual concern. Negotiators can engage before, during, and/or after the eruption of actual conflicts and specific disputes. Typically, successful negotiators create value by sharing information, networking, managing process, generating ideas, learning, identifying common ground, managing conflict over perceived differences, solving problems, resolving disputes, making decisions, reaching beneficial agreements, and determining viable next steps.

Based on this description, one might expect negotiations to proceed based on a uniform collection of principles and assumptions using a common set of steps and techniques. Experienced negotiators and third-party neutrals know that is not the case. For example, to some, the phrase 'traditional negotiations' describes a singular, easily understood pattern of distributive bargaining behaviors. Instead, 'traditional negotiations' merely reflects the particular traditions of the negotiators. Those who traditionally engage in distributive negotiations usually begin by identifying what they think is an ideal endpoint (their 'position'). They then craft proposals intended to achieve

1 The author has drawn from some of his prior published works when preparing this chapter. When doing so, the author generally did not cite himself except when he was joined by a co-author in a prior publication.

that endpoint and use bargaining power to seek an outcome as close as possible to that endpoint. Most often, for one party to win as much as possible, the other party must proportionally lose. As you might imagine, this win-lose, power-based, 'divide the pie' approach is associated with a significant risk for any party that highly values an ongoing working relationship.

In some parts of the world, a 'serious' traditional negotiator is someone who intends to be taken seriously. In other parts of the world, one traditional negotiator asking his or her counterpart whether they are 'serious' is really a request for a bribe in connection with their negotiation. These divergent traditions about what it means to be serious demonstrate potential pitfalls awaiting inexperienced 'traditional negotiators.'

Those who adopt what are perceived to be nontraditional styles of negotiation often adhere to divergent negotiation principles and assumptions in addition to engaging in different bargaining behaviors. For example, in contrast to distributive negotiators who define success by the extent to which they attain their predetermined positions, adherents to integrative bargaining models often measure success by the extent to which they satisfy joint and separate interests. An interest is an answer to the question, 'Why do you care so much about the issue you are negotiating?'

Distinctions between how negotiators measure success cause them to engage in different behaviors to achieve success. For example, successful integrative negotiators often engage more in collaborative behaviors than distributive negotiators and share more information with their counterparts about what they are trying to achieve. They also tend to seek solutions that lead to mutual gains rather than distributive win-lose outcomes. These distinctions have an impact on how negotiators might value the use of ODR tools and how they might use those tools.

1.2 ADR and Negotiation[2]

The intersection of *ODR* and negotiation is best understood in the context of *ADR* and negotiations.

ADR is defined as '*appropriate* dispute resolution' in the second paragraph of this chapter. Readers who are used to seeing ADR defined as '*alternative* dispute resolution' might have thought it was a typo. It was not. In litigious cultures like the U.S., the phrase '*alternative* dispute resolution' can imply that courts, administrative agencies, and other public sector adjudicative forums (hereafter, simply 'courts') should be the preferred, default mechanism to manage conflict and resolve disputes. By defining ADR as

2 For a brief treatment of the history of ADR in the U.S., *see* Michael McManus and Brianna Silverstein, *Brief History of Alternative Dispute Resolution in the United States* (November 2011), www.cadmusjournal.org/article/issue-3/brief-history-alternative-dispute-resolution-united-states.

'*appropriate* dispute resolution', we flip this on its head and view courts as a mechanism of last resort rather than the place to start.

Nevertheless, there are situations in which courts *can* be the preferred forum. For example, when one or both parties legitimately need a precedential or binding neutral opinion about a specific legal question. Or when a party perceives a need for public vindication or an all-or-nothing outcome. Or when public policy is best served by a public sector adjudication. Or when such factors matter far more than cost, speed, privacy, and relationship.

In most other situations, forums that do not result in public sector adjudication can be appropriate to consider first, especially when parties are willing to utilize a third-party neutral as they negotiate ways to manage conflict and resolve disputes. ADR is the umbrella term used to describe these '*appropriate* dispute resolution' forums, including:[3]

- **FACILITATION** – Someone with no stake in the outcome – the facilitator – helps participants accomplish goals by managing group process. They refrain from rendering opinions about the substance of the dispute. Facilitators provide structure, help participants develop and abide by ground rules, and remain focused. Facilitators also might manage discussion, group dynamics, conflict, communication, negotiation, problem solving, and the decision-making process.
- **CONFLICT COACHING** – Depending on the situation, a conflict coach confidentially helps coachees effectively engage in, manage, and/or resolve conflict. Because the conflict coach normally helps only one individual or entity be more successful in a conflict involving two or more disputants, the conflict coach is not a neutral participant. The conflict coach helps coachees clarify sources of conflict, the scope and nature of what might be addressed, interests, options, strategies, various negotiation skills and approaches, and possible consequences of alternate paths forwards.
- **ORGANIZATIONAL OMBUDS** – An organizational representative who investigates and tries to resolve complaints about that organization. When an investigation indicates that the problem resulted from a system failure, Ombuds might suggest reforms. When appropriate, Ombuds also might help a complainant see that the organization acted appropriately. Negotiation is one of many tools used by Ombuds.
- **CONCILIATION** – A neutral person tries to reduce tensions and improve disputant communication during negotiation to obtain a process agreement for resolving the dispute.
- **MEDIATION** – A third-party neutral helps disputants manage their negotiation process and achieve a mutually agreeable outcome. Mediators do not render

3 Source: Michael J. Wolf, Dispute Resolution Spectrum, https://prezi.com/dpp50exzeqvl/adr-related-odr-tools/. When reviewing this list, readers will notice the absence of some ADR tools, such as arbitration, which are more closely associated with litigation rather than negotiation.

decisions on the merits and many mediators refrain from even speculating about outcome.

- **FACT FINDING** – A third-party subject matter expert conducts an informal investigation and makes factual determinations. Sometimes, the fact finder helps parties use the determinations to negotiate a mutually agreeable outcome.
- **EARLY NEUTRAL EVALUATION** – Parties deliver an informal presentation of their best case to a third-party neutral. The ENE neutral normally responds with an expert evaluation of the relative merits and risks of each party's case and provides a non-binding, objective assessment that the parties can use to negotiate a constructive outcome.
- **SETTLEMENT CONFERENCE** – A third-party neutral, often a judge other than the presiding one, serves as a mediator or neutral evaluator in pending litigation. The settlement judge might offer an informal advisory opinion, after which the parties attempt to negotiate a settlement. If settlement is not reached, litigation usually continues before the presiding judge.
- **SUMMARY JURY TRIAL** – A highly structured presentation by litigation party representatives who offer a summary of their best case to a group that often thinks it is a real 'jury'. A third-party neutral (who the mock jury members usually think is the judge) serves as the process administrator and applies relaxed rules of evidence. After the 'hearing', the party representatives jointly debrief the mock jury, assess the relative strengths & weaknesses of their case and meet with the process administrator. The process administrator might be a subject matter expert, a mediator, or a retired judge who helps the parties negotiate a resolution to the matter.
- **MINI-TRIAL** – Party representatives present a summary of their best case directly to a panel composed of a third-party neutral and principals from each party. Relaxed rules of evidence apply, but unlike a summary trial, there is no mock jury. At the conclusion of the summary presentation, the third-party might express an expert view or advisory opinion. The third-party also might function as a mediator to help the other panel members negotiate a solution.
- **MED-ARB** – A third-party neutral first serves as a mediator to help parties negotiate a solution. If parties fail to achieve a complete solution, the third-party becomes an arbitrator (think 'private judge'). The third-party might seek additional evidence before rendering a decision, which is usually binding.
- **REG-NEG** – An alternative to traditional procedures that government agencies use to propose changes to rules and regulations. Reg-Neg brings together representatives of the agency and various stakeholders to negotiate the proposed changes.

This list is not all-inclusive. In addition, sophisticated negotiators and dispute resolution practitioners modify and blend aspects of these ADR tools to create hybrids to best meet the participants' specific, case-related needs.

Those who design, develop, and deliver expert ADR services must consciously consider the critical distinctions between various traditional and non-traditional negotiation styles. Negotiators generally expect ADR providers to help them manage risk by adapting to the negotiators' preferred bargaining styles, definitions of success, and methods. Quite often, third-party neutrals must design, develop, and deliver conflict management processes and dispute resolution services to minimize adverse impact on parties' long-term bargaining relationships. These are all considerations when third parties help negotiators integrate ODR tools into their bargaining process.

1.3 ODR and Negotiation

To summarize the preceding discussion, negotiation is how people strategically engage each other about matters of mutual concern. ADR is a set of process tools that third-party neutrals use to help negotiators be more successful. These core concepts frame the way that ODR is described in this chapter.

ODR is a set of technology tools and techniques that negotiators use to be more successful and that third-party neutrals use to be more effective helping negotiators be more successful. Put another way, ODR is a label applied to a collection of software, online services, and interactive technology-related processes that enhance negotiators' ability to be successful by minimizing barriers such as time, place, cost, and process. One way to understand ODR tools is to group them in three buckets: function driven, process derived, and process driven.[4]

Function-driven ODR tools help negotiators and third-party neutrals perform specific, essential functions of their roles. Negotiators can use function-driven ODR tools to convey information, generate and assess options, make a proposal, summarize information, see a remote participant, express preferences, interact, caucus with a remote team member, collaborate, perform administrative tasks, etc. If a third-party joins the negotiations, function-driven ODR tools can help that person perform her or his role as well, such as establishing groups, assigning rights and privileges, encouraging or discouraging certain behavior, etc.

Process-derived ODR tools enable participants to move through a negotiation process in a logical, often pre-defined, yet flexible manner. A third-party neutral can join the process at an appropriate time and use the process-derived ODR tool to mimic basic ADR models.

Some function-driven and process-derived ODR tools are sufficiently complex to require someone other than the negotiators and third-parties to configure and

4 *See* Daniel Rainey, *Culture of the Code* (March 2009), www.mediate.com/articles/culture_in_code.cfm.

administer them. Observing the use of both function driven and process derived applications makes it easy to see how Katsh and Rifkin's 'fourth party' concept[5] works – the ODR tool becomes an entity, a virtual fourth party at the table, with which negotiators must engage.

Process-Driven ODR tools were the subject of NSF-funded research by University of Massachusetts-Amherst and the ADR team leader at the U.S. National Mediation Board. Well-designed process-driven ODR tools present users with only those options that are appropriate for the stage of the process in which negotiators find themselves. For example, if information should be shared across the table at a certain stage of the process, a process-driven ODR tool might prompt the negotiator to consider sharing information. Or if it is best practice during brainstorming to make no judgements about others' ideas, a process-driven ODR tool would not present negotiators with the option to make online comments.

The practical implications of developing process-driven ODR applications is significant. Using the Katsh and Rifkin fourth party concept again, if the application is driven by a process model, the negotiators and third-party neutral spend less time and energy administering the fourth party (the software or online service) and more time interacting with each other. There would be fewer process choices to make, less software administration to manage, and fewer chances to make unwitting choices with unintended adverse consequences. Process-driven ODR tools offer a way to build in the parties' process requirements at the time the software and online services are designed. This can result in ODR tools that keep intact the essence of the negotiation process while adding value to the outcome. If successful, process-driven applications can make the fourth party a much less volatile and risky influence on negotiations.

The most important distinguishing feature of ODR is the way that negotiators and third-party neutrals use the software, online services, and technology-related processes. This makes ODR a rapidly evolving concept with fuzzy edges. Due to the variety of traditional and non-traditional negotiation styles, the multitude of ADR methods, and the rapidly evolving world of technology, the number and complexity of intersections between ODR and negotiation continues to grow at a dizzying pace. Today, negotiators can use ODR tools to schedule interactions,[6] generate and organize ideas,[7] safeguard and

---

5 *Cf.*, Janet Rifkin, *Online Dispute Resolution: Theory and Practice of the Fourth Party*, 19 Confl. Resolut. Q. 1 (Winter 2001), at 117-124. https://onlinelibrary.wiley.com/doi/abs/10.1002/crq.3890190109.

6 *E.g.*, with Doodle (www.doodle.com), a user can select available dates and times and then use email to send out a link that recipients use to identify their availability. The sender then selects the best date/time for everyone and sends out a notice with a calendar invite.
Note: Software and online services mentioned in this chapter usually represent only one of many similar products in the commercial marketplace at the time this chapter was written. Most such products are superseded by superior options over time as needs evolve, technology improves, and the marketplace matures.

7 *E.g.*, using FacilitatePro (www.facilitate.com) and ThinkTank (www.groupsystems.com/).

share files,[8] share screens, solve problems, offer and respond to proposals, work toward agreements, make decisions, manage implementation, manage relationships, survey constituents and stakeholders,[9] and engage remotely using video,[10] audio,[11] and data conferencing.[12] This list is far from inclusive, and it will continue to expand in response to evolving goals and barriers inherent to negotiations.

Some of what is commonly referred to as ODR consists of commercial, off-the-shelf software and online services. Other times, ODR tools are specifically developed to enhance a particular type of negotiation, conflict management, or dispute resolution. Experienced practitioners understand the term ODR to even include technology-enabled in-person processes during which negotiators are *not* using the Internet and therefore not technically 'online'.

One size certainly does not fit all! ODR is often, but not always, interactive. It can help enable collaboration among negotiators who are ready for a cooperative process. Best practice is to insert ODR technology only to the extent and in a way that is likely to enable negotiators to gain greater value from the engagement. For example, consider two people on opposite sides of the Atlantic who have an eBay dispute over a sweater not delivered in time for a birthday. These two people probably will have different ODR needs than 5,000 disbursed stakeholders to a boundary waters environmental matter straddling the Minnesota-Canadian border. Disputants in several million eBay-type commercial disputes might benefit most from custom-designed, technology-centered ODR that enables asynchronous remote negotiation while minimizing transaction costs and human interaction. In contrast, stakeholders to a complex environmental matter might benefit more from an integration of off-the-shelf, human-centered ODR tools that enable a combination of multiparty face-to-face and remote negotiations despite its higher transaction costs and likely need for extensive human interaction.

One important takeaway is that negotiators and third-party neutrals should avoid getting too attached to any particular ODR tool, regardless of how amazing it might seem today. The speed of evolution in software and online services will continue to escalate, rapidly replacing the latest and greatest in the contemporary marketplace. Focus should remain on the functional criteria that cause ODR tools to add value to the process and outcome of negotiation. ODR is really about how to use appropriate the technology and related techniques to become more successful performing the core functions of a negotiator and third-party neutral. That is the focus of the next section.

---

8 *E.g.*, using Dropbox (www.dropbox.com), Microsoft OneDrive (https://onedrive.live.com/), and Google Drive (https://drive.google.com).

9 *E.g.*, using SurveyMonkey (www.surveymonkey.com).

10 *E.g.*, using Cisco's WebEx (www.webex.com), Zoom (www.zoom.us), Google's Duo (https://duo.google.com/), Microsoft's Teams (https://teams.microsoft.com/_),and a plethora of similar online services.

11 *E.g.*, using Skype (www.skype.com).

12 *E.g.*, using LogMeIn's Join.Me (www.Join.me).

2 WHY AND WHEN TO CONSIDER USING ODR IN NEGOTIATIONS

Like any powerful tool, we should only pull ODR out of our toolbox when it is best tool for the job. Generally, consider introducing technology to the negotiation/ADR mix when it (1) appears likely to add meaningful value to the parties' process and/or outcome and (2) is *highly* unlikely to do harm.

Different types of negotiations have distinctive characteristics for which ODR might add net value. When considering whether to use ODR in a particular type of negotiation process, the first and most comfortable approach is to use technology tools that mirror techniques and processes which are common in face-to-face negotiation.

Distributive negotiators might imagine using technology to develop better positions, deliver better proposals, exercise more bargaining power, win more (and cause others to lose more), etc. Interest-based negotiators might imagine using technology to more efficiently identify issues and interests, do a better job sharing interest information, collaboratively generate a better collection of options, work with their counterparts to rate and rank those options, achieve stronger consensus, attain better outcomes, and map a more efficient path toward successful implementation.

Time, place, cost, process, and outcome using ODR in Negotiations. Negotiators' skills and best practices, even when combined with expert ADR, do not always enable negotiators to overcome problems inherent in almost all negotiations: time, place, cost, process, and their impact on outcome. ODR tools are valuable when they help bridge these gaps in ways that improve negotiated outcomes by increasing the likelihood of achieving meaningful results while reducing significant risks and maintaining important relationships. Well-designed ODR tools also can improve the process of negotiation by enhancing in-person and remote participation while addressing legitimate concerns about privacy and security, access and control, reliability, ease of use, speed, and affordability.

What would you include in a photo of people negotiating? Many of us would imagine two or more people sitting face-to-face at a table.[13] ADR has been thoroughly integrated into that paradigm. Yet as domestic and global organizations consolidate and migrate, problem solvers and key decisionmakers often find themselves far removed from a physical table around which they are asked to sit. The recent Covid-19 pandemic has become another barrier to face-to-face negotiation. Even before the pandemic created a new normal, enhanced private sector competition and scarcity of public sector resources required organizations to run leaner, sometimes working multiple shifts in multiple geographic locations to maintain competitive status in the global marketplace. And the

---

13 This portion is adapted from Michael J. Wolf, Jon Numair, and Jack Yoedt, *Essential Collaborative Technology Tools for the 21st Century: FMCS TAGS System*, 2 Pepp. Disp. Resol. L.J. Iss. 3 (2002), https://digitalcommons.pepperdine.edu/drlj/vol2/iss3/2.

global marketplace means that manufacturers, suppliers, distributors, retailers, and consumers often are a world apart from each other.

ODR creates opportunities for negotiators to work in all four quadrants of the time-place relationship: (1) same-time/same place, (2) same-time/different-place (including multi-location modalities), (3) different-time/same-place, and even (4) different-time/different place. ODR can offer solutions for a variety of time and place issues as well as associated challenges of scheduling negotiations and negotiators.

Another reason to consider using ODR is its potential to mitigate the financial cost of negotiations. These costs can be substantial, especially for organizational and institutional parties. Consider the out-of-pocket costs of an in-person, multi-day session involving negotiators from several locations: airfare, hotel, ground transportation, food, incidentals, meeting room rental, coffee, and snack service. Less visible but potentially far more costly, especially for workplace and business negotiations, is participant compensation and the productivity-related cost of lost opportunity. Add to that the cost of inviting a third-party neutral to the table. Out-of-pocket costs associated with that person normally are paid for by the negotiators, their principals, or sometimes taxpayers.

ODR tools can minimize financial costs by enabling negotiators to remotely engage each other. ODR tools can enable a negotiator to engage others at a time that is most convenient for that negotiator (asynchronously) rather than require engagement only at a common time (synchronously). ODR tools can minimize financial costs by minimizing or eliminating the need to travel, enabling negotiators to attend to other critical matters, and completing some or all their work more efficiently with less wasted time and less lost opportunity. As a result, a time-place cost-benefit analysis of ODR might intrigue even the most skeptical negotiator.

If not handled well, negotiations can impair critical relationships with customers, coworkers, employees, neighbors, and other stakeholders. Resulting lost productivity and lost opportunity can be costly yet difficult to directly measure. There is ample anecdotal evidence that appropriate use of ODR tools can make a substantial, positive difference concerning these factors.

ODR and synchronous, in-person negotiations. Negotiators sometimes express concern that using ODR might cause them to lose the benefits of in-person negotiations. Such benefits should not be underestimated or undervalued. Nor should the significant process barriers that typically accompany in-person negotiations.

For example, even when negotiators are face-to-face, objectives are oftentimes unclear. The 'right people' might not be present. Certain participants tend to talk a lot when in fact there is little value in what they say. Other negotiators might possess a critical element of the solution but not offer it in-person because they are conflict adverse or have other legitimate reasons for not actively participating in face-to-face engagements. Some negotiators attack each other rather than the problem. Even worse than bad process, many negotiations have no discernible process whatsoever. Negotiators often do not actively listen to one another, they talk for the wrong reasons, and fail to follow through on promised actions. Session documents tend to be issued late (if at all) and sometimes fail to accurately reflect the content.

The dynamics of synchronous, in-person negotiations can become extraordinarily complex in multiparty disputes as well as in multifaceted disputes, multicultural disputes, and multilingual disputes. Appropriate inclusion of special needs participants can introduce yet another type of challenge. Elements identified in this paragraph and earlier in this section often do not exist in isolation. The combination of such confounding dynamics during negotiation can be almost insurmountable without the application of best practices, exquisite skills, and appropriate resources, including the software and services collectively referred to as ODR.

Evaluation apprehension and production blocking are serious process barriers during in-person negotiations. For example, employee Joe is about to enter a meeting with his boss Mary. Just before they walk into the conference room together, Joe tells Mary about a great idea that he wants to offer the group. As they cross the threshold, Mary's reply is brief, 'We can't do that.' Ten minutes later, a wonderful facilitator stands at the flip chart and asks the group to begin brainstorming their best ideas. Joe might wonder about his job security and hesitate to offer his 'great' idea to the group. This is referred to as evaluation apprehension.

Production blocking is an equally debilitating process barrier during in-person negotiations. Trainers are fond of saying that the best ideas occur at the fringe. Yet few people want to be perceived as being at the fringe. People want to be respected for their ideas, but most also want to be liked and respected by their peers. Peers often ostracize those who are perceived as being at the fringe. Someone who is concerned about smirks and chuckles is not as likely to offer out-of-the-box ideas. This is called production blocking and, like evaluation apprehension, can cause even the best ideas to lay dormant.

There are good reasons to generally prefer a synchronous, in-person format for negotiations. There also are good reasons to be cautious about the accompanying process barriers and explore whether appropriate use of ODR tools might achieve superior process and outcomes. Certain ODR tools can be used to specifically prevent these types of process barriers from arising, and to overcome those that do arise both in-person and during remote negotiations.

ODR and negotiating on behalf of an organization. Individuals who negotiate on their own behalf might be the primary stakeholders in the outcome of their negotiation. Compare this to negotiators who primarily serve in a representative capacity on behalf of an organization. In the latter case, negotiators might be negotiating on behalf of others who serve in a leadership capacity of their organization and consider themselves to be among the primary stakeholders. The negotiators might have an interest in how ODR impacts time, place, and process, but organizational leaders, and sometimes their constituents, might have a stronger interest in factors like cost and outcome. These distinctions can bend and blur. For example, when the negotiator is expected to bear some of the transaction costs, like U.S. lawyers in personal injury cases. This can result in a complex allocation of interests between negotiators and organizational stakeholders when considering whether and when to use ODR.

ODR and negotiating broad-impact matters. At times, individuals and organizations are significantly impacted by negotiations yet they are not active participants in the process and are not directly represented by active negotiators. An example would be a hypothetical neighborhood organization negotiating with a refinery over a groundwater pollution environmental dispute. ODR tools might offer negotiators the only viable, cost-effective way to become aware of and attend to key interests of residents, others who live nearby, lenders, builders, insurers, suppliers, municipalities, and health care facilities. In fact, using ODR in such negotiations might be the best way to satisfy negotiators' moral and ethical obligations to properly represent the interests of key stakeholders. Similar complexity in stakeholder analysis can apply to regulatory negotiations (often referred to as 'reg-neg'), class action settlements, organizational strategic planning processes, and a virtually unlimited number of other situations in which negotiators' choice of whether and how to use ODR can impact a broad range of stakeholder key interests.

Private sector, public sector, and hybrid ODR providers. Why and when to use ODR is not always a case-by-case determination. Before 1999, eBay customers had few if any viable options to resolve disputes in connection with buying and selling merchandise through eBay. Since that time, ODR has been the only viable option available to most eBay customers.[14] For most eBay users, the only question has been whether to pursue a complaint about an eBay transaction. If they pursue the complaint, they generally must use the eBay online Resolution Center. As of 2016, eBay was using ODR to handle 60 million disputes per year.[15]

ODR has slowly been adopted by public sector institutions such as courts, government agencies, and certain membership organizations like state bar associations acting under

14 *See* discussion later in this chapter starting at note 96 below.

15 *ODR Platforms: eBay Resolution Center* (14 April 2016), ODR 2016, The 15th ODR Conference, 23-24 May 2016, The Hague, https://20160dr.wordpress.com/2016/04/14/odr-platforms-ebay-resolution-center/.

the umbrella of government oversight.[16] The question of why and when to consider using ODR to negotiate resolution of disputes pending before public sector institutions implicates interests of not only the parties to the dispute, but also the public sector entity itself and the public-at-large. Cost to the taxpayer might be one such consideration that concerns the public-at-large. Efficiencies created by the appropriate use of ODR might be a consideration that concerns the public sector entity before which the dispute is pending. Another important interest is the ODR tool's effectiveness at resolving disputes that otherwise would require additional public sector resources. An especially critical interest is whether ODR is being used in a way that helps process and outcomes be perceived as fair and just, thereby helping the legal system be trusted as a justice system.

The legitimate interests of private and public sector ODR providers in cost, efficiency, and effectiveness[17] can at times compete with legitimate interests of disputants who use the ODR tools. Especially when disputants have few if any viable options but to use ODR, transparency and public interest standards should govern the determination of whether and when disputants are asked to consider using ODR to negotiate resolution of their disputes.

Difficult and consequential determinations to use ODR. When the decision about whether to use ODR and what specific ODR tool is particularly difficult and consequential, consider adopting an analytical tool that evolved from recommendations offered by the late Frank E.A. Sander,[18] professor emeritus and Associate Dean of Harvard Law School. Sander and his frequent writing partner, Professor Stephen Goldberg, recommended a rigorous, multi-part analysis for ADR that can be adapted to the use of ODR in negotiations.[19] First, ask what considerations might inform the determination of the negotiators:

---

16 ODR in the courts is ably treated in another chapter of this book. Also *see Travis County Uses ODR to Fight Traffic on the Roads and in the Court*, www.tylertech.com/resources/case-studies/travis-county-uses-odr-to-fight-traffic-on-the-roads-and-in-the-court; Amy J. Schmitz, *Expanding Access to Remedies through E-Court Initiatives*, 67 Buff. L. Rev. 89 (2019), https://digitalcommons.law.buffalo.edu/buffalolawreview/vol67/iss1/3; *ODR for Courts,* JTC Resource Bulletin, Version 2.0 (29 November 2017), https://www.ncsc.org/__data/assets/pdf_file/0031/18499/2017-12-18-odr-for-courts-v2-final.pdf; *Case Studies in ODR for Courts*, JTC Resource Bulletin, Version 2.0 (Jan. 28, 2020), https://courttechbulletin.blogspot.com/2020/03/jtc-resource-bulletin-case-studies-in.html; and resources listed at www.ncsc.org/odr.

17 These are just a few of the foremost considerations when implementing ODR tools to enable negotiated solutions in court-connected disputes. Other publications contain a broader sample of considerations, such as *Considerations in Implementing Court ODR Systems* v.1, Michigan Supreme Court, State Court Administrators Office, Office of Dispute Resolution (6 January 2020), https://courts.michigan.gov/Administration/SCAO/OfficesPrograms/ODR/Documents/Resources/ODRConsiderations.pdf.

18 http://franksander.com/.

19 Frank E.A. Sander and Stephen B. Goldberg, *Fitting the Forum to the Fuss: A User-Friendly Guide to Selecting an ADR Procedure*, 10 Negot. J. 49, Program on Negotiation, Harvard Law School (January 1994), https://doi.org/10.1111/j.1571-9979.1994.tb00005.x.

- Subject matter
- Value attributed to the potential outcome (financial and otherwise)
- Environmental factors (human, physical, historical, cultural, etc.)
- Source of recommendation (principal, agent, other)
- The other negotiator(s) – identity, perceived behavior, skills, and desired behavior
- Timing
- Other

Second, ask what goals the negotiators are trying to achieve. For example,

Speed – Resolve quickly or delay the inevitable	Achieve something important and/or prevent other from doing so
Cost – Minimize or cause other to incur	Recovery – maximize own or minimize other's
Increase/decrease access to negotiated solutions	Vindication critical?
Transparency and information – promote and share, or maintain privacy	Future behavior – encourage or discourage
Relationships – improve, maintain, or inconsequential	Compliance – encourage or avoid
Constituencies – engage or not	Power imbalance – manage?
Interests (integrative) or rights & obligations (distributive) – preferred approach	Neutral opinion or decision – get or avoid (and why)
Focus of attack – focus on the problem or the person	Precedent – set or avoid (and why)

Third, ask what barriers might prevent negotiators from achieving their primary goals. For example,

Geographic separation of negotiators and/or principals	Unresolved question of fact or law – preventing resolution?
Negotiators' time zones and time of availability	Important principle at stake?
Financial cost of various face-to-face and remote options	Constituent resistance?
Based on relevant considerations and goals, what process alternatives are most likely to achieve goals?	Dispute between negotiator and principal?
Communication – ineffective so far?	Expect 'all or none' outcome
Strong emotions – getting in the way?	

Assign numerical values to the relevant factors, e.g., 0, 1, 2, or 3. Then thoughtfully distinguish and rate each relevant factor and rank the assessed factors based on the ratings. In general, use only the highest rated factors to determine whether to use ODR tools concerning the matter at hand.

If ODR appears worth exploring, the next step is to decide which ODR tool(s) might add the greatest value to the negotiations. This would be far easier if there was one trusted repository of information about ODR characteristics and a group of trusted, dispassionate experts who could inform negotiators about which ODR tools best satisfy the needs identified by applying the aforementioned assessment process. Hopefully, such resource people will exist in the future. Until then, negotiators can identify characteristics from the following list that might address the key goals and barriers identified above. Negotiators can then work with a trusted advisor to explore the best ODR options.

ODR Assessment Criteria – Consider the characteristics of ODR tools that might create value for negotiators.

Engage with other negotiators - Remotely &/or in-person - In real time &/or at their time	Sufficiently private & secure
Collaborate with teammates	Control over settings & risk characteristics
Supports integrative &/or distributive styles - Transmit proposals & counterproposals - Identify & clarify issues - Identify & share interests - Generate & manage ideas & options - Organize, categorize, prioritize, & align content	Enables appropriate remote participation
Electronic charting & mind mapping	Reduces risk of loss
Securely manage & appropriately share resources	Reliable
Build & maintain records	Transparency of process
Build & document agreements	Integration with other technology & negotiators' existing process
Draft, edit, view & electronically sign agreements	Low learning curve (practitioner + parties)
Accessible	Low transaction cost
Affordable	Negotiators can learn, practice, partner, share, mentor, assess
Can help overcome one or more process barriers	Consistent with negotiators' professional responsibility
Can help maintain/improve relationship issue	Other

3 How Negotiators Use ODR

The field of ODR is relatively young yet continues to grow and mature at an ever-accelerating pace. The commercial tools referenced in this article are likely to change dramatically in a brief period of time. Some will be upgraded, others discontinued, and new innovations will sweep old ideas aside before they even become old. Today's most prominent ODR software and services will become tomorrow's afterthoughts. ODR tools that negotiators adopt several years from now might not include any of the online services identified in this section.

As a result, this chapter does not attempt to catalogue or evaluate the universe of contemporary ODR tool used by negotiators. Readers of this chapter will gain more value from focusing on the types of tools available and ways that they can add the most value to negotiations. Specific software and online services are mentioned as examples without any intent to recommend one over another.

3.1 *First, Some Security Recommendations*

Negotiators should be especially mindful of security when working online. Jeff Greene, director of the National Cybersecurity Center of Excellence at the National Institute of Standards and Technology (NIST), recommends[20] limiting the reuse of access codes, use one-time PINs or meeting identifier codes, and consider multi-factor authentication. For synchronous online sessions, Greene suggests using a 'green room' and auto-notification, which is like ringing a virtual doorbell requesting permission to enter the online meeting space; allowing sessions to begin only after the host(s) joins; identifying and monitoring all attendees; disabling unneeded software features; and only recording the session if necessary [and with everyone's permission].[21]

In addition to the NIST guidance, negotiators should consider whether they need an ODR tool that can enable end-to-end encryption and encrypted recordings; 'locks' an online workspace's virtual door after everyone has entered; and performs other important security tasks. Negotiators also should be mindful of nation(s) in which their online data might be stored and the sources of legal, administrative, and contractual authority governing their online workspace. Some stark differences exist between Europe, the Americas, and elsewhere.

Negotiators should thoroughly examine, learn, configure, and test online services' security settings whenever possible. Especially before negotiating extremely sensitive matters, each negotiator should ensure that their operating system, mobile equipment,

20 Preventing Eavesdropping and Protecting Privacy on Virtual Meetings, www.nist.gov/blogs/cybersecurity-insights/preventing-eavesdropping-and-protecting-privacy-virtual-meetings (17 March 2020).

21 *Ibid.*

all applications, and any virtual private networks (VPNs) are updated and patched.[22] Beware of scams, disinformation campaigns, and phishing attacks! Test, test, and then test remote access scenarios before going 'live'. See the CISA document cited in the previous footnote for additional recommendations applicable to organizations and individuals.

Two final thoughts about security. First, security characteristics of hosted services often change in response to attempted hackers. Even negotiators who are comfortable with technology should consider periodically consulting with a reliable IT security expert about best ways to secure hosted services used as ODR negotiation tools.

Second, most negotiators should try to be a bit relaxed about security at the same time they use common sense and appropriate vigilance when working online. A lot of communication between negotiators is not particularly sensitive and it is often of little interest to potential hackers. Experienced hackers might have an easier time stealing sensitive information from an email account, cellphones, and cloud storage sites than surreptitiously eavesdropping on a live videoconference, especially if negotiators familiarize themselves with their ODR tools and heed best practice guidance.

3.2 How Negotiators Use Online Workspaces

The Internet is filled with online workspaces that were not designed specifically as ODR tools, yet negotiators can use them to perform one or more functions listed above. Creative negotiators can use online workspaces to initiate negotiations or trigger an ADR process, collect and exchange submissions and responses, pay fees, upload and securely share files, and use threaded discussion tools to engage in joint and separate sessions. One of the best features of the most popular online workspaces is ease of use (which might be why they become popular!). Negotiators and third-party neutrals can even carve out secure online workspace to store their notes, time and billing records, and confidential materials. An experienced negotiator or ADR practitioner can manage multiple matters in separate, clearly marked online workspaces and use a common set of templates, calendars, task lists, etc., across all workspaces.

Developers might offer their online workspace as a 'collaboration tool'. That can be an attractive term if the negotiators can envision collaborating with each other. But many negotiators might be put off by the term 'collaboration' and instead want an ODR tool designed for 'dispute resolution' or 'complaint handling'. Little if anything might distinguish online *dispute resolution* from online *collaboration* or online *complaint handling*. But negotiators who perceive themselves as combatants or gladiators will

22 *CISA Insights Risk Management for Novel Coronavirus*, The U.S. Cybersecurity and Infrastructure Security Agency (6 March 2020), https://assets.documentcloud.org/documents/6798491/CISA-Insights-Risk-Management-for-Novel.pdf.

prefer one label while other negotiators will utilize a different lens and different language. Trained leaders and professional negotiators are likely to understand that the real challenge is how to *end* the battle rather than how to continue engaging in a costly process that too often results 'success' being defined by how much the other side loses rather than how much either party wins. Real leaders understand that wars generally do not end by firing one more figurative bullet. Wars, like other conflicts, almost always end through negotiations.

From the standpoint of a negotiator or ADR practitioner looking for a useful ODR tool, the process environment for online *collaboration* is often virtually identical to that of online *dispute resolution* or online *complaint handling*. The primary difference usually is labels. In fact, early adopters of ODR tools discovered that online collaboration services can be configured to function as effective online dispute resolution tools and online complaint handling tools. Negotiators can use online collaboration services such as FacilitatePro,[23] iMeetCentral,[24] WebEx Teams,[25] and eRoom[26] to initiate online negotiations, collect and exchange party submissions and responses, upload and securely share documents, and engage in virtual caucuses and joint sessions using text-based threaded discussion tools.

As of this writing, Skype[27] and Teams[28] are Microsoft's dominant online collaboration solutions. Slack[29] is Team's primary competitor and it is preferred by many.[30] Both Slack and Microsoft Teams combine instant messaging, screen sharing, video conferencing, audio/video calling, file storage, and document collaboration into a single, integrated app that negotiators can use to prepare settlement agreements. Slack and Teams both try to seamlessly integrate as many other online tools as possible into their platforms. That way, users can adopt one platform as home base for their online presence and, with a click, utilize other online tools in a common or familiar interface. This can be useful for ODR negotiators and third-party neutrals who want to develop a rich, persistent, online workspace for multiple online negotiations.

A sophisticated negotiator or ADR practitioner with proper training and experience can customize an online workspace to be accessible, secure, simple, functional, and appropriate to the dispute at hand. Unfortunately, such negotiators and ADR

---

23 *See* FacilitatePro at www.facilitate.com.

24 *See* iMeetCentral (formerly Central Desktop) at https://imeetcentral.com/.

25 *See* WebEx Teams at www.webex.com/team-collaboration.html.

26 *See* eRoom at www.opentext.com/products-and-solutions/products/enterprise-content-management/documentum-platform/documentum-eroom.

27 In a pinch, negotiators can use Skype on just about any device to freely transmit files containing settlement language while simultaneously using Skype's free audio and video calling features to ensuring that the deal is understood, agreed and final. Skype is a peer-to-peer service, so file transmission can be more secure than e-mail.

28 https://products.office.com/microsoft-teams/group-chat-software.

29 https://slack.com/.

30 For a 2020 comparison, *see* www.chanty.com/blog/slack-vs-microsoft-teams/.

practitioners remain rare in today's marketplace, which is a barrier to more rapid adoption of these types of online workspaces for use as ODR tools.

3.3 *How Negotiators Use Visual and Double-Blind Bidding*

Suppose Tom Tennant believes that Linda Landlord improperly withheld part of his security deposit. A brief visit to a lawyer provided Tenant with some useful information. He learned what might be a reasonable range of recovery, and that no lawyer would find it worthwhile to represent him. However, in this hypothetical, Landlord participates in a property owners' association that licenses Smartsettle One.[31] Tenant clicks the Smartsettle One link on the association website, creates credentials to open a new case, and reviews the standard agreement form in which only a dollar amount must be entered. Tenant dons his negotiator cap, enters an initial demand, and enters his 'hidden walkaway', i.e., the lowest amount Tenant would take to resolve the matter.

By email, Landlord receives notice of the dispute and a link to login and respond. Landlord sees Tenant's demand, but not Tenant's hidden walkaway, which always remains confidential. Landlord agrees to negotiate with Tenant, enters an optimistic counteroffer and also enters a hidden walkaway that reflects the maximum she is willing to pay to resolve the matter. Tenant receives an email with a link to review Landlord's counter. Tenant responds by reducing his demand to a number that Landlord will never see, but which would result in a binding settlement if it overlaps Landlord's counter. It did not. Landlord receives an email notice and logs in a second time, enters a more realistic counteroffer, and in fact it overlaps Tenant's reduced demand. Case settled! Without any human intervention, the parties have used this ODR tool to negotiate a resolution to the dispute.

Smartsettle One was designed using an algorithm that capitalizes on the 'maximin' game theory. It presumes that each disputant's problem-solving behavior is driven by a singular desire to maximize his or her minimum gain. That might be a reasonable assumption about negotiators who have narrow bargaining boundaries, are well informed, and understand their level of risk and uncertainty. Especially for negotiators who both know that they possess a relatively unattractive BATNA[32] and maybe an ominous WATNA,[33] an online service built on a maximin game theory algorithm can be extremely valuable. Arguably, it is less useful in complex matters where negotiators have multiple and possibly competing goals, or where they are not well informed, have an attractive BATNA, or an inconsequential WATNA.

31 https://smartsettle.com/.
32 BATNA is an acronym for "Best Alternative to a Negotiated Agreement."
33 WATNA is an acronym for "Worst Alternative to a Negotiated Agreement."

Now imagine a scenario where 'Isabel' is injured while a passenger in an acquaintance's car. Isabel has $5,000.00 in medical bills (so far) and expects more.[34] The driver's insurance policy covers up to $15,000 for bodily injury but the carrier has not returned Isabel's phone calls. Isabel is not a lawyer, she has no experience with such matters, and she has no idea how to pursue a claim against an insurance carrier.

No lawyer seems interested in Isabel's case, so she asks the court clerk for advice. The clerk quietly suggests that Isabel negotiate a settlement with the insurance carrier. The clerk scrawls a web address on a scrap of paper and hands it to Isabel.

Isabel goes home and enters the web address in her browser. She learns that she and the carrier can submit up to three double-blind bids through this website and settle if any pair of bids 'cross', i.e., a demand and an offer are within a specified percentage or dollar amount of each other. The website explains that only the party submitting each bid will know the amount of a bid unless the parties settle or authorize disclosure for the purpose of negotiating a deal. Isabel also learns that, for an extra fee, a neutral facilitator can help the parties negotiate an agreement. To Isabel's amazement, she incurs no cost unless the case settles or unless the parties retain a facilitator.[35]

Isabel follows the simple online instructions and waits. Shortly thereafter, an e-mail informs her that the insurance carrier agreed to try the online service. Isabel securely logs into the website and demands the policy limits – $15,000. The carrier knows the policy limits (of course), but not the amount of Isabel's demand. The carrier offers $3,000. The website automatically notifies Isabel that their bids did not 'cross' or match, and it is time for Round 2. Isabel demands $12,000; the carrier offers $5,000. Once again, the website automatically notifies Isabel that their bids did not 'cross' or match and it is time for Round 3. Isabel's final demand is $8,000; the carrier's final offer is $9,000.

The website algorithm again compares each submission. This time Isabel and the carrier receive a notice that they reached a settlement for the amount of Isabel's final demand ($8,000). Isabel's $200 fee to the website host is based on the amount of the settlement.

This type of double-blind bidding tool can be valuable for at least a narrow slice of ODR negotiators and should be considered in appropriate matters.

---

34 Based on a scenario posted on a blog that is no longer accessible when last checked on 26 April 2020 at 10:13 PM ET. www.negotiationlawblog.com/2007/08/articles/conflict-resolution/man-vs-machine-automated-online-negotiated-settlements/.

35 That might not be the case for all vendors, but it appears to be CyberSettle's business model. *See* www.cybersettle.com.

3.4 *How Negotiators Use Full Service ODR Workspaces*

Imagine an ideal full service ODR platform. It would be a one-size-fits-all solution from cradle-to-grave of every possible negotiable matter. It has a shallow learning curve, no cost-barriers to entry, no language barriers, minimal technical requirements, and minimal support requirements. It is ubiquitous online and in person. It is safe, secure, and intuitive. It seamlessly guides negotiators when needed, and it is guided by negotiators when appropriate. Third parties like mediators, facilitators, arbitrators, and fact finders enter and exit when needed. Its functions include initiation, scheduling, billing, payment, video, text, audio, integrative/collaborative modalities, and distributive/conflictive modalities. It minimizes the need for costly administrators and tech support. Artificial Intelligence (AI) enables it to automatically adapt to process requirements of single-party, multi-party, one-on-one, and team engagements. It automatically morphs from interpersonal to intra-organizational to interorganizational to international matters. It senses and adapts to cultural elements that can cause negotiations to fail. Above all, it does no harm.

Such an idealized ODR tool does not exist ... yet. Nor is it likely to exist in the near future. But more than a few developers have tried to create full service ODR platforms targeted to a broad segment of the marketplace. It would be unfair to apply simplistic terms such as 'success' or 'failure' to these efforts. For their moment in time, and for their market segment, several are worth noting.

Juripax, developed by siblings then living in the Netherlands and Germany, offered negotiators and third parties online dispute resolution environments. Juripax was a leader among several online service providers that, for a relatively small fee,[36] enabled users to create secure workspaces in the Cloud. Juripax permitted customization of the online workspace by applying modules for divorce, employment, e-commerce, and small claims. Each negotiator began by establishing an account, electronically signing an agreement to engage, and using asynchronous tools to conduct intake and other preliminary processes. A third-party neutral then remotely guided the negotiators through the remainder of the process. This ODR platform sometimes was used together with a telephone connection, online video and/or audio communication tools, and even in-person meetings if appropriate to reach negotiated resolutions more effectively.

Juripax used standardized yet customizable online forms and procedures to minimize cost, time, and learning curve. It utilized asynchronous text-based methods of communication to maximize accessibility, minimize bandwidth and accommodate participant time zones and differential availability. Asynchronous communication also helped minimize online ranting – often called 'flaming' – and gave negotiators a chance to take a deep breath before replying to a potentially provocative remark. Rather than rely

36 In early 2012, users could reserve a single use Juripax workspace for as little as $20.00 US.

on a user manual, Juripax developers made best efforts to be intuitive for nontechnical users.

Divorce can give rise to the most complex array of legal and human factors in any negotiation. In a 2011 study of 126 Dutch participants in online divorce mediation, both parties perceived the online negotiation process and outcome as equally fair.[37] Men were more likely to express concerns about monetary and time costs of using ODR tools to negotiate the terms of their divorce, whereas women expressed greater concern about the potential adverse impact on emotions and important relationships. The researchers found mediated online negotiation of divorce to be a viable alternative to more traditional modes of negotiating terms of divorce.

Researchers also determined that Dutch parties in employment disputes who used Juripax to submit confidential intake data in preparation for in-person mediated negotiation sessions were better prepared, more likely to engage on a more level playing field, felt more empowered to make decisions on their own, and engaged with a more resolution-focused mindset. Research also demonstrated a 30-40% time and cost savings.[38]

Two other full service ODR platforms are worthy of special mention. One is British innovator Graham Ross's 'The Mediation Room'.[39] Another is Modria,[40] developed by Colin Rule after he created and administered at what was then the world's largest online dispute resolution systems at eBay and PayPal.[41] Both ODR tools have withstood the test of time better than many others.

Modria is an online service designed to expedite negotiated resolutions in a high volume of relatively low value disputes and do so at a low transaction cost to the system administrator. Modria was designed to lead negotiators step-by-step through an online negotiation process in disputes concerning debt, landlord/tenant, small claims, divorce, and even child custody. It enables negotiators to upload files, engage in asynchronous focused communication, exchange and respond to proposed solutions, and draft agreements. If necessary, the negotiators can engage a third-party neutral in separate and joint online sessions within the secure confines of the ODR tool. When linked to a court system, court staff can use Modria to manage caseloads with real-time dashboards, pre-configured reports, and data export options.

---

37 M. Gramatikov and L. Klaming, *Getting Divorced Online: Procedural and Outcome Justice in Online Divorce Mediation* (1 February 2011). Tilburg University TISCO Working Paper. Available at SSRN, https://papers.ssrn.com/sol3/papers.cfm?abstract_id=1752903.

38 Source documents for characteristics of Juripax were posted on www.juripax.com, but that site ceased to exist after Juripax was acquired by Modria.

39 www.themediationroom.com.

40 www.tylertech.com/products/modria. Modria stands for Modular Online Dispute Resolution Implementation Assistance. After several years in independent operation, Modria was acquired by Tyler Technologies.

41 Julia Wilkinson, *Colin Rule: From eBay Conflicts to Global Peace Initiatives*, eCommerceBytes.com (26 June 2011), www.ecommercebytes.com/cab/abu/y211/m06/abu0289/s05.

Several lessons can be learned from experience with these full service ODR workspaces. First, ODR tools can enable viable negotiated solutions to matters that heretofore might have resulted in litigated disputes. Second, ODR tools can be designed for high volume, narrowly prescribed disputes between people and organizations that do not have an ongoing relationship. These ODR tools also can be designed for higher value, lower volume caseloads in which ongoing relationships are essential to the solution. Third, regardless of whether ODR tools are purely commercial, or court-connected, or a hybrid model, it is essential to design systems that account for the types of negotiators, conflicts, and issues that might be addressed, as well as the negotiators' conflict management cultures.

3.5 *How Negotiators Use Video Conferencing*

Successful negotiation requires effective communication. Negotiators who are separated by time and/or space should appraise the best forms of communication for the matter before them. Negotiating high volume, low value disputes might require a different form of communication than low volume, high value conflicts. Without dwelling on Mehrabian's '7-38-55 rule,' suffice it to say that even though his research might be misconstrued,[42] significant value can be derived from appropriate exposure to voice, face, body language, and other elements of communication in addition to our words. This is especially true for negotiators who must manage complex conflicts in which trust is key or which involve ongoing relationships.

High definition video can be an effective tool to convey these additional communication elements between negotiators in remote locations. Unfortunately, bandwidth severely limited the utility of video during early days of the Internet. As a result, hosts of online video services before the 21st century sometimes used separate, dedicated, expensive ISDN connections.[43] Even ISDN video was marginally acceptable at best and quite often unreliable. The U.S. Department of Defense was an early adopter of ISDN to enable video between DoD locations.[44] Unfortunately, even the DoD internal video service failed on a regular basis. When it did work, it was often difficult to even

42 *Cf.*, Jeff Thompson, *Is Nonverbal Communication a Numbers Game?*, www.psychologytoday.com/us/blog/beyond-words/201109/is-nonverbal-communication-numbers-game; *How Much of Communication is Really Nonverbal*, https://vivipins.com/how-much-of-communication-is-really-nonverbal/; *Busting The Myth 93% of Communication is Nonverbal*, www.spring.org.uk/2007/05/busting-myth-93-of-communication-is.php.

43 ISDN is an acronym for Integrated Services Digital Network.

44 *Cf.*, LCDR Margaretmary Torelii Weidert, USN, *Integrated Services Digital Network (ISDN)*, June 1985, Naval Postgraduate School, CA, https://apps.dtic.mil/dtic/tr/fulltext/u2/a159578.pdf.

make out who was in the picture much less their facial expressions, body language, hand gestures, etc.[45]

Fast forward to the 21st century. Worldwide electronic communication infrastructure changes have been dramatic. According to some sources, the number of Internet users tripled between 2005 and 2017, at which time 48% of the world's 7.4 billion people had access.[46] Another source pegs the North American percentage in 2019 at 94.6, European percentage at 87.2, and worldwide at 58.8.[47] We have seen videoconferencing tools become more ubiquitous as Internet bandwidth envelops the earth.

Examples of hardware-based market leading vendors in 2020 include Polycom,[48] LifeSize,[49] and Cisco.[50] Leading online video service providers change rapidly, but currently include Zoom,[51] WebEx,[52] and GoToMeeting.[53] In the next several years, it is reasonable to expect a new crop of vendors to rise to the top of this busy marketplace. Each vendor tries to distinguish itself by offering a range of features and options at different price points.

Negotiators need not agree on which features are most important to their online work, and a complete feature comparison will surely cause readers of this chapter to stop reading. With that said, "Best-in-class video conferencing services let users share screens, remotely access one another's desktops, chat via text, exchange files, [and] communicate via digital whiteboards."[54] When used as an ODR tool, the best video products can be secure, affordable, useful from almost any device with a screen and Internet connection, allow joint and separate sessions, permit recording, and prevent recording. The most useful video systems enable remote negotiators to know who is 'present' in the online space, integrate video with other ODR tools, distribute differential participant permissions, and provide real-time access to tech support.

3.6 *How Negotiators Use Electronic Charting*

Electronic charting ODR tools enable users to digitize integrative negotiations and move them to the Cloud. Online services such as FacilitatePro[55] use a familiar flipchart

45 This was the frequent personal experience of this author, whose work included mediating DoD matters during that time.
46 https://en.wikipedia.org/wiki/Global_Internet_usage.
47 www.internetworldstats.com/stats.htm.
48 www.polycom.com.
49 www.lifesize.com, owned by Logitech (www.logitech.com).
50 www.cisco.com/assets/sol/tp/cop15/4340_cisco_COP15_page.html.
51 www.zoom.us/.
52 www.webex.com/, owned by Cisco (www.cisco.com).
53 www.gotomeeting.com/, owned by LogMeIn (www.logmein.com).
54 *The Best Video Conferencing Software for 2020*, www.pcmag.com/picks/the-best-video-conferencing-software (18 March 2020).
55 www.facilitate.com.

paradigm, allowing authorized users to securely login from virtually any online device with a browser. Negotiators can clarify issues, identify interests, and generate possible solutions. In real time or their own time, negotiators can organize and rate/rank ideas, and then collaboratively work toward solutions. When used with groups or teams of negotiators, electronic charting tools can add even greater value by enabling individual anonymity. Postings are thereby evaluated based on intrinsic value rather than by the identity of the source. The technology is designed to enable negotiators to detect best opportunities for consensus, avoid options that are least likely to gain support, and improve the chance of adopting the *best* solutions, not simply *good* solutions.

Negotiators who are first exposed to electronic charting can benefit from a brief orientation. Especially when administered by someone who is familiar with the ODR tool and the parties' negotiation culture, negotiators generally need no training to effectively use the tool.

3.7 How Negotiators Use Mind Mapping

'An outline' means different things to different people. Years ago, my daughter came home one day from elementary school with an outline in hand. It began with a big circle in the center of her page containing the main topic, with lines emanating to a swirl of multi-colored shapes around the edges of the page, each containing a distinct concept and idea.

This technique is called 'mind mapping'. It is preferred by many adults, not just children. Innovators have digitized the concept in such popular software as XMind,[56] Mindjet's MindManager,[57] iMindMap.[58] and FreeMind.[59] MindMeister[60] takes what my daughter did on paper and hosts it in a secure, shared workspace on the Internet. In both synchronous and asynchronous mode, negotiators can login from almost any device with a browser and Internet connection, review ideas posted by others, build on their ideas, comment on their ideas, and add new ones. The experience is graphical, intuitive, and can be fun!

Such ODR tools can improve the quest for creative negotiated solutions by breaking the bonds of visual linearity. These tools also can reduce cost, expedite the process, enable engagement in real time or negotiators' own time, preserve anonymity when appropriate, and make geographic location less relevant.

---

56 www.xmind.net/.

57 www.mindjet.com/.

58 www.imindmap.com/.

59 http://freemind.sourceforge.net/wiki/index.php/.

60 *See* the MindMeister online service at www.mindmeister.com.

3.8 How Negotiators Draft, Edit, View Settlement Agreements Online

ODR tools can help negotiators draft, edit, view, and even sign a settlement agreement.

Join.Me,[61] GoToMeeting,[62] WebEx,[63] and Zoom[64] are examples of intuitive online tools that negotiators can use to create, edit, and share documents across the Internet in real time. Each is amazingly simple to use, low cost or no cost, and requires only a browser or free phone app plus an Internet connection. These ODR tools also enable negotiators to engage through the Internet by video, voice, and text chat, display a presentation file, and even allow negotiators to collaboratively share ideas on a virtual whiteboard. The meeting host should be familiar with how to administer their tools of choice, but most negotiators only need orientation rather than training to use them.

These can be great tools for *synchronous* engagements, i.e., when negotiators are available at the same time but not all in the same place. When negotiators are not in the same place and cannot engage in real time, they might need ODR tools that enable *asynchronous* engagement. Tools like FacilitatePro, iMeetCentral, eRoom, Microsoft Teams, Slack, Google My Drive,[65] and Microsoft Word for Office 365[66] might be better in those situations. These ODR tools enable each negotiator to login at their convenience and even return periodically to view and respond to what other negotiators might have contributed to the persistent online content. These tools can automatically notify each negotiator when a change is made so they can login, review and add new content, update existing content, comment on changes, etc.

3.9 How Negotiators Electronically Sign Settlement Agreements Online

After negotiators achieve a settlement from remote locations and fully agree on language, they still must print and apply ink signatures to a paper document before mailing or faxing to the other party, who must do the same and return a fully executed copy to the first party.

Or do they?

61 www.join.me/.
62 www.gotomeeting.com.
63 www.webex.com.
64 www.zoom.us.
65 https://support.google.com/a/users/answer/9310248?hl=en&ref_topic=9296420.
66 https://support.office.com/en-us/article/collaborate-on-word-documents-with-real-time-co-authoring-7dd3040c-3f30-4fdd-bab0-8586492a1f1d.

Depending on jurisdictional requirements, negotiators can use an online service like DocuSign,[67] AdobeSign,[68] or dozens of other e-sign services available to electronically execute and finalize agreements online. This can simplify and expedite completion of the agreement and minimize costly administrative tasks associated with offline forms of negotiation.

Leading online e-signature services use similar intuitive protocols. One negotiator electronically transmits the completed document to the other negotiator(s) and copies him/herself through the e-signature website. Each signer receives an email message, clicks a link in the message, and e-signs the document. The website automatically saves the document with everyone's e-signature as a PDF and sends a fully executed copy to the signatories and anyone else specified.

3.10 *How Public Sector Mediators Use ODR in Negotiations*

3.10.1 FMCS

Congress established the Federal Mediation and Conciliation Service (FMCS) in 1947 to help prevent, manage, and resolve conflicts, primarily collective bargaining matters between employers and labor organizations.[69] FMCS mediators are schooled and highly experienced at using distributive ADR techniques to help negotiators overcome impasse and achieve agreements. Since the 1960s, FMCS mediators also have used integrative negotiation and problem-solving techniques to help parties resolve complex and sensitive workplace disputes, environmental disputes, and other matters critical to the economic health and social welfare of the United States and its citizens.[70] Past FMCS leaders like Dr. Jerome T. Barrett helped pioneer the use of integrative techniques at FMCS.[71] He taught these techniques to his peers and developed foundational materials that still form the basis for FMCS integrative ADR work today.

---

67 www.docusign.com.

68 https://acrobat.adobe.com/us/en/sign.html.

69 www.fmcs.gov.

70 Source: Former FMCS Commissioner Jim D. Chandler (deceased).

71 Source: Former FMCS Commissioner Jerome T. Barrett. Most ADR practitioners are familiar with the commercially successful works of Harvard Program on Negotiation co-founders Roger Fisher and William Ury, including their masterpiece *Getting to Yes: Negotiating Agreement Without Giving In* (New York: Penguin Books, 1983). The cornerstone of this slim yet influential book is the same set of powerful interest-based technique as those used by FMCS. Interest-based techniques like those developed at FMCS and popularized by Fisher and Ury underlie the tenants of 21st century ADR in the U.S. and throughout much of the world. It is remarkable to note that Professor Ury's early experience included anthropological research concerning conflict resolution in the New Guinea highlands. From there, Ury's research took him to the coal mines of Kentucky to study conflict resolution in the context of labor-management relations. https://www.mixcloud.com/internationalinstituteforconfl/idn-podcast-no-101-william-ury-on-negotiating-toward-a-better-world-nov-23/. Could Professor Ury's early exposure to labor relations, and possibly the interest-based techniques utilized by FMCS mediators, have influenced Ury's later work or contributed to 'Getting to Yes' and co-founding the Harvard Negotiations Project?

In 1999, FMCS Director C. Richard Barnes established a new department and named it Mediation Technology Services (MTS). Barnes temporarily assigned a small team of mediators to MTS to explore ways that technology might help FMCS customers better prepare for meetings and negotiations, retain better records, communicate better with constituents, minimize the impact of geographic separation, and save time, travel, and money.[72]

The MTS team explored hundreds of commercially available hardware and software tools in its efforts to discover which might most effectively help integrative and distributive negotiators solve complex problems, make important decisions, and take action that makes a difference. Over the course of about a year, MTS developed what FMCS named the 'TAGS System', an acronym for Technology Assisted Group Solutions.

At its inception, the FMCS TAGS System consisted of a network of servers, mobile computers, electronic conferencing facilities, plus commercial software and online services. A specially trained subset of FMCS's 200 federal mediators integrated TAGS ODR tools with their traditional skillset to help negotiators during integrative negotiations and problem solving, distributive negotiations, online surveys, strategic planning, focus groups, conventions, conferences attended by hundreds of negotiators, online meetings, assisted negotiations in grievances and EEO complaints, negotiation elements of labor-management committee meetings, organizational development processes, negotiation elements of collaborative labor-management initiatives, and even a statewide election of union officers.

Feedback from early adopters helped FMCS determine that negotiators who used the TAGS ODR tools engaged more openly and honestly, shared knowledge and opinions more constructively, generated better ideas, and built a stronger commitment to joint action. FMCS also determined that its TAGS ODR tools helped users conduct shorter, more productive, problem-focused engagements and helped minimize transaction costs associated with group decision-making.[73] FMCS has continued delivering ODR services and other 'eServices' for more than 20 years.[74] Renewed emphasis has been placed on FMCS's ODR services since the spread of the Covid-19 pandemic.[75]

3.10.2 NMB

Congress established the National Mediation Board (NMB) to help maintain the flow of interstate commerce by offering representation, mediation and arbitration services to employers and labor organizations in the airline and railway industries.[76] The ADR

72 The MTS team was led by the author of this chapter.

73 For a more detailed treatment of the TAGS initiative, *see* Michael J. Wolf, Jon Numair, and Jack Yoedt, *Essential Collaborative Technology Tools for the 21st Century,* cited at note 13 above.

74 www.fmcs.gov/services/resolving-labor-management-disputes/eservices-tags/.

75 www.fmcs.gov/services/resolving-labor-management-disputes/eservices-tags/online-mediation/.

76 www.nmb.gov.

Team at the NMB began to research ODR tools in the early 2000s and implement ODR tools in 2005.

One of the NMB's early successes involved a major air carrier and its pilots' association that used ODR tools to draft several settlement agreements in connection with a mediated dispute resolution process. Their online workspace allowed them to securely edit settlement agreements with automatic version tracking, upload and download supporting documents, maintain a trail of interpretive comments to minimize future disputes, and work asynchronously from virtually anywhere. They succeeded in a surprisingly brief period of time while minimizing travel, out-of-pocket costs, and lost productivity.[77]

In another example of the NMB's early use of ODR tools, representatives of a major rail carrier and its engineers' union used separate and joint online workspaces hosted by the NMB.[78] The parties used the online workspace to prepare for critical negotiations over numerous collective bargaining disputes. During the course of two years, the parties used the online workspace in between face-to-face meetings, together with the collaborative mind mapping software FreeMind. They used the ODR tools to post and maintain an ongoing issues list, a running record of issues discussed, documentation of how various issues were resolved, relevant contract language and voluminous side agreements. Within the secure workspace, they used an online forum for secure threaded discussions, an online calendar and task list to manage action items between dispute resolution sessions, and a 'Team' tab to manage contact information and ensure the security of their information. The system automatically sent a descriptive e-mail notice to all authorized users whenever something changed in the workspace.

Although only tangentially related to ODR and negotiation, the NMB began experimenting with online arbitration during the same time period. In the early days, the NMB sent out pre-configured laptop computers and video cameras to each party and the arbitrator who was scheduled to conduct an online case. The online arbitration hearings were conducted with technology support from the NMB staff. At the conclusion of each hearing, users returned the equipment so it could be reconfigured and sent out for the next case. As of 2020, the NMB still offers its Online Arbitration program in addition to its Online Video-conferencing Center for Railway Labor Act matters at no cost to the parties and NMB arbitrators.[79]

---

77 Source: The author of this chapter, who was the NMB ADR Team member who facilitated this engagement.

78 *Ibid.* At the time that the NMB parties were using this ODR tool, it was called Central Desktop. Following change in ownership and focusing the ODR on a new market segment, it was renamed iMeetCentral (https://imeetcentral.com/).

79 https://nmb.gov/NMB_Application/?s=online.

3.10.3 FLRA

The Federal Labor Relations Authority (FLRA) is an independent administrative federal agency that administers the labor-management relations program for 2.1 million non-postal federal employees, approximately 1.2 million of whom are represented in 2,200 bargaining units worldwide.[80] In 2010, the FLRA's Collaboration and Alternative Dispute Resolution Office (CADRO) started using ODR tools in appropriate cases. In one such case,[81] a labor dispute had already mushroomed into complex, large scale litigation. Both parties understood that failure to achieve a negotiated solution would surely result in significant legal costs, risk of substantial loss, and years of likely appeals regardless of who might initially prevail. Both parties seemed to understand that resolving the legal disputes had little chance of solving the persistent problems which gave rise to the legal disputes. They also clearly saw that, after a multi-year battle, victory would likely to be defined by whether the other party suffered a net loss greater than their own. As a result, the parties requested ADR assistance from CADRO and offered to cover the FLRA ADR provider's travel costs ... from Washington D.C. to Alaska.

It was a beautiful time of year for an expenses-paid visit to the Land of the Midnight Sun, but an 8000-mile round trip journey and a two-week absence from family and office did not fit well with the ADR providers' other responsibilities at that moment. So, the ADR providers hosted the parties' use of Join.Me[82] to link the ADR providers' Washington DC office with negotiators located in Alaska, Oregon, and elsewhere. During the course of two weeks, the negotiators and the ADR providers used the ODR tool and POTS[83] to engage in day-long joint and separate audio-video sessions, securely transmit files back and forth, identify and clarify issues, collaboratively build electronic charts used to generate and organize ideas and options, and engage in screen sharing to draft and edit negotiated language. The negotiators reached several dozen written agreements and fully resolve all issues that gave rise to the pending litigation.[84]

4 ORIGINS OF USING ODR IN NEGOTIATIONS[85]

The adoption of ODR tools used in negotiations has become a worldwide movement. Like the combustion engine, electricity, human flight, and mapping the human genome,

80 www.flra.gov.

81 A version of this example first appeared in Michael J. Wolf, *Collaborative Technology Can Improve Access to Justice*, 15 NYU J. of Legis. and Pub. Pol. 759 (2013). *See* https://nyujlpp.org/wp-content/uploads/2013/01/Wolf-Collaborative-Technology.pdf.

82 www.join.me/.

83 Plain Old Telephone Service.

84 Source: The author of this chapter, who was the lead ADR provider in these negotiations.

85 *See* www.pewtrusts.org/en/research-and-analysis/articles/2019/06/04/online-dispute-resolution-moves-from-e-commerce-to-the-courts and www.okbar.org/barjournal/aug2019/obj9006rule/.

ODR did not begin in one place by one person. There is more than one legitimate origin story, told in more than one language. The following is only one such story.[86]

4.1 1980s

Early adopters started using DOS-based ODR tools even before the Internet as we now know it could host such engagement. University of Arizona Emeritus Professor Jay Nunamaker was one of the earliest researchers and developers of what many people now refer to as ODR.[87] With the support of IBM and University of Arizona, he began decades of empirical research in the early- and mid-1980s on 'group decision support systems' (GDSS).[88] GDSS are interactive computer-based systems that enable negotiators to think more creatively, communicate more effectively, make better decisions, find the best available solutions, and solve complex problems that are semi-structured or unstructured in nature. If a distinction ever existed between GDSS and contemporary ODR in negotiations, such a distinction would not be useful today.

Dr. Nunamaker led teams of academic researchers, mentored more than 80 PhD candidates, and concurrently led a team that developed commercially available GDSS software. In 1989, Nunamaker started a company named Ventana to bring *Plexsys* to market. He later changed the name of the company and the GDSS to *GroupSystems.* As of 2020, GroupSystems markets GDSS by the moniker *ThinkTank.*[89] During the course of three decades, Nunamaker's GDSS has been adopted by industry, military, government, and universities at more than 2,500 locations.

4.2 1990s

During this era, Mike McCall and Julia Young independently developed software with functions similar to GroupSystems. They established their own software development

86 Idea: Create a collaborative online process to knit together the various origin stories and make that compendium available to the public while we still have access to those who can tell the story firsthand. Maybe establish a website called 'ODR Origin Stories.' Make it the Wikipedia of origin stories about ODR research and applications. Divide it into several sections such as 'Firsthand Accounts,' 'What Others Told Us,' 'Observations and Recommendations,' etc. The field is still young enough that new origin stories are still being written, so this should have a projected life of at least a decade.

87 University of Arizona profile of Jay F. Nunamaker at https://profiles.arizona.edu/person/nunamake; also *see* https://eller.arizona.edu/people/jay-f-nunamaker.

88 J.F. Nunamaker, Lynda M. Applegate, Benn R. Konsynski, *Computer-Aided Deliberation: Model Management and Group Decision Support*, 36(6) Oper. Res. 1988, at 811-966. *See* https://scholar.google.com/citations?hl=en&user=_kOnaK0AAAAJ&view_op=list_works&sortby=pubdate for a list of more than 250 research publications attributed to Dr. Nunamaker, which have been cited more than 29,000 times as of 2020. Other published research remains sparse concerning the efficacy of early ODR tools.

89 www.thinktank.net.

and consulting firm known as Facilitate.com.[90] This also was the early name given to their ODR software and online services, which now is called FacilitatePro.

One of the earliest hosted online collaboration services that evolved into ODR was eRoom Technologies. It started in Cambridge, Massachusetts in 1996.[91] Negotiators and ADR practitioners found eRoom most useful to manage robust online caseloads, facilitate secure document sharing, communicate before and during negotiation sessions, manage version control, billing, and reporting.

Cybersettle was another early entrant in the world of ODR. The company was founded in 1996 as a vendor of online claims settlement services based on an automated double-blind bidding system.[92]

Not to be confused with Cybersettle, Smartsettle[93] has offered an ODR service since 1995. It combines a process referred to as 'Visual Blind Bidding' with collaborative technology tools that draw from mathematician John Nash's Nobel Prize winning game theories.[94] Smartsettle offers a facilitated version of its online service called 'Smartsettle Infinity' designed to fairly and efficiently resolve complex matters such as divorce and multiparty business disputes.[95] Its other online service, as described in Section 3.3 above, 'Smartsettle One' is an online, self-help tool that negotiators can use to quickly resolve simpler matters such as small claims and consumer disputes.

The year 1995 was also when Pierre Omidyar founded AuctionWeb to link up buyers and sellers of merchandise via the Internet.[96] Soon, he changed the name to eBay. In 1997, eBay began to publicly rate sellers.[97] Future buyers could use the rating system to decide whether to trust a particular seller. An unintended consequence of implementing the rating system was disputes. A lot of them! In 1999, Steve Abernethy and Ahmed Khaishgi launched SquareTrade to became one of the first ODR services for negotiating the resolution of e-commerce disputes, mostly at eBay.[98] Abernethy and Khaishgi utilized online negotiation software to automate an asynchronous dispute resolution process, ultimately for about two million online sellers and buyers. But due to a change to eBay's customer feedback system, SquareTrade ended its ODR services and became a vendor of warranty services. In 2003, eBay and sister company PayPal then established their own ODR services developed by then-eBay Director of ODR Colin Rule. By the time

90 www.facilitate.com.

91 eRoom Technologies was purchased by Documentum, which was purchased by EMC2, which was purchased by Dell, which subsequently spun off Documentum and eRoom to OpenText. *See* www.emc.com/products/detail/software2/eroom.htm.

92 *See* description of CyberSettle at Note above.

93 www.smartsettle.com.

94 http://en.wikipedia.org/wiki/Nash_equilibrium.

95 http://vimeo.com/31214934.

96 www.ebayinc.com/history.

97 https://community.ebay.com/t5/Announcements/Upcoming-Changes-to-the-Feedback-System/ba-p/26161783.

98 https://en.wikipedia.org/wiki/SquareTrade. Allstate acquired SquareTrade in late 2016 for $1.4 billion.

Rule left eBay in 2011 to establish Modria, Rule and his team built an ODR negotiation system that was resolving sixty million eBay disputes per year by 2016.[99]

While SquareTrade was forming the eBay ODR system, the WIPO Arbitration and Mediation Centre began to offer an ODR service for the negotiated resolution of disputes between Internet trademark holders, service right holders, and domain name registrants. The Internet Corporation of Assigned Names and Numbers (ICANN) authorized the Centre to resolve disputes according to ICANN's Uniform Domain Name Dispute Resolution Policy and for a number of country code top-level domains. The Centre's ODR service has enabled the negotiated resolution of thousands of cases during the past two decades.

5 Path to Tomorrow: Opportunities Disguised as Challenges[100]

So far, this chapter has been a snapshot of contemporary ODR in negotiations and how we got here. This section contains prognostication about the future of ODR in negotiations.

In the near future, online services will mature and their default configuration will become more intuitive, safe, and secure. They will utilize non-proprietary data repositories and better integrate with negotiators' existing data sources. Speaking of integration, the best ODR tools will securely integrate with each other and with other online tools that negotiators use to initiate, schedule, bill, pay, and engage using video, text, and audio. AI will enable the best ODR tools to effortlessly morph between collaborative and conflictive modalities. ODR tools will become easier to incrementally modify and upgrade each time the leading-edge advances. Multi-lingual negotiations will be supported by online services that accurately translate in real time without human intervention.

In the near future, innovative online services will continue to change hands, consolidate, and replace expensive proprietary ODR software. Technical requirements for user equipment will continue a downward trajectory. Entry-level user equipment will continue to improve hardware elements necessary for useful online engagement. AI will enable no-cost or lower-cost support and minimize the need for costly system administrators. Sophisticated negotiators and third-party neutrals will be able to tweak

99 www.ecommercebytes.com/cab/abu/y211/m06/abu0289/s05. Jaap Van den Herik and Daniel Dimov, *Can the eBay's Community Review Forum Fairly Resolve Disputes?* (4 November 2011). Proceedings of the 23rd Benelux Conference on Artificial Intelligence, Vol. 4, pp. 263-272, November 2011. Available at SSRN: http://ssrn.com/abstract=1955505. Tyler Technologies acquired Modria to apply ODR in local courts and government tax offices to solve relatively low complexity disputes that have less need for lawyers, accountants and other human input. www.artificiallawyer.com/2017/06/07/ebay-odr-co-modria-sells-up-legal-tech-consolidation-mounts/.

100 'A relevant Talmudic principle is referred to as "its ruin is its remedy" (in Hebrew, kilkulo zehu tikuno).'

ODR tools to comport with their bargaining culture and best practices. Third parties like mediators, facilitators, arbitrators, and fact finders will seamlessly enter and exit when invited by negotiators. More third parties will become skilled and experienced at initiating an ODR process on behalf of negotiators.

In the near future, it is not difficult to imagine that more than one trusted neutral source will greatly expand the portion of its website devoted to ODR. Candidates might include mediate.com, Association for Conflict Resolution,[101] Harvard Program on Negotiation,[102] National Center for Technology and Dispute Resolution,[103] National Center for State Courts,[104] and the American Bar Association Section on Dispute Resolution.[105] Maybe it will become a collaborative effort of several such organizations. In addition to the ODR general education pages that some of these sites have already, it could grow a library of practice tips specifically for ODR negotiators and third-party neutrals. The site could contain pragmatic information about ODR functionality and security, user experience stories from ODR negotiators and third-party neutrals, ODR third-party practitioner bio information,[106] and reviews of the mushrooming list of potential ODR tools for negotiators. The site could contain wikis for shared content creation, blogs for community commentary, instructional videos, and educational webinars.

While finishing this chapter, many in-person meetings either were cancelled or moved online due to the Covid-19 (Novel Coronavirus) pandemic. Meetings that moved online exposed participants to the same types of software and online services used in ODR negotiations. An optimistic view is that this will cause a large spike in the number of people who recognize the value of ODR tools for both real time (synchronous) and 'my time' (asynchronous) negotiations. If implemented correctly, participants will experience secure connections from almost anywhere at a lower net cost (or at least cost-neutral) and in ways that can overcome process barriers of traditional negotiations. This has potential to dramatically increase the rate at which negotiators express interest in adopting ODR tools.

In the not so near future, virtual reality, augmented reality, and 3D holography will invade the ODR workspace. Cisco, BT, Deutsche Telekom, Vodafone, and EE are each

101 https://acrnet.org/.

102 www.pon.harvard.edu/.

103 http://odr.info/.

104 www.ncsc.org/.

105 www.americanbar.org/groups/dispute_resolution/.

106 A fledgling effort has already begun at www.onlinemediators.com/, which appears to be affiliated with mediate.com.

developing what might be called holographic Telepresence.[107] Imagine being there without physically being there. It might change the whole concept of negotiating online.

In the not so near future, rapid developments in AI will help ODR tools seamlessly guide negotiators when needed and be guided by negotiators when appropriate. AI will enable ODR tools to adapt to process requirements of single-party, multi-party, one-on-one, and team negotiations. AI will enable ODR security settings to automatically adapt for intra-organizational, inter-organizational, and international matters. Eventually, AI might even sense and adapt to cultural elements that distinguish process requirements in various parts of the world, and in diverse types of matters in the same part of the world.

5.1 *Fragmentation*

ODR faces potentially serious challenges as we navigate a path toward tomorrow. One such challenge is what some refer to as 'fragmentation'. Research indicates that people tend to reinforce each other's world views by engaging in political conversation with ideologically similar people.[108] When they seek information online, many if not most express preferences for sources that comport with their belief systems. Economic self-interest encourages online providers to use advances in monitoring algorithms to direct individuals to sources the individuals prefer. The outcome is an Internet that further polarizes groups which already believe differently.

One logical consequence is the potential weakening of the social fabric that motivates people with differing views to seek common ground and work together for mutual success. Instead, they are more likely to engage in high risk, low reward conflict even when doing so might fail to serve stakeholders' best interests. This has obvious consequences for negotiators and third-party neutrals, whether on- or off-line. Importantly, fragmentation can result in an enhanced view of the dichotomy between 'us' and 'them'. Everyone becomes viewed as either an ally or an enemy. There is no in-between, and there is no mutual respect or trust for 'them'. That loss of respect and trust extends to the other negotiator(s), the process, the third-party neutral, and even the technology. The cumulative effect will be greater challenges achieving the best negotiated agreements, whether on- or offline. Researchers might help us determine whether we are already seeing the effects of this dynamic.

---

107 Challenges in bringing Holographic Telepresence Technology to the masses (14 June 2019, https://becominghuman.ai/challenges-in-bringing-holographic-telepresence-technology-to-the-masses-91e5742d7faf; https://mdhhologram.com/telepresence/. Also *see* https://lookingglassfactory.com/product/8k; and https://hypervsn.com/blog/holographic-technology-at-ces-2020.html.

108 Jonathan Bright, *Explaining the Emergence of Political Fragmentation on Social Media: The Role of Ideology and Extremism*, 23 J. Comput. Mediat. Commun. 1 (January 2018), at 17-33. https://doi.org/10.1093/jcmc/zmx002.

Fragmentation is not a problem specific to ODR in negotiations, but it can adversely affect the adoption of ODR, the perceived success of ODR in negotiations, and retard the trajectory of ODR development.

5.2 *Transition From Dispute Resolution to Conflict Management*

In general, people appear to be conflict adverse. They seem to view disputes as failed transactions that should end as soon as possible. Most dispute resolution processes and ODR tools are designed accordingly.

Some disputes are nothing more than failed transactions and probably should end as soon as possible. These might be relatively low value, high volume cases like eBay or property tax appeals. But other disputes can be relatively high value, low volume like family or business dissolution, collective bargaining agreements, B2B matters, estate contests, certain neighborhood disputes, personal injury cases, and class action cases.

High value, low volume matters might start off as a conflict and only become a dispute if the conflict goes badly. All conflicts need not go badly! Well-managed conflict need not result in a dispute if the negotiators treat the conflict as a constructive opportunity to achieve important goals. Conflict management processes and associated ODR tools can be designed accordingly. This would enable ODR negotiators and third-party neutrals to manage conflict in a way that more effectively maximizes value, minimizes risk, and lowers barriers to success.

One challenge will be to develop a culture in which we appropriately distinguish dispute resolution from conflict management and develop ODR tools based on each paradigm. Dispute resolution will remain largely reactive intervention, while conflict management will be more proactive and preventive. Conflict management ODR tools will not be broadly adopted until negotiators and third-party neutrals learn to distinguish between dispute resolution and conflict management and become skilled at successful behaviors for each. This will be a bigger challenge than developing better ODR tools for negotiators.

5.3 *Access to ODR By Parties to U.S. Court Cases*

When Americans seek legal redress, many adamantly exclaim that justice requires they have their day in court. Instead, most parties to criminal and civil court cases in the U.S. might benefit more from access to ODR.

We might not think of these as opportunities for online dispute resolution, but consider the facts. In a 2015 *Landscape* Report based on a representative sample of non-domestic civil cases, the National Center for State Courts found that:[109]

- "(N)early two-thirds (64%) were contract cases, and more than half of those were debt collection (37%) and landlord/tenant cases (29%). An additional 16% were small claims cases involving disputes valued at $12,000 or less and 9% were characterized as 'other civil' cases involving agency appeals and domestic or criminal-related cases."
- "(T)hree-quarters (75%) of all judgments were less than $5,200."
- The value of three-quarters of judgments entered in contract cases following a bench trial was less than half of those in small claims cases ($1,785 versus $3,900).
- "For most represented litigants, the costs of litigating a case through trial would greatly exceed the monetary value of the case. In some instances, the costs of even initiating the lawsuit or making an appearance as a defendant would exceed the value of the case. ... The cost and delays of civil litigation greatly outpace the monetary value of most cases filed in state courts, effectively denying access to justice for most litigants and undermining the legitimacy of the courts as a fair and effective forum to resolve disputes."
- At least one party was self-represented in 76% of the cases (usually the defendant).
- Half of the cases were disposed in less than four months, but about ¾ took on average more than one year to resolve!

The *Landscape* Report helps frame the American access to justice crisis, in which we see the American legal system drifting away from its ideals of justice for all.[110] Americans suffer from differential access to legal representation and differential access to the courts. For decades, 'having your day in court' has been an illusion for most and a right for few. At most, a judge or jury decides only 2-3% of criminal and civil cases. Most civil cases in the United States settle[111] and at least 90% of criminal defendants in U.S. courts plead

109 *The Landscape of Civil Litigation in State Courts*, National Center for State Courts (2015), at iii, vi.

110 *Cf.*, Michael J. Wolf, *Collaborative Technology Improves Access to Justice*, cited at note 81 above, at 763. Also *see* a plethora of resources listed at www.americanbar.org/groups/legal_aid_indigent_defendants/resource_center_for_access_to_justice/.

111 Theodore Eisenberg and Charlotte Lanvers, *What is the Settlement Rate and Why Should We Care?* (2009), Cornell Law Faculty Publications, Paper 203, http://scholarship.law.cornell.edu/facpub/203; and John Barkai, Elizabeth Kent, and Pamela Martin, *A Profile of Settlement*, American Judges Assn. (undated), http://aja.ncsc.dni.us/courtrv/cr42-3and4/CR42-3BarkaiKentMartin.pdf. Comparable data for other nations has been difficult to find, but at least one source claims without citation that most European Union civil cases are *not* settled. Helmuts Kleins, *Comparison of Common Law (US) and Civil (EU) Litigation Practice* (19 November 2018), www.petefowler.com/blog/2018/11/19/comparison-of-common-law-us-and-civil-eu-litigation-practice.

guilty.[112] These settlements and guilty pleas result from time-sensitive negotiations for which ODR could offer substantial benefits.

More granular data might help ODR developers and providers better understand how to appropriately interact with the culture of each jurisdiction. In addition, it might be useful to work with court administrators to help parties understand their roles as negotiators rather than just think of themselves as litigators. Based on the characteristics of average state court cases, it also might be useful to partner with national or global firms that specialize in developing ODR tools for high volume, low value cases.[113] Offering to partner with the National Center for State Courts and similar organizations in other parts of the world could help ODR developers and providers learn from experiences that precede their own efforts as well as share best practices with others. This can also increase the chances of serving associated public interests that might otherwise not be adequately addressed.

5.4 *Orientation, Education, Skills Training and Assessment*

A constant stream of orientation, education, skills training, and assessment will be required to fully realize the potential of ODR in negotiations.

Some of us recall when the average person could not distinguish 'mediation' from 'meditation'. It has taken almost 40 years for the term 'mediation' to become mainstream (although many people still seem to not know the difference between arbitration and mediation). The acronym 'ADR' still is not mainstream. A concerted, long-term orientation campaign will help the public generally understand what we mean when we suggest using ODR in negotiations.

Some individuals should receive more than orientation so their decisions and actions will better support the appropriate use of ODR in negotiation. Examples of those who should receive a deeper education about using ODR in negotiations include judges, court personnel, community-based dispute resolution center staff and volunteers, HR personnel, landlord-tenant organization staff and volunteers, certain university faculty, ADR practitioners, labor leaders and staff, certain administrative agency employees, elected officials, appraisal district employees, lawyers, CPAs, software developers, and IT security experts to name a few.

---

112 *Only 2% of federal criminal defendants go to trial, and most who do are found guilty*, Pew Research Center (11 June 2019), www.pewresearch.org/fact-tank/2019/06/11/only-2-of-federal-criminal-defendants-go-to-trial-and-most-who-do-are-found-guilty/ (based on data from the Administrative Office of the U.S. Courts). Also *see* Jeffrey Q. Smith and Grant R. Macqueen, *Trials Continue to Decline in Federal and State Courts. Does It Matter?*, 101 Judicature 4 at 28 (2017), https://judicialstudies.duke.edu/wp-content/uploads/2018/01/JUDICATURE101.4-vanishing.pdf, citing Jed S. Rakoff, *Why You Won't Get Your Day In Court*, N.Y. Rev. Books (24 November 2016) www.nybooks.com/articles/2016/11/24/why-you-wont-get-your-day-in-court/ (noting that 'fewer than 1 percent' of state court cases go to trial).

113 For a sample of such organizations, *see* 'List of Vendors' section at www.ncsc.org/odr.

Skills training is necessary to use certain ODR tools appropriately and competently as a negotiator and as a third-party neutral. But the largest group of users might be those who are 'one-off' negotiators. Their skills training, if any, should be quite different than those who spend a fair amount of professional time negotiating business or legal matters. Aspiring ODR practitioners will gain greatest value from training that focuses on their special needs as third-party neutrals. IT support personnel should receive training about how to enable and how to secure ODR tools specifically for diverse types of online negotiations.

This combination of orientation, education, and skills training can help increase negotiators' appropriate utilization of ODR tools. Several existing ODR tools can even be excellent vehicles through which orientation, education, and skills training can occur!

Might there be interest in developing a consultant cadre of ODR negotiation experts? This could be a national or global, well-trained, diverse, highly experienced team of individuals who have a strong negotiation and ADR background, combined with an up-to-date working knowledge of technology that can support online negotiations. Members of this group would need to receive constant education and training to remain at the leading edge of the field. In addition to working as a consultant, advisor, mentor, and coach in the application of ODR to negotiations, members of this group could be called upon to deliver orientation, education, and skills training to others. They also could inform developers about specific unmet needs in the marketplace and help field-test new products.

5.5 Multicultural and Multi-lingual Participants

Many of us tend to unconsciously develop solutions that are culturally specific without realizing they are not universally applicable. The resulting sting of insult can be inadvertent yet intense.

That can be a more difficult problem than the challenge of multilingual environments. Automated translation functionality is already incredible yet still imperfect. Even human translators can misunderstand intended meaning, unique regional dialects, and nuances. Sometimes, intended meaning can only be captured by correctly interpreting a combination of facial expressions, hand gestures and body language. Even when we think we speak the same language we still get it wrong. And just like in-person, online humor can be mistaken for insult, online exasperation can be misconstrued as anger, and a head-nod of understanding can be misinterpreted as agreement. These issues will expand as ODR tools become more relevant to negotiators around our planet.

Developers have made remarkable progress building ODR tools that negotiators use today. As they create the next generation of software and online services, ongoing efforts should focus on how to better address issues arising with multi-lingual and multicultural participants.

5.6 *Financial and Public Policy Questions*

This subsection unfortunately contains a series of tough questions without offering insightful recommendations. Thought leaders have already begun discussing some of these questions and will need to keep them on their agenda so as to guide ODR development on an upward trajectory.

Who will bear the cost to develop ODR tools that are most beneficial to the interests of negotiators and those whom they might represent? If the answer is 'commercial developers,' will financial rewards create sufficient incentives for the developers to create the breadth and depth of ODR tools at a pace that best serves the community of users?

Cost is already a barrier to equitable availability of some of the most useful ODR tools. What if ODR becomes an even more costly negotiation tool of an ADR-based private justice system that is only accessible to those who can afford private justice? How might that affect the public sector legal system and broader access to justice issues?

What is the best way to handle potentially competing and conflicting interests between: (1) negotiators who use ODR tools, (2) private sector ODR developers, and (3) ODR system hosts and administrators? For example,

- Privacy issues might arise if ODR system hosts collect and store user (negotiator) data that might be discoverable and thereby create a risk of adverse impact on legitimate interests of negotiators and those whom they might represent.
- Security features that are switched off by default because the ODR tool host's commercial interests cause them to cater to social media users more than ODR negotiators?
- An ODR system stores data on servers in a nation whose laws and practices do not protect user data consistent with reasonable user expectations.
- Lack of funding in the legal system causes court administrators to select ODR tools that minimize caseloads at the expense of better case resolutions or more equitable access by people without representation by lawyers.

How might negotiators' rapidly increasing interest in ODR tools affect the existing community of ADR providers? Will there be a greater or lesser need for ADR providers? Will relatively less capable yet technologically proficient ADR practitioners gain a larger share of the market at the expense of highly capable traditional ADR practitioners who cannot or will not integrate technology into their practice? Will the '4th party' become the dominant player in the ADR marketplace?

Powerful ODR tools are neither intrinsically good nor evil, but the impact of how they are implemented might create net positive or negative outcomes. Consider the recurring public discourse about Facebook, Twitter, Instagram, Microsoft, Amazon, Alibaba and other entities that some people think can quietly steer a nation or even this planet one direction or another. This is not a suggestion that we make plans to regulate negotiators' ODR tools. But thought should be given to how the public interest intersects with the interests of individual negotiators, ADR and ODR providers, online system administrators, courts, and administrative agencies. These can make for exciting discussions at forums, conferences, and of course online.

5.7 Remote Engagement

Are in-person negotiations always better than online? Advocates for in-person negotiations might argue that face-to-face is necessary to derive full meaning from the process of communication. They would point out that words are not the most important source of meaning. Being face-to-face enables listeners to listen with their brain and not just their ears as they observe the speakers hand gestures, body language, facial expression, and tone of voice. They would argue that face-to-face is the best way to convey emotional content from which the listener can determine veracity, identify weaknesses, derive the speaker's true meaning, figure out how to expand the pie, satisfy more interests, etc.

That might be a pretty compelling argument against using ODR in many types of negotiations unless ODR is packaged with high-definition video and someday something close to virtual reality or 3D holography. On the other side of the issue are those who might assert that properly implemented technology, sometimes combined with the expertise of a third-party neutral, can effectively communicate meaning and emotional content that goes well beyond mere words. They might add that contemporary ubiquitous video technology does a fine job when used appropriately by skilled negotiators and ODR practitioners. They might even point out that sometimes a lack of face-to-face engagement can minimize opportunities for misunderstanding and other barriers that often arise during in-person negotiations. They will watch for you to nod your head when they explain this is sometimes why it is best to use caucuses rather than do everything in joint session.

These types of views about ODR will continue to surround discussions about certain types of negotiations, especially those which are complex, sensitive, concern matters of high value, and involve ongoing relationships. They should guide negotiators and process advocates as they consider when and how to best use ODR in negotiations. They should guide developers as they consider what ODR tools might be best received in the marketplace. And they should guide public policy leaders who want ODR to develop in a way that best serves a balance of public and private interests.

5.8 *Diversity and Expansion of 'ODR'*

It is easy to become complacent when we find a comfort zone in which we have mastered both the technology and the process of using ODR in negotiations. The longer we reside in that comfort zone, the more we can focus on achieving important outcomes and less on what it takes to master the technology and process.

But the world around us will discourage such complacency. The world of online technology will undoubtedly continue its unstoppable trajectory. That includes the general development and adoption of new electronic hardware, software, online services, and artificial intelligence. Creative minds will ensure that this results in more viable, diverse, and expansive uses of ODR that support the process of negotiation. That is great despite the requirement that we will need to regularly exit our comfort zone to take advantage of the ODR tools that enable the most successful negotiations. It is best to do so frequently so change is incremental and easier to integrate into existing successful negotiation processes.

5.9 *Evaluate Value of ODR*

Most evaluative information about the value of ODR tools is anecdotal and not from neutral, dispassionate sources. A story tied to a well-known name is great for marketing but not the best way to establish an empirical basis upon which to assign value.

An independent, trusted, neutral, global group from academia, negotiators, and third-party neutrals should be formed to establish evaluative mechanisms for ODR negotiation tools. The group's mission could be to help decisionmakers select the most useful ODR tools for specific applications. Doing so would support a vision of a world in which users adopt the best collection of ODR tools to achieve the most successful negotiated outcomes. The group could establish and propagate a set of criteria and standards against which to assess the utility of software and online services that can be used as ODR tools. They could enlist the aid of others to empirically measure ODR tools against the standards, after which they could publish results and field commentary.

This would not be a one-and-done initiative. The group would need to constantly reevaluate its membership, mission and vision, assessment criteria and standards, funding, test results, communication channels, etc., and reinvent itself as the field changes.

5.10 *Apology*

Apology has been found to be immensely important to resolve certain types of conflicts, such as medical malpractice cases. Apology is not simply saying 'I'm sorry.' Effective apology generally involves acknowledgement of the behavior in question, ceasing that behavior, expressing true regret for engaging in the behavior, and making a heartfelt commitment to not repeat the behavior.

How do negotiators effectively convey an apology in ODR-enabled negotiations and how do third-party neutrals help them do so? What if any ODR tools are most likely to be effective conveying a meaningful apology? Answers to such questions can be crucial to the adoption of ODR tools when negotiating certain types of matters.

5.11 *General Technology Issues in ODR-Enabled Negotiations*

Each portion of Section 5 has been about opportunities and challenges that negotiators and third-party neutrals might encounter at the intersection of ODR and negotiations. To conclude this discussion, here are several technology considerations that are more general in nature:

- Differential access – Pursue the future in a way that improves the chances that people of moderate means and in all parts of the world gain fair access to ODR tools so they can achieve equitable standing during online negotiations.
- Security – Take steps to ensure that future users are not deterred by breaches of ODR tools sanctioned for use in negotiations. In part, this might require developing ODR tools that contain AI elements and/or designing ODR tools for use by non-technical experts who are not knowledgeable or skilled at configuring a secure online environment.
- Reliability and Trustworthiness – Be mindful that someone's confidence in *all* ODR tools can be adversely affected by just *one* believable story about someone else's nightmare using an unreliable ODR tool or untrustworthy ODR provider.
- Differential comfort using technology – Not every ODR tool should be designed for the digital immigrant, but do not require that everyone be a digital native to use ODR tools.
- Integration and Interoperability – Users are more likely to adopt technology that is like that which they are already comfortable. An intuitive interface that feels and works like someone's other iPhone apps or someone's existing Android apps might be adopted more quickly than an interface that looks and feels foreign. Also, if you want someone to seamlessly negotiate using an ODR tool, try to tightly – yet securely – integrate it with other software and services negotiators are likely to use, especially those they are likely to use during negotiations.

- Differential advantages inherent in using technology - Would you consider trying negotiation tools that are affordable, easy to learn, low risk, and they might even give you an unfair advantage when you engage with negotiators who do not use those tools? ODR tools that satisfy these criteria might make it easier to convey the value proposition for using ODR to negotiate. A related recommendation is to market ODR tools in nontechnical language that enables negotiators to appreciate the value without extensive explanation.
- Escalating pace of change - Consider updating existing ODR tools at the pace of mobile phone apps rather than PC software. Infrequent updates, which are associated with substantial change, will create a risk that negotiators are pushed too far outside of their comfort and competence zone.
- Negotiators who use ODR tools might need to consider which jurisdiction governs unresolved matters. Those who use a hosted ODR tool might be subject to the terms and conditions associated with the host and therefore have nothing to decide. In other cases, what if Negotiator 'A' participates from Denmark and Negotiator 'B' logs in from New York City? Or what if both login from New York City but one negotiator is from Denmark, where the subject matter of the conflict arose? Or what if there is a tangential participant who agrees to login briefly from London and then everyone agrees to use a mediator who remotely participates from Panama? To make it even more interesting, the next time everyone logs in to continue the negotiation, participants could be in different locations than last time. It would be wise to decide in advance what jurisdiction governs: (1) processing and storage of online data, (2) whether the mediator can be compelled to testify or provide documents in connection with subsequent litigation, and (3) the ultimate resolution of subject matter disputes.

6 Closing Remarks

It has only been about 30 years since anyone began to consider how technology might assist negotiators to be more successful strategically engaging each other about matters of mutual concern. Progress made in the past 30 years has been nothing short of incredible. The next 30 years could be even more remarkable. It is easy to envision negotiators and ODR having a long and splendid future together.

Chapter 15 ODR and Mediation

Noam Ebner and Daniel Rainey

1 Introduction: ODR and Mediation

Online mediation has enjoyed a distinct place in the field of ODR. Online Dispute Resolution was born of the realization that virtual commercial interactions created conflict of a different nature than that created by face-to-face interaction, and that realization led to the development of ODR systems designed to handle large volumes of cases that fell into easily classifiable repeating groups. Even with this focus on e-commerce and its special environment, mediation was a feature of all early ODR platforms. As we will discuss in this chapter, the ODR field's response to such online commercial conflict tended toward a funnel-type system design involving assessment, direct negotiation, computer-assisted mediation, work with human mediators, and final resolution.

Things are very different now, almost a quarter of a century into the development of ODR. Even before the restrictions on in-person interactions imposed by the Covid-19 pandemic, use of information and communication technology tools outside of e-commerce was on the rise in various legacy dispute resolution modes, including mediation. It is fair to say that the practice of mediation was evolving toward the general acceptance of the integration of technology into traditional mediation practice. With the advent of the Covid-19 pandemic, to use a Star Trek analogy, we went immediately to light speed. Accordingly, it is time for a more specific exploration of online mediation, both as a standalone process and within the wider context of ODR.[1]

In this chapter, what do we mean when we say 'ODR,' and what do we mean when we say 'online mediation?'

There is currently something of a debate about whether mediation must be conducted entirely online in order to be considered ODR, or whether the integration of technology into face-to-face processes also qualifies. Initially, for many but not all practitioners working in the 1990s, ODR implied the use of online tools, used beginning to end, to resolve conflict created online, primarily in e-commerce. While the field has advanced beyond that limited grasp of ODR, it has maintained its focus on 'online processes' rather

1 An interest in the increased use of ICT in dispute resolution generally can be seen in the currently active ODR Task Force of the American Bar Association. There are three Work Groups: one for Best Practices, one for Courts, and one for Private ODR (including mediation). For information on the Task Force and Work Groups, refer to www.americanbar.org/groups/dispute_resolution/.

than on 'technology-assisted' processes; in other words, discussions and study of mediation in the world of ODR focus on the use of technology as a communication channel for the mediation process, rather than any other use technology could have in mediation. In a recently published review of the application of technology to the mediation process, Ebner and Carrel describe how the field of ODR has focused on online processes, and the field of Alternative Dispute Resolution (ADR) has focused on technology-bereft processes, effectively leaving the notion of incorporating technology into traditional mediation rooms an unexplored gap in practice.[2] There has been some movement, even in the realm of e-commerce, to acknowledge the possibility of integrating technology into face-to-face processes. In its report on Working Group III-ODR, UNCITRAL noted:

> [ODR] can assist the parties in resolving the dispute in a simple, fast, flexible, and secure manner, without the need for physical presence at a meeting or hearing. ODR encompasses a broad range of approaches and forms (including but not limited to ombudsmen, complaints boards, negotiation, conciliation, mediation, facilitated settlement, arbitration and others), and the potential for hybrid processes comprising both online and offline elements.[3]

Many of the elements driving the development of e-commerce ODR have transferred to court ODR, the arena of ODR currently seeing the most rapid development. As mediation's central role in court ODR, particularly in the United States,[4] becomes established,[5] the focus remains on online processes with an added spotlight on process automation. It is accurate to say that the early tendency to define ODR in relation to its use in e-commerce created

> a tendency to think of ODR as the wholesale overtaking of the mediation process by computer programs, pushing aside mediators, stripping off

---

2 Carrel, A. & Ebner, N. (2019). "Mind the Gap: Bringing Technology to the Mediation Table," *Journal of Dispute Resolution* 2019(2), 1-45.

3 United Nations Commission on International Trade Law (UNCITAL), Working Group III – ODR, *Technical Notes on Online Dispute Resolution,* United Nations, New York, 2017, p. 1.

4 In other locales, online mediation is a component, or a building block, of comprehensive court ODR systems, rather than the centerpiece. For example, the U.K.'s transition to an online court system did not offer novel mediation services beyond previously existing telephonic mediation. For discussion of the different building blocks available in court ODR, and their application in different locales, *see* Ebner, N. & Greenberg, E. (2020). "Strengthening ODR Justice," *Washington University Journal of Law and Policy* 63, 65-118.

5 For a review of court ODR, *see* "Case Studies in ODR for the Courts," NCSC, available at https://www.ncsc.org/__data/assets/pdf_file/0023/18707/2017-12-18-odr-case-studies-revised.pdf.

nonverbal communication, and, to some, perverting the course of alternative justice.[6]

A tendency toward this view of technology's role in mediation may be developing in court ODR, but interestingly the first detailed study of an ODR program designed for a court system did not mention artificial intelligence or de-humanization – it focused on improved user access, with the assumption that easy access to an ODR for the courts would be a positive development.[7]

Increasingly, practitioners are comfortable suggesting that ODR includes both fully online mediation and the injection of ICT into the various steps of the mediation process conducted in a mixed online and face-to-face environment. As Rainey suggested, "ODR in the broader sense, is simply the intelligent application of information and communication technology to any conflict engagement process."[8] However, it is hard to tell where the terminological needle will settle, and what will be the lingering effect of the Covid-19 pandemic when we settle into a 'new normal'. While we expect the primary effects of the Covid-19 era to be in the realm of acceptance of online process conduct, we anticipate that the increase in mediators' overall comfort with technology will lead to exploration of its use in the traditional mediation room.

All that aside, this chapter will focus not on 'ODR' in any broad sense, but on 'online mediation' in its strictest sense: mediation that is conducted, primarily beginning to end, in an online environment. That focus will highlight issues, problems, and opportunities that exist in any ODR process, but which are sharpened to distinction in a process that fully relies on communication and cooperation. While context is important, these elements are relevant to online mediation whether conducted in e-commerce or court-ODR, or by private mediators taking their practice online.

Bernie Mayer[9] has noted how closely the field of conflict resolution is identified with the role of the neutral, and most specifically with mediation. He has suggested that while the field offers many other roles, services, and areas of expertise, its identification with mediation has offered it numerous advantages, as well as significant constraints.

---

6 Rainey, D. (2016). "Conflict Engagement and ICT: Evolution and Revolution," *The International Journal of Online Dispute Resolution* 3(2), 80.

7 *See* "Utah Online Dispute Resolution Platform: A Usability and Performance Report," James E. Rogers College of Law, University of Arizona, available at https://law.arizona.edu/utah-online-dispute-resolution-platform-usability-evaluation-and-report (last accessed September 2020), and Cueto, E. (2020). "Online Court Pilot Gets Low Marks Ahead of Wider Launch," Law360, 13 September 2020, available at www.law360.com/access-to-justice/articles/1309437/online-court-pilot-gets-low-marks-ahead-of-wider-launch?nl_pk=77322a31-1bbc-4e35-8532-8a4ef2d22451&utm_source=newsletter&utm_medium=email&utm_campaign=access-to-justice&read_more=1 (last accessed September 2020).

8 *Ibid.*, Rainey, p. 81.

9 Mayer, B.S. (2004). *Beyond Neutrality: Confronting the Crisis in Conflict Resolution.* San Francisco, CA: Jossey-Bass.

ODR, it would seem, is not quite as closely identified with mediation as ADR in general might be. This may be due to the multiple influences on the rapid evolution of the ODR field. Indeed, the two best-known success stories of the field, cited in just about every paper written on ODR, involve online arbitration (ICANN's UDRP) and online assisted negotiation (the primary process of eBay's dispute resolution process). It may be that elements unique to the online environment are more conducive to processes other than mediation, and technological functions better suited for assisting processes other than mediation. For example, automation functions may be particularly helpful for automated and assisted negotiation, allowing management of large volumes of similar-type cases/claims. Some applications of ODR in these realms involve technology providing parties enough support or assistance *on its own* to work things out *without* involving a human mediator. However, automation and boilerplating of resolution process-flows may be less helpful in 'retail' mediation, if one can apply that term to the every-case-is-unique practice of sole practitioners or small firms.

Similarly, mediation may not be ODR's central identifying feature or signature process, given that a heavy focus on automation, artificial intelligence, and robo-practitioners in the literature and in ongoing conversations among the dispute resolution community is a sign of the times. When Katsh and Rifkin, in their seminal ODR book,[10] originally conceptualized technology's role in dispute resolution as being the 'Fourth Party', they did so with a relatively narrow frame in mind. Katsh notes, "In its original ... incarnation, the Fourth Party primarily assists the third party neutral, generally providing conveniences and efficiencies."[11] Janet Rifkin echoes this non-robotic view of the fourth party,[12] and both suggest that the future will bring greater advances in information processing. The future they predicted is here, automation and intelligent agents are on the rise, and parties are increasingly assisted by the Fourth Party without the involvement of a human third party.

All this notwithstanding, online mediation is certainly significant within the world of ODR. In 2005, Melissa Conley Tyler reported mediation to be the most common individual service offered by ODR service providers (closely followed by arbitration). However, out of the 115 operating ODR service providers she identified, mediation was offered only by about 50 providers (many of whom offered other services in addition to mediation).[13] More recent reviews of service providers[14] seem to support this general

10 Katsh, E. & Rifkin, J. (2001). *Online Dispute Resolution: Resolving Disputes in Cyberspace.* San Francisco, CA: Jossey-Bass.

11 Katsh, E. (2012). "ODR: A Look at History." In *Online Dispute Resolution Theory and Practice.* Mohamed S. Abdel Wahab, Daniel Rainey, and Ethan Katsh, eds., The Hague: Eleven International Publishers, p. 32.

12 Rifkin, J. (2001). "Online Dispute Resolution: Theory and Practice of the Fourth Party," *Conflict Resolution Quarterly* 19(1), 117-124.

13 Conley Tyler, M. & Bornstein, J. (2006). "Accreditation of Online Dispute Resolution Practitioners," *Conflict Resolution Quarterly* 23(3), pp. 383-404.

14 Pearlstein, A., Hanson, B. & Ebner, N. (2012). "ODR in North America." In M.S. Abdel Wahab, E. Katsh & D. Rainey (Eds.) *ODR: Theory & Practice.* The Hague: Eleven International Publishing.

observation: Online mediation is an important element in the array of ODR services offered, but the ODR field is not (and never was) synonymous with online mediation.

However, as ODR breaks its original boundaries and online mediation is implemented in new contexts, mediation might regain the primacy in ODR that it enjoys in ADR in general. The shakeup the Covid-19 era has brought to all justice systems, consumer environments, and professional practice, the world over may support this shift.

To explore these issues, we open this chapter with a brief discussion of the development of mediation within the wider context of ODR growth. Subsequently, we provide a snapshot of the field's *status quo* with respect to stakeholders, modes of communication and technology utilized, as well as the prevailing trends. In the third section of this chapter, we address substantive and process issues for online mediation: mediation process models, stages, practitioner skills, professional issues, ethics, and practitioner standards.

2 Historical Development and Early Experiments

Katsh, Rifkin, and Gaitenby[15] described several notable online mediation projects undertaken during the ODR field's early, experimental phase, including:

a. The Online Ombuds project, a pilot ODR program established in 1996,[16]
b. The Maryland Family Mediation project, another early initiative funded by the National Center for Automated Information Research (NCAIR),[17]
c. The Cybertribunal project at the University of Montreal School of Law,[18] and

15 Katsh, E., Rifkin, J. & Gaitenby, A. (2000). "E-Commerce, E-Disputes, and E-Dispute Resolution: In the Shadow of eBay Law," *Ohio State Journal on Dispute Resolution*, 15, pp. 705-734.

16 In 1999, it conducted a pilot program for mediation of eBay disputes, an experiment which laid the groundwork for eBay's extensive employment of online negotiation and mediation which continues to this day. Over a two-week period, 225 buyers or sellers responded to an offer for free resolution of buyer-seller complaints. The complaints dealt with feedback, non-delivery of goods and other common eBay issues. Using e-mail for shuttle communication between the parties, due to parties' comfort with the medium, the mediator invited the other party to participate, asked to hear each side's stories, and proceeded to conduct a mediation process similar to face-to-face processes. *See* a sample transcript of one such process in Katsh & Rifkin (2001). 144 cases, or about 2/3 of the complaint cases, were actually mediated (others were unsuitable for mediation or resolved themselves). Out of these, 46% ended in agreement. *See* Katsh *et al.* (2000); Ponte, L. & Cavenagh, T. (2005). *Cyberjustice: Online Dispute Resolution (ODR) for E-Commerce.* Upper Saddle River, NJ: Prentice Hall.

17 In 1996, the Center for Law Practice Technology at the University of Maryland's School of Law initiated a mediation project for family and health care disputes. This project, however, never quite got off the ground. *See* Granat, R.S. (1996). "Creating an Environment for Mediating Disputes On the Internet," Center for Law Practice Technology at the University of Maryland School of Law. A working paper for the NCAIR Conference on On-Line Dispute Resolution, Washington, DC; Katsh *et al.* (2000); Getz, C. (2007). *Closing the Distance with Technology: Report on Phase I of the Technology-Assisted Family Mediation Project.*

18 This later developed into e-Resolution, a commercial service provider providing online mediation as well as arbitration for domain name disputes, which operated until 2002. *See* Katsh & Rifkin (2001).

d. SquareTrade, which provided online mediation services to eBay as a commercial venture, building on previous work by the Online Ombuds project.[19]

Less known were the ODR mediation programs pursued by the National Mediation Board and by the Federal Mediation and Conciliation Service's TAGS program.[20]

After these initial experiments and projects, the field developed toward offering online mediation services to the general public. Among the early service providers were Internet Neutral,[21] e-Resolution,[22] and Online Resolution.[23] They dealt with a wide range of dispute types, including business-to-business and business-to-consumer commercial disputes, workplace conflicts, and insurance issues. The number of cases that actually went to mediation in those early years was probably low;[24] indeed, many of the early mediation service providers closed shop after only a few years. However, other service providers took their place, and the number of initiatives continued to grow.[25]

3 CURRENT STATE OF THE ART OF ONLINE MEDIATION

Even before the great transition of many professional services online rendered by Covid-19, mediation was being provided online all over the world by both local and global providers. As envisioned, online mediation is truly a process enabling dispute resolution across cultures, jurisdictions and borders. As early as 2003, Abernethy

19 SquareTrade offered a process in which parties to eBay feedback disputes began their contact with each other through automated negotiation, followed up by assisted negotiation. Only if agreement was not reached through these processes, were parties offered the use of a live mediator. Although most cases settled through the automated stages of the process, SquareTrade conducted many human-led mediations. (*See* Rule, C. (2002). *Online Dispute Resolution for Business: B2B, E-Commerce, Consumer, Employment, Insurance, and Other Commercial Conflicts.* San Francisco, CA: Jossey-Bass Inc Pub.) According to Steve Abernethy, president of SquareTrade, during the period between 1999-mid-2003, 80% of the cases involving online mediation resulted in agreement. While there are no firm numbers available on the volume of cases actually mediated by SquareTrade, there were certainly many thousands. Their operations continued until 2008, after which eBay integrated the feedback dispute resolution process into its in-house dispute resolution operations. eBay continues to implement a hybrid processes beginning with automated negotiation and continuing on to optional human mediator intervention in the event of no agreement. *See* Abernethy, S. (2003). "The Square Trade Experience in Online and Offline Disputes," *Proceedings of the 2003 United Nations Forum on ODR.*

20 In 1997, the National Mediation Board (NMB) began the process of integrating technology into its work in the airline and railroad industries in the United States. Mediation of contract negotiations, workplace disputes, and arbitration of workplace disputes were conducted in part using a variety of ICT platforms. Simultaneously the Federal Mediation and Conciliation Service (FMCS) developed its TAGS program, a portable suite of network-connected computers that could be used remotely or in face-to-face contract negotiation or mediation sessions.

21 *See* Beal, B.L. (1999). "Online Mediation: Has Its Time Come?," *Ohio State Journal on Dispute Resolution* 15.

22 Pearlstein *et al.* (2012).

23 Rule (2002).

24 *See* Beal (1999).

25 *See* Conley Tyler & Bornstein (2006); Pearlstein *et al.* (2012).

related that SquareTrade's processes had involved participants from over 120 countries, and were conducted in five different languages. The geographical spread of service providers since then has resulted in online mediation making headway in all regions of the world.[26] Increased activity across borders and an increase in access to mediation and other dispute resolution approaches was one driving force behind the attempt by UNCITRAL to establish international agreement on how to deal with cross border ecommerce disputes.[27] Similarly, increased use of mediation for non-commercial cross border disputes as addressed by the creating of the 'Singapore Convention', the United Nations Convention on International Settlement Agreements Resulting from Mediation.[28] Working groups on both of these projects discussed the role of ODR in transcending geographic and political boundaries for resolving such disputes.

3.1 Organizational Structures for ODR Mediation Services

This section will focus on the prevailing trends and applications in offering mediation services involving the use of ICT.

3.1.1 Regional versus Global

Some service providers hold themselves out as global practitioners, not limiting themselves to any one region.[29] Others, while not explicitly limiting the scope of their operations, do so implicitly by including comments on their websites referencing particular areas, organizations and legal issues, by the language/s in which services are offered, by a country-specific domain name or by the language of the website itself. Still other service providers limit themselves explicitly to specific countries or areas.[30]

---

26 *See* Conley Tyler & Bornstein (2006). Also *see* Abdel Wahab, M.S., Katsh, E. & Rainey, D. (Eds.) (2012). *ODR: Theory & Practice* (1st. ed.). The Hague: Eleven International Publishing; dedicated chapters of the book described ODR's spread and development in six regions: North America, Europe, Australia, Asia, Latin America, and Africa.

27 *See* UNCITRAL Technical Notes on Online Dispute Resolution, available at https://uncitral.un.org/sites/uncitral.un.org/files/media-documents/uncitral/en/v1700382_english_technical_notes_on_odr.pdf (last accessed 18 March 2021).

28 *See* UN Singapore Convention, available at https://uncitral.un.org/en/texts/mediation/conventions/international_settlement_agreements (last accessed 3 August 2020.

29 Examples of early providers taking this route are Juripax and TheMediationRoom; more recently, Youstice and Modria adopt this approach.

30 *E.g.*, Cybersettle (limiting comments), emediation.nl (language and domain name), and the British Columbia Family Mediation Project (explicit geographical limitation). An interesting provider in this regard is ODRWorld.com which operated in the mid-2000s. This platform did not limit the geographic scope of its operations, but the same service provider also operated separate platforms such as ODRChina, ODRMalaysia, ODRAustralia. and ODRIndia, servicing these countries specifically. In essence, ODRWorld contextualized its services by offering services to diverse regions in South East Asia and Australia.

3.1.2 Individual Practitioners versus Institutional 'Service Providers'

From the start, examination and discussion of online mediation (and ODR in general) has tended to focus on 'service providers' rather than on 'practitioners'. This probably had multiple reasons.

First, this was indeed the actual business model most often employed; many of the early ventures in online mediation were indeed run by a service provider who kept a roster of mediators. OnlineResolution kept a roster of 600 mediators and arbitrators, and SquareTrade had about 300 mediators on its roster.[31] The sites themselves were operated as businesses performing intake of cases, collection of fees, and assignment to mediators from the roster; in addition, they provided training and support to their neutrals.

Second, it is the nature of Internet commerce that individuals or small teams set up a website and present it as the face of a large-scale business. This is not necessarily an effort to pull the wool over anyone's eyes; on the web, your catchy name and web domain are part of your branding strategy. 'InternetMediationTeam.com' will always be more effective than NoamtheMediator.com.

Third, is that the previous point is particularly true given the market and clients that were being targeted. Early service providers aimed to engage with e-commerce entities and integrate themselves into their b2b and b2c operations. A corporate veneer and framework seemed more conducive to success in this area.

Fourth, continuing on the previous points, much of the focus (particularly the early focus) of ODR was on *scale*. ODR was seen as particularly effective for handling large volumes of similar disputes; the service-provider model fits that niche.

Finally, with much of the focus on new technological platforms for delivering mediation, early developers were more likely to be business organizations rather than individual practitioners due to issues of scale, cost, and expertise.

On the practitioner side, a contributing factor to this model's prevalence in ODR's early phases was that many individual practitioners simply did not hang out an online shingle. It may be that some individual practitioners were, behind the scenes, sole operators of an online mediation service providing site. However, no visible presence of small-shop mediation practitioners was identified on the web in Conley Tyler's 2005 mapping out of the field. These began to appear toward 2010, and their numbers have steadily increased since then. By 2015, individual or small-shop mediator websites offering online mediation alongside their traditional co-located processes (without trying to cloak themselves in a larger organizational veneer) were commonplace; by the end of the decade, they were everywhere.[32] Three converging factors drove this shift.

31 *See* Rule (2002).

32 In September 2020, Mediate.com's practitioner directory included 335 professionals self-identifying as 'online mediators.

First, mediation is ever a competitive market, supply-driven rather than demand-driven,[33] in which every edge a mediator can gain in attracting cases is of great value. Second, as mediators and the general population became increasingly adept and comfortable with technology, taking mediation processes online seemed more of a logical next step than a huge, daunting leap to which customers would never agree. Third, the constantly increasing availability of low-to-no cost platforms for communication remove a significant barrier to practicing online that existed in ODR's early days. One no longer required the expertise or funding to design a proprietary platform; with an email account and familiarity with Zoom or Skype, one was set to mediate, even if there were serious concerns about privacy, data security, access, etc.

While many individual practitioners were a part of this slow development, the prevailing attitude toward online mediation among practicing mediators during ODR's first couple of decades, and even at their end, remained that of reticence. Without in-the-room, face-to-face interaction, and the human touch presumably inherent to these, ODR would 'never work'. Writing as late as 2019, Carrel and Ebner summarized the attitudes toward online mediation that they encountered in discussions with practitioners:

> One powerful argument that often comes up in these conversations can be summed up as 'If it ain't broke, don't fix it!' Our time-tested processes work, mediators tell us, and they help parties more often than not. Why change things?[34]

While not unsympathetic to that attitude, they pointed out its fundamental unsustainability:

> As practitioners of these same time-tested processes ourselves, we cannot help but recognize the power of this approach and its underlying truths. However, powerful as it is, maintaining this approach cannot assure that what worked yesterday will not be 'broke' tomorrow.[35]

Tomorrow, it seems, has arrived, in the sense that Covid-19 effectively rendered traditional mediation 'broke' for a while, just as it did all professional activity requiring

33 Mayer (2004); Velikonja, U. (2009). "Making Peace and Making Money: Economic Analysis of the Market for Mediators in Private Practice," *Albany Law Review* 72, pp. 257-291.
34 Supra n.2 at 9.
35 *Ibid.*

face-to-face interaction. Facing this 'broke', most mediators' response was to conduct mediation remotely.[36]

While it is hard to make predictions about the post-Covid-19 era while mired deeply in its middle, we certainly expect to see many more practitioners offer online processes as one modality of their services than in the past. Going a bit further out on a limb, we anticipate that the online transition necessitated by Covid-19 will turn out to be a watershed event, in terms of practitioners' adoption of online processes. Indeed, in a number of dialogue sessions conducted separately by each of the authors of this chapter involving practitioners and advocates, the prevailing attitude is that once the Covid-19 crisis has passed, online mediation will be part of normal practice going forward. Having practiced mediation online, mediators have discovered that it does work.[37] Furthermore, throughout this period online mediation has been setting down educational roots of its own. All mediators trained during Covid-19 have conducted their training and simulations online. Academic courses on mediation and ADR taught during this period were also all taught online; moreover, many of them have added (previously untaught) substantive units regarding online mediation and negotiation together with including discussion of the effects of the online environment as part of the debrief phase of courses' simulations. Having studied and simulated mediation solely in an online environment, these trainees and students are unlikely to reject it as a mode of practice in the future. To tie all of these threads together, we predict that in the future, choice between online, in-person, or hybrid modalities of mediation will result from case features or exigencies, service provider models, and party and mediator individual *preferences*, rather than stemming from sweeping statements regarding (in)efficacy of online mediation or inimitable qualities of in-person interactions.

3.1.3 Alternative Models: Licensing and Partnering

There are some developing models of practice bridging the previous two categories of regional/global and of institutional service provider/individual practitioner. These

36 Indeed, as we worked on this chapter during the period of social distancing and sheltering in place necessitated by the Covid-19 epidemic in early 2020, we've seen the trends and forecasts we had originally made in this section regarding the increase in practitioner adoption of online mediation accelerate to saturation over the course of just a few days' time. As businesses in the US and around the world shut down, and people avoided travel and gatherings, we've witnessed an *ad hoc* wholesale embrace of online mediation (primarily, though not exclusively, videoconference-based) by practitioners around the world. Over half a year later as we finalize the manuscript, this remains the status quo in most of the US, and only in a few US states and a limited number of countries around the world have mediators resumed in-person meetings. This extended duration of the period during in which mediation has been conducted online, or not conducted at all, has resulted in most mediation practitioners dipping their toe in the waters of online mediation; many have dived in and gained significant experience with this mode of process-conduct during this period.

37 For another such summary of mediators coming to this recognition, *see* Creo, R.A. (2020). "Zoom, Zooming, Zoomed into the Future: Moving to Optimist from Skeptic on Online Mediation," *Alternatives to the High Cost of Litigation* 38(8), 119-122.

involve service providers who have developed advanced platforms offering their use to individual practitioners. This might be done by offering 'rooms' to individual mediators on an *ad hoc* or an ongoing basis, much in the way a face-to-face mediation center might rent out its meeting room to an individual practitioner. Early examples of this model include TheMeditionRoom and Juripax.[38] CREK, a recent entry into the ODR marketplace continues this approach by offering a 'virtual mediation case room' for a monthly fee.[39]

Another model involves a more robust connection between the institutional service provider and individual practitioners, in which the former sets the latter up with a dedicated 'space' on their platform, branded according to the practitioner's preferences (for example, Trokt[40]). There have also been instances of service providers selling country-specific or language-specific licenses or concessions, and other types of partnership.

3.2 *Contexts of Online Mediation Application: Mediatability*

What case types are *particularly* suited to be resolved via online mediation? Early service providers considered complaint handling, e-commerce, and low-value cases between geographically distant parties to be most suitable for online resolution. This likely stemmed from the original framing of ODR's promise by its early proponents. However, the targeting of these areas is far less predominant today (perhaps with good reason, given early service providers' lack of commercial longevity). Reviewing the websites of practitioners and service providers today, it is clear that a much wider and more general net is being cast regarding dispute type and context. Some providers do not limit customers' imaginations to any particular context at all; others highlight the multiple contexts in which they intervene.

To understand the spread of online mediation – in the past, and in the future – it is important to remember three things. The first, is that the use of online mediation processes never developed in line with commonplace intuitive notions as to 'what should/could be mediated online'. These limiting preconceptions were breached early in online mediation's history, as people became increasingly accustomed to taking their activities online. The second, is that many online mediation processes take place after disputes have already entered a settlement-through-ODR process. With ODR in general casting a *very* wide net, different types of cases find themselves funneled through to online mediation even though these might never have reached mediation, either online or in-person, as a first choice. The third is that the Covid-19 period has provided a

38 *See also* Rule (2002).
39 CREK, available at https://crekodr.com/ (last accessed September 2020).
40 Trokt, available at www.trokt.org/ (last accessed September 2020).

natural experiment – and a professional myth-buster – in that it saw mediation in *all* contexts conducted online; it may not be so simple, or logical, to redraw lines of distinction that have been shown to be insignificant in practice.

3.2.1 Online Mediation: Not What You Would Expect

In a dynamic very reminiscent of the growth of traditional mediation as an area of practice, it would be difficult, even in a pre-Covid-19 world, to isolate a dispute area in which online mediation is *not* offered or would not be considered suitable by an online mediator. While individual practitioners or readers might pose areas in which they might intuitively question the e-channel's suitability, these areas are clearly shrinking. Whereas original thinking on ODR envisioned it flourishing as a tool for resolving disputes-at-a-distance, settling online business and other transactional disputes, online mediation has jumped those conceptual fences and is offered in other areas. ODR in general has long left behind the conception that it is only suitable for disputes originating in online activity.[41] In addition, it has been shown to be a powerful tool for resolving disputes where geography is not a factor limiting participants' ability to convene face-to-face, and disputes in which emotional, relational and social issues are at least as important as transactional elements.

Two areas demonstrating this last notion are online family mediation and workplace mediation. Somewhat counter-intuitively, family mediation has always been an area of interest for online mediation.[42] Two projects – one conducted by Juripax in 2008, and the other conducted by The British Columbia Mediator Roster Society between May 2009 and February 2010, and expanded in 2019 – are good indicators of the benefits of online mediation for family cases. Both projects saw high settlement rates, which were complemented with high rates of party satisfaction and willingness to utilize online mediation in the future.[43] Similarly, workplace mediation, while long envisioned as suitable when involving organizations spread out across the globe, or between members of virtual teams working at a distance,[44] is receiving an increased amount of attention as a

41 *See* Conley Tyler & Bornstein (2006); Rule (2002).

42 *See* Granat (1996); Rule (2002).

43 Bollen, K & Euwema, M.C. (2010). *Online Mediation in Divorce Cases.* Leuven: Catholic University of Leuven; Getz, C. (2010). *Evaluation of the Distance Mediation Project: Report on Phase II of the Technology-Assisted Family Mediation Project.* Victoria, BC: British Columbia Mediator Roster Society.

44 *See* Rule (2002); Ebner, N. (2008). "Online Dispute Resolution: Applications for e-HRM." In T. Torres-Coronas & M. Arias-Oliva (Eds.) *Encyclopedia of Human Resources Information Systems: Challenges in e-HRM.* Hershey, PA: Idea Group Reference Publishing.

tool for settings involving close-quarters relationships.[45] A study conducted by Juripax found that adding an online element to workplace mediation processes contributes to their effectiveness by eliminating asymmetry in hierarchal workplace disputes (such as between subordinates and supervisors).[46] We note these two areas of practice as contexts in which cases will naturally involve up-close, emotional, and personal issues between parties who know each other well. While certainly not the cases for which ODR was originally envisioned, they (and other areas sharing similar characteristics, such as elder care mediation, health care mediation or others) might prove to be areas of significant growth for online mediation practice.

3.2.2 Online Mediation: Not Always First Choice

Traditional mediation usually assumes a breakdown in communication or other negotiation difficulties between parties, or, if introduced early in a conflict, assumes that a mediated discussion will be more productive than direct negotiation. This is in contrast to an assumption embedded in both ODR for e-commerce and ODR for the courts. In those venues, ODR platforms are developed using a DNMEA model (Diagnosis, Negotiation, Mediation, Evaluation, Appeal) in which mediation is engaged only after dispute diagnosis and direct negotiation.[47]

Outside of e-commerce and the courts, online mediation practitioners' general interest-based approach, and a preference for autonomous decision making, leads increasingly to a state-of the-art in which mediation – regarded as effective, and perhaps the best communication or negotiation fixer-upper – is viewed as the process of first choice.[48]

As traditional mediators enter the online mediation market, the emphasis on technology as a communication medium, rather than technology as a dispute resolution tool in its own right – will likely tip the balance back toward human intervention as

45 The topic of organizational and workplace topic received an impressive amount of attention at Cyberweek 2010. *See* http://adrhub.com/forum/topics/odr-for-organizational (last accessed 20 February 2011). In 2019, Laboratoire de cyberjustice launched a program to introduce ODR in workplace disputes in Canada: www.cyberjustice.ca/ Also *see* Parlamis, J., Ebner, N. & Mitchell, L. (2016). "Looking Back to Leap Forward: The Potential for E-mediation at Work." In K. Bollen, M. Euwema & L. Munduate (Eds.) *Advancing Workplace Mediation Through Integration of Theory and Practice* (3rd volume in *Industrial Relations and Conflict Management* series). The Netherlands: Springer Verlag.

46 Bollen, K. & Euwema, M.C. (2009). *Angry at Your Boss or Fearing Your Employee? Negative Affect in Hierarchical Conflicts and the Moderating Role of E-Supported Mediation.* Kyoto: IACM.

47 Rule, C. (2020). "Online Dispute Resolution and Future of Justice," available at www.colinrule.com/writing/future.pdf (last accessed in September 2020).

48 *See* Sander, F.E.A. & Rozdeiczer, L. (2006). "Matching Cases and Dispute Resolution Procedures: Detailed Analysis Leading to a Mediation-Centered Approach," *Harvard Negotiation Law Review* 11.

default, as opposed to automated intervention as default and human intervention as a backup.[49]

3.2.3 Covid-19 Era Effects: The Proof is in the Pudding, in a Pinch

January-February 2020 (in Asia and Europe) and March-April 2020 (in the US and South America), saw the shutdown of government services such as courts, and the curtailing of private business activities. With very few exceptions, all these resumed activity online, sometimes with a nigh-instantaneous transition. The authors were witnesses, participants, and occasional consultants to this transition in the fields of dispute resolution, participating in countless practitioner conferences, trainings, webinars, roundtables, one-on-one conversations and listserv discussions discussing online video-based mediation. To the best of our recollection (and, this section is being written only days and weeks after these conversations), not *once* did anybody involved say '...except for context X. You can't do X mediation, or mediations related to X, online'. This was particularly notable given the sharp rejection of online mediation, in general or in particular contexts, by many practitioners through the end of 2019 as discussed above. Beginning in 2020, online mediation is fully applied, albeit in a pinch, across all contexts in which mediation is practiced.

3.3 *Online Mediation: Advantages and Challenges, Suitability and Conditions*

There have been many attempts to provide an overview of the advantages and disadvantages of online mediation. We will summarize those that provide practical considerations pertinent to the mediatability of certain disputes arising in diverse contexts.

---

49 Court ODR and e-commerce ODR may continue to remain exceptions to this. However, these terms encompass a great many variations. Court ODR is not monolithic; jurisdictions, court systems or even individual courthouses create their system through picking and choosing from a variety of ODR 'building-blocks' to create the system preferred for their needs. *See* Ebner & Greenberg (2020). In some cases, the outcome is a mediation-centric or a mediation-only ODR system. *See*, for example the Franklin County Municipal Court ODR Project, which is essentially a negotiation platform with a mediator waiting in the wings in case parties need help, or a mediation platform with a preliminary stage of unfacilitated conversation, depending on how you look at it. There are no other automated elements such as analysis, diagnoses, party education, etc. *See* the project's website here https://sc.courtinnovations.com/OHFCMC/; *see also* National Center for State Courts joint Technology Committee Resource Bulletin: Case Studies in ODR for Courts, version 2.0, January 2020, available at www.ncsc.org/__data/assets/pdf_file/0020/16517/2020-01-28-odr-case-studies-v2-final.pdf (last accessed 15 September 2020).

3.3.1 Advantages of Online Mediation

3.3.1.1 Advantages for Parties

- Online mediation can be conducted synchronously or asynchronously, across different media. Mediators can employ more than one medium, in order to tailor a process to the parties' needs.[50] As a result, online mediation is convenient. Parties set their own timetable, and, when employing asynchronous communication, can participate at their own convenience.
- Parties gain access to mediator expertise beyond that which might be available in any given geographical region.[51]
- There are different models for pricing online mediation services, and pricing of online services is often no different than that of face-to-face services. However, there certainly is enhanced cost *effectiveness*, given that parties save on travel cost and the loss of productivity associated with travel time.

3.3.1.2 Process Advantages

- In asynchronous processes, the slowed-down pace can allow the mediator a more intentional application of the mediator's toolbox. This enhances opportunities for nuance and subtlety. Mediators might find it easier to tweak and reframe messages. They can create opportunities for behind the scenes contact with each party to a greater degree than face-to-face processes allow, as private communication reduces threats to perceived neutrality. Working with asynchronous methods, mediators can conduct simultaneous caucusing, saving process-time. Further utility can be achieved due to the elimination of those caucuses which face-to-face mediators conduct for the sole purpose of showing even-handedness.[52]
- In text-based communication, records are preserved and reviewable, allowing for more seamless processes and joint frames of reference.

---

50 For discussion of media choice, *see* Mor, S., & Suppes, A. (2014). "The Role of Communication." In M. Benoliel (Ed.) *Negotiation Excellence: Successful Deal Making* (2nd ed.). Singapore: World Scientific Publishing, p. 381; also *see* Schneider, A. & McCarthy, S. (2017). "Choosing Among Modes of Communication." In C. Honeyman & A.K. Schneider (Eds.) *The Negotiator's Desk Reference (Vol.2)*. St Paul, MN: DRI Press.

51 Katsh & Rifkin (2001) discuss the basic functions of any ODR system as convenience, expertise, and trust. As this section has shown, the first two are inherent in many models of providing online mediation services. The third requires more specific attention. *See* Ebner, N. & Zeleznikow, J. (2015). "Fairness, Trust and Security in Online Dispute Resolution," *Hamline Journal of Public Law and Policy*, 36(2), 143-160.

52 Rule, C. (2000). "New Mediator Capabilities in Online Dispute Resolution," available at www.mediate.com/articles/rule.cfm (last accessed 18 March 2021).

- In text-based mediation processes, gender-based cues are diminished, reducing bias.[53] Similarly, other cues related to race, accent, or national origin, to name just a few triggers of unconscious bias,[54] are diminished.
- Text-based communication also minimizes the effects of 'good talkers' gaining the upper hand or of dominant figures causing others to reduce their participation levels.[55]
- The limiting effect of text-based communication on emotive communication has been suggested as an advantage in e-negotiation and online mediation as reducing confrontational dynamics, although this is certainly issue for debate.[56]
- Where it is appropriate, ODR platforms can be configured to allow for anonymous input for brainstorming or idea generation, removing some of the potential points of anxiety regarding 'speaking up' in sessions.
- Parties and mediators can engage in text-based discussion without the immediate time pressure and other dynamics associated with synchronous, face-to-face conversations.
- External experts can be consulted with, or brought into the process as necessary, regardless of their geographical location and without disrupting the process' dynamics.
- In synchronous online processes, reductions in travel time and scheduling challenges offer flexibility to the mediation process, in the sense that it allows parties to choose between the one-session-process commonly practiced in traditional mediation the US,[57] and multiple sessions spread over a week or several weeks,[58] as practiced elsewhere in the world.

---

53 Bhalla, M.A. (2020). "Gender Identity & Text-based, Online Mediation," *McGill Journal of Dispute Resolution* 6(3), 57-75.

54 Greenwald, A.G., McGhee, D.E. & Schwartz, J.L.K. (1998). "Measuring Individual Differences in Implicit Cognition: The Implicit Association Test," *Journal of Personality and Social Psychology* 74(6), 1464-1480.

55 Thompson, L.L. (2001). *The Mind and Heart of the Negotiator* (2nd ed.). Upper Saddle River, NJ: Prentice Hall.

56 *See* Victorio, R.M. (2000). "Internet Dispute Resolution (IDR): Bringing ADR into the 21st Century," 1 *Pepperdine Dispute Resolution Law Journal*, 2, 279-300; Ebner, N *et al.* (2009). "You've Got Agreement: Negoti@ting Via Email." In C. Honeyman, J. Coben & G. De Palo (eds.), *Rethinking Negotiation Teaching: Innovations for Context and Culture.* St. Paul, MN: DRI Press.

57 *See, e.g.*, Lande, J. (2020). "The Evolution to Planned Early Multi Stage Mediation," *Kluwer Mediation Blog*, available at http://mediationblog.kluwerarbitration.com/2020/08/28/the-evolution-to-planned-early-multi-stage-mediation/.

58 Considering this model might also be beneficial given the phenomenon known as Zoom fatigue, the sense of depletion and exhaustion parties feel when participating in extended videoconferences. For more on this challenge, see Greenberg, E. & Ebner, N. (2020). "Designing Binge-Worthy Courses: Pandemic Pleasures and COVID Consequences," *Negotiation Journal* 36(4).

- In processes where language could be a barrier to communication, an increasing number of platforms offer real-time translation for all parties.[59]

3.3.1.3 Advantages for Society

- Online mediation is a helpful building block in a suite of responses to the access to justice crisis faced by many countries around the world.[60]
- Online mediation offers significant environmental benefits over traditional mediation, which convenes parties at a single location.[61]

3.3.2 Disadvantages of Online Mediation

3.3.2.1 Disadvantages for Parties

- In cases where parties file a case and are contacted by a mediator assigned by a service provider, it is challenging for parties to connect with mediators or to assess them. Parties cannot rely on local reputation, and there may be few Internet resources to assist them. This is an issue in both face-to-face mediation and online mediation – what makes a 'good' mediator? Is it situational and based on the mediator's knowledge of a specific area of expertise? Is the amount of training the mediator has undergone a marker for competence? Does the number of cases a mediator has handled have any relation to her or his competence? Adding the use of technology to the mix of the mediator's duties adds yet another challenge to this complicated issue.
- Experienced face-to-face negotiators, able to steer interactions (including mediated interactions) through communication techniques, conversation dominance, volume or body language, may be handicapped online;
- Archived materials, preserved as video or text are always out there. Once a party posts something in a discussion forum or participates in a recorded videoconference, their words are out of their hands forever. While many service providers are explicit about their security procedures, there are no certain guarantees in Internet security. As one of our colleagues once observed, when you say 'cloud computing' you are really saying 'someone else's computer'.

---

59 Platforms like Kudo (https://kudoway.com/) and the webinar version of Zoom (https://support.zoom.us/hc/en-us/articles/360034919791-Language-interpretation-in-meetings-and-webinars) offer the opportunity for simultaneous translation.

60 *See* Ebner & Greenberg (2020).

61 *See* Ebner, N. & Getz, C. (2012). "ODR: The Next Green Giant," *Conflict Resolution Quarterly* 29(3), 283-307.

3.3.2.2 Process Disadvantages

- The most oft-discussed process disadvantages are the perceived lack of warmth, empathy, immediacy, rapport, and other attitudes and affects that make face-to-face mediation so successful. These issues are encountered not only in text-based communication, but in video communication as well, albeit to a lesser extent. While efforts are made to explain how to compensate for these in online communication, and even to utilize certain characteristics of online communication to achieve gains on these elements beyond what face-to-face communication permits, this is still, in many aspects and to many communicators, an uphill battle.[62]
- Messages conveyed online, and particularly those conveyed through text, are prone to misinterpretation[63] and misattribution;[64] they are prone to triggering deterioration in trust.[65]
- The online venue challenges the function served by apology in mediation, given that party sincerity cannot be gauged without contextual cues.[66]
- Face-to-face mediation is transparent regarding the question of who is speaking with whom, at any given moment. As different forum dynamics play out (with all parties convened around a table, parties switching in and out of a mediation room as the mediator caucuses with each of them separately, or mediators conducting shuttle diplomacy between parties ensconced in separate meeting rooms) parties have a clear picture of where the mediator is, and who they are speaking to at any given moment. Asynchronous communication, along with mediators' ability to establish private communication with each party separately with the click of a button, increases potential for mediator manipulation and for worries about mediator neutrality. This uncertainty, particularly when left unaddressed, might cause suspicion and loss of trust.[67]

---

62 *See* Ebner, Chapter 4. Also *see* Ebner, N. (2012). "ODR and Interpersonal Trust." In M.S. Abdel Wahab, E. Katsh & D. Rainey (Eds.) *ODR: Theory & Practice*. The Hague: Eleven International Publishing. *See* Morris, M., *et al.* (2002). "Schmooze or Lose: Social Friction and Lubrication in E-Mail Negotiations," *Group Dynamics: Theory, Research, and Practice* 6(1), 89-100; Ebner, N. (2007). "Trust-Building in E-Negotiation." In L. Brennan & V. Johnson (eds.), *Computer-Mediation Relationships and Trust: Managerial and Organizational Effects*. Hershey, PA: Information Science Publishing; Ebner *et al.* (2009); Carrier, L., Spradlin, A., Bunce, J. & Rosen, L. (November 2015). "Virtual Empathy," *Computers in Human Behavior* 52, 39-48.

63 Thompson (2001).

64 Nadler, J. & Shestowsky, D. (2006). "Negotiation, Information Technology, and the Problem of the Faceless Other." In L. L. Thompson (Ed.), *Negotiation Theory and Research*. New York: Psychology Press.

65 Ebner (2007).

66 *See*, for example, the Cyberweek 2010 discussion forum led by Sam Edwards, Eileen Barker and Michael Cote. available at http://adrhub.com/forum/topics/media-effects-online (last accessed 14 September 2020).

67 The literature on ODR in general is rich with discussions of advantages and disadvantages of ODR, much of which is applicable to online mediation. For further discussion focusing specifically on online mediation, *see*, for example, Granat (1996); Ponte & Cavenagh (2005).

- More generally, online mediation involves reduced social presence and a sense of distance. Michael Moore's 'Theory of Transactional Distance' explains the challenge this poses in the context of distance education. He suggests that distance education's true challenge is not simply a geographic separation of learners and teachers. Rather, it is a substantive pedagogical challenge dubbed 'transactional distance'. Transactional distance includes both physical distance (bridged using technology) *and* social distance. To the degree that transactional distance rises, dialogue become more difficult. The more transactional distance is bridged, the more dialogue becomes robust. This notion appears to be valid in the context of mediation, suggesting that the existence of transactional distance presents an inherent barrier that mediators must overcome to produce strengthened relationships and durable resolutions.[68]

3.3.3 Suitability for Online Mediation

What elements of a case make it suitable for online mediation? We suggest augmenting traditional mediation suitability-tests[69] with the following considerations:

- Are disputants geographically distant from each other (such as is common in e-commerce), or from their preferred neutral?
- Did the dispute itself arise from an online transaction or interaction?
- Is travel to face-to-face mediation impossible, cost prohibitive, or a factor likely to rule out mediation for any other reason?
- Does the dispute include trans-jurisdictional issues, making choice of law or court-decision enforcement difficult?
- Are the parties unwilling, or unable, to meet with each other face-to-face?
- Do scheduling issues or party preferences make it difficult or impractical for parties to convene for face-to-face mediation?
- Is a party or a mediator disabled in a way that challenges travel or convening?
- Do concerns regarding inter-party violence or intimidation make convening in the same room a risky prospect?[70]
- Have parties participated in online mediation in the past?
- Are parties reasonably adept with online communication platforms?
- Will face-to-face mediation in this case incur prohibitive environmental costs?

---

68 *See* Moore, M.G. (1993). "Theory of Transactional Distance." In D. Keegan (Ed.) *Theoretical Principles of Distance Education*. New York: Routledge, pp. 22-38.

69 For example, *see* the suitability factors listed in MacFarlane, J. (2003). *Dispute Resolution: Readings and Cases* (2nd ed.). Ontario: Emond Montgomery.

70 *See*, regarding emotionally charged family situations, Getz (2010), available at www.mediatebc.com/sites/default/files/Distance-Mediation-Project--Evaluation-Report.pdf (last accessed 14 September 2020). Also *see* Rogers, S. (2008). "Online Dispute Resolution: An Option for Mediation in the Midst of Gendered Violence," *Ohio State Journal on Dispute Resolution* 24(2), 249-380, regarding restorative-justice oriented processes in cases of gender-based violence.

- Finally, in the Covid-19 era, we would be remiss for not including a final question: will face-to-face mediation in this case pose individual or public health risks?

Even one positive answer to these questions is likely to tilt the scales in favor of convening the process online; provided, of course, that mediation is a suitable process in the first place.[71] As time passes, the question of what constitutes a 'proper' case for online mediation becomes more and more irrelevant. Given the centrality of online communication and information handling in our lives, it is hard to imagine a conflict that simply could not be handled using some technology. As mediators and parties become increasingly comfortable doing everything from banking to finding life-partners online, they will certainly become increasingly comfortable with online mediation. Post-Covid-19, we anticipate the 'suitability' lines blurring even further.

3.3.4 Preconditions for Online Mediation

The previous section describes considerations likely to make choice of online mediation beneficial. However, online mediation cannot take place unless certain preconditions are met:

- Parties and mediator must have regular access to the Internet and computers or mobile devices. This may seem anachronistic to many readers who are so welded to their devices that they are virtually cyborgs; however, this is still not true in many areas in the world, and other situations - such as weather conditions or travel - can affect anyone. Even in developed areas, affordable data (particularly, sufficient data to support videoconferencing) is also a prerequisite.
- Parties must be competent and comfortable with technology of the type the mediator proposes to employ. Whereas competency can be directly affected by training, it is hard to directly affect a party's *dis*comfort with an online medium; in some cases, this might rule out online mediation.
- A shared language or adequate online translation services.[72]
- A contextually appropriate degree of privacy and security.[73]

71 For further discussion of this issue, *see* Summers Raines, S. (2004). "The Practice of Mediation Online: Techniques to Use or Avoid when Mediating in Cyberspace," *The Third Annual Forum on Online Dispute Resolution*, Melbourne, Australia; Ponte & Cavenagh (2005); Getz (2010).

72 Increasingly, applications like Kudo allow for instant translation into a variety of languages, allowing for real-time, multi-lingual mediation online, with video, document sharing, screen sharing, etc. In the foreseeable future, mediation across multiple languages could be relatively simple and inexpensive. While free programs such as Google Translate or Skype Translator are not yet precise enough to convey meaning and intent at the level required in mediation, they are improving all the time.

73 Summers Raines (2004). *See also* Draper, C. & Raymond, A. (2019). "Ethical Technology Risk," *The International Journal of Online Dispute Resolution* 6(2), 144-153. For discussion of the terminology associated with security and other related concepts in online processes, *see* Ebner & Zeleznikow (2015).

3.3.5 Choice of Technology

As Colin Rule[74] put it,

> Technology, like stage lighting for a play, should not be the focus – if people walk out of a play talking about the stage lighting then odds are either the play or the lighting was not a success.

Behind the scenes of every play, though, hours can go into discussing the placing of every light bulb and fog machine, often trying to figure out how to render the sources invisible and natural, letting the viewers focus on the actors. Indeed, the ODR field has seen examples of entities getting lost in their technology and paying a price. It has also seen examples of constantly adapting technology to suit users' comfort zones and capabilities in a world setting all these in constant flux.

While one could fill an entire chapter describing the nuances of different technologies that could be used for ODR, this section will avoid that, heeding another of Rule's admonitions: anything written about technology is certain to look silly (or, at best, quaint) after two or three years. Many pages in the ODR literature, and the wider literature on computer-mediated communication, have been filled with the advantages and disadvantages of text or video communication, or with commentary on email-based communication as opposed to dedicated platforms serving as the basis for communication. In this section, it seems sufficient to recall the original thinking regarding the role and nature of technology in ODR, and connect that to comments on the current state of the art and developing trends with regards to technology.

One critical process-issue is the question of whether a platform for online mediation should provide for synchronous or asynchronous communication. This conversation is often intertwined with the question of whether the focus should be on text or on video. In fact, though, one can achieve near-synchronous processes through any text-based platform (including email) although some lend themselves to being fully synchronous (*e.g.*, chat, instant messaging) and others are more commonly encountered as asynchronous (forum discussion posts, email[75]). Discussing text interactions, Katsh and Rifkin[76] recommended against real-time, chat-type interactions. They found that mediators felt rushed, pressured to respond quickly and were less able to control the flow of information between disputants. In addition, this style of communication focuses parties on the text itself, denying mediators the opportunity to use the on-

74 Rule (2002), p. 245.

75 It would be more accurate to call email semi-synchronous, given it can and often is used in as synchronous a manner as text messaging, and the way it is used is more a matter of user choice rather than the nature of the medium. *See*, Ebner, N. (2014). "Negotiating via E-Mail." In M. Benoliel (Ed.) *Negotiation Excellence: Successful Deal Making* (2nd ed.). Singapore: World Scientific Publishing.

76 Katsh & Rifkin (2001).

screen opportunities offered by the Fourth Party. By combining text, images and design, they suggested mediators can better provide resolution-oriented surroundings.[77]

While service providers sometimes advertise that they used synchronous methods such as instant messaging and chat, the market practice, so far as text-based processes are concerned, have gravitated, or evolved, toward asynchronous methods. Often, the process is asynchronous on multiple levels – with platforms providing each party with their own private room, allowing multiple people on each side (*e.g.*, a party, her lawyer, her business partner, her husband) to contribute their opinions at their convenience, before the lead party posts a message in the main conference area or forum, visible to the other party and the mediator.

Katsh, Rifkin, and Gaitenby[78] have advised against reliance on email, and others have argued that email is very easy to 'misuse', resulting in accidental sharing of information in an inappropriate manner.[79] Rather, they prescribed use of software providing a sense of a shared space as well as opportunities for whole-screen usage. This recommendation necessitated a certain sacrifice on the 'convenience' side of the trust-convenience-expertise triangle discussed by Katsh & Rifkin.[80] Parties would need to go to the mountain by accessing a platform, instead of the mountain coming to their inbox. This approach has often been incorporated in ODR platform design in a balanced manner; systems often rely on dedicated software while also using email as a notification method and a convenient portal to the system.

As individual practitioners began taking their mediation practice online in the late 2000s, many used email as a primary form of communication. They seemed to have read the triangle a different way: Convenience is paramount – and email is simplest. Viewing the triangle from the perspective of these practitioners, they offer process expertise, not technological expertise, and process expertise is what they are offering. Finally, it would seem that the issue of security, long considered by service providers dealing with the corporate world to be of the utmost concern (and one good reason to avoid email), was simply not that much of an issue to the individual practitioners' target market of people with individual transactional or marital disputes. People trust their email with a great deal of personal information; why should their disputes be any different? This difference in approach reduced individual practitioners' operating costs, and allowed them to enter a market that had traditionally been perceived to have a prohibitive technological entry-barrier.

It was only as the second decade of the 20th century unfolded that the age of videoconferencing in online mediation solidly arrived. Low-to-no cost videoconferencing platforms of sufficient quality to conduct reasonably good quality,

---

77 *Ibid.*, pp. 143-145.

78 Katsh *et al.* (2000).

79 *See* Draper & Raymond (2019).

80 Katsh & Rifkin (2001).

albeit never hiccup-free, conversations became readily available. Their use in mediation proliferated as soon as their simplicity threshold reached the point at which a party could click on a link sent to them by the mediator and immediately enter a videoconference, without any need to download and install software. In practice, Zoom's platform quickly became the most popular choice amongst video-based mediators, and this platform has certainly been the most frequently adopted by online transitioning practitioners in the Covid-19 era.

The state-of-the-art of online mediation on the eve of the Covid-19 era included many platforms based on text, and many others relying on video. The widespread adoption of video-based online mediation in the Covid-19 area may cause this balance, and the field's developmental thrust, to shift course. And, of course, if there is anything one *can* predict regarding technology, it is that a new one is always waiting in the wings, ready for its moment to come on stage. In this regard, we note contemporary experiments being conducted with telepresence,[81] human controlled robot-mediators,[82] and artificially-intelligent agents mediating between humans.[83] Who knows what will follow?

4 Substantive and Process Issues in Online Meditation

4.1 Process Model

All practice of mediation stems from practitioners' worldviews. This is epitomized by the debate regarding problem solving vs. transformative models of practice,[84] but also ripples through other process model discussions such as Riskin's[85] grid of mediator orientations, strategies and techniques. In considering online mediation, discussions of 'why?' and 'what?' have been overshadowed, to a large extent, by the 'how?' This section will

81 Exon, S.L. & Lee, S. (2019). "Building Trust Online: The Realities of Telepresence for Mediators Engaged in Online Dispute Resolution," *Stetson Law Review* 49(1), 109.

82 Druckman, D., Adrian, L., Damholdt, M.F., Filzmoser, M., Koszeigi, S.T., Seibt, J. & Vestergaard, C. (2020). "Who is Best at Mediating a Social Conflict? Comparing Robots, Screens and Humans." Paper presented at the 33rd Annual Conference of the International Association for Conflict Management, Virtual Conference, July 2020.

83 Haring, K.S., Tobias, J., Waligora, J., Phillips, E. & Tenh, N.L. (2019). "Conflict Mediation in Human-Machine Teaming: Using a Virtual Agent to Support Mission Planning and Debriefing." Presented at the 28th IEEE International Conference on Robot & Human Interactive Communication 14-18 October 2019, New Delhi, India.

84 Bush, R.A. & Folger, J.P. (2005). *The Promise of Mediation: The Transformative Approach to Conflict* (2nd ed.). San Francisco, CA: Jossey-Bass.

85 Riskin, L.L. (1996). "Understanding Mediators' Orientations, Strategies, and Techniques: A Grid for the Perplexed," *Harvard Negotiation Law Review* 1; Riskin, L.L. (2005). "Replacing the Mediator Orientation Grids, Again: Proposing a 'New New Grid System'," *Alternatives to the High Cost of Litigation* 23(8), 127-132.

include a few brief comments in the hopes of reminding practitioners that, with all due respect, technology only lights the stage.

The terms resolution, settlement, autonomy, and agreement all form the backbone of online mediation terminology much as they do in traditional mediation. However, terminology aside, worldview matters. Perhaps the shortest way to frame the question to be addressed in this section is: how does the online environment affect process issues that we hold to be substantive? Does the Fourth Party lean toward one process model over another, or toward any one quadrant of Riskin's grid? These two issues are certainly not identical, but they are intertwined at the practical level, and the few research findings at our disposal have implications for both of them.

To approach these issues, we should first note a couple of comments related to the evolution of ODR and online mediation. ODR was developed with an eye toward high-volume cases sourcing from e-commerce settings. These initial settings certainly lend themselves to the boilerplating of disputes noted by Bush and Folger as a hallmark of the problem-solving approach,[86] and may have had some effect on the way ODR terminology and technology developed.

As we have seen, online mediation first oriented itself around text-based, primarily asynchronous platforms and processes, and has only relatively recently veered toward rapid adoption of video platforms. The medium is never neutral; communicating through any medium has implications for how messages are transmitted, and how they are received.[87] This cannot help but affect the substance of a process. What is the impact? We only have a partial answer, given that the media effects of text interaction have been explored whereas video-based communication has received far less attention.

Research suggests that the use of asynchronous text-based media leads to more task-oriented and depersonalized communication styles than in face-to-face interactions.[88] This connects to the research indicating that people have (at least) two distinct information-processing modes: an *analytical-rational mode* and an *intuitive-experiential mode*. The former type of people tend to rely more heavily on logic and deductive thinking and their associated tactics (*e.g.*, development of positions and limits, use of logical argumentation, and the presentation of facts). People who adopt an intuitive-experiential mode rely more heavily on intuition and experience and their associated tactics (*e.g.*, appeals to emotion, the presentation of concrete personal stories, and the use of metaphors).[89] Asynchronous, text-based communication does not lend itself equally to these contrasting information-processing styles. Not only does this create a somewhat uneven playing field, favoring individuals who tend toward

86 Bush & Folger (2005).

87 Ebner (2014).

88 Kemp, N.J. & Rutter, D.R. (1982). "Duelessness and the Content and Style of Conversation," *British Journal of Social Psychology* 21.

89 Gelfand, M.J. & Dyer, N. (2000). "A Cultural Perspective on Negotiation: Progress, Pitfalls, and Prospects," *Applied Psychology: An International Review* 49(1), 62-99.

analytical-rational expression, it leads the conversational dynamics into expression of positions, arguments and facts.

The implications of this for online mediation might be that, left to its own devices, a conversation aimed at discussing a dispute conducted though asynchronous, text-based media might easily tend toward a problem-solving orientation, with a narrowly defined problem to be solved, and be addressed by parties and mediator through an evaluative approach. This may be particularly important for text-based ODR systems that are developed based on assumptions central to e-commerce ODR and for ODR as it is being adapted for the courts.[90]

Indeed, the little research that has been in this area tends to uphold the assumptions that text-based asynchronous mediation will be problem-solving, narrow, and evaluative.

Anne-Marie Hammond[91] conducted an experiment based in a series of text-based online mediation simulations. Her findings were based on surveys and focus groups conducted with the mediators and with the parties. Some of her findings have important implications to the topic of worldview, orientation, and media effects. In her study, most of the mediators, who typified their 'normal' (*i.e.*, face-to-face) approach as a hybrid facilitative/evaluative approach, reported that they were able to maintain this style of mediation in the online setting. However, mediators who defined their 'normal' approach as being of a more facilitative nature reported that in the online setting they were more directive and also tended to use more problem-solving techniques – hinting at their being more evaluative. Most explained these shifts as necessary to 'maintain momentum'. Others said they were more active in order to be heard in the non-reactive silence of online communication. Interestingly, some disputants commented that they would have preferred even more proactive and directive mediator interventions.

These findings are telling indeed: something in the online text-based environment is conducive to mediators becoming problem solving and directive, while at the same time conditioning parties to accept or desire this approach. This would seem to be a practical implication of the task-oriented mindset and the analytical-rational – favoring mode online communicators – mediators and parties alike – are subtly nudged into by the medium.

Another way in which the online, text-based environment leads mediators away, on a very practical level, from a transformative approach and toward a problem-solving

---

90 It is more widely significant, when you consider that most of the literature written on ODR and specifically on online mediation have, until very recently generally assumed a text-based interaction. It is not uncommon to encounter some of these text-oriented assumptions being applied out of context, as if they were truisms about ODR or online mediation in general, regardless of communication channel. Further research is needed in order to update our knowledge regarding online mediation to the different media effects caused by communication via video. For further discussion of this issue, *see* Ebner, N. & Thompson, J. (2014). "@Face Value? Nonverbal Communication and Trust Development in Online Video-Based Mediation," *International Journal of Online Dispute Resolution*, 1(2), 103-124.

91 Hammond, A.M.G. (2003). "How Do You Write 'Yes'? A Study on the Effectiveness of Online Dispute Resolution," *Conflict Resolution Quarterly* 20(3), 261-286.

approach is that the low degree of interactivity in asynchronous modes of communication[92] shifts focus away from the conversational dynamic and onto the issue at hand. This aspect of communications theory underlies Hammond's description:

> There was 100 percent agreement by mediators that the asynchronous nature of online communications helped them to focus on the broader picture of the conflict and not just the moment-to-moment interactions. For example, they did not have to concern themselves with interruptions from disputants. 100 percent (of the mediators) also agreed that having time to craft their responses enabled them to express their questions and comments effectively. All considered that this advantage led them to design more effective interventions. (at 275)

This unanimity is very telling in terms of understanding which orientation the online text-based environment is more conducive to. Transformative mediation processes are focused, to a large extent, on precisely those moment-to-moment interactions which mediators reported as being handily eliminated by the communication medium. Similarly, transformative mediation is *not* focused (or is even 'anti-focused') on 'well-crafted and effective mediator comments and questions' in the sense that we assume the study's respondents intended ⊠ comments and questions that channel disputants away from their conflict and toward resolution. Such comments and questions get in the way of the transformative process.

Given the boilerplating of disputes, and the nature of asynchronous text-based communication, it would hardly seem likely that an eBay feedback dispute could be handled with a transformative approach. And yet, Susan Summers Raines,[93] perhaps the most experienced eBay-cases mediator of them all, suggests that this is not necessarily the case. At the least, transformative elements can be adopted in an online mediator's approach, as they remain mindful of opportunities to highlight opportunities for empowerment and recognition along the road to resolution.

Taking the above into account, it would seem that the best summary is that technology is not neutral. Text-based, asynchronous communication nudges mediators into adopting problem-solving mindsets, and into using increased degrees of evaluative and directive methods.

---

92 *See* Ebner *et al.* (2009).

93 Summers Raines, S. (2005). "Can Online Mediation be Transformative? Tales from the Front," *Conflict Resolution Quarterly* 22(4), 437-451.

The effects of video-based mediation remain to be uncovered. Research on the use of video conferencing for online mediation specifically is thin – exceedingly so.[94] Some insight can be gleaned from the little that has been written on videoconferencing interactions in other areas.[95] While these can provide some practical advice for 'what works?' it is too early to engage in discussion of videoconferencing and mediator worldview and process models. As time passes, we hope to see specific focus on the impact of video platforms on mediation processes and mediator practices.

One way or another, mediators need to consider that the medium might lead them into acting at odds with their worldview. Once aware of this, they should be able to realign themselves to use technology in such a manner so that is supports their worldview.

In addition to the 'be aware' suggestion, we add another: 'set your stage carefully.' While it might be most practical to find a technological platform that 'works' (in terms of comfort, convenience, etc.), and then to adopt a process model that compliments it or makes best use of it, mediators aiming to be consistent and congruent with their own worldview might be well advised to take the opposite tack. Beginning with a reflection on their approach, mediators then need to find a platform or communication medium that allows for maximum application of this approach, and continue by allowing their approach to inform the way they advertise their services, train parties in the use of their platform, and conduct mediation processes.

Different worldviews, different approaches to mediation, and different levels of comfort with various styles (cultural and structural), were acknowledged in the drafting of the Singapore Convention on Mediation. One of the lingering questions in international mediation is whether mediated settlements are enforceable, or can be set aside. The Convention, in Article 5, stipulates that a judge in any signatory country can set aside a mediated settlement if there is a 'gross violation' of mediator or mediation standards. However, there is no universal set of standards against which to judge

---

94 *See* Ebner & Thompson (2014). Most of the writing on this topic is informative yet anecdotal in nature. *See, e.g.*, Leone, G. (2013). "5 Lessons Learned from Running Over 100 Mediation Simulations on Skype," available at www.mediate.com/articles/LeoneGbl20130104.cfm (last accessed 15 September 2020); also *see* Creo (2020).

95 For example, Ebner has written on the impact of videoconferencing in negotiation; *see* Ebner, N. (2017). "Negotiating via Videoconferencing." In C. Honeyman & A. Schneider (Eds.) *The Negotiator's Desk Reference*. St. Paul, MN: DRI Press. There is some research on the use of web video in human interaction more generally; *see* Wainfan, L. & Davis, P. (2004). "Challenges in Virtual Collaboration, RAND Corporation"; Guo, Z., D'ambra, J. & Turner, T. (March 2009). "Improving the Effectiveness of Virtual Teams: A Comparison of Videoconferncing and Face-to-Face Communication in China," *IEEE Transactions on Professional Communication* 52(1), 1-16; Julsrud, T., Hjorthal, R. & Denstali, J. (September 2012). "Business Meetings: Do New Teleconferencing Technologies Change Communication Patterns?," *Journal of Transport Geography* 24, 396-403.

settlements. This has led to Goncalves, Bogacz, and Rainey to suggest creation of a code of disclosure to establish mediation-specific standards, understood and approved by the participants.[96]

4.2 *Process Issues*

4.2.1 Process Stages

Beyond the general worldview/approach discussion above, not all stages of any particular process-model a mediator employs are substantially affected by the online medium. Reviewing the process, it would seem that the stages most affected are the early steps of the process, which we will discuss briefly in this section.

4.2.2 Preparation

The pre-process preparation phase requires more intentionality and investment than face-to-face interventions. In addition to any substantive preparation mediators might routinely conduct for any given mediation, there are particular medium-related preparatory actions e-mediators should not neglect. Mediators would do well to use this stage to build rapport with parties, which will later translate into in-process trust.[97] They need to find ways to personalize themselves to the parties, eliminating distance and creating social presence, such as through means of introduction, sending a picture or a welcoming video, making an initial phone call to lend voice to the interaction, etc. They should evaluate parties' comfort and experience in the online environment, and the degree to which they are adept with any particular platforms or communication methods to be used in the actual process. If necessary, they might conduct a test run to make sure that everything and everyone functions well. Finally, they should prepare and share with parties a backup communication plan, for use in the event that the primary channel fails for any reason.[98]

4.2.3 Agreement to Mediate

The usual language of a mediator's typical agreement to mediate should be adapted to incorporate issues pertaining to the online environment, which might include costs for video- or tele-conferencing, methods of accepting and binding signature of documents, etc.[99] It should include anything parties need to know about the platform's security, the

---

96 *See* United Nations Convention on International Settlement Agreements Resulting from Mediation, Art. 5 (1)e, United Nations, New York, 2019, p. 6; and Goncalves, A., Bogacz, F. & Rainey, D. (2019). "Beyond the Singapore Convention," *International Journal of Online Dispute Resolution* 6(2), 164-169.

97 Morris *et al.* (2002).

98 For more on preparing for online mediation, *see* Jani, S. & Getz, C. (2010). *Mediating from a Distance: Suggested Practice Guidelines for Family*. Victoria, BC: British Columbia Mediator Roster Society.

99 *Ibid.*

data they provide it, recording of video or preservation of text, etc. Keep in mind that in face-to-face mediation, signing the agreement to mediate is often preceded by an explanation of its content in simple language. In text-based online mediation, it might seem superfluous to do so; as this is seemingly doing the same thing twice. Mediators must find a way to verify that the agreement is understood and accepted. This might be a good reason for using simple-to-understand language in the agreement itself, or for sending the agreement to parties well in advance, providing sufficient time to ask any questions they have before the process is due to begin.

4.2.4 Introduction to Mediation

Parties to online mediation not only need an introduction to the concept and nature of mediation, they also need to understand the nature and rules of the online venue employed for the mediation process. Providing parties with a tour of the platform or some initial training in its operation increases their satisfaction and comfort levels. Parties' sense that their mediator is competent with the technological platform and has a clear road map for the process affects their degree of trust in the mediator.[100] Combined, these issues would suggest the utility of a new process stage, in which parties are walked through the platform (individually or jointly), and given an introduction to the online environment as it is used for mediation. Elements of this might include a site tour and tutorial, communication ground rules, instructions for participation, comments regarding language, reminder of time zone differences, expectation-setting related to synchronous or asynchronous communication, and technical support available to parties. This stage might be waived if the mediator is using a platform that both parties are familiar with, such as a commercial videoconferencing platform.

4.3 Mediators' Skills

What would constitute a full skill-set for online mediators? Raines[101] suggests that there is no need to re-invent the wheel: online mediators require the same general skill-set of a face-to-face mediator, with added competencies made necessary by technology. By contrast, the report of the Distance Mediation Project stated very clearly that "Distance mediation employs different skills, and involves a different mediation 'style' rather than simply new tools in the mediation tool box",[102] and noted that mediators expressed desire

100 *See* Hammond (2003).

101 Summers Raines, S. (2006). "Mediating in Your Pajamas: The Benefits and Challenges for ODR Practitioners," *Conflict Resolution Quarterly* 23(3), 359-369.

102 Getz (2010), p. 3.

for specialized training in skills unnecessary for face-to-face settings.[103] It could be posited that by using the face-to-face mediator's skill-set as the baseline and considering what needs to be tweaked or added, we are setting mediators up for confusion and for misapplication of techniques. In the end, combining both of these approaches probably offers a better picture of what is needed: All tools in traditional mediation need to be closely re-examined for suitability and application online.

Some skills necessary for providing face-to-face services are simply not necessary in some online venues. Text-based mediators do not need skill in communicating via their own body language, or in interpreting others. In a training aimed at preparing new mediators to conduct processes online via text, including the topic of body language communication in the curriculum might be handicapping students rather than helping them. Similarly, skills associated with designing a face-to-face setting for the meeting, choosing suitable seating arrangements, etc. are only very loosely comparable to web-platform design.

Other skills will need to be 'tweaked': Mediators skills in process and time – management will need to take different time dynamics into account, as mediation is conducted asynchronously. Speed and pace have different effects online.[104] Mediators' understanding of what happened 'during sessions' as opposed to 'in-between sessions' may need to adapt to ongoing, asynchronous processes which are always, to some extent, 'in-session'. They need to accommodate familiar communication skills such as active listening, reflecting and reframing, to the online environment.[105] Videoconferencing-based mediators will require understanding of nonverbal communication and body language – focusing on the unique ways these play out over video.[106]

Still other skills are unique to the online setting: Mediators will not only require new skills with technology, they will need to be skillful at helping *others* find their way around technology, and at making them feel at ease with it.

In a previous paper focusing on online negotiation,[107] Ebner and his colleagues have highlighted four skill-sets required for text-based e-negotiators: dealing with writing ability, message management, relationship management and content management. While too detailed to summarize in this section, we note that text-based online mediators would do well to acquire those skills. Moreover, they should be addressed in any online mediation training given that even if the primary interactional mode a

103 This debate is somewhat reflected in the variety of approaches to online mediation training available today; *see* discussion of this issue, below.

104 Brett, J.M., *et al.* (2007). "Sticks and Stones: Language, Face, and Online Dispute Resolution," *Academy of Management Journal* 50(1).

105 *See* Hammond (2003); Ebner (2007).

106 *See* Ebner & Thompson (2014).

107 Ebner *et al.* (2009).

mediator prefers is video-based, they will often find themselves supporting it through text interaction with parties.

Beyond those abilities borrowed from the skillset of online negotiators, online mediators require special skills for online process management and party management. Here are some examples:

- *Technological expertise*: A mediator must be adept with the videoconferencing equipment they conduct their sessions through. If they rely on text communication, typing and texting skills, and/or adeptness with a talk-to-text conversion program, are core capabilities.
- *Social norms*: Online mediators must be able to practice 'netiquette' and to understand and cope with the effects of its infractions.
- *Psychology of the medium*: Mediators need to learn the psychological effects of communication at a distance.[108]
- *Trustbuilding*: Mediators need to have a solid understanding of trust dynamics and of how interparty and mediator-party trust is affected and challenged by the online media. This ranges from how to build it to how to maintain it. The devil, it seems, is in the details. Rifkin[109] notes how trust can erode as a result of mediator response time being slower than parties' expectations. Hammond[110] reports that lack of mediator skill with the technological platform resulted in eroded trust. Katsh, Rifkin, and Gaitenby[111] suggested a structural challenge: the one-shot interactions common to the Internet make trust difficult to form and maintain. Given these challenges, mediators need to be proactive in building rapport and trust.[112]
- *Dealing with increased anger*: Mediators must understand the dynamics of online escalation, and how to deal with incidents of interparty flaming. These dynamics, combined with the ease of dropping out of a process, necessitate a higher level of repeated validation and empathy, as well as empowerment. Angry words and flaming escalation can ripple toward the mediator as well, requiring them to acquire thick skin: with social norms lower in online communication, expressions of anger, attacks, and flaming are sometimes directed at the mediator.[113]
- *Maintaining schedules and engagement*: Particularly in text-based processes, mediators should set, and adhere to, regular schedules for checking-in and participating.[114] By doing so, they counter the ease of procrastination associated

108 *See* Jani & Getz (2010).
109 Rifkin (2001).
110 Hammond (2003).
111 Katsh *et al.* (2000).
112 Braeutigam, A.M. (2006). "What I Hear You Writing Is ... Issues in ODR: Building Trust and Rapport in the Text-Based Environment", *University of Toledo Law Review* 38, 101. Also *see* Thompson & Ebner (2014).
113 Summers Raines (2006).
114 Hammond (2003).

with online processes, or simply of party drop-out.[115] This also offers a partial remedy to the difficulty of displaying mediator engagement. In Hammond's[116] discussion of online mediation experiments, the desire for more mediator engagement showed up as an issue regarding trust, satisfaction with the process, disputants' ability to see the others' perspectives and empathize, and more. Limited in terms of their ability to use bodily cues or active listening, text-based mediators require new ways to show engagement. Braeutigam[117] suggests mediators initiate constant, regular communication to bring some sense of synchronicity, presence, and listening to the asynchronous interaction.

- *Asynchronous communication*: Mediators need to understand the dynamics of asynchronous communication, and the pitfalls it presents in mediation processes. The anxiety and doubt that accompanies waiting for the other party to respond are a natural breeding ground for distrust and anger. Mediators should find ways to reflect this dynamic and explain it to parties when it seems to be affecting the process. Another problem with asynchronous communication is that as time passes, people forget things. Raines[118] recommends that mediators intentionally use many summary statements, to overcome the effects of time passing in asynchronous communication.[119]
- *Providing signposts*: Mediators are often both more experienced with the communication platform than parties, and have the advantage of being able to tailor it to their preferences.[120] Mediators should recognize points in the process and/or areas on the platform which tend to confuse people, and preempt this confusion through clear instructions regarding where parties need to go, what they need to do there, and when they need to do it by.[121]

4.3.1 Communication and Language Skills

Communication skills in asynchronous, text-based negotiation have been well explored;[122] less so, is their use in mediation. In this section, we address several issues that have been raised in the online mediation literature as particularly important from the third-party perspective.

Active listening: Much of a mediator's active listening toolbox, so important for trust- and empathy-building, relies on contextual cues that are not part of text-based communication. Mirroring or reflecting parties' words back to them is another element

115 Ebner (2014); Summers Raines (2006).
116 Hammond (2003).
117 Braeutigam (2006).
118 Summers Raines (2006).
119 *Ibid.*
120 *See* Hammond (2003).
121 For other elements recommended for the mediator's skill-set, *see* Katsh & Rifkin (2001), pp. 147-162.
122 Ebner *et al.* (2009).

that does not translate easily to the text-based online environment. Hammond[123] noted that some mediators reported difficulty with mirroring. Elsewhere,[124] Ebner has noted that reflecting is challenging primarily as it seems superfluous online: If a party's words appear in a forum thread or an email trail, what good will it do to repeat them back to them the way we do in face-to-face mediation? And yet, active listening and reflecting serve the same purposes online as they do in face-to-face settings, and mediators cannot afford to pass up these valuable tools for showing empathy and generating trust. A good way for a mediator to demonstrate online listening is to stress, in words, that they have read the party's message. For example, 'I read your message carefully' or 'Reading your letter last night, I realized…' might seem like casual opening lines, but they convey a powerful message: 'you have been heard.'

While demonstrating *listening* in online mediation may take some creativity, word processing can actually make *reflecting* relatively simple. Cutting, pasting and editing make creating a paraphrased summary of a party's statements an easy task.

Questions: When using questions to further understand a party's position and needs, we can utilize the benefits of word processing to connect our question to specific parts of another's message. This not only makes the question more to the point and part of the flow of conversation, it also incorporates elements of active listening and reflecting. Instead of writing 'When do you need the money paid?' we might write

> In your last email you wrote 'I am pressed for time and need the money ASAP.' I appreciate that you are in a real rush, however, I also heard your opposite say it will take her a little while to get money together, if indeed you both agree to payment being made. Can you tell me a bit more about our timeframe?

Reframing: Katsh, Rifkin and Gaitenby[125] suggest that reframing is particularly tricky online: it can be done only after the narrative has already unfolded (parties have already sent out, and read, they accusatory or escalatory email) ⊠ the mediator cannot jump in in the middle with a reframing word or sentence. This is reinforced by written word's characteristic of being recorded and re-accessible; parties can read their opposites annoying email message, ruminate on it over time and enter consecutive, spiraling, anger cycles – all before forming a devastating reply of their own.[126] Parties might employ methods to make their angry or toxic statements stand out and aggravate even more, for example by changing by font size, writing in ALL CPAS, or coloring a sentence in red. In asynchronous communication, mediators must be on the ball in order to interject

123 Hammond (2003).
124 Ebner (2007).
125 Katsh *et al.* (2000).
126 *See* Nadler & Shestowsky (2006).

reframing messages before things fly out of hand. Summers Raines[127] suggested that shuttle diplomacy, in which all messages are sent to the mediator rather than being exchanged between parties with the mediator looking on, is particularly helpful for dealing with angry messages. Depending on their approach, mediators might reframe one party's messages before moving them on to the other party, or discuss the message and its potential effects with the sender, reframing it together with them, before moving it on.[128]

Language issues are an immense challenge in online communication,[129] and skills with written language are a must-have in any online mediator's toolbox.[130] The lack of contextual cues such as body language and tone of voice in text-based communication leave parties and mediator's straining to infer meaning from any cue they can get[131] and in particular, attention returns to the actual wording of the text itself. This, as opposed to face-to-face communication in which we infer most of a messages meaning from non-verbal cues.[132] With the written word spotlighted, shades of meaning, subjective interpretation and cultural differences turn every sentence written into a powerful tool for dispute resolution – at the same time it becomes a potential process-wrecker. Accuracy becomes paramount. While pre-written language can be employed and helpful, overly generic language can lend the sense that the mediator is not really present, engaged and listening.[133] The emotional content of language, and the way it affects the framing of the dispute, has also been found to affect the likelihood of resolution.[134] All these issues challenge constructive conversation even when parties speak the same language; when issues of multiple languages and translation arise (and, these are likely to be encountered in transboundary processes that online mediation facilitates so well) communication challenges are compounded.[135]

---

127 Summers Raines (2006).

128 Rule (2002).

129 Rule, C. & Villamore, C. (2004). "The Importance of Language in Online Dispute Resolution," *ICC International Court of Arbitration Bulletin, 2004 Special Supplement.* 21-26.

130 Rifkin (2001).

131 Ebner (2007).

132 Mehrabian, A. (1971). "Nonverbal Betrayal of Feeling," *Journal of Experimental Research in Personality* 5(1), 64-73.

133 *See* Rule & Villamore (2005).

134 Friedman, R. *et al.* (2004). "The Positive and Negative Effects of Anger on Dispute Resolution: Evidence from Electronically Mediated Disputes," *Journal of Applied Psychology* 89(2); Brett, J.M. *et al.* (2005). "Tortoise or Hare? A Study of the Speed to Resolution in Online Disputes." Paper presented at the IACM 17th Annual Conference. Available at http://ssrn.com/abstract=602021 (last accessed 28 April 2011).

135 As noted, supra n. 59, translation software has yet to evolve to the level that professionals can rely on them for precise translation, far less for enabling the nuanced use of language discussed in this section.

4.3.2 Professional Issues

4.3.2.1 Training

It is safe to say that while there is wide agreement that mediators using online tools require specialized skillsets, as discussed in the previous section, and that these require special training, there are no widely accepted standards for training content or style, or indeed many training opportunities at all. Rule,[136] for example, suggested that ODR practitioners should go through a process of studying, participation in simulations, mentoring by an experienced practitioner, participation in discussions on ODR ethical issues with seasoned practitioners and sharing of standard, pre-formed language to be used in ODR processes with other practitioners for feedback.

However, given the prevailing service provider structure, widespread training did not evolve (as it did, for example, with general ADR training), throughout most of ODR's history. Any training of online mediators was conducted by service providers in-house. For example, SquareTrade's mediators were trained in-house, and received coaching on individual cases from SquareTrade's dispute resolution specialist support team.[137] Other service providers engaging a roster of mediators, such as Online Resolution, trained their mediators in use of the online platform.

While NCTDR was the first entity to offer ODR education to the general public, this was more of an introductory course than a training package aimed at professionals. TheMediationRoom was probably the first entity to offer training courses on conducting online mediation processes aimed at practitioners. The British Columbia Distance Mediation Project has suggested that its guidelines for distance mediation[138] might serve as the basis for any training program in online mediation. These guidelines – intended as a supplement to basic mediation training – include considerations for suitability of online mediation for specific cases, technology selection, managing confidentiality and security, online communication skills and more.

As the use of technology in mediation has increased, there have developed a number of training courses designed to teach online skills to mediators. Some institutionalization of online mediation training is in the offing; for example, in Virginia, the Self-Represented Litigants Committee of the Supreme Court's Access to Justice Commission is preparing a technology module as part of its continuing mediation education (CME) program for court-referred mediators.[139]

---

136 Rule (2002).

137 Abernathy, S (2003). "The Square Trade Experience in Online and Offline Disputes," *Proceedings of the 2003 United Nations Forum on ODR.*

138 Jani & Getz (2010).

139 In addition to professional training, a number of courses on ODR are offered in the frameworks of academic programs in the fields of conflict resolution and law, including courses taught by the authors at Creighton University, Southern Methodist University, Dominican University, and the McGeorge School of Law at the University of the Pacific.

There is certainly much to explore in terms of content and methods for online mediation training at the professional and pedagogical level. Practically speaking, experience with general ADR development has shown that regulation and accreditation of practice and of practitioners often spurs development of training programs.[140]

The sudden use of online tools by mediators necessitated by the Covid-19 pandemic has spawned numerous online ODR and e-mediation training opportunities. The debate regarding the relationship between the skillsets of mediation and of online mediation is reflected in these offerings. Some trainers offer a full-blown training course geared toward online practice, whereas others offer to teach mediators all they need to expand their practice to include online mediation in a two-hour webinar, essentially a tutorials on how to use Zoom or WebEx for the purposes of mediation. If e-mediation training is going to be meaningful in the long run, it will be necessary to develop more robust training programs that address skill sets, practice, ethics, and best practices.

Recently, several sets of guidelines for training and practice design have been published: The International Council for Online Dispute Resolution (ICODR) has published recommended standards for training;[141] and the International Mediation Institute (IMI) Task Force on ODR has issued standards for trainers, practitioners, and organizations engaged in online mediation.[142] While many of these documents apply to ODR in a broader sense then online mediation alone, they are likely to inform the content of future training programs.

4.3.2.2 Regulation and Accreditation

The question of whether ODR regulation is desirable, or even possible, has been discussed with some particular attention being paid to online mediation. As Sarah Cole and Kristen Blankley[143] summarized this somewhat prickly issue,

> Policymakers who regulate traditional mediation attempt to balance four general goals: fairness, effectiveness, quality, and access. To the extent that regulation of online mediation is necessary, potential regulators of online mediation should add to that list: access to technology, effectiveness of process as compared to traditional mediation, and quality of mediator services.

However, note Cole and Blankley, not only does this give rise to internal dissonance as these goals might prove to be mutually incompatible, they are challenged by one

140 As of this writing, none of the certification programs for court referred mediation that are sanctioned by state supreme courts require even a unit on ODR, much less a serious discussion of online practice. Specific, or separate, regulation of online practice will likely change that.

141 *See* https://icodr.org/training/.

142 *See* www.imimediation.org/about/who-are-imi/odr-tf/.

143 Cole, S.R. & Blankley, K.M. (2006). "Online Mediation: Where We Have Been, Where We Are Now, and Where We Should Be", *University of Toledo Law Review* 38, 193.

formidable external consideration: the Internet, by its very nature, resists regulation. They suggest that regulators prioritize carefully and aim for small gains rather than sweeping regulation of the field.

The issue of regulation relates to and overlaps with that of accreditation. One means of regulation is by setting up accreditation barriers to practicing in the field. Despite the relative novelty of the field, the question of practitioner accreditation has already been explored, likely due to the interminable discussion of ADR accreditation. Indeed, Conley Tyler and Bornstein[144] begin their survey of accreditation models for ODR with an overview of accreditation models in the ADR field. While their discussion regards ODR in general and not mediation specifically, many of their suggestions are particularly relevant to practitioners of this process. They surveyed six organizations and service providers conducting some form of accreditation or screening process for practitioners, including government entities and commercial bodies, examining them for entry hurdles to accreditation as well as for requirements posed to practitioners seeking to maintain their accreditation. Beyond regular ADR criteria, all of these entities stressed the need for a new knowledge-base and skill-set regarding online interactions.

Other questions regarding accreditation include who should be accrediting, and who should be accredited. Should 'online mediation skills' be incorporated into the accrediting criteria for currently existing accrediting bodies, raising the bar for *all* mediators seeking accreditation? This suggestion merits serious consideration in the aftermath of the Covid-19 era, as it has been empirically demonstrated that, given the right circumstances, all mediation practice will transition online.

Alternatively, special bodies (private market or government entities) could accredit online mediators, conferring the status of 'ODR specialist' as a status within a general ADR accreditation. Zooming in even closer – these bodies could testify that a particular mediator has studied one or more specific skill sets.

Whoever is conferring accreditation, who are they to accredit? Should individuals be accredited to practice, or agencies should be accredited to offer services? This was seen as a key question in the past.[145] Rule[146] noted how most of the early discussion regarding standards, regulation, and accreditation focused on the organization rather than on

144 Conley Tyler & Bornstein (2006).
145 *Ibid.*
146 Rule (2002).

individual practitioners. Focusing on the nature of online activity, he explained, ODR organizations are identifiable and locatable (through their website, address, management structure, etc.) whereas individual neutrals might be anywhere in the world, subject to different jurisdictions and legal obligations.[147]

However, given ODR's shift, described above, from its 'service provider' – heavy era, to the present abundance of private practitioners of online mediation, accrediting service providers might not have much impact on the online mediation service provision market. Certainly, a centralized model accrediting service providers could add an additional level of oversight. Even if organizational accreditation was preferred, the question of whether individual mediators should undergo accreditation *in addition* also merits consideration. One way or another, imposing a preference for organizational accreditation would stifle individual entrepreneurship and, practically speaking, it is likely that the ship has sailed on this possibility.

4.3.2.3 Ethics

The need for guidelines on ethics in ODR has been under discussion since an early stage in the field's evolution. Many organizations and institutions, professional and governmental, set up committees and drafted papers, as Conley Tyler[148] notes:

> The American Bar Association established a task force to look at ways of ensuring that ODR services remain effective and ethical (Rule 2002:116). The Online Sector of the Association for Conflict Management prepared Proposed Guidelines for Online Dispute Resolution (Wiener 2001:4). In Australia, NADRAC 2002 provides draft practitioner standards for ODR and the Department of Justice Victoria has commissioned a study into accreditation of ODR practitioners.

These have been more recently augmented by the National Center for Technology and Dispute Resolution's (NTCDR) Ethical Principles for ODR,[149] the International Mediation Institute (IMI) Task Force on ODR's standards for trainers, practitioners,

147 These are but a few challenges related to implementing governance on the field of online mediation, as a subset of the ODR field. For discussion of these and other governance challenges, *see* Ebner, N. & Zeleznikow, J. (2016). "No Sheriff in Town: Governance for the ODR Field," *Negotiation Journal* 32(4), 297-323. Some effort has been made to adapt the 'norms' for mediators working face-to-face into online mediation practice. In 2007, the American Bar Association (ABA), the Association for Conflict Resolution (ACR), and the American Arbitration Association (AAA), issued joint Model Standards of Conduct for Mediators. In 2016, a set of comments were appended to the Model Standards, many of which focused on ODR; *see* Rainey, D. (2016). "Model Standards of Conduct for Mediators: Annotated for Online Dispute Resolution Practice," *The International Journal of Online Dispute Resolution* 3(1), 30-40.

148 Conley Tyler & Bomstein (2006).

149 *See* http://odr.info/ethics-and-odr/.

and organizations engaged in online mediation, and other such documents,[150] many of which pertain, partially or in whole, to online mediation specifically This flurry of commissions and papers has been strongly counterpointed by the activity of service providers. Based on our own tracking of service provider websites over the years,[151] we can report that most service providers have not made (or, at least, did not publicly share) original statements of professional ethics, nor do they state their compliance with *any* of the documents referred to above, or refer to them at all.

4.3.2.4 Co-Mediation

As a final professional issue, we will note co-mediation. While prominent in many traditional mediation practices and debates, this practice has been greatly diminished in online mediation practice. We have not identified a single service provider or individual practitioner who has mentioned this mode of practice on a website, nor found mention of it in the literature on online mediation.

This is not to say that anything in ODR automatically rules out co-mediation. For example, a 2018 conference on 'Justice Reimagined' in Liverpool featured an ODR session with a simulation mediating the issue of Brexit; the third party was, in fact, a combination of an AI driven platform and three third parties working together. Additionally, there is nothing inherent in online mediation, conducted by video, email, text platform or any other medium, that would eliminate the capacity for 'seating' two mediators 'up front', 'at the table'. It certainly may be that issues of cost-efficiency might be at play here, along with a desire to keep the interaction-through-technology as simple as possible without compounding the challenges by having another address to add to the email, another computer susceptible to crashing, or another bad internet connection knocking out a video transmission. One might also consider whether there is something in the Fourth Party's assistance that renders the mutual assistance provided one another by co-third parties unnecessary. Perhaps a sharper question to pose would be whether the underlying justifications for, and benefits of, co-mediation are is in any way truly affected by the online environment, or whether mediators' preferences in this regard change as they take their practice online, reshaped by the effects of technology on their professional approach.[152]

---

150 *See* http://odr.info/standards/.

151 For example, for the past eight years Ebner has tasked students to survey ODR service provider sites and report on their disclosures regarding ethical standards (as well as anything related to this, such as accreditation, mediator standards of practice, etc.). Students often complain about the difficulty of this assignment given that they needed to identify and review numerous sites before finding anything report-worthy beyond 'no mention'. This is not to cast any practitioner or service provider as unethical; however, particularly in an unregulated field, we find this omission noteworthy.

152 In conversations with community mediators, Ebner has learned of two community mediation centers that maintained their co-mediation format in remote mediations conducted during the Covid-19-era. In the context of the considerations discussed in this section, it will be interesting to learn whether the centers' adherence to this model survives the era, and whether it is implemented in post-era online mediations.

5 CONCLUSION

Online mediation has been in a growth phase over the past few years, as individual and small-shop practitioners added online convening to their traditional practice. Even before the advent of the Covid-19 era, it was clear that traditionally accepted boundaries regarding areas of practice were fading, and that online mediation would likely continue to develop even in contexts requiring an extra dose of mediation's human touch, such as those that trigger high emotions and involve meaningful relationships. The experiences of mediation practitioners transitioning online during the Covid-19 era all but promises expansion of online mediation. As this expansion occurs, mediators would do well to review the knowledge gained to date regarding online communication and process management. We hope that some of the rapidly-expanding cadre of online mediators will conduct their practice with an eye to contributing knowledge to this growing field of practice by conducting experiments of their own, documenting their experiences, and sharing these with the online mediation community.[153]

While online and face-to-face mediation are certainly closely related, this chapter has demonstrated a wide range of elements characterizing online mediation as a distinctive mode of practice. These distinctive elements might tend to blur in the future, as interactions-at-a-distance continue to become increasingly ubiquitous, and online communication becomes second nature. However, even as the salience of some of the elements described in this chapter recedes, future research might surprise us with new areas of significant distinction between the two processes. We might discover, for example, distinct types of practitioners choosing to engage in each type of mediation. Individuals who would not consider practicing mediation face-to-face may find themselves very comfortable helping people to work their problems out screen-to-screen, and vice versa. It would be interesting to compare indicators of success across both modalities; we would anticipate that practitioners' success practicing one type will not necessarily predict their success practicing the other. Finally, we might discover that different types of people, voluntarily participating as parties, prefer one modality over the other. All this, however, is subject to the caveat that predicting the future of anything technology-related is, at best, a shot in the dark.

153 Six months into this era, the insights of online-transitioned mediators remain largely anecdotal, and understandably so. For the most part, practitioners' focus has been on mastering technology, leading one of the authors to formulate and self-promote Ebner's Law of Online Mediation in the Covid-19 Era: "As any conversation between mediators continues, the probability of it morphing into a discussion of Zoom settings approaches 1." As time goes by, mastery of the platform is achieved, and the novelty of its bells and whistles fades, we expect Ebner's Law to fail, practitioner's attention to return to substantive issues and non-technological nuances of practice. At that point, we hope to see more systematic investigation and fieldwide conversations taking advantage of the natural experiment in online mediation that Covid-19 era has imposed.

For now, however, we can enjoy the notion that we are at a tipping point. As Clay Shirky has written, "Communications tools don't get socially interesting until they get technologically boring."[154]

Communication platforms maturing for a number of decades, primarily email and text platforms, have all been converging to the point of being 'technologically boring' across society. The Covid-19 era has accelerated that process, and has catalyzed the ascension of videoconferencing to the 'technologically boring' title.

What follows next, in the realm of mediation, in terms of the ways mediators and parties actually put these technologies to work, is bound to be professionally and socially fascinating.

---

154 Shirky, C. (2009). *Here Comes Everybody: The Power of Organizing Without Organizations.* New York: Penguin Books, p. 105.

Chapter 16 ODR and Peacetech

Colin Rule

Over the past 20 years technology has reconfigured global society. Those of us in the field of Online Dispute Resolution (ODR) have witnessed these changes firsthand. Global networks, mobile devices, and social media have transformed (and are continuing to transform) the way humans interact with one another worldwide. The changes to date have been significant, but if current trends hold, they are likely only the beginning. The technological innovations coming in the next decade (e.g. artificial intelligence, augmented reality) will outshadow anything we have experienced to date.

The theory and practice of ODR, laid out thoroughly in this book, describes how technology can help people prevent, manage, and resolve disputes. ODR has focused on expanding access to justice by continually improving the understanding and efficacy of technology in resolving disagreements. As each new innovation emerges the community of ODR practitioners examines its capabilities and fits it into the ODR framework and toolbox.

But ODR is not the only field that has emerged from the change wrought by technological innovation. As ODR was growing and evolving over the past two decades the field of peacetech was following a similar path. Just as technology has created new possibilities for expanding access to justice through ODR, it has also created new possibilities for expanding peace through peacetech.

I've been lucky enough to witness this development as part of my role as a founding board member at the Peace Tech Lab (PTL), which is a spinoff from the United States Institute of Peace (USIP) in Washington, DC. USIP is funded by the United States government to promote the study and practice of peacebuilding around the world. In 2014 USIP decided to spin off its Technology, Media, and Peacebuilding program into a separate nonprofit, which became the Peace Tech Lab. PTL has since emerged as one of the leading innovators in the peacetech space, incubating new ventures and holding Peace Tech Exchanges in conflict zones around the world to support budding peacetech innovators and innovations.

ODR was born when technology was married with dispute resolution. Peacetech was born when technology was married to peacebuilding. ODR has experienced waves of innovation and contraction as new companies spring up that push practice forward, but then subsequently run out of money and shut down (a process Joseph Schumpeter described as *creative destruction*). Peacetech has similarly sparked many new ventures, most of which fail – but each venture moves the ball forward, and new companies then sprout up from the bleached bones of the old. This cycle of birth and death is the chaotic process that generates innovation.[1]

The growth of ODR has accelerated over the past decade in parallel with the acceleration of technological innovation. Now, in the midst of a global pandemic where face-to-face interaction has been sharply curtailed, ODR has suddenly become the new normal. Peacetech has gone through a similar transformation as the virus closed traditional channels for diplomacy and peacebuilding. Without technological channels for communication (e.g. email, videoconferencing, social media) the virus would have stranded many peacebuilders around the world, leaving them isolated and ineffective. Technology has enabled these peacebuilding efforts to continue functioning even as we are all quarantined. It is hard to imagine how our societies would be able to function at all during this crisis without technology-enabled channels for communication. The pandemic has highlighted how essential technology has become, and it is now clear that even when the pandemic eases we will never go back to the world as it was prior to Covid-19.[2]

1 THE FIELD OF PEACEBUILDING

Much as the field of Alternative Dispute Resolution (ADR) has decades of face-to-face experience undergirding its practice, the field of peacebuilding has a similarly strong and deep foundation. As promoted by organizations like the United States Institute for Peace and the United Nations, the practice of peacebuilding is based on decades of honoring the rule of law, building sustainable economies, promoting good governance, and reinforcing social well-being. Peacebuilders help displaced people in conflict zones return to their homes; peacebuilders facilitate fair elections in communities that have never held elections before; peacebuilders help negotiate compromises over scarce resources like water and land.

Peacebuilding interventions are aimed at addressing the core factors that can promote instability and conflict, leading to outbreaks of violence. These interventions can focus on initiatives like promoting secure and sustainable livelihoods for all groups of citizens, enhancing social and community cohesion, and encouraging entrepreneurship and economic development. Decades of experience have identified the key indicators of a society's strength or vulnerability in terms of susceptibility to conflict. The practice of

1 Reier, Sharon. "Half a Century Later, Economist's 'Creative Destruction' Theory is Apt for the Internet Age: Schumpeter: The Prophet of Bust and Boom," in The International Herald Tribune, 10 June 2000. www.nytimes.com/2000/06/10/your-money/IHT-half-a-century-later-economists-creative-destruction-theory-is.html, last visited 30 August 2020.

2 Peace Direct. "Digital Pathways for Peace: Insights and Lessons from a Global Online Consultation." Peace Direct, 2020. www.peacedirect.org/us/wp-content/uploads/sites/2/2020/08/PD-LVP-Tech-Report.pdf, last visited 30 August 2020.

peacebuilding assesses and monitors each of these key indicators, taking proactive action to deliver tangible improvements in any areas that prove vulnerable.

Peacebuilders come from many different backgrounds. Some start out as community organizers, elected leaders, private sector entrepreneurs, or heads of non-governmental organizations. But no matter their background, peacebuilders focus on tackling the sources of conflict before they escalate into violence and social strife. As Bill Ury, co-founder of the Program on Negotiation at Harvard Law School, put it: 'Wars are predictable – and preventable.' Peacebuilders track these key indicators and craft strategies to improve them when they encroach upon the danger zone, all in an effort to prevent societies from spinning out of control and getting sucked into violent conflict. But even though the field has matured over decades, monitoring these indicators remains an imprecise art.[3]

2 Peacebuilding and Early Intervention

One of the longstanding objectives of peacebuilding has been effective early intervention. To be able to detect escalating situations reliably and consistently and prevent them boiling over into violence is almost like the equivalent of achieving cold fusion in the peacebuilding space – long pursued but never fully achieved. Assessments are traditionally based on qualitative instead of quantitative data, which makes accurate prediction difficult.

For the last decade the rise of technology has given the peacebuilding community new hope that maybe this long held objective could finally bear fruit. As a result, large government agencies have launched well-funded initiatives to try to crack the nut. The United Nations, the CIA, and the US Defense Department have all announced efforts to analyze the enormous volume of unstructured digital information pouring out of blogs, twitter, marketplaces, and global networks to predict where conflict might arise. The Defense Department's *Information Volume and Velocity Program* uses pattern recognition to detect trends in the ocean of unstructured data on the internet that could point to emerging flashpoints, and the *Open Source Indicators Program* at the Central Intelligence Agency (CIA) aims to anticipate 'political crises, disease outbreaks, economic instability, resource shortages, and natural disasters' before they intensify into violent conflict. CIA's funding of and collaboration with private companies like Palantir

3 Himelfarb, Sheldon. "Peacebuilding Reboot" in Building Peace: A Forum for Peace and Security in the 21st Center. Issue #5: #Peacetech. Alliance for Peacebuilding, March 2015. www.scaruffi.com/peace/peacetech.pdf, last visited 30 August 2021.

are also aimed at making sense of the waves of unstructured data that wash on shore 24×7 from the internet.[4]

But it is not certain that these large initiatives will be successful in achieving these long sought after breakthroughs. Silicon Valley has demonstrated that large numbers of smaller initiatives can be more nimble and inventive in their approaches, and a presence on the ground in these conflict environments may help these smaller initiatives frame challenges in new ways, leading to new opportunities to resolve conflict. Cross-discipline collaboration between developers, data experts, and conflict specialists in hot zones can effectively pinpoint the key elements in ways that do not require the investment of billions of dollars. Also, individuals in societies riven by conflict are not willing to cede peacebuilding efforts to large public initiatives because they cannot afford to wait; their lives, and the lives of their loved ones, are on the line. It is primarily the work of those innovators that has led to the growth of the field of peacetech.

3 THE RISE OF PEACETECH

Peacetech is peacebuilding accelerated by technology. Peacetech initiatives are aimed at monitoring and improving the same conflict drivers that face-to-face peacebuilding has traditionally targeted, but using technology to take those efforts to the next level. Using technology, peacetech delivers insights into underlying data that may be difficult or even impossible for on-the-ground peacebuilders to assess (including inter-ethnic and interreligious tensions, gender violence, resource disputes, minority rights, corruption, or repression).

The peacetech field is still young, and as a result it is not yet mainstream. Many questions remain about how new technologies should be used in peacebuilding work, and how best to ensure that these technologies do no harm in conflict zones. Ambiguities around roles and boundaries between offline and online organizations are currently being debated and negotiated.

But that has not slowed peacetech's rise. The UN has been promoting the transformative power of technology for at least the past decade, and many organizations now make peacetech a central component of their work. In addition to the Peace Tech Lab at USIP, peacetech research centers have emerged at Stanford, Harvard, and MIT, as well as at dozens of other academic and non-governmental organizations. The ICT for Peace Foundation was established in 2005 to promote the

4 Himelfarb, Sheldon. "Can Big Data Stop Wars Before They Happen? Number Crunching and Pattern Recognition May Hold the Key to Predicting and Preventing Conflicts. But First, Peace-Builders Need to Change the Way They do Business," in Foreign Policy, 25 April 2014. https://foreignpolicy.com/2014/04/25/can-big-data-stop-wars-before-they-happen/, last visited 30 August 2020.

use of technology for peacebuilding, and it works closely with the UN to develop and strengthen the technological capacity of peacebuilding efforts around the world. However, because the pace of innovation within academia, government, and nonprofits cannot keep up with the speed of technological innovation, there is a growing realization that the private sector must play a key role in advancing the field.

4 The Emergence of the Peacetech Industry

This dynamic has led to the birth of a new market category: the peacetech industry. Startups and large companies are now developing business models focused on leveraging technology to empower disenfranchised groups, de-escalate violence, and constrain hateful speech and fake news. Peacetech entrepreneurs are entering the peacebuilding space with futuristic ideas about how to tackle old problems. Some of these ideas will become scalable business plans with the potential to transform peacebuilding practice.

These new private entities see the challenge of peacebuilding very differently from public and NGO actors. They are creating a market for peacebuilding services that can democratize access to information and produce innovations that save lives and create jobs. Individuals living in conflict zones are eager to innovate using technology designed to address the instability harming their families and friends. The emergence of this new market space represents the mainstreaming of peacetech, and it offers exciting possibilities for broader engagement in peacebuilding efforts.[5]

Government funded peacebuilding projects operate in an inefficient market. There's little incentive to innovate because all of the funding decisions are made by donors or bureaucrats. The private sector has traditionally avoided peacebuilding because most investors believe there's no money to be made in preventing wars. But that sentiment is changing. Violence and instability harms businesses' bottom lines, exacting a quantifiable price. By creating a market for peacetech services the private sector is beginning to craft funding models that can deliver sustainable innovation at the pace of technological innovation. Large players, like big defense contractors, now pay close attention because competition in their industry is intense and they must always look for ways to differentiate themselves from their competitors.

Experimentation is also key to innovation. Constant experimentation enables promising ideas to rise to the top and expand market share while less promising initiatives fall away. Private ventures are focused on action and impatient with overanalysis and slow progress. Peacetech ventures focus on key factors that promote

5 Cerf, Vinton, with Sheldon Himelfarb. "Can the Peacetech Industry Save the Internet?" CNN Opinion, 29 September 2018. www.cnn.com/2018/09/29/opinions/technology-harm-better-application-help-world/index.html, last visited 30 August 2020.

the rise of violence, like food insecurity or natural disasters. Peacetech entrepreneurs are always evaluating new tools to determine how they can be useful in achieving desired outcomes, whether that means artificial intelligence, blockchain, or social media mining. Whatever approach proves effective in preventing social and economic disruption will be embraced; if a particular approach does not achieve measurable results through A/B testing it is quickly discarded. What matters most is efficacy, so innovators explore every option to see what works best (e.g. blogs, social media, digital TV and radio programs, multimedia, webinars, podcasts, competitions, or some other as yet uninvented channel). Peacetech has little patience for 'feel good' projects with no tangible, measurable impacts. Thus rapid iteration is the best way to ensure that peacetech tools become more effective over time.[6]

Many of the innovators who created large internet companies like Google, Facebook, and Amazon were explicit at the outset that they wanted to 'move fast and break things' when they launched and grew their companies. As a result, these companies did just that – they broke things – and now in hindsight we can see some of the negative impacts that were unleashed by that rapid, disruptive change. Those early entrepreneurs made a lot of money from the disruptions they unleashed, but they also now acknowledge a measure of responsibility for the chaos that ensued. They are eager to invest some of the money they made to address the problems caused by the internet's explosive growth, but they are unwilling to provide resources to public or NGO initiatives that are a) unlikely to be sustainable over the long run without significant continued donations, or b) likely to innovate at the glacial pace of public or nonprofit organizations. These technology leaders have firsthand experience with the rapid pace of innovation in the private sector, and as a result they are much more willing to invest in a peacetech startup than to donate to a large peacebuilding NGO.

Vint Cerf (considered the Father of the modern Internet) and Sheldon Himelfarb (CEO of the Peace Tech Lab) summarized this perspective in an op-ed on CNN.com:

> We can and must embrace the unprecedented opportunities we have to solve the most intractable and ongoing conflicts that continue to plague our world, but we will only succeed if we beat technological swords into plowshares for the good of humanity.[7]

6 Varghese, Anand, with Sheldon Himelfarb. "Peace, Inc. - To Make their Mark, the Architects of Peacebuilding's Bleeding Edge Need to Leave the Government Payroll and Start their Own Industry," in Foreign Policy, 27 January 2015. https://foreignpolicy.com/2015/01/27/peace-inc-tech-government-industry-defense-funding/, last visited 30 August 2020.

7 Cerf, Vinton, with Sheldon Himelfarb. "Can the Peacetech Industry Save the Internet?" CNN Opinion, 29 September 2018. www.cnn.com/2018/09/29/opinions/technology-harm-better-application-help-world/index.html, last visited 30 August 2020.

5 Parallels Between ODR and Peacetech

The fields of ODR and peacetech mirror each other in several ways. If ODR is the application of information and communications technology to help people prevent, manage, and resolve their disputes, peacetech is the application of technology to prevent violence and address the underlying causes of violent conflict. Many have observed the close relationship between peace and justice. Painted broadly, ODR focuses on the justice side, while peacetech focuses on the peace side. But the two are inextricably intertwined (hence the motto 'no justice, no peace').

Both peacetech and ODR innovators frequently describe their work as focused on conflict management and resolution. From certain angles dispute resolution practice can even be seen as a component of peacemaking and peacebuilding (hence Lincoln's quote that 'as a peace-maker the lawyer has a superior opportunity of being a good man.') Some peacebuilding efforts even include formal dispute resolution processes as part of the overall de-escalation strategy introduced into conflict zones.

ODR usually focuses on two party disputes over a specific issue (such as an ecommerce dispute, a commercial disagreement, a divorce, or a workplace issue). Dispute resolution arose in the shadow of the law, and the legal framing for disagreements shapes ODR processes and protocols. ODR outcomes often have a clear path to enforcement. In contrast, peacetech operates on a more systemic, social level. The roots of social conflict are harder to synthesize and fully encapsulate. Instead of two or three parties conflicts may involve thousands or millions of parties. Enforcement of outcomes and agreements achieved may be complex, and fragile. Some describe peace as the absence of conflict, but conflict is omnipresent in human interaction, so it never really goes away. A more accurate definition may be to frame peace as the result of effective conflict management. But in both ODR and peacetech the core challenges of de-escalation and joint problem-solving are the same, just at a different scale.

In the ODR field we know that technology can help parties be at their best. It can provide cooling distance, structure communication to keep negotiations on track, and help parties achieve insight into and empathy for the other side. Peacetech can leverage many of the same dynamics. In addition to focusing on improving core metrics associated with social conflict, technology can create new opportunities for civic participation and engagement that also promote understanding of the other side's perspective.

Just like ODR can feel weird and dehumanizing to face-to-face mediators and arbitrators, peacetech can feel weird and dehumanizing to experienced peacebuilders who are used to doing their work in person. Many offline dispute resolvers were initially skeptical about the value of bringing technology into the peacebuilders' toolbox, similar to the reticence judges, lawyers, and face-to-face dispute resolvers felt about ODR in the early days. The ODR field talks about 'third parties' (human neutrals, like mediators and arbitrators) partnering with 'fourth parties' (technology tools that also have a seat at the negotiating table). Peacebuilding practitioners have to navigate how they can and should collaborate with technology in their work. Similar to the growth of ODR, peacetech began with smaller efforts, and once those efforts gained traction the activity and scale of peacetech initiatives began to expand. Each successful project helps convert skeptics into true believers. It is hard to argue with results.

Another similarity between dispute resolution and peacebuilding is the difficulty of measuring the beneficial impact of projects. Peacetech promoters are frequently put into the difficult position of proving a negative: if an intervention prevents escalation from happening, some may remain unconvinced that escalation would have occurred without the intervention. Technology can help by collecting data to document these benefits more clearly, as well as modeling the damage that would have occurred without the intervention, thereby strengthening the rationale for continued investment.

Just as technology has transformed disputant expectations around dispute resolution, technology is creating new expectations amongst stakeholders in conflict zones. Large internet companies are putting powerful tools in the hands of individuals that can help them to create and share data in transformative ways, and those users now expect to be able to utilize those tools to build peace. ODR innovations were not driven by mediators and arbitrators (or lawyers and judges) – they were driven by the parties themselves, who were utilizing technology in other areas of their lives and then expected to use it to resolve their disputes as well. This same expectation drives the introduction of technology into peacebuilding. Once you experience the power and reach a tool like Facebook or Google or Twitter or YouTube provides, a little bell goes off in your mind – and that bell cannot easily be unrung.

Some practitioners see ODR and ADR as being in opposition, as if neutrals and parties have to pick one or the other. But this is a false dichotomy. In reality ODR and ADR work most effectively when they operate in concert. Just like we do not live our lives entirely online or offline we do not need our dispute resolution processes to be entirely online or offline. Peacetech innovators are similarly utilizing hybrid approaches that marry online and offline techniques, which can maximize reach and minimize risks of exclusion. The ability to switch between offline and online tools has made peacetech platforms more flexible and adaptable in diverse cultural and geographic contexts.

Many of us in ODR are fond of saying that ODR is just ADR accelerated by technology. In a similar fashion peacetech is just peacebuilding accelerated by technology. ODR is ADR; it shares the same objectives, approaches, and theoretical foundations. In the same way peacetech is peacebuilding; it also shares the same objectives, approaches, and theoretical foundations. But as ODR opens many new possibilities for the practice of dispute resolution, peacetech opens just as many (if not more) new doors for the practice of peacebuilding.

6 How Does Peacetech Work?

Online dispute resolution can be broadly divided into two main segments: algorithmic ODR, which leverages the power of computer processors and data to resolve disputes, and facilitative ODR, which focuses on mediating human-to-human interaction to promote understanding and increase the likelihood of resolution.

Peacetech can be analyzed through a similar breakdown. One segment of peacetech focuses on using data and the algorithmic power of computers to glean insights that were previously inaccessible: hotspots at risk of escalation, complex data mapped across geographies to identify patterns, or worrisome trends in social media postings that might indicate a risk of escalation and violence. Another segment of peacetech focuses on the facilitation of human-to-human communication: how to use technology to empower marginalized or silenced groups to promote understanding and empathy, or how to use technology to connect disparate communities of peacebuilders so they can cooperate for greater effectiveness.

We will now examine these two segments of peacetech innovation, algorithmic and facilitative, and then analyze what lessons can be gleaned for ODR practice (and vice versa).

7 Algorithmic Peacetech: Using Technology to Generating Insight and Understanding

Fundamentally, computers are algorithmic engines. Since the 1970s computer processors have doubled their computational power about every two years. That fact translates into an exponential growth rate in the power of computers to crunch numbers at scale. Now, with the arrival of quantum computing, we may see this trend continue for at least another decade or more. This means that technology is going to get much, much faster and more powerful within our lifetimes.

How best to leverage these new capabilities is still an open question, but peacetech innovators are constantly experimenting to sketch out what is possible. Could big data analyzed by advanced technology have predicted the genocide in Rwanda, or the massacre of Bosnian Muslims, before they occurred? Could machine learning have predicted the Green Revolution in Iran, or the Orange Revolution in Ukraine, or the rising tide of violence against the Rohingya in Myanmar? If effective early intervention in conflicts is the 'cold fusion' breakthrough of peacebuilding, how can the growing algorithmic power of computers help us achieve it?

Number crunching and pattern recognition may hold the key to preventing wars before they break out, but to get there peacebuilders must change the way they do business. This awareness is already spreading through the peacebuilding community.

There is now a recognition that conflict prevention is no longer limited to diplomatic overtures and military threats. It also requires monitoring and data analysis to examine the root causes of violence, not only between governments, but also between non-state actors such as tribes, religious groups, and social movements.[8]

Crafting effective algorithms is one thing, but the lifeblood of algorithms is data, and peacetech innovators are working hard to collect and structure that data so that algorithms can make sense of it. Peacetech initiatives are crowdsourcing information collection and utilizing mobile and satellite technologies to map out hotspots on the ground. They are also absorbing billions of tweets, posts, images, and videos in real time to glean actionable insights. These efforts have already vastly improved early warning systems, but they have the potential to exert much greater impact over time as the data sets get larger.

Data is the new currency of technology, even more than money. Marc Andreesen, co-creator of the Netscape browser, said that software is going to eat the world. Now, as Martijn van Attekum has observed, artificial intelligence (AI) is going to eat software. The capacity to gather, structure, and learn from staggeringly large data sets is a defining strength of peacetech. Peacetech can use tools such as satellite imaging, GPS, and mobile devices to track, analyze, and present data via interactive maps to pinpoint outbreaks of violence and determine where interventions should focus their efforts. Similar approaches are now being used to identify Covid-19 hotspots to target outbreaks. Crisis mapping, crowdsourcing, and early warning systems can provide the right information to the right parties at the right time to enable an effective conflict intervention, and the ability of technology to process this information instantly can greatly increase the value of that information in preventing escalation.[9]

Feeding AI algorithms structured, accurate data can generate insights and actionable information. The complexity and sophistication of these programs can detect patterns and correlations that are beyond the capacity of the human brain to comprehend. This contrasts starkly with prior peacebuilding approaches, which relied upon individuals on the ground all over the world to gather information and draw conclusions from that information before sharing it. Algorithms can consume enormous amounts of raw data, much of it submitted by individuals, and then make connections that the collector of the information was unable to detect. For example, community members can provide information on cases that were not properly handled by the authorities (such as the *I Paid a Bribe* app, at ipaidabribe.com) and then algorithms can aggregate that information into clear patterns of misbehavior that can be systematically targeted and resolved. Each

8 Himelfarb, Sheldon. "Peacebuilding Reboot" in Building Peace: A Forum for Peace and Security in the 21st Center. Issue #5: #Peacetech. Alliance for Peacebuilding, March 2015. www.scaruffi.com/peace/peacetech.pdf, last visited 30 August 2021.

9 van Attekum, Martjin, with Jie Mei and Tarry Singh. "Software Ate the World, Now AI is Eating Software," in Forbes, 29 August 2019. www.forbes.com/sites/cognitiveworld/2019/08/29/software-ate-the-world-now-ai-is-eating-software/#795d67985810, last visited 30 August 2020.

contributor cannot see the patterns on the ground, but by submitting their individual data to a wider pool algorithms can cull out actionable information that benefits everyone.

8 Facilitative Peacetech: Using Technology to Improve Communication and Connection

The promise of big data and machine learning are impressive, but it may be that the even greater impact of technology on peacebuilding is in the area of computer facilitated communication. The wave of citizen-led protests that sprung up around the world in 2019 was spurred largely by the ubiquity of mobile devices and increasing use of encrypted messaging apps and social media platforms. Activism in online campaigns is powering the global climate change movement, and technology is proving essential in helping refugees around the world connect with one another and amplify their claims to political and economic rights.

As Bob Taylor, the creator of ARPAnet (the precursor to the internet), put it:

> Computers were first born as arithmetic engines, but my own view, and the view of some other people as well, is that they're much more interesting and powerful as communication devices because they mediate human-to-human communication.[10]

Social media platforms, blogs, podcasts, and online forums are amplifying previously marginalized voices and promoting peace through storytelling. These technology-enabled communications channels connect geographically separated users into communities focused on related themes, and bring greater attention to the voices of individuals with lived experiences of conflict.

Peacebuilders are now able to tap into large and powerful online communities, where they share knowledge, mobilize with like-minded actors, and drive social change. These online spaces can promote the creation of new partnerships and networks that are effective in building peace. Innovations and progress in one area can be shared through these networks with peacebuilders in other regions, which helps build momentum behind collective action, fostering a wider digital culture around peace and peacebuilding.[11]

Algorithmic peacetech approaches are highly dependent on continued innovations in processor design and storage technology, but facilitative technologies do not have to be

10 Rule, Colin. *Online Dispute Resolution for Business.* Jossey-Bass, 2003. www.amazon.com/Online-Dispute-Resolution-Business-Employment/dp/0787957313, last visited 30 August 2020.

11 Peace Direct. "Digital Pathways for Peace: Insights and Lessons from a Global Online Consultation." Peace Direct, 2020. www.peacedirect.org/us/wp-content/uploads/sites/2/2020/08/PD-LVP-Tech-Report.pdf, last visited 30 August 2020.

cutting edge in order to be effective. Traditional communication technologies like video, radio, and animation can also be effective in promoting peace and understanding. It is important to note that, like ODR, peacetech is not synonymous with the internet. The internet is one powerful tool in the peacebuilder toolbox, but there are many others that have been around for a long time, like radio, television, film, and the telephone, that should not be overlooked.

The expanding reach of global networks enables peacebuilders to reach across borders, changing the relationship between government and its citizens. Technology is empowering new voices and creating new communities around the world that are devoted to reforming the relationship between governments and citizens by expanding inclusivity and social equity. Technology can reinforce democracy and create new opportunities for civic engagement, which can empower marginalized groups and enhance government accountability.

Technology offers critical opportunities for building more inclusive democratic societies. This inclusivity can contribute to more effective security and peace efforts. For example, Afghan women have used social media platforms like Twitter to engage government stakeholders on women's inclusion in the Afghan peace process, enabling previously marginalized stakeholders to reclaim agency in shaping their collective future. Digital technology is increasing the visibility of youth-led peacebuilding movements and promoting positivity around youth as agents of change. An in-person training often maxes out at 30 participants, but technology can enable ten times more participants to access a training via social media and videoconference.[12]

Most governments are unable to allow for citizen participation in crucial decisions around the allocation of budgets, the occupation of land, and the management of resources. There may be no physical space large enough to enable the majority of a population to participate in a public meeting, and conflicting schedules often inhibit this kind of widespread involvement. Civic participation software, however, can help increase engagement from citizens in the activities of government. Virtual spaces remove logistical barriers, facilitating collaboration among large numbers of people.

Digital technology can also help engage communities in hard-to-reach areas and include them in peacebuilding activities. If the new mantra of engagement is 'nothing about us without us' the use of technology can help to deliver on that objective by expanding the reach of peacebuilding projects beyond geographic limitations. Online forums can include individuals from various levels of society to tackle political, social, economic, and judicial challenges while respecting core principles of inclusivity, ownership, dignity, sustainability, and knowledge-sharing.

---

12 Petersen, Jes Kaliebe. "Communication and Connection in Afghanistan" in Building Peace: A Forum for Peace and Security in the 21st Center. Issue #5: #Peacetech. Alliance for Peacebuilding, March 2015. www.scaruffi.com/peace/peacetech.pdf, last visited 30 August 2021.

Technology provides inherent operational benefits. Technology makes it possible to connect directly with communities affected by conflict without putting your staff members in harm's way. Technology is also helpful in ensuring accountability of project funds. Peacetech can enable organizations to gather data from conflict-prone communities even without having individuals on the ground in those communities. Anonymous online participation can also get people talking about taboo topics like sexual violence and abuse, and to create confidential communities of support once the silence is broken.[13]

Technology can also play an important role in mobilizing people and raising awareness. Physical spaces devoted to civil society may be shrinking, but online mobilization is filling the gap. Technology has proven effective in supporting activists in their efforts to resist authoritarian governments. Social media can link peace movements across geographies and allow consensual decision-making and resource sharing. Activists are using Facebook to schedule protests, Twitter to coordinate on the ground in real time, and YouTube to show the world what happened. Virtual exchanges make person-to-person connections that can vastly expand the diversity of young people with access to cross cultural experiences. Digital intercultural dialogues can promote deep listening and effective communication.

9 CHALLENGES IN PEACETECH

It is easy to get excited about all of the potential for these peacetech applications, but it is important to note that introducing technology into vulnerable societies carries significant risks as well.

If you ask the average person on the street about the impact of technology on global civil society they're more likely to bemoan its debasement of civic dialogue than to point to its benevolent impacts. It is undeniable that malevolent actors around the world are intentionally using technology tools for their own purposes, such as fomenting conflict, division, and disinformation. Every day brings new stories about the ways technology is being used to recruit terrorists, spread disinformation, and urge people who feel threatened to respond with violence. Technology can open opportunities to seed mistrust and social instability in open societies. Certain groups see the incitement of anger and mistrust as being in their interest, which creates a risk that the enmity they encourage will spill from online forums to offline violence.

And it's not just non-state actors that are engaging in this behavior. Some governments are enacting laws and regulations that use technology to further

13 Peace Direct. "Digital Pathways for Peace: Insights and Lessons from a Global Online Consultation." Peace Direct, 2020. www.peacedirect.org/us/wp-content/uploads/sites/2/2020/08/PD-LVP-Tech-Report.pdf, last visited 30 August 2020.

exacerbate digital divides and inhibit the rights and freedoms of certain groups within society. Technology is being abused by authoritarian states to promote censorship, surveillance, and marginalization of targeted groups. Government restrictions through regulations and policies are leading to censorship, surveillance, and internet shutdowns, which threaten the freedom and rights of online users and further shrink civil society.

Technology can also raise complex issues around ethics, privacy, and security. Even benevolent technological initiatives can unintentionally expose users to surveillance or sanction if the platforms are compromised or monitored by unauthorized entities. These risks should be considered in the design phase of each peacetech project, and staff should be trained to follow security best practices and to be on the lookout for warning signs. It can be difficult for small organizations to prevent these incursions from well financed government or military hackers, but if technology is going to be utilized its designers must pay close attention to preventing these kinds of unintended consequences.

These malevolent uses of technology are increasingly challenging peaceful societies, which underscores the popular perception that technology is dangerous and destabilizing. Let's examine two of the primary challenges technology can introduce into peacebuilding efforts: the use of technology to promote conflict and repression, and the digital divide.

10 Combatting the Use of Technology to Promote Conflict and Repression

In 2013 a group of Ethiopian bloggers and journalists created a blog to express their interest in evolving Ethiopia into a more open, inclusive, and democratic country. They called their blog *Zone 9*, which was an ironic reference to the eight zones of Ethiopia's notorious Kaliti prison. Their collective writing was intended to demonstrate the possibility of a more open civic life. They chose to publish on the internet both out of necessity (it was the only public forum easily available to them) and because their online presence connected them to a global community of writers, thinkers, and translators with similar ideas.

Given Ethiopia's history of imprisoning journalists and intellectuals they almost certainly knew there were taking a risk, but they probably did not realize that they would be arrested and charged with a range of offenses under Ethiopia's 2009 Anti-Terrorism Proclamation. The evidence used against them – and the reason they were legally charged with criminal intent – was that they had received training in the use of digital security and encryption tools from an online group called the Tactical Technology

Collective, which intended for this training to support peacebuilders around the world. While some of the members of the Zone 9 group were eventually released, several of the journalists remain imprisoned to this day.[14]

This example shows that while technology has the potential to connect local peacebuilders to likeminded activists around the world, many governments do not perceive this to be a good thing. In the name of preserving social order some governments are using the very same technologies leveraged by peacetech innovators to engage in surveillance and repression. A number of countries today are quashing the rights of democratic activists and using anti-terror laws to preserve non-democratic rule, punishing those who seek to leverage digital communication tools for the expression of their universal rights.

One example of how technology can contribute to violence was Facebook's experience in Myanmar. Facebook is so widespread in Myanmar that many internet users there can only access the internet through Facebook. However there is still very low digital literacy in Myanmar, and many citizens find it difficult to distinguish real news from disinformation. Over several years Facebook users were continuously exposed to a steady stream of hateful content targeted against minority groups in the country, and the volume of this content drastically increased in 2017. Made up stories claimed that the minority Rohingya Muslim population was stockpiling weapons and planning to attack the majority Buddhist population. This led to a call for decisive action against the Rohingya, and in August 2017 a military crackdown sent hundreds of thousands of Rohingya Muslims fleeing across the border into Bangladesh. Because of Facebook's prominence in Myanmar it became clear that the social network had played a key role in facilitating this misinformation campaign and had done little to combat it. Facebook commissioned its own internal investigation into the crisis, which corroborated that its platforms (including WhatsApp, Facebook, and Instagram) were used by conflict actors in Myanmar and that Facebook was guilty of slow playing its response before and during the attacks. Facebook subsequently hired hundreds of native speakers in Myanmar and changed its policies around hate speech, but the misinformation campaign has continued and there are fears that the crisis is in danger of re-escalating.[15]

It would be a mistake to presume from this example that technology is somehow inherently bad and that there is something in the expansion of technology that will inevitably promote hatred and misunderstanding. There were misinformation campaigns in Myanmar before Facebook got there, and no one in Facebook's

---

14 Sigal, Ivan. "The Shrinking Space for Online Civic Engagement" in Building Peace: A Forum for Peace and Security in the 21st Center. Issue #5: #Peacetech. Alliance for Peacebuilding, March 2015. www.scaruffi.com/peace/peacetech.pdf, last visited 30 August 2021.

15 Peace Direct. "Digital Pathways for Peace: Insights and Lessons from a Global Online Consultation." Peace Direct, 2020. www.peacedirect.org/us/wp-content/uploads/sites/2/2020/08/PD-LVP-Tech-Report.pdf, last visited 30 August 2020.

headquarters encouraged these developments. But that does not absolve technology providers from responsibility for these outcomes.

There are plentiful examples of how technology is being misused by bad actors, and even when technology itself is considered neutral; it is still a tool that users can deploy to achieve their ends, whether those ends are good or bad. So the question is: how can we maximize technology's potential for good and limit its harm? There is a race between those who would use technology to promote peace and those who would use it to create conflict, and in many regions the latter group is winning. The answer is not less technology on the peace promotion side, but rather greater investment to shift the race in favor of technology for good.

11 THE DIGITAL DIVIDE

In its infancy, ODR was often criticized for exacerbating the digital divide. If ODR was dependent on technology, the argument went, and only rich people could afford the technology, then ODR was essentially building a justice system only for rich people. This criticism was fair when ODR was dependent on expensive laptops and costly broadband data connections. But as access to technology has expanded, particularly through the launch and scaling of mobile devices, and internet access has grown from 50% of the population to more than 90%, those criticisms have waned. Now technology is seen as one of the most effective ways to expand access to justice, because most lower income individuals have easier access to justice through their mobile devices than through face-to-face channels.

For peacetech the criticism is still an apt one, however. In designing an ODR system for a developed country most everyone in the society has access to the internet in one form or another. But looking at conflict zones around the world, the story is quite different. As Ann Mei Chang, Chief Innovation Officer at Mercy Corps, puts it,

> Today, only 40 percent of the world's population is online. The number is growing rapidly, but those who do not have Internet access are disproportionately poor, rural, older, and female.

The use of technology in peacebuilding processes has the potential to disenfranchise populations that lack access to it, and those populations are often already marginalized by other factors. Chang continues:

> Who will be left behind by technology? One of the most significant barriers to internet access is affordability. With more limited financial resources women are disproportionately affected by high prices and face more barriers to access.

> The internet can be a global shared space where all are welcome and where the quality of your ideas leaves a greater impression than the color of your skin. Is the internet a model for peace for the peaceful world we strive to build? Can it be a place where clashing views can be shared peacefully? Perhaps, but to realize such a possibility we must ensure all voices are included.[16]

There are many obstacles to the use of technology in building peace, including structural barriers like poverty, weak infrastructure, and low digital literacy. These dynamics keep large segments of the global population from leveraging these tools. Poor infrastructure, high cost, and a lack of accessibility and training are widening social inequalities, and that may lead to future conflict. Digital divides disproportionately affect marginalized groups like women and minorities. Offline power imbalances are being replicated in online environments, and these balances translate into harassment and targeting by trolls.

But peacetech does not have to be expensive or technologically sophisticated in order to be effective. In the mid-1990s community centers in North Belfast used mobile phones to counter rumors and keep communities connected during sectarian violence. African social activists pioneered advocacy efforts in 2004 organizing social justice campaigns using mobile text and SMS technology. In countries like Afghanistan only a small fraction of Afghan mobile phone users have frequent access to data, but peacetech programs are using text messaging to communicate and share in groups using numerical or text keywords in local languages.[17]

Also, if past experience is an accurate predictor of the future, the cost for technology will continue to drop as a result of innovation and technological advances. A decade ago the One Laptop per Child (OLPC) project attempted to create inexpensive laptops (less than $100 apiece) that could be distributed to children around the world. Now India is distributing tablets to school children that are much more powerful than the OLPC laptops – and they only cost $5 apiece. Concerns around the digital divide must be taken seriously, but further efficiencies and innovations in the technology sector are helping to resolve those concerns a little more every day.[18]

---

16 Chang, Ann Mei. "The Digital Revolution: Who Gets Left Behind?" in Building Peace: A Forum for Peace and Security in the 21st Center. Issue #5: #Peacetech. Alliance for Peacebuilding, March 2015. www.scaruffi.com/peace/peacetech.pdf, last visited 30 August 2021.

17 Peace Direct. "Digital Pathways for Peace: Insights and Lessons from a Global Online Consultation." Peace Direct, 2020. www.peacedirect.org/us/wp-content/uploads/sites/2/2020/08/PD-LVP-Tech-Report.pdf, last visited 30 August 2020.

18 Robertson, Adi. "OLPC's $100 Laptop Was Going to Change the World – Then It All Went Wrong," in The Verge, 16 April 2018. www.theverge.com/2018/4/16/17233946/olpcs-100-laptop-education-where-is-it-now, last visited 30 August 2020.

12 Conclusion

As the former Swedish Foreign Minister Margo Wallström noted,

> Progress will depend on our capacity to join forces with the people who are currently working to create a better future. The times we live in suggest that technology will be at the heart of this work.[19]

Peacebuilders must combine the knowledge of social scientists, data scientists, conflict resolution experts, technologists, and engineers to envision the future of peacetech. We are witnessing the birth of a new world where access to information and capital are democratized and the playing field is radically leveled. Those who want to build peace must leverage these changes to improve the efficacy of our efforts to prevent and reduce violence. Peacetech innovators are on the front lines of that effort.

Technology is not inherently good or bad. Technology is only a tool to achieve a desired outcome. It is people's decisions that have the power to use or misuse technology. It is important to confront the dilemmas and dangers posed by expanded use of technology, and to identify the risk of unintended consequences to new tech tools. But the potential benefit of these tools outweighs the risks, especially if collaborative efforts between public and private entities can promote best practices, pass regulations, and work to civilize cyberspace.

More research into the effectiveness of peacetech in conflict-affected settings is needed. This should be a priority for funders and governments alike. Quantitative, long-term research will help us capture lessons learned and share best practices so that negative impacts can be avoided and/or mitigated, and ensure future peacetech initiatives do not need to reinvent the wheel.

The stakes are higher in peacetech than in ODR. There are negative impacts from a lack of fair and efficient redress in commercial and civil matters, certainly. But the devastation and misery of war is urgent on an entirely different level. Experimentation in ODR is easier because most of the unintended impacts are manageable. Peacetech initiatives must abide by higher standards as unintended impacts can quickly spiral out of control should things go wrong.

The scope of technologies relevant to peacebuilding is vast: information and communications technology, new media technology, big data, crowdsourcing, online mapping, digital video, radio, social networking – the list goes on. But these technologies do not and cannot cause peace. Instead, projects that encourage peace can use these technologies to achieve their objectives more effectively. We need to document

---

19 Wallström, Margot. "Plugging Governments into Peace" in Building Peace: A Forum for Peace and Security in the 21st Center. Issue #5: #Peacetech. Alliance for Peacebuilding, March 2015. www.scaruffi.com/peace/peacetech.pdf, last visited 30 August 2021.

effective peacetech practices and leverage them in new projects, as opposed to concluding that introducing technology is always beneficial. As Foreign Minister Wallström further summarized it,

> Technology in itself cannot resolve conflicts. But in a world where nearly everyone has or will soon have access to communication technologies, the question is whether we will be able to resolve conflicts without technology.[20]

Much like ODR, peacetech can enhance trust, encourage mutual action, and increase engagement. It can generate innovative solutions that strike at the root causes of conflict and insecurity. Peacetech can provide peacebuilders user-friendly scalable tools to help them expand their reach and be more effective, similar to the benefits ODR is delivering in the judicial system. By sharing lessons between the two fields, and studying the similarities and solutions, we can ensure that both will create a more just and peaceful world.

13. Additional Sources

The following sources were used in addition to the sources cited in the footnotes.

- Byrnes, Ciara. "Welcome to PeaceTech, The Movement to Use Technology to End Violent Conflict and Extremism." Fast Company, 11 August 2015. www.fastcompany.com/3047534/welcome-to-peacetech-the-movement-to-use-technology-to-end-violent-conflict-and-extremism, last visited 30 August 2020.
- Martin-Shields, Charles. "Proving (Digital) Peace" in Building Peace: A Forum for Peace and Security in the 21st Center. Issue #5: #Peacetech. Alliance for Peacebuilding, March 2015. www.scaruffi.com/peace/peacetech.pdf, last visited 30 August 2021.
- Peacetech Lab, "Our Unique History," www.peacetechlab.org/history, last visited 30 August 2020.
- Quihuis, Margarita with Mark Nelson, and Karen Guttieri. "Peace Technology: Scope, Scale, and Cautions" in Building Peace: A Forum for Peace and Security in the 21st Center. Issue #5: #Peacetech. Alliance for Peacebuilding, March 2015. www.scaruffi.com/peace/peacetech.pdf, last visited 30 August 2021.
- Synkov, Dmitriy. "Tools and Trends in Peace and Technology" in Building Peace: A Forum for Peace and Security in the 21st Center. Issue #5: #Peacetech. Alliance for Peacebuilding, March 2015. www.scaruffi.com/peace/peacetech.pdf, last visited 30 August 2021.

20 *Ibid.*

- Wikipedia, Zone 9 bloggers. https://en.wikipedia.org/wiki/Zone_9_bloggers, last visited 30 August 2020.

Chapter 17 Artificial Intelligence and the Future of Dispute Resolution

The Age of AI-DR

Orna Rabinovich-Einy and Ethan Katsh

1 Introduction

This chapter addresses the rise of artificial intelligence (AI) and its implications for the field of dispute resolution. In recent decades, digital technology has re-shaped alternative dispute resolution into online dispute resolution (ODR). In the last few years, ODR has spread to courts, further blurring boundaries between formal and informal dispute resolution, as well as between online and offline avenues of redress.

More recently, AI has begun to infiltrate dispute resolution, mostly in the realm of AI-based prediction. With the maturing of ODR and the spread of AI, we can expect the overlap between the two to further evolve in both private and public dispute resolution, giving rise to a new form of dispute resolution, AI-DR.

AI is increasingly being employed in a variety of legal and ADR settings and its role can be expected to grow further in the near future. The questions that remain open are the design choices that will be made with respect to AI and the means that will be employed to maximize its contribution and curb the challenges associated with AI-based decisions, recommendations, and predictions. Dispute resolution processes need not only to be efficient but to be fair, trustworthy, and accountable and must be perceived as such if they are to sustain their legitimacy and fulfill their societal role.

In the sections that follow, we describe the relevance and current use of AI in dispute resolution, while drawing on particular examples to illustrate the promise and limitations of such use, which can be expected to expand dramatically in the next decade.

2 Why AI?

2.1 What Is AI?

Artificial intelligence has made huge leaps in recent decades. Several decades ago, Moore's law posited that computer processing power would grow exponentially, doubling every 18 months. We have already experienced computers outperforming humans in games such as chess, Go and Jeopardy,[1] and increasingly algorithms decide our most basic needs – whether we will be approved for a loan,[2] hired for a job[3] or receive a refund.[4] Algorithms are influencing whether freedom will be taken away, as tools such as COMPAS advise judges on a defendant's risk level and the chances of reoffending, in deciding whether to release or arrest them.[5] AI is also writing some of the news we read,[6] recommending books, movies, and music for us,[7] and will soon be driving our cars.[8]

It is already evident that AI is having a sweeping impact on every aspect of our lives. Yet most of us know very little about it and how it operates. The concepts are complex and not always distinguishable – AI, algorithms, learning algorithms, deep learning, machine learning, and more. These are all overlapping but not identical in meaning. For our purposes, however, we will refer to most of these terms under the umbrella term of 'AI'.

AI is a set of algorithms derived from an array of calculations. Computer algorithms are automated instructions, ranging from the simple to the highly complex. The first generation of algorithms worked much like recipes, with a set of instructions that resulted in a foreseeable result.[9] Over the years, algorithms evolved and came to rely not just on inputs that were designed to operate as triggers, but also on unstructured data that allowed them to change, adapt, and grow. This is what is sometimes referred to as a 'second generation' of machines.[10] In this new, advanced generation we define AI as the ability of machines to perform actions, reach outcomes, anticipate problems, learn to adapt to new circumstances and to solve complex problems without human intervention or supervision.[11]

The combination of the huge increase in computational power in recent years combined with the availability of Big Data to serve as training data is what has buoyed

---

1 Elizabeth Gibney, *Google AI Algorithm Masters Ancient Game of Go*, 529 Nature News 445 (2016); John Markoff, *Computer Wins on 'Jeopardy!': Trivial, It's Not*, N.Y. Times (16 February 2004), www.nytimes.com/2011/02/17/science/17jeopardy-watson.html.

2 Joshua A. Kroll *et al.*, *Accountable Algorithms*, 165 U. Pa. L. Rev. 633, 633 (2016).

3 Pauline T. Kim, *Data-Driven Discrimination at Work*, 58 William & Mary L. Rev. 857, 860 (2017).

4 Chavie Lieber, *Amazon Might Ban You If You Return Too Much*, Racked (23 May 2018), www.racked.com/2018/5/23/17384044/amazon-bans-shoppers-returns (last visited on 17 May 2020).

5 Megan Stevenson, *Assessing Risk Assessment in Action*, 303 Minn. L. Rev. 103 (2018).

6 Jihii Jolly, *How Algorithms Decide the News You See*, Columbia Journalism Rev. (20 May 2014), https://archives.cjr.org/news_literacy/algorithms_filter_bubble.php (last visited on 17 May 2020).

7 Ben Ratliff, *Slaves to the Algorithm: How Music Fans Can Reclaim their Playlists from Spotify*, The Guardian (19 February 2016), www.theguardian.com/books/2016/feb/19/slave-to-the-algorithm-how-music-fans-can-reclaim-their-playlists-from-spotify (last visited on 17 May 2020).

8 Although at present, semi-autonomous cars present more of a challenge than fully autonomous ones. *See* Tracy Hresko Pearl, *Hands on the Wheel: A Call for Greater Regulation of Semi-Autonomous Cars*, 93 Ind. L. J. 713, 717-721 (2018).

9 Richard Susskind, Online Courts and the Future of Justice 266-268 (2019).

10 *Id.*, at 271-272.

11 Michael Kearns & Aaron Roth, The Ethical Algorithm: The Science of Socially Aware Algorithm Design 6-7 (2020).

these developments. In some cases, the algorithms use experience to look for patterns learned from the data.[12] In others, they draw on unstructured data and the goal is for the machine to cope with unforeseen circumstances by simulating natural intelligence to solve complex problems.[13] The ability to change and adapt to new circumstances is termed 'intelligence'.[14]

AI enjoys some important advantages over human activity through these new capabilities, but it also suffers from severe drawbacks and challenges. In the following sections we explore the potential contribution and appeal of AI for the dispute resolution world, as well as the sources of concern and disadvantages associated with the implementation of AI in dispute resolution processes and systems.

2.2 *Why Would We Want AI in Dispute Resolution?*

The dispute resolution field has traditionally relied on human resolution in a physical space. Resolving disputes in modern times has therefore depended on the pace of human decision-making and the capacity of physical courts. These characteristics have made dispute resolution costly, lengthy, and out of reach for many.[15] While few could afford the high costs associated with adversarial litigation, the prospect of pro se litigation had been an unattractive one given the complex nature of court proceedings.[16] Such a setting clearly benefitted those with power, resources, and the relevant knowledge and expertise.[17]

Against that backdrop, alternative dispute resolution (ADR) emerged in the 1970s, ultimately resulting in the widespread institutionalization of the mediation process in courts in the U.S., and, later, in many other jurisdictions worldwide.[18] Mediation was supposed to provide a cure to the ills of the court system – both by freeing the courts from their heavy backlog and allowing easier access to litigation. It was also hoped to provide an alternative that would not only be less costly and quicker than litigation but

12 *Id.*

13 The distinction between ML and AI is somewhat blurry as it is not always possible to distinguish between structured and unstructured data.

14 *See* definition of 'artificial intelligence' in the Encyclopedia Britannica, www.britannica.com/technology/artificial-intelligence (last visited on 19 May 2020).

15 Jerold S. Auerbach, Justice Without Law? 95 (1983) (describing the legal system of the time as 'a horse-and-buggy [system] near collapse in an urban industrial society').

16 James E. Cabral *et al., Using Technology to Enhance Access to Justice*, 26 Harv. J.L. & Tech. 241, 256 (2012).

17 Marc Galanter, *Why the "Haves" Come out Ahead: Speculations on the Limits of Legal Change*, 9 L. & Soc'y Rev. 95 (1974).

18 Carrie Menkel-Meadow, *Regulation of Dispute Resolution in the United States of America: From the Formal to the Informal to the 'Semi-formal', in* Regulating Dispute Resolution: ADR and Access to Justice at the Crossroads 419 (Felix Steffek & Hannes Unberath, eds. 2013).

would also allow parties direct participation and remedies that addressed their needs and interests, preserved relationships and expanded options beyond legal rights and remedies.[19]

Over time, the expectations surrounding ADR were fermented. Critics bemoaned the privatization of the judicial system, allowing efficiency-related considerations and the private interests of parties to outweigh the public interest in the development of the law, declaration of societal values, and the protection of rights of disempowered groups in society.[20] The fear was that access was being preferred over justice and efficiency over fairness.[21] A clear distinction was understood to exist between public proceedings based on procedural due process and substantive legal norms on the one hand, and quicker and simpler private processes that enjoy procedural and substantive flexibility on the other hand. This distinction was blurred with the emergence of a more legalized version of mediation in courts as well as the permeation of ADR-like tools and practices into the work of judges.[22] Managerial judging and judicial dispute resolution became the norm, accelerating the growth of the vanishing trial phenomenon.[23] Despite growth of ADR, there was no surge in non-adversarial mediation processes, as most ADR processes were being practiced in court, in the presence of lawyers and by lawyers or former judges resulting in a thin, efficient, and rights-based version of mediation.[24]

The spread of ADR, the emergence of the internet and the growth of digital technology, created a new arena in which dispute resolution processes were needed but inaccessible. For e-commerce-related disputes, the prospect of convening physically was often out of reach, and new tools and processes were soon developed to fill this vacuum.[25] Online equivalents of negotiation, mediation, and arbitration evolved and became increasingly sophisticated as technological capabilities developed and social perceptions and preferences related to use of online tools also changed.[26] These new dispute resolution processes that were being offered online came to be known as online dispute resolution or ODR.

Initially, the understanding was that ODR processes were the online equivalents of familiar ADR processes that were designed to address online disputes. Over the course of the last two decades, this definition broadened substantially in three respects. First, ODR was no longer seen as merely mimicking existing processes, but as an opportunity to

19 Carrie Menkel-Meadow, *The Trouble with the Adversary System in a Post Modern, Multicultural World*, 38 Wm. & Mary L. Rev. 5, 17-18 (1996); Nancy A. Welsh, *Making Deals in Court-Connected Mediation: What's Justice Got to Do with It?*, 79 Wash. U. L.Q. 787 (2001).

20 Owen M. Fiss, *Against Settlement*, 93 Yale L.J. 1073 (1984).

21 Orna Rabinovich-Einy & Ethan Katsh, *The New New Courts*, 67 Amer. U. L. Rev. 165, 181 (2017).

22 Orna Rabinovich-Einy, *The Legitimacy Crisis and the Future of Courts*, 17 Cardozo J. of Conf. Res. 23, 33-40 (2015).

23 *Id.*, at 34-35; Rabinovich-Einy & Katsh, *supra* note 21, 181-184.

24 Rabinovich-Einy, *supra* note 22, at 36-37.

25 Ethan Katsh & Orna Rabinovich-Einy, Digital Justice: Technology and the Internet of Disputes 7, 33 (2017).

26 *Id.*, at 37-38.

refashion dispute resolution processes by drawing on the unique qualities of digital technology.[27] Second, ODR was no longer seen as consigned to the realm of online disputes and began to gradually expand to offline disputes, such as consumer complaints, tax appeals, and insurance claims. In addition, in the last few years, a major growth area for ODR has been the courts.[28] ODR is now no longer seen as a transformation in medium for ADR processes, but as an umbrella term covering both court proceedings and alternatives, public and private.

ODR in the courts offered an opportunity to re-design the litigation process, including the ways in which alternatives, such as negotiation and mediation, were being administered. Through novel designs, ODR could improve access to justice by reducing complexity, improving efficiency, and lowering costs.[29] The structure associated with software and pre-fixed language and options offered to parties was also viewed as a means for leveling the playing field between parties and enhancing consistency by third parties – whether operating in a facilitative role or in an adjudicative one.[30] Another advantage exemplified by some ODR processes through the use of structured options and language is that they could also steer parties away from adversarial conduct and language more effectively than oral interventions in the face to face settings, focusing parties on interests and options rather than rights and positions.[31] Alongside the expansion of court ODR, online processes have continued to evolve in e-commerce, developing from product marketplaces to the 'gig economy' and smart contracts.[32]

To date, use of AI in alternatives to litigation has been limited. In formal court proceedings, the most well-known example is the reliance on COMPAS and other similar AI-based predictive algorithms. Such tools assist judges in assessing pre-trial danger and post-trial recidivism, which support judicial decision-making on pre-trial release or on sentencing.[33] In informal ODR, algorithms are used mainly in supporting parties' own decision-making either in the initial diagnosis phase at the outset of the process, or later on in considering common outcomes in similar cases and circumstances on such matters as child support.[34] Also, algorithms are sometimes used in a negotiation or mediation to assist parties in drafting court documents and in devising

27 *Id.*, at 33.

28 Rabinovich-Einy & Katsh, *supra* note 21, at 188-203.

29 *Id.*, at 207-208.

30 *Id.*, at 208-209.

31 *Id.*, at 194.

32 Orna Rabinovich-Einy & Ethan Katsh, *Blockchain and the Inevitability of Disputes: The Role for Online Dispute Resolution*, 2019(2) J. of Disp. Resol. 47, 49 (2019); Ethan Katsh & Orna Rabinovich-Einy, *Dispute Resolution in the Sharing Economy*, Internet Monitor (30 January 2015), https://medium.com/internet-monitor-2014-platforms-and-policy/dispute-resolution-in-the-sharing-economy-573f6369e3e8 (last visited on 17 May 2020).

33 Gary Calionese & Lavi M. Ben-Dor, *AI in Adjudication and Administration*, Brook. L. Rev. 1, 7-14 (forthcoming, 2020).

34 *See* discussion of Civil Resolution Tribunal's 'Solutions Explorer' and of Rechtwisjer's child support calculator below.

joint agreements based on their input in online exchanges.[35] A primary growth area for AI has been the realm of legal tech. It is evident to all those involved in ODR that the role of AI in ODR, including court ODR and court proceedings more generally, will grow dramatically because of its potential to further enhance the strengths of ODR and remedy some of the problems associated with the current dispute resolution landscape – the need for enhanced efficiency and, in certain instances, improved accuracy.

Clearly, use of AI is highly efficient since it relies on automation and inevitably fulfils tasks much more quickly than any human can and at a much larger scale. Indeed, that is where the appeal of algorithms lies – the ability to handle mass decisions at high precision and low costs.[36] Not only can it handle vast amounts of data and process it efficiently but one of the primary advantages of AI is its ability to detect correlations in large datasets that no human can.[37] These correlations can be used for AI-based decision-making, recommendations, predictions, and other tools.

Indeed, AI can facilitate human decision-making by incorporating tools that assist parties' understanding of their own situation and options, improve parties' presentation of the conflict, enhance decision makers' familiarity with decisions rendered under similar circumstances in previous instances, as well as provide decisionmakers with options for language and reasoning.[38] One should bear in mind, however, that to perform these functions through AI, one would need sufficient training data, e.g., examples of previous non-AI–based decisions, options, language choices and the like, all of which would need to be granularly analysed per case types.[39] This is a challenge because, at least in the ADR field, sessions are private and outcomes often remain unpublished, and not easy to come by.[40]

AI has the potential to improve the effectiveness of dispute resolution – it can study third party interventions and discern successful ones, it can identify features of common solutions to specific disputes and identify sources of repeat conflicts. Where the efficiencies of AI-based decision-making or predictions are combined with ODR and allow for dispute resolution to take place asynchronously from afar, away from the physical limitations of time and space associated with courtrooms and even mediation or arbitration sessions, then time and cost savings as well as convenience and access are all the more pronounced. Also, ODR, because it involves automatic documentation of

35 *See id.*

36 Maxi Scherer, *International Arbitration 3.0 – How Artificial Intelligence Will Change Dispute Resolution?*, *in* Austrian Yearbook on International Arbitration 504 (Klausinger *et al.*, eds., 2019).

37 Ari E. Waldman, *Power, Process, and Automated Decision-Making*, 88 Fordham L. Rev. 613, 619 (2019).

38 Dave Orr & Colin Rule, *Artificial Intelligence and the Future of Online Dispute Resolution*, available at www.newhandshake.org/SCU/ai.pdf.

39 *See id.*

40 Scherer, *supra* note 36, at 509.

exchanges, can make training data for algorithms more readily available, reducing the difficulty of obtaining dispute resolution data for such purpose.[41]

AI can enhance both efficiency and accuracy. By allowing for prediction of outcomes of certain disputes or claims, use of AI could make negotiations in the shadow of the law swifter and more accurate and bring parties closer together. While parties have always assessed the probable outcome in their case and bargained in its shadow, algorithmic capabilities for studying vast amounts of data present new possibilities in this realm. The prospects of analysing large amounts of data could provide important information that parties may miss and serve as a reality test curbing unfounded expectations. At the same time, where parties have differing access to such technology and to relevant databases, the potential for efficient bargaining may deteriorate into one-sided, imbalanced outcomes.

AI could also fortify efforts to address other types of problems in current dispute resolution processes. One such problem has been human bias, as exemplified in third party facilitation and decision-making. All humans, even those committed to egalitarian values, have unconscious biases and these biases inevitably impact their decision-making.[42] Over the years, much research has been devoted to the phenomenon, and in uncovering its potential and actual impact in court proceedings and their alternatives.[43]

Research has uncovered the impact of parties' social identity on the outcome of their claims, documenting persistent judicial outcome disparities in cases involving minorities.[44] In ADR, research has been inconclusive, to a large extent due to methodological weaknesses but there has been ongoing speculation on the disparate outcomes informal processes have on the types of outcomes reached through such processes by members of disempowered groups.[45] Despite attempts to eliminate bias and level the playing field, these efforts have had limited success in the face of ongoing pressures to streamline decision making and in light of the spread of informal decision making, conditions under which stereotype-based decision making tends to thrive.[46]

---

41 While the digital trail created in ODR was initially viewed as a limitation, the advantages of automatic documentation soon became clear. *See* for example Orna Rabinovich-Einy, *Technology's Impact: The Quest for a New Paradigm for Accountability in Mediation*, 11 Harv. Neg. L. Rev. 253 (2006).

42 Anthony G. Greenwald *et al.*, *Measuring Individual Differences in Implicit Cognition: The Implicit Association Test*, 74 J. Personality & Soc. Psychol. 1464, 1465-1466 (1998).

43 Jerry Kang *et al.*, *Implicit Bias in the Courtroom*, 59 UCLA L. Rev. 1124, 1169-1186 (2012).

44 *See*, for example, David C. Baldus *et al.*, *Racial Discrimination and the Death Penalty in the Post-*Furman *Era: An Empirical and Legal Overview, with Recent Findings from Philadelphia*, 83 Cornell L. Rev. 1638, 1675-1722 (1998).

45 Gilat J. Bachar & Deborah R. Hensler, *Does Alternative Dispute Resolution Facilitate Prejudice and Bias? We Still Don't Know*, 70 SMU L. Rev. 817, 829-830 (2017).

46 Avital Mentovich, J.J. Prescott & Orna Rabinovich-Einy, *Are Litigation Outcome Disparities Inevitable? Technology and the Future of Impartiality*, 71(4) Ala. L. Rev. 893 (2020).

Both in court and in ADR, outcome disparities can be viewed as 'inaccuracies', perhaps of the sort AI could effectively pre-empt.

The introduction of technology into dispute resolution, it was thought, could make a difference, in more effectively curbing implicit bias.[47] Such expectation was in line with a somewhat naïve view of technology as being neutral and value free in the early days of digital technology and internet communication. Indeed, the hope was that the introduction of technology in various realms would not only make processes more efficient but would also make them less biased.

Reality has proven somewhat nuanced. On the one hand, with current uses of ODR, there is in fact some indication that outcome disparities along group identity lines may be reduced, at least where identity is less salient and judicial decision-making is more structured than in a less formal face-to-face court encounters.[48] On the other hand, it has also become clear that technology is no panacea and that behind the code are humans, and that technological processes inevitably reflect human values and choices, and, consequently, biases as well.[49]

The question arises what happens to dispute resolution when decision-making or facilitation is not made by humans from afar through a platform, but human decision-making is displaced by a machine? With AI, as with technology more generally, early voices believed that the shift to algorithmic decision-making would eliminate the problem of human bias and enhance accuracy of legal outcomes and informal resolutions.[50] Over time, however, these hopes quickly dissipated, at least under current AI design, as we discuss further below.

2.3 *Why Would We Worry About AI in Dispute Resolution?*

Reservations about use of AI in dispute resolution typically fall in one of two categories: those concerned with losing important qualities of human dispute resolution processes with the implementation of AI, and fears about unique characteristics of AI that could detract from the effectiveness or fairness of dispute resolution, as well as exacerbate existing drawbacks of various dispute resolution processes.

In terms of the first concern, the question arises to what degree can AI replicate the ability of humans in dispute resolution to perform their roles. Some writing has been devoted to the role of lawyers – to what extent can the expertise offered by lawyers be

47 Scherer, *supra* note 36, at 510.

48 Mentovich, Prescott & Rabinovich-Einy, *supra* note 47.

49 Kroll *et al., supra* note 3, at 680; Cathy O'Neil, Weapons of Math Destruction: How Big Data Increases Inequality and Threatens Democracy 25-27, 59-60 (2016); Scherer, *supra* note 36, at 511.

50 *See for example* Jerry Kang, *Cyber-Race*, 113 Harv. L. Rev. 1131 (2000).

performed through AI.[51] Some have predicted that a significant portion of what lawyers do today, ranging from document review to legal advice and court outcome prediction, could in the future be performed by machines.[52] Others have been more skeptical, but there is already some indication that some tasks can and will become the domain of algorithms. For those who view lawyers as problem solvers, then the range of activities that may not be covered by AI may seem more expansive, and include the exploration of interests, brainstorming, ensuring balanced participation, and generating creative options for resolution.[53] At the same time, even our relatively brief experience with ODR has demonstrated that software can, where appropriately designed, successfully fulfill at least some of these functions.[54]

With third parties, the concerns are somewhat different than with lawyers. Adjudicators (judges and arbitrators) are expected to render decisions that are derived from the application of rules to the parties' factual circumstances. The decisions should be fair, consistent, nonarbitrary, timely, and well-reasoned. This task is far from simple and is often open to a myriad of options that fall under the third party's discretion. How do we translate the complexities of human judgment, which involves elusive determinations of what comprises *ratio decidendi* as opposed to *dicta*, and how such rules should be applied (or distinguished) in each case (sometimes due to extra-legal considerations)?

Similarly, where AI supports direct negotiation between parties or guides human third-party facilitation, doubts color the ability of algorithms to emulate the richness of human communication skills, sensitivity, and creativity.[55] At the same time, AI proponents do not purport to displace human intervention by mimicking human capabilities and actions, but by doing 'something else'.[56] What precisely is entailed in the workings of AI seems to be the main conundrum.

---

51 Dana Remus & Frank S. Levy, *Can Robots Be Lawyers? Computers, Lawyers, and the Practice of Law* (27 November 2016). Available at SSRN: https://ssrn.com/abstract=2701092 or http://dx.doi.org/10.2139/ssrn.2701092.

52 *See id.*; *see also* Richard Susskind & Daniel Susskind, The Future of the Professions (2015).

53 For some discussion of the limitations of current AI on some of these realms, *see* Scherer, *supra* note 36, at 513. There are, however, technologies aiming to succeed in some of these realms. *See* for example Samiha Samrose *et al.*, *CoCo: Collaboration Coach for Understanding Team Dynamics during Video Conferencing*, 1(4) ACM Hum. Comput. Interact. Art. 39 (2017), https://hoques.com/Publications/2018/2018-UbiComp-coco-collaboration-coach.pdf (last visited on 21 May 2020) (describing a technology that provides feedback in group dynamics on the level and quality of participation of each participant in an effort to ensure more balanced participation).

54 *See* for example Smartsettle's algorithm as discussed in *infra* Section 3.

55 *See* for example, Scherer, *supra* note 36, at 513 (demonstrating the limitations of algorithms in terms of creative writing).

56 Jamie Condliffe, *AI Is Learning to See the World—But Not the Way Humans Do,* Mit Technology Review (30 June 2016), www.technologyreview.com/2016/06/30/159029/ai-is-learning-to-see-the-world-but-not-the-way-humans-do/ (last visited on 17 May 2020).

A principal challenge has to do with the accuracy and transparency of algorithm-based outcomes and here we approach the second (and related) type of concerns voiced with respect to the employment of AI in dispute resolution (as in other contexts). Since we no longer rely on predetermined 'recipes' for their operation, it is often extremely difficult, at times impossible, to decipher how an algorithm reached a decision, what values, norms, and principles guided such decision, and whether it was erroneous or biased.[57]

Algorithms run on models and models inevitably simplify reality, and therefore are bound to make mistakes. Sometimes, these are not mistakes, but biases. Models reflect human values and as such often reflect our own biases and stereotypes.[58] Technology may seem objective, but in fact obscures the 'values in the design', and the related, potentially skewed, outcome.[59] Even where we can discern that an outcome might be flawed, it is quite difficult to uncover whether such problems stem from the data from which the algorithm 'learned' or from the meaning assigned to such data by the machine.[60] In some instances, even the programmers find it difficult to explain 'why and how the algorithm arrives at the predictions it makes'.[61] There have been efforts to address biased algorithmic outcomes by working on their definition of 'similar' individuals, by treating individuals belonging to disempowered groups in the same way as the overall population, and by examining whether principles of fairness were followed in the algorithmic decision-making process.[62] Nevertheless, concerns over lack of transparency and accountability of AI systems continue.

The opaque nature of algorithms has given rise to concerns over their 'black box' character and lack of accountability.[63] One way to approach such concern would be to limit use of AI to those instances where cost of error is high. But when is the cost of errors low? And who bears such costs? It is true that human decision-making can be similarly flawed and biased, and therefore it could be expected that machines, engineered by

57 While critics tend to attribute algorithms' opacity to the lack of transparency by large corporations and government (*see* Frank Pasquale, The Black Box Society: The Secret Algorithms that Control Money and Information (2015)), others believe that even those who have access to the code cannot always explain the operation of an algorithm (*see* David Auerbach, *The Code We Can't Control*, Slate (14 January 2015), https://slate.com/technology/2015/01/black-box-society-by-frank-pasquale-a-chilling-vision-of-how-big-data-has-invaded-our-lives.html (last visited on 17 May 2020)).

58 O'Neil, *supra* note 50, at 25-27, 59-60.

59 Helen Nissenbaum, *Values in Technical Design*, *in* Encyclopedia of Science, Technology, and Ethics lxvi, lxvi (Carl Mitcham ed., 2005).

60 Ryan Calo, *Artificial Intelligence Policy: A Primer and Roadmap*, 51 UC Davis L. Rev. 399, 411-412 (2017). For an analysis of the different levels on which the harms of automated decision-making may occur, *see* David Lehr & Paul Ohm, *Playing with the Data: What Legal Scholars Should Learn About Machine Learning*, 51 U.C. Davis L. Rev. 653 (2017).

61 Scherer, *supra* note 36, at 511.

62 Min K. Lee *et al.*, *Procedural Justice in Algorithmic Fairness: Leveraging Transparency and Outcome Control for Fair Algorithmic Mediation*, 3 ACM Hum-Comput. Interact. 182:3 (2019), http://minlee.net/materials/Publication/2019-CSCW-Al_ProceduralFairness.pdf.

63 Pasquale, *supra* note 59.

humans, would replicate some of the biases and problems associated with human decision-making as explained above.

In one book, the author describes the dangers associated with algorithms that operate at mass scale, across domains and make consistent errors that impact individuals who belong to disempowered groups – minorities, immigrants, the poor, and the uneducated.[64] Members of such groups have limited ability to challenge algorithmic decisions, few resources to devote a long and difficult battle and are often inclined to accept such outcomes as consistent with a history of maltreatment. Clearly, human decision-making can also be erroneous and biased, but it can also evolve, while machines, on the other hand, depend on the introduction of change by the humans who develop them.[65] Not only does AI operate on what are opaque and often discriminatory correlations, but the data that feeds into such AI-decision or recommendations constitutes a breach of our expectations of privacy,[66] and ultimately, the reliance on an unreasoned decision defies some of what many of us view as a fundamental element of decision-making.[67]

While use of AI continues to spread to more and more domains, questions over the fairness of these systems and their effect on different segments of society, continue. These concerns have stimulated various entities, public and private, to generate principles, best practices and ethical guidelines for the use of AI in the justice arena.[68] In all of these guidelines fairness, transparency, and accountability of AI systems feature prominently as central elements of ethical algorithmic design.[69] Transparency and fairness are the cornerstones of legitimacy, which is the goal of all dispute resolution processes. Legitimacy is what makes individuals bring their disputes before a dispute resolution forum, participate in the process, and abide by the final resolution. Where the workings of an algorithm remain opaque and the standards by which it reached its outcomes are not disclosed, it is difficult to see how a proceeding can meet the widely accepted underpinnings of legitimacy.[70]

---

64 O'Neil, *supra* note 50, at 8, 97, 111; *see also* Solon Barocas & Andrew D. Selbst, *Big Data's Disparate Impact*, 104 Calif. L. Rev. 671 (2016).

65 O'Neil, *supra* note 50, at 204.

66 Waldman, *supra* note 37, at 619-621.

67 Scherer, *supra* note 36, at 512.

68 The European Commission for the Efficiency of Justice, for example, published an ethical charter on the use of AI in justice systems, *see*: *European ethical Charter on the use of Artificial Intelligence in judicial systems and their environment* (European Commission For The Efficiency Of Justice (CEPEJ), 2018), https://rm.coe.int/ethical-charter-en-for-publication-4-december-2018/16808f699c (last visited on 15 May 2020); *see also* a Berkman Center study comparing mapping AI principles: Jessica Fjeld *et al.*, *Principled Artificial Intelligence: Mapping Consensus in Ethical and Rights-based Approaches to Principles for AI*, Berkman Klein Center for Internet & Society (2020), https://cyber.harvard.edu/publication/2020/principled-ai?fbclid=IwAR0TbxO1xBRYypSjYNBi2G4YgVK28IuA01BsNyRLXgltGwnQ4zpxk4nKpcY (last visited on 15 May 2020).

69 *See also* Calo, *supra* note 62, at 411; Kearns & Roth, *supra* note 11.

70 Rabinovich-Einy, *supra* note 22, at 25.

In the dispute resolution literature, there is often reference to perceived legitimacy, which is derived from parties' perceptions of the process they relied on to settle their dispute – the quality of the process (was it impartial, fair, and balanced), the quality of interpersonal treatment from the third party (did the third party treat the disputants with respect, did s/he listen to the parties) and the opportunity for voice for the parties (did the parties feel they were heard, were given an opportunity to tell their story, and were understood).[71] Clearly, though, perceptions of legitimacy grounded in procedural requirements cannot displace the need for substantive measures of fairness and equality.[72] However, the role of procedure in shaping people's perception of fairness has proven central and therefore must be examined in the AI context as well.

The major studies on procedural justice were, for the most part, performed in the face to face setting. There is reason to think that the while parties' perceptions of the quality of the process will rise, the perceived quality of interpersonal treatment may decrease.[73] With respect to opportunity for voice, the introduction of AI could have an impact in both directions. On the one hand, parties may feel there is no person at the other end and therefore their story is not truly being considered. On the other hand, the change in the nature of the process and being able to asynchronously consider what information to present, at one's leisure, without the pressure of real time synchronous communication, could make individuals feel that they had a better opportunity to convey their story.[74]

The few studies conducted in the online setting shed some light on the impact that AI in dispute resolution could have on perceptions of legitimacy, but more research is needed. What the studies that have been conducted on the legitimacy of AI-based decision-making in the dispute resolution (or a close) context show, is that we cannot refer to decision-making as a whole.[75] We need to adopt a contextual approach, referring to the nature of the task for which AI is employed, the subject matter it relates to, and the weight such intervention carries – a recommendation versus an authoritative decision. All of these studies demonstrate that under certain conditions and in particular contexts, AI-based decision making may surpass human decision-making in terms of party perceptions.

Above all, and beyond party perceptions, hovers the deep moral question regarding the delegation of human decision-making to machines over dispute resolution, certainly in the public court context, but also in the private arena where questions of power

71 Rabinovich-Einy & Katsh, *supra* note 21, at 174.
72 Waldman, *supra* note 37, at 628-629.
73 Mentovich, Prescott & Rabinovich-Einy, *supra* note 47.
74 *Id.*
75 Lee *et al.*, *supra* note 64, at 182:1; Ayelet Sela, *Can Computers Be Fair?*, 33 Ohio St. J. on Disp. Resol. 91 (2018); Min K. Lee, *Understanding Perception of Algorithmic Decisions: Fairness, Trust, and Emotion in Response to Algorithmic Management*, Big Data & Soc. (2018), https://journals.sagepub.com/doi/full/10.1177/2053951718756684; Theo B. Araujo *et al.*, *In AI We Trust? Perceptions About Automated Decision-Making by Artificial Intelligence*, AI & Soc. (2020), https://pure.uva.nl/ws/files/50211045/Araujo2020_Article_InAIWeTrustPerceptionsAboutAut.pdf

asymmetry and opacity can play an even more pronounced role. As we discuss below, it seems that AI is slowly making its way into the dispute resolution arena without deep reflection on the normative boundaries of such a move taking place. Use of AI in the dispute resolution context thus far has been quite limited, certainly where decision-making is involved, but change is clearly underway, and AI can be implicated in the disputation world in much richer ways than mere dispute resolution.

3 How AI?

As with other technological advancements, AI applications are not only generating advancement, but often cause disruption and conflict. Automated decisions on loans, job applications and medical coverage may seem arbitrary and capricious. Other times, such decisions may in fact seem deliberate but biased. In both cases, making such claims is a difficult task considering the opaque nature of the workings of AI, often undecipherable even to those engineers who developed the algorithm.

Other problems also abound. One algorithm mistakenly labeled African Americans as gorillas.[76] In another case, a Facebook yearly summary of photos 'insensitively' brought up the memories of a recently deceased child.[77] In yet a third story, an algorithm mistakenly flagged a crime victim as a fraudster because his spouse had switched their health insurance right before the incident occurred.[78] These problems, disputes or mishaps are typically unintentional. Indeed, unforeseen consequences in large scale, automated interventions should be expected. The pace and volume of disputes and legal claims can be expected to rise given the large volume of AI-based interactions.[79] This will make AI-based dispute resolution, legal advice, and prevention efforts all the more necessary in order to deal with such problems.

Many contemporary AI-based applications are providing legal assistance which in the past was obtained from human lawyers, ranging from will[80] and contract drafting,[81] through the provision of legal analysis and advice,[82] to assistance in filing lawsuits and

---

76 Katsh & Rabinovich-Einy, *supra* note 25.

77 *Id.*

78 Virginia Eubanks, Automating Inequality: How High-Tech Tools Profile, Police, and Punish the Poor 1-3 (2017).

79 Nicole Lewis, *AI-Related Lawsuits Are Coming*, Shrm (1 November 2019), www.shrm.org/resources andtools/hr-topics/technology/pages/ai-lawsuits-are-coming.aspx.

80 "Ailira," Facebook page, www.facebook.com/ailira/ (last visited on 11 May 2020) (a low cost will-drafting app).

81 "Robot Lawyer LISA", Facebook page, www.facebook.com/pg/RobotLawyerLISA/services/?ref=page_internal (last visited on 11 May 2020); *HirePeter is an artificial intelligence business lawyer that uses blockchain technology to notarise, store contracts and generate legal templates*, CH & co. (8 July 2016), https://fintank.chappuishalder.com/case-studies/hirepeter-ai/ (last visited on 11 May 2020).

82 "Visabot Helps you Cut Green-Card Red Tape", Venturebeat https://venturebeat.com/2017/07/11/visabot-helps-you-cut-green-card-red-tape/ (last visited on 11 May 2020).

in pursuing other redress avenues.[83] In courts, some ODR processes offer AI-based assistance for parties, at least in the initial phase of diagnosis of their claim and the avenues of redress that are available to them. In the Civil Resolution Tribunal in British Columbia, parties use the 'solutions explorer' to locate important information, resources, and template letters in certain types of disputes.[84]

Other AI technologies target lawyers, improving their performance through algorithmic assistance, and allowing them to focus on their human strengths. The now celebrated Ross Intelligence assists lawyers in conducting legal research, including case law, while avoiding overturned or criticized cases.[85] Others offer document review and due diligence tools.[86] Some platforms also offer automated contract analysis and negotiation tools, as well as automated document review boasting enhanced accuracy and efficiency at reduced costs.[87]

Lawyers and non-lawyers are also harnessing AI for predicting case outcomes, deciding on a winning strategy, or refining arguments, all based on statistical analyses of big data.[88] Clearly, analysis of cases across judges, case types, and the like is not new and large law firms with significant resources could always employ some form of data analysis. Nevertheless, the employment of AI in this context has changed the landscape dramatically by allowing for large scale studies to take place of judicial[89] and arbitral decisions,[90] as well as mediated cases[91] and lawyer success rates before judges.[92] Similar

83 " The World's First Robot Lawyer", Donotpay, https://donotpay.com/ (last visited on 11 May 2020).

84 "Solution Explorer", Government of B.C., https://civilresolutionbc.ca/how-the-crt-works/getting-started/strata-solution-explorer/ (last visited on 19 March 2021). For a similar diagnosis feature, *see* The Ohio State tax appeals system created by Modria, "Do I have a strong case for my appeal?", https://ohio-bta.modria.com/resources/ohio-bta-diagnosis/strongcase.html (last visited on 21 May 2020).

85 "The Intelligent Legal Research Choice", Ross Intelligence, www.rossintelligence.com/ (last visited on 11 May 2020). Other applications such as Casetext are now claiming superiority over Ross, *see* "Casetext v. Ross Intelligence", Casetext, https://casetext.com/ross-vs-casetext/ (last visited on 11 May 2020).

86 "The Most Powerful and Accurate Contract Analysis Software", Kira Systems, https://kirasystems.com/benefits/ (last visited on 11 May 2020).

87 https://leverton.ai/; https://ebrevia.com/#homepage; www.thoughtriver.com/; www.lawgeex.com/; www.luminance.com/ (last visited on 11 May 2020).

88 AI is being used for prediction purposes outside the court setting as well, most notably in the administrative realm. The Internal Revenue Service, for example, is using AI to predict cases of possible tax fraud by drawing on previous tax records and other data. *See* Cary Coglianese & Lavi M. Ben Dor, *AI in Adjudication and Administration*, Faculty Scholarship at Penn Law 20 (Forthcoming in the Brooklyn Law Review, 2020), https://scholarship.law.upenn.edu/cgi/viewcontent.cgi?article=3120&context=faculty_scholarship, at 20.

89 Daniel M. Katz, *A General Approach for Predicting The Behavior of The Supreme Court of The United States*, 12(4) PLoS ONE (2017); Scherer, *supra* note 36, at 508-509 (describing one such research conducted on Supreme Court decisions in 2017 with a 70% accuracy rate, as well as a 2016 study concerning decisions of the European Court of Human Rights with a 79% success rate).

90 "Boundless Legal Intelligence", ArbiLex, www.arbilex.co/welcome (last visited on 20 May 2020).

91 "Analytics", Decisionset, www.decisionset.com/analytics.html (last visited on 12 May 2020).

92 "The World's Largest Litigation Database", Premonition, www.losingisexpensive.com/ (last visited on 12 May 2020).

tools are also being used to study potential jury members demographics, history, and online persona in an attempt to predict who should be selected to the jury.[93]

In addition, there are decision-support tools and processes that are already in use in the ODR arena. Most notably, automated negotiation, one of the early developments in the ODR field, uses automation to support party to party direct negotiation on a designated platform. In this type of process, parties are asked to provide input on their 'side of the story' and the software plays an active role in assisting them to frame their account of what were the circumstances that gave rise to the conflict as well as the desirable outcome to settle the dispute. The algorithm can highlight to parties what outcomes were reached in similar cases, incentivize parties to bargain collaboratively,[94] and offer parties optimization of their outcome based on preferences they disclosed privately.[95]

Beyond decision-support, we are starting to see examples of automated decision-making in dispute resolution, but these are rare. One of the earliest examples were the 'automated blind-bidding' processes for the resolution of disputes over money. Two pioneers in the field were Cybersettle and Smartsettle. Each side would disclose to the software what its true reservation price was and if such amounts were within a given range of one another then the platform would split the difference and announce that a settlement was reached. Otherwise, the platform would inform the parties that the reservation prices were too far apart, and neither would find out what was the true reservation price of the other side. With both platforms, the algorithm could 'decide' the dispute and deliver an outcome, according to the agreed upon parameters for its performance and the input provided by the parties.

In terms of AI in U.S. courts, there is currently no 'automated justice' in the sense that a machine is solely responsible for the outcome of a case with no human involvement.[96] That said, perhaps surprisingly, in the courts the criminal arena has been in the lead in terms of AI use in the form of risk assessment tools being used by courts in pretrial arrest

---

93 *Voltaire Uses AI and Big Data to Help Pick Your Jury*, Artificial Lawyer (26 April 2017), www.artificiallawyer.com/2017/04/26/voltaire-uses-ai-and-big-data-to-help-pick-your-jury/ (last visited on 13 May 2020).

94 Smartsettle is an automated negotiation tool that employs blind bidding. Parties can state to the other side what their reservation price is but also disclose a secret reservation price that leans more towards their adversary (which the algorithm can draw on, if the openly stated reservation prices do not overlap). The algorithm is programmed to reward parties for bargaining more collaboratively by revealing a number that is closer to their true reservation price by declaring an agreed-upon amount that is closer to the collaborative party's stated price than the less collaborative party's offer. *See* Katsh & Rabinovich-Einy, *supra* note 25, at 35-36.

95 Once parties reach a settlement on Smartsettle infinity product which is a multi-interest negotiation tool, they can choose to have the algorithm optimize the resolution by creating an alternative outcome that improves at least one party's overall satisfaction with the agreement without detracting from that of the other side. This is possible because the parties secretly disclose to the algorithm their preferences regarding each of the issues that are being negotiated. *See id.*, at 48-49.

96 Calionese & Ben-Dor, *supra* note 33, at 3.

decisions as well as for punishment and parole purposes, weighing various factors such as the defendant's age, nature of current charge, substance abuse, their personality, and their social circle's criminal history (depending on the stage at which the tool is being used).[97] While these risk assessment tools have been challenged on due process grounds[98] and critiqued for being structurally biased,[99] their use has become widespread.

Finally, by studying patterns in big data and predicting the circumstances under which undesirable outcomes may occur, AI can be used to prevent such outcomes from occurring. We see such uses in various arenas, some, such as policing and fraud detection, were mentioned above. Other examples include use of AI in healthcare to improve health services and improve the accuracy of disease detection. The preservation of dispute resolution data, which used to be an anomaly and occurs automatically in ODR, makes the analysis of dispute data and the detection of patterns a prime candidate for algorithmic intervention.

4 Toward a Future Dispute Resolution Landscape

AI is here, but is still in its infancy. It is our contention that a growing part of what we now know as judging, resolving disputes informally, legal work, and the administration of justice, whether delivered online or in the physical setting, will involve AI and will become part of AI-DR.

While AI holds a promise to resolve many of the long-standing problems associated with the dispute resolution landscape – its backlog and inefficiencies, its high costs and complexity, and even some of its imprecision and biases, AI introduces new problems and challenges. The history of technology is a history of unintended consequences. New and unforeseen biases, reduced levels of privacy, and a lack of transparency feature prominently in the criticisms of AI. These challenges have been met with some responses in the form of ethical design of AI, which may mitigate some of these concerns and engender increased accountability and legitimacy.

Legitimacy is the organizing principle of the dispute resolution arena. If it is to be sustained in the emerging AI-DR setting, we need to understand its sources and design dispute resolution processes that are both perceived as legitimate and meet objective criteria for sustaining legitimacy. While the guidelines emphasize such objective

97 *Id.*, at 9.

98 881 N.W.2d 749 (Wis. 2016) – State V. Loomis, *Supreme Court of Wisconsin.* In another cases, the Indiana Supreme Court condoned the use of another algorithmic risk assessment tool since the decision was grounded is other separate factors and since the tool did not displace judicial discretion. *See* Calionese & Ben-Dor, *supra* note 33, at 13

99 Carolyn McKay, *Predicting Risk in Criminal Procedure: Actuarial Tools, Algorithms, AI and Judicial Decision-Making*, 19/67 The University of Sydney Law School (2019), https://papers.ssrn.com/sol3/papers.cfm?abstract_id=3494076&dgcid=ejournal_htmlemail_university:of:sydney:law:school:legal:studies:research:paper:series_abstractlink; O'Neil, *supra* note 50, at 97-103.

measures, they leave more to be desired in terms of disputants' perceptions – the types of activities they trust machines to perform, in what types of cases, and under what conditions. It might be surprising to find that algorithms feature most prominently at the moment in the criminal setting in decisions on defendants' liberty, but have yet to be employed in small scale, repetitive, and simple civil disputes. Similarly, one would expect more AI development in the informal dispute resolution arena.

A final point which the rise of AI-DR seems to crystallize is the further erosion of boundaries in the dispute resolution landscape. With the introduction of ADR into courts, the boundaries between formal and informal dispute resolution began to fade. Later, as ODR began to be adopted in courts, the boundaries between online and offline arenas diminished. And now, as AI is being introduced into all these settings, boundaries are further eroded: all of these processes can involve technology and automation, at various stages, displacing some of the roles and functions assumed to be inherently the domain of humans.

Chapter 18 Application of the General Data Protection Regulation and Cybersecurity Requirements to Digital Dispute Resolution

Kathleen Paisley

Dispute resolution as it is practiced today outside the courts is a digital process. The increasingly wide-spread use of the internet and other digital means to facilitate international trade and commerce both between businesses and between businesses and consumers has caused online or digital dispute resolution mechanisms (referred to interchangeably as '**ODR**' or 'digital dispute resolution') to become the dominant means of resolving disputes outside the traditional court setting (and even court proceedings are becoming increasingly digital).

With dispute resolution processes of all types becoming increasingly digital, access to, and processing of, potentially large amounts of data seamlessly without regard for geography becomes an essential component of the dispute resolution process.

The digitalization of dispute resolution has significant benefits in terms of time, cost, and other efficiencies, as well as reducing the impact on the environment. However, while the wide-spread use of technology acts as a facilitator of dispute resolution, it also poses certain constraints on the process including those related to security and applicable regulations. While these risks and regulations are obviously not unique to arbitration, arbitration is also not immune from them.

It is therefore important that data security and protection issues be addressed and managed during dispute resolution proceedings and the purpose of this chapter is to consider these issues with a focus on ODR.

The data being processed as a result of ODR includes both personal data, as well as confidential and potentially sensitive (and valuable) commercial information. This emphasizes the importance of legally compliant data processing and good data security and management as an inherent part of digital dispute resolution.[1]

---

1 For a robust discussion of these issues *see*, IBA-ICCA Roadmap to Data Protection in International Arbitration, Consultation Draft (February 2020); Annexes to the IBA-ICCA Roadmap to Data Protection in International Arbitration, Consultation Draft (February 2020), www.arbitration-icca.org/projects/ICCA-IBA_TaskForce.html (the 'Roadmap' and the 'Annexes'). As the co-chair of the taskforce, many of the ideas addressed herein find their genesis in the Roadmap and the Annexes and the author acknowledges her co-chair, Melanie Van Leeuwen, and all the members of the Task Force.

With the learnings of the pandemic firmly in sight, the use of technology to facilitate traditional offline arbitration, mediation and other dispute resolution processes is becoming more robust with entire proceedings being undertaken digitally and hearings held remotely even in major cases due to travel bans and health risks. When live hearings and meetings become possible again, this practice is unlikely to cease as the dispute resolution community and its users have now become accustomed to digital proceedings and remote hearings and have realized that in many cases (although not all) an in-person hearing may not be necessary. Further, even before the pandemic caused merits hearings to be held remotely, the use of email and digital platforms for the exchange of submissions and documents and the use of remote hearings for procedural matters and post-hearing submissions was a common occurrence.

In order for ODR to be an effective dispute resolution tool it must ensure that the data processed is done so securely and in a legally compliant manner. This means that measures to ensure reasonable security and compliance with relevant laws, most notably data protection laws, including the European Union's ('**EU**')[2] General Data Protection Regulation ('**GDPR**'),[3] are put in place.

There is no exception from the application of data protection and privacy laws for ODR. Where the GDPR or another similar data protection law applies during an ODR procedure, the processing of personal data will need to comply with the data protection laws. As a result, data protection compliance adds another layer to the legal regimes and rules applicable to ODR, alongside the law applicable to arbitral seat (in the case of arbitration), the merits, the rules and any other applicable rules or procedures such as the IBA Rules of Evidence.[4] To give just one example, in an arbitration where the GDPR or another similar data protection law applies, data protection rules will need to be applied alongside the arbitration rules and potentially the IBA Rules of Evidence in deciding the scope of permissible of data disclosure.

2 '**European Union**' or '**EU**' refers to the current 27 EU Member States: Austria, Belgium, Bulgaria, Cyprus, Croatia, Czech Republic, Denmark, Estonia, Finland, France, Germany, Greece, Hungary, Ireland, Italy, Latvia, Lithuania, Luxembourg, Malta, Poland, Portugal, Romania, Slovakia, Slovenia, Spain, Sweden and the Netherlands. This chapter refers throughout to the EU, although both the ODR Regulation and the GDPR also apply in the EEA countries: Iceland, Liechtenstein and Norway. On 31 January 2020, the United Kingdom withdrew from the EU. After the United Kingdom's withdrawal from the EU, the applicable data protection laws in the UK are the Data Protection Act 2018 ('UK DPA 2018'), and the UK General Data Protection Regulation ('UK GDPR'). These rules are discussed by the UK Information Commissioners Office (ICO) at https://ico.org.uk/for-organisations/dp-at-the-end-of-the-transition-period/data-protection-now-the-transition-period-has-ended/the-gdpr/.

3 Regulation (EU) 2016/679 of the European Parliament and of the Council of 27 April 2016 on the protection of natural persons with regard to the processing of personal data and on the free movement of such data, and repealing Directive 95/46/EC (General Data Protection Regulation), ***OJ L 119, 4 May 2016*** ('**GDPR**').

4 IBA Rules on the Taking of Evidence in International Arbitration (International Bar Association, 2010) ('**IBA Rules**'); Commentary on the Revised Text of the 2010 IBA Rules on the Taking of Evidence in International Arbitration (2010).

Other chapters of this book aptly describe the means by which this digitalization has taken place and its legal and practical implications for many types of dispute resolution mechanisms. This chapter focuses on how data protection and related data security requirements impact the digitalization of dispute resolution across methods and place certain constraints on the process and how those limitations can be managed effectively at both a macro and micro level. Adequate security measures and data protection compliance are required across ODR mechanisms and the purpose of this chapter is to provide guidance as to the impact that may have on the structuring of effective ODR procedures and their use.

This chapter is divided into five sections:

- Section 1 considers how data protection impacts ODR
- Section 2 addresses when the GDPR applies to ODR and who is subject to its rules
- Section 3 considers the application of the GDPR to the resolution of consumer disputes, including disputes between online traders and consumers in the context of the EU's ODR Platform
- Section 4 addresses the key obligations the GDPR imposes on ODR Participants and considers the specific ways in which the digitalization of the dispute resolution process is impacted by data protection principles
- Section 5 addresses data security
- Section 6 provides concluding remarks and some modest proposals

In considering these issues, it is important to keep in mind that while data protection principles apply across the board, the manner in which data protection impacts the digital dispute resolution process is contingent on the nature of that process and the amount and type of personal data processed as a result. Further, the extent of security required will depend on what is adequate and reasonable in the circumstances.

For example, the amount of personal data processed in a typical mediation or other means of non-binding dispute resolution and dispute avoidance is typically lower than that processed in an arbitration and hence the data protection and cyber security risks are reduced as a practical matter due to the fact that less personal data is typically exchanged. Further, the impact of data protection differs when ODR mechanisms are employed in a commercial dispute, as opposed to the consumer context. Moreover, in the context of EU consumer disputes, the impact of data protection principles on the operation of the EU's ODR platform for consumer disputes, which acts as a referral mechanism, may differ from the potential ADR procedures ultimately employed to resolve any dispute filed on the ODR Platform after its referral.[5]

Further, smart contracts and blockchain technology can be used to create fully automated technology driven dispute resolution systems programed into the smart contract. Where effective, smart contracts with block chain assisted dispute resolution are an example of technology-based ODR mechanisms where a fully-fledged application of cutting-edge technology is utilized to resolve disputes without resort to traditional dispute resolution processes. As a result, the use smart contracts and block chain technology may reduce the data protection issues created by traditional ODR mechanisms because, where they are effective, they allow for dispute resolution in an largely anonymous or pseudonimized manner without the use of significant personal data.

On the other hand, to the extent that the digitalization of dispute resolution expands the amount of personal data being processed, this may increase the data security and data protection risk. This can be the case for example with the use of big data and artificial intelligence, for example to predict results, where large amounts of personal data is often processed. This does not mean such mechanisms should not be employed, but rather that data security and data protection compliance should be considered when developing and employing big data and artificial intelligence.

The terms 'ODR procedure' or 'digital dispute resolution' are used in this chapter broadly to refer to any dispute resolution or avoidance process with a digital component, and it is important to keep in mind that the data security and data protection principles described herein apply to all forms of arbitration and ADR and to offline proceedings.[6] Further, the term 'data protection' is used to refer to the laws applicable to the processing of personal data, which in some jurisdictions is referred to as privacy.

5 *See* Regulation (EU) No 524/2013 of the European Parliament and of the Council of 21 May 2013 on online dispute resolution for consumer disputes and amending Regulation (EC) No 2006/2004 and Directive 2009/22/EC (Regulation on consumer ODR) OJ L 165, 18 June 2013, pp. 1-12 ('ODR Regulation'); *see also* Directive 2013/11/EU of the European Parliament and of the Council of 21 May 2013 on alternative dispute resolution for consumer disputes and amending Regulation (EC) No 2006/2004 and Directive 2009/22/EC (Directive on consumer ADR) OJ L 165, 18 June 2013, pp. 63-79, at Rec. ('ADR Directive'); European Commission Privacy Notice, Online Dispute Resolution, https://ec.europa.eu/consumers/odr/main/?event=main.privacyForConsumer2.show ('EU Commission ODR Platform Privacy Notice').

6 *See* GDPR, fn 3, at Rec. 15.

1 How does Data Protection and Cybersecurity Impact ODR?

The GDPR and other similar data protection regimes are based on the principle that the processing of personal data by a third party is prohibited unless expressly allowed by the terms of those laws.

Data protection and privacy laws apply to the 'processing' of 'personal data' falling within their jurisdictional scope and grant the individuals whose personal data is being processed important rights with respect to that processing.[7]

The goal of data protection legislation is to protect the privacy of individuals (often called 'data subjects') by ensuring that there is a lawful basis for the processing of their personal data; they are notified of the processing including the purpose and legal basis for the processing; the volume and type of personal data that is processed is minimized; and the processing is done in a secure manner, during a limited time frame, and they are afforded certain important rights with respect to that processing.

Where applicable, the data protection laws are of a mandatory nature and apply across the board whenever personal data is processed – their application does not depend on the context or nature of the data processing exercise but rather on the simple fact that personal data is being processed.

The GDPR, for example, clarifies expressly that its application is 'technologically neutral' and does not depend on the techniques used to process the data and that it applies to the processing of personal data by automated means, as well as to manual processing.[8] This includes the processing of personal data in the context of dispute resolution whether online or offline, and the European Union has stated expressly that the GDPR and its predecessor the Data Protection Directive[9] apply to ODR procedures in the consumer context.[10]

Although the application of the data protection laws is mandatory, the fundamental right to the protection of personal data is not an absolute right and the laws should be applied proportionally. The proportionate approach is focused on the potential impact on the data subject and is found throughout most modern data protection laws. Under the GDPR, for example, proportionality requires the consideration of the nature, scope, context and purposes of processing and the risks posed to the data subject, taking into

---

7 *See* GDPR, fn 3, Art. 4.

8 GDPR, fn 3, at Rec. 15.

9 Directive 95/46/EC of the European Parliament and of the Council on the Protection of Individuals with Regard to the Processing of Personal Data and on the Free Movement of Such Data, OJ L 281/31, 24 October 1995 ('**Data Protection Directive**').

10 *See*ODR Regulation, fn 5.

consideration the nature and extent of the personal data being processed.[11] It is important to keep in mind that data protection and the related data security requirements are focused on the rights and interests of the data subjects, who in the case of commercial ODR as such are often not the parties to the dispute, but rather their employees, contractors or other individual whose evidence is provided during the proceeding.

Where applicable, data protection and privacy principles pertain to everyone who processes personal data during an ODR procedure, including the parties, their legal representatives, the dispute resolution provider and the neutrals ('**ODR Participant**' or '**Participant**'), as well as those who work for them (or with them) during the process. However, each Participant may not be covered by the same data protection law or in the same way and some may not be covered at all.

The means that in any ODR procedure one or more data protection laws may apply to the different Participants imposing on them different and sometimes conflicting obligations. Considering what data protection law, if any, applies to the processing of personal data by the different Participants in an ODR proceeding demonstrates the potential complexities that arise in applying data protection laws to cross border dispute resolution.

Assume for example you are a mediator or arbitrator or counsel in an ODR proceeding where one of the parties is based in the EU or a country with a similar data protection regime. Or one of the neutrals? Or the administering institution? Or yourself? What does this mean for the ODR procedure and how is this impacted by the increasingly cross border and digital nature of dispute resolution as a result of the globalization of the economy?

From a financial perspective, a personal data breach or other GDPR violation can be expensive. For example, in the context of a data breach, there will be costs involved in investigating and remedying the causes and, to the extent necessary, in notifying and corresponding with the supervisory authorities and affected data subjects. In the event of harm, civil liabilities may be incurred and damages may have to be paid. In addition, of course, there is the possibility that a regulator or court may impose a regulatory fine. It is therefore not surprising that there are many insurance products available, which might

11 *See*, for EU, *EDPS Guidelines on assessing the proportionality of measures that limit the fundamental rights to privacy and to the protection of personal data*, European Data Protection Supervisor, https://edps.europa.eu/sites/edp/files/publication/19-12-19_edps_proportionality_guidelines2_en.pdf (19 December 2019); *see also* Handbook on European Data Protection Law, European Union Agency For Fundamental Rights (2018).

help ODR Participants mitigate relevant risks. Cover may also be available as part of, or as an add-on to, professional liability insurance taken out by arbitrators, lawyers and others.[12]

From a legal perspective, it is beyond the scope of this chapter to address these issues under all possible data protection and privacy laws that may apply of which there are hundreds. This chapter will therefore consider how these issues would be addressed under the EU's GDPR. The GDPR is used as an example because:

- when it does apply, the GDPR is among the most comprehensive data protection laws in force to date, applicable broadly to virtually every action (or inaction) with respect to personal data in a typical ODR proceeding, including arbitration, mediation and all forms of ADR provided that personal data is processed during the ODR procedure;
- due to the soft enforcement mechanisms employed by the GDPR particularly in the context of data transfer, even where it does not apply as a matter of law, the GDPR may be applied to the processing of personal data in an ODR proceeding by contract or by procedural agreement or direction when someone involved in the proceeding is subject to the GDPR;
- where the GDPR applies, it may impose serious potential fines,[13] civil liability including class actions, and criminal penalties; and
- even where it does not apply by law or by contract, the GDPR provides a good reference for understanding the data protection laws generally because the principles contained in the GDPR and its predecessor the Data Protection Directive form the basis for many of the data protection rules around the globe today (with the notable exceptions of the United States, China and Russia).

This chapter uses the GDPR to identify issues that may arise when data protection laws are applied in an ODR context and sets out measures to increase the likelihood that the processing of personal data is undertaken in a manner that is consistent with applicable data protection regimes while at the same time reducing the impact on the process itself. The application of data protection to international arbitration is further addressed in the IBA-ICCA Roadmap to Data Protection in International Arbitration and its Annexes.[14]

This is not to suggest that these issues have been harmonized or that the GDPR is of universal application. Indeed, even in the EU, it is important to consider the national laws

---

12 At this relatively early stage and in the absence of lengthy claims experience, it has not proved easy for insurers properly to quantify the risk, and as a result, premiums may vary substantially. An important point is that there is some debate about whether regulatory fines can be insured against. That is clearly a matter for the relevant national law, but many jurisdictions may take the view that it is illegal, or contrary to morals or public policy, to allow an individual or entity to insure against such fines. It is therefore not uncommon for policies to be sold on the basis that they will cover fines 'to the extent allowed by law'.

13 Under the GDPR potential fines for non-compliance may rise to 4% of global gross revenue or EUR 20 million, whichever is higher. GDPR, fn 3.

14 *See*, Roadmap, fn 1.

of the relevant EU country. Although the GDPR is a European regulation that should be consistently applied throughout the EU without the need for national implementing legislation, the GDPR itself allows Member States discretion (described as a 'margin of manoeuvre') and the possibility to implement derogations in several areas potentially relevant to ODR procedures.[15]

This chapter makes reference to the guidance provided by the European Data Protection Board ('**EDPB**'), which is an independent European body composed of representatives of the national data protection authorities and the European Data Protection Supervisor.[16] The EDPB is tasked with the consistent application of data protection rules throughout the European Union, and promotes cooperation between the EU's data protection authorities. References in this chapter to the 'Working Party' are to the Article 29 Working Party, which proceeded the EDPB under the Data protection Directive and the guidance of which remains in place unless overruled.

The Working Party and the EDPB have issued or endorsed four pieces of guidance that are of particular relevance to this discussion and will be referred to herein.[17] For ease of reference, they are as follows:

- Working Document on Pre-trial Discovery for Cross Border Civil Litigation, (Article 29 Data Protection Working Party, endorsed by the EPDB) ('Disclosure Guidelines')[18]
- Guidelines 2/2018 on derogations of Article 49 under Regulation 2016/679 ('Transfer Guidelines')[19]
- Guidelines 3/2018 on the Territorial Scope of the GDPR ('Territorial Guidelines')[20]
- Guidelines 07/2020 on the Concepts of Controller and Processor in the GDPR ('Controller Guidelines')[21]

---

15 *See, e.g.*, GDPR fn 3, at Rec. 10.

16 *See* https://edpb.europa.eu/edpb_en.

17 *See*, Roadmap, fn 1.

18 Working Document on Pre-trial Discovery for Cross Border Civil Litigation, Data Protection Working Party, 00339/09/EN WP 158, 2009 https://ec.europa.eu/justice/article-29/documentation/opinion-recommendation/files/2009/wp158_en.pdf (endorsed by the EPDB) ('Disclosure Guidelines').

19 Guidelines 2/2018 on derogations of Art. 49 under Regulation 2016/679 https://edpb.europa.eu/sites/edpb/files/files/file1/edpb_guidelines_2_2018_derogations_en.pdf. European Data Protection Board (May 2018) ('Transfer Guidelines').

20 Guidelines 3/2018 on the Territorial Scope of the GDPR, /edpb.europa.eu/sites/edpb/files/files/file1/edpb_guidelines_3_2018_territorial_scope_after_public_consultation_en_1.pdf, European Data Protection Board (November 2019) ('Territorial Guidelines').

21 Guidelines 07/2020 on the Concepts of Controller and Processor in the GDPR European Data Protection Board (September 2020) ('Controller Guidelines').

2 When Does the GDPR Apply to ODR and Who Is Subject to Its Rules?

The GDPR and other similar data protection laws have a broad jurisdictional scope extending beyond the borders of the EU. Further, the GDPR's influence is further expanded by the soft enforcement mechanisms put in place to ensure compliance after data is transferred outside the EU. The extent of coverage is exemplified in the digital context where data flows freely and borders are difficult to define.

Appreciating the potential application of the GDPR to digital dispute resolution requires understanding who and what is covered by the GDPR, and what rules apply to those who fall within its scope and in which contexts. The purpose of this section is to consider when and how the GDPR applies to those involved in an ODR procedure, keeping in mind that when it is applicable to processing by some Participants, it may not apply, or may apply differently, to data processing by other Participants. However, when the GDPR applies to even one Participant, as a practical matter compliance may require others involved also to follow the rules. Moreover, while considerations will differ in the case of other data protection laws beyond the GDPR, many of the requirements are similar in the many other laws throughout the world inspired by the GDPR or the Data Protection Directive.

2.1 When Does the GDPR Apply?

While data protection laws typically regulate data processing by entities or persons established within a jurisdiction, the scope of the GDPR is broader. The GDPR applies to the processing of personal data either:

- Where a controller or a processor is established in the EU and the processing takes place in the context of the activities of that establishment, whether or not the processing takes place in the Union; or
- Where a controller or processor is not established in the EU, but the data processing relates to the offering of goods or services (whether free or paid for) or the monitoring of behavior of data subjects in the EU (also referred to as targeting).[22]

The EDPB has underlined that the application of these principles:

> aims at determining whether a particular processing activity, rather than a person (legal or natural), falls within the scope of the GDPR. Consequently, certain processing of personal data by a controller or processor might fall within the scope of the Regulation, while other processing of personal data by

22 GDPR, fn 3, Art. 3.

> that same controller or processor might not, depending on the processing activity.[23]

2.1.1 EU Establishment

The first question in deciding whether data processing during a digital dispute resolution process falls with the GDPR is whether it is undertaken in the context of an EU establishment, and the EDPB has said that this analysis should be undertaken on a case-by-case basis in light of the specific processing activities at issue.[24]

While the GDPR does not define what constitutes an establishment, Recital 22 states that an

> [e]stablishment implies the effective and real exercise of activities through stable arrangements. The legal form of such arrangements, whether through a branch or a subsidiary with a legal personality, is not the determining factor in that respect.[25]

If an establishment exists, the second question is whether the relevant data processing activities are undertaken in the 'context of the activities of the establishment' which is a fact-based enquiry. The EDPB recommends that non-EU entities assess their processing activities,

> first by determining whether personal data are being processed, and secondly by identifying potential links between the activity for which the data is being processed and the activities of any presence of the organisation in the Union. If such a link is identified, the nature of this link will be key in determining whether the GDPR applies to the processing in question.[26]

If these two prongs of the test are met, the GDPR applies to all processing of personal data in the context of the activities of the EU establishment 'regardless of whether the processing takes place in the Union or not'.[27]

Applying these criteria, when considering whether their activities may be subject to the GDPR, ODR Participants would typically consider first, whether they are undertaking activities in the EU through stable arrangements, and, if so, whether the data processing activities at issue are being carried out in the 'context' of those activities. If the answer to

---

23 Territorial Guidelines, fn 20, at p. 5.
24 *Id.*
25 GDPR, fn 3, at Rec. 22.
26 Territorial Guidelines, fn 20, at p. 8.
27 *Id.*, at pp. 7-9.

both questions is affirmative, all data processing activities taking place in the context of that establishment are covered by the GDPR wherever they take place in the world.[28]

For example, an arbitrator or mediator is based in the EU. All of his or her data processing activities that take place in the context of that establishment would be covered by the GDPR regardless of where they take place in the world and whether the data processing is digital or manual. The same is true for parties, lawyers, institutions, and any others involved in the process with EU establishments.

Further, even if a Participant has its primary base of operations outside the EU, for example in the United States, if it also undertakes activities in the EU though stable arrangements, all data processing undertaken in the context of those arrangements would also be subject to the GDPR. For example, arbitrators and mediators based outside the EU who are tenants or door tenants of a barristers chambers in the EU should consider whether that relationship constitutes 'stable arrangements' in which case all their data processing activities undertaken in the context of those activities are covered by the GDPR. Further, although the UK has left the EU, these rules are applied under the UK DPA 2018 and the UK GDPR.

Having a website accessible in the EU is not, by itself, sufficient to create an 'establishment' in the EU, although what constitutes 'stable arrangements' in the context of remote services provided from outside the EU is unclear.[29] However, as described in the next section, even where there is no EU establishment, these services may be caught by the GDPR.

2.1.2 No EU Establishment

Where a data controller or processor does not have an EU establishment, the GDPR also applies to the processing of personal data of data subjects who are in the EU, where the processing activities are related to:

> (a) the offering of goods or services, irrespective of whether a payment of the data subject is required, to such data subjects in the Union; or (b) the monitoring of their behaviour as far as their behaviour takes place within the Union.[30]

---

28 Special rules apply to international organisation institutions, which includes, for example, the Permanent Court of Arbitration and the WIPO. Because they are subject to privileges and immunities that may make the GDPR inapplicable in certain circumstances, entities established under international law or by an agreement between countries are treated as though they are outside the European Union such that transfer to them is prohibited absent adequate safeguards. *See* GDPR, fn 3, Art. 4(26) defining international organisations), Art. 46 (1) (addressing transfers to international organisations).

29 Territorial Guidelines, fn 20, at pp. 5, 9-10, citing CJEU, *Verein für Konsumenteninformation v. Amazon EU Sarl*, Case C 191/15, 28 July 2016, Para. 76 (hereafter "Verein für Konsumenteninformation").

30 GDPR, fn 3, Art. 3 (2).

This is often referred to as 'targeting'.

The EDPB has stressed that determining whether targeting has taken place is a highly fact-specific inquiry and that national law should be taken into account where appropriate.[31] Further, some activities of a data controller may be considered to be targeting subject to the GDPR and others not.

The EDPB has provided factors to be considered in making this determination, none of which should be considered in isolation. Further, unhelpfully, none of examples given relate to dispute resolution. In the context of ODR, the factors to be considered in deciding whether targeting has occurred may vary between ODR that is related to commercial disputes between businesses and where it concerns online consumer relationships where a data subject is targeted.

It is important to note that in cases where a data controller or processor falls within the targeting criteria but does not have an EU establishment, they must appoint a representative in the EU and any EU supervisory body may bring actions again them.

2.1.2.1 Commercial Disputes between Businesses

In the context of commercial dispute resolution between businesses employing ODR mechanisms, an important question is whether the targeting of legal persons, as opposed to natural persons, constitutes a triggering event or whether the targeting must be of data subjects, *i.e.* natural persons.

For example, a virtual mediator from outside the EU with no EU establishment promotes her services to EU-based businesses as a result of which she is appointed as a mediator of a business dispute during which virtual mediation she processes personal data of data subjects in the EU. Would this be covered by the GDPR because she targeted EU businesses as opposed to data subjects? Would the application of the GDPR differ if the resulting virtual mediation was about the data subject (for example an employee issue) or rather about a commercial transaction where the data subject was simply a witness or identified in the evidence?

A plain reading of Article 3(2)(a) of the GDPR supports the view that the mediator's activity as such may not be considered targeting because her efforts were not directed at 'data subjects' themselves, but rather the company, which is a legal person.[32] Although it does not say so expressly, this interpretation is also supported by language the EDPB's Territorial Guidelines, although different interpretations are possible and no direct authority is available.[33] For example, the Territorial Guidelines provides, albeit in a different context, 'the location of the data subject in the territory of the Union is a determining factor for the application of the targeting criterion as per Article 3(2).'[34]

---

31 *See*Territorial Guidelines, fn 20, at p. 13.

32 GDPR, fn 3, Art. 3 (2).

33 *See* Territorial Guidelines, fn 20, at pp. 14-16.

34 *Id.*, at p. 14.

As the EDPB has not taken an express view on this issue, caution is warranted especially as the geographic component of ODR procedures becomes less important. Further, the GDPR does not distinguish between personal data generated in the professional or personal context. Moreover, even if the virtual mediator or other ODR Participant is not themselves subject to the GDPR, the EU business who engaged the mediator's services will require a lawful basis to transfer the personal data to them outside the EU, and the application of the data transfer provisions may entail the mediator becoming subject to the main provisions of the GDPR in any event, which is referred to as soft enforcement and is discussed later in this chapter.

2.1.2.2 Consumer Disputes

In cases where an online merchant offers good or services through a website based outside the EU resulting in a purchase or use of those goods or services by individuals in the EU, the EDPB has described factors that will be considered in deciding whether this should be considered targeting such that the GDPR applies.[35] These include, for example:

a. paying a search engine to provide a referencing service to facilitate access to its site by consumers in the EU, or launching marketing and advertisement campaigns directed at an EU country;
b. the international nature of the activity, such as certain tourist activities;
c. use of language/currency other than that generally used in the trader's country, especially the language/currency of one or more EU Member States; and
d. offering the delivery of goods in EU Member States.[36]

However, the Territorial Guidelines note that the mere accessibility of a website in the Union is not sufficient to amount to targeting.[37]

The offering of services also includes the offering of 'information society services', which are defined as

> any information society service, that is to say, any service normally provided for remuneration, at a distance, by electronic means and at the individual request of a recipient of the services.[38]

These include, but are not limited to, websites, apps and other online services provided the services are offered to a data subject, *i.e.* to an individual, in the EU.[39] Although

35 *Id.*, at p. 17.
36 *Id.*
37 *Id.*, at p. 18.
38 *Id.*, at p. 16.
39 *Id.*

payment is irrelevant, the Territorial Guidelines provide that offering goods or services to individuals in the EU requires intentionally, rather than inadvertently or incidentally, targeting individuals physically in the EU regardless of nationality or residence.[40]

With respect to monitoring, the Guidelines state that although the recitals to the GDPR mention monitoring in relation to tracking behavior on the internet, tracking through other technologies or networks involving personal data processing should also be taken into account when deciding whether the processing amounts to 'monitoring behavior' and provides examples such as wearable and smart devices.[41] Further, the Territorial Guidelines clarify that 'monitoring' requires a specific purpose for the collection and reuse of the relevant data about the individual's behavior in the EU.[42]

If the activity that is the source of the dispute is covered by the GDPR, g, the next question is whether ODR that is undertaken in relation to the sales of goods or the offering of services or monitoring that is caught by the targeting criteria would also be subject to the GDPR.

The EDPB has said in the Territorial Guidelines that

> [p]rocessing activities which are 'related' to the targeting activity which triggered the application of Article 3(2) fall within the territorial scope of the GDPR. The EDPB considers that a connection is required between the processing activity and the offering of good or service, but both processing by a controller and a processor are relevant and to be taken into account.[43]

Although they do not address dispute resolution, review of the Territorial Guidelines would suggest that where the subject matter of the ODR procedure itself arises out of the targeted activity this would be related to the activity and subject to the GDPR. The ODR is directly related to, and a consequence of, the targeted activity, and it seems likely that the GDPR would be applied in this context.

For example, an online retailer based in the US offers the sale of goods through a website that is directed at Belgium and is in Dutch and/or French, has a Belgian .be extension, offers deliveries to Belgium and otherwise the sales meet the targeting criteria. The online retailer offers an ODR solution to address complaints about those sales. Under these circumstances, the sales would likely be considered to be targeting and the ODR procedure covered by the GDPR because it is related to the targeted activity.

---

40 *Id.*

41 *Id.*, at p. 19.

42 *Id.*, at p. 20. The Territorial Guidelines provide some examples of what activities amount to 'monitoring' for these purposes, including: (a) behavioral advertising; (b) geolocation, in particular for marketing purposes; (c) online tracking through use of cookies or other tracking techniques (*e.g.* fingerprinting); (d) personalized diet and health analytic services online; (e) CCTV; (f) market surveys and other behavioral studies based on individual profiles; and (g) monitoring or regular reporting on the status of an individual's health.

43 Territorial Guidelines, fn 20, at p. 21.

2.1.3 Summary

Whenever any data processing activities by an ODR Participant falls within the jurisdictional scope of the GDPR, those data processing activities will be covered by the GDPR. This includes both where the personal data processing for ODR occurs in the context of an EU establishment and is related to targeting or monitoring. However, this does not make the proceeding as a whole or the data processing of others in the process subject to the GDPR. Nevertheless, the rules established by GDPR and described below in the context of data transfer are such that whenever any Participant is covered by the GDPR, this will often impact others in the ODR procedure through soft enforcement mechanisms.

2.2 What Is Covered by the GDPR?

The GDPR and other similar data protection laws around the world impose a set of rules and other obligations that must be complied with whenever 'personal data' is 'processed'.

2.2.1 Personal Data

'Personal data' means any information relating to a natural person allowing that person to be either directly or indirectly identified.[44] Thus, even if the individual is not named, the GDPR applies and gives the data subject rights if s/he can be identified based on the information provided. Businesses and other legal persons are not data subjects.[45]

The notion of personal data under the GDPR is wider than the US concept of Personally Identifiable Information (PII). The GDPR applies to personal data of individuals contained in both personal and business-related documents (such as emails, texts, WhatsApp messages), provided that an individual is identified or identifiable, and the EU Commission expressly included an individual's business email address as example of personal data covered by the GDPR.[46]

Information that is clearly 'about' someone also constitutes personal data. This includes opinions or assessments (for example, as to their credibility as a witness), whether subjective or objective, true or false, provided the individual can be identified.

A substantial portion of information exchanged during a typical ODR procedure therefore contains data that qualifies as personal data under the GDPR and would be covered by its rules.

44 GDPR, fn 3, Art. 4 (1).
45 *Id.*, at Rec. 14.
46 *What is Personal Data?*, European Commission, https://ec.europa.eu/info/law/law-topic/data-protection/reform/what-personal-data_en [https://perma.cc/CJ52-ZQVB] (archived 31 May 2018).

2.2.2 Data Processing

The GDPR covers all 'processing' of personal data and defines 'processing' broadly to include the 'collection, recording, organisation, structuring, storage, adaptation or alteration, retrieval, consultation, use, disclosure by transmission, dissemination or otherwise making available, alignment or combination, restriction, erasure or destruction of personal data.' Hence, data processing includes not only active steps such as collecting, using and disseminating data, but also passive operations such as receiving, holding, organizing and storing data.[47]

As mentioned above, the GDPR further clarifies that its application is 'technologically neutral' and does not depend on the techniques used to process the data and that it applies to the digital processing of personal data.[48]

Under such a wide definition, virtually any activity undertaken during a ODR procedure relating to materials including personal data is likely to be considered processing covered by the GDPR, even if it involves digital processing, archiving or storage of documents without any human intervention provided it is undertaken in the context of, or related to, data processing activities coming within the GDPR's scope.

2.2.3 Summary

The scope of personal data processing activities covered by the GDPR is broad and covers many aspects of ODR procedures whether they be fully or partially digitalized. These rules are similar in many data protection laws around the globe.

The GDPR and other data protection laws impose important rights and obligations on the processing of personal information during digital dispute resolution that would not otherwise be considered confidential or sensitive, including in the case of the GDPR business communications (emails, texts, Whatsapp messages).

This means that the impact of data protection obligations on ODR procedures should be addressed and considered in structuring digital disputes resolution processes and during the course of individual ODR proceedings. If done in a considered way, these requirements may be implemented in a manner that does not disrupt ODR.

2.3 What Obligations Apply?

The GDPR imposes different obligations depending on whether the individual or entity engaged in the processing qualifies as a (1) data controller, (2) data processor, or (3) joint controller.[49]

---

47 *What Constitutes Data Processing?*, European Commission, https://ec.europa. eu/info/law/law-topic/data-protection/reform/what-constitutes-data-processing_en [https://perma.cc/Q85B-NJ33] (archived 19 March 2018).

48 GDPR, fn 3, at Rec. 15.

49 *See* Controller Guidelines, fn 21.

These categories are of key importance because they determine the degree of responsibility and liabilty for data protection compliance as follows:[50]

- Data controllers have primary responsibility and liabilty, alone or jointly, for compliance with the GDPR and for being able to demonstrate compliance.[51]
- Joint controllers are jointly responsible for data protection compliance.[52] Data subjects have the right to seek compensation from joint controllers in the same way as from any independent controller. Each joint controller is liable *vis-à-vis* the data subject for any damage caused by the processing, unless the joint controller can establish that they are not responsible for the event giving rise to the damage. Any arrangement made between joint controllers is irrelevant in relation to the data subject, although it may allow the joint controller to seek compensation from the other joint controller(s).[53] In addition, joint controllers are each fully accountable to the regulatory authorities for any failure to comply with their responsibilities.[54]
- Data processors are only responsible for following the data controllers' instructions and for complying with the GDPR's requirements for data transfer, data security, and for notifying the data controller in the case of data breach and for keeping a record of its activities.[55]

The decision as to what category of obligations apply is based on who controls the purpose and means of the processing. It is important to keep in mind that this may change during a data processing operation and that someone can be a controller for certain processing activities and a joint controller for others within the same operation. For example, in an ODR proceeding, it is possible a Participant will act as a controller for certain parts of the process and a joint controller for others depending on whether it decides the purpose and means of the processing alone or jointly with others.

2.3.1 Controllers

A data controller is the person or entity that decides the purpose and means of the processing.[56] In the context of dispute resolution procedures, it is likely that absent special circumstances, most Participants in the proceeding would be considered data controllers or joint controllers because it is inherent in their function as counsel,

50 *See id.*, at p. 3.
51 *See* GDPR, fn 3, Art. 26 (3) and Art. 82 (2). The language of the GDPR leaves room for the view that controllers may be also be held accountable for the actions of others even when they are not joint controllers. *See* Art. 82 (2).
52 *See id.* Art. 26 (3).
53 *See id.*
54 *See id.*
55 *See* Controller Guidelines, fn 21, at p. 29.
56 *See* GDPR, fn 3, Art. 4 (7).

neutral, party, or institution that they determine the purpose and means of the data processing within the scope of their activities.

For example, the EDPB has taken the view that lawyers should typically be considered data controllers by reference to the following hypothetical:

> The company ABC hires a law firm to represent it in a dispute. In order to carry out this task, the law firm needs to process personal data related to the case. The reasons for processing the personal data is the law firm's mandate to represent the client in court. This mandate however is not specifically targeted to personal data processing. The law firm acts with a significant degree of independence, for example in deciding what information to use and how to use it, and there are no instructions from the client company regarding the personal data processing. The processing that the law firm carries out in order to fulfil the task as legal representative for the company is therefore linked to the functional role of the law firm so that it is to be regarded as controller for this processing.[57]

Furthermore, the UK Information Commissioner's Office (ICO), which applies the UK DPA 2018 and the UK GDPR, has taken the view that solicitors are data controllers.[58]

This is supported by the fact that the ODR Regulation provides expressly that ODR advisors, ADR providers, and the European Commission are all data controllers when they are active on the ODR Platform and the European Commission has taken the view in its Data Privacy Notice that they are all joint controllers when it comes to the operation of the ODR Platform.[59]

2.3.2 Joint Controllers

The GDPR introduces the concept of joint controllership, which was not set forth in the Data Protection Directive. The concept of joint controllership was developed by the European Court of Justice under the Data Protection Directive and has now been codified in the GDPR. Joint controllers jointly determine the 'purpose and means' of processing and are jointly and severally responsible for data protection compliance.[60]

57 Controller Guidelines, fn 21, at p. 21.

58 EU Working Party, 'Opinion 1/2010 on the concepts of "controller" and "processor"', WP 169, 16 February 2010, at 28; ICO, 'Data controllers and data processors: what the difference is and what the governance implications are', Data Protection Act 1998, pp. 40-43.

59 *See* ODR Regulation, fn 5; EU Commission ODR Platform Privacy Notice, fn 5.

60 *See* GDPR, fn 3, Art. 26.

Joint controllers are required to establish arrangements setting forth their respective responsibilities for complying with the GDPR, the principle components of which should be communicated to the individuals whose data is being processed.[61]

Whether ODR Participants can be considered joint controllers involves a factual assessment of their influence on the purposes and means of the processing. The Controller Guidelines gives important insight into the means that will be applied to decide whether controllers can be considered to be joint controllers. In considering this issue, it is important for ODR Participants to realize that the EU data protection authorities have stressed that the standard applied to decide this key compliance issue is specific to data protection law rather than the plain meaning of the words.[62]

In deciding whether there has been joint participation in the decisions on the purpose and means of the processing, the EDPB in the Controller Guidelines looked to both what it referred to as common decisions and converging decisions and gave a broad meaning to the concept of joint controllership, as follows:

- the purpose of the processing need not be the same or common provided the entities involved pursue purposes which are closely linked or complementary;
- joint participation in a decision does not require a common decision, but can also result from converging decisions. Converging decisions are those that complement each other and are required for the processing to take place and have a tangible impact on the determination of the purposes and means of the processing; and
- joint controllers need not be involved in determining all the purpose and means, rather different entities may be involved at different stages of that processing and to different degrees and controllers may act jointly for certain activities and individually for others. Importantly, joint controllership can exist even where a party does not have access to the personal data processed.[63]

The Controller Guidelines also provide a series of examples of individual versus joint controllers for different types of data processing activities.[64] Reference was not made to dispute resolution, but the following example may be helpful:

> Example: Research project by institutes
>
> Several research institutes decide to participate in a specific joint research project and to use to that end the existing platform of one of the institutes

61 European Commission, *What is a Data Controller or a Data Processor?* https://ec.europa.eu/info/law/law-topic/data-protection/reform/rules-business-and-organisations/obligations/controller-processor/what-data-controller-or-data-processor_en.

62 *See* Controller Guidelines, fn 21, at p. 3.

63 *See id.*, at pp. 19-20.

64 *See id.*, at pp. 20-23.

> involved in the project. Each institute feeds personal data it holds into the platform for the purpose of the joint research and uses the data provided by others through the platform for carrying out the research. In this case, all institutes qualify as joint controllers for the personal data processing that is done by storing and disclosing information from this platform since they have decided together the purpose of the processing and the means to be used (the existing platform). Each of the institutes however is a separate controller for any other processing that may be carried out outside the platform for their respective purposes.[65]

Moreover, the Guidelines also contain a useful flowchart for applying the concept of joint controllership.[66]

In the context of platforms such as those used in ODR procedures, the EDPB has said that a joint decision to use a common platform for a common purpose would be considered to fall within the concept of joint control when the purpose and means of the processing through use a platform is jointly determined, including where the 'entities involved pursue purposes which are closely linked or complementary'.[67]

In the context of digital dispute resolution, the parties decide to engage in ODR for the purpose resolving disputes under a certain system, as a result of which personal data is processed using that system by other ODR Participants who are data controllers and who have an impact on the purpose and means of the processing for purposes of the procedure. Further, in certain cases a platform is used and the decision to use the platform is taken jointly or by order either for a specific case or as part of an ODR procedure.

In deciding whether this results in a joint controller relationship for the personal data that is processed during the ODR procedure as such (or for part of it), all factors will have to be considered on case-by-case basis, keeping in mind that in the context of ODR specifically, the European Commission's Data Protection Notice for the ODR Platform takes the view that the ODR advisor, ADR provider, and the European Commission are joint controllers when they use the ODR Platform given the nature of those activities.[68]

In practice, there may be a lack of clarity concerning whether Participants in an ODR procedure are joint controllers for all or part of the process. The possibility of ODR Participants becoming jointly responsible for data protection violations and of being

---

65 *Id.*, at p. 21.

66 *Id.*, at p. 46.

67 *Id.*, at p. 19. The EDPB has also noted that there can be "situations where various actors successively process the same personal data in a chain of operations, each of these actors having an independent purpose and independent means in their part of the chain. In the absence *of joint participation in the determination of the purposes and means of the same processing operation or set of operations*, joint controllership has to be excluded and the various actors must be regarded as successive independent controllers."

68 *See* ODR Regulation fn 5; EU Commission ODR Platform Privacy Notice, fn 5.

exposed to joint and several liability for violations, stresses the need for GDPR compliance and building ODR systems and procedures keeping the GDPR and data protection principles in mind.

Where ODR Participants consider that they may be considered to be joint controllers, they are required to put in place arrangements defining their responsibilities for compliance and the EDPB recommends this be done through a binding instrument. The GDPR states expressly that these arrangements should cover data subject rights and notification, and the Controller Guidelines suggest that such arrangements should also cover

> the general data protection principles, the legal basis of processing, security measures, data breach notification obligations, data protection impact assessments, the use of processors, third country transfers and contacts with data subjects and supervisory authorities.[69]

In the context of ODR, this can be done either on a case-by-case basis through the use of procedural mechanisms such as terms of reference, data protection protocols, and procedural orders, or by building mechanisms into the procedure itself.[70]

Importantly, the EDPB states that, as discussed below in the context of notice, that

> each joint controller has the duty to ensure that they have a legal basis for the processing and that the data are not further processed in a manner that is incompatible with the purposes for which they were originally collected by the controller sharing the data.[71]

2.3.3 Data Processors

Data controllers can engage data processors to undertake the processing of personal data on their behalf. The GDPR defines a data processor as a 'a natural or legal person, public authority, agency or other body which processes personal data on behalf of the controller'.[72]

In determining whether an ODR Participant operates as a data processor or as a data controller, the question will be whether the ODR Participant:

1. Acts on behalf of the data controller when processing the personal data and
2. Does not decide the purpose and means of the data processing.

69 *See* Controller Guidelines, fn 21, at p. 4.

70 *See* Roadmap, fn 1.

71 *Id.*

72 *See* GDPR, fn 3, Art. 4(8).

It is this second criteria that creates a challenge for considering ODR Participants to be only data processors as opposed to controllers, because it is inherent in the function of most Participants that they are able to decide the purpose and means of the processing as the EDPB has indicated for lawyers.

In the traditional ODR context, whether this standard is met, for example, by data analysts and other e-discovery professionals, will depend on who takes the decisions with respect the purpose and means of the processing and will be influenced by number of factors, such as whether the controller has set forth instructions for the processing taking away the processors ability to control the purpose and means of the processing. These same considerations are likely to apply to decide to increasingly automated forms of dispute resolution.

Under the GDPR, data controllers, including those involved in ODR procedures, can only engage data processors who commit to comply with its terms in an enforceable agreement in the manner established in the GDPR. These agreements must set out

> the subject-matter and duration of the processing, the nature and purpose of the processing, the type of personal data and categories of data subjects and the obligations and rights of the controller,

and shall 'stipulate, in particular, that the processor [...] processes the personal data only on documented instructions from the controller'.[73]

The EDPB stresses that data processing agreements should include specific, concrete information as to how the requirements of the GDPR will be met and which level of security is required for the personal data processing that is the object of the data processing agreement, rather than as a formality that can be fulfilled simply by restating the content of Article 28 GDPR. Moreover, a controller is responsible for continuously assessing the sufficiency of the guarantees provided by the processor and should be able to prove that it has taken all of the elements provided in the GDPR into serious consideration.[74]

2.3.4 Summary

As dispute resolution becomes increasingly automated and digitalized, the question may be posed whether, and if so when, this will have an impact on data protection compliance. This will likely depend on the nature of the ODR system including the nature and types of data processed and the means of doing so. To the extent that ODR procedures simply mirror traditional dispute resolution but in a digital format, for the most part, the

---

73 *Id.*, Art. 28(3); Territorial Guidelines, fn 20, at p. 28.

74 Controller Guidelines, fn 21, at p. 4.

Participants are likely to be considered to be data controllers or joint controllers as the EU has said in the context of the ODR platform.[75] However, as ODR systems become more automated and digitalized such that in certain contexts they do not process personal data at all or they do so in a manner such that Participants no longer control the purpose and means of the processing, this may fundamentally change data protection compliance in ODR. This could be the case with smart contracts, for example, where, to the extent that personal data is processed, users do not control the purpose and means of the processing which has been predetermined in advance by the block chain technology.

3 How Does the GDPR Apply to Consumer ODR?

The European Union has established an online ODR platform for disputes between consumers and traders based in the EU, Iceland, Norway and Lichtenstein (all of which are referred to herein as the 'EU' for simplicity). The EU's Online Dispute Resolution platform ('ODR Platform'), which came into force in 2016, is operated by the European Commission, and follows on from rules established by the previous ADR Directive.[76] Pursuant to the ODR Regulation, all online retailers and traders in EU are required to provide customers with an easily accessible link to the ODR platform, as well as to provide consumers with a direct contact e-mail address.

Importantly for the purposes of this chapter, the legislation establishing this platform addresses data protection expressly. The EU has not provided guidance on the application of the GDPR to ODR or other forms of out-of-court dispute resolution generally, however, in the case of the ODR Platform for consumer disputes, the ODR Regulation provides expressly that processing under the Regulation is 'subject to guarantees of confidentiality and should comply with the rules on the protection of personal data', and further that

> those rules should apply to the processing of personal data carried out under this Regulation by the various actors of the ODR platform, whether they act alone or jointly with other such actors.[77]

75 *See* Commission Notice on the ODR Platform for Consumers, fn 5, at Para. 3.
76 *See* ODR Regulation, fn 5, ADR Directive, fn 5.
77 *See* ODR Regulation, fn 5, at Rec. 27.

3.1 *Purpose of the ODR Platform*

To give a bit of background on the EU's approach to consumer ODR, the EU has said that

> ODR offers a simple, efficient, fast and low-cost out-of-court solution to disputes arising from online transactions. However, there is currently a lack of mechanisms which allow consumers and traders to resolve such disputes through electronic means; this leads to consumer detriment, acts as a barrier, in particular, to cross-border online transactions, and creates an uneven playing field for traders, and thus hampers the overall development of online commerce.[78]

In an attempt fill this void, the ODR Platform allows consumers to submit contractual disputes arising from online transactions to the platform and to start an ADR procedure online through ODR mechanisms. In some EU Member States, traders can also use the platform to submit complaints against consumers, provider the selected ADR provider has authority to address such disputes but this is no mandatory.

It is important to note, however, that disputes are not resolved through the platform, rather the ODR Platform acts as a referral mechanism by recommending an appropriate dispute resolution body to the parties, which then must agree on a provider. If they do not agree, the process stops. If they do agree, the ODR Platform automatically submits the complaint to the agreed ADR provider and may allow further communications between them through the ODR Platform. However, the further processing of the complaint and any resolution is addressed by the agreed ADR provider, not the ODR Platform.

3.2 *Procedure Under the ODR Platform*

When a consumer submits a complaint through the ODR platform, the relevant online trader is automatically notified and has a period of 10 days within which to reply. Should the trader decline to take part in the ODR procedure, the complaint is automatically closed within 30 calendar days, without further action.

If the trader replies, both parties have thirty calendar days from the submission of the complaint to agree on a dispute resolution body. The ODR Platform will provide recommended dispute resolution bodies, however the parties may choose other bodies. If the parties cannot agree on a particular dispute resolution body, the complaint will automatically close within 30 calendar days without further action.

78 *See id.*, at Rec. 7.

The platform operates on the basis of the consent of both parties on its use to facilitate the dispute resolution process. Therefore, although online traders are under a legal obligation to make a link to the ODR website accessible from their sales platform, they are not required to co-operate with a consumer who submits a complaint through the ODR platform - or even respond to the complaint. The EU Commission operates the ODR Platform but is not otherwise involved in the process and disputes are not decided through the platform.

If the parties agree on a dispute resolution body, the ODR platform will provide the body with the consumer's complaint. The ADR body then has three weeks to inform the parties whether it accepts jurisdiction to handle the complaint.

If the dispute resolution body accepts jurisdiction, it will handle the complaint in line with its usual procedures, and must offer a suggested solution within 90 days, in accordance with its own procedures and practices. The final decision of the dispute resolution body will be available to access on the ODR Platform. Whether or not the suggested solution is legally binding on the parties depends upon the rules of the dispute resolution body handling the complaint.

3.3 *Application of the GDPR to the ODR Platform*

The ODR Regulation states expressly that the processing of information through the ODR Platform must comply with the personal data protection laws, which apply to the processing of personal data carried out by the various actors of the ODR platform, whether they act alone or jointly with other such actors.[79]

The ODR Regulation establishes rules for the application of the data protection rules to the ODR Platform and expressly provides that ODR advisors, ADR providers, and the European Commission are all data controllers.[80] Further, the European Commission's Data Protection Notice for the ODR Platform provides that they are all considered to be joint controllers when operating within the Platform itself and clarifies that the GDPR applies to all processing outside of the Platform, as follows:

> The dispute resolution procedure on the platform is an example of 'joint controllership', where the responsibility for ensuring data protection is allocated between the Commission, the ADR entities and ODR advisors as clarified in Article 12 of the ODR Regulation. Where ADR entities and ODR contact points decide to keep some data related to disputes handled on the platform in national files outside of the ODR platform, the Regulation (EU) 2016/679 on the protection of natural persons with regard to the processing

79 *See id.*, at Rec. 27.
80 *See id.*, Arts. 12 (4)-12 (6).

> of personal data on the free movement of such data (GDPR) will apply, if such processing takes place outside the platform.[81]

Thus, the European Commission's Notice takes the view that for the processing on the ODR Platform as such, the Commission, the ADR entities and ODR advisors would be considered joint controllers and that the GDPR applies to information processed in any ADR proceeding conducted outside the ODR Platform. Further, the ODR Regulation provides specifically that ODR advisors, ADR providers, and the European Commission are all data controllers.

While the ODR Regulation and the ODR Platform apply only where both the trader and the consumer are based in the EU, as discussed above, the GDPR also applies to consumer ODR where the dispute is between a trader established outside the EU and the data subject is in the EU, whenever data subjects are *targeted* for the provision of goods or services or intentionally monitored and the ODR relates to those goods or services or monitoring. Further, as discussed in this section, where the GDPR applies, the EU has said that ODR Participants would generally be considered data controllers and potentially joint controllers.

3.4 Summary

While the EU has not taken a view on the application of the GDPR in the context of commercial business-to-business ODR, the EU has stated expressly that the data protection laws apply to consumer ODR and that the Participants are data controllers and potentially joint controllers. It is likely that the same view would apply to commercial business-to-business ODR and other forms of ADR and arbitration. This makes it important that all ODR Participants are aware of their obligations when the GDPR applies to them. These issues will be discussed in the next section and apply to both consumer and business-to-business disputes alike and to all forms of ODR.

81 *See* Commission Notice on the ODR Platform for Consumers, fn 6, at Para. 3.

4 What Data Protection Principles Apply to Digital Dispute Resolution?

Digital dispute resolution will often be covered by the GDPR and similar data protection legislation.[82] Not only do these laws have broad jurisdictional reach, that reach is extended by so-called soft enforcement mechanisms especially those surrounding data transfer. This makes it important that all those involved in digital dispute resolution are aware of the requirements of data protection compliance.

Data protection obligations apply irrespective of the type of ODR procedure, including arbitration, mediation, dispute resolution boards, expert determination, standing mediation, consumer ODR, smart contracts and others. The extent of their impact will vary depending on the type and amount of personal data exchanged and the geographic scope of the process, but the rules apply.

The GDPR and similar data protection impose independent legal obligations with corresponding responsibility and liability on each ODR Participant, and potentially joint and several liability if they are deemed to be joint controllers. Further, it is often the case that some involved in an ODR proceeding will be covered by the GDPR or a similar data protection law and others are not. As a practical matter, this creates overlapping and potentially conflicting data protection rights and duties on those involved an ODR process, including parties, their counsel, institutions,, neutrals, arbitral secretaries, experts and vendors, each of whom may have individual (or joint) responsibility and liability for GDPR compliance.

This stresses the importance of creating ODR procedures that take into account the main principles of the GDPR and similar data protection laws where doing so would not unnecessarily conflict with the other goals of the ODR procedure. This can be done on a case-by-case basis or, where appropriate, data protection considerations can be reflected in the ODR procedure itself through the rules or other means.

With that in mind, this section considers the main data protection obligations that are potentially applicable to personal data processing activities and controllers during an ODR procedure. This section discusses in a non-exhaustive manner the main touch points where data protection affects digital dispute resolution processes and how this can be managed either within an ODR procedure specifically or in developing such processes generally. Each sub-section begins with a snapshot of the issue followed by more detailed analysis under the GDPR.

---

82 It is also important to note that ODR Participants who are 'established' in the EU and who process personal data 'in the context of those activities' should bear in mind that they will have general obligations under the GDPR that apply across their data processing activities in the context of that establishment. These include having a publicly available and easily accessible privacy notice, for example, on their website, putting data subjects on notice of the processing of their data in the manner set forth in the GDPR. They will also need to put in place GDPR-compliant data security measures, data breach procedures, and ensure that data subjects rights are complied with in all their data processing activities.

4.1 Overview of Data Protection Principles

The main data protection principles that form the basis for the GDPR, the Data Protection Directive and similar data protection laws find their genesis in these principles as enshrined in the Universal Declaration of Human Rights, the EU Convention on Human Rights, OECD Data Protection Guidelines and the Council of Europe Data Protection Convention (Treaty 108) that proceeded them.[83] The GDPR codifies these basic principles in Article 5 requiring data controllers to comply with six principles, namely that personal data shall be:

1. processed lawfully, fairly and in a transparent manner in relation to the data subject ('lawfulness, fairness and transparency');
2. collected for specified, explicit and legitimate purposes and not further processed in a manner that is incompatible with those purposes; ... ('purpose limitation');
3. adequate, relevant and limited to what is necessary in relation to the purposes for which they are processed ('data minimisation');
4. accurate and, where necessary, kept up to date; every reasonable step must be taken to ensure that personal data that are inaccurate, having regard to the purposes for which they are processed, are erased or rectified without delay ('accuracy');
5. kept in a form which permits identification of data subjects for no longer than is necessary for the purposes for which the personal data are processed; ... ('storage limitation');
6. processed in a manner that ensures appropriate security of the personal data, including protection against unauthorized or unlawful processing and against accidental loss, destruction or damage, using appropriate technical or organizational measures ('integrity and confidentiality').
7. The controller shall be responsible for, and be able to demonstrate compliance with, paragraph 1 ('accountability').[84]

These principles are then implemented through the other provisions of the GDPR. Further, in order to ensure compliance, the GDPR imposes restrictions on transfer outside the EU and grants data subjects important rights.

The GDPR is of mandatory application, but does not create absolute rights. Rather, its rules should be applied in a proportional manner focusing on the potential impact of the processing on the data subject. In the ODR context, this means that consideration should be given to the risks that the processing poses to data subjects (not necessarily the parties) and the extent to which the data subjects are themselves involved in the ODR procedure, the type and amount of personal or sensitive data being processed, how the personal data

83 International Network of Privacy Law Professionals, *A Brief History of Data Protection: How Did it all start?*, https://inplp.com/latest-news/article/a-brief-history-of-data-protection-how-did-it-all-start/.

84 GDPR, fn 3, Art. 5.

was collected, and what were/are the data subject's expectations about the processing of that data based on the notices they have been provided. At the same time, the parties' rights and interests at stake in the ODR procedure, as well as those of third parties that may be impacted, should be considered.

For example, applying the GDPR's principles proportionally would generally mean that standard business-related personal data (such as business email communications) related to the dispute may be treated differently than sensitive health-related data or social security and tax information concerning an individual. This does not mean that the data protection principles do not apply, but rather that the manner in which they are applied may vary – for example the degree of data security or data minimization required may differ depending on the sensitivity of the data. But in all cases, adequate protection including data minimization, data security and compliance with data transfer rules must be afforded to the data subject and his or her personal data even in business communications. This has been confirmed in the Disclosure Guidelines.[85]

With that in mind, in the context of ODR, the data protection principles with the most potential impact on ODR are:

- Notification
- Lawful Processing
- Lawful Data Transfer
- Data Minimization
- Data Subject Rights
- Data Breach Obligations
- Record Keeping
- Data Retention

Data security is discussed separately in the next section as the requirement for data security applies both to personal data under the GDPR and to other data exchanges in ODR.

4.2 Notice

Providing notice to the data subject of the processing of his or her personal data is an important part of the GDPR and other similar data protection legislation. Unless an exemption applies, data controllers, including ODR Participants, are required to provide data subjects with notice of the processing, its purpose and the lawful basis for

85 *See* Disclosure Guidelines, fn 18.

the processing that is concise, readily accessible and easy to understand, using clear and plain language, but the precise mode and format of the notice depends on what is appropriate in the circumstances.[86] The information shall be provided in writing, or by other means, including, where appropriate, by electronic means.

Snapshot

All data subjects whose data is processed during an ODR Proceeding including in the evidence and the pleadings should be notified of the processing including the lawful basis and purpose of the processing and other mandatory information. This obligation applies to all data controllers unless an exemption applies. To make this notification requirement manageable, a notification obligation on the parties can be built into the process either on a case-by-case basis or as part of the rules.

4.2.1 What Must Be Notified?

Articles 13 and 14 of the GDPR set out the information that should be notified to the data subjects.[87] This includes the controller's contact details, the purpose and the legal basis of the data processing, the recipients or categories of recipients of the data, whether the data will be transferred and if so, on which lawful basis, the period for which the personal data will be retained, or if that is not possible, the criteria used to determine that period; the existence of the data subject rights, including the right to withdraw consent if consent is the basis for processing, and their right to lodge a complaint.[88]

4.2.2 Who Must Be Notified?

Notification must be made to the data subject.[89] The data subject is the person who is identified or may be identified from the data being processed, which in the case of ODR will include the party representatives, counsel, and the witnesses, as well as all those referred to in the Memorials and the evidence (including, for example, emails), or whose identity could be inferred from that information. They are all data subjects and have a right to be notified of the processing. This can create logistical and confidentiality concerns, which is why the GDPR contains an exemption from the notification requirement in the case of data controllers that did not originally collect the data (referred to herein as secondary processors). Many of these exemptions may apply in the case of ODR where many Participants will not have originally collected the personal data.

86 GDPR, fn 3, Art. 12, Rec. 58, 59, 63; *see also* Guidelines on Transparency under Regulation 2016/679, (Art. 29 Data Protection Working Party, 17/EN WP 260, 2018), https://edpb.europa.eu/our-work-tools/our-documents/guideline/transparency_en (endorsed by the EDPB).

87 GDPR, fn 3, Arts. 13 and 14.

88 *See id.*

89 *See* Disclosure Guidelines, fn 18, at p. 11.

In the context of employee information, for example, notice of the processing will often have been given at the time of employment. Sometimes that notice will mention dispute resolution, but often it will not. Further, employees whose data is collected for the arbitration may be put on notice at that time of the processing for the ODR procedure, but that notice will not cover the many others whose personal data will be included in the data for the ODR procedure (some of whom may be associated with the opposing party or other third parties). This challenge to notification of data subjects whose data is used for dispute resolution was expressly identified in the Disclosure Guidelines but not resolved.[90]

4.2.3 Who is Required to Notify?

ODR Participants who are data controllers have notification obligations both when they collect the information themselves and when they receive it from others, such as, for example, when arbitrators or mediators receive information in the context of an ODR procedure that has been collected by another, for example, the parties or their counsel.

When data is received from others, which as noted by the EDPB is often the case in dispute resolution,[91] the secondary data controller is not required to notify the data subject when (i) the data subject already has the information; (ii) providing the information to the data subject would be impossible or would involve a disproportionate effort or would render impossible or seriously impair the achievement of the objectives of the processing (for example in confidential ODR); (iii) the data controller is required by law to obtain or disclose the personal data; or (iv) the data controller is subject to an obligation of professional secrecy regulated by EU or EU Member State law that covers the personal data.[92]

Many of the exceptions to the notification requirement found in the GDPR are likely to apply to secondary processing by ODR Participants, especially when the ODR procedure is confidential. However, even if separate notification is not required by the secondary processor, the content of the notice provided by the original data controller may be important because it determines the scope of permissible processing. Where personal data is processed during an ODR procedure by Participants who did not originally collect the data, the processing for the ODR proceeding should not be incompatible with the initial purpose as notified to the data subject.[93] This has been confirmed in the Controller Guidelines in the context of joint controllers.[94]

The purpose limitation means that original data controllers, including ODR Participants, who collect and process personal data may only process it for a specific

90 *Id.*
91 *Id.*, at pp. 11-12.
92 *See* GDPR, fn 3, Art. 14 (5).
93 *See* GDPR, fn 3, Rec. 50 Art. 6 (4).
94 *See* Controller Guidelines, fn 21, at p. 4.

and legitimate purpose that have been notified to the data subject and in the case of secondary processors, purposes that are not inconsistent with that purpose.[95] This means that ODR Participants falling within the GDPR or other similar data protection regime who are data controllers should consider the purpose of the processing, as notified to the data subject, and take a view as to whether processing for the ODR procedure is compatible with that original purpose.[96]

This is a highly case and fact specific analysis. For example, the use of employee and business-related information in an ODR procedure of a claim in which the data subject's actions are at issue may well be linked to the purpose for which the data was collected, and, depending on the employee's role, expected in the context in which it was collected. In making this determination, although not determinative, it is helpful if the data subject was informed in advance of the possibility that his or her personal data could be used in a later dispute resolution procedure.

4.2.4 Considerations for ODR

Although many of the exceptions to the notification requirement are potentially applicable to secondary processing by ODR Participants, especially when the ODR procedure is confidential, each ODR Participant will need to decide this on a case-by-case basis as the notification obligation applies to each data controller individually. Views may differ based on where the ODR Participant is established and what law applies, where the personal data was collected, where the data subjects are located and where the data is processed.

One possible solution is for the ODR Participants to agree who will be responsible for providing the data subjects with notice. Where the controllers are considered to be joint controllers, these arrangements are required.

More broadly, new ODR tools and practices, as well as existing institutional rules and practices, could embed a notification requirement and potentially other data protection-related compliance into their rules and systems. For example, the party presenting the personal data could be made responsible for ensuring that data subjects are provided with adequate notice and that further processing during the ODR proceeding is consistent

---

95 GDPR, fn 3, Art. 6(4).

96 *Id.* In deciding whether the purpose is compatible, the following is to be considered:
a. any link between the purposes for which the personal data have been collected and the purposes of the intended further processing;
b. the context in which the personal data have been collected, in particular regarding the relationship between data subjects and the controller;
c. the nature of the personal data, in particular whether special categories of personal data are processed ... or whether personal data related to criminal convictions and offences are processed;
d. the possible consequences of the intended further processing for data subjects;
e. the existence of appropriate safeguards, which may include encryption or pseudonymization.

with that notice. This may not be practical, however, when the data subject is employed by or has a relationship with the opposing party or the personal data is from a third party with whom the party presenting the personal data as part of its case does not have a relationship. Depending on the circumstances, embedding this into the ODR procedure itself arguably would allow other data controllers involved in the process to rely on this notice.

4.3 Lawful Basis

The premise of the GDPR and the many laws that have followed the EU's approach to data protection is that the processing of personal data by a third party (including during an ODR procedure) is prohibited unless allowed by the law. Every data controller, including in the ODR context, therefore must have a lawful basis for the processing of personal data during the proceeding. In the context of ODR, a lawful basis will be required for the processing during the proceeding of any (i) personal data; (ii) special category data and (iii) criminal offense data. Lawfulness also requires that the personal data is not be processed in a manner that is otherwise unlawful.

Snapshot

All data processing of personal data for an ODR proceeding must have a lawful basis, which must be notified to the data subjects. The lawful basis for the processing of personal data that is best suited for ODR is likely to be when it is necessary for the legitimate interests of the data controller (in this case one or more ODR Participants) or a third party, except where such interests are overridden by the interests or fundamental rights and freedoms of the data subject requiring protection of his/her personal data. In addition, there must be a separate lawful basis to the extent that the data processing includes 'special category' data, which is also referred to as sensitive data. The lawful basis for the processing of 'special category' data that is best suited for ODR is likely to be when it is 'necessary for the establishment, exercise or defence of legal claims.' Where possible, consent should be avoided as a lawful basis for both personal data and special category data because it can be difficult to obtain and can be withdrawn at any time in which case it is difficult to rely upon another lawful basis. The processing of criminal offence data poses challenges and is usually only allowed under the control of an supervising authority.

4.3.1 Personal Data

The GDPR contains no express provision allowing the processing of personal data for dispute resolution, which means that data processing for ODR will need to be justified under one of the general permissible bases set forth in the GDPR.[97]

97 Note that there are other bases for lawful processing, but we only mention those that are most likely to be the suited to ODR of commercial disputes taking into account the circumstances.

Given that consent forms such an important part of arbitration and other ODR procedures, it is important to mention at the outset that consent provides a lawful basis for data processing, which consent must be informed consent for the processing of personal data and explicit consent in the case of sensitive data.[98] However, there are significant legal constraints on relying on consent as a basis for processing personal and sensitive data.

This led the EU Working Party to describe consent as a 'false good solution' in the dispute resolution context because it is difficult to obtain (especially from employees) and must be as easy to withdraw as to give. Further, once consent has been withdrawn or refused, processing on the basis of consent cannot continue and it is difficult to then rely on another lawful basis for processing.[99]

In the specific context of discovery for US litigation, the Working Party noted the difficulties of a litigant getting valid consent both from employees and contractors, which confirms that, in the context of ODR, the consent must be of the data subject themselves.[100] This is not to say that consent should never be employed, but rather that it should only be used as a basis for processing when all these considerations are acceptable under the circumstances, which may be the case, for example, in some circumstances for consumer ODR where the claimant and the data subject are the same.

An alternative lawful basis for the processing of personal data in the context of ODR is where it is necessary for the purposes of the legitimate interests of the data controller (in this case one or more ODR Participants) or a third party, except where such interests are overridden by the interests or fundamental rights and freedoms of the data subject requiring protection of his/her personal data.

This means that there are three elements to a finding of legitimate interests as a basis for lawful processing, namely:

- identifying a legitimate interest;
- confirming that the processing is necessary to achieve it; and
- balancing it against the individual's interests, rights and freedoms.[101]

98 'Consent' of the data subject means any freely given, specific, informed and unambiguous indication of the data subject's wishes by which he or she, by a statement or by a clear affirmative action, signifies agreement to the processing of personal data relating to him or her (GDPR Art. 4(11)). *See, e.g.*, Guidelines on Consent under Regulation 2016/679 (Art. 29 Data Protection Working Party, 17/EN WP259 rev.01, as revised and adopted on 10 April 2018) (endorsed by the EPDB).

99 EU Working Party, 'Working document on a common interpretation of Article 26(1) of Directive 95/46/EC of 24 October 1995', WP 114, 25 November 2005, at 11.

100 *See* Disclosure Guidelines, fn 18, at p. 9.

101 *See* GDPR, fn 3, Art. 47.

The legitimate interests relied upon can be those of the controller or of third parties, and may include commercial interests, individual interests or broader benefits to the society or others.[102]

While not required by the GDPR, data controllers should consider undertaking a legitimate interests assessment whenever relying upon legitimate interests as the lawful basis for the processing of personal data in order to comply with their obligation of accountability.[103] This should be updated if events occur that might affect the original assessment.[104]

In the context of ODR, this may be part of being able to show compliance if issues are raised about the processing of personal data during an ODR procedure and, as discussed below in the context of compliance generally, where legitimate interests are relied upon it is helpful if ODR Participants are able to produce to the competent authority a contemporaneous legitimate interests assessment.

In the Disclosure Guidelines,[105] the Working Party supported the use of legitimate interests as a basis for the processing of personal data in the context of litigation, as follows:

> Clearly the interests of justice would be served by not unnecessarily limiting the ability of an organization to act to promote or defend a legal right. The aim of the discovery process is the preservation and production of information that is potentially relevant to the litigation. The aim is to provide each party with access to such relevant information as is necessary to support its claim or defence, with the goal of providing for fairness in the proceedings and reaching a just outcome.
>
> Against these aims have to be weighed the rights and freedoms of the data subject who has no direct involvement in the litigation process and whose involvement is by virtue of the fact that his personal data is held by one of the litigating parties and is deemed relevant to the issues in hand, e.g. employees and customers.
>
> This balance of interest test should take into account issues of proportionality, the relevance of the personal data to the litigation and the consequences for the data subject. Adequate safeguards would also have to be put in place and in particular, there must be recognition for the rights of the data subject to object

102 *See, e.g.*, UK Information Commissioner's Office, *How do We Apply Legitimate Interests in Practice?*, https://ico.org.uk/for-organisations/guide-to-data-protection/guide-to-the-general-data-protection-regulation-gdpr/legitimate-interests/how-do-we-apply-legitimate-interests-in-practice/.

103 *See, id.*

104 *See, id.*

105 *See* Disclosure Guidelines, fn 18.

> [to the processing ...] and, in the absence of national legislation providing otherwise, there are compelling legitimate grounds relating to the data subject's particular situation.
>
> As a first step controllers should restrict disclosure if possible, to anonymised or at least pseudonymised data. After filtering ('culling') the irrelevant data – possibly by a trusted third party in the EU – a much more limited set of personal data may be disclosed as a second step.[106]

These considerations also apply to ODR. This therefore supports the use of legitimate interests as a lawful basis for data processing in the context of ODR provided the personal data is minimized (as discussed below) and provided the rights and freedoms of the data subject do not outweigh those of the parties to the dispute. In balancing these interests, it was expressly noted that the fact that the data subjects in a disputes context are generally not parties to the dispute should be taken into consideration.

4.3.2 Special Category Data

Special categories of data (previously referred to in the Data Processing Directive as 'sensitive data') are those that reveal

> racial or ethnic origin, political opinions, religious or philosophical beliefs, or trade union membership, and the processing of genetic data, biometric data for the purpose of uniquely identifying a natural person, data concerning health or data concerning a natural person's sex life or sexual orientation.[107]

For example, in certain contexts photographs may be considered special category data.

The processing of special category data requires a basis for processing the personal data *and* a separate basis for processing special category data.[108] This means that the lawful bases set forth in the previous section for the processing of personal data should apply as well as an additional basis for the processing of the special category data discussed in this section.

Such additional bases include where explicit informed consent has been given, which is a higher standard than that discussed and discounted in the Disclosure Guidelines for personal data.[109]

106 *See id.*, at pp. 9-10.
107 GDPR, fn 3, Art. 9 (1).
108 *See, ICO Guidance on Special Category Data*, https://ico.org.uk/for-organisations/guide-to-data-protection/guide-to-the-general-data-protection-regulation-gdpr/lawful-basis-for-processing/special-category-data/.
109 GDPR, fn 3, Art. 9 (2) (a).

Further, special category data may be processed where 'processing is necessary for the establishment, exercise or defence of legal claims or whenever courts are acting in their judicial capacity.'[110] The GDPR provides that this applies 'whether in court proceedings or in an administrative or out-of-court procedure'. Where applicable, this standard provides a lawful basis for the processing of special category data for ODR proceedings and is discussed further before in the context of data transfer..

4.3.3 Criminal Convictions and Offences, or Related Security Measures

It is not uncommon for information related to criminal convictions or offences to be raised in the context of ODR. For example, allegations may be made of fraud or corruption. In addition to requiring a lawful basis for the processing of the personal data, the processing of personal data relating to criminal convictions and offences, or related security measures, must be carried out under the control of an supervising authority or if the processing is authorized, by EU or Member State law.[111] In the context of ODR, this means that the processing of data related to criminal activity should only be allowed after specific consideration.

4.4 Data Transfer

This chapter has referred to 'soft enforcement' as a means of extending the scope of the GDPR's influence beyond its already robust jurisdictional reach. It is fair to say that the most effective means of soft enforcement is through the data transfer restrictions. The aim of limiting data transfers is, in general, to ensure that the data processing falling within the GDPR's jurisdictional scope remains sufficiently protected and that the rights of data subjects in relation to their data are not prejudiced by transfer out of the EU.

Snapshot

All transfer of personal data to a third country or an international organization must have a lawful basis, which should be notified to the data subjects. Under the GDPR, transfer is possible only where the third country has an 'adequacy decision,' appropriate safeguards are put in place to ensure adequate data protection (including standard contractual clauses), or a derogation from the GDPR's third county transfer requirements applies. The same requirements apply to 'onward transfers' from the first recipient of a data transfer to a third party, even if the two are established in the same third country. Where possible, putting standard contractual clauses in place will facilitate the third country transfer of personal data in the context of ODR procedures. Where this is not feasible, the legal claims derogation applies to data transfers provided they are (1) occasional, (2) necessary and (3) undertaken in the context of a formal legal procedure.

110 *Id.*, Art. 9(2)(f).
111 *Id.*, Art. 10.

The notion of what constitutes transfer of personal data is broadly construed and is likely to include, among other things, uploading or downloading of documents from a cloud server, opening emails and storing them on a server, laptop or computer outside the EU. For example, whenever EU personal data is downloaded or reviewed from outside the EU (for example on a platform or during a remote hearing), this likely constitutes transfer of personal data outside the EU, even if the document is not saved. Note that if the processing is covered by the GDPR, the use of the data from outside the EU would not be subject to transfer restrictions (for example during travel). Some countries, for example Russia and China, apply a more stringent transfer regime referred to as localization, essentially prohibiting most data transfers out of the jurisdiction.

Transfer of personal data beyond the EU to those that are not covered by the GDPR requires an additional legal justification even if there is a lawful basis for processing: either the third country has an 'adequacy decision' (*i.e.* a determination by the EU Commission that its data protection regime is sufficiently robust), appropriate safeguards are put in place to ensure adequate data protection, or a derogation from the GDPR transfer requirements applies.[112]

This means that all ODR Participants, whether they are considered to be data processors or data controllers, will need to have a lawful basis before transferring any personal data outside the EU to countries without an adequacy decision. In the ODR context, it is important to recall that international organizations such as the Permanent Court of ODR, the World Bank, and the International Court of Justice, which are established under international law or by an agreement between countries, are treated as though they are outside the EU for purposes of the data transfer rules.[113] This means that transfer to such organizations will require compliance with the data transfer rules and the restrictions on onward transfer may apply even if they are located within the EU.

The Working Party has explained that the exceptions allowing data transfers follow a cascade approach, as follows:

- First, transfer is lawful to countries that are considered to provide adequate protection; may take place if there is an adequacy decision;
- Second, for data transfers to countries without an adequacy finding by the EU, transfer is allowed provided 'adequate safeguards' are be put in place where feasible;
- Third, where adequate safeguards are not feasible, the GDPR provides a list of specific circumstances in which date transfer is permissible; and
- Lastly, where the express derogations do not apply, it is possible to rely on so-called 'compelling legitimate interests' as a basis for transfer, provided the standard is met and notification is required both to the data subjects and the supervisory authority.

112 GDPR, fn 3, Arts. 44-46.

113 *Id.*, Art. 4(26) defining international organisations, Art. 46(1) addressing transfers to international organisations.

The same requirements apply to 'onward transfers' from the first recipient of a data transfer to a third party, even if the two are established in the same third country.[114]

The first question to be asked is whether the country to which data transfer would be made for ODR has an adequacy decision. At the date of publication, the following countries had adequacy decisions in place allowing the free transfer of data: Andorra, Argentina, Canada (commercial organizations), Faroe Islands, Guernsey, Israel, Isle of Man, Japan, Jersey, New Zealand, Switzerland and Uruguay, and adequacy talks are ongoing with South Korea.[115]

Where a country is not the subject of an adequacy decision, the controller or processor should consider whether appropriate safeguards can be put in place to ensure that the rights and remedies of data subjects are protected. In the context of digital dispute resolution, these safeguards may be provided through the adoption of the so-called 'standard contractual clauses.' When these are in place, transfer is generally allowed provided the restrictions on onward transfers are respected.[116]

These standard clauses must be adopted verbatim to provide a valid legal basis for transfer. By entering into standard contractual clauses, the non-EU entity agrees to be bound by the main provisions of the GDPR as a condition of the transfer and they give data subjects a right of action against the non-EU entity.[117]

The use of standard contractual clauses was recently addressed by the European Court of Justice in the Schrems II decision.[118] While the Court upheld the use of standard contractual clauses, it added an important caveat. The Court clarified that when using standard contractual clauses, data subjects must be afforded a level of protection essentially equivalent to that guaranteed within the EU by the GDPR. The Court specified that

114 *Id.*, at Rec. 101; Territorial Guidelines, fn 20.

115 European Commission, *Adequacy of the Protection of Personal Data in Non-CU Countries*, https://ec.europa.eu/info/law/law-topic/data-protection/data-transfers-outside-eu/adequacy-protection-personal-data-non-eu-countries_en.

116 *See* GDPR, fn 3, Rec. 101.

117 Commission Decision 2001/497/EC of 15 June 2001 on standard contractual clauses for the transfer of personal data to third countries, under Directive 95/46/EC, OJ L 181, 4 July 2001, p. 19 (EU controller to non-EU or EEA controller); Commission Decision 2004/915/EC of 27 December 2004 amending Decision 2001/497/EC as regards the introduction of an alternative set of standard contractual clauses for the transfer of personal data to third countries, OJ L 385, 29 December 2004, p. 74 (EU controller to non-EU or EEA controller); Commission Decision 2010/87/EU of 5 February 2010 on standard contractual clauses for the transfer of personal data to processors established in third countries under Directive 95/46/EC of the European Parliament and of the Council, OJ L 39, 12 February 2010, p. 5 (EU controller to non-EU or EEA processor) (Note that the standard contractual clues were promulgated under the Data protection Directive, but remain valid until replaced or overruled).

118 *Data Protection Commissioner v. Facebook Ireland Ltd*, Maximillian Schrems, Case No. C-311/18 [2020] (Grand Ct.) (Ir.) ('**Schrems II**').

> the assessment of that level of protection must take into consideration both the contractual clauses agreed between the data exporter established in the EU and the recipient of the transfer established in the third country concerned and, as regards any access by the public authorities of that third country to the data transferred, the relevant aspects of the legal system of that third country.[119]

This language was addressed at countries with wide-scale surveillance activities.

In the absence of an adequacy decision or an appropriate safeguard, a transfer of personal data to a third country outside the EU can only take place under the specific derogations provided for in the GDPR. Of most relevance to ODR, these derogations include situations in which:

i. there is explicit consent of the data subject (which is a higher standard than informed consent); or
ii. (ii) the legal claims derogation applies.

Explicit Consent. The concerns discussed above about consent in the context of lawful processing also apply to the use of consent as a basis for transfer and it is even more difficult to obtain consent for transfer as it must be explicit. The Disclosure Guidelines expressly questions the use of consent as a basis for transfer of data in the context of disputes.[120]

Necessary for Legal Claims. Like is the case for the processing of special category data, data transfer is allowed where 'necessary for the establishment, exercise or defence of legal claims'. However, in the context of data transfers, an additional requirement is added, namely that the transfers are

> occasional and necessary in relation to a contract or a legal claim, regardless of whether in a judicial procedure or whether in an administrative or any out-of-court procedure, including procedures before regulatory bodies.[121]

Contract or Legal Claim. The EDPB has stated that the concept of a contract or legal claim as used in the context of data transfers covers a range of activities and that

> data transfers for the purpose of formal pre-trial discovery procedures in civil litigation may fall under this derogation. It can also cover actions by the data exporter to institute procedures in a third country for example commencing

119 Court of Justice Press Release, Schrems II, https://curia.europa.eu/jcms/upload/docs/application/pdf/2020-07/cp200091en.pdf.
120 *See* Disclosure Guidelines, fn 18.
121 GDPR, fn 3, Art. 49(1), Rec. 111.

> litigation or seeking approval for a merger. The derogation cannot be used to justify the transfer of personal data on the grounds of the mere possibility that legal proceedings or formal procedures may be brought in the future.[122]

Further, the EPBD has stated that the

> combination of the terms 'legal claim' and 'procedure' implies that the relevant procedure must have a basis in law, including a formal, legally defined process, but is not necessarily limited to judicial or administrative procedures ('or any out of court procedure').[123]

The EDPB did not explain further what it mean by a 'formal, legally defined process'. For purposes of ODR, formal arbitration, mediation and ODR under the EU scheme would seem to fall within this concept, but other less formal ODR procedures may not if they are not 'legally defined' and do not have a 'basis in law'. However, the trend in favour of digital dispute resolution and ADR and the EU's endorsement in the context of consumer dispute would support the inclusion of such mechanisms within this definition.

Necessity. The EDPB has said that the 'necessity test' requires a 'close and substantial connection between the data in question and the specific establishment, exercise or defense of the legal position'.[124] European case law (on the Data Protection Directive) indicates that the concept of 'necessity' must be given its own independent meaning in relation to data protection, to fully reflect the objectives of data protection legislation.[125]

To quote the EDPB,

> whilst there may be a temptation for a data exporter to transfer all possibly relevant personal data in response to a request or for instituting legal procedures, this would not be in line with this derogation or with the GDPR more generally as this (in the principle of data minimization) emphasizes the need for personal data to be adequate, relevant and limited to what is necessary in relation to the purposes for which they are processed.[126]

122 *See* Transfer Guidelines, fn 19, at p. 11.
123 *Id.*
124 *Id.*, at p. 13.
125 *Id.*, at p. 13, Case C-524/06 *Heinz Huber v. FRG* [2008] ECR I-9705.
126 Transfer Guidelines, fn 19, at p. 13.

The EDPB elaborated further as follows:

> In relation to litigation proceedings the WP29, predecessor of the EDPB, has already set out a layered approach to the question of whether the personal data should be transferred, including the application of this principle. As a first step, there should be a careful assessment of whether anonymized data would be sufficient in the particular case. If this is not the case, then transfer of pseudonymized data could be considered. If it is necessary to send personal data to a third country, its relevance to the particular matter should be assessed before the transfer – so only a set of personal data that is actually necessary is transferred and disclosed.[127]

Occasional transfer. In addition to the rules set forth in the legal clams derogation, in the context of data transfers another criteria is added, namely it is limited to 'occasional transfers'. The EDPB has said that in deciding whether this criteria is met, 'data exporters would need to carefully assess each specific case' and that:

> such transfers may happen more than once, but not regularly, and would occur outside the regular course of actions, for example, under random, unknown circumstances and within arbitrary time intervals. For example, a data transfer that occurs regularly within a stable relationship between the data exporter and a certain data importer can basically be deemed as systematic and repeated and therefore not be considered occasional or not-repetitive. Besides, a transfer will for example generally be considered to be non-occasional or repetitive when the data importer is granted direct access to a database (e.g. via an interface to an IT-application) on a general basis.[128]

The sentence in italics implies that where personal data is made available through a platform during an ODR procedure, this may not be considered an occasional transfer and hence not covered by the legal claims derogation for data transfers. However, the EU has supported on-line platforms in the context of consumer disputes albeit within the EU.

4.4.1 Considerations for ODR

Where possible, data transfer obligations can be managed during an ODR procedure involving Participants that are not subject to the GDPR by putting in place standard contractual clauses with those Participants. To avoid this being debated on a case-by-case basis, consideration could be given to building a general requirement into ODR

127 *Id.*
128 *Id.*, at p. 4.

procedures that both the Parties themselves and those they appoint or engage to be involved in the process who are not subject to the GDPR are willing to enter into standard contractual clauses in order to permit free data transfer throughout the process. Where this is not feasible, the preferred alternative is the legal claims derogation, the availability of which requires the data transferred to be necessary and occasional, which does not always square easily with its application to ODR.

4.5 Data Minimization

Data minimization is an important principle underlying the GDPR. Data minimization requires that personal data processing is limited to that which is 'adequate, relevant and limited to what is necessary in relation to the purposes for which they are processed ("data minimisation")'.[129]

Snapshot

The processing of personal data for an ODR proceeding should be minimized. This means that the personal data processed must be limited to that which is necessary for the purposes of the ODR procedure, non-duplicative, personal data should be redacted or coded where this is feasible, and confidentiality measures should be put in place where possible to protect the personal data.

The EPDB has indicated that the layered approach to the minimization of documents discussed above in the context of data transfer is part of the general data minimization requirement, which would mean that it also applies to documents containing personal data that are processed during an ODR procedure even if they are not transferred outside the EU. The EDPB said that

> whilst there may be a temptation for a data exporter to transfer all possibly relevant personal data in response to a request or for instituting legal procedures, this would not be in line with this derogation or with the GDPR more generally as this (in the principle of data minimization) emphasizes the need for personal data to be adequate, relevant and limited to what is necessary in relation to the purposes for which they are processed.[130]

It is important to keep in mind that the GDPR is not concerned with the amount and volume of data that is exchanged, just the extent to which it includes personal data. In this context it is important to recall, however, that all evidence by which an individual is

129 GDPR, fn 3, Art. 5 (1) (c).
130 Transfer Guidelines, fn 19, at p. 13.

identified or identifiable is considered personal data, even it is contained in a business document such as a work email address. This would mean that before these documents are processed for an ODR proceeding (including by a party before bringing a claim, counsel in preparing or defending a claim, or any other Participant during the process) any documents containing personal data should be reviewed first for relevance and to be sure it is non-duplicative, any unnecessary personal data should be redacted, and a determination should be made whether they are 'necessary' to make out the claim. These requirements should be applied in a proportional way taking into account the underlying risk to the data subject from their use in the proceeding.

Documents that are duplicative or ancillary should be excluded and the personal data that is not necessary for the ODR procedure should be redacted. This can be achieved by using coding mechanisms including as part of artificial intelligent review of the data. The EDPB clearly favors redaction and encryption. However, even with technological advances, redaction measures may be time consuming and expensive. It therefore remains to be seen the extent to which data minimization and redaction takes place earlier and becomes more prominent in the context of digital dispute resolution as a result of data protection compliance.

One way to minimize the personal data processed during a digitalized dispute resolution process is to limit the amount of documentary evidence that is relied upon as part of the process. In the context of ODR, the less adjudicatory the process, the fewer documents that will be reviewed as part of the procedure, as a result of which the personal data processed will be minimized. For example, the amount of personal data processed as a result of mediation or a dispute resolution board is reduced compared with a formal arbitration, which is even more relevant when an arbitration or litigation would require data transfer to third countries for the reasons discussed in the previous section.

4.5.1 Considerations for ODR

The use of mediation and other forms of non-adjudicatory ODR require fewer documents and therefore operate to minimize the data processed to resolve a dispute where they are successful. Further, where arbitration is used, efforts have been made to limit the amount of disclosure required as part of the arbitral process, which assists in minimizing the amount of personal data that is processed. However, it is important to keep in mind that data minimisation obligations apply across the board during an arbitration or other ODR procedure, not just during disclosure. Data minimization argues against processing documents that are duplicative or ancillary and applying redaction techniques to eliminate personal data where feasible, and favors approaches geared at focusing the parties on the matters in dispute and the evidence required to prove those claims and looking first to the documents in their possession.

4.6 Data Subject Rights

The GDPR and other similar data protection laws grant data subjects important rights, which will need to be respected during an ODR procedure.[131]

Snapshot

All data subjects whose data is processed during an ODR procedure are granted important rights by the GDPR and other similar data protection laws. Requests to exercise these rights can be made of any ODR Participant who is a data controller or joint controller including, for example, the parties, counsel, neutral and the institution. Further, right requests may come from any individual whose personal data is handled during the process. This could be individual parties, witnesses, experts, or even persons not directly involved in proceedings but about whom personal data has been adduced (e.g., an employee of a party but who is not involved in the proceedings directly). Putting in place an agreed means to address these requests before they are raised will avoid such requests disrupting the process.

The GDPR requires data and joint controllers, including ODR Participants, to put in place a system for addressing any concerns raised by data subjects and to notify them of how these rights can be exercised. Given the impact that the exercise of these rights may have on the ODR procedure, ODR Participants should consider in advance how they will be addressed.

The rights most likely to be exercised in the context of an ODR procedure include:

1. the 'right to erasure' or 'to be forgotten,' (except when the processing is required for, among other things, the establishment, exercise or defence of legal claims);[132]
2. the right to restrict processing (except when the processing is required for, among other things, the establishment, exercise or defence of legal claims);[133]
3. the right to object to the processing of their data (except when the processing is required for, among other things, the establishment, exercise or defence of legal claims);[134]
4. the right to correct inaccurate personal data;[135]
5. the right of access and to obtain a copy of the personal data being processed (also referred to as a 'data subject access request').[136]

4.6.1 Rights to Erasure, Restriction of Processing and to Object

A data subject has the right to request erasure of his or her personal data when:

131 *See* GDPR, fn 3, Arts. 15-21.
132 *See id.*, Art. 17.
133 *See id.*, Art. 18.
134 *See id.*, Art. 21.
135 *See id.*, Art. 16.
136 *See id.*, Art. 15.

- the processing is no longer necessary for the intended purpose;
- the data subject withdraws his or her consent;
- the data subject objects to the processing and there are no overriding legitimate grounds for the processing;
- the processing is unlawful; or
- erasure is necessary for compliance with a legal obligation.[137]

In addition to erasing the data, when a controller has shared the data with others, the controller must take reasonable steps, including technical measures, to inform the controllers processing the data of the data subject's request to erase this personal data.

A data subject can also request a restriction on the processing of his or her personal data when:

- the data subject contests the accuracy of the data;
- the processing is unlawful and the data subject does not want to exercise the right to erasure;
- the controller no longer needs the data for the purposes of the processing but the data subject needs the data to defend a legal claim; or
- (if) a decision on a complaint lodged by the data subject is pending.[138]

A data subject also has the right 'to object, on grounds relating to his or her particular situation, at any time to processing of personal data concerning him or her' which is based on either the public interest or the legitimate interests of the controller.[139] This is important in the ODR context because, as discussed above, legitimate interests of the controller will often form the preferred lawful basis for personal data processing in the context of an ODR proceeding and this right to object is therefore important.

In understanding the potential impact these rights could have on dispute resolution, it is important to consider that the GDPR exempts processing 'for the establishment, exercise or defence of legal claims,' which would include many ODR proceedings, from the data subject's rights to erasure,[140] the right to obtain a restriction of processing,[141] and to the right to object to data processing,[142] but not the other rights. Interestingly, unlike in the context of sensitive data processing and data transfer, the GDPR does not refer to a necessity requirement.

The fact that these rights are expressly subject to a limitation for processing for the establishment, exercise or defense of legal claims makes it easier to manage these rights

137 *See id.,* Art. 17, Rec. 65.
138 *See id.,* Art. 18.
139 *See id.,* Art. 21.
140 *See* GDPR, fn 3, Art. 17(3)(e).
141 *See id.,* Art. 18 (2).
142 *See id.,* Art. 21 (1).

during an ODR procedure especially if measures are agreed in advance. This does not preclude such requests being made by data subjects, but does make it easier to address them when this exception is deemed to apply.

This raises the question again, as discussed above in the context of data transfer and special category data, what is caught by the phrase 'processing for the establishment, exercise or defense of a legal claim' and to what extent this would apply to less formal ODR procedures. Moreover, this exception for legal claims does not apply to either the right to rectify personal data or to data subject access requests.

4.6.2 Rectification

The GDPR grants data subjects

> the right to obtain from the controller without undue delay the rectification of inaccurate personal data concerning him or her. Taking into account the purposes of the processing, the data subject shall have the right to have incomplete personal data completed, including by means of providing a supplementary statement.[143]

The Working Party has recognized the tension between this right and the requirements of data processing for the purpose of dispute resolution in the litigation context and has said:

> These rights may only be restricted ... on a case by case basis for example where it is necessary to protect the rights and freedoms of others. The Working Party is clear that the rights of the data subject continue to exist during the litigation process and there is no general waiver of the rights to access or amend.
>
> It should be noted however that this right could give rise to a conflict with the requirements of the litigation process to retain data as at a particular date in time and any changes (whilst only for correction purposes) would have the effect of altering the evidence in the litigation.[144]

Notwithstanding this statement, the GDPR does not exempt processing 'for the establishment, exercise or defence of legal claims' from the right to rectification. This will therefore have to be addressed on a case by case basis when requests for rectifications are made in ODR proceedings and, while recognizing the tension, the

143 *See id.*, Art. 16.

144 Disclosure Guidelines, fn 18, at p. 12.

Working Party did not provide insight into how it may be reconciled. Common sense would say that when evidence has been adduced in during an ODR procedure it cannot be rectified as such, but other means may be used to identify the concerns raised by the data subject without hindering the process.

4.6.3 Data Subject Access Requests

The most common form of data subject right request is a Data Subject Access Request. Given its importance, Article 15 of the GDPR is set forth in full below:

1. The data subject shall have the right to obtain from the controller confirmation as to whether or not personal data concerning him or her are being processed, and, where that is the case, access to the personal data and the following information:
   (a) the purposes of the processing;
   (b) the categories of personal data concerned;
   (c) the recipients or categories of recipient to whom the personal data have been or will be disclosed, in particular recipients in third countries or international organizations;
   (d) where possible, the envisaged period for which the personal data will be stored, or, if not possible, the criteria used to determine that period;
   (e) the existence of the right to request from the controller rectification or erasure of personal data or restriction of processing of personal data concerning the data subject or to object to such processing;
   (f) the right to lodge a complaint with a supervisory authority;
   (g) where the personal data are not collected from the data subject, any available information as to their source;
   (h) the existence of automated decision-making, including profiling, referred to in Article 22(1) and (4) and, at least in those cases, meaningful information about the logic involved, as well as the significance and the envisaged consequences of such processing for the data subject.
2. Where personal data are transferred to a third country or to an international organization, the data subject shall have the right to be informed of the appropriate safeguards pursuant to Article 46 relating to the transfer.
3. The controller shall provide a copy of the personal data undergoing processing. For any further copies requested by the data subject, the controller may charge a reasonable fee based on administrative costs. Where the data subject makes the request by electronic means, and unless otherwise requested by the data subject, the information shall be provided in a commonly used electronic form.
4. The right to obtain a copy referred to in paragraph 3 shall not adversely affect the rights and freedoms of others.[145]

---

145 GDPR, fn 3, Art. 15.

Like with other data rights requests, all data subjects whose data is processed during an ODR proceeding may file a data subject access request of any ODR Participant who is a data controller or joint controller at any time during the process, including, for example, the parties, counsel, the neutral (s) and the institution. Further, these requests may come from any individual whose personal data is handled during the process. This could be individual parties, witnesses, experts, or even persons not directly involved in proceedings but, as recognized in the Disclosure Guidelines,[146] about whom personal data has been adduced (e.g., an employee of a party but who is not involved in the proceedings directly). Putting in place an agreed means to address these requests before they are raised will avoid such requests disrupting the process.

ODR Participants should be aware that upon receipt of a valid data subject access request, while they must provide an individual with access to their personal data that they hold, the data subject's right to obtain a copy should not adversely affect the rights or freedoms of others.[147] This may include (but should not necessarily be limited to) any potential adverse impact on data protection rights, trade secrets and intellectual property of others.[148]

When reviewing a data subject access request ODR Participants should therefore consider carefully what impact meeting the request might have on others (both ODR Participants and third parties). This may include identifying and implementing steps to reduce any potential adverse impact. For example, ODR Participants are allowed to redact personal data relating to other individuals and to ensure they right of access to those documents (or portions of them) strictly necessary to meet the exact terms of the data subject's request rather than adopting a blanket (and likely less time consuming) approach to responding.

Adopting a tailored approach balancing different stakeholders' rights can be time consuming, but is the preferred way to ensure that competing rights are respected while allowing the ODR Participant to comply with a data subject access request.

Data subject access requests is an example of an area where national law of the EU Member States may be important. The GDPR permits derogations in this area, and many national laws tailor (and curtail) the GDPR considerably in specific circumstances. For example, Ireland has a broad exemption excluding all out-of-court procedures from all data subject rights.[149] National courts have also suggested that striking a balance between different stakeholders' interests might involve obtaining undertakings to restrict the onward transfer of any information disclosed in response to the subject access request.[150]

146 *See* Disclosure Guidelines, fn 18.
147 *See* GDPR, fn 3, Art. 15(4).
148 *See e.g., id.,* Rec. 63.
149 *See* Number 7 of 2018, IRISH DATA PROTECTION ACT 2018, Section 60 (3) (a) (iv).
150 *B v. General Medical Council [2018] EWCA Civ 1497*, 28 June 2018 (UK).

National law may also provide further guidance (or obligations) on how to handle other difficult situations such as where personal data of one individual is mixed with another ('mixed data') in documents otherwise responsive to a data subject access request. In the UK, national law provides that requests involving mixed data will still need to be complied with if the third-party data subject has consented to disclosure of their personal data or it is reasonable to disclose the information notwithstanding that consent has not be obtained to do so.[151] In all cases, it will be necessary to balance the various interested parties' positions when dealing with the request.

There are also common derogations in national laws excluding the production of privileged documents from data subject access requests. The existence and scope of these exclusions will need to be considered on a case by case basis given variations between Member State laws. It is important to remember, however, that many documents held by ODR Participants will not be privileged (e.g., witness statements submitted to the Tribunal). That said, some local laws, such as the UK Data Protection Act 2018, provide exemptions for information in respect of which a duty of confidentiality is owed by a legal adviser to their client even if it is not privileged.[152]

If an ODR Participant considers that a data subject should be provided with access to their data, it should be produced in a structured, commonly used and machine-readable format (the right to data portability).[153] As is always the case when transferring personal data, secure means must be used to provide materials when responding to a data subject access request. For example, sending attachments to an unencrypted email may not be sufficiently secure. Consideration should therefore be given as to what measures are appropriate in the circumstances, depending on the amount and type of data.

4.6.4 Considerations for ODR

As has been discussed above, in most ODR procedures there will be multiple data controllers and many data subjects, all of whom can file data subject access rights from those data controllers, which may involve sensitive information related to the ODR procedure and decision making. This would argue in favour of, to the extent possible, putting in place a system in advance to consider how data subject rights requests will be addressed and by whom. For example, it may make sense that data subjects who are employed by, or have a contractual or other relationship with, a party be required to make any data rights request first from that party. However, it may be difficult to preclude the data subject from making a follow-up request to other data controllers, but this approach would limit the impact on them. This is similar to the approach suggested above for notification and requires either advance agreement among the Participants or to be embedded in the process ether systematically or by tribunal order.

151 UK DPA 2018, Sch. 2, Para. 16(2).
152 *Id.*, at Para. 19(b).
153 *See* GDPR, fn 3, Art. 20.

Where controllers are considered to be joint controllers, these types of arrangements among them are required.

4.7 Data Breach Notifications

Whenever a data breach occurs, the GDPR provides express rules and a strict timeline for when and how the data breach should be notified. However, even when those rules do not apply, notification may be required as part of the ethical duties and other obligations and good practices applicable to counsel, the neutral (s) and the institution.

Snapshot

The GDPR and other similar data protection regimes impose strict requirements for data breach. The question of whether notification is required and to whom turns on the extent to which the data breach results in a risk for the rights and freedoms of the data subject. Note that risks to legal persons, companies, are irrelevant. However, ODR Participants may have other obligations to notify a data breach under applicable legal or ethical requirements or as a matter of good practice. In the case of neutrals in particular, this can create concerns that notification may be used as a basis to derail and delay the process.

The GDPR contains strict notification requirements in the case of a data breach, which apply to ODR Participants during the course of the ODR proceeding.[154]

Data controllers are required to notify the supervisory authorities of 'a data breach that is likely to result in *a risk for the rights and freedoms* of the data subject within 72 hours of discovery of the breach'.[155] Data subjects must also be notified of the breach without undue delay if the data breach 'presents a *high risk* for the rights and freedoms of individuals'.[156] If the data breach only presents 'some risk' for individuals, only the data protection authority will need to be notified and not the individual data subjects.

The data breach notification must include the cause and nature of the breach (if known) and recommendations for how the potentially affected individuals can mitigate the risks of the breach. The burden to prove the absence of risk in a data breach rests on the data controller. Even where no notification is required, a record of the breach must be kept.

4.7.1 Considerations for ODR

Data breach is the most likely way that ODR will come to the attention of the supervisory authorities or trigger data subject claims. Given the tight time lines and large fines, it will

154 *See id.*, Arts. 33-34.
155 *See id.*
156 *See id.*

be important for the ODR Participants to consider in advance, before any breach occurs, exactly what will trigger a breach notification and the process for how data breach notifications will be given, by whom and to which authority. The fines for violating the data breach notification requirements may run up to EUR 10 million or 2% of annual global turnover (gross revenue), which bears out the importance of adopting a rigorous data breach notification policy.[157] ().

Even where a data breach is not legally required to be notified under the data protection laws, there may be a need for an ODR Participant to notify the other ODR Participants of a breach either as an ethical matter or as a matter of good practice. The extent of the breach and the impact on the proceedings will often not be known immediately and a decision will need to be taken whether to notify others involved in the ODR proceeding in advance of having full information, being conscious of the fact that it is possible that this could be used to disrupt or delay the process.

This makes it important that the ODR Participants consider in advance the process that will be applied should there be a data breach. Who will need to be notified and when and what will the impact be on the process? Establishing a process and parameters for addressing data breaches in advance will help avoid disruption and may be required in the case of joint controllers..

4.8 *ODR Compliance/Recordkeeping*

The GDPR requires that controllers of data not only comply with the GDPR, but that they keep a record of their compliance.[158]

Snapshot

Data controllers should keep a record of their compliance with the GDPR, which can be shown to a data protection authority if requested. In the context of ODR, where Participants may have obligations of confidentiality and ethical obligations as counsel and neutrals, Participants should consider agreeing in advance how compliance will be documented in a manner that can be shown to a data protection authority if requested.

Data controllers are required to maintain records of their compliance efforts. This set forth in Section 5 (2) of the GDPR, and reiterated in Article 24:

> Taking into account the nature, scope, context and purposes of processing as well as the risks of varying likelihood and severity for the rights and freedoms of natural persons, the controller shall implement appropriate technical and

157 *See id.*, Art. 83(4).
158 *See id.*, Art. 5(2).

> organizational measures to ensure *and to be able to demonstrate that processing is performed in accordance with this Regulation.* Those measures shall be reviewed and updated where necessary.[159]

The EDPB has stressed the importance of accountability and that the

> aim of incorporating the accountability principle into the GDPR and making it a central principle was to emphasize that data controllers must implement appropriate and effective measures and be able to demonstrate compliance.[160]

4.8.1 Considerations for ODR

During the course of an ODR procedure, it will be up to each ODR Participant that is a controller both to ensure that they comply with their obligations under the GDPR and to keep adequate records demonstrating compliance.

Applying data protection in the context of ODR will not always be straight forward and will require protecting the rights of data subjects in a balanced and proportionate way and in light of the other important rights at stake in the ODR procedure. Being able to show that these obligations and rights were taken into consideration and applied contentiously will be a key component of establishing compliance. This makes it important that decisions on data protection issues during an ODR procedure be documented, including the rationale for the decision. If an issue is raised, such records may need to be shown to a regulator so it will important to maintain them in manner that they can be shared and to avoid any concerns about confidentiality and secrecy that can be raised in the context of an ODR procedure.

In the context of ODR, data protection compliance will rely on the Participants exercising good faith efforts to apply the data protection laws to the ODR procedure in a proportionate manner and documenting those efforts. This stresses the importance of keeping a record of compliance.

4.9 Data Retention and Destruction

Data retention and destruction are considered forms of processing under the GDPR. Under the GDPR, personal data may be retained to the extent that it is necessary for, and related to, the purpose of the processing, and data subject should be notified of the data retention policy applicable to his or her personal data.

---

159 *See id.*, and Art. 24.

160 Controller Guidelines, fn 21, at p. 4; citing Article 29 Working Party Opinion 3/2010 on the principle of accountability adopted on 13 July 2010, 00062/10/EN.

Snapshot

An ODR Participant should only retain personal data that is reasonable in light of the purpose of the processing, including not only the ODR itself and the enforcement of any award or settlement, but any attendant processing requirements for example to undertake future conflict checks and to comply with legal and regulatory obligations.

The GDPR provides that personal data be 'kept in a form which permits identification of data subjects for no longer than is necessary for the purposes for which the personal data are processed'.[161]

To demonstrate compliance with this principle, organizations with more than 250 employees are required to establish and document standard retention periods for different categories of information and to create a system for ensuring that they are complied with, and for periodically reviewing retention. Smaller firms, chambers and independent neutrals will need to be able to demonstrate compliance but will not need to comply with these specific requirements unless they are engaged in high risk processing. However, they will still be required to employ compliant retention policies and to regularly review the data held, and to delete (or anonymize) any personal data no longer required for processing.

4.9.1 Considerations for ODR

ODR Participants should take into account their stated purposes for processing the personal data in question when deciding how long it can be retained. ODR Participants can retain personal data for as long as required for the lawful purpose relied on for processing and for any related processing requirements.

ODR Participants should also consider whether they need to keep a record of a relationship with the individual once that relationship ends. The data controller may need to keep some information so that it can confirm that the relationship existed - and that it has ended - as well as some of its details. This applies, for example, for future conflict checks.

ODR Participants may also be required to retain personal data to comply with any legal or regulatory requirements, for example, for income tax and audit purposes.

161 *See* GDPR fn 3, Art. 5 (1) (e).

5 What Data Security Measures Should Be Applied to ODR Processes??

The GDPR requires all controllers and processors of personal data governed by its terms to implement 'appropriate' technical and organizational measures to secure the personal data.[162] This means that whenever the GDPR applies to personal data processed in an arbitration, adequate data security is *mandatory*.

Snapshot

All Arbitral Participants should apply reasonable and appropriate data security measures to the processing of personal data during an ODR proceeding. There is no one-size-fits-all solution to data security for ODR. Rather, what is 'appropriate' or 'reasonable' will depend on many factors including the ODR Participant's function, the amount of personal data being processed, whether any sensitive data is being processed, whether third party data transfer is required and if so, where, the size and type of organization (including number of employees and its premises and data systems), the type of processing being undertaken and whether data processors are employed, and the types of data being processed including how valuable, sensitive or confidential it is, and the damage or distress that may be caused if the data was compromised.

Article 5(1)(f) of the GDPR establishes the principle that personal data shall be:

> [P]rocessed in a manner that ensures appropriate security of the personal data, including protection against unauthorised or unlawful processing and against accidental loss, destruction or damage, using appropriate technical or organisational measures (integrity and confidentiality).[163]

Article 32 of the GDPR explains further that the following measures are required to secure all personal data covered by its terms:

1. Taking into account the state of the art, the costs of implementation and the nature, scope, context and purposes of processing as well as the risk of varying likelihood and severity for the rights and freedoms of natural persons, the controller and the processor shall implement appropriate technical and organizational measures to ensure a level of security appropriate to the risk, including inter alia as appropriate:
   a. the pseudonymization and encryption of personal data;
   b. the ability to ensure the ongoing confidentiality, integrity, availability and resilience of processing systems and services;

162 *See id.*, Art. 5 (1) (f) and Art. 32.
163 *Id.*, Art. 5 (1) (f).

c. the ability to restore the availability and access to personal data in a timely manner in the event of a physical or technical incident;
d. a process for regularly testing, assessing and evaluating the effectiveness of technical and organizational measures for ensuring the security of the processing.

2. In assessing the appropriate level of security account shall be taken in particular of the risks that are presented by processing, in particular from accidental or unlawful destruction, loss, alteration, unauthorized disclosure of, or access to personal data transmitted, stored or otherwise processed.[164]

The GDPR does not define the security measures required for compliance, deferring to the general notion that data controllers and processors, including ODR Participants, should 'implement technical and organisational measures' that are 'appropriate to the risks' presented by the processing, and taking into consideration the state of the art and costs of implementation, as well as the nature, scope, context and purpose of the data controller processing and the risks to data subjects.

Similarly, in its Disclosure Guidelines, the Working Party has said in the context of litigation that the data controller shall take all:

> [R]easonable technical and organisational precautions to preserve the security of the data to protect it from accidental or unlawful destruction or accidental loss and unauthorized disclosure or access. These measures must be proportionate to the purposes of investigating the issues raised in accordance with the security regulations established in the different Member States. These requirements are to be imposed not just on the data controller but such measures as are appropriate should also be provided by the law firms who are dealing with the litigation together with any litigation support services and all other experts who are involved with the collection or review of the information.[165]

In considering what constitutes adequate data security, the Information Commissioner's Office in the United Kingdom has issued helpful guidance.[166] The risk-based approach to data security adopted by the GDPR and more fully described in the ICO Guidance can helpfully be understood in light of the core functions of data security management outlined by data security professionals and adopted in the NIST framework for cybersecurity, which in the context of the GDPR must be understood more broadly to

164 *Id.*, Art. 32.
165 Disclosure Guidelines, fn 18, at p. 12.
166 *See* ICO, Security and Guidelines referred to therein https://ico.org.uk/for-organisations/guide-to-data-protection/guide-to-the-general-data-protection-regulation-gdpr/security/ ("ICO Guidance").

encompass all data security.[167] These functions include to Identify, Protect, Detect, Respond, and Recover from data security risks and breaches.

The GDPR lists a number of mechanisms that may be employed to reach that appropriate level of security, none of which are required, but which should be considered where appropriate:

- ***Pseudonymization and encryption*** – Pseudonymization and encryption are specified in the GDPR as examples of measures that may be appropriate depending on the circumstances.
- ***Confidentiality, integrity, availability and resilience*** – The GDPR instructs ODR Participants to consider the basic principles of 'confidentiality, integrity and availability' of the personal data they process. Sometimes referred to by data security professionals as the 'CIA triad', confidentiality, integrity and availability are three important elements of data security to be considered under the GDPR.[168] Any data security measures employed by ODR Participants should endeavor to ensure these principles are complied with both with respect to their systems and the data processed.
  - The GDPR also suggests that ODR Participants consider providing for 'resilience' in their processing systems and services. The ICO has explained that resilience in this context refers to whether systems can continue operating under adverse conditions, such as those that may result from a physical or technical incident, and their ability to be restored to an effective state.[169]
- ***Restore*** – The GDPR also asks ODR Participants to consider the ability of their systems to 'restore the availability and access to personal data in a timely manner in the event of a physical or technical incident'. The GDPR does not define what a 'timely manner' should be, but the ICO has suggested that this will depend on:
- who the data controller is;
- what systems the data controller has; and
- the risk that may be posed to individuals if the personal data the data controller processes is unavailable for a period of time.[170]

The ODR Participant should consider these issues when making their risk assessment and selecting their security measures. For example, something as straightforward as having an appropriate backup system should allow an ODR Participant to restore their systems, and therefore the personal data they hold, in a timely manner.

- ***Regular testing, assessing and evaluating*** – The GDPR also expressly suggests that adequate security requires ODR Participants to consider a process for regular testing,

167 *See* NIST, Cybersecurity Framework, www.nist.gov/industry-impacts/cybersecurity-framework.
168 *See* ICO Guidance, fn 164.
169 *Id.*
170 *See id.*

assessing and evaluating the effectiveness of their security measures. Circumstances will dictate the form and regularity of the testing; however, it is important to note that the requirement in the GDPR to test concerns 'the effectiveness of technical and organisational measures for ensuring the security of the processing' as whole.[171]

In applying these factors to ensure that ODR Participants, have 'appropriate' data security, Article 32(2) provides expressly that:

> In assessing the appropriate level of security account shall be taken in particular of the risks that are presented by processing, in particular from accidental or unlawful destruction, loss, alteration, unauthorised disclosure of, or access to personal data transmitted, stored or otherwise processed.[172]

This reflects both the GDPR's risk-based approach, and that there is no 'one size fits all' solution to data security.[173]

This means that what is 'appropriate' will depend on many factors including the ODR Participant's function, the size and type of organization (including number of employees and its premises and data systems), the type of processing being undertaken and whether data processors are used), whether third party data transfer is required and if so, where, and the types of data being processed including how valuable, sensitive or confidential it is, and the damage or concerns that may be caused if the data was compromised.

5.1 Considerations for ODR

Applying these principles, from a data protection perspective, the bottom line is that all ODR Participants should undertake the following with respect to their data security:

- Undertake a risk-based analysis considering the nature and amount of data being processed and document the findings;
- Employ security measures in that are appropriate in light of the risk;
- In deciding what measures to employ, take into account the state of technological development, but the cost of implementation can also be considered;
- Implement data security measures taking into consideration the existing data infrastructure and operational requirements, the nature and amount of data processed and the risk that might result from any data breach.

171 *See* GDPR fn 3, Art. 32.

172 *See id.*

173 *See* ICCA-NYC Bar-CPR Cybersecurity Protocol for International Arbitration (2019 Edition), www.arbitration-icca.org/projects/Cybersecurity-in-International-Arbitration.html. (the "Protocol").

In the context of data protection, the focus will be on the personal data being processed and how to minimize the risk to the data subject. However, the more valuable and sensitive data being processed during an ODR procedure will often not be personal data but rather confidential information, trade secrets, IP, and similar commercially sensitive information. Reasonable data security will also need to be applied to this data taking into account the factors discussed above.

Important initiatives have been undertaken towards ensuring cybersecurity in international arbitration, which are also applicable to other forms of ODR. These include the ICCA/NYC Bar/CPR Cybersecurity Protocol for International Arbitration (2019),[174] the IBA Cybersecurity Guidelines for Businesses (2018)[175] and the ICC Cybersecurity Guidelines for Businesses (2015).[176] These initiatives are not focused on the data security requirements of the GDPR specifically, but together with ICO Guidance and the NIST framework they are a useful resource for applying a risk-based analysis to data security during ODR procedures.

The Protocol is the only guidance geared directly at international arbitration, and may also be applied to other forms of ODR as appropriate. The protocol sets out 14 principles together with explanatory commentary and examples that provide guidance on establishing reasonable cybersecurity measures during an arbitration proceeding. These principles are very useful in considering what constitutes appropriate data security in the context of ODR and are set forth in an Annex to this article.

One way to address the data security requirements posed by ODR is through the use of digital platforms for the exchange of information. Platforms are often used in consumer ODR and they are becoming increasingly prevalent in all forms of digital dispute resolution. Many initiatives are underway to encourage the use of platforms for data exchanges during digital dispute resolution, including the Protocol for Online Case Management in International Arbitration prepared by the Working Group on LegalTech Adoption in International Arbitration.[177]

However, any platform or any other data security system is only as good as those who use it, and it is important that ODR Participants are aware of their data security obligations and apply them as no-one wants to be the 'weak link'. For example, when documents are exchanged through a secure platform with only limited access, care must be applied before downloading them and distributing them to numerous persons. Further, when travelling, care should be given to how data is accessed and carried to

174 *See id.*

175 *See* IBA Cybersecurity Guidelines (2018), www.ibanet.org/LPRU/cybersecurity-guidelines.aspx.

176 *See* ICC Cybersecurity Guide for Business (2015), https://iccwbo.org/publication/icc-cyber-security-guide-for-business/#:~:text=The ICC Cyber Security Guide, be managed as a result.

177 *See* Protocol for Online Case Management in International Arbitration, Working Group on LegalTech Adoption in International Arbitration, https://protocol.techinarbitration.com/p/1 (consultation draft) (2020).

avoid unnecessary risk. These are just examples, but many of the most serious data breaches have occurred through simple human error.

The bottom line is that applying adequate security measures has both technical and behavioral components, both of which are important in the context of ODR procedures.

6 CONCLUSION AND A MODEST PROPOSAL

The digitalization of the dispute resolution processes holds great promise for the avoidance of disputes and their expeditious resolution in arbitration, mediation, and across all types of existing ADR processes and those of the future. For this promise to be realized, however, it is important that as dispute resolution becomes increasingly digital and ubiquitous that proper consideration is given to the legal and practical constraints on that process including those related to data protection and data security.

Where data processing falls within the jurisdictional scope of the GDPR during an ODR procedure, defining responsibility is complicated by the facts that:

- During the course of any ODR proceeding Participants in the process may qualify as controllers or joint controllers or processors, and this may change over time and with respect to the various activities performed.
- Participants may be subject to different data protection regimes, which create different and potentially conflicting legal obligations with respect to how they each handle personal data during the proceeding.
- Even where the GDPR applies, each Participant may be established in a different Member States or outside the EU and consequently, may be subject to the jurisdiction of a different Member State supervisory authority which may take a different view of how the rules apply to the ODR procedure.
- This uncertainty with respect to the responsibilities of the various Participants for GDPR compliance stresses the importance of planning for GDPR compliance both in structuring the ODR procedure and during any ODR proceeding.

In concrete ODR procedures, it may not always be clear whether the Participants may be joint controllers for all or part of the process. The possibility of ODR Participants becoming jointly responsible for data protection compliance and of being exposed to joint and several liability for violations, emphasizes the importance of taking GDPR seriously and building ODR systems and procedures with the GDPR and data protection principles in mind.

Where ODR Participants consider that they may qualify as joint controllers, they are required by the GDPR to put in place arrangements defining their responsibilities for compliance and the EDPB recommends for this be done through a binding instrument.[178] In the ODR context this can be done through the rules of an ODR platform, terms of reference, procedural orders or data protection protocols, all of which are important means of managing data protection compliance during ODR proceedings.

If these considerations are properly taken into account both at the systemic level and in individual cases, reasonable procedures can be built into ODR processes that reflect these constraints without major disruption. This chapter has suggested a few such practical considerations:

- Where appropriate, consider the use of non-binding ODR such as standing mediation, dispute resolution boards, expert determination or traditional mediation at least as a first step before binding dispute resolution, which limits the amount of information to be processed during the ODR procedure and at the same time may avoid the dispute altogether or result in its early resolution.
- Build basic data protection compliance requirements into the ODR procedure either at a systemic level or on a case-by-case basis. This may include:
  - o Requiring parties to provide assurances that the data being presented in the ODR procedure may be processed during the proceeding in compliance with applicable data protection laws, including that it has been properly notified to data subjects and minimized before submission.
  - o Building reasonable data protection compliance measures into the ODR procedure itself including establishing the lawful basis and purpose of the processing, measures to comply with data subject rights and in the case of data breach, and the documentation of compliance.
  - o Ensuring that ODR Participants agree to enter into any reasonable measures requested either by the institution or as part of the process to ensure the free flow of information across borders during the ODR procedure, potentially including standard contractual clauses.
  - o Ensuring adequate data security for the ODR proceeding and deploying secure means to exchange information during the ODR procedure including the use of secure digital ODR platforms where appropriate and prescribing the means of such use to avoid the risks created by the digital exchange of information.

In the context of digital dispute resolution, the application of the data protection laws may not be straight forward and will center around the Participants exercising good faith efforts to apply the data protection laws to the ODR procedure in a proportionate manner and documenting those efforts. Further, the risks raised by data security and data breach in the digital context should be expressly addressed and appropriate

178 See Controller Guidelines, fn. 21.

reasonable measures adopted. This stresses the importance of considering these issues early and documenting compliance.

The important take away from this discussion is that practical compliance measures can be taken without damaging the fundamental tenets of dispute resolution or the way it is practiced in a digital environment. The expected result would be that the personal data processed for ODR is minimized and that it is processed and transferred securely based on a lawful basis and for a purpose that has been notified to the data subject where possible and further that measures are put in place to comply with data subject rights and in the case of data breach and to document compliance. If these measures are taken upfront either in developing the system or on a case-by-case basis, this need not disrupt the process unnecessarily and the compliance risk to ODR Participants will be reduced.

ANNEX

ICCA-NYC BAR-CPR CYBERSECURITY PROTOCOL FOR INTERNATIONAL ARBITRATION (Without Commentary)

Scope and Applicability

Principle 1 The Cybersecurity Protocol provides a recommended framework to guide tribunals, parties, and administering institutions in their consideration of what information security measures are reasonable to apply to a particular arbitration matter.

Principle 2 As a threshold matter, each party, arbitrator, and administering institution should consider the baseline information security practices that are addressed in Schedule A and the impact of their own information security practices on the arbitration. Effective information security in a particular arbitration requires all custodians of arbitration-related information to adopt reasonable information security practices.

Principle 3 Parties, arbitrators, and administering institutions should ensure that all persons directly or indirectly involved in an arbitration on their behalf are aware of, and follow, any information security measures adopted in a proceeding, as well as the potential impact of any security incidents.

Principle 4 The Protocol does not supersede applicable law, arbitration rules, professional or ethical obligations, or other binding obligations.

The Standard

Principle 5 Subject to Principle 4, the information security measures adopted for the arbitration shall be those that are reasonable in the circumstances of the case as considered in Principles 6-8.

Determining Reasonable Cybersecurity Measures

Principle 6 In determining which specific information security measures are reasonable for a particular arbitration, the parties and the tribunal should consider: (a) the risk profile of the arbitration, taking into account the factors set forth in Schedule B; (b) the existing information security practices, infrastructure, and capabilities of the parties, arbitrators, and any administering institution, and the extent to which those practices address the categories of information security measures referenced in Principle 7; (c) the burden, costs, and the relative resources of the parties, arbitrators, and any administering institution; (d) proportionality relative to the size, value, and risk profile of the dispute; and (e) the efficiency of the arbitral process.

Principle 7 In considering the specific information security measures to be applied in an arbitration, consideration should be given to the following categories:

(a) asset management;
(b) access controls;
(c) encryption;
(d) communications security;
(e) physical and environmental security;
(f) operations security; and
(g) information security incident management.

Principle 8 In some cases, it may be reasonable to tailor the information security measures applied to the arbitration to the risks present in different aspects of the arbitration, which may include:

(a) information exchanges and transmission of arbitration related information;
(b) storage of arbitration-related information;
(c) travel;
(d) hearings and conferences; and/or
(e) post-arbitration retention and destruction policies.

Process to Establish Reasonable Cybersecurity Measures

Principle 9 Taking into consideration the factors outlined in Principles 6-8 as appropriate, the parties should attempt in the first instance to agree on reasonable information security measures.

Principle 10 Information security should be raised as early as practicable in the arbitration, which ordinarily will not be later than the first case management conference.

Principle 11 Taking into consideration Principles 4-9 as appropriate, the arbitral tribunal has the authority to determine the information security measures applicable to the arbitration.

Principle 12 The arbitral tribunal may modify the measures previously established for the arbitration, at the request of any party or on the tribunal's own initiative, in light of the evolving circumstances of the case.

Principle 13 In the event of a breach of the information security measures adopted for an arbitration proceeding or the occurrence of an information security incident, the arbitral tribunal may, in its discretion:

(a) allocate related costs among the parties; and/or

(b) impose sanctions on the parties.

Principle 14 The Protocol does not establish any liability or any liability standard for any purpose, including, but not limited to, legal or regulatory purposes, liability in contract, professional malpractice, or negligence.

Chapter 19 Smart Contracts and Blockchain

Brandon Malone

1 Introduction

Automated contracts are not new. A form of automated contract has existed for at least as long as we have had vending machines. I insert a coin and a bar of chocolate drops out. The money now belongs to the owner of the vending machine, and I now own the bar of chocolate. A set or rights is created by a simple mechanical action.

The vendor does not know my identity, nor do I necessarily know the identity of the vendor, and yet a contract has been formed and executed automatically.

Developments in technology have increased the options for the automatic execution of contracts. 'Smart' contracts are now widely used in certain sectors, and as the technology develops, they have the potential to remove the 'middleman' (also known as lawyers and professional advisors) from the equation.

The sophistication of smart contracts reduces the scope for disputes, and in some applications, they all but remove the possibility of a dispute.

Will this result in a reduction in the need for legal services? Does this spell the end of the legal profession?

In the arbitration sphere, there are two distinct areas where blockchain will become increasingly relevant. The first is in the resolution of disputes arising under smart contracts. The second is the use of blockchain technology in the arbitration process (regardless of whether the underlying contract is a smart contract). In this chapter, I will examine the smart contract and blockchain concepts, and the consequences for the practice (and indeed the idea) of arbitration.

2 Smart Contracts

The concept of smart contracts has been around for some time now, having first been posited in the mid-nineties by the legal writer and cryptographer, Nick Szabo.[1] A smart contract, at the basic level, is an agreement recorded in whole or in part as computer code, which is capable of automatic execution of some or all of its terms. However, there is no settled definition of a 'smart contract'.

---

1 Szabo, N. (1997). Formalizing and securing relationships on public networks. *First Monday, 2*(9). Retrieved 6 September 2020, from https://firstmonday.org/ojs/index.php/fm/article/view/548/469.

More recently the term has become synonymous with the use of blockchain to implement contractual obligations. Whilst strictly speaking a smart contract can be created without using a blockchain platform, the use of blockchain adds a level of security and transparency that has allowed users to have faith the concept.

The term 'smart contract' can refer to two different concepts: 'smart contract code' and 'smart legal contracts'.[2] Smart contract code is an operational concept. It involves software, which is generally located on a blockchain ledger, and is stored verified and executed electronically. The execution of the code may result in a change in rights and obligations, including the transfer of property, However, it may be argued that smart contract code is not a 'contract' in the traditional legal sense at all.

'Smart legal contracts' refers to the application of smart contract code technology as a complement or substitute for legal contracts.

The distinction between the two concepts is important in the context of enforcement and arbitration, and I will explore the distinction in that context later on.

In their paper 'Smart Contract Templates: foundations, design landscape and research directions' Clack, Bakshi and Braine suggest the following definition as being broad enough to cover both concepts:[3]

> A smart contract is an automatable and enforceable agreement. Automatable by computer, although some parts may require human input and control. Enforceable either by legal enforcement of rights and obligations or via tamper-proof execution of computer code.

This is the definition used in this chapter, although the distinction between smart contract code and smart legal contracts is drawn where necessary. The definition has a number of components which themselves require definition.

> A smart contract is an automatable and enforceable agreement.

The first point to note in this definition is the use of the word 'agreement'. Where the smart contract comprises smart contract code only, there may be a question whether there is 'agreement' in the traditional sense, the *consensus in idem* required to form a contract, or at least whether the agreement can be said to be a true contract, expressing the intention of the parties. The idea of consent in a smart contract code may be

2 Stark, J. (7 June 2016). *Making Sense of Smart Contracts.* Retrieved from www.coindesk.com/making-sense-smart-contracts.

3 Clack, C.D., Bakshi, V.A., & Braine, L. (2016). Smart Contract Templates: foundations, design landscape and research directions. *arXiv: Computers and Society.* Retrieved 6 September 2020, from https://arxiv.org/pdf/1608.00771.

particularly difficult where contracts are being entered into automatically in accordance with a set of parameters.

The next part of the definition is that the contract is 'automatable' which is clarified as 'automatable by computer, although some parts may require human input and control'. This requires that unlike a paper or an oral contract, at least part of the contract can be executed automatically using computers: when certain conditions of the code are met, payment or ownership (or a right of access, etc) is transferred without the need for human intervention. Examples are discussed below.

The contract must be capable of enforcement in the normal way, through courts or arbitration or by 'tamper-proof execution of computer code'. The term 'tamper-proof' in this context refers to the use of blockchain technology, computer code which for practical purposes is not capable of being interfered with, and executes automatically when the agreed condition is met.

It should be kept in mind that smart contract code that is enforced through the execution of the code may not be legally enforceable in every instance. Whilst cryptocurrencies have by and large allowed users to escape the control of financial institutions, smart contracts do not allow the contracting parties to escape the consequences of the law.

If a smart contract purports to effect a change in legal rights and obligations which normally require a further formality, such as a formally executed deed, or recording in an external register, the smart contract may not be enforceable as a matter of law. Legal requirements will therefore normally prevail over code, whether or not that code is tamper-proof, and that is one of the issues which may slow that spread of smart contracts into new areas.

However, it is also true to say that the law is constantly evolving to meet developments in technology, and that there is a general trend towards business activity, including official and government business moving online.[4] It is not unreasonable to expect that the formal requirements of the past will continue to be replaced by electronic safeguards, and blockchain applications will have a major role in these developments.

It is therefore crucial for those of involved in dispute resolution to understand the scope and potential of blockchain and smart contracts, and the role that they play in the formation of legal relationships now and in the future.

---

4 *See* for example the electronic transaction legislation enacted in various jurisdictions following the publication of UNCITRAL Model Law on Electronic Commerce, uncitral.un.org/sites/uncitral.un.org/files/media-documents/uncitral/en/19-04970_ebook.pdf.

3 BLOCKCHAIN

To understand the potential of smart contracts, it is necessary to have a basic understanding of blockchain technology. Many lawyers find this to be a daunting subject, but whilst the technology is complicated, the basic concept is not. I do not propose to try and explain the technology in any detail in this chapter, but the concepts are set out below.

Consider the banknote: the dollar, the euro, the pound note. Over the years, banks have made it more and more complicated to make a copy of a paper bill. Once banks relied upon the difficulty of reproducing complicated engraved designs to defeat counterfeiters, and there have been many advances in banknote technology over the years. A modern banknote is likely to be made of specialised plastic, and to contain various security features like holograms, transparencies, and watermarks. It is more or less impossible for the average person to make a convincing copy.

Compare this to a digital token. It is the nature of a digital file that anyone with the most basic knowledge of computers can make an exact copy, simply by pressing the 'save as' button, or copying and pasting. Of course, there are many ways in which a file can be protected to prevent copying, but most of these methods can be overcome by someone with a reasonable knowledge of computer software, and do not present a challenge to sophisticated hackers.

In the context of a digital 'coin', there is little to stop a sophisticated user from spending that coin, retaining a perfect digital copy, and spending it again, and again.

This is where blockchain technology comes in: it prevents 'double-spending'. That is because the system is transparent, distributed, and operates on an 'add-only' basis, which is to say that only new information can only be added to chain of data, it cannot be altered, so there is always a complete and transparent record of transactions.

A key feature of a blockchain is that it is decentralised. A bank can see money coming in and out of an account, and it is the sole arbiter of whether money has been received or spent. It is a centralised ledger system. In contrast, the ledger in a blockchain is distributed. The whole of the ledger (which consists the blocks of data making up the chain) is kept on various computers across a network.

Because the ledger is fully distributed, there is no single point of failure, and no central controlling authority.

The information on the blockchain cannot be altered without the consent of the majority of the users on the network. Thus, one person cannot spend the same token twice, as the other ledger holders will reject the second transaction as invalid. There is a mutual self interest in ensuring that fraudulent transactions do not occur. That is because the value of the digital coin is dependent on faith in the system.

Transaction on the blockchain involve public and private keys which are mathematically related. A user of the system has a public key generated by the blockchain software and a private key, also generated by the software. A transaction is initiated by posting a message to the network encrypted using the private key. The other members of the network are able to verify that the transaction is genuine by using the initiator's public key. When 51% of participants on the network verify the transaction, it is added to the blockchain.

Verification of the transaction and the consensus of ledger holders to a new transaction is achieved by a 'proof-of-work consensus algorithm' (PoW algorithm).[5] A PoW algorithm functions by setting a complex mathematical problem. There are different types of such problems, but a commonly used one is known as prime number factorisation. Essentially this entails the computer working out which two very large numbers when multiplied together result in the very much larger number it starts with. This takes the programme some time (optimally around ten minutes or so, balancing a sufficient level of difficulty with a degree of convenience) and uses a lot of computational power. It is easy for another computer to take the two prime number it has produced and multiply them thus verifying that the work has taken place, and that the transaction is valid.

The new data block resulting from this exercise is added to the chain. The new block contains the data from the previous block, and in this way, it is possible to verify the order in which data has been added, thereby avoiding tampering with the record.

The result of this system is that there is one consolidated record that constitutes a single and shared version of the true history of transactions on the blockchain. This is essence of a blockchain currency, and Bitcoin was the first practical implementation of such a system.

With an understanding of the basic principle of blockchain technology, it is immediately apparent that this technology could be used to implement secure transactions with the blockchain providing both incorruptibility of the contract documents, with the terms recorded as data blocks, and a secure escrow system allowing automatic payment under the contract when performance is recorded.

These two characteristics, incorruptibility and automatic execution are separate advantages of using a blockchain implementation for contracts. A contract can be recorded using blockchain technology, and that will make it immutable and incorruptible. However, the use of blockchain does not render the contract 'smart'. Equally, it is not necessary to use blockchain far less crypto currencies to create a contract which executes automatically. However, the term 'smart contract' has come to imply the use of blockchain and automatic execution, and it is those types of contract, and their implications for dispute resolution and arbitration in particular that is the main focus of this chapter.

---

5 Markus Jakobsson, A.J. (1999). Proof of work and bread pudding protocols. In P. (Preneel, B. ed), *Secure Information Networks.* Boston: Springer.

4 USING BLOCKCHAIN TO IMPLEMENT CONTRACTUAL OBLIGATIONS

There are a number of use cases for smart contract which have gained popularity in recent years, including so called 'parametric' travel insurance, crop protection insurance (which is also parametric in nature), and stock trading. There are also a number of possible use cases which have been posited but not yet properly implemented. A few use cases are considered below:

4.1 Parametric Travel Insurance

The most impressive use of a smart contract is where performance is implemented without any third-party intervention. A good, and easy to understand example of this is the now discontinued 'Fizzy Axa' flight insurance policy.

Fizzy Axa was a form of parametric insurance. Parametric insurance does not pay out the actual loss incurred, but instead pays out a pre-agreed set sum in the event of a pre-defined circumstance occurring, that is, an event occurring within a predefined parameter.[6]

The subject matter of this particular parametric insurance policy was flight delay. In terms of a Fizzy Axa policy, a set premium was paid, and in the event of the flight being late by the defined period (two hours or more) the policy paid out automatically.

It is easy to see how a contract like this lends itself to smart contracting. Because the insurance was a parametric policy, there was no need to make an actual assessment of damages. The role of a loss adjuster in assessing the level of damages, and that of lawyers in arguing the correct amount are obviated by the scheme of the policy. Using blockchain technology and smart contracts allows claims to be paid out automatically.

That still leaves the question of whether the insured event has occurred. In the case of flight arrival times, this is quite easy to ascertain via various apps and website. The information is recorded by various airports and agencies, such as the Aircraft Situation Display to Industry (ASDI). The Fizzy Axa system connected to data streams, such as ASDI, and used that recorded landing time information to determine whether or not a claim event had occurred on a particular policy.

In the event of a flight being delayed by more than the agreed period, the system paid out to the policyholder automatically, by operation of a computer programme, without the intervention of any human operator.

It can be seen that the scope for disputes on such a contract are extremely limited. Either the flight arrives within two hours (or whatever the agreed period might be) of the scheduled time, and that is the end of the contract; or the flight arrives beyond the agreed period, and the payment due under the policy is paid automatically. Only in the event of

6 Parametric means 'relating to or expressed in terms of a parameter or parameters'.

there being some glitch in the system whereby an incorrect time is recorded for the arrival of the flight is there any real scope for disagreement. Conceivably an insured passenger might cause a delay on their own flight, so as to procure a payment, by feigning an illness, or locking themselves in the lavatory before takeoff, but on the whole, the system will run automatically.

Fizzy Axa has now been discontinued,[7] and some of the reasons for that are examined below.

4.2 *Crop Protection Insurance*

Another useful implementation of smart contracts in the insurance sector is that of crop insurance, and there are good examples in the citrus fruit industry.

Oranges are more valuable when they can be sold as whole fruit. If the crop is affected by frost, the skin can be damaged, and the flesh can become desiccated. The crop can no longer be sold as whole fruit and is instead used to produce orange juice.

In some parts of the world there is little or no chance of temperatures dropping below zero, but some places are more marginal, and frost can damage the crop.[8] Therefore, farmers take out insurance to protect against frost damage losses.

Like flight arrival times, temperature (and weather generally) is a data set that has long been recorded and made available online. It is easy to create a contract that pays out on the occurrence of a certain weather event, such as a drop in temperature below zero by reference to agreed weather stations, and where that is possible, it is relatively straightforward to code a smart contract that automatically pays out when the temperature has dropped below freezing.

Whilst a traditional crop protection policy will be based on actual damage incurred to the crop, as assessed in the report of a loss adjuster, in the smart contract scenario, the policy is parametric in nature, and pays out a fixed amount based on projections of the damage to the crop if an event occurs within the agreed parameters.

Whether the amount agreed in terms of the parametric policy covers more or less than the actual loss is a gamble for the insurer and the insured. From the insurer's point of view, there is an advantage in not having to pay loss adjusters, not having to carry out expensive investigations, and not becoming involved in litigation over the correct level of recoverable loss. The main advantage to the insured is the certainty of payment at the agreed level, and the immediacy of payment, which happens automatically by operation of the code when the specified weather event (in this case the temperature falling below zero) occurs.

---

7 https://coinrivet.com/axa-drops-ethereum-based-flight-insurance-platform/.

8 As a graduate of Citrus High School, Citrus County, Florida, the author has some direct knowledge of these things.

Crop protection insurance is a form of climate risk insurance. Parametric climate risk insurance is also available in respect of other indexed weather events, such as hail, rainfall, and drought.

4.3 *Blockchain Property Registers*

We are starting to see the use of blockchain to complete property transactions. In some areas, property titles are recorded electronically, which lends itself to blockchain transactions. In England there has been a trial of a house sale using smart contracts by HMLR (Her Majesty's Land Registry).[9]

The advantage of a system like this is that it allows instantaneous and secure transfer of title, and immediate confirmation of payment. The 'single consolidated ledger (register)' model avoids a situation that may arise where there is a physical register: the seller becoming insolvent after the funds have transferred to the seller, but before the registration of the title, casting doubt upon the true ownership of the property, and leaving the purchaser with no title and no way of recovering the price.

5 Difficulties in Implementing Blockchain Solutions

Whilst the potential of smart contracts is huge, there are barriers to their wide scale adoption and implementation. Some of these barriers are explored below.

5.1 *Legal Status of a Smart Contract*

Where a smart contract is of the smart legal contract variety, which is to say a traditional contract which is partly automated, there is little doubt that it is to be regarded as a contract in the usual sense.

However, since a smart contract is at least partly expressed in computer code rather than words, and since lawyers and their clients do not generally speak computer code, there is at least a question as to whether the parties are really consenting to the terms of the contract expressed in code.

Where the smart contract is purely code, there is a question whether the smart contract is really a contract at all.[10] The concern that such a contract may not be binding and enforceable (albeit it may be self-executing) suggests that it is sensible to give smart contract code a smart legal contract 'wrapper' so that the intention of the

---

9 www.ledgerinsights.com/uk-land-registry-successfully-completes-blockchain-trial/; www.gov.uk/government/news/hm-land-registry-is-making-it-easier-to-remortgage.

10 Durovic, M., & Lech, F. (2019). Enforceability of Smart Contracts. Italian Law Journal, 5(2), 493-511.

parties to consent to the creation of the contractual relationship is properly evidenced, at least until the law catches up with the technology.

5.2 *Knowledge and Understanding of the Product*

As noted above, the Fizzy Axa parametric insurance product was withdrawn by Axa in November 2019, around two years after its launch. Why did that happen? At the time, a spokesman for Axa said "The first Fizzy product didn't reach its commercial targets, notably because there wasn't enough market appetite yet and the right distribution channels weren't there either."[11]

It is difficult to say why there was insufficient market appetite for the Fizzy Axa product. It may simply be a case of inertia. It is certainly the case that we have not yet reached the stage of a widespread understanding of smart contracts in the general populace.

Axa have treated the Fizzy projects as a learning process and are pressing ahead with their climate risk parametric insurance through Axa Climate.

Parametric insurance seems like an idea that is likely to take off when insurers can get the business model worked out, and consumers get used to the idea. Other use cases may be more difficult.

5.3 *Trust*

The system of paper currency relies on trust in financial institutions. The purpose of Bitcoin was to get away from 'trust-based models' which rely on centralised financial institutions. As Satoshi Nakamoto put it in the original proposal paper for Bitcoin 'We have proposed a system for electronic transactions without relying on trust.'[12] Is it possible to do away with 'trust' in this context?

It is fair to say that there is still a degree of distrust in blockchain technology. There is certainly lingering wariness of cryptocurrencies. This is not entirely surprising. The identity of the person who invented bitcoin is not known, or rather the true identity of the person or persons using the pseudonym Satoshi Nakamoto, the creator of Bitcoin, is unknown. Various individuals have been identified as possible 'Satoshis' including Nick Szabo, who posited the smart contract idea and the inventor and entrepreneur Elon Musk, but no one has been confirmed as the true Satoshi.[13]

---

11 Axa stops selling blockchain flight delay product. Insurance Post, 7 November 2019.

12 Bitcoin: a peer-to-peer electronic cash system. Nakamoto, 31 October 2008.

13 Popper, N. (n.d.). *Decoding the Enigma of Satoshi Nakamoto and the Birth of Bitcoin.* Retrieved 8 August 2020, from www.nytimes.com/2015/05/17/business/decoding-the-enigma-of-satoshi-nakamoto-and-the-birth-of-bitcoin.html.

This obscurity of origin does little to enhance trust in cryptocurrencies. There have also been a number of cryptocurrency scams. These scams can take many forms. One such form is an ICO (Initial Coin Offering) scam, where investors are invited to invest in a new cryptocurrency.

The value of the original cryptocurrency, Bitcoin, rocketed from around $1,000 per bitcoin at the beginning of 2017 to $19,000 at the end of that year. Unsurprisingly, that kind of profit drew a lot of get rich quick investors who were less than expert in the field.

One company looking to take advantage of the boom was Benebit, who disappeared with $3 million of investors' money.[14] Another was Centra Token, which scammed $25 million from investors.[15]

Leaving aside scams, the whole concept of a cryptocurrency is a difficult one for some people to accept as something which has inherent value. Once, currency was linked to real assets (gold and other metals), either because it was actually made of a metal, or in the case of bank notes, was a promise to pay a certain value of gold or silver. That model has of course moved on and currencies are now generally fiat currencies meaning that there is more money in circulation than is held by the relevant central bank in precious metals and foreign currency. The value of the currency depends upon the confidence of the market in the nation's ability to meet its debt.

Whilst there may be insufficient gold and foreign currency reserves behind a currency, holders of a currency know that it is rare for a nation state to become bankrupt, and nations always have a tax base and natural resources.

The same cannot be said of crypto currencies, the value of which depends entirely upon the confidence of holders of the crypto currency and the willingness of others to accept it in satisfaction of obligations.

The chief advantage of a crypto currency is that there is no central bank or nation state standing behind it, but that, when it comes to trust and confidence, is also its principal weakness.

Nick Szabo has explored these issues in some detail on his blog, and has gone so far as to say that monetary metal is the nearest analogue that we have to Bitcoin in monetary history (although he has not yet explained why that is, and it is not easy to see the basis for that analogy given the abstract and intangible nature of cryptocurrencies).[16]

However, whilst metals have an inherent value, cryptocurrencies do not, and for these various reasons, there is still a lack of widespread understanding of and acceptance of crypto currencies. It has been argued that cryptocurrencies have an inherent value because they require energy to create (mine) them, and they are finite in that a limited number of coins can be created in respect of any given algorithm.

---

14 https://bitcoinexchangeguide.com/benebit-pulls-an-exit-scam-disappearing-with-3-million-in-ico-funds/.

15 https://blockchain.news/news/third-co-founder-crypto-firm-pleads-guilty-role-25-million-ico-fraud.

16 Nick Szabo's blog on the subject is at https://unenumerated.blogspot.com/.

Another concern is that crypto currencies are increasingly used in illegitimate activities like extortion, money laundering, terrorist financing, and tax evasion. This is an area that is being examined by the European Union and other authorities.[17] Ironically, it may be the utility of crypto currencies for illegitimate activities that guarantees their continuing value.

Now of course smart contracts do not necessarily use cryptocurrencies to function, but they are based on the same blockchain technology as cryptocurrencies, so there is a degree of scepticism due to that association.

Against this, it should be noted that smart contracts are generally based on the Ethereum algorithm, the origins (and inventors) of which are known.

As Houben and Snyers put it in their paper on cryptocurrencies and blockchain.

> It would not be wise to discourage future innovations in this respect by submitting blockchain and fintechs exploring its use cases to burdensome requirements, simply because of one of the applications using blockchain technology, cryptocurrencies, is used illicitly by some.[18]

It is reasonable to suppose that as familiarity with blockchain technology grows, acceptance of blockchain implementations will grow. The trust issue is one which is likely to be overcome in the longer term.

5.4 Oracles: Interface with the Physical World and Existing Systems

There are many postulated use cases for smart contracts. However, many of them are not practical, or not yet practical because of difficulties achieving automatic execution. This happens either because the performance conditions cannot be recorded automatically, or because implementation cannot be achieved online.

Smart contracts, and blockchains generally rely on data from outside of the network in order to confirm whether the test of the 'if' in the code has been met and that accordingly the 'then' consequence is to be implemented. They obtain the information required to know whether the condition has been met, and communicate that action is to be taken in execution of the contract through the use of 'oracles'.

In ancient Greece, the oracle was a priest or priestess who acted as a medium through whom advice or prophecy was sought, the most famous being the Pythia, the oracle of Apollo at Delphi. A blockchain oracle serves as a medium between the smart contract,

17 Houben, R. A. (2018). *Cryptocurrencies and Blockchain: Legal Context and Implications for Financial Crime, Money Laundering and Tax Evasion.* Brussels: European Parliament.

18 *Ibid.*

and the real world, providing external data, such as the temperature in a specific location, or whether a particular payment has been made.

There are a number of different types of oracle:[19]

Software Oracles

These oracles handle data from an online source, an agreed data stream, such as temperature, flight arrival times, the price of a commodity. The software oracle extracts data from the stream and pushes to the smart contract.

Hardware Oracles

A smart contract may need information directly from the physical world. For example, RFID sensors attached to packages in a supply chain contract.

Inbound Oracles

An inbound oracle provides data from the outside world to the smart contract. The examples given for software and hardware oracles above are inbound oracles.

Outbound Oracles

These oracles give smart contracts the ability to communicate with the outside world. Such an oracle might authorise the release of funds from a bank account when delivery of a produced has been confirmed (using an inbound hardware oracle for example). Another example could be a smart contract sending data to a smart lock, which opens when the smart contract records receipt of payment.

Consensus Oracles

This is where data is gathered from human-based predictions, and more than one source is used.

The role of oracles is summarised well by Shermin Voshmgir, the director of the Research Institute for Cryptoeconomics at the Vienna University of Economics:

> Oracles provide the external data necessary for the smart contract and trigger smart contract executions when predefined conditions are met. Oracles are services that find and verify real world occurrences and submit this information to a smart contract, automatically triggering state changes on the blockchain. The primary task of oracles is to provide these values to the smart contract in a secure and trusted manner. These data flows stem either from software (Big Data application) or hardware (Internet of Things).[20]

19 Beniiche, A. (2020). A Study of Blockchain Oracles. ArXiv, abs/2004.07140.

20 Voshmgir, S. (2020). *Token Economy: How the Web3 Reinvents the Internet.* Berlin: BlockchainHub.

In the Fizzy Axa example, the condition of the contract (late arrival) is recorded automatically through an established data stream, a software oracle. However, unlike the role ascribed to the ancient oracles, inbound oracles are not all knowing and all seeing. In a traditional car insurance contract, establishing the existence of the insured event, let alone the losses arising is far more difficult and no current software or hardware oracle can calculate the losses accruing to an injured pedestrian (for example). Even if it were possible to pre agree a set level of compensation in the event of an accident, it is not currently possible for the cause of the accident to be established automatically, and therefore there cannot be automatic execution.

Similarly, at the other end of the transaction, there are difficulties with implementation, and there limits to the capabilities of outbound oracles.

5.5 *Coding Errors and Exploitable Vulnerabilities*

Most people are not able to communicate using computer code. The average lawyer is not able to code, let alone the average contracting party. Commercial contracts can run to dozens, hundreds and sometimes thousands of pages, packed with complex legal concepts. Is there scope for something to be lost in translation between the lawyer and the code? With the best will in the world, there is always going to be the possibility that the coder attempting to translate a complex contract into electronic form is going to make a mistake. Who is liable if such a mistake results in loss?

An example of an error in drafting, which resulted in a loophole, or exploitable vulnerability in a smart contract is the infamous DOA hack. DOA stands for distributed autonomous organisation. A DOA is a computer code through which a set of smart contracts are connected together as a governance mechanism.

A DOA was set up by a company known as slock.it (since acquired by the company Blockchains). The slock.it project concerned peer to peer sharing/renting, combining blockchain smart contracts with the internet of things to create a Universal Sharing Network (USN). So for example, if I have a connected electric car, such as a Tesla, I might rent it out directly using the USN system, bypassing middlemen such as car rental companies, and ultimately when such vehicles become autonomous, bypassing companies like Uber. It is an idea with a lot of potential.

Slock set up the DOA as decentralised investment club to fund the project. However, they encountered a major problem.

The DOA works on the basis that investors purchase Ethereum 'coins' ('Ether') which go into the fund in return for DOA tokens. Despite setting it up, Slock did not own the DOA, but was rather one of the projects which the DOA would fund. Other investors could pitch projects to the fund, and after an initial sift, approved investment proposals went to the coin holding community to vote on the project. A project receiving sufficient votes, the required quorum, got investment from the fund. Any profit generated by the project would be returned to the participating investors as Ether, with the whole thing recorded on the blockchain.

It can be seen from this structure that the DOA is similar in nature to a joint stock company, with voting on major decisions, and the consequent possibility that a minority of holder might be suppressed by a majority. Accordingly, the creators of the DOA introduced the equivalent of minority shareholder rights into the code, so that a minority holder in the fund would be able to retrieve their funds where a project that the minority did not want to be part of is approved by the majority.

The solution was to split the DOA with the minority Ether holders' funds being place in a 'child' DOA. Built into the code was a requirement that where a split was called for, there was a 48-day delay during which the funds could not be withdrawn or placed in a child DOA controlled by the minority fund holder.

A coder found a loophole in this procedure. Once a split in the fund had been called for, the code was written in such a way that the Ether was transferred to the child DOA immediately, but the balance of the fund was not updated until a later stage. The coder was able to call for the split multiple times before the code reached the stage of checking the balance (known as a 'recursive call exploit').

The 'hack' was noticed quite quickly, and due to the delay period built into the code, the problem became apparent before the funds were actually transferred. At this stage, the coder who had found and exploited the vulnerability, wrote a letter to the DOA community, styling himself 'the Attacker' and asserting that since the code was the sole measure of the participants rights, and he had simply done something that was permitted by the code, the Ether now rightfully belonged to him.[21] He asserted that he had decided to participate in the DOA having considered the code and come to the conclusion that splitting the fund resulted in a reward of additional Ether. Thus, he was, as he put it 'making use of this explicitly coded feature as per the smart contract terms'. He quoted the DOA terms which state 'The DAO's code controls and sets forth all terms of The DAO Creation,' and asserted that any attempt to 'fork' the code to reverse the transaction would be a violation of his rights in terms of the smart contract, and that any such action would destroy confidence in the Ethereum blockchain and in the field of blockchain and smart contracts generally.

The amount obtained through this 'hack' was 3,641,694 Ether (about $1.5 billion at the time of writing). There was therefore significant interest in rectifying the problem from the other investors. The community had to decide, within the remainder of the 48 day period, whether to do nothing and allow 'the Attacker' to remove the funds, introduce a 'soft fork' in the code which would have had the effect of rendering the stolen funds in the child DOA worthless, or to introduce a 'hard fork' in the code,

21 The text of the open letter to the DOA community is available online at https://pastebin.com/CcGUBgDG.

which would have overwritten the history of the blockchain, reversing the transactions which arose after the attack started.

Interestingly, there was considerable amount of support for the first option, allowing the transaction to stand, on the basis that 'the code is the law' and everything that is permitted by the code (including the exploitation of a vulnerability) is legal within the blockchain. They accepted the Attacker's arguments.

However, the majority of the members were of the view that the situation had to be addressed. After attempting a number of solutions, a hard fork in the code was agreed as the best solution, and the funds were returned to the investors.

It is difficult to analyse this situation from the point of view of traditional legal principles. The Attacker believed and asserted that he had legal advice to the effect that what he had done was perfectly within his rights. If the 'contract' between the parties was that the code itself was the sole measure of their rights, then perhaps there was something in that.

The DOA case illustrates the need to consider and cater for all eventualities, so as to avoid unintended consequences.

5.6 Catering for Variables

Some contracts are very straightforward. Parametric flight insurance, for example is a fairly simple 'if, then' scenario: if the flight arrives late, you get your money.

The DOA contract was, on the face of it, a straightforward arrangement. However, the possibility of someone making repeated calls to split the fund before the balance of the fund was checked was missed, leaving an exploitable vulnerability. No doubt it seemed obvious to the lawyers who put the scheme together that no one should be able to generate additional entitlements by splitting the funds multiple times, but if the ultimate arbiter of the parties rights is the code, the code has to be right first time every time and that means anticipating every variable.

Some contracts are much more complicated than the DOA. For an example, consider a construction contract for the erection of an office block. The number of possible variables that might affect the execution of the works are almost impossible to map out, let alone the consequences of those variables.

To give a common example, how does one code a smart contract to deal with the situation where bad weather is delaying the works, but the contractor is also behind in the programme because one of the contractor's subcontractors has become insolvent, one of its suppliers is withholding delivery because of late payment, and its contract manager is off sick? Is it possible to create algorithms to cater for the various eventualities that might arise on such a contract? That seems unlikely without a step change in the computer power available to technologists, and the level of investment of time and effort would be disproportionate to the gains of having a smart contract in a situation like this.

5.7 *Difficulty in Coding Subjective Tests*

Some performance criteria and contractual events are easy to code. Whether or not there has been a frost in a particular place is a question that is easily ascertained from weather stations. Whether or not payment has been made can be verified by reference to banking systems, or cryptocurrency blockchains.

Some legal concepts are much more difficult to express in computer code. Perhaps the most obvious is 'reasonableness'. The question of whether a party to a contract has exercised 'reasonable endeavours' in the performance of an obligation is something which is more or less impossible to code in a way that will allow automatic execution of the contract.

Similarly, obligations of 'good faith' are difficult to express in terms of ones and zeros. Indeed, any contractual term that relies on a subjective test to assess performance rather than objectively ascertainable events will be difficult if not impossible to code. The decision as to whether performance of such a term has been achieved involves subjective judgement.

At present, the only way to deal with such a provision is to have an external input to the smart contract. So for example, where a shipment of a commodity is to comply with a certain standard, and compliance with that standard is a matter of expert opinion and cannot be ascertained objectively, it will be necessary for there to be external input (the decision of the expert) before the contract can be implemented.

5.8 *Human Nature*

It is human nature to desire a 'day in court' when a dispute arises. The idea that the outcome of a contract is predetermined, and that disputing parties' rights and obligations can be determined automatically, by the operation of a computer programme, can be a difficult for the average person to digest. This issue is explored in the next section.

6 Enforcing Smart Contracts and Disputes

Where there is a 'pure' smart contract, and every eventuality is catered for in the code, there is limited scope for a dispute to arise: there are only 'if-then' consequences.

In such a smart contract, a dispute can only arise where there is a coding error, or an interface error such that performance is falsely reported as having occurred. There is also the possibility that a smart contract has been induced by misrepresentation. Disputes may also arise in relation to enforcement where performance cannot be completed electronically.

At the beginning of this chapter, I referred to the distinction between 'smart contract code' and 'smart legal contracts'. If the smart contract is of the 'smart contract code' type and is not part of wider 'smart legal contract', there will be no disputes clause, and indeed there is a question whether there is any contract that may form the basis of a legal dispute. The 'contract' is implemented by the code.

6.1 Coding Error

It is of course possible for there to be an error in the code, as there was in the DOA hack referred to above. In the DOA hack, the code was sequenced in such a way that it was possible to call for the fund to be split multiple times before the system checked the balance. The DOA attacker argued that this was a feature of the system, not a coding error, and that the additional funds accruing to him were nothing more than his entitlement under the smart contract.

In the DOA hack, the error was so severe and the consequences for the general Ethereum community so damaging that a solution was found. It is notable that the solution was found without recourse to any supervisory court.

Perhaps, if the DOA attacker had had the courage of his convictions, and genuinely believed that this exploitable vulnerability in the code was intended by its creators, he have gone public, and attempted to enforce his rights in a court.

In the event, the rest of the community was comfortable that this was an unintended error in the code and took collective action to remedy it.

A coding error which effects only one, or a small number of parties is unlikely to get the consensus needed for a 'hard fork' in the code as occurred in response to the DOA hack. In such a scenario, it may be necessary to look to the lawyers and coders who prepared the smart contract for a remedy, but it may be possible to seek relief from the other contracting party, if the innocent party is able to find a court willing to accept jurisdiction.

The difficulty with pure smart contracts which consist only of 'smart contract code' is that they do not sit comfortably with traditional notions of contract law and may not even be expressed in words. This presents a challenge to a court attempting to ascertain and enforce parties' rights.

6.2 *Interface Errors*

As discussed, in a pure smart contract situation, if the code has been correctly programmed, there should not be real any scope for dispute. However, for a smart contract to execute automatically, unless is it a purely financial contract based on cryptocurrencies, there must be some interface with the real world, an oracle.

For example, the data stream used by crop protection parametric insurance comes from weather stations monitoring local weather. If that monitoring station is damaged, or manipulated, it will provide false data, and that data may result in a false implementation of the contract: paying out when there has been no temperature event within the agreed parameter, or failing to pay out when there has been.

A pure smart contract is not set up to deal with such an aberration. It proceeds on an 'if-then' basis only.

Similarly, if the output of the smart code contract is not payment (or delivery of an electronic asset) but delivery of a physical asset, the code cannot implement the contract automatically. Transfer of title to the property can be achieved electronically, but delivery of possession of the property must take place physically or 'off chain' as it is known.

7 RESOLVING SMART CONTRACT DISPUTES

7.1 *Disputes under Smart Legal Contracts*

Where the smart contract is a smart legal contract, the situation is relatively straightforward. A smart legal contract is simply a contract which has aspect of its implementation automated. Accordingly, it can be enforced like any other contract via litigation or arbitration.

Of course, the nature of a smart legal contract is that some of the issues arising may be very technical and difficult for parties to argue. The role of technical expert witnesses becomes particularly important, and it may be argued that specialist lawyers, familiar with coding principles, and perhaps even specialist arbitrators and judges are required to deal with such disputes.

Equally, it may be argued that a contract involved a smart legal contract, is a dispute like any other, and it is simply a matter of ascertaining the parties' rights and applying the law.

Parties will include arbitration in such contracts just as they would in any other contract, or will choose litigation, expert determination, or whatever method of dispute resolution they prefer.

7.2 *Disputes in Respect of Smart Contract Code*

The situation is more complicated where there is no traditional contract wrapper to the smart contract provisions, and the whole of the 'contract' is constituted by code. The question arises, is such a smart contract a contract at all?

The whole ethos behind the creation of blockchain technology is a move away from centralisation and the need for intermediaries: the centralisation of financial authority in the hands of governments and financial institutions, and the centralisation of authority of commercial transactions in the hands of the state (the courts).[22] Cryptocurrencies remove financial institutions from the concept of money. Do smart contracts take the law out of the hands of the courts (and arbitrators)? Is 'contracting without the state' possible?

At a basic level, smart contract code is concerned with the rights and obligations of contracting parties. The contract may not be expressed in traditional terms. It may be difficult to find usual concepts of contract law such as offer and acceptance or consent within the code. It may even be impossible to identify the parties. Ultimately, however, the purpose of smart contracts code is to affect the transfer of value. It is implicit in smart contract code that the rights and obligations of the parties to the smart contract are altered by their participation in the code.

It may be asked is smart contract code a contract in and of itself where the code is the full expression of the parties' relationship or is it merely an implementation of an unwritten agreement. Different legal systems may approach the concept from different angles.

It is submitted that on a proper analysis, this type of code only smart contract is a contract as commonly understood. It is therefore capable of being litigated, and arbitrated, although in the absence of words, it may only be possible to submit such disputes to arbitration by agreement after the dispute has arisen.

In its 'Legal Statement on cryptoassets and smart contracts'[23] the UK Government's UK Jurisdiction Taskforce gave the following view on smart contracts under English law:

> Should smart contracts be treated as contracts for legal purposes? Contract law is concerned with the enforcement of promises. It might be argued that the automaticity of smart contracts, and the mechanistic way in which computer code operates, means that there is strictly no need for a party either to promise performance or to resort to the law to enforce a promise by their counterparty: the code will simply do what it has been programmed to do. Even if that is

22 Di Matteo, C. A. (2020). *The Cambridge Handbook of Smart Contracts, Blockchain Technology and Digital Platforms.* Cambridge: Cambridge University Press.

23 UK Jurisdiction Taskforce. (2019). *Legal Statement on Cryptoassets and Smart Contracts.* London: United Kingdom Government.

> right, however, we do not think it is a good reason for treating smart contracts as being different in principle from conventional contracts.

A similar approach was advanced by Lord Hodge, a UK Supreme Court Justice in his paper Law and Technological Change[24] as follows:

> At their simplest, [smart contracts] involve an instruction to the computer that if X happens then the computer is to act to make Y the result. ... In such a simple form, there should be no problem in upholding the existence of a contract in legal systems such as the common law (in which I include in this context Scots law), which assess the intention of the contracting parties objectively, so long as the parties were aware, when contracting, of the nature of the arrangement which they were entering into.

If it is correct that smart contracts including smart contract code are contracts as commonly understood, then it is open to the courts, and arbitral tribunals to apply concepts of contract law to such contracts, to look at the context in which they have been agreed, to imply terms, to strike down unconscionable terms, and where the governing law permits, to take account of duties of good faith and considerations of force majeure.

An interesting question is whether the parties to smart contracts will resort to the courts or arbitration. For some users of smart contracts, particularly the cryptocurrency enthusiasts and evangelists who hold the immutability of the blockchain and its consequential independence from centralised authorities as an article of faith, the idea of submitting to a central power such as a court, or even an arbitral tribunal applying laws is anathema.

In the DOA situation, the Ethereum community bent over backwards trying to avoid recourse to the courts, and eventually implemented a hard fork in the blockchain, which sacrificed the principle immutability of the code, but at least avoided the external intervention of a court thereby maintaining the independence of the system.

It may be reasonable to expect that there will be instances of wronged parties simply accepting their loss as a necessary sacrifice to the wider benefits conferred by a decentralised system.

However, as smart contracts gain wider currency, and less evangelical businesses make use of them, it seems likely that courts and tribunals will be called upon to settle disputes arising out of smart contracts, and with wider currency, it is likely that contracting parties will wish to use their preferred dispute resolution process including arbitration.

---

24 Hodge, L. (2019). *Law and technological change.* Edinburgh: British Irish Commercial Bar Association.

How arbitration is incorporated into a contract comprised purely of code is a difficult question. It seems likely that some sort of traditional contract wrapper would be required to achieve this.

8 The Suitability of Arbitration for Resolving Smart Contract Disputes

To the extent that there is a question of whether smart contracts are truly contracts, it might be questioned how arbitration is a suitable method to resolve disputes arising out of them. However, if one accepts the emerging consensus that smart contracts fall within the commonly accepted definition of a contract then there are many factors that make arbitration an attractive dispute resolution method for resolving smart contract disputes, and these are the usual factors that make arbitration attractive. The flexibility of the arbitration process may prove particularly useful in dealing with the novel issues arising out of smart contract disputes.

Arbitration is of course particularly well suited to resolving disputes involving technical subject matter, and there are already institutions dedicated to technology disputes, such as the Silicon Valley Arbitration and Mediation Center which has a 'Tech List' of arbitrators and mediators.[25] The possibility of having arbitrators from a technical or mixed technical and legal background may be particularly advantageous where all or part of the contract is expressed in code. In Poland, a new body called The Arbitration Court of the Blockchain and New Technologies Chamber of Commerce has been established as a specialist tribunal to deal with disputes arising out of blockchain applications.[26] Dubai International Financial Centre is also focusing on blockchain disputes.[27]

The international enforceability of arbitral awards through the New York Convention is another attractive factor given the international nature of blockchain transactions.

The confidentiality afforded by arbitration may be particularly beneficial to technology disputes where the subject matter is commercially sensitive. The ability to select a seat with strict confidentiality rules[28] confers an advantage over court proceedings. Of course, in investor state arbitration, the trend is towards transparency, and the requirement for transparency can be incorporated by agreement.

25 *See* https://svamc.org/tech-list/.
26 https://blockchaincourt.org/.
27 Bilbow, A., Opportunities for Blockchain Arbitration 17 July 2019, www.cdr-news.com.
28 Such as, for example, Scotland (*see* Rule 26 of the Scottish Arbitration Rules forming Schedule 1 to the Arbitration (Scotland) Act 2010).

9 USING BLOCKCHAIN IN ARBITRATION

Arbitration may be used to resolve problems thrown up by blockchain technology and smart contracts. Might that technology be used to improve arbitration? One can envisage a number of use cases for blockchain and perhaps also smart contracts in the arbitration sphere.

It has been suggested that in a smart contract situation, a dispute may be referred to an arbitrator automatically as part of a smart contract process which requires the contract to be paused, and a completed dispute form sent to the other contracting party.[29] The arbitration then proceeds, and the smart contract recommences when the award has been issued. This represents a fairly limited interface of blockchain and arbitration.

Some characteristics of blockchain technology may be of particular relevance to the arbitral process. In particular, the incorruptibility of data stored using blockchain, and its self-authenticating properties may be very useful at the enforcement stage, although it is fair to say that the drafters of New York Convention did not anticipate the advent of blockchain, and some innovation may be required.

Similarly, blockchain allows for a complete an unalterable record of the pleadings and evidence. In 2019, China's leading search engine Baidu launched a blockchain solution for legal arbitration, utilising the immutability of blockchain to provide a trustworthy log of evidence from the source.[30] This would guard against the uncommon, but not unheard of phenomenon of parties tampering with pleadings and evidence on document servers. The use of cryptographic hashes in blockchain technology mean that an alteration as slight as the deletion of a comma will result in a very different hash, which will immediately flag up an attempt to alter content.

Cryptocurrencies may have applications for deposits, and escrow accounts, although the volatility of some cryptocurrencies would have to be considered and addressed, perhaps through an arbitration specific crypto coin with the valued pegged to a reserve currency.

Ultimately, it seems unlikely that blockchain is going to have a massive impact on the *conduct* of traditional arbitrations as it is, for the most part merely enhancing elements of the traditional process.

Where smart contracts and blockchain are the subject matter of an arbitration, then that is going to have a significant impact on the capabilities of the tribunal to understand the subject matter and dispose of the dispute.

---

29 *See* the process set out in the website of the Blockchain Arbitration Forum: http://blockchainarbitrationforum.org/dispute-resolution/.

30 Wood, M. (September 2019). *Baidu Launches Judicial Arbitration Blockchain*. Retrieved from Ledger Insights: www.ledgerinsights.com/baidu-judicial-arbitration-blockchain/

However, it is the potential of blockchain technology to replace traditional dispute resolution, including arbitration, altogether, that is likely to have the biggest impact and that is explored in the next section.

10 Blockchain *Instead* of Arbitration

Perhaps the greatest potential impact of blockchain upon arbitration is where blockchain solutions are replacing traditional dispute resolution. There has been a lot of discussion as to whether robot arbitrators based on artificial intelligence are going to replace human arbitrators,[31] and that is considered below.

The more immediate threat is not artificial intelligence, but crowd sourced justice, as manifested in for example the Kleros project. On its website, Kleros describes itself as 'an open source online dispute resolution protocol which uses blockchain and crowdsourcing to fairly adjudicate disputes'.[32]

The idea of Kleros and other online juror sites is that they rely on the wisdom of the masses. The system works by referring disputes to online jurors who make a decision on the case. If the decision of an individual juror coincides with the decision of the majority, the juror is rewarded with a percentage of their investment. If they decide 'incorrectly' they lose a percentage of their investment. There is therefore an incentive to come to the 'right' decision ('right' in this context meaning the decision that most jurors reached). Kleros relies on game theory incentives.

From a traditional arbitration lawyer's point of view, there are so many immediately obvious problems with the Kleros system that it is difficult to take it seriously. Who would advise their client to subject their contract to such a random and theoretical system of dispute resolution?

And yet Kleros is gaining traction, and the driver is low value claims where traditional dispute resolution is uneconomical.

In their 'Long Paper'[33] setting out the system Kleros states:

> Cryptocurrencies are giving many the possibility of having their first bank account to send and receive money in a secure way. Cryptocurrencies are helping millions achieve financial inclusion. Kleros will do the same in access

---

31 *See* for example the articles by Sophie Nappert and Paul Cohen, March of the Robots, available at https://globalarbitrationreview.com/article/1080951/the-march-of-the-robots and *ROBOTS REDUX: Blockchain, AR and Quantum Computing Explained to Lawyers, Their Impact on the Arbitral Process, and Why The Time To Act Is Now.* Retrieved from www.researchgate.net/publication/335776761_ROBOTS_REDUX_Blockchain_AR_and_Quantum_Computing_Explained_to_Lawyers_Their_Impact_on_the_Arbitral_.

32 kleros.io/about/.

33 Clement Lesaege, W. G. (March 2020). *Kleros Long Paper v1.0.0.* Retrieved from Kleros.io: https://kleros.io/static/yellowpaper_en-28d8e155664f3f21578958a482f33bd1.pdf.

> to justice by enabling dispute resolution in a large number of contracts that are too costly to pursue in court. Just as Bitcoin brought 'banking for the unbanked', Kleros has the potential to bring 'justice for the unjusticed'.

This statement chimes with a truth that we all know: there is a value of dispute below which level is it not worth instructing lawyers, not worth going to court or arbitration, because is it uneconomical. There is certainly a value, and is in absolute terms quite a high value, below which it is not worth going to international arbitration.

There is therefore a market which is not catered for, an unmet need for cheap and effective dispute resolution. Systems like Kleros, and perhaps in due course Artificial Intelligence systems have the potential to fill that gap.

The question is whether this is the thin edge of the wedge? If, where the amount in dispute is low, parties are willing to forego their day in court, willing to forego detailed reasoned awards explaining the outcome, will they become accustomed to the idea?

What is a low value dispute? If the perception of 'low value' shifts upwards, will these new systems eat into the remunerative work being done by lawyers as well as catering to the 'unjusticed'? Time will tell, but there are other factors, developments in technology likely to have a more profound effect on smart contracts and the practice of arbitration on the near horizon.

11 FUTURE GAZING

For decades now we have been told that the end of the legal profession is nigh, and that lawyers, judges, arbitrators are all going to be swept away in a tide of automation and artificial intelligence. This has not come to pass, and commentators regularly assert that machines will never replace lawyers, and robots will never replace arbitrators, although they do all concede that we are starting to see Artificial Intelligence (AI) programmes predicting the outcomes of certain types of cases with remarkable accuracy.

Earlier in this chapter, two major limitations on the utility of smart contracts, and the ability to resolve disputes arising under them automatically were noted. The first is that smart contracts, reliant as they are upon if-then propositions, are not capable of dealing with complex concepts of law, such as reasonableness and good faith. The second is their limited ability to interface with the physical world.

Advancements in computer technology have the potential to overcome these problems with the consequence that disputes arising under such contracts are more likely to be avoided because of the smart contract's increased capacity to cater for variables. Where disputes do arise, the potential to deal with them in an automated way will be greatly enhanced.

11.1 Smart Contracts, Quantum Computing and Artificial Intelligence

For a smart contract programme to be capable of dealing with abstract legal concepts and catering for the endless variables in a complex contract would require a massive increase in computing power and capability. Of course, computing power is constantly growing. Moore's law holds that computers become twice as fast at half the price, every two years, and this has generally proved true to date.

Quantum computing combined with AI is going to increase the rate of progress exponentially. Traditional computers use silicon switches to store data. A switch may be on or off, represented by 1 or 0. That value is known as a 'bit' of data. In quantum computing the switch is capable of being on and off at the same time. This is known as a quantum bit, a 'qubit'. Multiple qubits increase computing power exponentially. The aim of quantum computing research is to achieve 'quantum supremacy'. This is where a quantum computer is able to carry out a task that a traditional computer cannot.

Google and NASA claim to have achieved quantum supremacy with their Sycamore computer.[34] They report that this computer has carried out a calculation in 3 minutes 20 seconds, that would take the most advanced supercomputer 10,000 years to complete. In other words, it is 1.5 billion times faster than a traditional supercomputer. The effect of such an advance in computing power on current technology is incomprehensible.

There is some debate as to whether or not what the Sycamore computer has achieved is truly to be regarded as quantum supremacy.[35] It is also important to understand that the calculation carried out by Sycamore was a random number generation exercise, not a practical computer application. It is, therefore, fair to say that we are currently in the early dawn of quantum computing, and it will be a number of years before they are of practical use.

However, when quantum computers come of age, they will impact on smart contracts, arbitration, and the practice of law generally, in a number of ways. In the first place, the sheer computing power of a quantum computer will allow it to overwhelm all current computer encryption, meaning that current computer security, and the encryption underpinning blockchain applications such as cryptocurrencies and smart contracts will be compromised. New quantum computer–based encryption will become necessary.

The other major consequence of this exponential increase in computing power is the effect that it will have upon artificial intelligence technology. As things stand, AI has little impact on the day-to-day practice of the law and does not have the capacity to materially enhance the functionality of smart contracts.

---

34 Arute, F. A. (2019, October 23). *Quantum Supremacy using a Programmable Superconducting Processor.* Retrieved from Nature: www.nature.com/articles/s41586-019-1666-5.

35 Cho, A. (2019, October 23). *IBM Casts Doubt on Google's Claims of Quantum Supremacy.* Retrieved from sciencemag.org: www.sciencemag.org/news/2019/10/ibm-casts-doubt-googles-claims-quantum-supremacy.

However, the capabilities of AI are advancing at a pace that some find alarming. The billionaire engineer and inventor, Elon Musk has predicted that the so-called technological singularity, when machine intelligence surpasses human intelligence and accelerates at an incomprehensible rate could occur by 2025.[36] That is a controversial point of view, but if a fully functioning quantum computer can be developed, the technological singularity cannot be too far behind.

The combined effect of quantum computing and advances in AI on automation and the capacity of smart contract programmes to deal with a wide range of contractual situations are not possible to predict with any accuracy. What can be said is that at the moment, there is little point in trying to create smart contract capable of dealing with complex contractual relationships because the time effort and computing power needed is disproportionate to the cost savings to be gained. When computing power becomes, for practical purposes, unlimited, that drag on progress disappears. A computer that is capable of mapping and catering for every conceivable outcome in a complex contractual situation, and interfacing with the real world through advanced robotics and all seeing oracles has the potential to replace some lawyers, to say the very least.

12 Conclusions

Amara's law states that 'we tend to overestimate the effect of a technology in the short run and underestimate the effect in the long run'[37] There is a good deal of complacency in the legal profession about the likelihood of technology threatening the traditional role of lawyers in drafting contracts and resolving disputes.

There is a huge amount of hype around all things blockchain, and there are parallels with the dotcom bubble of the late 1990s. One company saw its share value surge 394% simply by adding the word 'blockchain' to its name.[38]

Whilst we can already see instances of smart contracts replacing intermediaries and obviating disputes (in parametric insurance policies for example), there has been little effect on the legal profession to date.

In the short term, it is reasonable to suppose that there will be an increase in demand for specialist smart contract drafting lawyers, who are able to code, or know enough about code to ensure that the tenets of the contract are reflected in the code. It is also

36 Elon Musk claims AI will overtake humans 'in less than five years', The Independent, 27 July 2020. Retrieved from www.independent.co.uk/life-style/gadgets-and-tech/news/elon-musk-artificial-intelligence-ai-singularity-a9640196.html.

37 Ratcliffe, S. (ed.) (2016). *Roy Amara 1925-2007, American Futurologist.* Oxford Essential Quotations (4th ed.). Oxford: Oxford University Press.
The Cambridge Handbook of Smart Contracts, Blockchain Technology and Digital Platforms (Cambridge Law Handbooks) (p. 18). Cambridge University Press. Kindle Edition.

38 Bloomberg, 27 October 2017. Retrieved from www.bloomberg.com/news/articles/2017-10-27/what-s-in-a-name-u-k-stock-surges-394-on-blockchain-rebrand.

reasonable to suppose that, as the use of smart contracts increases, there will be growth in disputes arising out of smart contracts that have gone wrong, and that will require a specialist breed of arbitrators and arbitration lawyers who understand the concepts involved.

With advances in AI and quantum computing, it is reasonable to suppose that increasingly complex contractual relationships will be reduced to smart contract form, and that this too will increase the need for code competent lawyers and arbitrators.

However, at some point in the future, when AI scientists have broken through the technical singularity, and quantum computing scientists have achieved true quantum supremacy, will the demand for lawyers survive? When the average desktop computer, or perhaps even the average smartphone is able to hold the whole of the accumulated knowledge of the human race on its tiny circuits, has intelligence surpassing the greatest human minds, and can communicate with you naturally and fluently, will the world need more or fewer lawyers?

Smart contracts are not going to take away lawyers' jobs and obviate the need for arbitration in the short term. On the contrary, the expansion of the use of smart contracts is going to increase the need for specialist lawyers and arbitrators. The longer-term picture is not clear, but it is highly probable that the convergence of smart contract technology, increasing powerful artificial intelligence applications, and quantum computing will be disruptive to the arbitration sector.

Elon Musk made an interesting observation on what he saw as a refusal to take the dangers posed by AI seriously:

> My assessment about why AI is overlooked by very smart people is that very smart people do not think a computer can ever be as smart as they are. And this is hubris and obviously false.

Whilst there is no immediate existential threat to the practice of arbitration, there is every likelihood that advances in technology combined with existing pressures on cost and efficiency will drive demand for automated contracts, and automated dispute resolution in lower value disputes. This will result in an expansion of justice as lower value, commercially unviable disputes become capable of being resolved economically. It is at least possible that when such programmes are accepted in respect of lower value disputes that the definition of 'lower value' shifts to include higher value work, currently carried out by lawyers.

Of course, the availability of technology capable of arbitrating a dispute does not mean the users of arbitration will wish to deal with machines rather than humans, but on any view, it is important that lawyers and arbitrators understand how emerging technologies may impact the practice of arbitration, and engage with those technologies.

Chapter 20 ODR in Canada

Karim Benyekhlef and Nicolas Vermeys

1 Introduction

Contributing a chapter to a book on a topic such as online dispute resolution (ODR) presents an interesting conundrum since the concept of ODR, as any reader perusing this tome can confirm, has many definitions. Therefore, as we explained in a previous edition of this very publication,[1] testifying as to the implementation and impact of ODR in a given country – in the present case, Canada – will depend on the definition one chooses to adopt to circumscribe the very notion of *online dispute resolution*.

If ODR is interpreted broadly – as some argue it should[2] – as being the use of online environments to facilitate communications and dispute resolution,[3] then it could be stated that ODR has made tremendous strides within the Canadian legal environment. After all, numerous courts, tribunals, mediation associations, and arbitration chambers have incorporated online tools into their practices.[4] However, if we accept a more conventional definition of ODR as being a process that 'utilizes the Internet as a more efficient medium for parties to resolve their disputes through a variety of ADR methods',[5] and that 'brings disputing parties together "online" to participate in a dialogue about resolving their dispute',[6] then ODR's impact on the Canadian legal landscape – while undeniable – remains limited.[7] Finally, if ODR is merely seen as an online transposition of *alternative dispute resolution* (ADR) systems and processes, which, as

---

1 N.W. Vermeys and K. Benyekhlef, "ODR and the Courts", in M.S. Abdel Wahab, E. Katsh and D. Rainey (eds.), *Online Dispute Resolution: Theory and Practice*, The Hague, Eleven International Publishing, 2012, p. 295.

2 A. Lodder, "The Third Party and Beyond. An Analysis of the Different Parties, in Particular the Fifth, Involved in Online Dispute Resolution", (2006) 15(2) *Information and Communications Technology Law* 144. G. Kaufmann-Kohler and T. Schultz, *Online Dispute Resolution: Challenges for Contemporary Justice*, The Hague, Kluwer law international, 2004, p. 5.

3 J. Hörlne, "Online Dispute Resolution", in R. Bernstein, J.A. Tackaberry and A.L. Marriott, *Bernstein's Handbook of Arbitration and Dispute Resolution Practice*, Volume 1, 4th ed., London, Sweet & Maxwell, 2003, p. 782, para. 12-004.

4 We provided a detailed example of this in a 2016 study for the Government of Quebec. *See*: N. Vermeys and E. Amar, with the collaboration of V. Gautrais, "Le dépôt technologique des documents", 2016, available at: www.cyberjustice.ca/files/sites/102/WP15-1.pdf.

5 This definition is taken from the syllabus of an online course offered at Harvard. *See*: http://cyber.law.harvard.edu/olds/ecommerce/disputestext.html.

6 *Ibid.*

7 This will be addressed in Section 2 of this article.

their name clearly states, serve as an alternative to the Court system,[8] then – outside a few exceptions[9] – ODR has simply failed to leave its mark in the field of dispute resolution within Canada.

We would of course reject this last conception of ODR since it implies that courts cannot take part in the ODR movement. We believe this to be inaccurate since, as Thomas Schultz put it:

> Cybercourts are simply court proceedings that use exclusively (or almost exclusively) electronic communication means. They should be, and often are, considered to be part of the ODR movement, for two reasons. First, because the ODR movement emerged because of the clash between the ubiquity of the Internet and the territoriality of traditional, offline dispute resolution mechanisms. The term ODR is thus opposed to offline dispute resolution mechanisms, not to courts. Online ADR is only one part of ODR. Second, courts do not only provide litigation. As I said before, there also is court-based mediation and non-binding arbitration.[10]

This is especially true in Canada where court annexed ADR is more and more common. For example, Quebec courts offer judicial settlement conferences, which are a form of mediation.[11] The small claims division of that province's provincial court also offers mediation services to litigants prior to trial.[12] As we shall see in the fourth part of this article (Section 4 – Rebirth: How Virtual Tribunals are Creating a Golden Age of ODR in Canada), this trend is also true for online dispute resolution where courts are

8 "ODR draws its main themes and concepts from alternative dispute resolution (ADR) processes such as negotiation, mediation, and arbitration. ODR uses the opportunities provided by the Internet not only to employ these processes in the online environment but also to enhance these processes when they are used to resolve conflicts in offline environments. [...] Like ADR [...] at its core is the idea of providing dispute resolution in a more flexible and efficient manner than is typical with courts and litigation". E. Katsh and J. Rifkin, *Online Dispute Resolution*, San Francisco, CA, Jossey-Bass, 2001, p. 2. *See also*: J. Hörlne, "Online Dispute Resolution", in R. Bernstein, J.A. Tackaberry and A.L. Marriott, *Bernstein's Handbook of Arbitration and Dispute Resolution Practice*, Volume 1, 4th ed., London, Sweet & Maxwell, 2003, p. 782, para. 12-004.

9 *See* Section 2 of this article.

10 T. Schultz, "An Essay on the Role of Government for ODR: Theoretical Considerations about the Future of ODR", *Proceedings of the UNECE Forum on ODR 2003*, p. 5, available at: www.mediate.com/Integrating/docs/Schultz.pdf.

11 *See* Sections 161 through 165 of the *Code of Civil Procedure*, CQLR c C-25.01. As explained in section 162 of the Code: "The purpose of a settlement conference is to facilitate dialogue between the parties to help them better understand and assess their respective needs, interests and positions, and explore solutions that may lead to a mutually satisfactory agreement to resolve the dispute." For an analysis of the effectiveness of these processes, *see*: J.-F. Roberge, *The Feeling of Access to Justice and the Amicable Settlement Conference. Research report on the experience of litigants and lawyers at the Quebec Superior Court and the Court of Quebec*, University of Sherbrooke, 1 December 2014, available at: www.tribunaux.qc.ca/c-superieure/pdf/rech_exp_justiciables_cs_cq.pdf.

12 *See*: www.justice.gouv.qc.ca/en/your-disputes/small-claims/mediation-at-the-small-claims-division/.

incorporating classic ODR mechanisms such as online negotiation and mediation into their processes. Of course, before addressing the present and future of ODR in Canada, one must understand its past. This article will therefore start with presenting how ODR emerged in the country (Section 2 – Montreal: The Birthplace of ODR Systems), and how it evolved to where it is today (Section 3 – Growing Pains: Hits and Misses in the Development of ODR Platforms in Canada).

2 Montreal: The Birthplace of ODR Systems

At first glance, discussing ODR from a national perspective seems counterintuitive since the online nature of ODR tools and platforms lends itself to international and cross-border applications. Therefore, it's difficult to speak of truly and uniquely Canadian ODR practices or applications. That being said, as stated by Arthur Pearlstein, Bryan Hanson and Noam Ebner in a previous edition of this book,

> Canada has been home to ODR initiatives since the mid-to-late 1990s, and is increasingly becoming home to a lively ODR scene [thanks to] innovative practice initiatives and research [...] led by practitioners and academics across Canada.[13]

In fact, it remains undeniable that the ODR movement has some Canadian roots, as its emergence can notably be traced back to work undertaken by researchers at the *Centre de recherche en droit public* (the CRDP),[14] under the guidance of one of the authors of this article.[15] This research led to the launch of three of the very first ODR platforms in the World: the Cybertribunal (Section 2.1), eResolution (Section 2.2), and ECODIR (Section 2.3).

2.1 The Cybertribunal

While opinions vary as to the exact moment ODR was created, and who should be credited with its 'invention',[16] Canadians can boast that the Cybertribunal, the first ODR platform in the Western World to offer the now classic process of what is

13 A. Pearlstein, B. Hanson and N. Ebner, "ODR in North America", in M.S. Abdel Wahab, E. Katsh and D. Rainey (eds.), *Online Dispute Resolution: Theory and Practice*, The Hague, Eleven International Publishing, 2012, p. 443, at p. 459.

14 *See* www.crdp.umontreal.ca/.

15 Karim Benyekhlef.

16 As Richard Susskind explains, "This phenomenon emerged in the 1990s as a branch of ADR". *See* R. Susskind, *Online Courts and the Future of Justice*, Oxford, Oxford University Press, 2019, p. 61.

described in the UNCITRAL Technical Notes on Online Dispute Resolution as 'negotiation; facilitated settlement; and a third (final) stage',[17] was developed on Canadian soil. While other contemporaneous initiatives, such as the Online Ombuds Office[18] and the Virtual Magistrate,[19] could also be credited with initiating the ODR movement, these systems mostly relied on an email interface and arbitration, rather than offering an online platform integrating a slew of services including negotiation, mediation and arbitration.[20]

The inception of the Cybertribunal can be traced back to 1996, a defining year in the ODR 'movement'. On 22nd May of that year, Henri H. Perritt Jr. organized what was, in our knowledge, one of the very first – if not the first – seminars on the topic of 'Electronic Dispute Resolution'.[21] In parallel to this event, researchers at the CRDP started to work on the first book in French to focus on how the then nascent Internet would impact legal relationships.[22] In preparing the initial draft of this publication, an important problem came to light: with the Internet opening up to the general public, cross-border disputes related to informational transactions would inevitably occur. This created somewhat of a problem since, if a conflict were to arise between – for example – a Canadian consumer and a U.S. merchant, there was no clear way of establishing how it would be addressed. Which national law would apply? Through which medium should this dispute be resolved? In other words: which mode of dispute resolution could best allow for the treatment of disputes that arose in cyberspace?

A hypothesis soon took form: As these disputes were born on the Internet, they should be resolved using this same medium. Of course, since traditional courts had no online presence or foothold at the time, and since their very dominion over online disputes was the subject of much debate,[23] there became a need to go beyond the strict framework of traditional dispute resolution in order to avoid the judicialization of online conflicts. This is how the idea of incorporating the principles of alternative dispute resolution (ADR) within an online platform first emerged.[24]

---

17 *UNCITRAL Technical Notes on Online Dispute Resolution*, section 3, Art. 18.

18 *See* E. Katsh, "The Online Ombuds Office: Adapting Dispute Resolution to Cyberspace", available at: www.umass.edu/dispute/ncair/katsh.htm.

19 *See* J. Osen, "The Virtual Magistrate", (1996) 9 *Network Security* 18.

20 *See*: K. Benyekhlef and F. Gélinas, "Online Dispute Resolution", (2005) 10-2 *Lex Electronica* 1, 88-91, available at: www.lex-electronica.org/docs/articles_87.pdf.

21 Among the participants were Karim Benyekhlef, Ethan Katsh, Lawrence Lessig, A. Michael Froomkin, Pamela Samuelson and David Post. *See* H.H. Perritt Jr., "Electronic Dispute Resolution NCAIR Conference Washington, D.C.", (1996), available at: https://mediate.com/articles/perritt.cfm. For the conference program, *see* "Dispute Resolution Conference", available at: www.umass.edu/dispute/ncair/.

22 P. Trudel, F. Abran, K. Benyekhlef and S. Hein, *Droit du cyberspace*, Montréal, Thémis, 1997.

23 *See* J.P. Barlow, "A Declaration of Independence of Cyberspace", (1996), available at: www.eff.org/cyberspace-independence.

24 For more on this topic *see*: K. Benyekhlef and F. Gélinas, "Online Dispute Resolution", (2005) 10-2 *Lex Electronica*, available at: www.lex-electronica.org/s/939.

Two years later, thanks in part to a $300,000 grant From the Government of Quebec's *Information Superhighway Fund*,[25] the Cybertribunal was officially launched. As explained by its instigators, the platform was based on the following postulates:

- With the spread of various information transactions on the Internet, conflicts will arise that traditional national law will not be able to handle owing to the a-territorial nature of cyberspace;
- In the open environment of cyberspace, no authority can claim to have a monopoly over establishing or enforcing rules. Parties are often able to move elsewhere to escape rules that do not suit them;
- Mediation and arbitration processes, as well as other dispute resolution methods, at least partially help to establish frameworks and processes through which rules may be applied in cyberspace;
- Appropriate dispute prevention and resolution mechanisms, based not on government regulations but on other mechanisms designed to ensure effectiveness, are a necessary component of the framework for transactions in cyberspace.[26]

Of course, the Cybertribunal was not a virtual tribunal *per se*, as it was not a body created by parliament in concordance with the relevant constitutional dispositions,[27] but it did serve to settle a number of disputes. Although this number remained relatively low,[28] the platform did help to demonstrate that online dispute resolution was a viable means of

25 This fund was created on 1 June 1994.

26 K. Benyekhlef and F. Gélinas, "Online Dispute Resolution", (2005) 10-2 *Lex Electronica*, p. 3, available at: www.lex-electronica.org/s/939.

27 *See* Sections 92 and 101 of *The Constitution Act*, 1867, 30 & 31 Vict, c 3.

28 In all, approximately 50 cases were settled using the platform.

settling certain types of what can be qualified as low intensity disputes,[29] i.e., claims for which the complexity of the issue at hand remains relatively low.[30]

That being said, the launch of the first Canadian platform did not come without its detractors. In fact, the legal community being what it is, the initiative did not receive the warmest welcome from those within said community both locally and abroad. Among the criticisms, two arguments were most recurrent:

1. It is not possible to develop online mediation and arbitration procedures because of legal considerations;[31]
2. The principles of ADR require that both parties be present in the same place and at the same time in order to achieve conditions conducive to the dispute resolution process.

The first argument was proven to be unfounded since this new approach to dispute resolution was not intended to change the standards of litigation, but rather to provide a new tool and an effective way to resolve a novel type of dispute where the courts, for reasons relating to competency, distance and costs,[32] were simply out-of-reach. While most would argue that free and swift access to a neutral and competent judge remains the better mechanism to attain justice, the choice has never been between an ideal system

29 For an analysis of the concept of 'low intensity' claims, *see* K. Benyekhlef and E. Amar, "Some Reflections on the Future of Online Dispute Resolution. From e-platform to Algorithms", in I. Barral (dir.), *La resolución de conflictos con consumidores: de la mediación a las ODR*, Madrid, Editorial Reus, 2018, 229, at p. 232.

30 Most legal literature will use the expression 'low-value, high-volume cases' to qualify these types of claims as they usually have low monetary values. While the expression has garnered much support, we feel it presents a skewed view of these types of cases. As we've stated elsewhere: '"low-value, high-volume" is a somewhat difficult term to define because it will vary according to income level and priorities – and that's not even taking into account disparities between countries.' *See* K. Benyekhlef and N. Vermeys, "'Low-Value, High-Volume' Disputes: Defining the Undefinable", (2014) *Slaw*, available at: www.slaw.ca/2014/01/29/low-value-high-volume-disputes-defining-the-indefinable/. It should be noted that this position was shared by the United Nations Commission on International Trade Law's (UNCITRAL) Working group on online dispute resolution. *See*: Report of Working Group III (Online Dispute Resolution) on the work of its twenty-eigth session (Vienna, 18-22 November 2013), p. 6: "In relation to the term 'high-volume', it was said that for a user of the Rules, the fact of whether or not the dispute arising out of that individual's transaction was one of a number of disputes would not be relevant [...] Following discussion it was decided to delete the words 'high-volume' from the preamble. [...] In relation to the term 'low-value' [...] in the preamble, diverging views were expressed in relation to whether that term ought to be defined. On the one hand, it was said that providing a definition would increase clarity as to when the Rules applied, and was said to be particularly relevant in that context from a consumer-protection standpoint. It was also said that any abuse of the use of the Rules would be limited if its scope was indeed limited to low-value transactions. On the other hand, it was said that creating a definition would be exceedingly difficult, not least because the definition of 'low-value' could change over time and across borders; in that respect, the Working Group recalled its agreement at its twenty-fourth session that such a definition ought not to be included in the Rules, but indicative information set out in guidelines".

31 With regard to the first argument, we invite the reader to read T. Schultz, *Réguler le commerce électronique par la resolution des litiges en ligne. Une approche critique*, Brussels, Bruyant, 2005.

32 For more on this issue *see*: C. Lavarone-Turcotte, *La resolution en ligne des conflits de consummation à l'aune de l'accès à la justice*, Montreal, Thémis, 2015.

and ODR, but rather between a system that is inaccessible for financial and geographical reasons and an accessible although imperfect way of settling a dispute.

As for the physical presence argument, it too was proven to be somewhat fallacious for two reasons. First, the very nature of the disputes that the platform sought to resolve – i.e. online disputes – already implied lack of presence as they were rooted in the use of the Internet. Second, never was it claimed that online dispute resolution prohibits the parties from meeting in person.

2.2 eResolution

On the heels of the conceptual success of the Cybertribunal, a decision was made to try and carry out a larger scale project. Hence was born eResolution, a public-private ODR venture aimed at settling domain name disputes.

In the early days of the Internet, conflicts quickly arose between trademark owners and domain name holders. Since domain names did not fall within any classic categorizations of intellectual property, certain individuals started to register domain names that corresponded with the trademarks of large companies. While some were doing this in good faith, others – later labelled 'cybersquatters' – would do so with the sole intention of either causing harm to the trademark owner or reselling said domain name at a profit.

Several considerations need to be highlighted in order to better understand how cybersquatters came to be. Let us remember that companies in the early 1990s did not realize the scale and importance that the Internet was going to take on for their business needs. In fact, many viewed the web as an academic tool, and a fad. They therefore did not feel it necessary to register 'their' domain names, i.e., those that were identical to their trademarked brands. However, since, as alluded to above, the domain name registration process does not require any sort of proof of ownership of the industrial or intellectual property rights associated with a given brand name, anyone willing to pay the registration fee could claim ownership of an otherwise protected trademark.

In order to put a stop to this emerging crisis,[33] the Internet Corporation for Assigned Names and Numbers (ICANN) felt it necessary to create a system through which domain name disputes could effectively and affordably be resolve. Therefore, in 1998, the United States National Telecommunications and Information Agency (NTIA), mandated the World Intellectual Property Organization (WIPO) to come up with such a system.

33 While the term crisis might seem strong, one must understand that the cybersquatting problem was then seen as a big enough threat that the US government saw it fit to adopt the Anticybersquatting Consumer Protection Act (ACPA), 15 U.S.C. § 1125(d).

The report[34] published by WIPO the following year as an answer to the NTIA's request drew much criticism, most notably because it granted WIPO a monopoly on domain name dispute resolution and allowed trademark holders to be granted the domain names they sought (or claimed were theirs) with ease, without consideration for criticism, parody, or other rights stemming from laws pertaining to freedom of expression. Therefore, a group composed of Canadian[35] and American[36] academics approached ICANN in order to offer their services in developing what was perceived as a 'fairer'[37] method of settling domain name disputes through an ODR platform based on the Cybertribunal. Concurrently,[38] ICANN adopted a series of official documents; the Uniform Domain-Name Dispute-Resolution Policy,[39] followed by a set of rules and procedures.[40] These rules established who could legitimately register a given domain name, and under what conditions.[41]

The requirements set out in the Procedures made it necessary to somewhat depart from the ODR processes implemented in the Cybertribunal platform, and create a new and unique platform that would be capable of resolving highly complex and numerous[42] domain name disputes online.[43] The eResolution process worked as follows:

- The complainant would have to sign onto the eResolution platform and fill out a form giving their personal information, information regarding the domain name holder (the respondent), information pertaining to the litigious domain name, and the grounds for the transfer or cancelation request. They could also upload evidentiary documents onto the platform.
- The respondent was then notified and was invited to also fill out the relevant forms and produce necessary evidence.
- Once both parties had filed the necessary documents, the appointed expert or three-person panel (depending on the case) would be given access to the documents.

34 "Final Report of the WIPO Internet Domain Name Process", (1999) available at: https://archive.icann.org/en/wipo/wipo-report.htm.

35 Karim Benyekhlef.

36 Ethan Katsh, Michael Froomkin, David Post and Janet Rifkin.

37 On the notion of fairness in cybersquatting cases, *see* M. Geist, "Fair.com: An Examination of the Allegations of Systemic Unfairness in the ICANN UDRP", (2001) available at: http://aix1.uottawa.ca/~geist/geistudrp.pdf; and M. Geist, "Fundamentally Fair.com? An Update on Bias Allegations and the ICANN UDRP", (2002) available at: http://aix1.uottawa.ca/~geist/fairupdate.pdf.

38 The full timeline is available at: www.icann.org/resources/pages/schedule-2012-02-25-en.

39 Available at: www.icann.org/resources/pages/policy-2012-02-25-en.

40 The archived Rules are available at: https://archive.icann.org/en/udrp/udrp-rules-24oct99.htm.

41 On this topic, *see* F. Gélinas, "U.D.R.P.: Utopie de la Décision Rapide et Pondérée ou Univers du Droit Réduit au Pragmatisme?", in V. Gautrais (dir.), *Droit du commerce électronique*, Montréal, Theémis, 2002, p. 577.

42 As of the date of the WIPO Final Report ("The Management of Internet Names and Addresses: Intellectual Property Issues", available at: https://archive.icann.org/en/wipo/FinalReport_1.html), nearly 7.2 million domain names had been registered.

43 K. Benyekhlef, "Online Consumer Dispute Resolution: A Narrative Around (And an Example of) Postmodern Law", (2016) 21 *Lex-Electronica.org* 57, 73.

- The expert's (or the panel's) decision would then be uploaded onto the eResolution website and sent to ICANN so that, if necessary, it could proceed to transfer the website to the complainant.[44]

Launched on 1 January 2000, eResolution would go on to handle nearly 500 domain name disputes in just under two years,[45] including some implicating very well-known brands (iphone.com, royalbankonline.com, universalpictures.com, starfrit.com, croatiaairlines.com, 2pac.com, cisco-online.com, federalcourtofcanada.com).

2.3 ECODIR

On 8 June 2000, a few short months after the launch of eResolution, the European Commission adopted its 'Directive on electronic commerce',[46] which opened the door to online dispute resolution initiatives:

> (1) Member States shall ensure that, in the event of disagreement between an information society service provider and the recipient of the service, their legislation does not hamper the use of out-of-court schemes, available under national law, for dispute settlement, including appropriate electronic means.
> (2) Member States shall encourage bodies responsible for the out-of-court settlement of, in particular, consumer disputes to operate in a way which provides adequate procedural guarantees for the parties concerned.
> (3) Member States shall encourage bodies responsible for out-of-court dispute settlement to inform the Commission of the significant decisions they take regarding information society services and to transmit any other information on the practices, usages or customs relating to electronic commerce.[47]

While this directive obviously did not apply to Canada, Canadian expertise was sought to lead an international and multidisciplinary team of researchers[48] charged with developing an ODR platform that was more than a simple online transposition of

44 K. Benyekhlef and F. Gélinas, "Online Dispute Resolution", (2005) 10-2 *Lex Electronica* 1, 117-126, available at: www.lex-electronica.org/docs/articles_87.pdf.

45 eResolution decisions are available here: www.disputes.org/index.htm.

46 Directive 2000/31/EC of the European Parliament and of the Council of 8 June 2000 on certain legal aspects of information society services, in particular electronic commerce, in the Internal Market, Official Journal L 178, 17 July 2000, pp. 0001-0016; available at: https://eur-lex.europa.eu/legal-content/EN/TXT/HTML/?uri=CELEX:32000L0031&from=EN.

47 Art. 17 of the Directive.

48 Isabelle de Lamberterie, from the *Centre national de la recherche scientifique* in France, Yves Poullet of the *Centre de recherches informatique et droit* at the University of Namur, and the technical team behind eResolution.

existing dispute resolution mechanisms. This team took on the task of analyzing European initiatives in the field of consumer law that used alternative methods of dispute resolution in order to establish the underlying issues pertaining to the use of ADR.[49] This allowed for the conceptualization of a web-based platform for the online resolution of consumer disputes that would fall within the parameters set forth by Article 17 of the Directive.

This platform, which would come to be known as ECODIR (for 'Electronic Consumer Dispute Resolution') became one of the most complete ODR tool suites of its time, and its process was simple. It consisted of two steps: First a private negotiation between the parties, and if said negotiation failed, they could call upon a mediator.

In order to treat both parties equally and fairly, the platform revolved around the use of forms. This provided for a better understanding of the problem and avoided getting lost in details that were unnecessary for the proper resolution of the dispute. Upon signing up on the platform, the consumer was asked to fill out an initial form aimed at describing the issue. He would then be invited to propose a settlement using a second form. This information was then made available to the merchant who was granted access to the same forms to make a counter proposal, and so on. Parties were given 18 days to settle the issue on their own using this mechanism before the mediation phase would be initiated. Like during the negotiation phase, the mediator who was called upon to intervene in the case had a set of functionalities at his disposal that made it possible to hold the mediation process entirely online. These included access to a secure and private space to exchange with the parties, as well as the possibility of filing documents relevant to the dispute in order to discuss them with the parties.[50]

Despite being well received by stakeholders after its initial launch in October of 2001, ECODIR never really became more than the successful completion of a research project. While the reasons the platform did not reach the heights of further incarnations of the ODR process it helped to create are numerous, the fact that the European Commission had not earmarked funds for the deployment of such a platform within its service offering to European consumers surely stands out as one of the main barriers to its success.

49 This lead to the drafting of two studies: I. de Lamberterie *et al.*, "Le 'Online' dans le règlement extrajudiciaire des conflits entre consommateurs et entreprises. Étude de faisabilité", 2000; and Y. Poullet *et al.*, "Evaluation of the Legal Issues involved in the Implementation of an Extrajudicial Dispute Settlement System", 2000.

50 For a more detailed analysis of the ECODIR process, *see*: L. Caplin, *Online Cross-Border Consumer Dispute Resolution: An Assessment of Its Potential and Analysis of the ECODIR Project*, Master's Thesis, 2004, pp. 64 and ss.

3 Growing Pains: Hits and Misses in the Development of ODR Platforms in Canada

Although it has a relatively small population of 37.59 million people,[51] Canada is the second largest country in the world and represents 6.7% of the planet's landmass.[52] As others have pointed out, this therefore 'creates a setting that is well positioned to achieve vast benefits from the integration of ODR principles into the resolution of disputes across many contexts'.[53] After all, certain populations and areas of the country have historically been underserved by the courts given their geographical isolation.[54] Keeping this in mind, and with the Cybertribunal and ECODIR serving as proofs of concept as to how ODR platforms could be deployed and used, and with eResolution – as well as some American endeavors such as SquareTrade –[55] further demonstrating that these same platforms could be financially viable, both private and public entities started developing and offering their own ODR platforms and services. While some tried to come up with new and novel ODR processes,[56] and to serve some of the aforementioned isolated communities,[57] others simply built on established methods to try and position themselves in this emerging market.[58]

During the first decade on the 21st century, the Canadian ODR landscape was therefore populated with a number of new offerings (Section 3.1), some more successful than others. While reasons for the lack of success of most platforms are numerous, two stood out – and continue to stand out to this day – as major hurdles (Section 3.2): *the lack of incentives to take part in ODR*, and *the lack of a proper business model for ODR service providers*.

51 Statistics Canada, "Population and Demography Statistics", (2019), available at: www.statcan.gc.ca/eng/subjects-start/population_and_demography.

52 "Countries in the World by Area", (2019), available at: www.nationsonline.org/oneworld/countries_by_area.htm.

53 A. Pearlstein, B. Hanson and N. Ebner, "ODR in North America", in M.S. Abdel Wahab, E. Katsh and D. Rainey (eds.), *Online Dispute Resolution: Theory and Practice*, The Hague, Eleven International Publishing, 2012, p. 443, at p. 459.

54 *See*, for example, T.C.W. Farrow, "What is Access to Justice", (2014) 51(3) *Osgoode Hall Law Journal* 957.

55 *See* S. Abernethy, "Building Large-Scale Online Dispute Resolution & Trustmark Systems", (2003) *Proceedings of the UNECE Forum on ODR 2003*, available at: www.mediate.com/Integrating/docs/Abernethy.pdf.

56 *See*, for example, the bling bidding processes put forth by Smartsettle. *See*: www.smartsettle.com/.

57 For example, Civil Resolution Tribunal staff 'have undertaken specialized training in cultural competency, particularly Indigenous cultural competency, assisting parties with mental health issues, and communicating effectively with distraught or angry parties.' *See*: S. Salter, "Civil Resolution Tribunal To Start Accepting Small Claims Under $5,000 June 1, 2017", (2017), available at: www.cbabc.org/News-Media/News/2017/Civil-Resolution-Tribunal-to-Start-Accepting-Small.

58 This was the case of the now defunct Novaforum. *See*: www.candoo.com/novaforum/procedures.html.

3.1 Canadian ODR Offerings

When discussing Canadian ODR offerings, the issue becomes that of establishing the boundaries of our dataset. After all, to once again quote Arthur Pearlstein, Bryan Hanson and Noam Ebner:

> Canada has an impressive history in alternative dispute resolution (ADR). There are many member organizations, educational initiatives, mediation centers, and individual practitioners throughout the country. This serves as a strong foundation on which to integrate ODR elements into ADR practices, in addition to new development.[59]

Keeping this in mind, to present an expansive view of all ODR offerings in the country seems unmanageable, especially when using the broadest definition of ODR put forth in our introduction, i.e. 'the use of online environments to facilitate communications and dispute resolution'.[60] Therefore, rather than to embark on this impossible endeavor, we thought it more pertinent and prudent, no matter their importance, to disregard ODR researchers,[61] enthusiasts,[62] supporters and users, and to limit ourselves to actual Canadian actors in the ODR process: platform developers (Section 3.1.1) and ODR service providers (Section 3.1.2).[63]

3.1.1 ODR Platform Developers

As we will see in Section 3.1.2 of this article, a number of ODR service providers have emerged across Canada, some using platforms that were built in-house, while others have relied on tools developed by United States[64] or international[65] companies with a foothold in Canada. This is not to say that there are no 'truly' Canadian ODR platform developers,

59 A. Pearlstein, B. Hanson and N. Ebner, "ODR in North America", in M.S. Abdel Wahab, E. Katsh and D. Rainey (eds.), *Online Dispute Resolution: Theory and Practice*, The Hague, Eleven International Publishing, 2012, p. 443, at p. 458.

60 J. Hörlne, "Online Dispute Resolution", in R. Bernstein, J.A. Tackaberry and A.L. Marriott, *Bernstein's Handbook of Arbitration and Dispute Resolution Practice*, Volume 1, 4th ed., London, Sweet & Maxwell, 2003, p. 782, para. 12-004.

61 *See*, for example, Concordia University's Internet Research Center, available at: http://interneg.concordia.ca/index.php; of Queen's Conflict Analysis Lab, available at: https://conflictanalytics.queenslaw.ca/.

62 For example, Osgoode Hall Law School has developed a certificate in ODR. *See*: www.osgoodepd.ca/wp-content/uploads/2019/11/2020-OPD-Certificate-in-Online-Dispute-Resolution_NewDates.pdf.

63 These actors are usually referred to as the 5th and 6th parties in the ODR process. *See* A.R. Lodder, "The Third Party and Beyond: An Analysis of the Different Parties, in Particular the Fifth, Involved in Online Dispute Resolution", (2008) 15(2) *Information and Communication Technology Law* 143.

64 For example, certain providers rely on Equivant. *See*: www.equivant.com/contact-us/.

65 For example, British Columbia's Civil Resolution Tribunal platform (https://civilresolutionbc.ca/) was built on a software developed by Salesforce. *See*: www.salesforce.com/.

but these are few and far apart. In fact, our research has only allowed us to identify three such entities: Smartsettle, the Cyberjustice Laboratory, and relative newcomer Siësde.

– **Smartsettle** (http://www.smartsettle.com/)
As explained by Arthur Pearlstein, Bryan Hanson and Noam Ebner:

> Smartsettle is a series of negotiation support systems developed by Canadian company iCan Solutions, Inc. Led by Ernest Thiessen, the Smartsettle team has developed systems aimed not only at helping parties exchange offers or identify middle ground, but at allowing them to identify opportunities for creating and gaining value that so often goes unnoticed in many traditional negotiations. Parties inform the platform of their real preferences and priorities, beyond what they are willing to share with the opposite party. In the event that parties reach agreement on their own, the platform can conduct an analysis of the agreement to see if it maximizes each party's gains, and offer the parties improved solutions which are at least as good as the one they reached on their own – and usually better. Parties can, of course, reject these offers and stay with their own solution; however, the advantages of the computer-optimized solution are usually very obvious to both parties.[66]

The company's main platform, Smartsettle Infinity, is presented as 'the world's most advanced negotiation system', as it 'can do what human minds alone cannot – model the problem, manage preference information, and quickly optimize solutions'.[67] Its other offering, Smartsettle ONE,[68] was one of the first systems to offer blind bidding,[69] and has been used to settle disputes across the globe.[70]

---

66 A. Pearlstein, B. Hanson and N. Ebner, "ODR in North America", in M.S. Abdel Wahab, E. Katsh and D. Rainey (eds.), *Online Dispute Resolution: Theory and Practice*, The Hague, Eleven International Publishing, 2012, p. 443, at p. 459.

67 *See*: www.smartsettle.com/smartsettle-infinity.

68 *See*: www.smartsettle.com/smartsettle-one.

69 Blind bidding can be defined as "an ODR negotiation process used to determine the quantum of an economic settlement for cases in which there is no question of liability or fault. Similar to an auction mechanism, it allows for parties to participate in an automated negotiation process in order to achieve a resolution." *See*: Department of Justice, Dispute Prevention and Resolution Division, "Dispute Resolution Reference Guide", (2012), available at: www.justice.gc.ca/eng/rp-pr/csj-sjc/dprs-sprd/res/drrg-mrrc/10.html.

70 For example, it was recently used to settle a much-publicized dispute in the UK. *See*: N. Hilborne, "Robot Mediator Settles First Ever Court Case", (2019), available at: www.legalfutures.co.uk/latest-news/robot-mediator-settles-first-ever-court-case. It should be pointed out that, while Smartsettle's technology is referred to as 'artificial intelligence' in this article, such claims are debated by certain experts. *See*: A.R. Lodder and E.M. Thiessen, "The Role of Artificial Intelligence in Online Dispute Resolution", (2003) *Proceedings of the UNECE Forum on ODR 2003*, available at: http://citeseerx.ist.psu.edu/viewdoc/download?doi=10.1.1.97.9137&rep=rep1&type=pdf.

– **The Cyberjustice Laboratory** (https://www.cyberjustice.ca/)[71]
Created in 2010 by professors Karim Benyekhlef (Université de Montréal) and Fabien Gélinas (McGill University), the Cyberjustice Laboratory is a hub for thought and creativity, where justice processes are modelled and re-imagined. More specifically, the Laboratory analyses the impact of technologies on justice and develops concrete technological tools that are adapted to the reality of justice systems. Benefitting from multidisciplinary academic expertise, the Laboratory's team is energized by a number of dynamic students as well as by seasoned researchers and professionals. In addition to its permanent team at the Université de Montréal and McGill University, the Laboratory has a pool of experts located around the world. Its international team brings together researchers from different universities and research, as well as local, national and international partners.

Among the Cyberjustice Laboratory's offerings is its 'Platform to Aid in the Resolution of Litigation electronically', or PARLe, a

> customizable platform [...] that facilitates dispute resolution before low-intensity cases go before the courts, and facilitates online dispute resolution in a timely and efficient manner using self-help tools and online negotiation, mediation or adjudication.[72]

Although it benefitted from multiple enhancements financed by numerous partners over the years, PARLe was initially created thanks to a research grant received from the Quebec Government to develop a 'platform to resolve litigation stemming from conflicts born on the Internet'[73] that could be built on the successful deployment of the Cybertribunal, eResolution, and ECODIR. What set PARLe apart from its predecessors, however, is the fact that the platform was never meant to be privately operated. Although PARLe offers negotiation, mediation, and adjudicative tools like previous platforms, it was not conceived as an alternative to the courts, but rather as a process that courts could use to alleviate strained dockets, and, more importantly, grant access to justice for a slew of neglected low intensity claims.[74]

---

71 For transparency reasons, we wish to remind the reader that the authors of this article are both members of the Cyberjustice Laboratory.

72 Cyberjustice Laboratory, *A Tale of Cyberjustice*, Montreal, 2020, p. 135.

73 This was the wording found in the initial grant application presented to the Quebec Ministry of Government Services (*Ministère des services gouvernementaux*).

74 It should be noted that PARLe is currently behind Quebec's PARLe project (www.opc.gouv.qc.ca/a-propos/parle/), the French Medicys platform (www.medicys.fr/), Ontario's Condominium Authority Tribunal (www.condoauthorityontario.ca/en-US/tribunal/) and the Quebec entity for the protection of health, safety and employment standards (CNESST)'s online system (www.cnesst.gouv.qc.ca/en).

– **Siësde** (https://siesde.com/)
SIËSDE Dispute Resolution Technologies 'is an interdisciplinary, legal tech company, based from the IBM Centre in Toronto, focused on developing dispute resolution technologies, system processes and solution generation specific to family law'.[75] The company's mandate is described as

> break[ing] down very complex and difficult legal processes into smaller and more manageable modules that can be streamlined, simplified and systemized, with the assistance of technology, for the sole purpose of minimizing, if not resolving human and legal disputes.[76]

As explained on SIËDE's website:

> SIËSDE Dispute Resolution Technologies, innovates, creates and prototypes legal and dispute resolution technologies specific to Family Law and Alternative Dispute Resolution processes such as mediation and collaborative law.
> SIËSDE's Platform of Technologies streamlines the family law process and facilitates problem solving technologies and dispute resolution tools for both professionals and the general public.[77]

The company offers a series of software solutions aimed at settling family law disputes, including a 'Digital Financial Disclosure Platform that minimizes client process times and maximizes professional efficiency', negotiation tools that allow 'professionals to link client files and lead clients visually through their negotiations', etc.

3.1.2 ODR Service Providers

Since the first Canadian ODR platform was launched in 1998, numerous ODR experiments followed with different degrees of success. As the number of platforms is now relatively substantial, it is difficult to present a detailed account of every project to have been launched over the years. Therefore, rather than to address the minutia of every current and past platform, we have chosen to present a table enumerating some of the most well-known ODR endeavors of the last 20 years. In order to present as much information as possible in an objective manner, we identified a series of criteria to be evaluated. We invite the reader to refer to the following elements in order to understand the scope of the analysis of each criterion:

75 *See*: www.crunchbase.com/organization/si%C3%ABsde#section-overview.
76 *Ibid.*
77 https://siesde.com/.

- **Ownership:** What type of institution owns the ODR platform? Is it a publicly funded platform offered by a foundation, a university, a government entity, or is it a privately-operated service? In the latter case, is the service for profit or not?
- **Headquarters:** Where in Canada is that institution headquartered? (City and province).
- **Jurisdiction:** In which jurisdiction does the platform operate? Does it only settle disputes in a given province, across the country or even internationally?
- **Dispute types:** Which type(s) of dispute does the platform deals with? Does it only serve a certain type of public (e.g. consumers) or does it ofer services in multiple legal areas and to different types of litigants?
- **Services:** Which services are available to users through the platform? Does it offer the classic negotiation-mediation-arbitration model or only some elements of it? In certain cases, as we will see, arbitration will be replaced by adjudication as some of the identified platforms are associated with governmentally sanctioned tribunals.
- **Price:** How much does it cost to use the ODR platform? While a few platforms are free, most do have the parties cover part or all of the operating costs and, some do aim to make a profit.

Platforms followed by the † symbol are those that are no longer in operation.

Table 20.1 List of Canadian ODR Service Providers[1]

Name	Ownership	Headquarters	Jurisdiction	Dispute Types	Services	Price
BidSettle†[2]	Private, for-profit	Saint-Lambert, Quebec	Across Canada	Civil[3]	Negotiation	Percentage
Canadian Commercial Arbitration Center4	Private, non-profit	Montreal, Quebec	Worldwide	Business	Arbitration	Multi.[5]
Canadian International Internet Dispute Resolution Centre[6]	Non-profit foundation[7]	Vancouver, British-Columbia	Worldwide	Domain name	Negotiation Adjudication	$425 (USD)[8]
Civil Resolution Tribunal[9]	Public, Government entity[10]	Victoria, British-Columbia	British-Columbia[11]	Multiple[12]	Online Help Negotiation Mediation Adjudication	Between $50-$200 (CAD)[13]

1 As they were covered in section 1 of this paper, the Cybertribunal and eResolution have not been catalogued in this list.
2 While the company is still in operation, it no longer offers ODR services. *See*: www.bidsettle.com/about-us/.
3 The platform settled disputes between individuals (civil disputes, grievances, unpaid invoices).
4 Although the CCAC's current practices do not necessarily promote the use of ODR, its previous incarnation, the Quebec National and International Commercial Arbitration Centre or CACNIQ did use online mechanisms. *See*: N. Solovay and C.K. Reed, *The Internet and Dispute Resolution*: Untangling the Web, New York, Law Journal Press, 2013, pp. 3-61.
5 *See*: https://ccac-adr.org/en/administrative-fees.
6 The platform has been active since 7th November 2019. *See*: https://ciidrc.org/canadian-organization-takes-on-global-domain-name-disputes/.
7 *See*: https://ciidrc.org/about-ciidrc/.
8 The service charges a non-refundable filing fee of USD $425 as well as case fees that can vary between USD $1050 and USD $2835. *See*: https://ciidrc.org/how-it-works/fee-schedule/.
9 The service is available since 13 July 2016. *See*: https://www2.gov.bc.ca/gov/content/housing-tenancy/strata-housing/resolving-disputes/the-civil-resolution-tribunal.
10 *See*: *Civil* Resolution Trib*unal Act*, SBC 2012, c 25.
11 *Ibid*.
12 Motor vehicle injury, Small claims, Strata property, Societies and cooperative associations. *See*: https://civilresolutionbc.ca/.
13 *See*: https://civilresolutionbc.ca/resources/crt-fees/.

Name	Ownership	Headquarters	Jurisdiction	Dispute Types	Services	Price
CNESST[14]	Public, Government entity	Montreal, Quebec	Quebec	Labor	Negotiation Mediation	Free
Condominium Authority Tribunal[15]	Public, Administrative body	Toronto, Ontario	Ontario	Condo[16]	Negotiation Mediation Adjudication	Multi.[17]
eQuibbly†[18]	Private, for-profit[19]	Toronto, Ontario	USA Canada	Civil Commercial[20]	Arbitration	Multi.[21]
Justicity[22]	Private, for-profit	Montreal, Quebec	Quebec[23]	Civil Commercial[24]	Mediation Arbitration	Multi.[25]

14 The tribunal was launched in 2020.
15 The tribunal was launched on 1st November 2017. *See*: www.condoauthorityontario.ca/en-US/news-and-media/new-authority-launches-online-resources-for-condo-owners-and-directors/.
16 Disputes about the issuance of records or to obtain an order requiring compliance with a settlement agreement reached previously on the CAT platform. *See*: www.condoauthorityontario.ca/en-US/tribunal/.
17 Costs vary between $25 for guided negotiation, $50 for assisted resolution (mediation), and $125 for a tribunal decision (adjudication). *See*: www.condoauthorityontario.ca/en-US/about-cao/fees/.
18 R. Ambrogi, "Online Dispute Resolution Site eQuibbly Shuts Down", (2016), available at: www.lawsitesblog.com/2016/03/online-dispute-resolution-site-equibbly-shuts-down.html.
19 *See*: https://web.archive.org/web/20140413204648/https://www.equibbly.com/faqs#head10.
20 *See*: https://web.archive.org/web/20140413204648/https://www.equibbly.com/faqs#head30.
21 There were three bundles of fees based on the complexity of the dispute ($149, $249 or $449 per party). *See*: https://web.archive.org/web/20140413215135/https://www.equibbly.com/pricing.
22 The platform was launched during the Covid-19 pandemic in 2020.
23 The platform technically does not specify jurisdiction, but as it is only offered in French, it remains mostly inaccessible outside of Quebec. Internationally, Justicity also has a foothold in France. See: https://justicity.fr/.
24 *See*: https://justicity.ca/offre/.
25 Fees range from $750 (CAN) for a half day to $1200 (CAN) for a day. The platform also offers multi-day options. *See*: https://justicity.ca/tarifs/.

Name	Ownership	Headquarters	Jurisdiction	Dispute Types	Services	Price
MyLawBC[26]	Public, government entity[27]	Vancouver, British-Columbia	British-Columbia	Multi.[28]	Negotiation Mediation	Free
Novaforum[29] †	Private, for-profit	Ottawa, Ontario	Worldwide	Commercial	Mediation Arbitration	$2 500 (CAN)[30]
PARLe-OPC[31]	Public, University	Montreal, Quebec	Qc.	Consumer	Negotiation Mediation[32]	Free
SmallClaimsBC	Non-profit	Vancouver, British-Columbia	British-Columbia	Small claims	Negotiation	Free
Sports Dispute Resolution Center of Canada[33]	Non-profit[34]	Montreal, Quebec	Canada	Sport disputes[35]	Facilitation Mediation Arbitration	Multi.[36]

26 The service is available since May 2016. *See*: https://mylawbc.com/assets/info/MLBCCommunicationKitSept2019.pdf.

27 MyLawBC is a non-profit organization created under the *Legal Services Society Act*, SBC 2002, c 30. *See*: https://mylawbc.com/info/lss.php.

28 The platform settles both family law (separation, divorce, abuse & family violence), and other civil (Missed mortgage payments, wills & personal planning) cases. *See*: https://mylawbc.com/.

29 Although Novaformu's website is still active, it has not been updated since 2000. For a description of the service as it existed at the time, *see*: N. Solovay and C.K. Reed, *The Internet and Dispute Resolution:* Untangling the Web, New York, Law Journal Press, 2013, pp. 3-64.

30 *See* G. Blackwell, "On-line ADR Helps Close Cases Quickly", (2003) *The Globe and Mail*, available at: www.theglobeandmail.com/technology/on-line-adr-helps-close-cases-quickly/article1049150/.

31 The service has been available since 7th November 2016. *See*: https://cyberjustice.openum.ca/actualites/2016/12/07/communique-de-presse-lancement-de-la-plateforme-parle-par-le-laboratoire-de-cyberjustice-et-loffice-de-la-protection-du-consommateur/.

32 www.opc.gouv.qc.ca/en/opc/parle/process/.

33 A. Pearlstein, B. Hanson and N. Ebner, "ODR in North America", in M.S. Abdel Wahab, E. Katsh and D. Rainey (eds.), *Online Dispute Resolution: Theory an*d Practice, The Hague, Eleven International Publishing, 2012, p. 443, at p. 459.

34 *See Physical Activi*ty and Sport Act, SC 2003, c 2, section 9.

35 *See* Physical Activity and Spo*rt Act*, SC 2003, c 2, section 10.

36 *See*: www.crdsc-sdrcc.ca/eng/fee-for-service-program.

3.2 Hurdles to the Development of ODR in Canada

The previous table allows us to draw a few conclusions regarding the evolution of ODR in Canada. First, the number of publicly funded ODR initiatives has grown at a much faster rate than private ODR offerings. Second, private ODR providers have had much more difficulty staying afloat then their public counterparts. In fact, of the four for-profit private ODR service providers we have identified (five if we count eResolution), only one is still advertising its services.[78]

As we've alluded to earlier, while there are many reasons that can explain this situation, two have stood out over time: *the lack of incentives to take part in ODR* (Section 3.2.1), and *the lack of a proper business model for ODR service providers* (Section 3.2.2).

3.2.1 The Lack of Incentives to Take Part in ODR

In order to become financially viable, ODR platforms operators have had to solve an important conundrum: how do you make people take part and invest in a nonbinding process? As we and others have posited elsewhere,[79] the success of eBay's ODR platform stems from the built-in incentive (most notably for merchants) to take part in the ODR process in good faith: those that do not will be excluded from the eBay community. Unfortunately, most other ODR platforms, especially those which do not benefit from public backing, offer no such incentives. For example, as mentioned earlier, and as we've described elsewhere,[80] the ECODIR platform presented in the first part of this article never managed to achieve numbers remotely similar to eBay's, even though it used similar technology, was aimed at a similar clientele and received backing from consumer watchdogs.[81] Although there are many factors that explain ECODIR's ultimate lack of success,[82] it quickly became obvious that, while consumers loved the

78 As of these writings, BidSettle stopped offering ODR services to concentrate on other offerings, while eQuibbly has officially closed down. As for the the NovaForum website, it has not been updated in 20 years. The only remaining player is Justicity, but as it was launched this year, it remains too early to tell how well the platform will do.

79 N.W. Vermeys and K. Benyekhlef, "ODR and the Courts", in M.S. Abdel Wahab, E. Katsh and D. Rainey, *Online Dispute Resolution: Theory and Practice*, The Hague, Eleven International Publishing, 2012, p. 295, at p. 307.

80 K. Benyekhlef, "Online Consumer Dispute Resolution: A Narrative Around (And an Example of) Postmodern Law", (2016) 21 *Lex Electronica* 57, 70.

81 *See* L. Caplin, *Online Cross-Border Consumer Dispute Resolution: An Assessment of Its Potential and Analysis of the ECODIR Project*, Master's Thesis, 2004.

82 K. Benyekhlef, "Online Consumer Dispute Resolution: A Narrative Around (And an Example of) Postmodern Law", (2016) 21 *Lex Electronica* 57, 72. *See also* L. Caplin, *Online Cross-Border Consumer Dispute Resolution: An Assessment of Its Potential and Analysis of the ECODIR Project*, Master's Thesis, 2004.

platform, merchants did not feel any incentive to accept an invitation to negotiate since they knew that they faced no repercussions should they refuse.[83] While recent European regulation has seen to offer a stronger incentive to parties to take part in private ODR initiatives should they find themselves in a dispute,[84] Canadian legislators have not necessarily followed suit. For example, in 2016, the province of Quebec adopted a new *Code of Civil Procedure* which now states that:

1. To prevent a potential dispute or resolve an existing one, the parties concerned, by mutual agreement, may opt for a private dispute prevention and resolution process.
   The main private dispute prevention and resolution processes are negotiation between the parties, and mediation and arbitration, in which the parties call on a third person to assist them. The parties may also resort to any other process that suits them and that they consider appropriate, whether or not it borrows from negotiation, mediation or arbitration.
   Parties must consider private prevention and resolution processes before referring their dispute to the courts.[85]

While stating that parties 'may opt for a private dispute prevention and resolution process' is a step in the right direction, it remains a far cry from the necessary incentive to force individuals into submitting their disputes to private ODR service providers.

3.2.2 The Lack of a Proper Business Model for ODR Service Providers

The funding model – or lack thereof – put forth by private platform administrators has historically constituted one of the biggest hindrances to the rise of ODR.[86] It goes without saying that, in neoliberal capitalist societies, private platforms need to be profitable to be sustainable. Therefore, development costs, administrative costs, mediator salaries, and so

---

83 P. Cortes, *Online Dispute Resolution for Consumers in the European Union*, London, Routledge, 2011, p. 73. The author quotes G. Kaufmann-Kohler & T. Schultz, *Online Dispute Resolution: Challenges for Contemporary Justice*, The Hague, Kluwer law international, 2004, p. 339.

84 Regulation (EU) No 524/2013 of the European Parliament and of the Council of 21 May 2013 on online dispute resolution for consumer disputes and amending Regulation (EC) No 2006/2004 and Directive 2009/22/EC. It should however be noted that statistics show that current legislative incentives remain insufficient. In fact, "In about 80% of disputes submitted to the ODR platform the case was closed automatically after 30 days because the trader had not reacted on the platform to the notification of the dispute and the invitation to propose an ADR entity to the consumer. Only in about 2% of cases did the parties agree on an ADR entity and was the platform therefore able to transmit the dispute to an ADR entity." *See*: Report from the Commission to the European Parliament, the Council and the European Economic and Social Committee on the application of Directive 2013/11/EU of the European Parliament and of the Council on alternative dispute resolution for consumer disputes and Regulation (EU) No 524/2013 of the European Parliament and of the Council on online dispute resolution for consumer disputes, COM/2019/425 final.

85 *Code of Civil Procedure*, CQLR c C-25.01.

86 *See* K. Benyekhlef, "Online Consumer Dispute Resolution: A Narrative Around (And an Example of) Postmodern Law", (2016) 21 *Lex Electronica* 57, 73; and P. Cortes, *Online Dispute Resolution for Consumers in the European Union*, London, Routledge, 2011, p. 75.

on, need to be built into a financing structure that transfers these costs to users. This leads to three possible scenarios: have the parties split the costs of ODR, have the losing party assume the costs, or have one party (in consumer cases, for example, the merchant) cover all costs.

Unfortunately, all three of these financing models contain major flaws. For example, in the province of Quebec, current estimations set the average cost of settling a consumer dispute online at roughly $150 (CAN).[87] While this amount is lower than the costs of going to trial,[88] and represents less than 10% of the amount of an average claim,[89] it will discourage the filing of many low intensity claim, those very types of claims that are ignored by the current court system, and that could therefore benefit most from ODR. This is obviously a problem if costs are shared, but even more problematic if the losing party has to absorb said costs. After all, a consumer who stands to lose the value of his or her claim as well as costs will feel disincentivized from using a given platform.[90] This last scenario also raises a seldom asked question: Who is the winner in a mediation? Isn't a mediated settlement, by definition, an understanding where both parties agree on the outcome? As this is the case, it becomes impossible to establish a 'winner' or a 'loser' in a win-win scenario.[91] Obviously, should the process move onto the third and final stage of arbitration or adjudication, then costs can be attributed by the deciding party, but as the nego-med-arb process was designed to limit the number of cases that actually reach that stage, this will seldom be useful.

The final option, therefore, is to have the cost of the proceedings be absorbed by the 'dominant' party (the merchant in a consumer case) when possible. This party can then incorporate ODR fees into the cost of doing business. Unfortunately, this also means that this party will be tempted to impose the choice of a given platform that it sees as being more amenable and, ultimately, a given third party (be it at the mediation or arbitration phase). Seeing as platforms, under this scenario, serve as a mere service provider for

87 These are the current numbers that we have been given by the *Office de la protection du consommateur*.

88 In Quebec, court fees for small claims matters range between $103 and $308 (CAN). *See*: www.justice.gouv.qc.ca/en/documentation-center/tariff-of-court-costs/small-claims.

89 The average claim on PARLe is around $2000 Canadian.

90 This also creates issues regarding predictability. As Jean-François Roberge and Veronique Fraser observed, predictability as to the outcome plays a strong role in a platform's acceptability. *See* J.-F. Roberge and V. Fraser, "Access to Commercial Justice: A Roadmap for Online Dispute Resolution (ODR) Design for Small and Medium-Sized Businesses (SMEs) Disputes", (2019) *Ohio State Journal on Dispute Resolution* (Forthcoming). Available at SSRN: https://ssrn.com/abstract=3299246, p. 17.

91 As David Larson explains: "Contrary to the adversarial approach of litigation, mediation emphasizes the importance of a "win-win" solution to the conflict with which both parties can feel satisfied". *See*: D. Allen Larson, "Artificial Intelligence: Robots, Avatars and the Demise of the Human Mediator", (2010) 25 *Ohio State Journal on Dispute Resolution*, 105, 154.

merchants, forum shopping for the most favorable platform becomes a risk.[92] There is therefore a clear conflict of interest between the fact that platform operators would then become financially beholden to merchants, and their obligation to be truly neutral during an ODR process opposing said merchants to third party consumers.[93]

As we've alluded to above, these and other reasons have made it difficult for private ODR service providers to strive in Canada. This has, however, allowed public ODR offerings to emerge.

4 Rebirth: How Virtual Tribunals are Creating a Golden Age of ODR in Canada

As referenced in our introduction, and as stated by Thomas Schultz, 'if we accept that courts can be part of the ODR movement if they provide dispute resolution online, we can think about the advantages that are specific to courts.'[94] The legal system can clearly benefit from the incorporation of ODR, and in a way, State-run ODR can serve to eliminate the hurdles private ODR initiatives still face, such as those of confidence and enforcement presented above.[95]

As we just stated, there have been few ODR success stories in Canada over the years.[96] While certain platform developers have prospered,[97] service providers have mostly failed to capture the conflict-resolution 'market' (for lack of a better word).

Although this is true in the private sphere, public ODR platforms are growing in popularity. Many courts and tribunal across Canada are currently studying how ODR could help make their processes more efficient and, at the same time, more accessible.

---

92 A similar observation has been made by Michael Geist in the case of domain name disputes. *See* M. Geist, "Fair.com: An Examination of the Allegations of Systemic Unfairness in the ICANN UDRP", (2001) available at: http://aix1.uottawa.ca/~geist/geistudrp.pdf; and M. Geist, "Fundamentally Fair.com? An Update on Bias Allegations and the ICANN UDRP", (2002) available at: http://aix1.uottawa.ca/~geist/fairupdate.pdf.

93 As one author puts it: "When not based on normative standards, dispute resolution is just another form of bureaucratic processing, the resolution of disagreements according to a set of tacit, often biased, intraorganizational, administrative norms (e.g., seller is always correct), that are defined by repeat players who 'capture' the system and use it for their private ends". *See* R.J. Condlin, "Online Dispute Resolution: Stinky, Repugnant, or Drab", (December 27, 2016). U of Maryland Legal Studies Research Paper No. 2016-40. Available at SSRN: https://ssrn.com/abstract=2873918, p. 5. This statement has been proven accurate in at least one reported case. *See* State of Minnesota, "National Arbitration Forum Barred from Credit Card and Consumer Arbitrations Under Agreement with Attorney General Swanson", (2009), available at: http://voiceofsandiego.org/wp-content/uploads/2013/05/arbitration2-052313-5.pdf.

94 T. Schultz, "An Essay on the Role of Government for ODR: Theoretical Considerations about the Future of ODR", *Proceedings of the UNECE Forum on ODR 2003*, p. 5, available at: www.odr.info/unece2003.

95 *Ibid.*

96 *See* K. Benyekhlef, "Online Consumer Dispute Resolution: A Narrative Around (And an Example of) Postmodern Law", (2016) 21 *Lex-Electronica.org* 57.

97 For example, Smart Settle has been around for decades. *See*: https://smartsettle.com/about-us/vision-speech/.

While most are years away from launching actual platforms, four such 'virtual tribunals' have seen the light of day in the past few years.

- **The Civil Resolution Tribunal** (https://civilresolutionbc.ca/)
  Established in 2012 through the adoption of the *Civil Resolution Tribunal Act*,[98] and subsequently launched in 2016, the Civil Resolution Tribunal (CRT) is an online court that allows for the resolution of disputes regarding small claims (up to $5,000), strata (condominium) disputes, motor vehicle injury disputes (under $50,000),[99] societies and cooperative association disputes, as well as shared accommodations and some housing disputes (under $5,000).[100]
  The CRT platform uses a customized version of Salesforce[101] to offer a process based on the classic ODR model of 'negotiation; facilitated settlement; and a third (final) stage'.[102] The current CRT process is as follows:

1. **Solution Explorer:** Plaintiffs are given access to the Solution Explorer, a free tool that helps them identify the right CRT application form for their type of dispute.
2. **Negotiation:** Parties are invited to talk through their dispute and try to reach an agreement.
3. **Facilitated settlement:** If parties cannot resolve their dispute by negotiation, a case manager will try to help them reach an agreement. Said agreement can be turned into an order, and be enforced like a court order.
4. **Decision:** If parties cannot reach an agreement by negotiation or facilitation, an independent CRT member will render a decision, which is enforceable like a court order.[103]

While numbers vary, roughly 450 disputes are filed every month. According to exit surveys, 65% of litigants would recommend the platform to a friend or relative with a similar issue.

- **The Condominium Authority Tribunal** (https://www.condoauthorityontario.ca/en-US/tribunal/)
  Established by part I.2 of Ontario's *Condominium Act*,[104] the Condominium Authority Tribunal (CAT) 'is a new online tribunal that helps to settle and decide

98 SBC 2012, c 25.
99 It should be mentioned that, as of these writings, the constitutionality of attributing the CRT jurisdiction over certain motor vehicle accident claims was successfully challenged. *See: Trial Lawyers Association of British Columbia* v *British Columbia (Attorney General)*, 2021 BCSC 348.
100 *See*: https://civilresolutionbc.ca/.
101 *See*: D. Thompson, "The Online Justice Experience in British Columbia", available at: www.scl.org/articles/3784-the-online-justice-experience-in-british-columbia.
102 United Nations Commission on International Trade Law, *UNCITRAL Technical Notes on Online Dispute Resolution*, New York, United Nations, 2017, Section III, Art. 18.
103 *See*: https://civilresolutionbc.ca/.
104 1998, SO 1998, c 19.

condominium-related disputes in Ontario'.[105] Working hand in hand with the Cyberjustice Laboratory,[106]

> [t]he CAT has developed an online dispute resolution system (CAT-ODR) to help people resolve their disputes conveniently, quickly and affordably, while encouraging everyone to work together in healthy condominium communities.[107]

Like the CRT's, the CAT's process was inspired by a classic ODR approach. However, it is presented in five main steps rather than four:
1. **Filing a case:** The plaintiff opens an online case file with the CAT.
2. **Joining a case:** The other party joins the case, which activates the negotiation stage.
3. **Negotiation:** The parties are invited to reach an agreement using online tools put at their disposal.
4. **Mediation:** If negotiation fails, a CAT mediator can be asked to join the case and help resolve the dispute.
5. **Tribunal Decision:** Should mediation prove to be unsuccessful, a CAT member will join the case and render a binding decision.[108]

The platform was initially launched in November 2017 and mainly focused on disputes about condominium corporation records (including the retention, sufficiency, and access to records by condominium owners). However, teams are constantly developing and adding new functions and tools to the platform to allow for other types of condominium-related disputes to be submitted.

As of these writings, while numerous cases have been filed using the platform, only 137 have made it all the way to the Tribunal decision stage.[109]

- **PARLe-OPC** (https://www.opc.gouv.qc.ca/a-propos/parle/)
  In 2016, Quebec's *Office de la protection du consommateur* (the Consumer protection agency, or OPC), the Cyberjustice Laboratory and the Department of Justice launched a joint pilot project aimed at helping Quebec consumers and merchants settle their disputes online rather than through the courts. The project – which has now become a permanent service offered by the OPC – uses the Cyberjustice Laboratory's Platform to Aid in the Resolution of Litigation Electronically or PARLe.

---

105 *See*: www.condoauthorityontario.ca/en-US/tribunal/.
106 *See*: www.cyberjustice.ca/en/actualites/2017/11/30/communique-le-tribunal-de-loffice-du-secteur-des-condominiums-de-lontario-choisit-la-plateforme-en-ligne-parle-du-laboratoire-de-cyberjustice-de-montreal/.
107 *See*: www.condoauthorityontario.ca/en-US/tribunal/.
108 *See*: www.condoauthorityontario.ca/en-US/tribunal/the-cat-process/.
109 *See*: www.canlii.org/en/on/oncat/.

While PARLe offers many different ODR tools, the OPC version of the platform is limited to negotiation and mediation. The PARLe-OPC process works as follows:

1. **Opening a consumer account:** A consumer with a grievance can contact the OPC to obtain connecting information to the platform. This is done to ensure that the consumer's case falls within the parameters of the service.
2. **Creating a file in connection with the problem:** The consumer logs on to the PARLe platform and fills out two forms, the first to explain the problem (defective product, hidden costs, etc.) and the second to specify the desired remedy (refund, rebate, etc.). Once the file is created, an invitation is sent to the merchant.
3. **Negotiation with the Merchant:** After receiving the consumer's proposal, the merchant can either accept the proposal or submit a counterproposal to start the negotiation process.
4. **Mediation:** If the parties consider that they cannot come to an agreement, or if no agreement is entered into 20 business days after the start of negotiations, a mediator can be asked to intervene in the file and help the parties find common ground.
5. Entering into an agreement and closing the file: Once an agreement has been entered into, a document that describes the details of that agreement is uploaded to the file.[110]

In rare cases when the process fails (the project boasts a 70% settlement rate), consumers are invited to submit their case to the small claims division of the *Cour du Quebec*. It should be pointed out, however, that most parties that do not reach a settlement are still content with how things unfolded and choose not to file a claim. In fact, 90% of all users claim to be satisfied with the process.

- **PARLe-CNESST** (https://www.cnesst.gouv.qc.ca/en)

  The CNESST (Commission des normes, de l'équité, de la santé et de la sécurité du travail)'s Labor standards division,[111] is the latest Canadian tribunal to offer an ODR platform. In fact, as of these writings, the platform has only been operational for a few months.

  With the help of the Cyberjustice Laboratory, the division's version of the PARLe platform provides for the application of the *Act Respecting Labour Standards*[112] ('ALS') and the management of resulting complaints that deal with dismissals not made for good and sufficient cause (i.e. unjustified dismissals),[113] as well as

110 *See* www.opc.gouv.qc.ca/en/opc/parle/process/. For a more detailed explanation of this process, *see* N. Vermeys and M.-F. Acevedo Lanas, "Online Dispute Resolution Platforms as a Public Service: How the Cyberjustice Laboratory's Platform to Aid in the Resolution of Litigation Electronically (PARLe) is Transforming the Canadian Justice System", in I. Barral Vinals (dir.), El sistema de ADR/ODR en conflictos de consumo: aproximacion critica y prospeccion de futuro, Barcelone, Atelier, 2019, p. 219.

111 The CNESST is made up of three major divisions (Labour standards, Pay equity, and Occupational health and safety). *See*: www.cnesst.gouv.qc.ca/Pages/accueil.aspx.

112 CQLR c N-1.1.

113 *Act respecting labour standards*, section 124.

prohibited practices.[114,115]

The CNESST process follows that of other implementations of the PARLe platform, but was obviously adapted to the specific context of employment disputes. The current PARLe-CNESST process is therefore as follows:

1. Creation of the file by the CNESST following a complaint by an employee;
2. Formulation of a proposal by the employee;
3. Verification by a mediator and invitation of the employer to join the file;
4. Negotiation (counter-offers) if necessary and possibility to proceed to mediation upon the request of one of the parties;
5. Mediation, when applicable;
6. Reaching of an agreement and creation of the resulting document.

As the platform was launched earlier this year, it remains too early to talk about statistics. However, as the SNESST is looking into broadening its ODR services, the system does seem to have met expectations.

The four previous examples serve to demonstrate what some authors have been claiming for years:

> [T]he courts can play an instrumental role in providing legitimacy through control. There are actually many advantages to utilizing an online court process (more traditional adjudication facilitated with technology) over a more informal ODR process. First, online courts have more predictable remedies in that the decisions are appealable and enforceable. Judicially mediated settlements are much easier to enforce as they can qualify as 'consent judgments' or as another form of enforceable instruments. Also, courts can benefit from the democratic accountability of judges. As an institution, judges have great symbolic capital in the field of dispute resolution. Additionally, online courts, as an arm of the state, have much greater authority to demand the accountability parties often desire from businesses than do private dispute resolution providers.[116]

For these and other reasons, and as we had stated in the previous edition of this book,[117] we believe that the future of ODR in Canada is inextricably linked to its incorporation into the publicly funded court system as a component of the legal process.

---

114 *Act respecting labour standards*, section 122 and following.

115 The division also deals with psychological or sexual harassment complaints, but those could not be settled using the platform as of these writings.

116 A. Pappas, "Online Court", *University of California, Los Angeles Journal of Law and Technology*, 2008, p. 17.

117 N.W. Vermeys and K. Benyekhlef, "ODR and the Courts", in M.S. Abdel Wahab, E. Katsh and D. Rainey (eds.), *Online Dispute Resolution: Theory and Practice*, The Hague, Eleven International Publishing, 2012, p. 295.

Furthermore, we would argue that, while current offerings mostly relate to what we define as low intensity claims (consumer disputes, housing disputes, traffic violations, etc.), courts and tribunals are now looking beyond these types of disputes to see how ODR can be harnessed to settle more complex disputes such as workers compensation cases.[118] We had already made this point in 2012,[119] and it remains true to this day.

5 CONCLUSION

Canada has been on the forefront of the ODR 'movement' since its inception in the mid-1990s, and while other countries have since caught up and are now exploiting ODR tools to offer private services to settle disputes or public platforms to increase access to justice, Canadian researchers remain active in finding new ways to improve these same ODR tools. For example, Canadian universities are currently leading a number of national and international research initiatives[120] to see how machine learning[121] and other

118 As we have seen, such is the case of Quebec's Commission des normes, de l'équité, de la santé et de la sécurité du travail.

119 N.W. Vermeys and K. Benyekhlef, "ODR and the Courts", in M.S. Abdel Wahab, E. Katsh and D. Rainey (eds.), *Online Dispute Resolution: Theory and Practice*, The Hague, Eleven International Publishing, 2012, p. 295.

120 One of these initiatives is the Autonomy through Cyberjustice Technologies and artificial intelligence (or 'ACT') project of which the authors of this article are the instigators. "The ACT partnership aims to leverage artificial intelligence (AI) to the service of justice stakeholders to improve conflict prevention and resolution. This project brings together a multidisciplinary and international team of 52 researchers and 44 partners representing a number of stakeholders including the world's leading research centres dedicated to the implementation and use of technologies in the field of justice (cyberjustice), litigants and legal professionals (justice stakeholders), as well as main users and developers of AI for justice in Canada." *See*: www.ajcact.org/en/ajc/presentation/.

121 Machine learning can be summarized as "[t]he capacity of a computer to learn from experience, i.e. to modify its processing on the basis of newly acquired information". *See*: https://en.oxforddictionaries.com/definition/machine_learning. Machine learning should be envisioned as a spectrum that ranges from relatively simple algorithms to complex self-teaching systems that could eventually mirror the human brain in their complexity (if not their structure). This later subset of machine learning is usually referred to as 'deep learning', i.e. "a sub-field of machine learning, where models inspired by how our brain works are expressed mathematically, and the parameters defining the mathematical models, which can be in the order of few thousands to 100+ million, are learned automatically from the data". *See* EDX, "Deep Learning Explained", (2018), available at: www.classcentral.com/course/edx-deep-learning-explained-8746. Deep learning relies on what are referred to as neural networks, an interconnected group of nodes said to be modeled after the human brain.

forms of artificial[122] and augmented[123] intelligence can be exploited to make the ODR process more efficient, accessible, and fair. Far from the idea of melding the third and fourth parties into a 'robot mediator' (which both AI and legal experts have continuously warned against[124]), this new field of research – which we have christened ODRAI for 'ODR aided by Augmented Intelligence' – is gaining tremendous grounds and should bear fruit in the coming years. As we've explained elsewhere:

> AI could be used to power case analysis tools,[125] or to 'offer a library of suggested approaches the disputants can utilize if they like'.[126] These and other 'predictive tools', as they are normally referred to, can offer information to parties on possible outcomes to their case, how similar cases faired, etc. For example, one could imagine that, through a study of similar facts and patterns found in other cases, an algorithm could give parties (including the mediator and tribunal) statistics as to the success rate of similar claims, the amount granted, etc.[127] These tools could facilitate settlements, make the tribunal's work easier, and create a certain predictability that is often lacking in ODR procedures.[128] In other words, incorporating machine learning capacities into

122 The classic definition of 'artificial intelligence' or, rather, the 'artificial intelligence problem' was drafted by those credited with branding the term, John McCarthy, Marvin L. Minsky, Nathaniel Rochester, and Claude E. Shannon. In their now famous paper, "A Proposal for the Dartmouth Summer Research Project on Artificial Intelligence", the authors defined artificial intelligence as: 'making a machine behave in ways that would be called intelligent if a human were so behaving'. *See*: J. McCarthy *et al.*, "A Proposal for the Dartmouth Summer Research Project on Artificial Intelligence", 31 August 1955. The paper has since been reprinted in AI Magazine Volume 27 Number 4 (2006), p. 10.

123 As Luc Julia explains, "[translation] AI should no longer signify 'artificial intelligence', but rather 'augmented intelligence'. [...] Whether we call them expert systems, machine learning, or deep learning, they are nothing else than what we humans have decided they are. All of these technologies serve the purpose of assisting us in accomplishing punctual tasks that are often repetitive and highly codified. They offer help to amplify our humanity and augment our physical or intellectual capacities but can in no way replace them. There is no artificial intelligence that escapes our control and will precipitate our extinction. There is augmented intelligence that must benefit from just regulation in order to support our own intelligence." *See*: L. Julia, *L'intelligence artificielle n'existe pas*, First Edition, Paris, 2019, pp. 118-151.

124 *See*, for example, J. Zeleznikow, "Can Artificial Intelligence and Online Dispute Resolution Enhance Efficiency and Effectiveness in Courts", (2017) 8 *International Journal for Court Administration* 30, 43.

125 A.J. Schmitz and C. Rule, *The New Handshake: Online Dispute Resolution and the Future of Consumer Protection*, Chicago, ABA, 2017, p. 133.

126 *Ibid.*

127 K. Benyekhlef and E. Amar, "Some Reflections on the Future of Online Dispute Resolution. From e-platform to Algorithms", in I. Barral (dir.), *La resolución de conflictos con consumidores: de la mediación a las ODR*, Madrid, Editorial Reus, 2018, 229, at p. 250.

128 For example, the Cyberjustice Laboratory is currently developing a chatbot aimed at helping parties in housing disputes. *See* K. Benyekhlef and E. Amar, "Some Reflections on the Future of Online Dispute Resolution. From e-platform to Algorithms", in I. Barral (dir.), *La resolución de conflictos con consumidores: de la mediación a las ODR*, Madrid, Editorial Reus, 2018, 229, at p. 247.

> ODR applications made available to the courts could go a long way in making the judicial system more accessible.[129,130]

In the meantime, however, while private ODR service providers continue their search for a business model that would make their platforms profitable, more and more Canadian courts and tribunals are looking into ODR processes as a means to help alleviate overburdened court dockets, improve access to justice, and - more generally - modernize a legal system that has come under fire by the public, and the courts themselves, as needing to harness technological changes in order to better serve its fundamental purpose.[131]

129 For an extensive presentation of how these tools could be employed, *see*: D. Thompson, "Creating New Pathways to Justice Using Simple Artificial Intelligence and Online Dispute Resolution", (2015) 1 *International Journal of Online Dispute Resolution* 1.

130 N. Vermeys and M.-F. Acevedo Lanas, "Online Dispute Resolution Platforms as a Public Service: How the Cyberjustice Laboratory's Platform to Aid in the Resolution of Litigation Electronically (PARLe) is Transforming the Canadian Justice System", in I. Barral Vinals (dir.), El sistema de ADR/ODR en conflictos de consumo: aproximacion critica y prospeccion de futuro, Barcelone, Atelier, 2019, p. 219.

131 Action Committee on Access to Justice in Civil and Family Matters, "Access to Civil & Family Justice - A Roadmap for Change", (2013), p. 15, available at: www.cfcj-fcjc.org/sites/default/files/docs/2013/AC_Report_English_Final.pdf.

Chapter 21 ODR and Innovation in the United States

*Amy J. Schmitz and Janet Martinez**

1 Introduction

Recent years have seen new technologies disrupting many established industries and institutions. A wide variety of breakthrough technologies, many highlighted in yearly reviews in the MIT Technology Review, are generating innovations that are changing how we live and work.[1] Moreover, Covid-19 has generated both large numbers of new disputes, as well as space for dispute resolution professionals to consider how they can fashion means for resolving and preventing disputes without travel or in-person meetings that could be unsafe due to Covid-19. As a result, developers and policymakers are scrambling to utilize technology to improve efficiency and provide business continuity.[2]

Consistent with this, processes associated with alternative or appropriate dispute resolution (ADR) are now yielding to a new age of online dispute resolution (ODR). ODR includes automated decision-making, as well as online negotiation, mediation, arbitration, community courts, and variations thereof. While ODR is not specifically defined in this book, a deluge of online options has developed over the past ten years, and now have accelerated in connection with Covid-19. Different benefits might emanate from setting parameters of the ODR field that are inclusive, or exclusive. Given the state of flux, we leave it to the reader to synthesize what advantages accrue from setting standards or opting for flexibility. What can be said is that ODR's efficiency, accessibility, and ease open new avenues to remedies.[3] Across many dispute domains, ODR allows individuals to resolve disputes more quickly, cheaply, and hopefully, fairly,

* We would like to thank Kelli Reichert, Henry Sivils and Claire Mendes for their research assistance.

1 *See* MIT Technology Review, Vol. 123, No. 2 (March-April 2020) p. 15 and previous annual reviews back to 2001.

2 Richard Susskind, Tomorrow's Lawyers: An Introduction to Your Future (Oxford: Oxford University Press 2013).

3 *Id. See also* Amy J. Schmitz and Colin Rule, The New Handshake: Online Dispute Resolution and the Future of Consumer Protection (Chicago: American Bar Association Section on Dispute Resolution 2017). *See also,* Amy J. Schmitz, *Building on OArb Attributes in Pursuit of Justice, in* Arbitration in the Digital Age: The Brave New World of Arbitration, 182-208 (edited by Maud Piers, Christian Aschauer, Karl-Franzens, Cambridge: Cambridge University Press 2018).

using technology as simple as the cellphone – without the costs or hassles of travel or time away from work.[4]

Accordingly, ODR has gained significant traction in the United States (U.S.). After canvasing ODR providers in the U.S., we found that commercial, small claims, and family disputes are leading the way in terms of ODR case types. A majority of ODR providers offer mediation and case management systems. These observations are based on our charting the seventy organizations and firms who identified themselves as ODR providers that offer services in the U.S. and volunteered listing with the National Center for Technology and Dispute Resolution (NCTDR). These are self-selected, without any independent review and verification, but do provide insight into diverse offerings by public, private, and nonprofit entities. See below Appendix A: Summary of Select U.S. ODR Providers, which is based on the larger chart that we compiled.[5]

Building on this momentum toward digitization, courts have joined the bandwagon by adopting ODR and developing e-courts.[6] Many jurisdictions in the U.S. are experimenting with ODR, with some, such as Utah, launching ambitious small claims e-courts seeking to replace in-person hearings.[7] This is just the tip of the iceberg, with over 50 courts also offering online processes for case types ranging from traffic tickets to divorce to small claims. (See Paul Embley, Ch. 9.) At the same time, groups such as the American Bar Association (ABA), the International Center for Online Dispute Resolution (ICODR), and the National Center for Technology and Dispute Resolution (NCTDR) are developing standards and best practices as we move to institutionalize ODR.[8]

In these efforts, efficiency is not the only goal. Our experience with ODR provides evidence that it may increase access to justice by allowing litigants to 'attend court' in a meaningful way.[9] Technology has opened new virtual doors to the courthouse for those that cannot afford the time and costs of in-person processes.[10] ODR seems to especially fill this need with respect to small claims, traffic, landlord-tenant, and similar smaller

4 Ethan Katsh and Colin Rule, *What We Know and Need to Know About Online Dispute Resolution,* 67 S.C. L Rev 329, 330 (2016). *See also,* Ethan Katsh and Orna Rabinovich-Einy, Digital Justice: Technology and the Internet of Disputes 1-25 (Oxford: Oxford University Press 2017).

5 See Amy J. Schmitz and Janet Martinez, ODR Providers Operating in the U.S. (August 27, 2020), at SSRN: https://ssrn.com/abstract=3599511.

6 Amy J. Schmitz, *Expanding Access to Remedies through E-Court Initiatives,* 67 Buffalo L. Rev. 101-173 (2019); Rebecca Love Kourlis et al., A Court Compass for Litigants (July 2016), http://iaals.du.edu/honoring-families/publications/court-compass-litigants.1%20-%20Nov.ashx.

7 *Id.*; *see also* Utah Courts Recent Press Notifications, Utah Courts (13 August 2020), www.utcourts.gov/utc/news/2020/08/13/to-tackle-the-unmet-legal-needs-crisis-utah-supreme-court-unanimously-endorses-a-pilot-program-to-assess-changes-to-the-governance-of-the-practice-of-law/.

8 ODR Standards, Principles, & Guidelines, at http://odr.info/standards/ (last visited March 14, 2021)..

9 J.J. Prescott, *Improving Access to Justice in State Courts with Platform Technology,* 70 Vand. L.R. 1993-1996 (2017).

10 *Id.* at 1995-1996. *See also* Schmitz, *supra* note 5, at 120-170.

dollar or less complex disputes.[11] Problem diagnosis built into ODR programs reduces the number of disputes from escalating into lawsuits, and online negotiation and mediation lead to consensual and quicker resolutions. Online court systems also encourage fee and judgement payments by incorporating automatic notices and payments into the process.[12] We are even seeing ODR used to resolve disputes over cryptocurrency and insurance in the blockchain.[13]

This book provides insight into the technical design, practice, social and legal policy of ODR. This chapter seeks to add to this story with a special focus on the U.S., and the most notable developments over the past ten years. Section 2 will provide insights regarding the growth of ODR in business to consumer (B2C) commerce, which includes ecommerce as well as B2C commerce more broadly. Section 3 will build on this picture of entrepreneurship and innovation with respect to ODR in the courts – supplementing Paul Embley's Chapter 10, with special emphasis on trends in the U.S. Section 4 considers how public and private institutions are now leading/embracing ODR. By institutionalization, we note how bar associations seek to govern ODR, and universities now teach ODR as it becomes mainstream in the dispute resolution ecosystem. Section 5 highlights cutting themes and reflections through the lens of dispute system design (DSD), considering how ODR is engaged from firms to courts to communities to governments. Section 6 concludes.

2 ODR IN B2C COMMERCE

ODR in e-commerce is discussed more generally in *ODR for E-Commerce: Legal Standards and Developments in Asia and Europe*, the chapter written by Pablo Cortés, Aura Esther Vilalta and Chittu Nagarajan. This section adds to that conversation with a special focus on e-commerce ODR in the U.S., taking note of how ODR more generally has evolved from its ecommerce roots at eBay. In the U.S., eBay is no longer the lonely star in the ODR horizon. Instead, others have joined in by using ODR to promote efficient claims resolution and build goodwill. Indeed, eBay learned that it could retain loyal customers and even inspire them to make more purchases where customers trust that they will get a remedy if a purchase goes awry.[14] Nevertheless, many ecommerce as well as other B2C commerce companies have continued to impose predispute arbitration

11 Schmitz, *supra* note 5, at 120-170.

12 *Id. See also* Amy J. Schmitz, *A Blueprint for Online Dispute Resolution System Design*, 21 No. 7 J. Internet L. 3-11 (2018); Amy J. Schmitz, *There's an "App" for That: Developing Online Dispute Resolution to Empower Economic Development*, 32 Notre Dame J. L. Ethics & Pub. Pol'y 1-45 (2018); republished in Russian with permission at Эми Дж. Шмитц «Для этого есть приложение!» // Посредничество и примирение. Медиация и право. 2018. №1-2 (45). С. 6-51.

13 Amy J. Schmitz and Colin Rule, *Online Dispute Resolution for Smart Contracts*, 2019 J. of Dispute Resol. 203-225 (2019).

14 Add from the book.

clauses in their consumer contracts – leading one to question their primary business goals. Trends nonetheless indicate that companies will continue to move customer service online, which often includes some variation or form of ODR – if not simply digital communication. Moreover, it is notable that B2C ODR in the U.S. remains largely unregulated, as distinguished from e-commerce ODR in Europe, as noted in the chapter referenced above.

2.1 E-Commerce Platforms

EBay is the original ecommerce example of ODR in the U.S. Before filing a complaint, eBay encourages users to attempt to work out the problem on their own.[15] If unsuccessful, the buyer is able to file a claim in the eBay Resolution Center.[16] This will inform the seller that there has been an issue, which will prompt negotiations between the seller and the buyer.[17] If the buyer is satisfied with the seller's solution, they can close the case.[18] If unsatisfied with the seller's response, or the seller has not responded in 3 days, the buyer has 21 days to report it to eBay to continue the process.[19]

At this point, eBay helps resolve the issue, typically within 48 hours.[20] If the goods did not arrive or are not as promised, the buyer usually gets her money back. In the case that the buyer loses a claim, they have 30 days to appeal that decision.[21] When appealing, a buyer can submit information to support their claim, such as photos of the item, tracking and shipping information, proof the item was sent to the wrong address, and police reports.[22] Typically eBay decides appeals within 48 hours of the submission.[23]

As a seller, the typical complaint is that a buyer has not paid for the item.[24] If the parties do not reach a resolution on their own, the seller can use the online Resolution Center to file a complaint.[25] The Resolution Center will help parties negotiate a

15 eBay, https://resolutioncenter.ebay.com (last visited 1 March 2020).
16 eBay, www.ebay.com/help/buying/resolving-issues-sellers/using-resolution-center-buyer?id=4636&st=3&pos=2&query=Using%20the%20Resolution%20Center%20as%20a%20buyer&intent=dispute%20resolution&lucenceai=lucenceai (last visited 1 March 2020).
17 *Id.*
18 *Id.*
19 *Id.*
20 eBay, www.ebay.com/help/buying/returns-refunds/ask-ebay-step-help-buyers?id=4701 (last visited 1 March 2020).
21 *Id.*
22 eBay, www.ebay.com/help/buying/returns-refunds/handling-disputes?id=4039 (last visited 1 March 2020).
23 *Id.*
24 eBay, www.ebay.com/help/selling/resolving-buyer-issues/using-resolution-center-seller?id=4642&st=3&pos=3&query=Using%20the%20Resolution%20Center%20as%20a%20seller&intent=dispute%20resolution&lucenceai=lucenceai (last visited 1 March 2020).
25 *Id.*

resolution, but if no resolution is reached after 5 days of opening the case, the final value fee will be credited back to the seller and the seller will be free to resell the item.[26]

Amazon also provides ODR under its Buyer Dispute Program.[27] Buyers who do not receive goods or receive goods not as described may file a claim against the merchant through Amazon.[28] Complaints must be filed within 30 days of final payment.[29] If the item qualifies for Amazon A-to-Z Guarantee, they have longer to submit a claim – with times varying based on whether the claim relates to digital or tangible goods.[30] Once a buyer submits a complaint, Amazon will contact the merchant and facilitate a resolution.[31] Amazon aims to resolve all complaints within 45 days.[32] Amazon may deny buyers' claims if the item matched the merchant's description, the buyer failed to respond for further information, or it appears that the complaint was filed for buyer remorse.[33] In the case that a claim is denied, the buyer may appeal.[34] If a seller loses a complaint, the seller has 30 days to file an appeal.[35] If a merchant is uncooperative, Amazon may restrict or terminate their account.[36]

Etsy, another ecommerce platform in the U.S., has a limited ODR system.[37] Etsy provides that if parties are unable to resolve a dispute, they can participate in Etsy's case system in which Etsy representatives have sole discretion to decide the disputes "in good faith and based solely on the interpretation of our policies."[38] Etsy nonetheless states that they are under no obligation to resolve any dispute and reminds users that they are not making judgements on any legal issues or claims.[39] The system covers claims regarding failure to deliver or to conform to item description.[40] Etsy will not decide claims regarding items damaged in shipping, items that match seller's description but not consumer's expectation, shipping costs, and more.[41] Furthermore, consumers must

26 *Id.*
27 Amazon, https://pay.amazon.com/help/201751580 (last visited 1 March 2020).
28 *Id.*
29 *Id.*
30 *Id.*
31 *Id.*
32 *Id.* If during the process, Amazon must contact the buyer and the buyer fails to respond within 5 days, the complaint may be cancelled.
33 *Id.*
34 *Id.*
35 Amazon, https://pay.amazon.com/help/81965 (last visited 1 March 2020).
36 *Id.* Merchants are expected to respond to all correspondents within 10 days.
37 Etsy, www.etsy.com/legal/terms-of-use#disputes (last visited 13 February 2020).
38 *Id.*
39 *Id.*
40 Etsy, www.etsy.com/legal/policy/cases-for-buyers/243306189901?ref=list (last visited 13 February 2020); Etsy, https://help.etsy.com/hc/en-us/articles/115015570547?segment=shopping (last visited 13 February 2020).
41 Etsy, www.etsy.com/legal/policy/cases-for-buyers/243306189901?ref=list (last visited 13 February 2020). Etsy reserves the right to terminate the dispute due to lack of party participation as well.

use F2F arbitration under New York law for any claims directly against Etsy.[42] The resort to arbitration reflects the prevalence of arbitration clauses in all types of consumer contacts in the U.S. in the wake of U.S. Supreme Court jurisprudence continually enforcing predispute arbitration under the Federal Arbitration Act.[43]

Facebook has created an ODR process through Commerce Manager, that is available to customers who buy from merchants who have a 'Facebook Page Shop' and facilitate purchases in which customers pay through Facebook or Instagram. This flows through the Purchase Protection plan, which generally would not apply to a business that just has a general Facebook Page, an individual selling on Facebook Marketplace, or merchants outside of the U.S.[44] Per Facebook's information page,

> Purchase Protection only applies when you purchase an item with shipping or checkout on Facebook. This means that items purchased with local pickup or with a peer-to-peer payment method (example: PayPal, payments in Messenger, Venmo) aren't covered.[45]

Specifically, Facebook's Purchase Protection policies with respect to purchases made through Facebook lays out what kind of purchases are protected (such as items not received, damaged, or if a merchant is not following their return policy) and what is not protected (such as vehicles, real estate, services, and more).[46] Claims are limited to $2,000 with a $10,000 lifetime coverage limit.[47] If a claim is found to be fraudulent, Facebook may disable the consumer's ability to make payments through Facebook or Instagram, or take additional action against the user's account.[48]

Under this policy, when a customer makes an inquiry, the seller has two business days to respond through either the Commerce Manager Inbox or through the business's email provided to Commerce Manager.[49] If the business corrects the issue, the customer has forty-five days from date of delivery to create a dispute claim for Facebook to review.[50]

42 Etsy, www.etsy.com/legal/terms-of-use#disputes (last visited 13 February 2020). If the claim against Etsy does not exceed $10,000 Etsy will pay for filing, administrative, and arbitrator fees, unless the arbitrator finds the claim was frivolous or made with improper intent. *Id.*

43 *AT&T Mobility, L.L.C. v. Concepcion*, 131 S. Ct. 1740, 1743-56 (2011).

44 Facebook, www.facebook.com/business/help/1167434420087941?id=353836851981351 (last visited 27 April 2020).

45 Facebook, www.facebook.com/help/228307904608701?helpref=faq_content (last visited 27 April 2020). Additionally, the purchase protection policy requires: "use onsite checkout on Facebook or Instagram to complete your payment for the purchase. Purchases made through third-party sites, local pickups, Messenger transactions, or through other messaging services do not qualify." www.facebook.com/policies/purchase_protection.

46 Facebook, www.facebook.com/policies/purchase_protection (last visited 12 February 2020).

47 *Id.*

48 *Id.*

49 *Id.*

50 *Id.*

Facebook then notifies the business to let them know a claim has been filed.[51] Facebook considers the following when evaluating a claim: (1) the order details; (2) communication between the parties; (3) information provided by the parties; and (4) the customer's past refund requests and purchase activity indicating fraudulent behavior.[52] This appears to be an online arbitration process, allowing for appeals within 10 days from the notification of the decision.[53] However, the decision reached in the appeal is the final decision.[54]

Overall, this shows that B2C ecommerce has embraced various forms of ODR for resolving consumer issues. Ecommerce giants such as Amazon and eBay started the trend, and others have followed – mainly with an eye toward improving efficient claims resolution and augmenting customer loyalty. Nonetheless, smaller businesses do not adopt ODR at the same rate as their larger counterparts due to lack of operational and technical infrastructure. The 'start-up' costs of developing ODR are not worth it for smaller businesses with fewer complaints. This suggests the need for a global ODR platform accessible to merchants and consumers for ecommerce remains.[55]

2.2 Sharing Economy and Facilitators

ODR has also helped resolve disputes within the sharing economy, and facilitating websites like Grubhub. Grubhub is a food delivery app that allows consumers to order food from any restaurants on the platform. If there is a minor issue, such as something wrong with the consumer's food order, they may contact the Grubhub customer care team through the app, online chat, or a phone call.[56] There is also an online space for consumers to provide feedback on their app.[57] Nonetheless, Grubhub requires arbitration for any disputes against Grubhub itself.[58] The agreement also has a class action waiver, preventing parties from being collectively represented.[59] The agreement requires that the arbitration be conducted by the American Arbitration Association ('AAA') in the county where the claimant resides.[60] If the controversy is less than $10,000, the arbitration will be conducted solely by sending documents to the arbitrator.[61]

Postmates is like Grubhub, as it also connects consumers with restaurants for food delivery. Postmates does not appear to offer ODR. Instead, Postmates includes an

51 *Id.*
52 *Id.*
53 *Id.*
54 *Id.*
55 Amy J. Schmitz and Colin Rule, The New Handshake: Online Dispute Resolution and the Future of Consumer Protection (Chicago: American Bar Association Section on Dispute Resolution 2017).
56 Grubhub, www.grubhub.com/help/faq (last visited 19 February 2020).
57 *Id.*
58 Grubhub, www.grubhub.com/legal/terms-of-use (last visited 19 February 2020).
59 *Id.*
60 *Id.*
61 *Id.*

arbitration clause with an opt-out provision, which limits the opt-out option to 30 days of account opening.[62] In other words, a customer would have to opt-out of arbitration within 30 days of account opening, or they will have to arbitrate any eventual disputes. The arbitration clause precludes any class actions or collective arbitration.[63] If the claimant is a resident of the U.S., the arbitration will take place in the county where the claimant resides.[64] If they are not a US resident, the arbitration will take place in San Francisco County, CA.[65]

Airbnb also requires a dispute resolution process ending in arbitration for any claims against Airbnb.[66] The dispute resolution process starts with an informal negotiation with Airbnb's customer service team, and if unresolved, binding arbitration with the AAA online.[67] There are two exceptions to the arbitration agreement: (i) copyright infringement or other intellectual property claims; or (ii) claims seeking emergency injunctive relief.[68] The location of the arbitration can be at any of the following locations:

> (1) in the county where you reside; (2) in San Francisco County; (3) in any other location to which you and Airbnb both agree; (4) via phone or video conference; or (5) for any claim or counterclaim under $25,000, by solely the submission of documents to the arbitrator.

Accordingly, arbitration remains the end-game for resolving disputes with Airbnb – as for others in the sharing economy.

2.3 Limited Liability Through Arbitration and Technological Distance

The above discussion indicates that the sharing economy uses arbitration, as is true of many B2C companies in the U.S. that continue to effectively hide behind predispute arbitration clauses. These clauses preclude consumers from bringing class actions in court. Some ecommerce platforms may offer ODR for claims among buyers and sellers on their platforms, but insist on regular arbitration for claims directly against the ecommerce company. Similarly, Facebook requires its users to arbitrate any claims against Facebook, although Facebook offers ODR for its Commerce Manager program involving other sellers.[69]

---

62 Postmates, https://postmates.com/legal/terms (last visited 19 February 2020).
63 *Id.*
64 *Id.*
65 *Id.*
66 Airbnb, www.airbnb.com/terms#sec201910_19 (last visited 19 February 2020).
67 *Id.*
68 *Id.*
69 Facebook, www.facebook.com/msqrd/terms (last visited 12 February 2020).

At the same time, other companies have been using technology to reduce customer service costs by aiming to eliminate most or all telephone or office support. For example, Groupon has very limited service options – focused on what they offer through their website or app. Dissatisfied consumers have fourteen days to seek a trade-in, and in some cases a refund, through the Groupon website.[70] The policies differ depending on if the voucher was for local uses, a getaway, goods, or GrouponLive.[71] For local vouchers, consumers who have not yet opened or redeemed the voucher may be able to get back the price the consumer paid if it is within three days after purchase.[72] For Getaways, consumers can be refunded for the coupon if the merchant is unable to accommodate the consumer's available booking dates.[73] For GrouponLive, all purchases are final unless stated otherwise.[74]

These are the limited 'choices' on Groupon's website in case an issue arises.[75] Groupon does not explicitly state that they use an online resolution system but it is apparent that one's choices for relief are limited to those listed on the website or app. It is difficult to reach live assistance on the telephone, and one may have to resort to direct messaging through Twitter for assistance.[76] Moreover, if one is unhappy with Groupon, they are again stuck with arbitration and a class action waiver.[77] Uber is likewise notorious for limiting access to assistance to the limited choices for remedies located in their app.[78] Even Zappos, which generally offers fine customer service, requires that consumers bring claims in arbitration, with no allowance to join a class action.[79] The tables may be turning on arbitration with the recent DoorDash case. 'Driven partly by a legal reformist spirit and entrepreneurial zeal', attorneys Lidow and Lenkner formed FairShake, a startup that automates initiation of an arbitration process. DoorDash, a food delivery app service, has predispute mandatory arbitration for claims by dashers,

---

70 Groupon, www.groupon.com/legal/grouponpromise (last visited 12 February 2020).

71 *Id.*

72 *Id.*

73 *Id.*

74 *Id.*

75 Groupon, www.groupon.com/faq#faqs:category-1040?crumbs=W3sidGV4dCI6IkZBUXMiLCJ1cmwiOiIvZmFxIyIsInBhdGgiOiIvZmFxIn0seyJ0ZXh0IjoiQXJ0aWNsZXMiLCJ1cmwiOiIvZmFxI2ZhcXM6Y2F0ZWdvcnktMTA0MD9jcnVtYnM9VzNzaWRHVjRkQ0k2SWtaQlVYTWlMQ0oxY213aU9pSXZabUZ4SXlJc0luQmhkR2dpT2lJdlptRnhJbjFkIiwicGF0aCI6Ii9mYXEjZmFxczpjYXRlZ29yeS0xMDQwP2NydW1icz1XM3NpZEdWNGRDSTZJa1pCVVhNaUxDSjFjbXdpT2lJdlptRnhJeUlzSW5CaGRHZ2lPaUl2Wm1GeEluMWQifSx7InRleHQiOiJGQVFzIiwidXJsIjoiL2ZhcSIsInBhdGgiOiIvZmFxIn1d (last visited 12 February 2020).

76 One author has experienced this.

77 Groupon, www.groupon.com/legal/termsofservice (last visited 12 February 2020).

78 Uber provides limited remedies through their app: "My promo code didn't work; I was charged a cleaning fee; I had a different issue with my charge; I was charged more than I expected; I was charged a different amount than in my receipt; I was charged twice on my payment method; My driver asked to be paid in cash." Jennifer Still, How to dispute an Uber charge using the mobile app or Uber's website, Business Insider (8 August 2019, 12:25 PM), www.businessinsider.com/how-to-dispute-an-uber-charge. It is nonetheless difficult to get a live person for assistance.

79 Zappos, www.zappos.com/c/terms-of-use (last visited 13 February 2020).

the delivery contractors. American Arbitration Association provides the arbitration service. FairShake filed 6000 claims on behalf of dashers, which called for DoorDash to pay over $9 million in arbitral case filing fees.[80]

In sum, while the nature of ecommerce allows for ODR to provide an avenue toward remedies, companies continue to find ways to shirk consumer claims. In particular, U.S. companies notoriously use predispute arbitration clauses in their consumer contracts as means for avoiding class actions, which make it more economical for individuals to pursue smaller dollar claims in particular.[81] Many businesses insist upon class action waivers in all of their consumer contracts to save litigation costs and veil claims from the public eye of the courts.[82] The presence of arbitration clauses is an important aspect of the 'U.S. story' because unlike the E.U., the U.S. insists on strict enforcement of predispute arbitration clauses under the Federal Arbitration Act (FAA),[83] even when statutory claims are at stake.[84] In addition, arbitrators in the U.S. rarely order class arbitration in the wake of the U.S. Supreme Court's ruling in *Stolt-Nielsen S.A. v. Animalfeeds Int'l Corp.*[85] Moreover, *AT&T Mobility L.L.C. v. Concepcion*, severely narrowed consumers' power to challenge class waivers based on traditional contract defenses.[86] The Supreme Court in *AT&T* held that the FAA preempts a state court from using unconscionability to condition enforcement of an arbitration clause on preserving consumers' ability to bring class-wide arbitration.[87] This was seen as a 'free pass' for companies to employ arbitration clauses with class waivers in the U.S.[88]

---

80 DoorDash sought to overturn the arbitration provision and substitute another arbitration firm; a federal judge ruled that the original provision stood. Michael Corkery and Jessica Silver-Greenberg, *Scared to Death by Arbitration: Companies Drowning in Their Own System*, The New York Times, 6 April 2020.

81 Brian T. Fitzpatrick, *The End of Class Actions?*, 57 Ariz. L. Rev. 161 (2015).

82 *Id.*, at 164-197.

83 *AT&T Mobility, L.L.C. v. Concepcion*, 131 S. Ct. 1740, 1743-56 (2011); *Stolt-Nielsen S.A. v. AnimalFeeds Int'l Corp.*, 130 S. Ct. 1758 (2010); *Rent-A-Ctr, W., Inc. v. Jackson*, 130 S. Ct. 2772, 2777-80 (2010).

84 *See Rodriguez de Quijas v. Shearson/Am. Express, Inc.*, 490 U.S. 477, 485-86 (1989) (overruling prior opinion to hold securities claims arbitrable); *Green Tree Fin. Corp. v. Randolph*, 531 U.S. 79, 89-92 (2000) (finding TILA claims may be subject to binding arbitration under the FAA).

85 *Stolt-Nielsen S.A. v. AnimalFeeds Int'l Corp.*, 130 S. Ct. 1758 (2010).

86 Peter B. Rutledge and Christopher R. Drahozal, *Contract and Choice*, 2013 B.Y.U. L. Rev. 1, 38 ("Of the arbitration clauses in the sample [of credit card agreements], forty-four of forty-seven clauses (or 93.6%) (covering 99.9% of the credit card loans outstanding) waived any right to class arbitration.").

87 *AT&T Mobility, L.L.C. v. Concepcion*, 131 S. Ct. 1740, 1743-56 (2011).

88 Consumers in that case filed a class action lawsuit against AT&T alleging that it had fraudulently advertised free phones. The AT&T consumers' standard cellular phone agreements included an arbitration clause that precluded arbitrators from ordering class relief or consolidation, but allowed for small claims court actions, the recovery of double attorney fees if an award exceeded the company's settlement offer, and the company's payment of arbitration costs. The California court struck down the class waiver, but the U.S. Supreme Court reversed that decision and admonished California's use of state contract law to hinder enforcement of class waivers. *See id.*, at 1748-55 (emphasizing that class action arbitration sacrifices informality); Sarah Rudolph Cole, *On Babies and Bathwater: The Arbitration Fairness Act and the Supreme Court's Recent Arbitration Jurisprudence*, 48 Hous. L. Rev. 457, 481-491 (2011) (highlighting how recent Supreme Court opinions curtail class action relief).

Legal economists may argue that the curtailment of legal action is beneficial to the extent that it generates cost-savings that companies may pass on to consumers through lower prices and better products and services.[89] However, public action is often necessary to uncover product defects, initiate recalls, and inform other consumers about systemic or firm-specific problems. Accordingly, class actions play an important role in providing information about consumer issues. They also allow individuals to assert small dollar claims in an economical manner, thereby making vindication of their rights feasible in such consumer cases.[90]

That is not to say that class actions are ideal.[91] Some have criticized class actions for failing to provide just compensation.[92] Additionally, some have noted that attorney's fees and litigation costs may deplete class awards and settlements, leaving the injured consumers with very little redress.[93] Accordingly, ODR is often very beneficial for consumers in the U.S.

Furthermore, companies like Amazon and eBay are reaping the rewards of customer goodwill and increased trust by providing ODR and it remains the hope that more companies will follow. ODR adds a significant portal to remedies for consumers in smaller dollar cases, and provides benefits for companies. Again, consumers feel more comfortable purchasing from companies that provide an avenue for obtaining remedies if the purchase goes awry. This seems especially important as ecommerce giants with loyal customers survive in the age of Covid-19.

3 ODR in the Courts

The quests for efficiency and access to justice have driven the insurgence of ODR in courts and e-courts, in the U.S. Courts on local and state levels have recognized that the justice system has not been working for many, leading some to miss out on remedies or otherwise forego their rights. With an entrepreneurial spirit, some courts

89 *See* Stephen J. Ware, *The Case for Enforcing Adhesive Arbitration Agreements - with Particular Consideration of Class Actions and Arbitration Fees*, 5 J. Am. Arb. 251, 254-264, 292 (2006).

90 *See* Amy J. Schmitz, *Curing Consumers' Warranty Woes Through Regulated Arbitration*, 23 Ohio State J. on Dispute Resol. 627, 635-645 (2008) (discussing functions of class actions).

91 Linda S. Mullenix, *Ending Class Actions As We Know Them: Rethinking the American Class Action*, 64 Emory L.J. 399 (2014).

92 *Id.*, at 418-427 (also explaining how class notices may disclose the total amount received through settlement but provide no information about payment of individual claims).

93 George Rutherglen, *Wal-Mart, AT&T Mobility, and the Decline of the Deterrent Class Action*, 98 Va. L. Rev. In Brief 24, 25-27 (2012).

have begun to act as laboratories in adopting, and in some cases creating, ODR programs for addressing particular case types.[94] This is an exciting time, as the National Center for State Courts (NCSC) is partnering with PEW Charitable Trust in assisting and assessing judicial ODR projects.[95] Much of the story is chronicled above by Paul Embley in Chapter 10 of this book. This section will, therefore, highlight particular themes in the U.S. experience: (1) leaders with resources are foundational; (2) pilots that learn from experience are essential; and (3) case types for which Access to Justice (A2J) has been lacking make sense for ODR.

Leaders such as judges. court administrators or advocates for the underserved, are significant stakeholders who can identify problems in the justice system and seek to solve them – in this case with ODR. When such leaders become champions for ODR, ODR pilots take off. For example, Utah has implemented an ODR program for small claims cases statewide.[96] An ODR Steering Committee was formed by the Utah Judicial Council in June 2016 to create means for improving access to remedies in small claims cases, but the project really gained traction once Justice Dino Himones of the Utah Supreme Court took the lead in supporting the effort.[97] The ODR program follows a stepped process, beginning with 'Education and Evaluation', moving to direct negotiation and then allowing for mediation if the parties are unable to resolve their dispute on their own.[98] Since the process has gone live in family court, the number of in-person hearings dropped 27%.[99] Additionally, 22% more cases were resolved than

94 Individual state, county, and city courts act as laboratories for new initiatives aimed at improving access to justice as well as judicial efficiency. This is one of the tenets of federalism. *New State Ice Co. v. Liebmann*, 285 U.S. 262, 311 (1932); *see also* Utah Courts Recent Press Notifications, Utah Courts (13 August 2020), www.utcourts.gov/utc/news/2020/08/13/to-tackle-the-unmet-legal-needs-crisis-utah-supreme-court-unanimously-endorses-a-pilot-program-to-assess-changes-to-the-governance-of-the-practice-of-law/.

95 *See* NSCS/PEW Charitable Trusts ODR Project Announcement, odr.info (10 July 2018), http://odr.info/ncscpew-charitable-trusts-odr-project-announcement/ (last visited 28 January 2019). Interactive Online Portals Offer Targeted Legal Resources on Demand, pew (4 January 2019), www.pewtrusts.org/en/research-and-analysis/fact-sheets/2019/01/interactive-online-portals-offer-targeted-legal-resources-on-demand (last visited 28 January 2019). The Pew Charitable Trusts is also funding teams from Stanford University and Suffolk University to train a natural language processor (NLP) to help people identify their own legal issues. An NLP is a type of AI that focuses on understanding context in speech. An NLP would be able to match legal terms with more commonly used words or phrases after further AI training. Erika Rickard, How Artificial Intelligence Could Improve Access to Legal Information, pew (24 January 2019), www.pewtrusts.org/en/research-and-analysis/articles/2019/01/24/how-artificial-intelligence-could-improve-access-to-legal-information (last visited 28 January 2019).

96 Melisse Stiglich, *Utah Online Dispute Resolution Pilot Project*, NCSC (December 2017), 1-3; *see also* Utah Courts Recent Press Notifications, Utah Courts (13 August 2020), www.utcourts.gov/utc/news/2020/08/13/to-tackle-the-unmet-legal-needs-crisis-utah-supreme-court-unanimously-endorses-a-pilot-program-to-assess-changes-to-the-governance-of-the-practice-of-law/.

97 *Id.*, at 6-7.

98 *Id.*, at 9.

99 Paul Embley, NCSC, Presentation at the First Int'l Forum on Online Courts, U.S. Courts and Online Dispute Resolution 13 (3 December 2018), https://assets.publishing.service.gov.uk/government/uploads/system/uploads/attachment_data/file/761379/US.pdf.

before the program began, and 36% fewer warrants were issued for failure to appear.[100] In the small claims/tax department, 93% of cases reached agreement with ODR, versus only 46% for those cases without help of ODR.[101]

The Utah project also demonstrates how projects aimed at addressing problems hold promise. Leaders in Utah adopted ODR after they saw the high number of default judgments in small claims courts. Their goal was to help empower defendants to engage in the process without the time and cost of attending court in person. As one court administrator explained, 'half the battle is getting people to appear in court.'[102] ODR saves the parties and court personnel from the time and hassles of in-court proceedings. It also allows parties and judicial mediators and judges to communicate at convenient times and places.[103] The example in Utah also shows how it is helpful to start with an ODR pilot, and build on lessons learned.[104] Moreover, Utah may show us how ODR can reimagine court rules as it has employed the concept of a 'regulatory sandbox' to allow for innovation.[105]

The expansion of ODR and easy e-court options for addressing traffic ticket disputes also exemplifies the importance of choosing case types for which in-person procedures generally 'do not work'. For example, in-person hearings for ticket cases are problematic. Who wants to take time off of work and expend resources while wasting hours in court waiting for a judge to hear their defenses for a traffic ticket? Michigan was one of the first U.S. states to launch an ODR pilot program in collaboration with Matterhorn, a private ODR provider, for resolving traffic disputes.[106] The core of the program is an online portal for defendants to submit their cases, including arguments contesting their tickets or explanations for why they cannot pay their fines. Police and prosecutors then review cases through the portal before a judge makes a decision.[107] In this way, the online format provides for the resolution of traffic disputes without the need for face to face court appearances.[108] This is especially important for out of state drivers, for whom in-person procedures would be too costly in light of the travel involved.

---

100 *Id.*

101 *Id.*, at 15.

102 Email from Clayson Quigley, District Court Program Administrator in the Greater Salt Lake City area, in the Administrative Office of Utah Courts, to Andrew Johnson, Research Assistance to Professor Schmitz, 9 August 2018 (on file with author).

103 *Id.*

104 *Id.*

105 *See* Utah Courts Recent Press Notifications, Utah Courts (13 August 2020), www.utcourts.gov/utc/news/2020/08/13/to-tackle-the-unmet-legal-needs-crisis-utah-supreme-court-unanimously-endorses-a-pilot-program-to-assess-changes-to-the-governance-of-the-practice-of-law/ (discussing the new regulatory 'sandbox' pilot in Utah).

106 John Nevin, *Online Ticket Review*, Michigan Courts News Release (8 June 2015), http://courts.mi.gov/News-Events/press_releases/Documents/Online%20Ticket%20Review%20news%20release.pdf.

107 *Id.*

108 Anna Stolley Persky, *Michigan Program Allows People to Resolve Legal Issues Online*, ABA Journal (1 December 2016), www.abajournal.com/magazine/article/home_court_advantage/.

The government also benefits from these ODR systems because they promote easy ticket payment for those defendants found in violation of a traffic law. Only 2%, or less, of the cases heard on Matterhorn are likely to end in default, compared to 20% of traditional cases.[109] Courts using Matterhorn are also likely to collect 80% of fines within twenty-one days, compared to collecting 80% of fines within three months in regular court.[110] Surveys and interviews also reveal that 90% of Matterhorn users find it 'easy to use', while more than a third of users said they would have been unable to participate in a F2F adjudication.[111]

Another ODR pilot astutely aimed at addressing a problem is the Franklin County Municipal Court Dispute Resolution Department's ODR program. It began with a focus on addressing individuals' disputes with the City of Columbus Division of Income Tax.[112] Again, this was the type of dispute for which F2F alternatives were inconvenient and costly considering the small sums often at stake.[113] Also, stakeholder leaders stepped in to champion the program and gather research that should help pave the way for improvements.[114]

Early surveys regarding the Ohio project revealed that 93% said that they would recommend ODR to others, and the Department reported that the ODR program shortened the time from case-filing to resolution.[115] The intervals between filing and commencing ODR were much shorter than they were in the cases outside of the ODR program.[116] The ODR pilot has saved the City of Columbus on costs of negotiating and mediating income tax small claims, and has increased its collection of unpaid taxes. This is especially true with respect to defendants from out of state, who generally defaulted in F2F processes. Accordingly, the program is addressing problems with access to remedies and collections, is supported by leaders, and seeks to continually learn from data collected.

The growth in family ODR provides another example of a case type that 'fits' ODR because the F2F options are often unpleasant, inefficient, or nonsensical in light of costs involved. ODR may provide the only means for accessing remedies in some family cases. First, in a divorce without children, there may not be a great amount of money at stake and individuals simply want a fast and cheap divorce without the complexities of in-person processes.[117] Second, many people do not want to see the person they are

109 *See* J.J. Prescott, *Improving Access to Justice in State Courts with Platform Technology*, 70 Vand. L. Rev. 1993, 1994-1996, 2033-2034 (2017).

110 *Id.*, at 2038.

111 *Id.*, at 2045.

112 Franklin County Municipal Court, www.courtinnovations.com/ohfcmc (last visited May 2017).

113 *Id.*

114 FCMC Data Project, https://sites.google.com/view/fcmcdataproject/data?authuser=0 (last visited 28 March 2020).

115 Franklin County Municipal Court Dispute Resolution Department, ODR 2016-17 Spreadsheet.

116 *Id.*

117 Rebecca Aviel, *Counsel for Divorce*, 55 B.C. L. Rev. 1099, 1126 (2014).

aiming to divorce. Indeed, running into the soon-to-be-ex during in-person mediation may cause pain and anger that inhibits a productive process.[118] Use of computer-mediated-communication and other technologies in managing family issues can therefore provide 'space' that helps parties focus on their interests while moving toward settlement.[119] This may be especially true where individuals seek face-saving, which is difficult in F2F processes.[120]

Third, family law processes often involve a plethora of legal documents. Indeed, it is overwhelming for one without an attorney to complete the documentation necessary for even a simple divorce, let alone for parenting plans and child support. Accordingly, platforms such as Turbocourt provide easy means for individuals to complete required forms by answering a series of questions – much like completing taxes using Turbotax.[121] ODR platforms can also offer opportunities to upload documents, respond to a mediator or other disputant over a chat or email mechanism, and integrate with a court so that ODR is part of an 'end-to-end' solution. At the same time, as younger generations get married and coparent, it has become increasingly clear that digital access is expected.[122]

In sum, judicial ODR projects have grown in the U.S., especially where stakeholder leaders have invested resources and power in bringing projects to fruition. These projects also have had success where they aim to address access to justice and payment problems. This seems to follow a simple functional analysis: processes are more likely to gather support where they 'function' by addressing a problem. We see this play out as ticket, small claims, and family dispute resolution move online more quickly than, for example, large commercial cases, in which there is less incentive to move online. That said, the current Covid-19 crises may change this calculus as all cases move online due to lack of the F2F alternative.

4 Institutions

Another new development in U.S. ODR has been the institutional interest in research and development of best practices. ODR interest is no longer limited to a small group that

---

118 *See* Dafna Lavi, *No More Click – Click in Here: E-Mediation in Divorce Disputes-The Reality and the Desirable,* 16 Cardozo J. of Conflict Resol. 479-542 (2014-2015).

119 Gary L. Welton, Dean G. Pruitt and Neil B. McGillicuddy, *The Role of Caucusing in Community Mediation,* 32(1) J. Conflict Resolut. 181-202 (March 1988). Leah Wing, Daniel Rainey, Borislava Simidchieva, Ethan Katsh, Lee Osterweil, and Lori Clarke. Unpublished research findings, 2009, on file with co-author (Leah Wing).

120 Leah Wing and Daniel Rainey, *Online Dispute Resolution and the Development of Theory,* in Online Dispute Resolution: Theory and Practice, 23-38 (edited by M. Wahab, E. Katsh, and D. Rainey, The Hague: Eleven International Publishing 2012); Amy J. Schmitz, *Remedy Realities in Business to Consumer Contracting,* 58 Ariz. L. Rev. 213-261 (2016).

121 Turbocourt, http://info.turbocourt.com/learn-more/individuals-families/ (last visited 18 February 2020).

122 Amy J. Schmitz, *There's an "App" for That: Developing Online Dispute Resolution to Empower Economic Development,* 32 Notre Dame J. L. Ethics & Pub. Pol'y 1-45 (2018).

meets once a year and talks about the future. The 'future' is now, and institutional recognition evidences the 'new normal' that involves technology in dispute resolution.

4.1 Pew Charitable Trust and NCSC

Research around ODR in the U.S. is ramping up. As noted earlier, the NCSC and PEW have been researching ODR.[123] For example, one of their early polls found that only 44% of those surveyed who earn $75,000 or more were likely to want an online resolution for tenancy disputes. Furthermore, they found that "poorer, older and also less educated people generally – according to this survey – seem less willing to engage with ODR."[124] This seemed to indicate that there might be less interest in ODR than expected. However, this is not entirely clear – and will certainly change as we see courts move online and ODR take shape during this period of Covid-19.

Even before Covid-19, PEW ODR research was underway.[125] PEW stated that its project aims were the following:

- Increase the availability and quality of free online legal tools that help everyone navigate complex problems and connect to resources.
- Develop, promote, and evaluate technologies that improve how people interact with state and local courts.
- Conduct research to identify policies that can improve outcomes for people involved in the civil legal system.
- Build partnerships with the private sector, policymakers, and other stakeholders to advance comprehensive improvement to the civil legal system.[126]

This research includes plans to work with selected group(s) and the NCSC with respect to RFP No. CLSM-2019-01.[127] The RFP lists many research questions and a rubric for working with pilot courts. PEW selected up to five pilot court sites, in consultation with NCSC, and is simultaneously conducting its own research in conjunction with the selected grant recipients.[128] NCSC will conduct process evaluations on a sample of pilot courts. Additionally, NCSC will evaluate and assist with stakeholder engagement to the extent outlined by Paul Embley in Chapter 10 of this book.

---

123 *Online Dispute Resolution Faces Major Challenges,* Artificial Lawyer, 19 March 2019, www.artificiallawyer.com/2019/03/19/online-dispute-resolution-faces-major-challenges-survey/ (last visited 10 May 2019).

124 *Id.*

125 The Pew Charitable Trusts, Civil Legal System Modernization, www.pewtrusts.org/en/projects/civil-legal-system-modernization (last visited 29 June 2019).

126 *Id.*

127 Outcome Evaluation for Online Dispute Resolution in State Courts, 31 May 2019 (as amended), www.pewtrusts.org/-/media/assets/2019/04/2019-clsm-rfp-01-amended.pdf (last visited 29 June 2019).

128 *Id.* Again, as noted above, this Article is not associated with the Pew project and I am not one of the selected researchers. However, this Article may be helpful for those who are conducting the research.

At the same time, the Pew Charitable Trusts is researching use of emerging technologies in dispute resolution. For example, PEW is funding teams from Stanford University and Suffolk University to train a natural language processor (NLP) to help people identify their own legal issues. An NLP is a type of AI that focuses on understanding context in speech. It is thus hoped that this NLP would be able to match legal terms with more commonly used words or phrases so that individuals could gather guidance without need for typing or dealing with more complicated computer processes.[129]

This is just one example of research with respect to emerging technologies. One can expect that there will be a surge in research regarding AI and use of 'bots' for helping people assess their problems and perhaps prevent litigation. Research should help pave the way to improving access to remedies and helping us reimagine justice in the U.S.

4.2 American Bar Association (ABA) Task Force

Given the importance of ODR for A2J, there is a great deal of interest in setting standards or best practices for ODR.[130] Technology is incorporated into ODR in a variety of ways from simple communication processes to automated negotiations and virtual juries of online volunteers.[131] With AI enhancements and the incorporation of blockchain technology, the potential for ODR has yet to be fully realized.[132] A great number of ODR cases are characterized as low-value, high-volume disputes, providing slighted consumers with access to justice when the costs of litigation are prohibitive.[133] ODR has also been growing in international cross-border disputes, allowing consumer redress without the impediments of litigation delay, significant monetary expense, and multi-jurisdictional issues like choice of law and enforcement.[134]

Still, it is unclear how to even define 'ODR' let alone how we can or should provide governance. For this reason the American Bar Association has established an ODR Task Force aimed at making the market more transparent to instill trust in its users. The ABA is not alone. There are several legal organizations and task-forces working to create guidelines and best practices for ODR. While some minimum standards have emerged from the numerous efforts to self-regulate, none have achieved global consensus.[135] As a

129 Erika Rickard, How Artificial Intelligence Could Improve Access to Legal Information, Pew (24 January 2019), www.pewtrusts.org/en/research-and-analysis/articles/2019/01/24/how-artificial-intelligence-could-improve-access-to-legal-information (last visited 28 January 2019).

130 Gralf-Peter Calliess and Simon Johannes Heetkamp, *Online Dispute Resolution: Conceptual and Regulatory Framework* 2-5 (TLI Think! Paper 22/2019, 2019), http://ssrn.com/abstract=3505635.

131 *Id.*, at 5-6.

132 *Id.*, at 6.

133 *Id.*, at 9.

134 *Id.*, at 9-10.

135 *Id.*, at 11-12.

result, there's been a growing trend in state regulation on the international, national, and regional level.[136]

The ODR Task Force in the U.S. is organized around three main 'Working Groups': (1) guidance with respect to best practices, and institutions' involvement in establishing and regulating such practices; (2) guidance with respect to special issues relating to Court ODR; and (3) guidance with respect to special issues relating to private ODR. For all these groups, there is an overall interest in exploring how institutions like the ABA should deal with resistance and facilitate best implementation of ODR. The task force is thus struggling with deciding how best to regulate, if at all. At the same time, groups are considering stakeholder building – internal and external to courts, and how to assess impact on legal education as well as the practice of law more generally.

The Task Force includes not only members of the ABA, but individuals from various backgrounds and vantage points, including ICODR, American Arbitration Association, Self-Represented Litigants Network, American Law Institute, and others. It even includes experts from outside of the U.S., and continues to consult with counterparts in other parts of the world. The Uniform Law Commission is also interested in joining the ABA Task Force's effort, as ODR becomes mainstream.

That said, it is unknown at the time of this publication whether the Task Force will succeed in developing guidance or best practices that will garner support. The courts and other major stakeholders are developing their own standards and metrics. Accordingly, it is essential for the Task Force to collaborate and team build. Development of institutional guidance with inclusive input and support will be necessary to build consensus for sound design, implementation and success in the long term.[137]

A starting point for these groups to promote ethical and effective ODR in the U.S., and throughout the world, is the ICODR principles and standards for ODR.[138] At the same time, certifications and audit systems may develop as public, private and nonprofit institutions seek to promote transparency around ODR. Transparency means not only that individuals have full information about a process at the outset, but the outcomes achieved. It also means that administrators should publish reports on the system and provide these reports to auditors with authority and expertise to assess whether the use of technology is not only saving time and money, but also assisting individuals to obtain fair redress in the courts and elsewhere.

136 *Id.*, at 12.

137 *See* Anjanette H. Raymond and Scott J. Shackelford, *Technology, Ethics, and Access to Justice: Should an Algorithm Be Deciding Your Case?*, 35 Mich. J. Int'l L. 485, 492 (2014).

138 The following list of ODR Standards is taken directly from the International Council for Online Dispute Resolution, ICODR http://icodr.org/index.php/standards/ and were based on the ODR Ethical Principles put forth in Leah Wing, *Ethical Principles for Online Dispute Resolution: A GPS Device for the Field*, 3 Int'l J. on Online Dispute Resol. 12-29, 11-15 (2016). *See also* the National Center for Technology and Dispute Resolution http://odr.info/ethics-and-odr/ (last visited 28 August 2018).

4.3 *Law Schools/Education*

While law schools have long offered courses in negotiation and dispute resolution to complement traditional civil procedure and trial practice classes, ADR (appropriate dispute resolution) is expanding to include ODR. A number of law schools now include modules as well as full courses.[139]

The NCTDR has received information from 14 colleges and universities that offer courses at least 50% focused on ODR. Of these, three are international. Course offerings in the United States span ODR policy, law, and practice in cases from consumers and claims facilities to family law and misdemeanors, as well as disputes involving social media and smart contracts on the blockchain. Students in these classes have the opportunity to use ODR platforms and experience simulations; to study technology in the context of system design; and write papers that address best means for using technology to assist in resolving a particular type of dispute.

For example, the authors share their respective programs about which they are most familiar. Stanford Law School offers Regulating AI, and Digital Technology and Law, plus Dispute System Design and Online Dispute Resolution. Regulating AI (which enrolls law, engineering and computer science students), surveys current and emerging legal and policy problems related to how law structures humanity's relationship to artificially-constructed intelligence. Digital Technology enables students to gain fluency across digital technologies (machine learning, internet structure, cybersecurity, encryption, and blockchain) and legal frameworks. The Dispute System Design course probes a number of systems from ecommerce to courts, claims facilities, and cryptocurrency, examines the stakeholders, goals sought, and processes provided. Other academic programs offer a hybrid of both alternative dispute resolution theory and practice and the digital fluency in development of artificial intelligence.

The University of Missouri Law School likewise offers a general Law and Technology course, as well as 'AI, Data Analytics and the Law', and two versions of 'Dispute Resolution in the Digital Age (DRDA)'. The two versions of DRDA include one for in-person J.D. students, and the other for the online LLM in Dispute Resolution. Both courses consider technology through the lens of dispute systems design and practice, including simulations using various ODR platforms, an examination of ethical dilemmas, and completion of a final project proposing a system design for addressing resolution of a chosen area of conflict. ODR is truly an interdisciplinary field that calls for mastering both process and outcome, as well as the engineering skill to optimize design and practice.

---

139 Schools that have posted their courses with the National Center for Technology and Dispute Resolution include Creighton University, Dominican University, Mitchell Hamline School of Law, Nova Southeastern Florida, Pepperdine School of Law, Santa Clara University, Southern Methodist University, Stanford Law School, University of Massachusetts Amherst, and University of Missouri School of Law (Columbia).

5 Dispute System Design

The innovative energy in the U.S. applied to dispute resolution highlights how ODR should follow best practices for dispute system design – how technology fits within one or more processes that prevent, manage, and resolve a stream of disputes (this subject is also treated in Chapter 3, Rabinovich-Einy and Katsh, 'Lessons from Online Dispute Resolution for Dispute Systems Design'). ODR may constitute one or all of the processes devoted to addressing disputes. For example, at eBay, all of the processes available to customers were found on the eBay portal: diagnosing whether and what kind of problem the customer experienced, facilitating a conversation between the buyer and the seller to resolve the issue, introducing third-party assistance (or mediation) followed by a third-party evaluation and decision. This progression of processes went from negotiation, in which the parties retained control over the process and outcome, to assisted negotiation with the benefit of a third party, to evaluation in which a third party assumed control of both the process and outcome.

This section lays out an approach to dispute system design, then uses four examples to illustrate a range of design using ODR. This author (Martinez) with colleagues developed an analytic framework with six elements: goals, stakeholders, context and culture, structures and processes, resources, and accountability.[140]

Specifying the goals of the system is the most critical of the design elements: what does the designer[141] seek to accomplish and what disputes will be addressed? Goals can include efficiency, compliance, access to justice, innovation, dispute prevention, reputation, and more, all of which are likely desirable. But someone, or some decision-making body, will need to decide which goals are most important. Articulating the priority goals will focus the process choice and provide a metric for evaluating the system's effectiveness. In the case of eBay, the goals were explicitly fast and fair resolution of the disputes.[142]

A second framework element is the identification of stakeholders, their interests, relationships, and relative power. Stakeholders include the people and organizations that create, host, use, and are affected by a system; ideally, they will be involved in the design from the start and share experience as users. Here as with eBay, stakeholders include eBay management, the buyer and seller 'users', and the broader ecommerce community.

140 Lisa Amsler, Janet Martinez, and Stephanie Smith, Dispute System Design (Stanford: Stanford University Press 2020), and Stephanie Smith and Janet Martinez, *An Analytic Framework for Dispute System Design*, 14 Harv. Neg. L.R. 123 (Winter 2009).

141 A designer is an individual or team, internal or external to the organization of interest, that designs or redesigns its dispute system.

142 Amy J. Schmitz and Colin Rule, The New Handshake: Online Dispute Resolution and the Future of Consumer Protection (Chicago: American Bar Association Section on Dispute Resolution 2017).

Context and culture comprise the third element – meaning the circumstance or situation in which a system is diagnosed and designed. By 'culture', we mean the implicit assumptions and values held by the surrounding community that help define the dispute. In the eBay example, the culture is clearly one that values technology and innovation, plus the dilemma whereby it was not physically or legally feasible to bring modest claims in a local court when the parties spanned the globe.

Structures and processes include examining how the processes are related to each other and the formal legal system, and include the range of process types described above: direct negotiation to third-party facilitation, mediation, or arbitration, and court adjudication. As a process option, ODR offers both a significant advantage on efficiency, and a difference in kind of experience.

Resources are critical. What financial, human, data, technological, information, and training resources are needed and available to support a system. Leadership from the top combined with understanding of the users' perspective, are both critical to understanding motives and building scale capacity.

Lastly, a system's accountability and success will depend on the degree of transparency around its operation and whether the system includes monitoring, learning, and evaluation components. Evaluation enables the organization to establish metrics on whether the system is functioning effectively in terms of its goals, participation, cost-benefit, quality neutrals, and user satisfaction. The Pew Trust ODR evaluation project described above will contribute significantly to the overall benefit of ODR.

The following table compares the design elements in four examples of ODR.[143] EBay manages over 60 million disputes a year in ecommerce.[144] Courts and tribunals across the country handle litigation over civil and criminal matters with a priority aim of offering access to justice; of these, civil claims, small claims, and family law, have lead in the development of court ODR options. (See Chapter 10 Paul Embry and Section II above.) NextDoor is a social media platform that enables geographically adjacent neighbors to communicate over issues relevant to their living environment. Disputes arise over property, services, reputation, and other issues.[145] Kleros is one of the leading firms to offer resolution of smart contract disputes.[146]

143 Martinez, JDR Winter 2020 pending.

144 Amy J. Schmitz and Colin Rule, The New Handshake: Online Dispute Resolution and the Future of Consumer Protection (American Bar Association Section on Dispute Resolution 2017).

145 Gordon Strause.

146 Amy J. Schmitz and Colin Rule, *Online Dispute Resolution for Smart Contracts*, 2019 J. of Dispute Resol. 203-225 (2019)

DSD Design Element	eBay	Court & Tribunals	NextDoor Social Media	Kleros
Goals	Fast and fair resolution for transaction problems	Justice, efficiency, streamlined user experience	Intervene on fake news, and bullying; Promote civility, politeness, and neighborliness	Fair, transparent, scalable, and self-administering
Stakeholders	eBay, consumers, sellers, and regulators	Court, court staff, judges, public, counsel, and litigants	Citizens/neighbors, journalists, and regulators	Commercial disputants, employment or insurance smart contracts, and coders
Context/Culture	High volume, low value, international/cross-border, transactional Relationships	Public, diverse, formal, various levels of literacy, education, and comfort with technology	Geographic proximity, personal relationships, different races, ages, and income levels	Online first, international diversity, informality, and high comfort with technology
Processes	Diagnosis, negotiation, facilitation, and evaluation	Settlement, mediation, early neutral evaluation, and trial	Discussion forums, technology-based coaching and advice, and facilitative process	Online evaluation, crowd-sourced jurors, and incentivized participation
Resources	eBay investments in the software and case management staff	Public funds, parties, public employees, and supporting non-profits	NextDoor investments in the software and case management staff	Kleros overall management, but designed to be self-sustaining
Evaluation	eBay teams using surveys, user experience research, and data capture and monitoring	Internal and external evaluation programs, and court satisfaction data	Surveys and user experience monitoring	Overall usage and growth of the Kleros caseload and user base
Designer	eBay	Court with external vendors and partners	NextDoor	Kleros and the worldwide developer community
Process selection for individual case	Specified in user agreement, initiated by consumer	Opt-in by filer/plaintiff	Required by NextDoor software	Can be initiated by either complainant or respondent

The goals of these four examples overlap significantly and are mostly compatible, but with a tension between giving primacy to fairness (eBay, Kleros, NextDoor) or efficiency (courts). Each example is comprised of multiple stakeholders with likely differentiated goals. The notion of process pluralism underscores the importance of multiple processes that would each meet some goals better than others. Both facilitative and evaluative options are offered, with a tilt toward facilitative with NextDoor and evaluative with Kleros. Context and culture capture both public and private interests, again calling for process options according to parties' priorities. In an individual case, process choice is usually made by the user/consumer with eBay, courts, and NextDoor. Resources and design leadership are primarily provided by the dispute resolution provider (eBay, courts, NextDoor, and Kleros). A combination of engaged stakeholder goal assessment, process choice according to rights or interests, and substantive and procedural transparency all contribute to system success.

This note on dispute system design is important for the U.S. story. We are in an incredible growth phase of ODR in the U.S., but the story will not end well if design principles are ignored. As noted above and in this last section, the systems with deliberate design show the most success in terms of advancing both fairness and efficiency. Accordingly, thoughtful design must remain at the foundation of ODR as we look to the future.

6 CONCLUSION

Innovation and entrepreneurship have yielded remarkable advances in ODR in the U.S. First, we have seen some ecommerce companies rise to the challenge and provide varied and large numbers of avenues to remedies. Second, exponential growth in judicial ODR has added a virtual door to the courthouse in many jurisdictions, and has thereby advanced access to justice as well as efficiency. Third, we have seen institutionalization of ODR in the U.S. in terms of ABA and NCTDR leadership, and universities taking on the challenge of teaching ODR to students, as well as training mediators who are moving online.

Nonetheless, ODR's contribution toward access to justice has not gone as far as it could in the U.S., especially with respect to B2C commerce. Indeed, it is surprising that there is so little ODR for commercial disputes in the U.S. Furthermore, there has not been enough attention to dispute system design, especially where the stakeholders do not have incentive and power to provide the best system to address concerns with access to justice. Additionally, there are areas 'ripe for the picking' – such as Veteran's and Social Security claims, worker's compensation, and other disputes that will likely move online (if they have not already done so in the age of Covid-19).[147]

We are at an unprecedented time in our history, and people are moving online regardless of their intention. ODR is a game-changer for many. ODR has the capacity and power to create connections despite forced physical disconnection. Furthermore, resources are flowing to support ODR in the wake of Covid-19, and institutions are busy articulating standards. We hope that dispute system design, and sound functional analysis, remain at the core to advance access to justice along the way. Concern, however, remains that urgency will throw caution to the wind, as policymakers and practitioners must move online in haste.

Appendix A: Summary of Select ODR Providers

This summation is based on the National Center for Technology and Dispute Resolution: ODR Providers list, mentioned above. Again, these are firms and organizations that have self-identified as providing ODR. Furthermore, we sought to identify the providers who operate in the U.S. We did not enroll in, and fully examine, the processes of each entity. Instead, we simply accessed these firm and organization websites and attempted to determine what processes, case types, and services were offered. We then compiled a chart with this information, which can be found at Schmitz, Amy J. and Martinez, Janet, ODR Providers Operating in the U.S. (August 27, 2020), available at SSRN: https://ssrn.com/abstract=3599511.

The following is a summary of findings from the larger chart on SSRN:

147 While beyond the scope of this article, it is worth noting the significant efforts of federal administrative agencies to use AI for improved governance in terms of their data management, adjudication, enforcement and accountability functions. David Freeman Engstrom and Daniel E. Ho, *Algorithmic Accountability in the Administrative State*, 37 Yale J. Regulat. 800-854 (2020); David Freeman Engstrom, Daniel E. Ho, Catherine M. Sharkey, and Mariano-Florentino Cuellar, "Government by Algorithm: Artificial Intelligence in Federal Administrative Agencies," Report Submitted to the Administrative Conference of the United States (February 2020).

CASE DOMAIN

Case Type	Number of entities	Percentage (n=70)
Commercial	21	30
Civil	14	20
Construction	1	1
Consumer	8	20
Copyright	1	1
Debt	2	3
Domain names	3	4
Divorce/family	13	19
Employment	3	4
Financial	2	3
Government	1	1
Insurance	1	1
Intellectual Property	1	1
International	1	1
Labor	1	1
Landlord/Tenant	2	3
Probate	1	1
Real Estate	1	1
Small Claims	15	21
Smart Contracts	2	3
Traffic	1	1
Trustee	1	1
Water	1	1
Warrants & Pleas	1	1
Unspecified	10	14

Disputes in the commercial, civil, small claims, and family areas dominated the focus of these ODR firms.

PROCESSES & SERVICES

Process*	Number of entities	Percentage (n=70)
Negotiation/settlement conference	20	28
Negotiation/algorithm	4	6
Mediation	41	58
Arbitration	21	30
Adjudication	1	1
ADR	7	10
ODR	33	47
ADR & ODR	9	13
Cloud	6	8
Communication	7	10
Complaint Portal	1	1
Crowd-sourced jurors	2	3
Directory	2	3
Predictive software analysis	3	4

*Non-exclusive

The most prevalent process option is mediation, followed by ODR, then roughly equal offerings of negotiation and arbitration. Curiously, firms had self-identified as 'ODR Providers', but did not all offer ODR.

SERVICES

Services*	Number of entities	Percentage (n=70)
Case Management	41	58
Rules for Parties	22	31
Rules for Neutrals	14	20
Secure	54	77

*Non-exclusive

Nearly 80% offered secure platforms, but not all. Nearly 60% offered case management, but this was not always explicit.

While this survey is informal and anecdotal, it does reflect where a business model is viable, and what case types, processes, and services appear to generate use of ODR.

Chapter 22 Mediation and ODR in Latin America and Argentina

Alberto Elisavetsky and María Victoria Marun

1 Introduction

In Latin America, different forms of alternative dispute resolution (ADR) methods such as mediation, conciliation and arbitration have been established in the last 30 years. For example, in Argentina, Law N° 24.573 was passed in 1995 to regulate the Mandatory Pre-judicial Mediation, in the federal capital, providing a significant boost to the establishment of alternative dispute resolution methods and expanding them throughout the country. This process has also been developed in other countries, such as Brazil, Chile, Mexico and Colombia, with different degrees of evolution, but with a focus on toning up the efficiency of the administration of justice, in many cases overwhelmed by the number of existing judicial cases in court, and respecting the right to justice of citizens

In Argentina, some years ago, a process was initiated to organize online dispute resolution (ODR), which is currently fully developed. Other countries in Latin America have begun a similar process with different levels of development.

2 Online Dispute Resolution in Latin America

We must recognize that in Latin America, in general, and Argentina, in particular, the subject of ODR is a space in construction with different levels of development of practices and frameworks between the countries of the region and also within each country.

For example, Brazil put in place an ODR system under the Mediation Law in 2015. Mexico is treating a project of law nowadays. The Mexican state is in transition between different systems of access to justice. The paradigm shift in labour justice in Mexico, in accordance with the text of sections XX and XXII Bis of section A of article 123 of the Constitution, since the reforms undertaken on 24 February 2017, legitimates two instances of access to justice, namely the administrative route in specialized conciliation centres, on the one hand, and the jurisdictional route in the courts of the judiciary, on the other. On 30 November 2018, the United States, Mexico and Canada agreed to modernize the North American Free Trade Agreement (NAFTA), in what is now known as the United States-Mexico-Canada Agreement (T-MEC or USMCA), which was approved and ratified by the chamber of senators of Mexico, on 19 June 2019, but pending ratification by the other two countries. This document in Annex 23-A, as general aspects and commitments, reflects Mexico's commitment in its labour legislation to the creation of independent organs responsible for conciliation and records of collective work contracts. The labour reform, published on 1 May 2019, sets the guidelines for initiating and implementing the conciliation process and presents an opportunity for a new system that envisions transparency, certainty and other forms of communication and resolution of social conflicts, where the subjects involved in labour relations will strengthen asymmetric communication in the formulation of peaceful agreements.[1]

The constitutional reforms introduced by the Mexican justice system almost a decade ago have evolved in two ways: making the jurisdictional apparatus efficient and integrating the other model of justice through voluntary mechanisms, mainly the active participation of the citizen.[2]

While ODR has long been a reality in the developed world, the situation in the Latin American region, particularly Argentina, is quite different. Only in the last few years have the preliminary results emerged and, hence, for ODR to evolve and permeate society, several challenges need to be addressed.

Argentina does not have a national framework for ODR. Thus, the implementation of ODR programmes in Argentina is far from easy because it is a big country with a federal system of government and some provincial states have their own ODR policies, while others have no such programme.

Litigation before national courts in Argentina entails a great deal of paperwork. For example, after filing the case the court in question receives it and creates the written case file folder. This process takes several days until the court dictates the first resolution opening the legal action and sorting out notification of the legal action to the defendant, who has to reply by a certain deadline.

This situation discourages litigants and weakens confidence in the judicial system. However, we realize that the government cooperates with the scientific and academic community as well as civil society. This will allow Argentina to address the complexity of the technological, social, economic, legal and cultural challenges that prevail and make ODR a national reality.

As noted earlier, Argentina does not have a national ODR programme, and each provincial state either has its own system or does not have one at all. For example, the province of Mendoza has not organized a mediation programme by a specific law. There is a partial organization in the judicial system. The province of Salta established its Mediation Law Nº 7324 in 2004. Alberto Elisavetsky, who is the founder of ODR Latin

1 Egla Cornelio Landero – José De Jesús Rodríguez Segura – Perfiles de las Ciencias Sociales, Volumen 7, Número 14, enero-junio 2020, 247-267 pp., available at: http://revistas.ujat.mx/index.php/perfiles, México, UJAT. ISSN: 2007-9362 – file:///C:/Users/vicky/Downloads/3803-19806-1-PB.pdf.

2 *Ibid.*

America and the CEO of a great academic team, began the ODR model in this province of Salta, in 2012 with the support of the Ministry of Justice. The project was established by Ministerial Resolution 118/2012.[3] Under the project, ODR Latin America would provide online and face-to-face training in developing technological skills in virtual mediation to more than 120 mediators of the register of the province. Among them were about 70 community workers, who successfully replicated the model in their locations, before it was shared with other provinces of Argentina.[4]

Later, the province of Córdoba and its Direction of Alternative Methods for Conflicts Resolution (Di.M.A.R.C.) joined the trajectory of training in ODR by ODR Latin America. The hours of the courses were homologated by Resolutions n° 083/2015 and 110/2015 for the mediators of their register.[5]

In 2015 the Direction of Mediation of the province of Buenos Aires came into being for training in ODR with online courses. This project was endorsed by Dispositions n° 535/2015 and 652/2015.[6]

ODR Latin America also assisted the government of the Autonomous City of Buenos Aires with the MEL Program (Online Mediation), providing the training programme and the state-of-the-art professional mediation software. This programme has been established as a social inclusion device that is simple and accessible.

3 Covid-19 Pandemic – The Influence on ODR

In 2020 the Covid-19 pandemic affected the normal administration of justice in most countries, and many private and government organizations sought the services of ODR Latin America to train e-mediators in carrying out online conflict resolution, developing taught courses (an activity that is still ongoing) in Spain, Ecuador, Mexico, Costa Rica, Brazil, Chile and in the Argentine provinces of Salta, Cordoba, Mendoza and Buenos Aires.

3 Elisavetsky, Alberto, "La mediación a la luz de las nuevas tecnologías", Ed. Printing Books 2019, p. 9.

4 http://gobierno.salta.gob.ar/index.php/2-uncategorised/21-mediacion-a-distancia – Ministry of Justice Government of Salta – Elisavetsky Alberto – http://institutoscamdp.com.ar/mediacion/2016/04/14/la-mediacion-a-distancia-puente-de-inclusion-social-elisavetsky/.

5 Mensaje de Di.M.A.R.C. Córdoba sobre Curso de Formación en Resolución de Conflictos y Nuevas Tecnologías Nivel I, available at: www.resolucionelectronicadedisputas.com/?tag=dimarc-.

6 Elisavetsky Alberto – "Programa de mediacion en linea", available at: http://odrlatinoamerica.com/programa-mediacion-linea-mel-del-gobierno-la-ciudad-buenos-aires/.

4 DIFFERENT TOPICS

4.1 ODR Mechanisms, Processes and Platforms – A Way to Update ADR

Since the beginning of the 1980s, governments, judicial leaders, civil society organizations and a number of external agencies have been committed to making regional efforts towards instituting reforms in the field of justice in Latin America.

> [...] Change has been introduced in the legal framework, the organization and resources for justice in most of the countries; In some cases tangible improvements have taken place.[7]

This change has been effected not only through the traditional means of expanding the infrastructure and resources of the institutions but also by adopting new ways of resolving conflicts. These include arbitration (mainly institutional) or mediation, developed within the formal system or in autonomous settings.[8]

The proliferation of ADR mechanisms (in Latin America) is a function of the remarkable explosion of world trade, commerce and finance in the past 20 years. With economic globalization, the volume of international commercial transactions has multiplied, and so have the numbers of international disputes appropriate for submission to ADR procedures of one sort or another.[9]

In the last few decades the impulse for change and implementation of reforms in information and communication technology (ICT) for the administration of justice has become evident.[10] This change has facilitated the gradual transformation of ADR in ODR, not only in the administration of justice, but also in the private areas of cross-border trade.

In Argentina, as mentioned previously, only a few provincial states apply ODR mechanisms in the judicial process, and governments do not use any specific platforms for ODR. For example in Buenos Aires, Cordoba and Salta online mediation is practised through a videoconferencing system, using Skype and other platforms, and in Mendoza,

---

7 L. Hammergren, *Quince Años de Reforma Judicial en América Latina: Dónde estamos y por qué no hemos progresado más*, in *Reforma Judicial en América Latina: Una tarea inconclusa*, Internacional Law Department, Ed. OAS), available at: www.oas.org/juridico/spanish/adjusti5.htm.

8 C. Hernández & R. Adelardi, *Perspectivas de uso e impacto de las TIC en la Administración de Justicia en América Latina*, Working Paper – in Spanish, Study Centre for Justice in the Americas (CEJA) and Microsoft (no year informed), p. 7, n. 4, available at: https://biblioteca.cejamericas.org/bitstream/handle/2015/3955/Libroblancoe-justicia.pdf.

9 Speech by W.D. Rogers, "Inter-American Development Bank Conference on Commercial Alternative Dispute Resolution in the XXI Century", *The Road Ahead for Latin America and the Caribbean*, 26-27 October 2000, Washington DC, available at: www.iadb.org/mif/v2/speeches/rogers.html.

10 C. Hernández & R. Adelardi, work cited.

some cases of family disputes have been resolved by some platforms and by phone and email.[11]

But in Argentina, there are some private platforms of high quality. *SIMEDIAR*, for example, is a pioneer in the field of remote conflict prevention and management and in the use of ICT and offers quick and low-cost options to resolve conflicts with an interdisciplinary team of RDL. It also provides training and updating services for ODR professionals.[12]

Another platform is *ODR Latin America*, which is a social network created, in 2008, to enable conflict resolution professionals to exchange knowledge and experience and learn about the application of ICT to the ADR field. The network now counts 5.500 users. This social network has promoted Latin American participation in international ODR forums, such as Cyberweek and e Marc.[13]

It should be recognized that laws and practices in places where the process of transformation has begun have had a high level of effectiveness, despite the lack of adequate platforms and mechanisms.

4.2 Legal Frameworks – An Important Issue

Argentina has a federal system of government with 24 provincial states. In 2010 the national government established, through Law N° 26589, the ADR system prior to the judicial process. Unlike the case in many other countries, ADR processes were adopted only a few years ago in Argentina, and each provincial state developed different policies concerning this subject. For example, in 2008, before Law N° 26589, the province of Salta established, through Law N°. 7324, three areas of application for the mediation system: a) *Judicial*, which takes place within the judicial processes and for matters already judicialized; b) *Extrajudicial*, which is performed with the intervention of a private mediator and registered and authorized by the secretary of Alternative Methods of Conflict Resolution, as a prior and mandatory requirement for the filing of the lawsuit; and, finally, c) *Social or Community mediation*, which is contemplated as a public and free service by the state. Other provincial states, such as Córdoba, Buenos Aires and Autonomous City of Buenos Aires, adopted similar systems to those of Salta.

Yet many provincial states do not have a framework for ADR. In Mendoza, although it is not regulated by law, extrajudicial mediation does apply within the judicial processes related to family and labour cases.

---

11 ODR in Mendoza – Judicial Power Mendoza – www.jus.mendoza.gov.ar/.../Mediacion... Distancia/88881e17-fc40-43e0-a1c9-b661b...

12 http://simediar.net/.

13 www.google.com.ar/search?ei=3p-XXMCxHZyi5OUP9LGM8A4&q=odr+latinoamerica&oq=ODR&gs_l=psy-ab.1.0.35i39j0i67j0l8.262635.263299..265979...0.0..0.117.336.0j3......0....1..gws-wiz.......0i71j0i131.fQ8zveiZTLw.

This situation has affected the way in which lawyers, mediators, judges, etc. have reacted. For example, most professional associations (lawyers, accountants, notaries, etc.) have dispute resolution centres that offer extrajudicial mediation service, but few professionals use this service, and some judges do not recognize the agreements reached in the field of extrajudicial mediation.

Other provincial states that have regulated both the judicial and the pre-judicial mediation do not have this problem. Besides, before using ODR mechanisms, legal practitioners have to set up the technological resources, and not everyone can or wants to do so.

This situation significantly influences the transformation of ADR, because this process shows varying levels of effectiveness. Salta, Córdoba, Buenos Aires and Autonomous City of Buenos Aires have begun a slow process of transformation by new frameworks that allow the application of ODR simultaneously with that of ADR when the cases require it. In regard to Mendoza, on 8 March 2012, the first online mediation was conducted successfully, marking the beginning of a slow process of applying ODR simultaneously with ADR, when the case required it.[14]

The citizenry presents high levels of dissatisfaction whenever confronted by the justice system. Most people mistrust the system as a whole. Thus, the legal and practising community are working in forums, conferences, etc., in order to review the situation for applying ADR and ODR in judicial processes and develop new frameworks for doing that.

It should be noted that laws and practices in places where the process of transformation has begun have been highly effective, and we believe that other provincial states will begin to use these methods very soon.

4.3 ODR and Consumer Protection

In Argentina, Law No 24240 on consumer protection was enacted in the mid-1990s. The application of ODR in the processes related to consumer conflicts began a few years ago in different ways:

1) *A new Process:* Claim by Internet to Consumer Defence: If a person conspired or hired a good or a service and the supplier company did not fulfil the assumed commitment, a claim can be registered on the website of the Federal Single Window of Consumer Protection, which will designate the most appropriate method to resolve the conflict (provincial jurisdictions, National System of Consumer Arbitration or Protected

14 ODR in Mendoza – work cited.

Consumption).[15]
2) Resolution *394/2018*. The figure of the 'defender of the client' is created, as better and more efficient tutelage, for consumers and their rights. This is a function of all providers that voluntarily implement this process for consumers, in order to provide a simple and expeditious solution to the complaints and/or claims of their users.[16]
3) *The Memorandum of Understanding of Complaints Handling* has been concluded between the National Consumer Affairs Center of Japan (NCAC) and ODR Latino-America, based in the Argentine Republic. According to the MOU, which has been effective since 1 January 2018, NCAC and ODR Latin America will cooperatively solve problems faced by consumers in transactions (for example, problems associated with international travels and cross-border online shopping) between Japan and Latin America (Argentina, Chile, Uruguay, Paraguay, Bolivia, Brazil, Peru, Columbia, Venezuela, Costa Rica and Mexico).[17]

The subject of consumer protection always features in academic and scientific forums, conferences, etc. The way is to get the ODR system for traditional commerce and e-commerce. In Argentina, the new process works as follows: through joint work between the National Mediation and Consumer Defence Departments, a claim can be initiated online free of charge and access provided to an instance of conciliation with the company or seller. The files are channelled through the Previous Conciliation Service in Consumer Relations (COPREC), which is a tool for enforcing the rights of consumers. The conciliations in consumer relations arise from the sanction of Law 26993. This process implies a major advance in the defence of consumers.

We recognize that laws and practices have a high level of effectiveness in consumer protection.

5 Conclusions

We believe that ODR is a space in construction in Argentina, because we began to work on ODR a few years ago, but different spheres (legal, economic, scientific, academic, technological, etc) are working a lot; for example, UNTREF (Tres De Febrero National University, Buenos Aires, Argentina) offers important academic alternatives, such as a degree programme in conflict resolution and mediation, providing the possibility of creating a professional profile for conflict operators, and a postgraduate programme in ODR, which is the only one in the world that is taught in Spanish (https://www.

15 Ed. Perfil, "Habilitan una pagina para reclamos por internet en defensa del cnsumidor", available at: www.perfil.com/noticias/sociedad/habilitan-una-pagina-para-que-consumidores-hagan-sus-reclamos-por-internet.phtml.
16 www.argentina.gob.ar/noticias/defensor-del-cliente-un-nuevo-instrumento-para-agilizar-la-respuesta-los-reclamos-de-los.
17 http://odr.info/mou-of-complaints-handling/.

untrefvirtual.edu.ar/oa.php?id=72). In addition, on 8 and 9 April 2019 we celebrated the first Latin American Meeting on Conflict Resolution 4.0.

All these activities will allow us to get new frameworks, processes and mechanisms for ODR because this is a necessity; people use ICT to a high degree of effectiveness. At least 65% of Argentines have access to the Internet, and 54% do so from their cell phones, while 52% of households in the country are connected by broadband, according to a report by the International Telecommunications Union (ITU), with support from the United Nations Educational, Scientific and Cultural Organization (UNESCO). According to ITU, Argentina has the second highest proportion of Internet users (64.7%) in the region, surpassed only by Chile (72.4%). Argentina is also among the Latin American countries with the largest number of people connected to mobile broadband, with 53.6%. ICTs have become simpler and cheaper. The Internet entails modifications in the new digital economy related to consumer and human rights, computer law, economic law, business law and international law, among others.

We thus envisage an important future in ODR for Argentina, and Latin America, in general; the paths of research and debates in academic and scientific forums and concrete actions, through new normative frameworks, lead us to this conclusion.

Chapter 23 ODR in Europe

Marta Poblet and Graham Ross

1 Introduction

18 years have passed since the first online dispute resolution initiatives were launched in Europe. Undoubtedly, the European contribution to the initial phase of ODR deployments has been significant: of the 46 ODR sites reported by Conley Tyler in 2003, 20 were based in European countries.[1] As with any new technology, the boom of ODR services in Europe over the past decade has nevertheless been accompanied by some delay in achieving its full potential, possibly as a result of an of underestimation by its original pioneers of the marketing effort and investment required to attract adequate numbers of early adopters. While ODR services rose to 38 sites in 2004, some of them were no longer, even at that time, providing services.[2] In addition, it has to be borne in mind that a review of the list shows that many were well established, and still continuing, ADR organizations or business associations who were at that time simply engaged in initiatives to examine the future that technology could offer rather than launching a committed and specific ODR service. Since 2004, Europe has, notwithstanding, continued to be not only at the forefront of ODR development and usage but also a leading centre for ODR research and discussion. Most important of all, Europe, or at least those countries that are members of the European Union, has introduced legislation that has the potential, not only to rapidly expand public experience of ODR, but, through ODR, expand use of mediation itself. At the same time, the Council of Europe, has issued guidance on the role of ODR and the quality of, and access to, justice itself. At present, the current state of the art of ODR in Europe constitutes an opportunity to instil realism into the enthusiastic forecasts whilst still making significant progress with making ODR services the default systems to resolve online

1 M. Conley Tyler, "Seventy-six and Counting: An Analysis of ODR Sites", in E. Katsh & D. Choi (eds.), *Online Dispute Resolution: Technology as the "Fourth Party"*, Proceedings of the UNECE Second Forum on Online Dispute Resolution. UNECE Center for Information Technology and Dispute Resolution, University of Massachusetts, 2003. Available at: https://scholar.google.com.au/citations?user=YFLUVq4AAAAJ&hl=en#d=gs_md_cita-d&u=%2Fcitations%3Fview_op%3Dview_citation%26hl%3Den%26user%3DYFLUVq4AAAAJ%26citation_for_view%3DYFLUVq4AAAAJ%3AJ_g5lzvAfSwC%26tzom%3D240.

2 M. Conley Tyler, "115 and Counting: The State of ODR 200", in M. Conley Tyler, E. Katsh & D. Choi. (eds.), *Proceedings of the Third Annual Forum on Online Dispute Resolution*, Melbourne, Australia, 5-6 July 2004Available at: https://scholar.google.com.au/citations?user=YFLUVq4AAAAJ&hl=en#d=gs_md_cita-d&u=%2Fcitations%3Fview_op%3Dview_citation%26hl%3Den%26user%3DYFLUVq4AAAAJ%26citation_for_view%3DYFLUVq4AAAAJ%3Au5HHmVD_uO8C%26tzom%3D240.

disputes as well as colonizing off-line domains. This paper offers an overview of the present situation of ODR in Europe and discusses effective development of ODR deployments to handle online, offline, national and cross-border disputes in Europe. To do so, we proceed by first defining the scope of ODR and reviewing developments impacting on ODR and existing services. We then continue by analyzing the major challenges faced by ODR in Europe and finally conclude by suggesting some future scenarios.

2 DEFINING THE SCOPE OF ODR

Since Katsh and Rifkin first referred to technology as the 'Fourth Party' in ODR schemes there have been successive proposals on how to define the scope of ODR.[3] That same year, a research team at the University Geneva published a first report as part of a small colloquium of experts ('ODR: Where Are We And Where Are We Going?') which put on the table the main technical and legal issues raised by the emerging ODR services that proliferated in a market where e-commerce transactions were gaining a significant volume.[4] These and other documents proposed different definitions of ODR.[5] Schultz, for example, raised the question of whether the term ODR was synonymous to the online provision of traditional ADR procedures or a sui generis method of dispute resolution.[6] Other issues were also addressed: would it be the case that to qualify the service as ODR would require all phases of the process to be online, or would a combination of online and offline phases suffice? (*Ibid.*); did ODR have to deal with disputes generated online or could it also include those that originate outside the domain?; are the different terms that have been used throughout this decade – Internet Dispute Resolution (iDR), Electronic

---

3 *See* E. Katsh & J. Rifkin, *Online Dispute Resolution: Resolving Conflicts in Cyberspace*, San Francisco, CA, JosseyBass 2001.

4 T. Schultz, G. Kaufmann-Kohler, D. Langer & V. Bonnet, "Online Dispute Resolution: The State of the Art and the Issues", E-Com Research Project of the University of Geneva, Geneva 2001.

5 *E.g.* Consumers International, "Disputes in Cyberspace 2001: Update of Online Dispute Resolution for Consumers in Cross-border Disputes", Consumers International Office for Developed and Transition Economies. Available at: www.consumersinternational.org; T. Schultz, "Online Dispute Resolution: an Overview and Selected Issues", United Nations Economic Commission for European Forum on Online Dispute Resolution, Geneva, 6-7 June 2002. Available at http://ssrn.com/abstract=898821; T. Schultz, V. Bonnet, K. Boudaoud, G. Kaufmann-Kohler, J. Harms & D. Langer, "Electronic Communication Issues Related to Online Dispute Resolution Systems", Proceedings of the Eleventh International World Wide Web Conference – Alternate Track CFP: Web Engineering, Honolulu, Hawaii, 7-11 May 2002. Available at: www2002.org/globaltrack.html; A.G. Hammond, "How Do You Write 'Yes'?: A Study on the Effectiveness of Online Dispute Resolution", *Conflict Resolution Quarterly*, (2003) Vol. 20(3), pp. 261-286; Conley Tyler (2003), Conley Tyler (2004); V. Bonnet, K. Boudaoud, M. Gagnebin, J. Harms & T. Schultz, "Online Dispute Resolution Systems as Web Services", *Journal of Alternative Dispute Resolution*, (2004) Vol. 3. Available at http://ssrn.com/abstract=899107; A.R. Lodder & J. Zeleznikow, *Enhanced Dispute Resolution Through the Use of Information Technology*, Cambridge, Cambridge University Press 2010. Schultz (2002).

Dispute Resolution (eDR) electronic ADR (eADR), online ADR (oADR) – interchangeable? These questions remain open to discussion.

In this chapter we adopt a flexible notion of Online Dispute Resolution (ODR) in which a dispute resolution service may qualify as ODR if it fulfils at least the two following conditions: (i) online technology providing assistance to the different parties – *e.g.*, disputing parties, mediator, adjudicator, arbitrator, facilitator, etc. – throughout the process; and (ii) the subject matter is defined by being either a grievance, complaint or dispute. In this perspective, therefore, a pure forum (not necessarily an ODR specific technology) can qualify as ODR if it meets condition number ii, but if it is dealing with a subject that is neither a grievance, nor a complaint or a dispute, then it should not be considered as ODR even if it includes online technology. These basic conditions notwithstanding, there are different degrees of sophistication of ODR services, ranging from those integrating basic technologies (*i.e.* email, chat, voice IP, etc.) to those using commonly available conferencing tools or have developed, or have taken a license of, software that actively aids and encourages resolution.

3 ODR in Europe: The Normative Background

An important background context to ODR in Europe is that the European Commission has over recent years taken steps to actively encourage the use of ADR for the settlement of cross-border disputes. For some years now the European Commission has acknowledged the necessity of an adequate legal framework in which ADR programs can thrive. In this regard, the protection of European consumers constituted one of the main priorities of the legislative work. As early as 1993, the Green Paper on Consumer Access to Justice in the Internal Market,[6] aiming at safeguarding the effectiveness of the legal framework providing consumer protection, already noted the proliferation of ADR services in European Countries dealing with consumer disputes, and notably arbitration schemes. These considerations led the Commission to adopt the 'Action plan on consumer access to justice and the settlement of consumer disputes in the internal market', which represented a clear step in favour of the use of ADR.[7] This communication affirmed that 'consumer access to justice' was being achieved with a

6 Commission's Green Paper, 16 November 1993, on access of consumers to justice and the settlement of consumer disputes in the single market – COM(93) 576 Final, p. 76.

7 Communication by the Commission on 14 February 1996, COM(96) 13 Final, "Action plan on consumer access to justice and the settlement of consumer disputes in the internal market".

variety of instruments, but it also concluded that this access did not always imply access to the courts and that it was possible to consider the available alternatives.

Similarly, the Commission Recommendation of 30 March 1998 on the out-of-court settlement of consumer disputes[8] sought to find a standard among the different types of ADR that the Member States had created over the years, laying down the principles applicable to out-of-court procedures for the settlement of consumer disputes. The Recommendation noted, for instance, the difference between the Scandinavian preference for an ombudsman and Spain's consumer arbitration scheme with a third-party arbitrator. This Recommendation was followed in 2001 by another Commission Recommendation on the principles for out-of-court bodies involved in the consensual resolution of consumer disputes.[9] This second Recommendation applies to procedures that involve an attempt to bring the parties together to convince them to find a solution by common consent (an aspect not being covered by the former Recommendation).

In a similar vein, three important ADR normative initiatives have crystallized in the last few years as regards civil and commercial matters:[10] the establishment of the European Small Claims Procedure,[11] the adoption of the Directive on Mediation in Civil and Commercial Matters[12] and the EU Directive on Alternative Dispute Resolution For Consumer Disputes[13] (together with its associated EU Regulation on Online Dispute Resolution For Consumer Disputes).[14] As regards the Regulation establishing the European Small Claims Procedure, its aim is to simplify, speed up and reduce the litigation costs of small claims that do not exceed € 2,000 in cross-border cases. Importantly for ODR, Article 8 of the Regulation states that 'The court or tribunal may hold an oral hearing through video conference or other communication technology if the technical means are available'. Secondly, in 2008, the European Directive on Mediation in Civil and Commercial Matters (Directive 2008/52/EC) was issued to facilitate access to

8 Commission recommendation on the principles applicable to the bodies responsible for out-of-court settlement of consumer disputes, COM(1998) 198 Final, available at: http://eur-lex.europa.eu/smartapi/cgi/sga_doc?smartapi!celexplus!prod!DocNumber&lg=en&type_doc=COMfinal&an_doc=1998&nu_doc=198.

9 Commission Recommendation on 4 April 2001 on the principles for out-of-court bodies involved in the consensual resolution of consumer dispute, available at: http://ec.europa.eu/consumers/ redress/out_of_court/adr/acce_just12_en.pdf.

10 This work was preceded by the 2002 EC Green Paper on alternative dispute resolution in civil and commercial law initiating a broad-based consultation, available at: https://www.euromed-justice.eu/en/system/files/20090128140854_GreenPaperonAlternativedisputeresolutionincivilandcommecialLaw.COM%282002%29196final.pdf.

11 Regulation (EC) No 861/2007 of the European Parliament and of the Council of 11 July 2007 establishing a European small claims procedure, available at: http://eur-lex.europa.eu/smartapi/cgi/sga_doc?smartapi!celexplus!prod!DocNumber&lg=en&type_doc=Regulation&an_doc=2007&nu_doc=861.

12 Directive 2008/52/EC of The European Parliament and of the Council of 21 May 2008 on certain aspects of mediation in civil and commercial matters, available athttps://eur-lex.europa.eu/legal-content/EN/TXT/HTML/?uri=CELEX:32008L0052&from=EN.

13 EU Directive 2013/11/EU.

14 Regulation (EC) No 524/2013.

mediation in cross-border civil or commercial disputes. It requires Member States to ensure that mediation training and provision is positively encouraged and that agreements resulting from mediation can be rendered enforceable. An important element is that the Directive requires that, when parties engage in mediation, any limitation period within which legal proceedings would ordinarily, under the laws of a Member State, have to be issued will be suspended to avoid parties not agreeing to mediation purely in order to preserve their legal remedies. Both these provisions provide an environment more conducive to the development and adoption of ODR solutions and services in cross-border disputes.

In the UK a new Civil Procedure Rule (Part 78) was put in place in April 2011 to implement the Directive. Part 78.24 enables parties to disputes coming within the scope of the Directive, and who have settled the matter by mediation, to obtain a Mediation Settlement Enforcement Order, which will enable the terms of the agreement to be enforced through the courts. An Order will only be made if applied for either by both parties or by one party presenting evidence of explicit consent of the other to making such an application. Since only mediations in disputes covered by the Directive have the benefit of this provision, and as all such disputes will be cross-border, which are more appropriate for being conducted online, this Rule effectively supports and encourages ODR itself.

These developments had an indirect impact on the drive to embrace ODR. However, a much more direct development was the EU Directive on Alternative Dispute Resolution for Consumer Disputes[15] and the linked EU Regulation on Online Dispute Resolution For Consumer Disputes.[16] These two pieces of EU legislation carried with them the hope that they will help the public to begin to become more familiar at least with the acronym of ODR itself. Together this European legislation effectively requires most businesses to act as the unpaid promoters of ODR. At least that was as anticipated albeit a lack of information being given to businesses about this law and a significant lack of enforcement to date has slowed down the extent to which it has so far impacted on the culture of consumer complaints.

Under the provisions of the Directive (which under EU law is required to be implemented through local legislation by Member States) all customers who have bought (offline or online) products or services for a purpose other than business, trade, profession or craft, and with whom the business had not resolved a dispute directly with them (and, with no value ceiling this can include high value transactions such as the sale of an ocean going yacht as well as building extensions, swimming pools etc) must now be informed by the relevant businesses of the web address of a provider of ADR that has been approved by a responsible authority in each country as satisfying certain standards required by the Directive. Since such standards include using a system that enables claims

15 *Ibid.*, p. 468.
16 *Ibid.*

to be raised, and information to be exchanged, online, the ADR provider must effectively also be an ODR provider.

Additionally, under the Regulation on Online Dispute Resolution For Consumer Disputes, which came into effect in February 2016, all European traders who sell online must now ensure that their website contains an easily accessible hyperlink to an EC designed and run ODR platform.[17]

The platform's goal is to 'make online shopping safer and fairer through access to quality dispute resolution tools'. The primary function of the platform is to take in the complaint and refer the consumer to an approved ADR provider in his or her country. The most recent data from the platform show that, in its second year of operation (February 2017 to February 2018), the serviced totalled more than 36,000 cases (50% more than in the first year) and an average of 2,700 complaints submitted per month. While this growth is promising, given the population of the EU at the time (before the exit of the UK) was around 500,000, this is still a far cry from mass adoption. More damning still, only 2% of cases reached an ADR service. As explained below, one problem is that very few businesses are aware of this new duty. Another problem is that companies are only required to point the consumers to an approved provider of ADR but not to actually participate in the ODR system of resolution.

The EU have published a study[18] on the level of compliance with the Regulation on Online Dispute Resolution in Consumer Disputes. This Report is disturbing in two ways:

1. 72% non-compliance through absence of any link more than a year after the law came into effect shows gross lack of effort by member governments in creating awareness.
2. The situation is even worse than the headline figures, since the 'mystery shoppers' who provided the core data were asked to find a link as if they already had a complaint. As a result, the Report claims that by placing the link within Terms and Conditions (or complaint handling pages), to where a consumer might navigate to if they already had a complaint, satisfies the 'easily accessible' requirement. This ignores and defeats the principle objective of this legislation which was to encourage growth in cross border online consumer purchases within the Single Market by building confidence BEFORE the purchase has been made and a complaint arisen, that an approved ODR service is available. It is well established that very few people bother to read Terms and Conditions unless they have a specific reason to do so.

Consumers deciding whether to buy from an EU trader will not, therefore, know of the EU's ODR platform if the link is not displayed on the home page. The reality is that as, out of the 28% with any link at all, 83% had it buried in various legal terms that would not be read by consumers, the true figure for compliance is thus less than 5%!

17 https://ec.europa.eu/consumers/odr.

18 https://op.europa.eu/en/publication-detail/-/publication/9cafdfce-b4a7-11e8-99ee-01aa75ed71a1/language-en/format-PDF/source-search.

No doubt in time the Regulation will start to be complied with, at least from the point of view of referring dissatisfied customers to ODR services and, given the acronym of 'ODR' has been adopted to describe the online requirements, one can look forward to greater public awareness.

4 ODR in Europe: The Early and Recent Story

4.1 Institutional Initiatives

Europe was the birthplace of the International Forum on ODR which began in 2002 with its first Forum at the Palais des Nations in Geneva. This had resulted from discussions between Daewon Choi of the United Nations Economic and Social Commission for Europe (UNECE) and Professor Ethan Katsh of the University of Massachusetts, and founder of the main ODR space on the web, www.odr.info. The Forum, referenced elsewhere in this book, also held its second Forum in Geneva in 2003. Although it no longer is associated with its institutional host, UNECE, this initial launch has resulted in the Forum becoming the main annual gathering point for all involved in the development of ODR. The Forum returned briefly to Europe in 2007, when it was held in Liverpool, and will return once again to Europe in 2012 when it is to be held in Prague. Professor Richard Susskind, IT Adviser to successive Lords Chief Justice in England and Wales since 1998 and a prolific and highly respected writer on the application of technology to the practice of law[19] gave a keynote speech at the Liverpool Forum in which he said "ODR has the potential to fundamentally change the way litigators function and to become mainstream."[20] He advised that progress would require not just the continuing activities of ODR advocates, practitioners, developers and commentators but, importantly, action by those in positions of influence who may have a more traditional approach and who do not readily see technology as an obvious contributor to the delivery of justice. Bringing those people 'on board', through focusing on how technology can help meet the wider needs of justice systems to cope with growing demand, was key to future uptake.

Another major initiative was the formation of the European Extra-Judicial Network (EEJ-Net). This was set up by the European Commission on the 16 October 2001, with the aim

19 *See e.g.*, R. Susskind, *Transforming the Law*, Oxford, Oxford University Press 2000. R. Susskind, *The Future of Law*, Oxford, Oxford University Press 2006; R. Susskind, *The End of Lawyers? Rethinking the Nature of Legal Services*, Oxford, Oxford University Press 2008.

20 As stated in a keynote speech given on the 20 April 2007 at the 5th International Forum on Online Dispute Resolution held at the University of Liverpool.

> [t]o establish a network of national bodies for the extra-judicial settlement of disputes in order to resolve cross-border consumer disputes quickly and effectively, making use of the new means of communication, particularly the Internet.

EEJ-Net comprised primarily, of the Trading Standards agencies (local government run consumer services) and retail and utility industry associations throughout Europe. The rationale of the initiative is that in order for the European Commission to operate a true single market, consumers should have similar redress no matter from which member country they purchase the goods and services. The different legal jurisdictions present a heavy barrier for consumers purchasing across borders and thus the need to focus on extra-judicial solutions. Whilst ODR itself was not the declared subject, it inevitably encompasses all of the processes discussed at the EEJ-Net meetings. There has over the years been much development of what is referred to as 'clearing houses' which essentially are services set up within particular industries and service groups to handle consumer complaints/disputes. All of these have over the years notified themselves to the EEJ Net.

The network became part of a wider network, the European Consumer Centres network (ECC-Net), with a broader remit covering information provision to the public on law and regulation in cross-border shopping as well as advice on ADR.

The European Consumer Centres Network was established in January 2005 by the European Commission and national governments. As a result of the enlargement of the European Union, the ECC-Net has expanded to include: Bulgaria and Romania in 2007, and Croatia in 2013. Today, there are 30 European Consumer Centres: 28 in the EU Member States, one in Norway, and one in Iceland.

Whilst these initiatives focused on consumer disputes, a significant development, with wider impact, took place in Vienna on the 29 and 30 March 2010, when the United Nations Commission on International Trade Law(UNCITRAL),in collaboration with Pace Institute of International Commercial Law, and Penn State Dickinson School of Law, hosted a Colloquium entitled 'A Fresh Look at Online Dispute Resolution and Global E-Commerce: Toward a Practical and Fair Redress System for the 21st Century Trader (Consumer and Merchant)'.

The outcome of the UNCITRAL Colloquium was that a proposal from the Pace Institute of International Commercial Law was presented to the 43rd session of UNCITRAL held in New York, from 29 June – 9 July 2010 and which resulted in the unanimous decision of UNCITRAL to form a Working Group on ODR.[21] The Working Group held its first meeting in Vienna on the 13th to the 17th December 2010.

---

21 https://undocs.org/en/A/CN.9/710.

UNCITRAL finalized and adopted at its 49th session in 2016 what is termed as the Technical Notes on Online Dispute Resolution.[22] These rules are non-binding, taking the form of a document listing the elements for an online dispute resolution process. Another initiative is the work done on ODR within the CEN framework. CEN (The European Committee for Standardization) is a Brussels based organisation that produces standards for products and services that are adopted by all EU member countries. Throughout 2008, a CEN Workshop committee met to produce recommended standards for ODR for adoption through a CEN Workshop Agreement (CWA). The CWA was published in 2009. The following phrases from the Foreword explain the intention:

> The objective of the CWA is to maintain the processes of ODR and offline dispute resolution in as close a synergy as may be practicable and to encourage and facilitate their future evolution in parallel to the maximum practicable extent. While these tools are becoming more and more important at international level for the out-of-court settlement of disputes, it is important to promote them in a proper way, using clear, simple and homogeneous rules on a pan-European basis. Without these rules, the heterogeneous procedures of the various ODR systems would create confusion among potential users. Moreover, ODR systems offer different user interfaces, and are unable to exchange information each other, preventing potential users from using their features within a multilanguage and cross-country business environments. This problem represents a barrier to the development of European e-business both from the consumers and the business perspectives.[23]

The existence of this CWA, and the recognition at CEN of the need to set standards, is further evidence of the significance that technology and ODR is being seen to play in dispute resolution.

Another European institution that has taken steps to tackle issues related to ODR is The Council of Europe. The Council is an international organisation focused on supporting human rights, democracy and the rule of law throughout Europe. The Council has 47 member states, including the 27 members of the European Union. It has responsibility for upholding the European Convention on Human Rights. Article 6 of the Convention sets out the human right of access to a public tribunal.

The Committee on Legal Affairs and Human Rights⊠ of the Council of Europe was asked to investigate the question of whether ODR and the increasing use of technology

22 https://uncitral.un.org/sites/uncitral.un.org/files/media-documents/uncitral/en/v1700382_english_technical_notes_on_odr.pdf.

23 CEN, Workshop Agreement on Standardisation of Online Dispute Resolution Tools). CWA 16026, November 2009. https://www.cen.eu/news/brochures/brochures/WorkshopODR.pdf.

and communications over the Internet for the resolution of disputes may conflict with the public's right to access to justice as enshrined in Article 6.

The Council of Europe is the body responsible for enforcement of the ECHR through the European Court of Human Rights. Research carried out as well as two hearings of the Committee, at which evidence was taken from three experts in ODR being Professor Arno Lodder of Vrije University, Amsterdam, Ms Iveta Havlova of Youstice.com and Graham Ross of ODRtraining.com.

The Report[24] of the Committee stated:

> both ODR and ICT, though not by any means panaceas, can help provide greater access to the judicial system by offering solutions to the problems of judicial inefficiency, the high cost of litigation, and geographical barriers. ODR and ICT nevertheless have some drawbacks, and member States should continue to invest in the development of safer, more effective, and more accessible ODR and ICT.

A Resolution was then adopted by the Parliamentary Assembly of the CoE, the key messages from which are:

- that the 47 member States be encouraged to promote awareness of, and further develop, mechanisms for ODR;
- that the extrajudicial enforcement of ODR decisions be promoted;
- that there be recognition of various challenges including inequalities in access to online resources, privacy and enforcement;
- that ODR procedures should contain safeguards compliant with Articles 6 and 13 (right to an effective remedy, particularly against authority) of the ECHR;
- that parties engaging in ODR procedures should, afterwards, retain the right to access a judicial appeals procedure satisfying the requirements of a fair trial pursuant to Article 6 of the Convention;
- that standards be developed for ODR, including ensuring that the process does not unfairly favour repeat players over one-time users, and establish a system of aceditation for ODR providers. (Some potential for duplication here with the system of accreditation already now in place under the EU Directive of an Alternative Dispute Resolution in Consumer Disputes 2013/11/EU)
- that technological developments be monitored in order to promote the use of ICT within courts.

The Online Civil Money Claims Pilot (OCMCP) is an online court initiative in England and Wales that followed the recommendations in two Reports, being that of the Civil

24 http://assembly.coe.int/nw/xml/XRef/Xref-XML2HTML-en.asp?fileid=22245&lang=en.

Justice Council's Advisory Group on Online Dispute Resolution for Low Value Civil Claims[25] (dated 15 February 2015) and the Final Report of Lord Justice Briggs on the Civil Courts Structure Review[26] (dated July 2016) which both recommended an online court for civil claims. The court deals with money claims up to £10,000 in value with generally no legal representation. Currently it is in a public beta phase meaning that anyone can issue in the court but it is still under development. As at August 2020 it only covers the issue of Claim and Defence through an intuitive journey thereafter reverting to the standard existing system. There are initial inroads into a segment encouraging the parties to resolve the dispute between themselves although no actual tools are provided.

Graham Ross came across a problem when taking out a case himself in that, despite a Defence having been sent to him, the system nevertheless invited him to apply for judgment on the basis that the system was unaware the Defence had been filed. When this was raised with the court staff it was discovered that the new online system despite only covering the early part of the case journey, did not 'speak' to the old, but still active, system and in which the Defendant had filed the Defence (the long established email address published on its website). Graham Ross alerted the court administrators who have now added a routine to check the old system before allowing judgement to be entered by default.

In another initiative, the UK's Ministry of Justice announced in 2020[27] that it is to provide £2m of funding to help with the development of new systems of online dispute resolution suitable for resolving the disputes of small businesses. The project leaders, LawTechUK Vision, will develop a 'sandbox' to help test new ideas for technology assisted resolution.

LawTech UK itself is a collaboration between an industry body called Tech Nation, the government-sponsored LawTech Delivery Panel and the Ministry of Justice.

Four initial projects were announced: a 'UK SME Dispute Resolution Platform', the LawTech Sandbox, a LawTech online hub and a guidance and training centre.

4.2 Publicly Funded Research Projects

The European contribution to ODR has been significantly assisted through European Commission funding support in one form or another. The e-Arbitration-t project[28] was a very early multi-partner collaborative project to develop the regulatory structure and

25 www.judiciary.uk/wp-content/uploads/2015/02/Online-Dispute-Resolution-Final-Web-Version1.pdf.

26 www.judiciary.uk/wp-content/uploads/2016/07/civil-courts-structure-review-final-report-jul-16-final-1.pdf.

27 www.lawgazette.co.uk/news/online-dispute-resolution-will-be-part-of-2m-lawtech-initiative/5104354.article.

28 www.e-arbitration-t.com.

the dynamic and intelligent infrastructure needed to allow simple and efficient distributed processes in electronic out-of-court dispute settlement systems.[29] More specifically a model was designed as an online arbitration service for disputes involving small to medium sized businesses. Public funding by the European Commission was significant (€ 860,000). However, the platform was never completed and the project disbanded at an advanced stage.

Similar vicissitudes affected the CC Form project. This project was funded under the EU's Information Society Technology program (IST-2001-38248) to support online customer complaint management. The project was set up to consider the foundation of a central European customer complaint portal, on which any consumer could, on one website, register a complaint against any party, and about any problem, and in any official EU language. All ODR and dispute handling services could register and the site would inform complainants and signpost solutions. The general view was that on completion of the online form by a complainant, the provider of the service complained of would be encouraged to participate in online dispute resolution on the basis this would significantly increase consumer confidence. The project was a collaboration of various partners led by FEDMA (The Federation of European Direct and Interactive Marketing). CCForm held its final workshop in Brussels in June 2003. Whilst an ontology was developed for customer complaint handling[30] it is not clear why no central website as the destination for all complainants as planned was put into place, but a contributory factor may have been the untimely death in a road accident of the project team leader, Peter Scoggins, shortly before the final conference.

Another early initiative in Europe that received public funding was ECODIR. This initiative was a commissioned research project of the Faculties of Law at the University of Namur, Belgium, the University of Montreal, Canada, and, latterly, University College Dublin, Ireland in the pilot phase, supported by the European Commission and the Irish Department of Enterprise, Trade and Employment. ECODIR is restricted to disputes in relation to online consumer transactions. It involves a three-step process of inter-party negotiation followed by mediation and then, if the mediation does not itself succeed, a non-binding recommendation of a solution is provided by the allocated mediator. In providing the recommendation, the mediator offers a solution based on the facts as presented by the parties, the rights and obligations of the parties in law and the principle of good faith. If the parties accept the recommendation, it may then be formalized in a settlement. It has handled to date 200 cases most with a value no more than € 350. ECODIR's formal pilot project commenced in 2001 and ended in June 2003, although the organisers have since kept the service active. Ecodir Ltd, an Irish Registered Company, is responsible for organising and managing the commercial operation of ECODIR. It is co-ordinated by the Faculty of Law at University College Dublin under

29 http://cordis.europa.eu/fetch?CALLER=PROJ_ICT&ACTION=D&CAT=PROJ&RCN=54082.

30 www.jarrar.info/CContology/index.htm.

the leadership of Professor Brian Hutchinson. "The ECODIR pilot project has shown that a real need exists for a low-cost mechanism for the resolution of low-value cross-border disputes."[31]

The Mediation Room[32] carried out a 25 case pilot funded by the Ministry of Justice in England in which two mediators employed by the court used a dedicated online mediation platform to undertake a selection of cases that were awaiting final hearing in the Small Claims Court. The Court handles cases with a value of no more than GBP 5,000. The parties are offered free mediation from mediators employed by the court. The platform replicates face to face mediation by providing discussion areas for open discussion between all parties and private discussion between each party and the mediator.

Finally, another EU funded initiative is the EMCOD project with the stated aim of broadening access to justice through the use of ODR. With this aim in mind, EMCOD built an open source software module to enable providers and users of ODR to measure comparatively the user experience and the costs and the quality of the dispute resolution processes within the context of universal norms of accessible justice. Participating providers would receive feedback of user experience and benchmarking data that it is anticipated will help direct further advances in ODR. Although the Handbook was published in 2012,[33] the planned pilot has not as yet taken place. Given 8 years have now passed since the project produced the book, it may not now take place. The project partners were TISCO (the Tilburg Institute for Interdisciplinary Studies of Civil Law and Conflict Resolution Systems), the Institute of Advanced Legal Studies, The Mediation Room.com, the Bulgarian Institute for Legal Development, the Autonomous University of Barcelona, the Research Centre for Legal and Economic Issues of Electronic Communications (CBKE) of the Faculty of Law at the University of Wroclaw, and the University of Haifa.

Other EU funded projects in the last few years are EUH2020 project CREA,[34] which aims at developing algorithms to improve cross-border civil proceedings, and the European Research Council funded project "Building EU civil justice: challenges of procedural innovations bridging access to justice."[35] At the time of writing, the project Nemesis, coordinated by Serafin.legal in France has also launched to "conduct innovative,

---

31 Caplin, L Online Cross-border Consumer Dispute Resolution: An Assessment of Its Potential and Analysis of the ECODIR Project - 2004. Avalable at thttps://books.google.ca/books?id=YkMHSQAACAAJ&ved=0ahUKEwi24pi_sMLRAhWDvRQKHbbVDm4Q6AEIHDAA.

32 www.themediationroom.com.

33 "Costs and Quality of Online Dispute Resolution", edited by Martin Gramatikov, Maklu 2012.

34 www.crea-project.eu/.

35 www.eucivil justice.eu/en/project.

interdisciplinary research on online dispute resolution".[36] Serafin.legal is also the developer of the open-source ODR platform FastArbitre.[37]

4.3 Private Initiatives

The new millennium saw the launch of the first UK based ODR services: InterSettle, e-Settle and We Can Settle, all in 2000. They were all blind bidding sites using privately developed software. They were all also founded by lawyers. InterSettle was run by Scottish solicitor, Stephen Moore, backed by eight of Scotland's leading litigation practices; We Can Settle was set up and run by two English solicitors, Anne Irving and Graham Ross; and e-Settle was set up by a consortium of barristers and solicitors who had secured significant investment funding of GBP 1.3 million.[38] The co-author's experience in We Can Settle was that it was difficult attracting the support of claimant lawyers to participate in a novel game-like service at the request of the insurer. This was an issue not so much of trust in the 'Fourth Party' but of trust in the insurer and the motive for making the request. The claimant lawyers were being asked to move out of their comfort zone into a form of negotiation with which they were totally unfamiliar. Many may have questioned their professional competence to do so. As a result, none of the pilots succeeded in changing practices. Following the US company, Cybersettle Inc, obtaining world patent rights to their version of blind bidding, (29 January 2003) and issuing 'cease and desist' letters, all three companies closed down their operations.

None of the three exist today. The Mediation Room did develop its own blind bidding engine and the British' Columbian company, iCan Systems Inc, has patented its own unique system of 'visual blind bidding' under the brand of 'Smartsettle ONE' which is fully operational. Blind bidding refers to a system in which some, but not necessarily all, offers and counter-offers in disputes in which the only issue to resolve is the amount of a payment to be made by one party to the other, can be submitted yet not be seen by the other party. Settlement is declared when the latest bids satisfy one of the applied algorithms, such as to the proximity of the bids to each other. This significantly reduces the time spent in the usual negotiation 'dance' with parties sitting on offers that are less than their bottom lines.

Smartsettle ONE encourages positive bidding rewarding the party that makes more effort to settle. Graham Ross, introduced the system to two litigants in a UK court in 2019. The case was issued in the new Online Civil Money Claims Court. After 3 months in the court process, including an unsuccessful court administered telephone mediation, the parties

---

36 https://cordis.europa.eu/project/id/890793.
37 https://github.com/Open-Justice/ODR.
38 A. Gould, "Blind Bidding Site On Trial", *Post Magazine*, 14 December 2000.

were able to settle the dispute (over unpaid fees for a counselling course) within an hour of first use of the Smartsettle ONE visual blind bidding tool.

This early history of blind bidding in the UK contributes generally to the controversial issue of patents in software. The argument runs that whilst, on the one hand, patents encourage investment to better facilitate creative development in software, on the negative side, in restricting rights to one rights holder and its own commercial policies, they prevent wider development. None of the three UK companies would have relished extensive litigation with Cybersettle, itself then owned by a major insurer and thus feared to have a 'deep pocket' so far as litigation was concerned. Cybersettle itself faced professional and cultural barriers current for any development in the legal arena that threatened to reduce legal cost through its impact, by speeding up the time to conclusion, on chargeable hours (unlike in the USA where claimant costs are more often based on the amount of the compensation awarded than time spent). The impact of such barriers became apparent subsequently when Cybersettle made two separate attempts to expand into the UK market, both of which resulted in failure. They initially set up a UK company in 2002, and promoted the service in the insurance industry press but, despite success in the USA, it failed to take a hold in the UK. In 2004, they entered into a marketing partnership with a UK firm of solicitors, Steeles,[39] but this terminated the following year. In 2007, Cybersettle announced, at the 5th International Forum on ODR held in Liverpool, a new European initiative being a strategic alliance with the Ireland based International Centre for Dispute Resolution (ICDR) of the American Arbitration Association. A year later at the 7th International Forum held in Victoria, British Columbia, Charles Brofman, CEO of Cybersettle Inc, gave a presentation announcing an ODR project that the Cybersettle/ICDR collaboration had launched in Italy for the GE Oil and Gas Company. This was an online med-arb process (a period of online mediation and, if that failed, an arbitral award would be made and declared on the online file) for disputes with suppliers in the oil and gas industry. A panel of Italian engineers was created to provide the arbitrators. In 2010 use of the system became included as a term of purchase in contracts by GE Oil and Gas.

In 2008, one of the then leading providers of ODR in Europe, Juripax, no longer operational, was asked by the Dutch Legal Aid Board to create an Internet application for online mediation in divorce cases. The aim of the research project was to verify whether online mediation is a good way to settle divorce cases. In total, twelve mediators were involved in the research project, all trained in the use of online mediation and the Juripax technology. A total of 126 parties filled out the evaluation questionnaire, comprising 56 couples and 14 individual respondents. Reactions to the project show significant gender differences. Women indicated, more than men that they would use an online tool again in the future. The data also showed that the online

39 www.lawgazette.co.uk/news/steeles-targets-pi/41113.article.

tool provided women with a (better) sense of 'justice' by giving them a voice and answers to important questions.

A partnering between the Hague Institute for the Internationalisation of Law (HIIL), the Dutch Legal Aid Board and the US firm Modria created Rechtwijzer, Rechtwijzer provided guided pathways for divorcing parties through an interactive experience that led to information specifically tailored to client needs. The systems developed to build online dispute resolution into the package. However in 2017, due to limited take-up users, Rechtwijzer closed its doors. Later the same year a new system of ODR was launched called Justice42, which has since been under development.

Recently there have been a number of new ODR services in Europe setting up in operation. A new smartphone App for consumer disputes, co-funded by the EU, was launched in 2020 called ADR4All, allowing consumers to file a complaint online and access dispute resolution services largely operating under the EU law on ODR. It covers all businesses and consumers worldwide and is supported by a back end multi-level administration and case management system.

In Ireland there has been the launch of An Olive Branch[40] which uses online technology to help parties in dispute to reframe, under guidance from lawyers, their claims and responses in a way more likely to achieve mutual resolution.

A Slovakian ODR solution, Youstice,[41] provides a graphic rich platform for logging and resolving consumer disputes. Consumers can engage with the retailer over a complaint and, if not resolved, a neutral can issue a solution. Unlike with the similar UK complaint service, Resolver,[42] Youstie requires to be adopted by the retailer before being used by a consumer. Resolver does not as yet include a dispute resolution service.

In August 2020 in the UK, Resolve Disputes Online,[43] a comprehensive case management and resolution platform, was awarded a contract by LawTechUK, a collaboration including the Ministry of Justice, to conduct a feasibility study for the development of an ODR system to help small to medium sized companies quickly resolve their disputes with slow paying larger corporation customers.

5 THE EUROPEAN LANDSCAPE IN THE 2010S

A broad overview of European ODR service providers was extracted from research undertaken by the ODR team within the framework of the White Book on Mediation

40 www.anolivebranch.com.
41 www.youstice.com.
42 www.resolver.co.uk.
43 www.resolvedisputes.online.

in Catalonia.[44] Desktop research of ODR websites was combined with interviews and electronic mail communications with experts on the field. The results were synthesized in Table 23.1 below.

The table summarized the basic features of some of the main EU ODR providers at the time.[45] As shown in the table, meditation was the most frequent service being offered online. In a few cases, services provide recommendations, arbitration, assisted mediation, and early neutral evaluation. Similarly, in some other cases there were ODR services providing ancillary services such as lists of mediators, training, or trustmarks. As regards functionalities, it was usual for these EU ODR services to have automated flows and, to some degree, structured forms, automated messages alerting on the different ODR steps, and confidential registers of cases. Almost unanimously, all ODR in the table relied on asynchronous communication between all parties, while some of them also include synchronous methods (*i.e.* videoconference or chat). As for the service models provided, the table also distinguished: (i) basic ODR, using state-of-the-art Internet tools; (ii) ODR services using proprietary technology; (iii) ODR services that also sell their software licences and (iv) ODR services that provide software on demand (SAAS).

The research excluded internal complaint management systems for aggrieved customers that were not including ADR mechanisms or, while having one, only provided a form to initiate the complaint, domain name dispute resolution systems, and online courts (also known as cybercourts). Likewise, the table did not show ODR websites providing services for domain name disputes, present in a large number of European countries. Finally, Table 23.1 does not report Negotiation Support Systems (NSS) that are closely related to some EU ODR services.

---

44 M. Poblet, P. Noriega, J. Suquet, S. Gabarró & J. Redorta, "Tecnologías para la mediación en línea, estado del arte, usos y propuestas", in P. Casanovas, J. Magre, Mª.E. Lauroba (eds.), *Libro Blanco de la Mediación en Catalunya*, Departament de Justícia, Generalitat de Catalunya, Barcelona 2010.

45 The original table reported roughly 40 ODR services from all over the world. *See* Poblet *et al.* (2010), pp. 943-1008.

Table 23.1 European ODR Service Providers (2010)

Product	*Aegi Solutions*	*Agència Catalana de Consum*	*Concilia Online*	*Confianza Online*	*Conciliazione On-Line*	*Der Internet Ombudsmann*	*ECODIR*	*eMediation.NI*	*Juripax*	*Mediar Online*	*Allegro*	*Mediation Room*	*Risolvi Online*
Provider	Centre de Médiation et Arbitrage de Paris	Agència Catalana de Consum	Camera di Commercio di Firenze	AECEM, AUTOCONTROL i Red.es	Camera di Commercio di Ancona	Der Internet Ombudsmann	International consortium	Emediation & Roelvink Advocatenkantoor	Juripax	Individuals and legal persons	Allegro	Mediation Room	Cammera Arbitrale di Milano
Country	France	Catalonia	Italy	Spain	Italy	Austria	Europe	Netherlands	Netherlands	Spain-Argentina	Poland	UK	Italy
Web	www.mediationetarbitrage.com	http://www.consumcat.net	http://www.conciliaonline.net/concilia/	http://www.confianzaonline.es	http://conciliazione.an.camcom.it/index.php	http://www.ombudsmann.at/	http://www.ecodir.org	http://www.emediation.nl/	www.juripax.com	http://www.mediaronline.com	http://allegro.onet.pl	www.themediationroom.com	http://www.risolvionline.com/
Domain	*G*	*G (B2C)*	*G*	*G*	*e-T (B2B, B2C)*	*e-T (B2C, C2C)*	*e-T (B2C)*	*G*	*G*	*G*	*e-T (B2C, C2C)*	*G*	*e-T (B2B, B2C, C2C)*
ODR Mechanisms													
Assisted negotiation							X				X		
Automated negotiation													
Mediation		X	X	X	X	X	X	X	X			X	X
Arbitration				X									
Adjudication				X									
Recommendation	X						X						
Early neutral evaluation	X												
Other services													
Mediators' list										X		X	X
Trustmark				X									
Training										X		X	
Other									Premediatio				
Functionalities													
Automated workflow			X				X		X	X	X	X	X
Registry of cases	X		X						X	X	X	X	
Structured forms				X	X		X		X	X			X
Automated messages	X		X				X		X	X	X	X	X
Confidential registers	X		X		X	X	X		X	X	X	X	X
Database													
Communication													
Asynchronous	X	X	X	X	X	X	X		X	X	X	X	X
Synchronous		X	X		X			X	X	X		X	
Algorithms													
Optimisation algorithm													
Cross-offers algorithm									X				
Service models													
Basic ODR		X		X		X							
Proprietary technology	X		X		X		X	X			X		X
ODR licence seller									X			X	
SAAS Provider			X							X			

[G: general; e-T: electronic transactions]

Source: Adapted from Poblet *et al.* (2010)

6 Towards Distributed Models of ODR: Blockchain Dispute Resolution

The ODR initiatives of the first decade of the 21st century in Europe leveraged different digital technologies and business models. Overall, the outcomes resulted in a mix of successes and failed promises, especially with regard to mass adoption by European businesses, consumers, and citizens at large. At present, another generation of projects is emerging and, very much like its predecessors, it is gradually building its services on top of state-of-the-art online technologies. This new stage of ODR services has received different labels, such "crowdsourced dispute resolution,"[46] "decentralized justice"[47] or, more specifically, "blockchain dispute resolution."[48]

A distinctive feature of the next generation of ODR services is the use of the blockchain. Blockchain is a distributed, immutable, and censorship-resistant ledger that records cryptographically signed transactions. The first implementation of the Blockchain was Bitcoin, the peer-to-peer payment system famously announced by Satoshi Nakamoto in 2008[49] and launched on January 2009. In 2014, the launching of the Ethereum platform ushered a new wave of innovations based on the use of smart contracts (self-executing software running on the blockchain). The new ecosystem of blockchain startups have leveraged smart contracts as a core component of decentralized applications (or dApps) for a growing number of sectors (finance, gaming, energy, logistics and supply chains, government, etc.). The value proposition of blockchain services is to enable automated transactions in a trustless environment where consensus algorithms replace traditional intermediaries. While the absence of these intermediaries may reduce transaction costs and potential disputes, smart contracts do not come dispute-free either. Rather, new types of disputes may emerge from different angles (e.g. defective software, manipulation of the data feeding the smart contract – the oracle problem – or, more generically, changing circumstances outside the smart contract that cannot be captured, updated, or properly executed.

Blockchain dispute resolution broadly refers to services and protocols managing disputes that arise in the socio-technical ecosystem of distributed ledger technologies. While these services and protocols are distributed in nature, a number of them have been developed by teams that have incorporated as legal entities in different European

46 N. Luz, M. Poblet, and N. Silva, "Crowdsourcing Dispute Resolution: Survey and Challenges", in P. Novais and D. Carneiro (eds.) *Interdisciplinary Perspectives on Contemporary Conflict Resolution*, pp. 279-295. IGI Global, 2016.

47 Kleros, *Dispute Revolution. The Kleros Handbook of Decentralized Justice*, available at: https://ipfs.kleros.io/ipfs/QmZeV32S2VoyUnqJsRRCh75F1fP2AeomVq2Ury2fTt9V4z/Dispute-Resolution-Kleros.pdf.

48 D.W. Allen, A.M. Lane, and M. Poblet, "The Governance of Blockchain Dispute Resolution", *Harvard Negotiation Law Review*, (2019), Vol. 25, pp. 75-101, 2019. *See also* M. Poblet, D.W. Allen, O. Konashevych, A.M. Lane, and C.A. Diaz Valdivia, "From Athens to the Blockchain: Oracles for Digital Democracy", *Frontiers in Blockchain*, (2020), doi: 10.3389/fbloc.2020.575662.

49 S. Nakamoto, "Bitcoin: A Peer-to-Peer Electronic Cash System", 2008, available at: https://bitcoin.org/bitcoin.pdf.

jurisdictions. This is the case, for example, of Mattereum,[50] offering arbitration of disputes in different property domains. Likewise, Kleros[51] and the Aragon Court[52] have incorporated in France and Switzerland, respectively, to develop crowdsourced jury services where networks of distributed jurors are randomly selected to resolve disputes. Both systems rely on protocols applying game-theoretical incentives for jurors to stake tokens and earn disputes by adjudicating tokens. Finally, in Germany, the Blockchain Arbitration Forum brings together researchers and practitioners in the blockchain space to facilitate the resolution of disputes in that space and advocate for more education on the legal ramifications of this emergent technology.

The blockchain space is still in its infancy and it is too early to conclude which directions the new ODR services are going to take. Yet, the teams and platforms currently being developed in Europe will surely constitute a fundamental piece in this nascent ecosystem.

7 CONCLUSIONS

It is safe to conclude from the preceding pages that Europe has played a major role to date in the development of ODR, starting with the emergence of the first entrepreneurial launches – chiefly with private blind biddings sites – and, on the institutional side, with the launch, in Geneva, of the International Forum on ODR, the annual event providing a privileged space for the emergence of a heterogeneous, international ODR community. Europe also introduced the first ODR specific legislation in the Regulation on Online Dispute Resolution For Consumer Disputes.

The EU public funding initiatives have also constituted a major driver for the development of ODR. However, some projects ended with no conclusive results in terms of prototypes or proofs of concept. In this line, some lessons could be also extracted at this point on how to adequately fill the gap between initial prototypes – raising high expectations – and the effective provision of ODR services to customers.

One minor, but nevertheless helpful lesson that comes out of the European experience over the first 20 years of the 21st century is the need for some pan-European co-ordination of all those involved in the development of ODR. The introduction of ADR within the judicial process must itself help increase the demand for, and awareness of, technology assisted ADR. It is believed, for the reasons set out in this paper, that not only has Europe made a substantial contribution in the past to ODR but, with the new developments in distributed ODR, will continue to do so at an increasing pace in the future.

---

50 https://mattereum.com/.

51 https://kleros.io/.

52 https://anj.aragon.org/.

Chapter 24 Online Dispute Resolution and Africa

*Ayodele Musibau Kusamotu**

1 Introduction

Africa is the most populous and largest continent after Asia. It has the youngest population of all the continents. Among its more than 1.3 billion people, Africa has more Internet users than North America and the Middle East. According to the United Nations (UN's) projections, half of the world's population will reside in Africa between 2015 and 2050 when the population is expected to more than double to 2.4 billion in 2050. The newly created African Continental Free Trade Area (ACFTA), the largest free trade area with 55 participating countries, has a combined gross domestic product (GDP) of US$3.4 trillion, and more than 30 million people are expected to be lifted out of poverty by its creation.

To benefit from the international economy, African nations must adopt new technologies. The governments will have to eliminate regulatory and political barriers to extend broadband access to citizens. In particular, to enjoy the benefits of the Internet, marginalized groups and women who hitherto have had no access must be provided with connectivity.

The Internet has transformed the way commerce, business, and human interaction happen around the world. Africans have become increasingly dependent on the World Wide Web and have found incredible ways of leveraging technology over the Internet to add value to small and medium-sized enterprises (SMEs) increasing job opportunities for the new generation. Electronic commerce can be a catalyst for development in Africa; however, the problem of the digital divide persists, with only about 13.5% of Africans having access to the Internet.

Given that online dispute resolution (ODR) is generally about the settlement of business disputes between consumers on the likes of eBay and other platforms, it has now spilled over into mainstream dispute resolution involving the courts. It is in this context that this article interrogates ODR amidst the ongoing Internet revolution in Africa and issues related to the application of ODR as a means of settling disputes in the continent.

* The author wishes to thank the lawyers of Kusamotu Firm for their assistance.

This article begins by discussing ODR and legal technology regulation, goes on to address ODR and the access to justice and concludes with suggestions for the future.

2 Online Dispute Resolutions in Africa and Legal Technology Regulation

There are a variety of definitions of ODR, but, essentially, it refers to the use and adaptation of traditional alternative dispute resolution (ADR) models (most commonly mediation, negotiation, and arbitration) to resolve disputes that arise online. These types of disputes can arise from contracts concluded through electronic or digital means. These include (but are not limited to) contracts concluded via email, short message service (SMS), or other automated systems.[1]

Although the use of ODR mechanisms has long been advocated, the advent of the coronavirus (Covid-19) pandemic has strengthened the case for exploring new ways to ensure that disputes between parties are resolved speedily and amicably without the need for physical meetings. Online resolution of disputes has also been used by parties through various mediums like Zoom, Skype, WhatsApp, Google Meetings, and other online platforms, both audio and visual.

For those African countries that are members of the Organization for the Harmonization of Business Law in Africa (OHADA), the Uniform Act on Arbitration Law and the Uniform Act on Mediation does not provide for online dispute resolution. The OHADA region also has the Common Court of Justice and Arbitration, headquartered in Abidjan, Cote D'Ivoire.[2]

In Uganda, the law allows for various ADR methods, including arbitration, conciliation, and mediation; ODR is a relatively new concept in Uganda, thus there are no laws specifically providing for it.

There have been attempts by the judiciary in Uganda to undertake digital transformation. The Judicature (Visual-Audio Link) Rules 2016[3] has gone a long way towards empowering the Ugandan courts to encourage alternative hearing methods. However, these online hearings are mainly confined to the higher courts and high-profile criminal matters. It is important to mention that the International Centre for Arbitration and Mediation in Kampala (ICAMEK) has arbitration rules[4] permitting the

1 http://ase-scoop.org/papers/IWLP-2016/3.Cupido_IWLP.pdf (last accessed on 2 September 2020 at 10:12pm).

2 www.ohada.org/index.php/fr/cour-commune-de-justice-et-d-arbitrage-ccja/ccja-en-bref (last accessed on 2 September 2020 at 10:34pm).

3 https://ulii.org/system/files/judicature-visual-audio-link-rules-si-no-26-of-2016a.pdf (last accessed on 3 September 2020 at 3:15am).

4 http://ugandabankers.org/the-international-centre-for-arbitration-mediation-in-kampala-commences-operations/ (last accessed on 8 April 2021 at 11:22am) / www.icamek.org/wp-content/uploads/2020/02/ICAMEK-ARBITRATION-RULES-2018.pdf (last accessed on 3 September 2020 at 4:14am).

use of ODR. The legal profession and the general Ugandan public are, because of the pioneering of ODR platforms in neighbouring countries, such as iResolve[5] in Tanzania, slowly accepting ODR.

As discussed previously, ODR is not provided for in the laws in force in most African countries; however, owing to exceptional circumstances preventing physical presence, there is nothing to prevent parties from choosing to resolve their dispute using technological means if all guarantees are offered to that effect. To date, the presence of Covid-19 has not fundamentally affected the functioning of institutions as ADR is taking place in strict compliance with the barrier measures enacted by the government and the use of online platforms.

In line with global practice, most African countries have enacted laws, policies, guidelines, and regulations governing the use of technology and covering e-commerce. These were enacted to regulate electronic signature and electronic evidence in such countries with the use of technology in commerce and dispute resolution. An example of such laws is the Evidence Act of 2011 of Nigeria,[6] which makes provision, in Section 84, for the admissibility of electronic/computer-generated evidence. Another example is the Republic of Guinea law L/2016/035/AN of 28 July 2016,[7] which aims to regulate electronic transactions in Guinea. These are few examples of the myriad of innovations resorted to by African countries to meet international standards.

In addition, there are various laws affecting technology in Uganda, including the Electronic Transactions Act, 2011,[8] the Electronic Signatures Act, 2011,[9] the Computer Misuse Act, 2011,[10] E-Transactions Regulations, 2013,[11] and E-Signatures Regulations, 2013.[12] The Electronic Transaction Act of 2011 is the major law governing e-commerce in Uganda, which stipulates the use, security, facilitation, and regulation of electronic communications and transactions and encourages the use of e-government services. The Electronic Signatures Act, 2011, provides for regulating the use of electronic signatures to ensure that transactions are carried out in a secure environment. The Electronic Signatures Regulations (Statutory Instrument No. 43 of 2013) provide further details to the Electronic Signatures Act (ESA) concerning licensing and

5 www.iresolve.co.tz/ (last accessed on 3 September 2020 at 3:45am).

6 www.refworld.org/pdfid/54f86b844.pdf (last accessed on 2 September 2020 at 10:48pm).

7 www.ictpolicyafrica.org/fr/document/68hrs1fphei?page=1 (last accessed on 2 September 2020 at 10:51pm).

8 https://ulii.org/system/files/legislation/act/2011/8/electronic_transactions_act_rtf_16395.pdf (last accessed on 3 September 2020 at 2:56am).

9 www.nita.go.ug/sites/default/files/publications/Electronic%20Signatures%20Act%202011%20%28Act%20No.%207%20of%202011%29.pdf (last accessed on 3September2020 at 5:18am).

10 https://ict.go.ug/2019/12/03/the-computer-misuse-act-2011/#:~:text=An%20Act%20to%20make%20provision,electronic%20environment%20and%20to%20provide (last accessed on 7 April, 2021 at 3:42pm).

11 www.nita.go.ug/sites/default/files/publications/Electronic%20Transactions%20Regulations%202013%20-%20SI%2042%20of%202013.pdf (last accessed on 3September2020 at 3:29am).

12 www.unwantedwitness.org/cyberpolicy/wp-content/uploads/2018/02/Electronic-Signatures-Regulations-2013-SI-43-of-2013-1.pdf (last accessed on 3September2020 at 2:19am).

recognition of certification service providers, providers of repository services, and the date and time stamp services. It also sets out the roles, responsibilities, and obligations of the various service providers and players in the e-signatures environment, provides for the handling of complaints and resolution of disputes that may arise between the players and lays down offenses and penalties for failing to adhere to the regulations.

Furthermore, most African countries have started enacting laws and regulations to provide for data protection. An example of such law is the Ghanaian Data Protection Act of 2012,[13] which establishes a data protection commission to protect individuals' privacy and personal data by regulating the processing of personal information, to outline the process of obtaining, holding, using, or disclosing personal information and related matters. The Data Protection Act requires that personal data be processed only if the purpose for which it is to be processed is necessary, relevant, and not excessive. These yardsticks must be used in measuring all claims by the data controller.

South Africa also has its Protection of Personal Information Act, 2013[14] which gives effect to the constitutional right to privacy by safeguarding personal information when processed by a responsible party subject to justifiable limitations.

Kenya has the Kenyan Data Protection Act of 2019,[15] which regulates the processing of personal data, protects the privacy of individuals, establishes the legal and institutional mechanism to protect personal data, and provides data subjects with rights and remedies to protect their data from the procession that is not in accordance with the act.

Egypt also enacted its Data Protection Law No. 151 of 2020, which protects the privacy of personal data and penalizes the sharing of data without the prior consent of the data owner; it also regulates overseas data transfers according to international General Data Protection Regulations (GDPR) that ensure personal data protection in Egypt and abroad and protects foreign investors, especially those from European Union (EU) countries.[16]

Uganda has the Data Protection and Privacy Act (2019),[17] which was largely inspired by the European Union (EU) General Data Protection Regulation (GDPR) and aims to "protect the privacy of the individual and of personal data". This act applies to all persons or entities processing personal data within and outside Uganda for those using personal data relating to Ugandan citizens. The regulator under this act has been carrying out

13 http://media.mofo.com/files/PrivacyLibrary/3981/GHANAbill.pdf (last accessed on 2 September2020 at 11:07pm).

14 www.justice.gov.za/inforeg/docs/InfoRegSA-POPIA-act2013-004.pdf (last accessed on 2 September2020 at 11:10pm).

15 http://kenyalaw.org/kl/fileadmin/pdfdownloads/Acts/2019/TheDataProtectionAct__No24of2019.pdf (last accessed on 2 September 2020 at 11:16pm).

16 www.mondaq.com/data-protection/968902/data-protection-law-no-151-for-2020-legal-alert-118 (last accessed on 2 September 2020 at 11:34pm).

17 https://ulii.org/system/files/legislation/act/2019/1/THE%20DATA%20PROTECTION%20AND%20PRIVACY%20BILL%20-%20ASSENTED.pdf (last accessed on 2 September 2020 at 11:59pm).

public awareness on the various obligations, and we await the testing of these provisions in the courts.

Although Nigeria is yet to enact a data protection law, it has in place the Nigeria Data Protection Regulation 2019,[18] whose provisions safeguard the rights of natural persons to data privacy, foster safe conduct of transactions involving the exchange of personal data, prevent manipulation of personal data and ensure that Nigerian businesses remain competitive in international trade. This is done through the safeguards afforded by a just and equitable legal regulatory framework on data protection that is in tune with global best practices.

A major challenge in almost all African countries in the use of ODR is the lack of reliable telecommunication infrastructure. Internet penetration in most African countries is still hovering at about 20%, the urban centres constituting the majority of this segment. Other challenges are technology apathy by parties and their legal representatives. The majority of systems in Africa are manual, and there is a need for a significant mind shift by all stakeholders. Implementation of existing policy and legislative frameworks is a recurring issue.

Most of the dispute resolution mechanisms in Africa involve physical interactions, resulting in serious delays in most hearings, and the government directives restricting public gatherings have greatly reduced the case disposal rate because of the reliance on physical hearings. It is now obvious that ODR can be used by parties to resolve their disputes amicably, and despite the general challenges with the use of technology in Africa, parties can still apply this medium to have access to justice at all times without the need for physical meetings.

3 Online Dispute Resolution and Access to Justice[19]

Recent events have clearly shown that only a small but steadily increasing number of courts have just begun implementing ODR court technology that provides a digital space for parties to resolve their dispute or case.

The use of technology in dispute resolution and justice administration in developing economies has been ongoing for nearly two decades; however, the outbreak of the novel coronavirus disease (Covid-19), which led to the suspension of judicial activities in courts in most African countries, has brought ODR to the fore. Thus, governments have been forced to adopt the use of remote or non-physical proceedings of dispute resolution.

---

18 https://ndpr.nitda.gov.ng/Content/Doc/NigeriaDataProtectionRegulation.pdf (last accessed on 7 April 2021 at 3:47pm).

19 A topic by Adedayo Adamolekun, Paul Kalejaiye and Oluwatosin Akinjide, all of the Law Firm of Kusamotu & Kusamotu, Nigeria.

Previously, the recognized methods of dispute resolution in Africa were litigation and ADR mechanisms like arbitration, mediation, conciliation, and negotiation. Nigeria, whose economy and the population is the largest in Africa, has been particularly forward-looking and set up the first court that is connected to an ADR centre in Africa –the Lagos Multi-Door Courthouse (LMDC). Generally, Nigerian courts are closely connected to the ADR centres. Of Nigeria's 36 states, 16 (sixteen) currently have legally established courts connected to ADR centres.[20]

ODR shifts dispute settlement from physical to online platforms which allow all parties, including the mediator, judge, arbitrator, and negotiator to connect and resolve disputes from anywhere in the world without being physically present at a particular location.

4 EXISTING OR PROPOSED LAWS, GUIDELINES, POLICIES, REGULATIONS, RULES, LAWS OR PRACTICE DIRECTIONS IN AFRICA PROVIDING VIRTUAL/REMOTE COURT HEARING

The emergence of Covid-19 created a pressing need to reassess all the previous modes of dispute resolution to ensure that parties can resolve their disputes without the need for their physical presence. This impacted the court systems in some countries in Africa, whose judiciary had to devise means of proceeding with the administration of justice without the need for parties to be present in courts. We shall now discuss some of the countries and courts in Africa that have already introduced remote-virtual hearings.

4.1 African Court on Human and People's Rights

The African Court on Human and People's Rights adopted a virtual hearing to facilitate the administration of justice amid the Covid-19. It also issued a practice direction for virtual sessions,[21] basically to provide for the safety of the judges, staff, and other court users and also for the timely and efficient disposal of cases. It provides mainly for the use of technology for case management, holding of court sessions and the conduct of public hearings, and for all hearings to be live-streamed on the court's YouTube channel on www.youtube.com/user/africancourt/channels/live. In line with the new practice direction, on 24 June 2020, the court announced that it held the four-week virtual

20 Morenike Obi-Farinde: ODR in Africa: The Emergent Face of Dispute Resolution Post COVID-19 – www.mediate.com/articles/obi-odr-africa.cfm# (last accessed 3 September 2020 at 11.00 am).

21 https://en.african-court.org/images/Basic%20Documents/Practice_Directions_for_Virtual_Sessions_EN.pdf (last accessed on 28 August 2020 at 10:43pm).

sitting of its 57th ordinary session and that the cases were adjourned to 26 June 2020 for judgment.[22] On 13 July 2020, the court also announced that it would deliver three judgments virtually on 15 July 2020.[23]

4.2 *Community Court of Justice, ECOWAS*

The Community Court of Justice, ECOWAS court also took measures to provide for remote hearing to ensure that the system of justice administration continued without any hitch or hindrance, either from the coronavirus pandemic or otherwise. This led to the issuance of its practice directions for electronic case management and virtual court sessions[24]on 22 May 2020 mainly to provide for the use of technology for the general case management system and court sessions. The court also published its cause list dated 3 July 2020[25] and stated that the cases on the cause list would be conducted virtually, with the meeting ID and password stated clearly on the cause list.

4.3 *East African Court of Justice*

This court is one of the organs of the East African Community established under Article 9 of the Treaty for the Establishment of the East African Community. The court was established in November 2001 with the major responsibility of ensuring adherence to law in the interpretation and application of and compliance with the East African Court Treaty. The court has also commenced virtual hearings via video conferencing for online hearings and delivery of rulings and judgments. The decision to proceed with virtual hearings is based on Rules 132 and 133 of the Court's Rules of Procedure 2019 on the use of technology in court proceedings and electronic sharing of documents, respectively. The court also issued extra guidelines to be followed by the parties.[26]As of 15 May 2020, the Appellate Division's Cause List had a total of 12 matters scheduled for

22 https://en.african-court.org/index.php/news/press-releases/item/356-african-court-on-human-and-peoples-rights-to-deliver-eight-judgments-on-friday-26-june-2020 (last accessed on 28 August 2020 at 10:48pm).

23 https://en.african-court.org/index.php/news/press-releases/item/358-african-court-on-human-and-peoples-rights-to-deliver-three-judgments-on-wednesday-15-july-2020 (last accessed on 28 August 2020 at 10:49pm).

24 http://prod.courtecowas.org/wp-content/uploads/2020/05/PD_ENG.pdf (last accessed on 28 August 2020 at 10:57pm).

25 http://prod.courtecowas.org/wp-content/uploads/2020/07/New-General-Cause-List-signed-and-dated-3rd-July-2020-1.pdf (last accessed on 28 August 2020 at 11:05pm).

26 https://www.eacj.org//wp-content/uploads/2020/04/GUIDELINES-FOR-VIDEO-CONFERENCE-PROCEEDINGS-OF-EACJ-MAY-2020-.pdf (last accessed on 28 August 2020 at 10:33pm).

hearing, including 5 Scheduling Conferences, 2 Hearings of the Reference and Application, 1 Hearing of Arbitration, 3 Rulings and 1 Judgment to be delivered.[27]

4.4 *Gambia*

The chief justice of Gambia established an Inter-Agency Task Force (IATF), approved the establishment of 2 virtual high courts for civil and criminal cases, and issued practice directives to the stakeholders. The first virtual court hearing in Gambia was held on 10 June 2020, and a total of 55 cases have been heard, 13 of them related to criminal matters and 42 to civil matters, as of 15 July 2020. The cases of detainees are heard daily before two virtual high courts. The chief justice of Gambia is considering adding two more high courts per day to the virtual court, totaling 4 (four) and extending the pilot to the magistrate level.[28]

4.5 *Ghana*

Ghana is actively trying to ensure the system of justice administration does not suffer during the pandemic or any other time. This led to the innovation of the e-justice platform by the Ghanaian judiciary. E-justice (also called paperless courts) seeks to automate the existing manual filing systems within the court's registry, i.e. from the filing of cases to the execution of court decisions. It is an electronic case management system for the registry side of the entire court process. The judges can also deliver rulings and judgments remotely.[29] Other novelties are the e-docket, a digital copy of the physical docket that contains all processes filed in a matter and that can be accessed remotely from the comfort of one's home; e-cause lists, which dispense with the physical presence of lawyers or their clerks at court premises to check on dates scheduled for their cases; and an entirely new digital and paperless working environment that most judges, lawyers, and court staff are still adapting to.[30]

---

27 www.eacj.org/?news=court-set-for-virtual-hearings-starting-next-week-with-the-appellate-division (last accessed on 28 August 2020 at 9:56pm).

28 www.gm.undp.org/content/gambia/en/home/blog/2020/undp-support-to-the-establishment-of-the-virtual-courts-in-respo.html (last accessed on 28 August 2020 at 9:46pm).

29 www.judicial.gov.gh/index.php/e-services/ejustice/f-a-q (last accessed on 28 August 2020 at 11:32pm).

30 www.africanwomeninlaw.com/post/a-judge-s-perspective-preparedness-of-the-judicial-service-of-ghana-post-covid-19 (last accessed on 28 August 2020 at 11:33pm).

4.6 Kenya

In Kenya, steps have been similarly taken to conduct proceedings and enable courts to continue regular business virtually. The judiciary sent out notices to lawyers that pending judgments and rulings would be delivered via Skype video link and sent by Gmail to lawyers' email accounts. On 7 May 2020, the chief justice of Kenya, Justice David Maraga, stated that more than 7,000 judgments were delivered online by Kenya's judiciary.[31] On 28 August 2020, the judiciary issued a notice that all court proceedings during the high court recess shall be conducted virtually and also gave the virtual links of the judges in charge of the courts.[32]

4.7 Nigeria

The first among such innovations in the Nigerian judiciary is the *Practice Directions for Remote Hearing of Cases,* issued by the Lagos State Judiciary on 4 May 2020,[33] which provides for electronic filing of court processes, hearing of some specific matters, and the delivery of court judgments and rulings using online/virtual platforms like Zoom and Skype. It also provides for the service of court processes on parties to a suit using online means, especially emails. The practice directions apply to new cases demanding urgency, pending cases involving urgent or important, and time-bound interlocutory applications such as bail applications, adoption of addresses, rulings, and judgments, or any other matter that the chief judge will approve.

Nigeria's first virtual court session held on 4 May 2020 at the Lagos State High Court, Ikeja Judicial Division, used the Zoom platform from where Justice Mojisola Dada delivered judgment and convicted the accused person of murder.[34]

Thereafter, the National Judicial Council (NJC), in a circular dated May 2020,[35] addressed the issue of virtual hearing amid Covid-19. The NJC laid down guidelines for virtual or remote court sittings. The circular provides that virtual court sittings (alternatively referred to as 'remote court sittings' or 'online court sittings') should be encouraged and promoted by the courts and counsel and that the courts should insist on such remote hearings for matters that do not require taking any evidence. All judgments, ruling, and directions may be delivered and handed down by the courts in and through remote court sittings. The NJC stated that collaborative platforms, like

31 https://allafrica.com/stories/202005070565.html (last accessed on 29 August 2020 at 12:01am).
32 http://kenyalaw.org/kl/index.php?id=8281 (last accessed on 28 August 2020 at 11:46pm).
33 https://lagosjudiciary.gov.ng/ (last accessed on 21 August 2020 at 2:36am).
34 http://saharareporters.com/2020/05/04/nigeria-holds-first-online-court-sitting-lagos-man-sentenced-death-murder (last accessed on 28 August 2020 at 11:55pm).
35 https://njc.gov.ng/30/news-details (last accessed on 21 August 2020 at 2:14am).

MS365, Zoom, Google Meetings, are equipped with electronic recording functionalities for recording virtual court proceedings and that the courts shall make use of
those functionalities for the recording of the proceedings in addition to any other recording methods that the court may wish to deploy.

In line with the aforementioned NJC guidelines and circular, other courts decided to pass similar practice directions, all to support virtual court hearings during the pandemic. These included the High Court of Federal Capital Territory, Abuja, which issued the Covid-19 Practice Direction 2020, on 8 May 2020,[36] and the Federal High Court, which issued its practice directions 2020 for the Covid-19 period on 18 May 2020.

The issuance of the practice directions on remote hearings engendered mixed reactions initially, as some sections were sceptical about the constitutionality of having court sittings outside the courtrooms. Pursuant to this, the Supreme Court of Nigeria, on 14 July 2020, at the hearing of the two separate suits filed by the attorneys general of Lagos and Ekiti states, ruled that virtual court sittings are not unconstitutional, null, or void. The Supreme Court was of the view that the suits filed were speculative and that they did not disclose how virtual proceedings had or would negatively affect anyone's interest or right.

Nigeria also launched its E-Government Master Plan, whose overall objective is to strengthen the efficiency and transparency of public service administration and drive digital literacy and technology awareness of government officials and citizens. This will no doubt enhance private participation in justice service delivery models.

4.8 South Africa

The South African judiciary also developed a system called the Court Online, an advanced cloud-based collaborative solution that is aimed at providing a platform for law firms and litigants to file documents to the courts electronically (e-filing). It is an end-to-end e-filing, digital case management, and evidence management system for the high courts of South Africa. It provides law practitioners with the opportunity to file documentation electronically online anywhere and anytime without being physically present at court. It also affords law practitioners the ease of managing their court appearance diaries and court evidence instantaneously online. Within the courtrooms and chambers, the judges shall make use of the system to adjudicate disputes electronically.[37]

36 www.fcthighcourt.gov.ng/download/COVID-19-PRACTICE-DIRECTION-2020.pdf (last accessed on 21 August 2020 at 1:19am).

37 https://www.judiciary.org.za/index.php/court-online (last accessed on 7 April 2021 at 4:50pm)

4.9 Tunisia

It was reported on 18 April 2020 that court hearings in Tunisia would be organized remotely from 2 May 2020 to avoid infection from the Covid-19 within courts and that the Department of Justice was preparing a law that would govern these remote trials.[38]

4.10 Uganda

Ugandan law allows for various ADR methods, including arbitration, conciliation, mediation, and litigation. ODR is a relatively new concept in Uganda. There are no laws specifically providing for ODR. There are attempts by the judiciary in Uganda to undertake digital transformation. The Judicature (Visual-Audio Link) Rules 2016 have gone a long way towards empowering the courts in Uganda to encourage alternative hearing methods. Uganda began virtual court hearings in April 2019 before the coronavirus pandemic.[39] However, these online hearings are mainly in the higher courts and concern high-profile criminal matters. In 2020 as a result of the coronavirus pandemic, courts are slowly adopting online hearings. For criminal matters, some persons on remand are currently being heard through online hearings. The High Court Civil Division has adopted online hearings, albeit on specific occasions.

4.11 Zimbabwe

Prior to the pandemic, Zimbabwe had already enacted the Judicial Laws Amendment (Ease of Settling Commercial and Other Disputes) Act, 2017, to provide for remote hearings and electronic filings of processes before the courts.[40] This law empowers the courts in Zimbabwe to utilize virtual hearings in the administration of justice.

5 Challenges of Virtual Court Hearings and Processes

Infrastructural inadequacies and lack of information technology equipment seem to be the major concern of the African judiciary regarding embracing virtual hearing in Africa. Issues such as power, Internet facilities, and other necessary information technology equipment had to be provided to enhance remote court proceedings.

Another challenge of virtual court hearings is the lack of information technology skills among judicial staff, counsel, and litigants. It was necessary to educate the judicial officers

38 https://allafrica.com/stories/202004190039.html (last accessed on 28 August 2020 at 12:48am).
39 www.xinhuanet.com/english/2019-04/15/c_137979447.htm (last accessed on 29 August 2020 at 12:54am).
40 http://extwprlegs1.fao.org/docs/pdf/zim171588.pdf (last accessed on 29 August 2020 at 1:08am).

as well as to sensitize the general public on the importance of technology in the dispensation of justice in the present time.

Internet connectivity issues in Africa are a major impediment to courts and counsel during court proceedings, and counsel and litigants with connectivity issues risk being unable to participate in court proceedings on the scheduled dates.

Funding is another constraint, as some counsel and litigants might not have adequate funds to participate in the remote court proceedings because of the amount of data that is involved in utilizing the online platforms through which the proceedings are conducted. For the judiciary, there is an additional cost to be incurred in using virtual hearing, which was not provided or budgeted for before the pandemic.

A virtual hearing will also be difficult to propose and adopt where a visit to *locus in quo* is required, especially in criminal cases. For civil cases, however, parties may agree on video recording of scenes.

Other challenges to virtual court processes are associated with rules and traditions that may no longer be relevant. For instance, oath-taking is mandatorily required to be performed before the commissioner for oaths. By law, non-signing of the oaths or written statements on oath before a commissioner for oaths renders them void. Again, notarization has often been a requirement in many judicial processes. With increased flexibility in court rules because of Covid-19, many courts are dispensing with notarization, wet signatures, paper filings, and other procedural bottlenecks, at least temporarily, to avoid their attendant undesirable consequences.

6 Going Forward

Current realities undoubtedly call for an urgent redesign of the form and manner in which disputes are resolved. In post-pandemic planning, courts will need to devise cost-effective and efficient means and mechanisms to meet the anticipated spurt in demand.

There is no better time to adopt the use of remote or non-physical proceedings in dispute resolution than now. Thus, courts should seriously implement ODR, permanently adopt virtual hearings for some case types, expand self-help resources on court websites, and further leverage a host of digital tools to meet the needs and expectations of a 21st-century African population.

An excellent opportunity has been presented for courts to modernize fast. It would inure to the benefit of self-represented parties who do not have to take time off work or school or find childcare or transportation or pay for parking to get to court for multiple hearings, which are often long drawn out.

Several jurisdictions are making the requisite legislative modifications and engendering regulatory frameworks to enable virtual court proceedings and dispute resolution. This is expected to facilitate the continued administration of justice, particularly concerning civil proceedings. Resolution of civil and commercial disputes, which is undoubtedly central to economic survival, must also not be relegated to the back-burner at this time.

Following the initiatives in various other jurisdictions of the kind discussed in the article, the time is ripe for greater use of ODR by deploying technology in the dispensation of justice in our court systems here in Africa.

Chapter 25 Online Dispute Resolution in China: Today and Future

Anyu Lee

With the continuous advancement of judicial reforms, China has witnessed the rapid development of diverse dispute resolution mechanisms. Not only has academic exploration and innovation been happening, but normative legal documents are also continuously being promulgated. As a result, local courts, industrial organizations and social autonomous institutions have gained from this rich experience. This chapter focuses on the current development status of China's online dispute resolution mechanism (hereinafter referred to as 'ODR') in the field of e-commerce and e-courts and summarizes the following six future trends for ODR in China:

- centralization of the platform for ODR
- user-friendly systems
- universality of rules
- diversity in types of mechanisms
- resource sharing
- intelligence of means in mediation.

In the 21st century, the development of information technology, has changed social production and people's ways of thinking. It has created new spaces for human life and expanded new areas of national governance. Using network dispute mediation technology to promote the modernization of the judicial system and judicial capabilities, we now face rare opportunities and many challenges. In the modernized system of internet + justice, we uphold the idea of shared co-governance and use the internet to build new ODR mechanism. This is one of the important signs of the modernization of judicial capabilities.

1 The Current State of ODR in China

In the age of the internet, the field of dispute resolution has been transformed by technology. However, the transformation is not simply applying modern technology to the traditional dispute resolution models, but rebuilding a new online model based on the internet to achieve better justice. Technology is the tool, efficiency is the goal, but justice is the purpose. The development trajectory of China's ODR mechanism is similar to that of its peers. There are three phases of evolution: the dispute resolution platform of e-commerce, the rise of the e-court and the integration of the previous two phases.

1.1 Internet Accelerates ODR Adoption

The internet has received a great deal of attention in today's society, not only because of the internet technology itself, but also because of its significant role and tremendous impact on the economy and society. According to the 'China Statistical Report on Internet Development', as of December 2015 the population of Chinese internet users had reached 688 million. Meanwhile, the population of mobile internet users has reached 620 million, and the proportion has increased to 90.1%. With the rapid development of the internet, the construction of infrastructure, the iterative update of information technology, big data, cloud computing, etc., there is already strong technical support to build ODR platforms. In the area of dispute resolution, information technology, as a 'fourth party',[1] has been a catalyst for new dispute resolution methods, platforms and mechanisms.

The information revolution and economic globalization have changed our original social, economic, geographical and cultural structures. The application of internet technology has influenced people's way of thinking, consumption and lifestyle. Chinese society has demonstrated a trend of revolution and reformation. The most important aspect of big data, cloud computing, intelligent hardware, augmented reality (AR), virtual reality (VR), 3D printing and other technologies is internet thinking, which includes fragmented thinking, innovative thinking, non-linear thinking and reunification of fragments. Big data analysis technology, one of the most significant economic tags in the era of 'internet+', inter alia, has become one of the prime movers of innovation in China's economic and social domains and a necessary epistemological tool in economics, as well as daily life.

1.2 ODR Application in E-commerce Dispute Resolution

In June 2004 a website under the auspices of 'chinaeclaw.com' and the former Policy and Law Committee of the China Electronic Commerce Association (CECA), the first specialized ODR institution, 'China Online Dispute Resolution Center', was established. Alongside the progress of China's 'Belt and Road' initiative, global economic integration and the momentum of China's internet, e-commerce too grew rapidly, and the rising trend has continued. In 2014, the overall scale of transactions in the Chinese e-commerce market reached 12.3 trillion RMB, demonstrating that it had become the

1 Ethan Katsh and Janet Rifkin, *Online Dispute Resolution: Resolving Conflict in Cyberspace* (2001).

world's largest online retail market with a transaction volume exceeding that of the United States. By 2015, the overall scale of transactions in the Chinese e-commerce market grew as high as 16.4 trillion RMB. Consequently, in order to resolve the increasing number of e-commerce disputes, major e-commerce platforms looked for their own online resolution mechanism. For example, Taobao, JD.com, Suning.com, Gome Online, Dangdang, Amazon and other e-commerce companies have resolved disputes through email, online chat and telephone customer services.

According to incomplete statistics, Taobao handled a total of 2.16 million rights protection cases in 2010. In the same year, Chinese people's courts (district courts) concluded 5.97 million civil cases of first instance. The number of disputes handled by Taobao is equivalent to one-third of the civil cases tried by the people's courts. In order to deal with millions of disputes between hundreds of millions of buyers and nearly tens of millions of sellers every year, Alibaba officially launched the social jury platform for the Dianping APP on 18 December 2012. Both parties to a dispute can choose no more than 15 jury members from the corresponding database. The procedure adds an employee-juror from Taobao to form a 31-person jury to handle e-commerce disputes according to the principle of majority. Throughout the year 2014, Taobao had resolved more than 7.1 million cases, and a total of 416,452 jury members had participated in the 'judgment'.

1.3 *Internet and Intelligent Courts*

E-courts, or online tribunals, are a new form of trial mode that does not simply apply network technology to court activities. Specifically, the e-court is a litigation trial mode in which all court hearings and related litigation procedures are conducted through electronic communication methods (audio, videoconferencing, webinars, network transmission methods, etc.). Note that the e-court is a new form in the e-era that fully integrates court hearings and information technology. The electronic court has not changed the traditional trial procedures but has transformed the traditional trial methodologies through network technology to make it convenient for litigant participants, thereby reducing litigation costs.

The contradiction between more cases and fewer cases is intensifying. Informatization and diversification are effective ways to use scientific and technological resources and integrate social resources to alleviate the court's 'more cases and fewer cases' contradiction. With the development of people's courts' informatization, the emergence of electronic courts (courts) has prompted people's courts to make full use of modern information technology to improve judicial efficiency. Since 2000, Chinese courts have actively explored online filing and electronic delivery and built the People's Court Informatization Version 2.0 with basic features of interconnection.

In 2015 the courts in China began to transform and upgrade, building a data-concentric 3.0 version of informatization for people's courts. The Higher People's Court of Jilin Province established an e-court as the search engine for the courts of the entire province. The e-court fulfils fundamental functions, such as online filing, online trial, online decisions and enforcement, online petition, online inquiry of case information, online disclosure, online office, online management and network interconnection. In addition, the Zhejiang Higher People's Court created the Zhejiang Court E-Commerce Online Tribunal, which has been piloted in the Hangzhou Intermediate People's Court, West Lake District People's Court, Binjiang District People's Court and Yuhang District People's Court, among others. The other regional courts are also speeding towards the establishment of e-courts.

In November 2014 the Supreme People's Court (hereinafter 'SPC') launched the 'China Judicial Process Information Online', which makes all civil judicial activities open and transparent, from the filing of the case to the final judgment. Since then, the litigant parties and attorneys can promptly receive push notifications in the eight major procedural steps by mobile phone text messages, voice messages, Weibo, WeChat, mobile phone apps, and other ways. As of the end of December 2015, the SPC disclosed 232,000 pieces of case information. In light of the SPC, all provincial courts have established unified provincial trial information disclosure platforms, and created a link to the China Judicial Process Information Online. Moreover, on 1 July 2016 the SPC set up a live broadcast platform for court hearings. In principle, all public hearings of the SPC are broadcast live through the internet.

Although the development prospects of the online ODR mechanism are unlimited, there are still unavoidable problems in the development of the ODR in China. First, China's ODR mechanism started comparatively late; the number of platforms are inadequate to meet their demands. The functions should be more comprehensive, and some research and development is repetitive. Secondly, there is no unified dispute resolution platform. The direct result is that the various dispute resolution resources cannot be shared among platforms. When the dispute resolution resources are scattered, their information cannot be interconnected. Third, dispute resolution talents are scarce, and the legal soundness needs to be effective. The ODR mechanism is jointly developed in an international background. China should stay ahead and establish a unified ODR mechanism as soon as possible to fully realize information intercommunication and resource sharing.

2 The Future Development of ODR in China

As a vital component of the social governance system, having a diversified dispute resolution mechanism has a positive effect on integrating social resources, mobilizing all parties in society and providing parties with more alternative dispute resolution possibilities. Recently, the SPC issued the 'Opinions on Further Deepening the Reform of Diversified Dispute Resolution Mechanisms' (hereinafter referred to as 'Opinions'), which unambiguously stated that "we must innovate ODR according to the 'internet+' strategic requirements, among others, to promote establishment of online mediation, online case filing, online judicial confirmation, online court trial, electronic supervision procedures, electronic judicial service, as an integrated information platform." Such regulations are also in response to Supreme Justice Zhou Qiang's opinion to "build a completely covered, mobile interconnected, and transparently people-friendly, safe and reliable intelligent information system by the end of 2017."

China's ODR mechanism effectively links the e-courts of the judicial system to other non-judicial ODR platforms. Through systematic design, an open, modular and diversified network has been constructed to resolve disputes at low cost and high efficiency. The ODR mechanisms aim to prevent and resolve disputes. ODR, as an important part of the diversified dispute resolution mechanism, demonstrates five dominant trends:

2.1 Trend One: Centralization and Diversification

China's ODR platforms are divided into three levels:

On the first level are the ODR platforms designed and founded by internet companies, such as Taobao's mass jury model dispute resolution platform, Sina's Weibo community mediation platform and the Internet Association Mediation Center's 'common sense law' mediation platform. On the second level is a unified ODR platform for the national court system. On the last level is a platform for the prevention and resolution of contradictions and disputes established by the comprehensive governance organs.

The future goals of the ODR platform of the national court system are as follows:

1) First, establish a centralized platform to facilitate resource integration and to build a nationwide unified ODR platform that will help the four court levels to connect specially invited mediators and provide integrated ODR services to the public on the basis of the internet. As the centralized platform can attract nationwide mediation resources, the supplies and demands of mediation services can be matched and connected through internet standard services throughout the country.

2) The second is to use the internet to expand the 'reorganization of institutions to

reconnect (*Chai Diao Dui Jie*) mechanism'. A variety of techniques will be adopted to promote the platform to the public. The relevant persons and organizations will quickly introduce the source of disputes resolution through the internet online platform in the high incidence areas, maintaining a close cooperation with the courts. It is planned that the online disputes of e-commerce websites, or of other online platforms such as Weibo, will be efficiently accepted and handled by online integration to ODR. The stakeholders will also strengthen the cooperation between the websites of various mediation organizations and the disputes acceptance websites of insurance companies to realize the simultaneous development of offline mediation and online mediation.
3) The third is to use the platform to enhance data collection and analysis. During the operation of the ODR platform, the non-confidential dispute data, user feedback data, user behaviour data and platform operation data will be processed through big data analysis and information mining technologies. The different levels of competent courts will analyse the dispute status, reorganization and reconnect data and the effectiveness of dispute resolution as well as the typical cases. Simultaneously, the system analyses and evaluates the mediator's workload and effectiveness; analyses the hotspots, operating situation and user needs of the ODR platform; and analyses and predicts the overall situation and development trend of conflicts and disputes.

The centralized ODR platform of national courts has four missions:
1) The first is unified display of resources. The ODR platform facilitates the integration of case resources, mediators' resources and training resources. It will work with the court information display system for unified electronic display through court websites, displays at different levels of courthouses, and touch-terminals.
2) The second is a unified connection mechanism. The ODR platform is designed with a unified data interface to ensure a seamless connection with the court system. Therefore, various procedures in case filing, mediation and litigation will be thoroughly interconnected. Furthermore, the unobstructed progress of pre-litigation mediation, mid-litigation mediation, and judicial confirmation will be thereby ensured.
3) The third is a unified training assessment. The ODR platform assists the courts to aggregate and integrate various training resources on the internet. The courts can design training courses on the basis of data analysis results and improve the mediators' professional capabilities in a targeted methodology. Also, the mediators' performance can be evaluated according to the users' feedback and training records.
4) The fourth is unified data management. The platform will process dispute data, dispute resolution process data, user feedback data, dispute resolution resource data, platform operation data, users access behaviour data, etc., whereupon the data will be accurate and effective, systemized, and analysed in depth. The aforementioned will provide adequate support for the courts and public's decision-making.

2.2 *Trend Two: Convenience and Efficiency*

The famous Italian jurist Capelleti summarized the fundamental concepts throughout modern civil litigation as procedural guarantees and access to justice. The people-friendly and convenient dispute resolution service provides the parties with a fast lane to justice.

Compared with traditional dispute resolution mechanisms, the outstanding advantage of ODR mechanisms is convenience, high efficiency and low cost. The parties and the mediators can choose any appropriate time and place to communicate via network communication tools. The procedures of application, evidence submission, cross-examination, mediation, court hearing and service of documents are all completed online, reducing the burden for litigation. Compared with traditional dispute resolution means, ODR is cheaper and more efficient.

Since the birth of the internet, the human footprint has expanded from the physical world to the virtual world. In the internet world, different types of online civil disputes, represented by online shopping disputes, have experienced vigorous growth. Most online civil disputes have a relatively small amount of subject matter, and the physical distance between the parties can be large. Solving civil disputes through litigation and alternative dispute resolution (hereinafter referred to as 'ADR') creates practical problems; e.g., "costs are higher than the subject amount." To overcome the challenges brought by online civil disputes, litigation and ADR, people began using network resources to resolve online civil disputes to further realize the dream of "online resolution of online disputes."

The ODR platform will provide support for parties to negotiate and choose a mediator, use simple methods or structured data to describe disputes, exchange evidence online, participate in mediation and apply for judicial confirmation. After the mediation, mediators and the mediation process can be evaluated and receive feedback. Through the ODR platform, the parties can utilize a standardized dispute resolution process approved by the judiciary and choose appropriate services from a large scale of dispute resolution resources according to the characteristics of the dispute type and the jurisdiction of the case.

2.3 *Trend Three: Universal Dispute Resolution Standardization*

The parties' recognition and trust in the ODR dispute resolution mechanism will be strengthened if the dispute resolution rules are more universal, authoritative and neutral.

Primarily, the rule makers should establish ODR procedural rules with procedural justice as priority. It is necessary to design a procedure that ensures the neutrality of the mediators or arbitrators, gives the parties adequate opportunities to represent themselves, clarifies the parties' right of disposal and reinforces procedural justice. It must be highlighted that the online document service adopts mainly electronic means; physical means are supplementary. Additionally, the validation of the online service of documents should be noted; what are the online file transmission methods and how to guarantee their security? Academia and practitioners should research and solve the legality and objectivity of electronic evidence at the first opportunity.

Secondly, the stakeholders should establish a system to guarantee the neutrality and impartiality of ODR mediators or adjudicators. The mediators' or adjudicators' expertise, educational experience, work experience, ODR training experience and other necessary information should be publicly available online. The mediator or adjudicator can be either randomly selected by the ODR software or based on the parties' recommendation. If a party believes that it may have grounds to challenge, the party may request the mediator or adjudicator to be replaced without cause.

Thirdly, the ODR website should contain an evaluation system for mediators or adjudicators. The parties can assess and score the mediator or arbitrator along with the case. Moreover, the relevant websites should also establish an evaluation mechanism for the mediator or arbitrator.

Fourthly, the national courts or other suitable bodies could establish an ODR mediator or adjudicator training mechanism. One of the advantages of ODR is that it has professional technical advantages in adjudication. A strict selection and training mechanism will ensure that mediators or adjudicators have relevant expertise, network technical background and dispute resolution capabilities. After completion of the training, adjudicators and mediators can obtain training qualification certificates.

2.4 *Trend four: Diversity in ODR Implementation*

In addition to online consultation, online mediation and online arbitration, there are other ODR processes, such as dispute review committees, review and supervision mechanisms, neutral fact-finding experts, early neutral evaluations, micro trials and dispute resolution consultants. However, these are not complete dispute resolving processes of the ODR but represent only a few ways of resolving a dispute, such as clarifying the facts or providing objective opinions. To some extent, online civil disputes have triggered the ODR mechanism. The diversity and complexity of online civil disputes have determined the varieties of the ODR mechanism.

China's integrated all-in-one ODR platform can include online litigation, online execution and even online petitions, thereby integrating all types of dispute resolution. It provides access for various dispute types and various industrial requirements. Moreover, it performs modular combination and offers personalized customization. The function of the platform is not limited to resolving disputes but also includes accumulating and analysing mass data. The co-construction and sharing of resources are technical support to conflict resolution, disputes prevention and control.

2.5 *Trend Five: Sharing of Resources*

The idiosyncrasy of the ODR mechanism is sharing and socialization. People can realize the rational allocation and resource sharing of legal and non-legal resources, official resources and private resources via ODR platforms.

First, the ODR could fully utilize private resources. Wherein the ODR platform actively mobilizes the participation of people's mediation organizations; administrative mediation organizations; experts from various industries, lawyers, psychologists, community workers, social volunteers and other social forces, it provides disputing parties with additional alternative dispute resolution channels.

The next step is to encourage enterprises and independent third parties to play a role in dispute resolution. For example, Taobao independently developed a set of dispute resolution platforms that absorbed the public jury model; Sina managed the foundation of a microblog community mediation platform; 'Mediation Online', the official cooperation website of the Beijing Mediation Alliance, accepts parties' mediation applications online. Other mediation institutions are also dedicated to developing their own ODR platforms.

The third is to set up e-courts on the model of the People's Court Informatization 3.0. The SPC's 'Five-Year Development Plan for the Informatization of People's Courts' proposed that China's 'smart courts' should focus on serving the people, adjudicating execution and judicial management. The characteristics of Chinese e-courts are highlighted by "full coverage, mobile internet, cross-border integration, deep application, transparent and convenient, safe and controllable." The local courts will speed up system construction, strengthen the security system and improve application effectiveness. By improving the 'Judicial Open Platform', the local courts will work better on the litigation service centre and the litigation and docking centre and provide better service by the '12368' public welfare service hotline. The aim is the "online mediation, online filing, online judicial confirmation, online court trial, electronic supervision, electronic document service" all-in-one ODR platform. Besides, one can make full use of rich case information resources to accurately reflect the dynamics of economic and social operations and provide references for the Communist Party and the government to make decisions. Additionally, judges can comprehensively promote the simultaneous generation, and in-depth application, of electronic files with cases that use intelligent services for judges to handle cases. This will reduce the burden of handling cases, while promoting the standardization of sentencing. Standing at the forefront of the times, it attaches great significance for the national courts to take full advantage of judicial artificial intelligence, which will lead to profound changes in the national courts. Namely, it plugs in the wings of science and technology to the courts to go higher in the quality and effectiveness of adjustment.

China's ODR mechanism will make full use of information technology to build a comprehensive and three-dimensional dispute resolution platform to promote the cross-border integration of various dispute resolution mechanisms and to lead the upgradation of traditional dispute resolution methods.

3 ARTIFICIALLY INTELLIGENT DISPUTE RESOLUTION IN CHINA

The Chinese government regards artificial intelligence technology as a critical national development strategy and has invested heavily in research and application resources. In the field of mediation, the application of artificial intelligence is manifested mainly in the construction and use of online mediation platforms. On the one hand, the application of artificial intelligence has effectively improved the efficiency of online mediation, promoted the standardized development of ODR mechanisms and enhanced the convenience of dispute resolution. On the other hand, it has also faced challenges such as incomplete 'deep learning databases' of mediation, lack of artificial intelligence expertise and technical support and threats to confidentiality in mediation procedures. Currently, the intelligence of China's online mediation platform is reflected mainly in the guidance of mediation procedures, helping parties recommend and contact mediators, cases classification and voice recognition. However, it facilitates online mediation work and carries relatively simple auxiliary tasks that are not of high intelligence. In addition, the online mediation platform also faces problems such as uneven regional development, low platform utilization and lack of legislation and security mechanisms. In the future development of online mediation, the first task is to strengthen the construction of the mediation platform, not only to enhance the intelligence of the mediation platform through technological innovation, but also to take into account the professional development of the mediation team, to achieve the synergy of 'artificial' and 'artificial intelligence'. The second task is to maintain a correct understanding of the concept, positioning artificial intelligence as a 'helper' in mediation. The third task is to improve the legislative provisions to ensure the healthy development of online mediation at the system level.

In recent years the influence of artificial intelligence on the judicial field has been ever increasing. In judicial practice, the emergence of intelligent case handling methods and the intelligence-assisted case handling systems such as e-courts, 'internet + mediation', 'rui' judges, the C2J (court to judge), have imperceptibly influenced traditional judicial trials and other dispute resolution mechanisms. The application of artificial intelligence technology in the judicial field has increased the convenience and efficiency of dispute resolution. Furthermore, China's existing judicial 'big data' foundation is unstable, and the lack of talents and technical support and other objective circumstances have hindered the utilization of artificial intelligence in dispute resolution. At present, artificial intelligence has become an important concern in the legal community. In 2016, the SPC put forward the development goal of founding an 'intelligent court' and version 3.0 of the People's Court informatization. In the same year, the state council included this goal in the country's information development strategy. In 2017, the SPC and the state council successively issued the 'Supreme People's Court Opinions on Accelerating the Construction of Intelligent Courts' and the 'New Generation Artificial Intelligence Development Plan' to further guide the construction of 'intelligent courts' by top-level design. Against this general background, the issues of how to apply science and technology to the modernization of justice for effective integration of technology and law, how to coordinate the relationship between the 'rigidity' of intelligent judgment and the 'diversity' of judicial practice, and how to take technical rationality and human culture into consideration of judicial judgment have assumed urgency.

3.1 Adoption of Information Technology: Different Models and Different Results

3.1.1 ODR Operation Model

According to the different types of online mediation promoters, the online mediation models in China can be divided into government-operated, court-operated, and civil organization-operated models. There are various construction methods under these different models.

3.1.1.1 Government Operated

The People's Mediation Law of the People's Republic of China (hereinafter referred to as the 'Mediation Law') stipulates that the judicial administrative department is responsible for guiding the people's mediation work. The judicial administrative departments of some provinces and cities have established an online mediation platform on their portals. For example, in Shanxi Province, Baoji City's 'People's Online Mediation Committee' has been built and upgraded on the Baoji City Justice Bureau's portal, the 'Baoji Judicial Window'. There are also other government-related functional departments that have set up online mediation platforms for specific types of disputes, such as the 'Labor and Personnel Dispute Mediation Service Platform' of the Jiangsu Provincial Department of Human Resources and Social Security, and the 'internet + mediation' model of local governments. In general, the operating procedures of these platforms are similar and can be briefly summarized as follows:

1. enter the platform network
2. register user name
3. choose the mediation organization or mediator

4. communicate with the mediator (telephone or online)
5. online or offline mediation
6. get mediation results.

Under this model, informatization construction is usually invested in by local governments. Afterwards, it will be opened to society in the form of public services. The biggest challenge of this public service platform is the volume of resources required for the continuous maintenance of software systems and the costs on account of reasonable technical support and consulting services in the use of the platform.

3.1.1.2 High Court Operated

Court mediation is a necessary component of China's civil litigation system, and the courts become the merited subject of online mediation. Several opinions of the Supreme People's Court on Further Deepening the Reform of the Diversified Dispute Resolution Mechanism of the People's Court state, "... promote the use of modern information technology in the diversified resolution mechanism." In the process of nationwide promotion of the construction of 'intelligent courts', after conducting online mediation practices in some courts in Zhejiang Province, Sichuan Province and Anhui Province, the SPC conducted trials in six pilot higher courts, including Beijing and Hebei, to explore the establishment of a provincial unified online mediation platform. Simultaneously, the SPC established e-courts in Beijing, Hangzhou and Guangzhou to form a seamless connection between network mediation, litigation and enforcement. The main challenge of the court model is that the expectations of the parties to the dispute cannot be effectively guided into the dispute mediation and that the success rate of the mediation is lower than expected, making it difficult for the court to obtain a return on investment in the mediation system.

3.1.1.3 Private Sector Operated

The 'internet + mediation' carried out by non-governmental organizations (NGOs) mainly include Taobao, Tmall's online dispute resolution centre, Sina People's Mediation Committee, Sina online dispute resolution platform, China Online Dispute Resolution Center (China ODR), and China Consumer Association's online mediation station (Online315). Consider Sina's online dispute resolution platform as an example. The platform provides an abstract summary of mediation services and forms standardized information and processes based on the differences in the display methods and business processes of mediation information in various courts in practice.

In terms of platform promotion, it adopts mainly three kinds of manoeuvres: first, placing touch terminals in the court litigation service hall and deploying an internet mediation platform to guide the parties into mediation when the parties are in the hall to file the case. Second, arranging quick access terminals, that is, small PCs, and internet mediation platforms in the communities and other dispute-prone places, as well as in road transportation dispute arbitration institutions. The terminal is connected to a monitor or TV for portable operation. Third, guiding the parties to participate in mediation through the official Weibo of the court. At the same time, a dedicated internet mediation platform user card is designed to help parties use the internet mediation platform more conveniently and efficiently. This type of mediation model is questioned by the public on the credibility and neutrality of the mediation agency. Meanwhile, there is also a lack of effective regulatory measures in the implementation of mediation agreements. At present, the main private mediation system is built by monopolistic platform operators, which provide mediation platforms. Consequently, the monopoly raises significant doubts about information security.

3.1.2 Difficulties of Adopting Artificial Intelligent ODR

3.1.2.1 Lack of Intelligence in Algorithm

According to the standard of whether the artificial intelligence products have the ability to identify and control, artificial intelligence products can be divided into weak artificial intelligence products and strong artificial intelligence products. Weak artificial intelligence products can make independent judgments and decisions within the set procedures and scopes but do not have independent identification and control capabilities. Weak artificial intelligence products are essentially manifestations of the programmers' and users' intentions. Strong artificial intelligence products have the ability to recognize and control; they can not only realize the instruction of the programmers and users, but can also exceed the scope of the designed and programmed programs to make independent decisions and implement corresponding behaviours and then realize their own purpose. In terms of the application of artificial intelligence in the judicial field, the utilization of weak artificial intelligence products is realized mainly in the auxiliary work for judicial activities through certain technologies, while the use of strong artificial intelligence products is reflected in the analytical tools for judicial judgment activities.

From the perspective of the current operational mode of online mediation, although the aforementioned models emphasize the application of artificial intelligence, weak artificial intelligence is mostly statistical and empirical. Its functions are preparing documents and textual templates, the main purpose being the establishment of a basic mediation platform, intelligent recommendation and contact with the mediators, dividing online and offline cases, recognition of documents, conversion of audio voices and other common, relatively simple auxiliary work. Combining artificial intelligence with legal big data, cloud computing and other technologies, the use of artificial intelligence technology to push similar cases, analyse laws and regulations, predict referee results and even simulate mediators and other substantive content has not been embodied or applied in the current online mediation system.

There are three main reasons for this situation. First, the existing legal artificial intelligence technology is immature, and the talent resource is limited. Technology and talent are the fundamental prerequisites for implementing artificial intelligence. However, artificial intelligence has not been applied in the legal field for a long time, and it is mostly used in the area of judicial trials. In the domain of mediation, artificial intelligence technology is still new. As a result, it is inevitable that the technology still needs perfection and that the application can be better developed.

In addition, compared with the litigation area, the talent pool in the mediation field is also smaller. There are fewer mediation talents who are both good at mediation and proficient in computer technology, a factor that largely limits the application and development of artificial intelligence technology in online mediation. Secondly, there is an ongoing conflict between the 'big data' requirements in artificial intelligence and the 'small data' reality in mediation. The current 'big database' in Chinese judicial trials is inadequate, especially in the area of mediation. From one point of view, the existing mediation mechanism in China is not fully developed, and the mediation agreement is not standardized enough to provide sufficient and effective sample materials for the establishment of a large mediation database. From another point of view, mediation itself is confidential, and mediation agreements should not be publicly available on the internet as reference documents. The conciliation of mediation and the relevant mediation documents have served as major obstacles to the establishment of the mediation 'big database'. Thirdly, the flexibility, diversity and humanity that characterize mediation limit the use of strong artificial intelligence. Compared with litigation, mediation has higher requirements on the 'people'. Whether the mediator is authoritative, has sufficient mediation skills and is erudite in persuasion with reasons will affect the conclusion of the mediation agreement. Mediation is not a black-and-white judgment. It stresses the combination of multiple factors such as psychology, reason, law and morality. In contrast to litigation, mediation requires more ingenuity. Even under the same or similar circumstances, different parties and different mediators may achieve distinctive results. Therefore, it is very difficult to find the 'greatest common divisor' in the case of mediation. If the judges, like the 'vending machine' are difficult to 'invent', then the mediator of the 'vending machine' is more difficult to find. For this reason, it is not easy for us to simulate the mediation behaviour of the mediators through the application of strong artificial intelligence technology, and any attempt made to use it is unlikely to achieve the desired effect.

3.1.2.2 Unbalanced Development in Regions

The development of online mediation is disproportional and insufficient in various regions, and the regional differences are radical. Correspondingly, the growth of artificial intelligence-assisted mediation is also imbalanced and inadequate in several regions, and the regional comparison is critical. Generally speaking, online mediation and artificial intelligence-assisted mediation all around the country has the following features: the eastern coastal area grows significantly faster than the mid-west inland area; the economically developed area develops sooner than the economically underdeveloped area; and where the government leaders attach importance to online mediation, there the progress is significantly faster than in other areas. For example, Shandong Province and Xiamen City, located on the eastern coast, have taken the lead in formulating local regulations for the settlement of diversified disputes. Among them, the Shandong Province Diversified Dispute Resolution Promotion Regulations have stipulated online mediation. Zhejiang Province, the cradle of e-commerce and internet economy, was the first to establish a commercial online court. Hangzhou West Lake District Court took the lead in conducting online court mediation. The national courts seek an in-depth advancement of the reform of the diversified dispute resolution mechanism and the exchange of experience of the model courts (referred to as the Ma'an'shan Conference). These five grass-roots model courts from Shanghai, Hangzhou, Shenyang, Kunming and Chongqing belong to national or regional economic centres. The advantages in economy, science and technology are obvious.

Regional differences have three primary causes of: the first is the economic level. Economically developed regions have higher fiscal revenues, and the government has invested more in platform construction; urban internet and other hardware infrastructures are comparatively complete, internet access is cheaper and more convenient; residents have a generally higher educational background, and the use of the internet has become the norm in daily life. This active online economic exchange has engendered an increasing number of online disputes. These factors constitute the premise and foundation for the development of online mediation. The second cause is psychological understanding. Anhui Province is located in the interior of the central region, but the province has taken the lead in promulgating special online mediation work rules, which is at the forefront of the country. This is inseparable from the local government and the courts attention and active promotion. However, there are also many areas that lack internet thinking, "the lack of understanding of the necessity and urgency of the 'online-ness' of diversified dispute resolution," "although there is a small scale of 'touching the network', there is no large-scale in-depth network access," "Hardware equipment has transformed to informatization, but the multiple dispute resolution work went no further than offline." If the location advantage and economic development level determine the starting point and threshold for the development of online mediation in various regions, the level of subjective awareness and the promotion of execution in these regions largely determine the potential and momentum of the progress in online mediation. The third cause is the support of power. The long-term development of online mediation requires the joint efforts of multiple powers such as government, courts, social organizations and industrial associations. Take online court mediation as an example. At present, courts do the most to promote online mediation. Court online mediation is not just a matter of the courts but involves government-related functional departments, enterprises and institutions, industry organizations, social groups and other units. It is not sufficient for the courts alone to promote online mediation. For the moment, apart from the court system, online mediation is not sufficiently coordinated with other units, and there is no higher-level unit (such as the first-level government, political and legal committee) at the administrative level or business executives to conduct overall coordination and linkage. The government, courts and related industries are all building their own online mediation platforms, each with a separate construction, with a low degree of resource and data sharing. The data barriers need to be broken. At the same time, there are repeated constructions. The trilogy of people's mediation, judicial mediation and administrative mediation is not coordinated harmoniously.

Within the court system, many courts have not included ODR, including online mediation, in their work evaluation objectives. The efforts invested into online mediation lack incentive and guiding mechanisms. In addition, although online mediation has developed rapidly in some places, the construction of their online mediation platform is treated as separate work. The practice of mediation in artificial intelligence reflects a situation with a low resource sharing rate, repeated construction and insufficient development. This is manifested mainly in the fact that the online mediation platform systems in different regions are designed and developed by different companies and there is no unified top-level planning and design. Multiple units in the same region have developed their own separate mediation platform systems.

3.1.2.3 Inconvenience and Less Usage

Online mediation has the advantage of breaking time and space constraints through the internet, saving transportation costs for the parties and improving the efficiency of dispute resolution. However, the online mediation system does not operate as conveniently as imagined, and the actual utilization rate is low. The online mediation platform is primarily used to accept cases on the platform in many places. The fact is that users "make appointment of schedule on the platform but conduct mediation outside the platform." Online mediation is often just 'going through the motions' and represents a mere formality.

Considering courts' online mediation as an example, the author learned during the investigation that there are very few cases of online court mediation. Even in Zhejiang, the province that leads the use of internet platforms to resolve disputes, some basic courts have not yet encountered any online mediation cases. In the pilot court for compensation of traffic accident damages, 'integrated online data processing' – Hangzhou Yuhang District Court – the number of online mediation cases is relatively low. Most relevant cases are online judicial confirmation cases. The factors that affect the use of online mediation are multidimensional and diversified, and mainly include the following:

(1) Type of dispute
The specific type of dispute determines how to settle it. The types of disputes that are suitable for online mediation and dispute resolution are relatively narrow. Most of them focus on simple cases where there are clear facts or, clear *cus fori* in debate, where parties find it inconvenient to present themselves in court, or where they are related to e-commerce.

(2) Influenced by participating entities
The use of online mediation is influenced by factors such as judges, mediators and parties. Concerning judges, some have insufficient understanding of mediation and despise mediation, let alone online mediation. Additionally, the ODR platform is currently at the trial stage. Out of prudence and other considerations, the courts must handle cases online to complete the entire process offline and complete the corresponding file documents. With the use of online mediation, judges and clerks must repeatedly serve the parties with communication and guidance, spending more time and energy on such activities. The relevant workload has not decreased but has rather increased. Concerning mediators, most prefer on-site mediation, which is more conducive to the control of mediation procedures and handling of unexpected situations. The use of online mediation is currently concentrated in the demographic of users who are middle-aged and younger, the generation of mediators born in the post-1970s, post-1980s and post-1990s. The older mediators are generally unwilling to use online mediation owing to their own limited computer skills and reluctance to accept the use of new technology. Concerning the parties, distrust of the internet and unfamiliarity with online operations are the main factors affecting their use of online mediation.

Today, there are many cases of fraud through telecommunications and the internet. The internet is vulnerable to hackers, viruses, etc., and its stability and security are not strong, leaving the public suspicious of online mediation. Some parties once posted screenshots of mediation videos on an online platform and commented on them, infringing on the privacy and portrait rights of others and causing the public to question the privacy of online mediation. Moreover, some older people who are not well educated, and who do not use computers, do not choose online mediation.

(3) Procedures dependent
Whether the online mediation system is easy to use, fast and user-friendly affects the use of online mediation. The registration procedures of some mediation platforms are cumbersome, and the unscientific design of the mobile phone message reminder

program for platform mediation information makes the online mediation experience of users unsatisfactory.

3.1.2.4 Lack of Supportive Laws and Regulations

Currently, the relevant regulations on online mediation are inadequate and incomplete. The level of normative effect is low. Besides, artificial intelligence is extremely rarely involved in online mediation. At the national level, the relevant regulations appear only in the 'Outline of the People's Court Reform' and 'Multiple Dispute Resolution Reform' issued by the SPC. These two documents are judicial documents and cannot be used as the basis for adjudication. At the local level, only two regions, Shandong Province and Xiamen City, have promulgated principal provisions on 'online mediation'. The Anhui Online Mediation Rules (hereinafter, the 'Rules) are the earliest specialized rules laid down by the court for online mediation. However, it is only an internal provision of the provincial court and lacks regulatory effect. In general, online mediation rules are imperfect, and the level of normative effect needs to be enhanced.

Although the Rules fill the loopholes in online mediation, namely the related concepts such as principles, scope of application, rights and obligations, mediation process, supervision and management, the specific provisions still need to be refined, and it is necessary to issue implementation rules or explanations for further clarification. For example, the Rules contain controversial definitions. They define the subject of 'online mediation' as "specially invited mediation organizations and specially invited mediators." In practice, the Rules exclude the online mediation conducted by courts or judges. Likewise, 'online mediation platform' fails to distinguish between the online mediation platforms established by the court on its own website and those established by the court on other subjects (such as Sina Court Channel). Furthermore, some provisions of the Rules are not operable in practice. For example, Article 33 of the Rules stipulates the responsibility of the operating entity of the website where the online mediation platform is located only in principle, but has no specific provisions on how to determine the responsibilities (e.g. how to deal with leakage of confidential information in mediation cases due to human factors such as improper management of the operating entity; job failure; property loss of the parties).

3.1.2.5 Lack of Guarantee Mechanism

The online mediation guarantee mechanism is not perfect. The human resources, property and other investment are insufficient. Therefore, the guarantee mechanism for artificial intelligence in online mediation is even more deficient. In terms of personnel arrangement, the human resource participation in online is inadequate. For example, the resident staff of the Hangzhou West Lake Court Chen Liaomin's Online Studio has only one judge and one clerk during the initial operation. Owing to the daily trial of the court and the heavy workload, the judge and the clerk basically sacrifice their rest time to complete the Online Studio tasks, including online mediation. In terms of funding guarantee, the construction of an online mediation platform entails a considerable financial commitment, which is also time-consuming and labour intensive. Many local Communist Party committees and governments do not pay enough attention to online mediation platforms, and projects that apply for such platform construction do not get easily approved. The long approval cycle thus means that funds cannot be transferred adequately and timely. In terms of hardware facilities, online mediation has certain requirements for computer operating systems, internet equipment, etc. In the early days, owing to the lag in court information construction, court hardware facilities in many regions could not meet the basic requisitions for online mediation, let alone the use of artificial intelligence to assist mediation. With the in-depth advancement of informatization construction and scientific and technological progress, the current situation has been significantly improved. However, the hardware facilities in some areas (such as old revolution areas, ethnic autonomous areas and underdeveloped areas) have not yet met the rudimentary requirements of online mediation. In terms of guarantee mechanisms, the online mediation assessment and evaluation mechanism, work incentive mechanism, talent training mechanism, etc. have not yet fully taken shape. Furthermore, many mechanisms are only macro-graphic concepts or assumptions and have not been implemented.

3.2 The Opportunities of Artificially Intelligent ODR

3.2.1 ODR's AI Revolution

Online mediation is a type of ODR mechanism. Generally speaking, online mediation refers to the judicial activities in which the parties communicate with each other, exchange opinions and evidence and, finally, reach a mediation agreement through network information channels such as chat software, email and electronic bulletin board (CBB) without the necessity of physically meeting one another. Compared with the traditional mediation model, online mediation has higher requirements on 'technicality'. For instance, the establishment of an online mediation platform requires mature internet communication technology. In addition, the diversification and long-term development of online mediation are inseparable from the application of artificial intelligence technologies such as big data and cloud computing. Therefore, the emergence of artificial intelligence is of considerable significance to the improvement of China's existing online mediation mechanism.

3.2.1.1 Improving Efficiency

The application of artificial intelligence in justice is reflected in two main ways: the first is to provide practical tools for assisting judicial activities, and the second is to provide new analytical tools to clearly and strictly demonstrate judicial judgment activities. In current judicial practice, the former has been widely applied in the automatic identification of parties' claims, legal provisions and legal documents, as well as the drafting of conventional legal documents and the diversion of cases. Since the ability of artificial intelligence to recognize information and the corresponding computing power is much more advanced than that of human beings, it can conduct preliminary analysis of cases in a short time and then generate formatted document materials in time, contact relevant mediation experts and classify mediation cases into online or offline. With the support of this technology, online mediation retains the advantages of traditional mediation, while ensuring better speed and efficiency of dispute resolution. Compared with the traditional mediation model, online mediation procedures are simple and flexible, free from the constraints of time, space, cost and other mediation subjects, and are more effective in providing a quick resolution of contradictions and disputes. For example, the judges of Beijing Second Intermediate People's Court used the WeChat platform to complete a labour dispute in just five minutes. Another example is the 'half-day acceptance and ten-day settlement' system of the Jiangsu labour and personnel dispute mediation service platform. After receiving the case information provided by the platform, the mediation expert will contact the applicant within half an hour and accept the application within half a day. Then the case will be handled within ten days. However, artificial intelligence is not commonly applied in judicial practice. There are only a few application scenarios for the use of artificial intelligence to assist judicial procedure: the 'intelligent' judgment system of the Beijing court, the criminal auxiliary intelligent case handling system of the Shanghai High Court and the data cloud centre of the Chongqing High Court. These systems have the ability to instantly 'unlock' legal facts and cases. They can even imitate the judge's thinking. After in-depth analysis of data and intelligent calculations, they will provide judges with effective case-handling regulations, sentencing information and other content in a short time. At present, the application of this technology is still being explored. In the long run, this technology should become the development direction of judicial artificial intelligence.

3.2.1.2 Encouraging Standardization

The rationale of artificial intelligence as a judicial judgment analysis tool lies in its ability to automatically extract the plot features and intelligently learn the judgment results of numerous judgment documents. It is able to establish a judgment model for specific cases. Based on the keywords selected by the judge or the facts provided, artificial intelligence will automatically process statistics, make real-time display of the judgment of similar cases as well as predict the substantial judgment of the case. Furthermore, it is able to present more accurate cases with similarities for the judge's reference. In addition, artificial intelligence can also play the role of supervising judicial judgments. If the judge's final judgment results differ greatly from those of previous cases, the artificial intelligence system will automatically send a warning. This means that artificial intelligence is more objective and neutral in judicial decisions and is less likely to be improperly interfered with externally. Applying this technology to dispute resolution mechanisms such as online mediation will ensure the efficiency of dispute resolution and also facilitate the realization of 'analogous judgments to analogous cases' and 'similar mediation to similar disputes', thereby promoting the standardization of dispute resolution mechanisms.

3.2.1.3 *Achieving Convenience and Quickness*

For the parties, ODR is more convenient and people friendly. Online mediation is a product of the combination of the virtual world constructed by the internet and traditional mediation practices. It inherits the internet's idiosyncrasy of 'virtuality' inherently. The virtuality of online mediation gives it the capacity to transcend constraints of time and space in traditional mediation and eliminates transportation costs, time costs, lost time of work, etc. so that parties can resolve disputes without leaving their houses. Taking Sina's Internet People's Mediation Committee as an example, all disputes within Weibo are determined by a community committee composed of 'netizens', forming a convenient right remedy model of "microblog disputes on the left hand and network mediation on the right hand." Compared with offline mediation, the online mediation procedure is more user friendly, convenient, fast and operable. The intelligent consultation function, case push notification function and case analysis function of the online mediation system also allow the parties to follow the progress of the case and make timely predictions on its outcome. In short, online mediation satisfies the needs of humanity and meets the requirements of people's convenience.

3.2.2 The Challenge of Artificial Intelligent ODR

3.2.2.1 *Lack of Adequate Database of Machine Deep Learning*

The essential function of artificial intelligence is to store the wisdom of experts for a long time in the form of data and to help people deal with various legal issues through in-depth analysis and intelligent calculation of various kinds of data. Therefore, big data is the premise and foundation for the development of artificial intelligence. If artificial intelligence is to be used as an analytical tool for judicial judgment in future judicial practice, it must be based on sufficient, objective, veritable and reasonably structured legal big data. However, China's large legal database is not yet completely built. On the one hand, the depth and breadth of the disclosure of judgment documents in China are not enough, and it cannot provide sufficient and complete sample materials for the establishment of legal databases. On the other hand, there is inadequate objectivity or authenticity of the existing data, making it difficult to provide clear reference for artificial intelligence. The underlying reasons are as follows: first, in practice, important contents such as tribunal panel discussions, *intime conviction* of judges and mediators cannot be fully reflected in legal documents. Secondly, because of the diversity and complexity of social life, the mediators have cognitive differences. Judging from the exploration of artificial intelligence in current judicial practice, most of the legal databases that artificial intelligence relies on are the current judgment documents in the relevant regions, and the sufficiency of data is extremely limited.

3.2.2.2 *Of Technology Development and Talents*

During the application of artificial intelligence, there are heavy demands on technology and talents. The implementation of artificial intelligence in the mediation leads to the establishment of a mediation team that is well endowed with common sense, proficient in law and familiar with computer software technology. However, in judicial practice, the mediation team is faced with the predicament that the mediation personnel do not have a suitable educational background or sufficient professional experience. Taking the popular people's mediation as an example, the current people's mediation team in China is composed mostly of village committees, residents' committees, unit employees, towns and street staff, NGOs and social organizations and retired judges and public prosecutors. A high proportion of these mediators are ordinary community workers and retirees. Although they have rich offline mediation experience, they are unwilling to accept or incapable of accepting new legal technologies and therefore hardly qualified to serve as online mediators. In addition, the smooth operation of the online mediation platform requires integrated technical guarantees. How to play the role of science and technology to provide the necessary auxiliary measures for online mediation, how to effectively complete the analysis and retrieval of cases and how to protect the privacy and confidentiality of the parties are common issues in online mediation.

3.2.2.3 *Resolution of ODR Itself*

Confidentiality is the most predominant feature of mediation. However, the operation of the online mediation platform may infringe on the privacy of the parties and threaten the confidentiality of the mediation and the mediation agreement, conflicting with the inherent requirements of mediation. As mentioned previously, the application of artificial intelligence should be based on big data. However, the establishment of large databases and the collection and sorting of related information will inevitably expose the parties' information. In addition, the permanent traces usually left by internet technology will also affect the confidentiality of mediation. Therefore, although online mediation has improved the efficiency and convenience of dispute resolution, it has violated the requirements for confidentiality in mediation.

3.3 *The Outlook of Artificially Intelligent ODR*

3.3.1 Adoption of AI in ODR

3.3.1.1 ODR Adoption of AI Mediator

Empirical research indicates that the current use of artificial intelligence in ODR platforms is mostly 'weak artificial intelligence'. Although one cannot deny the convenience of 'weak artificial intelligence' brought to online mediation, objectively speaking, the mere application of 'weak artificial intelligence' cannot effectively realize the value of artificial intelligence technology. Therefore, people must explore the use of 'strong artificial intelligence' in the ODR platform through technological innovation. Thereby, the online mediation platform will become more intelligent and will help the parties to resolve disputes more efficiently and conveniently. To meet this objective, there are two proposals: First, relevant authorities should improve the construction of the 'big database' of mediation. Big data is a prerequisite for the application of 'strong artificial intelligence'. Nowadays, big data construction in mediation is not comprehensive, and some regions have not even started the exploration. The construction of the 'big database' of online mediation must collect documents of people's mediation, industrial mediation commercial mediation in a consolidative manner without infringing on parties' confidentiality. Moreover, the construction should obtain effective data through effective classification and integration. These efforts will lay the foundation for intelligent comparison and intelligent computing. Secondly, the relevant parties must introduce scientific calculation and analytical methods. Scientific calculation and analytical methods are a prerequisite for intelligent analysis in the online mediation system. From the angle of the present calculation methods absorbed in the construction of the 'intelligent court', the biggest problem lies in efficiency and privacy. In judicial practice, most legal persons and legal companies lack precision in constructing artificial intelligence models and algorithms. These intelligent systems usually mark and analyse certain relatively distinguishable factors in specific types of cases (parties' region, gender, age, amount of money involved in criminal cases, length of sentence, etc.) and then predict the sentences in criminal cases and the side in civil cases that is more likely to win. In reality, owing to certain technical defects, the accuracy rate is low. For good measure, owing to technical secrets, artificial intelligence algorithms are mostly behind the veil. As a technology layman, one can only know the results but not the process. In building an online mediation platform, the authorities must learn the experience from the construction of the 'intelligent court', adopt the advice of technicians and legal workers. This will enable them to complete the necessary hardware technology improvement while introducing it into legal expertise. Consequently, people will summarize and refine common factors in the 'mass' mediation documents to enhance the accuracy and precision of the models and algorithms.

3.3.1.2 Mediators' Adoption of AI Technology

Mediation places high requirements on expertise. Making use of both mediation skills and common sense, mediators are far more humane than machines. Therefore, while developing and exploring the use of strong artificial intelligence in online mediation, the role of the mediator cannot be neglected. Overall, the construction of an online mediation platform must adhere to a development model that integrates 'people first' and 'combination of people and machine in mediation'. In the process of introducing and perfecting strong artificial intelligence, the professionalization of the mediation team should be highlighted simultaneously. The focus should be on cultivating mediators who are familiar with common sense, proficient in legal principles and regulations and master computer software technology to form a professional team of mediators to achieve a synergy between 'manpower' and 'artificial intelligence' to ensure that online disputes are resolved effectively.

3.3.2 Clarification of AI's Role in Dispute Resolution

In regard to the role of artificial intelligence in litigation, the theoretical and practical circles have reached a consensus: although artificial intelligence is much superior to judges in data storage, analysis and calculation capabilities, artificial intelligence is not competent to do judges' work and cannot replace judges. Judicial adjudication is a complicated task, which not only requires a large storage of vast knowledge and high legal expertise, but is also relevant to life experience, common feeling and general reason as well as other human experience. All of this cannot be simplified to a logical model. Therefore, artificial intelligence should become a judge's 'assistant' or 'staff' in litigation. Alternatively, it can help judges complete basic tasks such as voice and image recognition, litigation guidance, document classification and text conversion. For example, data analysis and cloud computing are used to select cases to assist judges in making decisions. The same happens in mediation. Moreover, the confidentiality and flexibility provided by mediation determine that a more cautious attitude will be adopted towards artificial intelligence in building online mediation platforms. While improving the application of artificial intelligence in routine work, users should be cautious about the inertia and dependence resulting from the process of exploring and developing strong artificial intelligence. Even if an 'intelligent mediator' can be developed in the future, human mediators have an irreplaceable role in online mediation. After all, online mediation changes only the form of mediation and not its internal requirements. Nor can it ignore the application of humanistic care in mediation.

3.3.3 Consideration of AI Factors in Laws and Regulations

Improving the system construction of online mediation follows the working strategy sequence of 'pilot first – experience summary – role models-driven – full-scale promotion'. The authorities can first practise in each pilot area, and after positive results have been achieved, they can promote the successful experience nationwide. If circumstances permit, the government can formulate policies and regulations at the national level. When the situation calls for it, the legislators can stipulate that relevant contents of online mediation will be clearly in the national legislation of diversification dispute resolution.

Taking online court mediation as an example, in the construction of intelligent courts, the national courts can promote the use of artificial intelligence in online court mediation in many places, encourage local areas to practise and explore first, and formulate the work rules of local court online mediation that reflect the characteristics of artificial intelligence. After experience has been acquired, the SPC will formulate uniform work regulations across the country. (1) Provincial courts or suitable municipal courts within districts may formulate relevant rules on their own. The courts may jointly formulate the rules with relevant government departments (public security departments, judicial administrative departments, industries and commerce administration departments, complaints handling departments, etc.), social groups (trade unions, women's federations, etc.), business organizations (internet companies, insurance companies, etc.) and other units and institutions. The cooperation will form a joint force for dispute resolution and promote the standardization and refinement of the system. The court must actively seek support from Communist Party committees, governments and People's Congresses to assist local legislation of the online diversified dispute resolution mechanism. (2) The SPC may formulate rules for online court mediation. On the basis of the experience acquired and summed up from various regions and when the time comes, the SPC will promulgate uniform work regulations. According to the needs of future social development, the legislators will then decide whether to raise the multiple dispute resolution mechanism in a national legislation proposal with due consideration of the legal system and local characteristics.

About the Authors

Mohamed S. Abdel Wahab is the Chair of the Private International law Department and Professor of Dispute Resolution at Cairo University; Vice President of the ICC International Court of Arbitration; Member of the ICCA's Governing Board; Vice-Chair, IBA Arab Regional Forum; Member of the CRCICA Advisory Committee; Member of the Advisory Board, Mauritius International Arbitration Centre (MIAC); Member of the Board of Trustees of the Chartered Institute of Arbitrators (CIArb); Court Member of the Casablanca International Mediation and Arbitration Centre (CIMAC); Dean and Member of the Advisory Council of the Africa Arbitration Academy; and Chair of the International Expert Advisory Committee of the Permanent Forum on China Construction Law.

Prof. Dr. Mohamed S. Abdel Wahab is former Vice Chair, Academic Forum for Investor-State Dispute Settlement (2018 -2020); former Court Member of the LCIA (2014-2019); former President of LCIA's Arab Users' Council (2016-2018); former Vice President of the IBA Arbitration Committee (2015-2018); former President of the Egypt Branch, Chartered Institute of Arbitrators (CIArb) (2018); former Member of the CIArb's Board of Management (2018); former Chair of the CIArb's Technology Sub-Committee (2012-2014); and Accredited Mediator of the Centre for Effective Dispute Resolution ('CEDR').

Prof. Dr. Abdel Wahab is a world-renowned authority on international arbitration and ODR; a Fellow of the NCTDR at the University of Massachusetts, Amherst, USA; and founding member of ICODR and member of its Governing Board. In 2021, Prof. Dr. Abdel Wahab was selected to feature amongst the top (64) world leading arbitration practitioners as part of the GAR/WWL Global Legal Elite in Arbitration.

Karim Benyekhlef has been a professor in the Faculty of Law at the Université de Montréal since 1989 and member of the Barreau du Québec (Québec Bar Association) since 1985. He has been seconded to the Centre de recherche en droit public (Public Law Research Center) since 1990 and served as its Director from 2006 to 2014. He was also the Director of the Regroupement stratégique Droit, changements et gouvernance (Strategic Law, Change and Governance Group), which brings together some 50 researchers, from 2006 to 2014. At the same time, he was the Scientific Director of the Centre d'études et de recherches internationales de l'Université de Montréal (CÉRIUM – the Université de Montréal's International Research and Study Centre) from 2009 to 2012. He is now the Director of the Cyberjustice Laboratory, which he founded in 2010. The Cyberjustice Laboratory has obtained in 2015 the award "Mérite Innovation" from the Bar of Quebec (Innovation Award). He holds the Chaire de recherche en information juridique Lexum (Lexum Research Chair on Legal Information) and serves as a member of CÉRIUM's science and advisory committees. He received in 2016 from the Bar of Quebec the distinction Advocatus Emeritus. He holds the 2019-2020 Alexandre Koyré Excellence Research Chair. He is the co-leader of the research group Law, cyberjustice and cybersecurity at OBVIA (International Observatory on the Social Impacts of AI and Digital Technology).

In 1995, Professor Benyekhlef founded the electronic law journal Lex Electronica, the very first French-language online law journal. He also initiated the first online dispute resolution projects (the CyberTribunal Project, 1996-1999; eResolution, 1999-2001; ECODIR, 2000-today). He now serves as Director of the Cyberjustice Laboratory, the work of which is designed to increase and facilitate access to justice. From 2011 to 2018, he lead a project funded by the Social Sciences and Humanities Research Council (SSHRC) of Canada in the context of the Major Collaborative Research Initiatives (MCRI) Program: Rethinking Procedural Law: Towards Cyberjustice, composed of an international team made up of some 30 researchers from over 23 different universities in Canada, the United States, Australia and Europe. He is now leading the project "Autonomy through Cyberjustice Technologies and Artificial Intelligence" (ACT Project) funded by the partnership program of SSHRC (2018-2024). ACT aims to increase access to justice through the use of artificial intelligence (AI). Over the next 6 years, ACT will be able to count on a multidisciplinary and international team of 50 researchers, as well as 42 partners including research centers, public institutions, legal professionals, representatives from civil society and private sector actors. He has published and directed more than 15 books, numerous articles and chapters contributions on information technology law, global law and international law.

Larry W. Bridgesmith J.D., is President of Accelerate Insite LLC, CEO of Legal Alignment LLC and a practicing lawyer in Nashville, Tennessee. Larry is a member of the International Academy of Mediators and a former member of the Dispute Resolution Section Council of the American Bar Association. He chairs the Tennessee Supreme Court Alternative Dispute Resolution Commission. Larry has practiced in the fields of labor, employment and dispute resolution for over 40 years and served in management roles for boutique and mid-sized law firms throughout his career.

He founded Lipscomb University's Institute for Conflict Management and served as its inaugural Executive Director. Larry is an adjunct professor in legal project management, conflict management and mediation at Vanderbilt University School of Law, Belmont University Massey Graduate School of Business, The Nashville School of Law and the Albany Medical School Alden March Institute for Biomedical Ethics. He coordinates the Program on Law and Innovation at Vanderbilt School of Law.

In 2013, Larry was awarded the Grayfred Gray Award for Public Service in Mediation by the Coalition for Mediation Awareness in Tennessee. In 2017, he received the Justice

Janice Holder Award and the Tennessee Bar Association President's Award for technology innovation in the legal system. Larry's current interests include legal technology development, access to justice for all and 'better, faster and cheaper' innovation in law, education and health care. He holds a Six Sigma Green Belt certificate. The American Bar Association chose his article Collaboration is the Future for its 2019 publication reprint.

Pablo Cortés is a full professor and has a chair in Civil Justice at Leicester Law School where he teaches and conducts research in the field of Alternative Dispute Resolution (ADR), civil procedure and consumer law. He is also acts as an online arbitrator-adjudicator for CEDR's aviation, telecommunications and water disputes schemes. He has published three books in the field of technology and dispute resolution, including most recently *The Law of Consumer Redress* (Cambridge University Press, 2018) and prior to that he edited *The New Regulatory Framework for Consumer Dispute Resolution* (Oxford University Press, 2016).

He has been invited to many international conferences and expert meetings, including by the UN Commission for International Trade Law (UNCITRAL), the European Commission and the European Parliament (Internal Market and Legal Affairs Committees). He is a fellow of the National Centre for Technology and Dispute Resolutions (http://www.odr.info/, University of Massachusetts) and in 2012 he was a Gould Research Fellow at Stanford University. He is a member of the Online Dispute Resolution (ODR) Taskforce of the International Mediation Institute and of the ODR Advisory Group of the Civil Justice Council, which first proposed the launch of the Online Court in England and Wales. He has been employed as a consultant for a number of organization, including to assist the European Commission during the drafting of the legislative proposals for the ADR Directive and the ODR Regulation.

Benjamin G. Davis is a retired professor of law at the University of Toledo College of Law. He graduated from Harvard College (B.A. cum laude 1977), Harvard Business School and Harvard Law School (JD-MBA 1983). He worked for three years as a development consultant in West Africa and a management consultant with Mars and Co in Paris, France. He was the American Counsel at the International Court of Arbitration of the International Chamber of Commerce for ten years where he managed arbitrations with parties from around the world, led the computerization of the case management system and developed fast-track arbitration. He rose to Director, Conference Programmes and Manager of the Institute of World Business Law of the International Chamber of Commerce before entering teaching in 2000 at Texas Wesleyan University School of Law. He is the creator and one of the organizers of the International Competitions for Online Dispute Resolution.

Ben is an expert with the United Nations Economic Commission for Europe. He has drafted shadow reports to the UN Committee for the Elimination of Racial Discrimination and the UN Committee Against Torture. He was the Assistant Reporter, American Bar Associate Task Force on Electronic Commerce and Alternative Dispute Resolution. He was the Co-chair of the Teaching International Law Interest Group of the American Society of International Law. He led the drive for a resolution on international law at the ASIL Centennial meeting March 30, 2006. He is a former Chair of the ABA Section of Dispute Resolution and a former Member of the ABA Standing Committee on Law and National Security. He has published widely and spoken around the world on topics related to international commercial arbitration, online dispute resolution, contracts, and public international law. He teaches Contracts, Public International Law, International and Domestic Arbitration, Alternative Dispute Resolution, Commercial Law, and International Business Transactions

Chris Draper, Ph.D., P.E., helps humans make fewer errors when using technology. This expertise was gained through a career of analyzing and reducing the operational risk of how humans interface with technology systems in industries including automotive, aerospace, biofuels, petrochemical, commercial real estate, law enforcement, and academia. Chris has been at the intersection of technology and dispute resolution since 2011 with roles including Managing Director of Trokt in Des Moines, Iowa, and as a Venture Partner with VU Venture Partners in San Francisco, California. With Trokt, Chris oversees the development and delivery of technologies that help equitably resolve and avoid disputes ranging from labor relations to construction arbitration, financial compliance to special needs education. As a Venture Partner, Chris evaluates the utility, viability, and investability of innovative or unproven technologies as a partner to the FrontierTech evaluation team. Chris serves on numerous startup and non-profit boards, and has led initiatives that include his service as Chairman of the American Bar Association's Online Dispute Resolution Task Force Working Group One, Co-Chair of the American Bar Association's Section of Dispute Resolution Technology Committee, and as a Fellow of the National Center for Technology and Dispute Resolution. Chris received a Bachelor of Science in Mechanical Engineering from the University of California at Berkeley and a Doctor of Philosophy from the University of Glasgow.

Noam Ebner is a professor of negotiation and conflict resolution at Creighton University. Previously, Noam taught for over a decade at universities around the world while practicing as an attorney, negotiator, mediator, and mediator trainer.

Noam has been working at the crossroads of conflict resolution and technology in practice, teaching and research for over fifteen years. A fellow of the National Center for Technology & Dispute Resolution, he is a regular speaker on issues related to technology's role in conflict and its resolution. His writing on ODR has been published in *Negotiation Journal, Conflict Resolution Quarterly*, the *International Journal on ODR*, and the *Journal of Dispute Resolution*, and other central books and journals in the negotiation and conflict field.

All of Noam's writing is available at http://ssrn.com/author=425153. He also curates a comprehensive bibliography of the ODR field, available at http://odr.info/publications/. Noam can be contacted at noamebner@creighton.edu.

Alberto Elisavetsky is Founder and Director of Online Dispute Resolution Latin-American, Director of Social Conflict Observatory, National University of Tres de Febrero Buenos Aires Argentina. Director of TECHNOLOGIES APPLIED TO THE CONFLICT RESOLUTION Posgraduate Course National University of Tres de Febrero Buenos Aires Argentina. Chairman of e-MARC Alternative Dispute Resolution Worldwide Online Spanish Congress. Scientific committee member of the Master in Conflict Resolution University Degli Studi Di Padova Italy. Co-Director of 'School mediation program' University of Las Palmas of the Gran Canaria Spain. Founder and CEO of 'Simediar' – an online mediation simulation project. Cyber week coordinator of the Spanish, Italian, and Portuguese chapters.

Lise Embley has written more than a dozen court technology topic whitepapers on behalf of the Joint Technology Committee as a technical writer for the National Center for State Courts. Some of her most widely read publications include *Judicial Perspectives on ODR, Courts Disrupted, Case Studies in ODR for Courts: A View from the Front Lines*, and *Marketing a Court Website: Helping the Public Find the Court Online*. Prior to NCSC, Lise was a business systems analyst in Silicon Valley where she learned concepts key to quality improvement analysis, an awareness that influences every aspect of her work. She has a passion for words, carefully selected, and for applying technology in innovative ways to improve processes and outcomes.

Paul Embley is the CIO and Technology Division Director at the National Center for State Courts. He began his career in Silicon Valley working for the 'who's who' of high tech (along with several of the 'who's no longer'). After 25 years in the for-profit sector, Paul shifted to public sector work on integrated justice. He has gleaned broad product lifecycle expertise from diverse and challenging projects in US states and territories, Australia, many EU nations, and several emerging democracies including Haiti and Nigeria. He continues to follow potential disrupters such as blockchain and machine learning/data science looking for ways those disrupters might be used advantageously in courts and with justice partners. He is currently involved in international, national, and localized technology initiatives for criminal and civil justice. Paul is a thought leader and recognized expert in US State Court utilization of ODR. He has participated in panels and delivered presentations at international ODR gatherings including Doha, London,

Auckland, and Zagreb, as well as many US conferences such as SXSW, the Court Technology Conference, eCourts and several others.

Clare Fowler received her Doctorate on designing dispute resolution systems for small businesses from Pepperdine University Graduate School of Education/Organizational Leadership and her Master's of Dispute Resolution from the Straus Institute for Dispute Resolution at the Pepperdine University School of Law. Dr. Fowler serves as Managing Editor at Mediate.com and as Director of Caseload Manager. She has also worked at Pepperdine Dispute Resolution Department and UO CRES as the Career Advisor. Clare has mediated and trains, focusing on workplace disputes. Dr. Fowler's dissertation was a phenomenological study of Workplace disputes. Her current book project is a guidebook for HR directors dealing with high conflict employees.

Frank Fowlie is the Commissioner with Athletics Canada. Frank is a member of the Board of Directors with the Canadian Sport Institute, Pacific. Dr. Frank Fowlie served as the Independent Mediator with the Organization for the Prohibition of Chemical Weapons (2015-2016) and as the Ombudsman at the International Organization for Migration (IOM) (2012-2015). He was the inaugural Ombudsman at the Internet Corporation for Assigned Names and Numbers. ICANN is the agency which administers the global domain name system which serves as the backbone for the Internet (2004-2011).

Frank also served as a Capacity Building Consultant with the World Bank in Pakistan, specifically working with the Ombudsman of the Province of Balochistan (2015). Frank is on the Mediation Roster with the Court of Arbitration for Sport and served six years as a Director of the Sport Dispute Resolution Centre of Canada (2009-2015). Frank served as the Chef de Mission for the Individual Olympic Athletes from East Timor at the 2000 Sydney Olympic Games.

Frank holds a Doctor of Conflict Resolution (DCR) from La Trobe University, Melbourne, and is a Fellow with the Centre for Information Technology and Dispute Resolution at the University of Massachusetts – Amherst. Frank holds the designation of Chartered Mediator. Frank was awarded the Canadian Peacekeeping Service Medal for his work with the UN in East Timor. In 2010 Frank was awarded the Lifetime Achievement Award from the University of Regina Alumni Association. Frank began his career as a member of the Royal Canadian Mounted Police.

Alma Abdul-Hadi Jadallah is an internationally recognized conflict prevention and mitigation expert. She is a recognized expert facilitator and mediator and coach serving on the roster of mediators for the European Union_ERMES, the Office of Compliance, Advisor, Ombudsman IFC – World Bank, and the UN Rosters of Mediators and Rapid Deployment for Crisis Intervention, and is a member of the International Consortium on

Closed Space (iCon), Center for International and Strategic Studies. Dr. Jadallah is the recipient of several business awards and honors including the 2017 Distinguished Alumni Award for the School of Conflict Analysis and Resolution at George Mason University.

As President and Managing Director of an award-winning woman owned firm, Kommon Denominator (KD) Inc.(www.kommondenominator.com), she designed and led global strategy and expansion, and drove strategic growth through the building of multiple alliances with a diverse number of institutions and businesses.

Dr. Abdel-Hadi Jadallah educated and trained hundreds of individuals across the globe in conflict assessment tools, mediation and facilitation skills, identity-based conflicts, intervention and process design, and monitoring and evaluation techniques. She has extensive experience in the Middle East and especially in Iraq where she has worked on a high-profile projects that included training of academic, civil society, religious leaders and youth from all Iraqi ethnic and religious communities in peacebuilding tools and skills. This work has resulted in the adoption of peace education programs in six universities across Iraq. She is currently working on developing the nexus for security and development in Iraq for UNDP. In 2018, she joined the Experts and Eminent Persons, ASEAN Regional Forum where she serves as an adviser to the Forum and US Department of State on women, peace and security, and conflict prevention.

Professor **Ethan Katsh** is one of the founders of the field of online dispute resolution (ODR). He is the director of the National Center for Technology and Dispute Resolution (NCTDR) and Professor Emeritus of Legal Studies at the University of Massachusetts. Along with Janet Rifkin, he wrote the first book on ODR, *Online Dispute Resolution: Resolving Disputes in Cyberspace* (2001). The frequently mentioned metaphor of technology as a 'Fourth Party' in dispute resolution was first proposed in that book.

Professor Katsh is a graduate of the Yale Law School and was one of the first legal scholars to recognize the impact new information technologies would have on law. He is the author of two books on law and technology, *Law in a Digital World* (Oxford University Press, 1995) and *The Electronic Media and the Transformation of Law* (Oxford University Press, 1989). More recently, he was co-author, with Orna Rabinovich-Einy of *Digital Justice: Technology and the Internet of Disputes* (Oxford University Press, 2017)

Professor Katsh was the recipient of the 2017 D'Alemberte-Raven Award from the American Bar Association Section of Dispute Resolution, the Section's highest award. He received the Mary Parker Follett award from the Association of Conflict Resolution and his scholarly contribution in the field of law and technology has been the subject of a Review Essay in Law and Social Inquiry. Professor Katsh received the Chancellor's Medal and gave the University of Massachusetts Distinguished Faculty Lecture in October 2006.

During 2010-2011, Professor Katsh was the Fulbright Distinguished Chair in the Humanities and Social Sciences at the University of Haifa (Israel). In 2014-2015, he was an Affiliate of Harvard University's Berkman Klein Center for Internet and Society. He has been Visiting Professor of Law and Cyberspace at Brandeis University and is co-editor of the International Journal of Online Dispute Resolution. Professor Katsh has served as principal online dispute resolution consultant for the Office of Government Information Services (OGIS), a federal agency mandated to provide mediation in Freedom of Information Act disputes. He was principal dispute resolution advisor to SquareTrade.com and was Chairman of the Board of Advisors of Modria.com. Professor Katsh has chaired the annual International Forums on Online Dispute Resolution and is Chait of the International Council for Dispute Resolution (ICODR).

Ayodele Musibau Kusamotu practices law with the firm of Kusamotu and Kusamotu in Lagos, Nigeria. He is a graduate of the University of Lagos School of Law and chairs the Information Technology and Communications Committee of the Nigerian Bar Association, Lagos Branch. He chairs the Africa Committee for InternetBar.org, is the Project Lead of Creative Commons Nigeria and is involved in assisting One Laptop Per Child in launch strategies for Nigeria. He was a member of the Presidential Task Force that drafted intellectual property legislation in 2001 and was an adviser to the Economic Community of West African States (ECOWAS) in negotiations with the European Union on economic partnership agreements.

David Allen Larson is a Professor of Law at the Mitchell Hamline School of Law and Senior Fellow at the Dispute Resolution Institute. He has been involved with online dispute resolution (ODR) since 1999 and is the System Designer helping create an ODR platform for the New York State Unified Court System. David is the John H. Faricy Jr. Chair for Empirical Studies, and a Fellow for the National Center for Technology and Dispute Resolution and the American Bar Foundation. He has 60 legal publications and has made more than 170 professional presentations in ten different countries. He is Chair Elect of the ABA Section of Dispute Resolution, Co-Chair of the Section's ODR Standards Task Force, and was a member of the ABA E-Commerce and ADR Task Force. He teaches Arbitration Law, Arbitration Skills, Disability Law, Employment Law, Employment Discrimination Law, Online Dispute Resolution (ODR) for the 21st Century, Labor Law, and Torts.

David worked at the Equal Employment Opportunity Commission Office of General Counsel, Appellate Division in Washington, D.C. and, on behalf of that Office, participated in drafting the Regulations and Interpretive Guidance for the Americans with Disabilities Act. He was founder and Editor-in-Chief of the 'Journal of Alternative Dispute Resolution in Employment' (CCH Inc.), an arbitrator for the Omaha Tribe and other disputes, and a Hearing Examiner for the Nebraska Equal Opportunity

Commission. He worked with the International Legal Resource Center (a partnership between the ABA Section of International Law and the United Nations Development Programme) and the ABA Central and East European Law Initiative (CEELI). David has been a tenured professor at four different universities and colleges and practiced with a litigation law firm. His articles are at http://ssrn.com/author=709717 and his profile is at http://mitchellhamline.edu/biographies/person/david-larson/.

Anyu (Andy) Lee is the president of Beijing eBridgeChina Research Institute, visiting professor at Qinghua University, Beijing, China and adjunct professor at East West Center, Honolulu, Hawaii, before this position, Prof. Lee was a professor at University of International Business and Economy in Beijing, China since 2010. Prof. Lee served as the chief scientist of the university's eCommerce Research institute and headed the university's Shenzhen Research Institute, which is a thinking tank founded jointly by the university and Shenzhen municipal government. Prior to the university position, Prof. Lee was the director of eCommerce technology research center at China Academy of Sciences for 10 years. Before coming back to China, Prof. Lee worked in Silicon Valley for over 12 years as an engineer and research scientist in various companies including LSI Logic, Silicongraphic, HP Lab. Prof. Lee founded Internet Image Inc. in 1997 and successfully merged with Intraware, a Nasdaq listed company. Prof. Lee was educated in Shanghai JiaoTong University (BS, MS), University of Arizona (MS), and Stanford University (PhD) with HP corporate fellowship.

Brandon Malone is an lawyer and international arbitrator based in Edinburgh and with Quadrant Chambers, London. He is a panel arbitrator for many arbitral institutions including AAA/ICDR, SIAC, DIAC, and CIETAC and has been appointed to deal with arbitrations under a variety of ad hoc and institutional rules.

Brandon is the founder and Chairman of the Scottish Arbitration Centre. He is also a member the ICC UK Arbitration and ADR Committee and a member of the ICC Commission. He is the Congress Chair of the XXVth ICCA Congress, which will be held in Edinburgh 26-29 September 2021 (see www.icca2021.scot).

Brandon has particular interests in construction, engineering, energy, and technology. He proposed and now chairs the ICCA-New York City Bar-CPR Institute Working Group on Cybersecurity in International Arbitration, and is a member of the International Task Force of the Silicon Valley Arbitration and Mediation Center.

Brandon was one of the founding members of the Scottish Society for Computers and Law. He is a member of the Scottish Civil Justice Council, and sits on the Council's ICT Committee. Further information about Brandon can be found at www.brandonmalone.com and www.arbitration.scot.

Janet Martinez is Director of the Martin Daniel Gould Center for Conflict Resolution where she teaches advanced negotiation, dispute system design and alternative dispute resolution law, practice & policy. Martinez practiced corporate law for ten years before moving to Cambridge, Massachusetts where she did research, writing, and teaching in negotiation at Harvard University's graduate schools of business, law, and government. In Cambridge, she was Senior Associate for the Consensus Building Institute, a nonprofit provider of dispute resolution services in the public and private sectors, both domestic and international. There, she facilitated policy dialogues for the United Nations, World Trade Organization, and Framework Convention on Climate Change; she currently serves on its board of directors. Martinez has coached and trained for Lax Sebenius since 2000 and now serves as senior advisor. Martinez' current research and consulting focus on dispute system design, online dispute resolution, international comparative dispute resolution, sustainable groundwater management in California, and illegal fishing/forced labor in the global fishing industry. Martinez holds a B.S. in Bacteriology & Public Health from Washington State University, J.D. from Golden Gate University, Masters in Public Administration from Harvard University, and Ph.D. from Massachusetts Institute of Technology. Recent publications include: (with Lisa Amsler and Stephanie Smith, *Dispute System Design: Preventing, Managing, and Resolving Conflict*, Stanford University Press, 2020), Janet K. Martinez, *Designing Online Dispute Resolution*, J. Disp. Resol, vol. 2020, number 1, p. 135-149, and Leah Wing, Janet Martinez, Ethan Katsh and Colin Rule, 'Designing Ethical Online Dispute Resolution Systems: The Rise of the Fourth Party' (2021).

Maria Victoria Marun is Attorney Mediator. Senior Lecturer in Law. University Teaching Specialist. Director at Center for Alternative Dispute Resolution of the Bar and Solicitors of the 3rd Legal Circumscription Mendoza. Argentina. University Professor. Trainer in School Law and Conflict Resolution in Educational Institutions. Founder member of ODR Latin Americа Academy. Member of the International Professional Mediators Forum. Professor of TECHNOLOGIES APPLIED TO THE CONFLICT RESOLUTION Postgraduate Course National University of Tres de Febrero Buenos Aires Argentina. Member of the Management Committee of Cyberweek 2013 to 2019 (Spanish chapter) and E-MARC (Spanish Speaking Worldwide Congress on Conflict Resolution).

Chittu Nagarajan is a pioneer in the field of ODR, a thought leader and a serial ODR Entrepreneur for the last 20 years. Her current venture is CREK ODR a 4th Generation ODR Technology Solutions Platform. Before CREK she Co-founded Modria – the world's leading online dispute resolution platform, was the Head of eBay and PayPal Community Courts and founder of one of the first ODR platforms – ODRIndia and ODRWorld. She is a Fellow of the National Center for Technology and Dispute

Resolution (NCTDR) at UMass – Amherst and a Founding Board member at the International Council for Online Dispute Resolution (ICODR). Her expertise in the ODR field includes research, teaching, policy making, auditing, analysis, systems design and execution.

Chittu is also the Managing Director of Contract Wrangler (India), a one of a kind Contract Management and Analysis Company in the Silicon Valley. She holds a Master's degree in Alternative Dispute Resolution to Ecommerce Disputes, a Graduate degree in Law and BA in History. She is a Certified Mediator and holds a Legal Practicing Certificate. She can be reached at chittu@crekodr.com.

Aura Esther Vilalta Nicuesa holds the Chair in Civil Law at the Open University of Catalonia (UOC). Researcher at the Internet Interdisciplinary Institute (IN3). PhD in Law from the University of Barcelona (cum laude and European Extraordinary Prize). Postgraduate Studies in Catalan Civil Law (UB). Diploma of Advanced Studies in Civil Law (UB). Master in Comparative Civil Law (UNICAM, It). Vilalta is fellow of the National Center of Technology and Dispute Resolution (NCTDR), member of the European Law Institute (ELI) and member of the Online Dispute Resolution Taskforce of the International Mediation Institute (IMI). Vilalta collaborates as well with the Scientific Excellence Unit 'Digital Society: Security and Protection of Rights' at the University of Granada. Vilalta is part of Advisory Commitee for the Catalonian Government of Generalitat – mediation committee of TERMCAT, Parenting Coordination committee of Dept. Justice – and Legislative Committee for Consolat de Mar. Vilalta has served as Spanish Delegate and ODR expert in Working Group WG III of UNCITRAL, United Nations. She has been Director of the Legal Department at the University School of Labor Relations in Lleida (EURL), lawyer (ICAB), mediator (AEPJMA and FMA), arbitrator for the Arbitration Tribunal of Barcelona (TAB) and arbitrator for the Chamber of Commerce of Madrid (CAM). Vilalta was appointed Deputy Magistrate in the Court of appeal in Barcelona during year 2008. Before, served as independent lawyer during 12 years. Her field of expertise is out-of-court dispute resolution and more in particular, online and consumer dispute resolution, e-contracts, dispute avoidance tools in online intermediary platforms, blockchain applied to contracts – smart legal contracts – and access to justice (A2J).

Kathleen Paisley is an international arbitrator with more than 30 years' experience in both commercial and investor-State arbitration. She is triple qualified with degrees from the Yale Law School, a Master's degree in Finance and has completed the Certified Public Accountancy exam. Kathleen has specific industry expertise in technology (both medical and non-medical), biotech, pharmaceuticals, semiconductors, construction, energy and hospitality. Ms. Paisley's areas of legal specialization include international law, intellectual property, data protection, cybersecurity, complex damages, competition/

antitrust and EU law issues related to arbitration. She brings a truly international approach to her work given her US nationality and training, European and US presences, and significant experience covering Asia, the Americas, Africa, and Europe. She is a member of the New York and DC Bars and has worked under the laws of England and Wales, Belgium and other civil jurisdictions. In addition to her practice, Kathleen also speaks and publishes regularly on arbitration and has the honor of serving on the major international arbitration task forces established by ICCA and others on damages (quantification), data protection (co-chair), cybersecurity, as well as the Sedona Conference Drafting Committee on arbitration and the Mixed Mode International Task Force (enforcement).

Mirèze Philippe joined the Secretariat of the ICC International Court of Arbitration (ICC) in 1984 and is a Special Counsel. She administered arbitration cases during several years before being entrusted with various projects, including building the NetCase platform for the conduct of arbitration in a secure online environment. She is in charge of practices, a legal training program and the internship program.

Mirèze is co-founder of ArbitralWomen (AW), an organization gathering and promoting female practitioners in the field of international dispute resolution. She is also member of various organizations promoting gender equality and equal opportunities for equal qualifications. Mirèze received the CPR 2018 Diversity Award for outstanding contributions to diversity in ADR.

She has been in the field of online dispute resolution since 2000 and built various platforms, namely for ICC and for AW alongside IT engineers. She was also member of the UNCITRAL Working Group III on ODR (report delivered in February 2016).

Mirèze is a Board member of various organizations: Co-Founder of ArbitralWomen and Board member (www.arbitralwomen.org); member of the Steering Committee of the Equal Representation in Arbitration Pledge (www.arbitrationpledge.com); member of the ICCA Diversity Task Force; member of the Council of the ABA Section of Dispute Resolution and of the ABA Online Dispute Resolution (ODR) Task Force; member of the Advisory Board of Arbitri (http://associationarbitri.com); Board member of the International Council for Online Dispute Resolution ('ICODR'); member of the Editorial Board of International Journal of Online Dispute Resolution ('IJODR'); Fellow of the National Centre for Technology and Dispute Resolution ('NCTDR') (http://odr.info/); Board member of ODR Africa Network (https://odrafrica.com). CV and articles available on www.arbitralwomen.org/author/mireze-philippe/.

Marta Poblet is an Associate Professor at RMIT University's Graduate School of Business and Law. She is one of the co-founders of the Institute of Law and Technology at the Autonomous University of Barcelona and past researcher at ICREA (Catalonia). She holds a JSD in law (Stanford University 2002) and a Master in International Legal

Studies (Stanford University 2000). Her research interests cover different areas at the intersection of law, political sciences, and technology. She is also interested in the connections between technology developments (AI, distributed technologies, human-computer interaction) and the different theories of democracy and citizenship. She has been the PI of a number of national and international research projects and has published over 80 scientific articles and book chapters on these topics.

Orna Rabinovich-Einy is a law professor at the University of Haifa. Her areas of expertise are online dispute resolution (ODR), alternative dispute resolution (ADR), and civil procedure, with research focusing on the impact of technology on dispute resolution, the relationship between formal and informal justice systems, and dispute resolution system design. She has published widely in these areas, including a book (co-authored with Professor Ethan Katsh) entitled 'Digital Justice: Technology and the Internet of Disputes,' published by Oxford University Press. Rabinovich-Einy holds a J.S.D. degree from Columbia University. She was admitted to the Israel (1998) and N.Y. (2001) Bar, and was certified as a mediator in New York (2003).

Daniel Rainey is a principal in Holistic Solutions, Inc. (HSI), and an adjunct faculty member in graduate dispute resolution programs and law schools. He is currently a Fellow of the National Center for Technology and Dispute Resolution, a member of the Board of Directors for the InternetBar.Org, and a founding member and founding Board Member of the International Council for Online Dispute Resolution (ICODR). He is the Co-Chair of Working Group 3 of the ODR Task Force for the American Bar Association Section of Dispute Resolution, and the Co-Chair of the International Mediation Institute's Online Mediator Competency Task Force. He also serves as a member of the Supreme Court of Virginia's Access to Justice Commission, Self-Represented Litigants Committee. He is one of the Editors-in-Chief of the *International Journal of Online Dispute Resolution.* He is also an author/editor of numerous book chapters and articles about ODR and ADR. In September 2017, he retired as the Chief of Staff for the National Mediation Board, and in October 2017, at the Association for Conflict Resolution annual conference, he received the Mary Parker Follett Award for innovation in dispute resolution.

Graham Ross is a UK lawyer and mediator with over 20 years' experience in IT and the law. Graham is the author of legal application software (accounts and time recording) and the founder of LAWTEL, the popular web-based legal information update service. Graham co-founded the first ODR service in the UK, WeCanSettle, and designed the blind bidding software at the heart of the system. Graham subsequently founded TheMediationRoom.com, for whom he designed their online mediation platform. Graham runs a distance training course on ODR (www.ODRtraining.com), is a member of the UK Civil Justice Council's ODR Advisory Group. Graham is also a Fellow of the National Center for Technology and Dispute Resolution at UMass and a Board Member of the International Council for Online Dispute Resolution. Graham is an advisor to Smartsettle of British Columbia, developers of e-negotiation tools.

Graham speaks regularly at international conferences on the impact of the law on the Internet and e-commerce and on the application of technology to ADR. Graham was host of the 5th International Conference on Online Dispute Resolution held in Liverpool, UK, in 2007 and ran a further conference in Liverpool in 2018. Graham was a team member of the EMCOD project which created a facility for the European Union for the measurement of justice through ODR.

Colin Rule is CEO of Mediate.com. In 2011 Colin co-founded Modria.com, an Online Dispute Resolution (ODR) provider based in Silicon Valley, which was acquired by Tyler Technologies in 2017. From 2017 to 2020 Colin served as Vice President of ODR at Tyler. From 2003 to 2011 Colin was Director of ODR for eBay and PayPal. Colin is the author of *Online Dispute Resolution for Business* and co-author of *The New Handshake: ODR and the Future of Consumer Protection.* He serves on the boards of the Consensus Building Institute and the PeaceTech Lab at the United States Institute of Peace. He is currently Co-Chair of the Advisory Board of the National Center for Technology and Dispute Resolution at UMass-Amherst and a Fellow at the Gould Center for Conflict Resolution at Stanford Law School. Colin co-founded Online Resolution, one of the first online dispute resolution (ODR) providers, in 1999 and served as its CEO and President. Colin also worked for several years with the National Institute for Dispute Resolution in Washington, DC and the Consensus Building Institute in Cambridge, MA.

Nicolas Vermeys, LL. D., CISSP, is the Dean of Programs at the *Université de Montréal*'s Faculty of Law, a researcher at the *Centre de recherche en droit public* (CRDP), and the associate director of the Cyberjustice Laboratory. Professor Vermeys is also a visiting professor of law at both William & Mary (USA) and the University of Fortaleza (Brazil). Pr. Vermeys is a member of the Quebec Bar, as well as a certified information systems security professional (CISSP) as recognized by (ISC)2. He is the author of numerous scientific articles, books and other publications relating to the impact of technology on the law in general, and to ODR in particular including *Droit codifié et nouvelles technologies* (2015), and *Responsabilité civile et sécurité informationnelle* (2010). He also spearheaded, in collaboration with his colleague Karim Benyekhlef, the conception, development and deployment of a number of ODR platforms in Canada and Europe. His research, which focuses on legal issues pertaining to artificial intelligence, information security, developments in the field of cyberjustice, and other questions relating to the impact of technological innovations on the law, has helped shape legislation and policy around the globe. He is regularly invited to speak on these topics in different fora, and has offered training and counsel in the field of ODR on numerous occasions to judges, lawyers, international bodies, and government organizations, both in Canada and abroad.

Professor **Amy J. Schmitz** joined the University of Missouri School of Law and the Center for Dispute Resolution as the Elwood L. Thomas Missouri Endowed Professor of Law in 2016. Previously she was a Professor at the University of Colorado School of Law for over 16 years. Prior to teaching, Professor Schmitz practiced law with large law firms in Seattle and Minneapolis, and served as a law clerk for the U. S. Court of Appeals for the 8th Circuit. Professor Schmitz teaches courses in Contracts, Lawyering and Problem-Solving, Online Dispute Resolution (ODR), AI, Data Analytics and the Law, Arbitration, International Arbitration, and Consumer Law. She has been heavily involved in ODR teaching and research for a long time and is a Fellow of the National Center for Technology and Dispute Resolution, as well as the Co-Chair of the ABA Technology Committee of the Dispute Resolution Section and the ODR Task Force. Professor Schmitz has published over 55 interviews as host of The Arbitration Conversation, and is joining the revered RESOLVING DISPUTES casebook. Recent speaking engagements include various webinars and events around ODR with the American Bar Association, Yale/Quinnipiac Speaker Series, ODR Forums in New Zealand, Paris and the U.S., Universities in Munich and Augsburg, Germany, Cyberjustice Lab in Montreal, Consumer Financial Protection Bureau in Washington, D.C.; Cyberspace Conference, University of Leicester in England; Stanford Law School; and many other universities and conferences throughout the world. She serves on the Association of American Law Schools Executive Committee on Commercial and Consumer Law, was an External Scientific Fellow of the Max Planck Institute Luxembourg, and is a researcher with the ACT Project exploring AI and ODR at the Cyberjustice Lab. She also has taught in France, South Africa, and Oxford, England, and has been an expert and liaison for the United Nations working group seeking to create a global ODR mechanism (UNCITRAL WG III). Professor Schmitz has published over 50 articles in law journals and books, and a book, The New Handshake: Online Dispute Resolution and the Future of Consumer Protection, with Colin Rule.

Richard Susskind OBE is the world's most cited author on the future of legal services. He is President of the Society for Computers and Law, Chair of the Advisory Board of the Oxford Internet Institute, and, since 1998, has been Technology Adviser to the Lord Chief Justice of England and Wales. The Founder of Remote Courts Worldwide (www.remotecourts.org), he also chaired the Online Dispute Resolution Advisory Group of the Civil Justice Council in England and Wales whose proposals on online courts have been adopted as judicial and government policy. Professor Susskind's work has been translated into 15 languages and he has been invited to speak in over 50 countries. He has written numerous books, including *The Future of the Law* (1996), *Transforming the Law* (2000), *The End of Lawyers?* (2008), *The Future of the Professions* (2015, with D Susskind) *Tomorrow's Lawyers* (2013, 2017), and *Online Courts and the Future of Justice* (2019). In the 1980s, he wrote his doctorate on artificial intelligence and the law at Balliol College, Oxford University. He holds professorships at Oxford University, UCL, Gresham College, and Strathclyde University. A Fellow of the Royal Society of Edinburgh and of the British Computer Society, and an Honorary Bencher at Gray's Inn, he was awarded an OBE in 2000.

Herb Waye M.B. MALT, is the Ombudsman for the Internet Corporation for Assigned Names and Numbers (ICANN). He has held the position for three years and was previously the Adjunct Ombuds for 10 years working for both previous Ombudsmen. Herb recently retired from active duty with the Royal Canadian Mounted Police after 36 years in law enforcement. Herb is also Associate Faculty at Royal Roads University where he teaches online the capstone practicum course to students finishing their Bachelor of Justice degrees in the university distance learning program. In 2007, Herb was conferred a Master of Arts in Leadership and Training (MALT) from Royal Roads University. He is a member of the International Ombuds Association, the International Ombuds Institute, and the Forum of Canadian Ombuds. He lives with his wife Christine on a small hobby farm near Ottawa Ontario, Canada.

Leah Wing is Co-Director of the National Center for Technology and Dispute Resolution (NCTDR), cofounder and board member of the International Council on Online Dispute Resolution, and Senior Lecturer II and Honors Director in the Legal Studies Program, Department of Political Science, University of Massachusetts Amherst, USA. Dr. Wing has taught dispute resolution since 1993 and served as a researcher on early experiments in online dispute resolution at NCTDR. She mapped the first application of mediation into an online system as a senior researcher for a National Science Foundation funded project. Her present research projects focus on ethical principles for online dispute resolution, crowdsourcing and spatial justice, and technological responses to digital harm doing. Leah led the crafting of Ethical Principles for Online Dispute Resolution with NCTDR and serves on the American Bar Association Dispute Resolution Section Technology Committee and on its ODR Task Force. She serves on the editorial boards of the *International Journal of Online Dispute Resolution* and *Conflict Resolution Quarterly* and has served two terms on the Association of Conflict Resolution Board of Directors. Leah has provided mediation training and consultation to more than one hundred organizations and institutions in the U.S. and internationally.

Michael Wolf creates significant value for workplace leaders by helping them improve engagement, grow collaborative cultures, solve complex and sensitive mission-critical problems, constructively manage conflict, and participate in collective bargaining. He also exercises expert ADR & ODR skills as a mediator, trainer, educator, facilitator, consult, conflict coach, conflict management system developer, and organizational leader.

Michael has worked in three U.S. federal agencies as ADR Director, EEO Director, unfair labor practice Settlement Official, Counsel for Dispute Resolution Technology, Federal Mediator, Director of Mediation Technology Services, and Special Assistant to the agency director. Earlier in his career, Michael spent more than a decade practicing labor and employment law and a brief time as a Congressional staffer.

He has held leadership roles in the American Bar Association, the Association for Conflict Resolution, ADR segments of the New Jersey and Texas bar associations, and the Steering Committee of the U.S. Federal Interagency ADR Working Group, Texas Mediator Credentialing Association, and New Jersey Association of Professional Mediators

Michael has been adjunct faculty at Catholic University Metropolitan School of Professional Studies, Pepperdine University Law School's Strauss Institute for Dispute Resolution, and at the University of Baltimore. He has been a guest instructor at Harvard's Kennedy School, Cornell's ILR School, George Washington University Department of Organizational Sciences, University of Syracuse Maxwell School of Citizenship and Public Affairs, University of Texas Business School, North Texas State University Business School, Sullivan University, and Rutgers University Dept. of Public Policy.

Michael is a graduate of the University of Wisconsin at Madison and Washington University School of Law in St. Louis, Missouri.

www.ingramcontent.com/pod-product-compliance
Ingram Content Group UK Ltd.
Pitfield, Milton Keynes, MK11 3LW, UK
UKHW050954290926
15470UKWH00006B/1821

9 789462 361836